THE COMPLETE GUIDE
TO HEALTH AND NUTRITION

THE
Complete Guide
to Health
and Nutrition

GARY NULL

Delta

Published by
Dell Publishing
a division of
The Bantam Doubleday Dell Publishing Group, Inc.
666 Fifth Avenue
New York, New York 10103

CONTENTS

ACKNOWLEDGMENTS

I wish to give special thanks to Adria Eisenmeyer, my verification editor; Cindy Eisenmeyer and Maya Randolph, my researchers; Julie Wiener and Emily Nesbitt, my editors; and a very special thanks to Cynthia Vartan, who saw this project through nearly five years of continued expansion.

INTRODUCTION

Gary Null's *Complete Guide to Health and Nutrition* is the most complete and authoritative popular work of its kind. Five years in the making, it explains fully and simply the basics of health and nutrition: what's in the food we eat, how it affects us, and how we can make ourselves healthier through good nutrition.

The *Complete Guide* is unique in the thoroughness and objectivity of its viewpoint. Nutrition arouses strong emotions in many of us, and some researchers let their emotions guide them toward one or another particular philosophy of health: "alternative" medicine, "holistic" therapy, "New Age" beliefs, or the orthodox, traditional methods of health care. And many of these adherents let their presentation of facts be guided by their opinions.

Gary Null lets his opinions be guided by the facts. Avoiding all prejudiced viewpoints, he gathers every important piece of research on every important subject: vitamins, minerals, fats, carbohydrates, protein. Thousands of books and articles have been read, and more than 2,000 experts in diverse fields have either been consulted or interviewed in establishing the real facts of each particular problem. From this mountain of material Gary Null has distilled a concise, accurate statement of everything that's known about health and nutrition. To get the same wealth of information you would have to consult thirty to fifty separate books in the same field.

But the *Complete Guide* is not simply a reference book; it is a source book for a healthier life. When all the facts support a particular position on some issue in diet and nutrition, Gary Null does not hesitate to state that position strongly and back it up with sound practical advice. He confronts all the complex health issues facing us today and answers the questions his readers will be asking. How much protein do I need? Is vitamin E really effective in treating heart disease? Which vegetables supply the highest fiber content? Questions like these are answered not only in authoritative explanations but in valuable charts and diagrams as well. And sensitive issues such as sugar and cholesterol are presented not only as matters of health but as economic and political issues.

With Gary Null's *Complete Guide to Health and Nutrition*, readers can stop guessing—and worrying—about what's in the food they eat. They can get all the knowledge amassed by scientific research, and learn how to apply that knowledge to their own lives.

Martin Feldman, M.D.
New York City, 1984

THE COMPLETE GUIDE
TO HEALTH AND NUTRITION

PROTEIN

And God said, Behold, I have given you every herb bearing seed, which *is* upon the face of all the earth, and every tree, in the which *is* the fruit of a tree yielding seed; to you it shall be for meat.

Genesis
1:29

If I were to do a word association test with you and I mentioned the word protein, the first thing to come to your mind would probably be meat.

After the term meat, no doubt you would mention chicken, hamburger, steak, veal—the flesh of an animal.

If I said, "high-protein diet," most likely you would imagine lots of red meat would be included.

If you are like most people, you probably have no idea how many grams of protein you need every day. You may have heard of the concept of complementing proteins but are probably vague about how it's done. And if you are like most people, you have no idea how to evaluate the net protein utilization of a particular food.

If you had to eliminate meat from your diet, would you be able to obtain enough quality protein?

In America today, we are faced with the notion that protein is synonymous with meat, our primary source, and that without a substantial amount of meat in the diet, we would be suffering from gross protein deficiencies. Many people believe they must eat meat every day, often three times a day. They'll consume ham or bacon for breakfast; luncheon meat such as salami, bologna, frankfurters, or hamburgers for lunch; and roast beef, fish, chicken, or steak for dinner. If you are an athlete, you will almost surely at some time in your training take high-protein supplements.

Serious problems arise as a result of the gross ignorance and misinformation prevalent on a subject so essential for good health. Very few people know what protein truly is, why we need it, what its best sources and its worst sources are, what are the toxic forms of protein and the toxic by-products associated with it, what is the most easily digested protein, how we should combine proteins, and how much protein we need as we age.

Family No. 1: The Typical American High-Protein Diet

If I were to ask you whether a seventeen-year-old and sixty-year-old woman require the same amount of protein, what would you say? As a point of fact, if you went into the average person's home and joined their family for dinner, you might sit down at the table with a mother, father, daughter, son, and possibly a grandparent. In all probability, all of them would receive the same amount of a protein food. This would usually be a meat/flesh item. But clearly the daughter and son, since they are growing, have a greater need for quality protein; the wife, who weighs fifty pounds less than her husband, has less need for protein than her husband; and the grandparent has still less need due to both age and the difficulty of digesting protein. Instead of offering each person the type and quantity of protein he or she needs for optimal health, we give protein in the same amount to every person irrespective of age or special circumstance.

When you are going in for surgery, when you are pregnant or lactating, or when you are under stress, exercising regularly, or growing, you require more protein than under normal conditions.

The average person's lack of knowledge on protein is as great as their ignorance concerning carbohydrates and the distinction between the empty calories from white sugar and the much better utilized calories from, for example, brown rice.

We must now take a careful look at protein to see what role it plays in our life.

To many Americans, good nutrition *means* protein. They know they need something called protein. As a result, they usually take too much. Most of our protein requirements could be met with about six ounces of complete protein a day. It's been estimated that the average American consumes upward of 100 grams of protein a day. That may be almost double what we actually need.

Let's sit down for dinner with that typical American family mentioned earlier. They associate meat with strength, well-developed musculature, and an active, hearty life. They think of their heroes—the athlete, the cowboy, the rugged outdoorsman—as meat eaters. And they believe the strength of these mythlike figures somehow derives from regular consumption of beefsteak.

The father, our host tonight, is proud that, as his income has increased, steak has appeared more and more frequently at his dinner table, replacing chicken, ground meat, veal, pork, and other cuts of meat that used to be less expensive. As part of the upper middle class, he feels proud that he can provide his family with the fruits of his labor. He urges his young son to "eat hearty"—and eating hearty means, to him, eating plenty of good, red meat. It doesn't occur to him that the diet he is urging on his offspring might be—at best—too much of a good thing.

The Advantages of Meat

Now in one sense, father does know best. Meat *does* have an advantage as a source of protein—not just father's favored steak, but all meats cut directly from the animal: veal, pork, lamb, chicken, turkey, etc. (This advantage does not necessarily hold for sausage, luncheon meats, hot dogs, chicken rolls, or other processed meats.) Meats are among the foods that supply *complete protein:* they contain all eight of the essential amino acids, the building blocks of protein. And they also supply other nutrients, such as iron and B vitamins, in which many vegetables are deficient. They contain fats we can use for energy, heat insulation, and a variety of metabolic functions. Many of our organs, including our nerves, can make good use of this fat (although unsaturated fats from vegetable or fish sources would be preferable).

However, father is probably not aware that, along with those amino acids, B vitamins, and saturated fats, his family is also taking into the body some unwanted visitors.

Chemicals in Your Meat

For instance, along with the roast beef that they are eating tonight, they might be obtaining some type of growth-stimulating hormones, even the banned DES—diethylstilbestrol—the artificial sex hormones that were given to women all over America in the 1950s and 1960s in order to prevent miscarriage. It was later found to be ineffective and to have carcinogenic consequences for the daughters and sons born to women who took it. DES was also fed to beef cattle because it slows down the animals' metabolism, making them fatter quicker. Though it is now banned for such use, illegal residues still appear.

That juicy roast beef would also supply them with unwanted antibiotics. These are administered to the cattle primarily because a large percentage of feedlot animals are fed as much as thirty pounds of grain a day, but they can only transform the food into three or four pounds of muscle and fat. That enormous overfeeding causes painful liver abscesses which in turn affect profits. So the cattle are simply given antibiotics such as oxytetracycline.

When animals are kept crowded together in close confinement, standing knee deep in excrement, fed twenty-four hours a day under bright lights on conveyor belts, they are prone to epidemic diseases such as respiratory ailments, foot rot, and diarrhea. For further protection, they are given additional medication such as streptomycin, another antibiotic.

Nor is that the only tampering. The cattle are also given tranquilizers so they will not mind their miserable, cramped existence, and will eat despite their lack of exercise.

The animals, of course, can pass on to the consumer, through their flesh, many of the chemicals that were given them to turn them into mechanized feeding machines. You can't really insulate yourself from this chemical abuse because there is no listing on the steak or roast beef of all the chemicals used—more than 2,700 chemicals are allowed in the processing of meats.

Eating these unwelcome additives along with your meat could have serious consequences for your health and that of your family. Imagine the mother of the family you are visiting sitting at the dining table eating that roast beef, as she has been eating it nearly every day for years. She believes that it provides her with strength. At the same time, suppose she has been suffering from localized infections and has been taking antibiotics on and off for twenty years. Between the antibiotics she has been taking deliberately, and those used in animal production coming through her food supply, it is entirely possible that the bacteria in her body have developed an immunity to many if not all the antibiotics she has tried. If she were to come down with a severe infection, the antibiotics might not work as a result. She could die from bacterial death due to antibiotic-resistant bacteria. She would not know that her bacterial infection had developed this resistance in part because of her constant ingestion of highly potent antibiotics. It is conceivable that the chemicals in the meat she was eating for strength could ultimately cause her to succumb to pneumonia or some other infection.

If the animals were kept in clean, spacious surroundings, these antibiotics would rarely be necessary. However, because of the manure and encrusted filth present in cattle and pig pens, they are a necessary precaution against rampant disease. Unfortunately, the fact they are used routinely no doubt encourages the agribusiness dealers who handle the cattle and hogs to be less interested in animal sanitation than antibiotics.

Nor are antibiotics and tranquilizers the only chemicals your hosts may be eating tonight with the roast beef. The cow that provided the beef had to eat to get so fat and juicy. Unfortunately, she is not likely to have eaten grains or soybeans grown on an organic farm—your hosts tonight don't buy their beef in health food stores. As a result, that cow —like most of us—gobbled down quite a quantity of pesticide along with her feed. Her metabolism stored it up and concentrated it in her flesh—especially the liver and fat tissues, but the rest of her body, too —to pass along to you.

What's Missing in Meat

Antibiotics and other chemicals are not the only obstacles to health our typical American family faces as a result of making meat the main element of each meal.

Let's look more closely at father's plate. Several slices of roast beef fill most of it. He may like his roast beef sliced thin, but he piles up the slices on his plate. There's hardly any room left on the side for his baked potato. Beside his plate, in a bowl so small you could hold it in the palm of your hand, sits a salad of iceberg lettuce and bottled dressing.

What he's getting in this meal is a high portion of fat and chemical residues. What he is missing is an adequate portion of vitamins and minerals.

True, the meat supplies complete protein—but possibly more than he really needs. And by the time he finishes a pound or so of roast beef, he's really not very interested in eating his vegetables, such as they are. He throws a few pats of butter onto his potato—still more saturated fat —eats the inside and discards the skin as waste. He doesn't realize he's throwing out a fine source of fiber and vitamin C—neither of which is to be found in his roast beef. And by eating so little salad, he's short-changing himself of magnesium—a mineral found in leafy greens and needed for the proper functioning of nerve tissue and of the muscles he thinks his meat is taking care of. Still more pertinent to a particular problem of his, he is losing another source of fiber.

Father's overreliance on meat at the expense of other foods—particularly whole grains, legumes, fruits, and vegetables—has led to a lack of fiber in his diet. Fiber is necessary for maintaining healthy bowel movements. It stimulates peristalsis, the rhythmic wavelike movements that move food through the intestine. Fiber also allows more moisture in the fecal matter so it does not stagnate.

Father has thought it to be completely natural for the past twenty years to be taking a laxative virtually every day. He does not realize he is addicted to them or that they actually contribute to his constipation.

As a result of lack of fiber, the transit time of food through his digestive system, instead of being twenty-four to thirty-six hours—normal for optimal health—is incredibly slow, often taking upward of ninety hours from the time it is ingested until it is passed through the body. During these ninety hours, disease-producing microorganisms can multiply, putrifying the protein in his intestines. Picture what happens to meat dropped by mistake behind the stove for four days and left there to rot. And don't forget that the body temperature is 98.6° Fahrenheit. The slowness and pressure of the progress of food through his intestines could contribute to him developing diverticulitis, small pouchlike bumps in the intestine where bacteria and putrified matter collect in a sort of chronic infection. It also causes poor absorption of the nutrients in the food he eats. All this because the amount of protein that he eats has replaced the more nourishing fiber-rich foods in his diet.

If he is not careful, he—or anyone in his family—could end up with cancer of the colon. In fact, the National Cancer Institute has released a five-year study that implicates high consumption of beef in cancer of the colon.

Summary

In the mind of most Americans, protein has almost a glamorous image, as the essence of nutrition.

We pay very little attention to how much we actually need based on our biological individuality. This amount varies with our weight, age, and the amount of stress we are under. Pregnant and lactating women also have increased protein needs.

While meat is an excellent source of complete protein and B vitamins, the typical American diet, with its emphasis on beef, pork, and processed meats, has serious drawbacks. Marbled beef, long considered the prestige meat, is high in saturated fats, as are pork and processed meats. Beef cattle are fed a wide range of growth-stimulating hormones, antibiotics, and tranquilizers. DES, now banned because of its carcinogenic effects, was one of these hormones. But there remain nearly 3,000 chemicals with which it is still legal to douse cattle, and any of these can affect your health. Antibiotics, for example, can alter your intestinal flora, and can become ineffectual when taken repeatedly. In addition, pesticides and other chemicals from cattle feed concentrate in the animals' flesh (particularly in the liver).

Finally, overreliance on protein at the expense of high-fiber foods (grains, beans, fibers, fruit) can cause constipation, diverticulitis, cancer of the colon, and other diseases of the intestines.

Dangers of a High-Protein Weight-Loss Diet

The teenage daughter sitting at the table is one of twenty million Americans who are regularly on high-protein crash reducing diets. She is under the impression that by eating a great deal of protein, she is consuming a minimum amount of calories, and so will lose weight. Nothing could be further from the truth. In point of fact, eight ounces of beef contains upward of 500 calories, because beef is only approximately 22 percent protein. It contains an appreciable amount of fat, and the rest is water. She could be eating three or four giant salads, including several vegetables, raw or cooked, crammed with high quantities of nourishing vitamins and minerals, for 300 to 400 calories. They would also provide her with adequate fiber bulk, which would make her feel full, in addition to aiding in peristalsis. Instead, she is following one of the many fad diets which have made small fortunes for their promoters while being of dubious benefit to their followers. (There are lots of high-protein diets; they've been around for generations now, always marketed as brand new. With all the mystique attached to protein by the American food industry, it is hardly surprising that protein should be touted as having magical weight-loss properties.)

She may or may not lose weight on whichever high-protein, low-carbohydrate diet she is trying tonight. But more important, what risks is she taking with the diet?

To begin with, a diet of all-the-meat-she-wants but little or no bread, vegetables, or fruit is seriously imbalanced nutritionally. She is losing all the benefits of fiber for health and for the feeling of fullness it brings without excessive calories. The diet is also forcing her body to use protein both from her food intake and the catabolism (breaking down) of her lean muscle tissue for the purpose to which it is least suited: providing energy.

As she read in the book that advised her to go on this high-protein diet, her body is in a state similar to that of starvation, called "ketosis." All the fat she is eating, along with the meat, is causing her body to produce compounds called ketones. At low levels ketones are relatively harmless. But eating too little carbohydrates is causing some toxicity effects. She's pleased to note that she's not particularly hungry—in fact, she feels somewhat nauseous on this diet. This is one effect of those ketones. There are at least forty known cases—as of 1977—of people on high-protein, low-carbohydrate diets (most using liquid protein) dying. The diet can contribute to a host of medical problems.

Is she losing weight effectively on this low-carbohydrate diet? There is some evidence that her body is primarily excreting water and salt, especially at the beginning of the diet. While losing several pounds the first few days has been encouraging, this probably won't last for long. For losing weight steadily and over the long term, she would do just as well on a diet high in complex carbohydrates and much lower in saturated fats; or on the traditional, balanced, low-calorie diet.

If she keeps up the diet long enough, she may be increasing her risk of heart disease. Meat, butter, and other foods high in saturated fats, cholesterol, and sodium have been implicated as contributors to coronary heart disease.

She is lucky that she is on a high-protein diet involving food rather than one involving liquid protein, however. Such a diet can also cause serious damage to your health. The liquid protein, usually from collagen or gelatin, is inferior to that found in eggs, dairy products, or meat. Several obese women died after following the liquid protein diet; it is strongly discouraged.[1, 2]

Challenging the Theory Behind High-Protein Diets

Both of these diets are based on the concept, first proposed in 1903, of "protein stores." Some of the promoters of these diets claim the body isn't hurt by eating excess protein—that it just stores the excess away for future use. But no one has yet discovered where the protein is stored; nor has the existence of "protein stores" been established in controlled experiments with human subjects. In fact, we have no protein stores as we do for fat and carbohydrate.

This means that the body must work overtime to dispose of excess protein. This can be quite stressful—especially on the kidneys. When the body metabolizes protein, a waste product called urea builds up in the blood. It has to be excreted through the kidneys. They need extra water to do the job, and can be harmed if they don't get it. It's especially dangerous for older people, whose kidneys may be weak to begin with, to eat too much protein. As we age, our kidney function decreases, yet grandmother is eating almost as much meat as her granddaughter on the high-protein diet!

The whole high-protein controversy spotlights once again the American tendency to fixate on *quantity* and forget about *quality*. No one nutrient group is intrinsically harmful or beneficial. What is important is the specific content of a particular food. Twenty-five grams of protein from poached eggs on whole grain bread have far more nutritional value than fifty grams from a poor-quality gelatin drink. They provide fiber, B vitamins, and minerals in addition to their protein content.

Summary

The typical American protein, fat, and sugar-laden diet leads many people, invariably, to become overweight.

Because we think so highly of protein, many people experiment with the high-protein, low-carbohydrate diets which become popular every few years.

These diets are often high in calories, because of meat's fat content; fresh vegetables and salads are much lighter fare, and their bulk (fiber), missing from low-carbohydrate diets, makes them filling.

A long-term high-protein diet can cause heart disease (because of the saturated fats) and kidney problems (due to the difficulty of disposing of urea, a waste product of protein metabolism and excess sodium).

There are several theories of weight loss on high-protein diets. The body goes into ketosis when not enough carbohydrates are consumed, causing it to use fats and also body protein for energy. High levels of ketones can be slightly toxic. The idea of protein stores is now discredited—your body has no extra stores of protein. That is why, normally, it uses carbohydrates and fats as fuel, protecting the protein used in building cells and excreting excess protein.

Poor-Quality Highly Processed Protein Foods

The young son is eating the same roast beef as the rest of his family tonight. For breakfast, they all ate bacon and eggs together. But for lunch, the son ran across the street from his school for a hot dog or hamburger—or maybe he bought one in the school lunch program. Having seen them advertised on television, the parents are convinced that these are completely natural foods and that their son is getting proper nutrition.

What they're not being told about the processed meat they think is perfectly nutritious is that it may be made in part from the carcass of a diseased animal.

When an animal has cancer, very often the meat cutters will cut out and throw away the cancerous organs—and then send the rest of the carcass on for processing. In one year alone, 2.4 million cattle whose livers were cancerous or tubercular were sent on for packaging as meat. Not a very appetizing thought!

Do you notice that the child seems a bit restless at the table? Depending on whether his hot dog was labeled all meat, frankfurters or wieners, or imitation frankfurters, he may also have ingested artificial flavoring in his lunch. Artificial flavors and preservatives can cause hyperactivity in certain allergic children. Monosodium glutamate, which can cause a headache and dizziness, may also have been present. Sodium nitrate, dextrose, water, and a wide variety of animal products are some other common ingredients. Under the law these products can contain upward of 15 percent nonmeat ingredients, including artificial flavorings, colorings, and preservatives.

Even all-meat frankfurters may contain pork, lamb, and goat in any proportion and up to 15 percent chicken. The child would probably not have found it appetizing to learn that his frankfurters could contain animal products such as beef lips, pork lips, snout, tail gristle, blood, and lungs. If there were chicken in it, it might take the form of ground chicken skin, chicken fat, or even pulverized chicken bone.

Mother thought she was saving money by giving her son less than a dollar for a hot dog lunch. She saw it as an inexpensive lunch for her children considering that it contained protein. It is important for her to learn that a) it's not quality protein and b) it's expensive protein. A hot dog may contain over 50 percent moisture. Thirty to forty percent of it is fat. That leaves around 10 to 13 percent of the hot dog as protein. *Consumer Reports* has calculated that the average cost of one pound of protein from hot dogs is from $6.98 to $7.94 a pound. That's no saving!

It's a bad buy in terms of health, as well. Hamburgers, hot dogs, bologna, and other sliced luncheon meats are extremely vulnerable to rampant bacterial growth. When the grinding machines break down the beef or pork into tiny pieces to make processed meats, that causes the cells to break down and the fluids in the cells to be released. The semiliquid medium that results is the perfect environment for bacteria to breed. In fact, food scientists generally agree that the bacteria count of the average piece of meat is about 10 million per gram. This means that putrefaction has begun to set in. *Consumer Reports* analyzed thirty-two brands of USDA-inspected hot dogs and found 40 percent of the brands tested had begun to spoil. Some bacteria are grown in airtight containers, and some airtight containers are not really airtight. Thus, that hamburger for lunch may be contributing to the child's vulnerability to infection.

Nitrites, Anemia, and Low Blood Pressure

The husband who likes his bacon in the morning with his eggs may not be aware that the morning protein is loaded with nitrites and other preservatives, as are the bologna, hot dogs, or salami his family eats for lunch.

Nitrites make meat red. In its natural form, the meat would otherwise turn to a putrid gray.

Have you ever noticed if you cut your skin, the blood first comes out red because of the oxygen in it, and then it oxidizes and turns purple? It loses oxygen and coagulates.

That is similar to what happens when they slaughter an animal. It turns bright red immediately after slaughtering, then purple-gray. As they process the meat it eventually becomes a gray-blue color.

Once they put sodium nitrite into meat, the nitrite is broken down into nitrous acid which combines with the hemoglobin in the meat to form a permanent red color.

Unfortunately for all of the people sitting at this table, there is no difference between the way the nitrites interact with the blood of the dead carcass and the way they might interact in the human beings who eat it. They function by inactivating a certain percentage of the red blood cells which carry oxygen through the body. In children this is especially dangerous because it can produce a condition called methemoglobinemia—inactivated hemoglobin. If too many red blood cells are inactivated, severe poisoning and sometimes death can result. This has actually occurred when children have eaten highly nitrited hot dogs —hot dogs containing as many as 200 parts per million of nitrites.

In addition to small children, anemic people are extremely susceptible to methemoglobinemia, as are people with low blood pressure.

In fact, the grandmother might have been to a doctor who used sodium nitrite as a prescription to lower her high blood pressure! The therapeutic dose that the physician probably gave her was about 30 milligrams, the amount legally allowed in one-third pound of meat or fish.

Even if you don't have high blood pressure, your blood pressure could be lowered for up to two hours after eating meat or fish containing legal levels of nitrites. That is only part of what the husband is not seeing which could account for his midmorning fatigue.

Suppose he's eaten four strips of bacon for breakfast, not an uncommon amount! The nitrite level could be extremely high in the bacon, so he's had a portion of his hemoglobin inactivated and he may be fatigued, tired, and sluggish—not energetic and competitive like that cowboy image he admires so much.

Nitrites and Cancer

Something else that would truly shock and surprise this family is that nitrites are known as one of the three ingredients which can combine in the stomach to form nitrosamines. Nitrosamines have been known to induce cancer in rats; every type of cancer in all types of rats. It only takes tiny amounts—as small as two parts per million. Experiments conducted at the Oak Ridge Laboratory by Dr. William Lijinsky showed that nitrosamines are one of the most formidable, versatile, cancer-causing substances ever discovered.

Nitrosamines are created when there is a mildly acid solution consisting of nitrites and amines together. Beer, wine, tea, cigarette smoke, fish, and cereals all contain amines. So do some prescription drugs, including oral contraceptives, antidepressants, tranquilizers, analgesics, nasal decongestants, antihistamines, and diuretics. Nitrites and amines come together to form nitrosamines in the stomach like a perfect test-tube case. Think of what happens when the husband has a beer with his ham sandwich. Nitrites from the ham sandwich combine with amines from the beer—and he's eating nitrosamines. The wife smokes a cigarette after her corned beef sandwich—and she's increased her cancer risk more than she knows.

Sodium and High Blood Pressure

Grandmother, as mentioned, has high blood pressure, and the rest of the family believes they have inherited a genetic predisposition for it.

In reality, grandma's high blood pressure may be caused entirely by her diet. The saturated fats contained in meat are not the only problem. She's lived in the United States all her life. Imagine how many hamburgers and hot dogs she's consumed over the years.

Did you know that a hamburger with relish, ketchup, and a pickle could contain over 3,000 milligrams of sodium? That hot dogs, too, are loaded with sodium, both from sodium nitrite and regular salt?

We only need, on the average, 250 to 800 milligrams of sodium a day. Many people get 10,000 to 15,000 milligrams!

The resulting epidemic of high blood pressure should be no surprise. All this extra sodium can damage the kidneys. Your kidneys filter waste materials from your blood and control blood pressure. They need the right level of sodium to function well.

This whole family is not only gorging themselves with more protein than they need—which can also hurt the kidneys—they are also consuming far too much sodium in the process.

Summary

Hot dogs, hamburgers, sausages, salami, bologna, and luncheon meats are as American as apple pie—but so are hyperactivity, high blood pressure, and cancer. Unfortunately, these phenomena are connected.

The connection is in the chemicals added to processed foods. Many children are sensitive to the artificial dyes, flavors, and preservatives in these foods. Hyperactivity or other allergic symptoms may result.

One group of coloring agents is particularly dangerous. Nitrites keep meat red by combining with hemoglobin—and they can affect human as well as porcine blood, causing a form of anemia called methemoglobinemia. Nitrites are used pharmacologically to lower blood pressure; they do the same thing whether in a pill or a hot dog. On the other hand, sodium nitrite or sodium chloride (table salt) can raise blood pressure and damage kidneys.

Still worse, nitrites combine with amines (present in cigarette smoke, fish, cereals, and many common prescription and over-the-counter drugs) to form highly carcinogenic nitrosamines.

Nor are there any advantages to eating processed meats. They are so high in water and fats that the small amount of protein they contain is actually quite expensive. Furthermore, they often contain ground-up remains of cancerous animals and unappetizing parts like lips, snout, tail, gristle, blood, and lungs.

Meat Consumption and Food Allergy

Still another problem may account for the "low moments" several members of this family experience during the day. Because they eat meat at virtually every meal (with the possible exception of the occasional peanut butter and jelly sandwich of which the youngest is still fond), they are eating both beef and pork every single day: pork in their bacon, sausages, luncheon meat, ham, pork chops, beef in their hamburger, roast beef sandwiches, steaks, etc.

Now there is a danger to eating *any* food every single day, a danger that has been discovered by physicians whose specialty is clinical ecology. This is the danger of food allergy addiction. It is possible to become allergic to the foods we eat most often, without being aware that an allergy is developing. This is because this type of allergy disguises itself as an addiction: like a drug or alcohol addict, we feel sick when we *don't* eat the food often enough. Even though it is really the food that is making us sick, it appears to us as if it is the food that makes us well! Food allergies can affect any organ of the body. They can make you feel tired, edgy, or nervous; they can give you a depression or a headache; they can cause arthritis, stomachache, and many other health problems.

It is very possible that, because they have been eating the same two foods every day for years, one or more members of this family are now allergic to either or both of them. Perhaps the son's mild hyperactivity is caused, not by food additives, but by allergy to the foods themselves. Perhaps the grandmother's high blood pressure is an allergic reaction, or the daughter's weight problem (which she is, ironically, trying to solve by eating almost *nothing but* beef and pork). This family would be able to find out whether this was the case if they varied their diet, rotating beef and pork with other sources of protein so they didn't eat any one food more often than every four or five days for three months. In this way they could test the effect of different foods on their metabolisms. And they could prevent many food allergies from developing by making sure to vary their diet from day to day instead of sticking so rigidly to the traditional meat and potatoes.

So this typical meat-eating family, who thought they were treating themselves to a nutritional plus by eating protein from beef or pork at nearly every meal, have in reality been doing themselves a substantial disservice. They are eating too many calories and excess saturated fat, increasing their cholesterol intake, consuming a high degree of sodium and nitrites in their hot dogs and hamburgers, and absorbing uncounted chemical additives, antibiotics, tranquilizers, color stabilizers, growth stimulating hormones, etc.—none of which they are aware of.

The Cumulative Effect of Food Additives

If tonight's dinner was the only meat they ate containing those chemicals, it would not be that serious. But what happens when they're consuming these foods every single day, and the effects are cumulative?

The body becomes a polluted reservoir. The family doesn't put water in their gas tank; they don't put mud in their carburetor; they don't put concrete in their radiator; they know what fuels the car needs to function properly. Yet they continue to put unhealthy, unnecessary, polluting products into their bodies and assume the body can tolerate it and that nothing wrong will occur.

If the human body were as simple a machine as our cars, we would quickly see the danger that is done. The effects are usually longer term in the body—in the shortening of our life span and the onset of chronic and degenerative disease.

Summary

The cumulative effects of meat eating are difficult to define. Unconsciously, we may become addicted to any food we eat every day: the result can be allergies whose symptoms can only be alleviated by continuing to eat the food frequently—or by going cold turkey.

No one knows the cumulative effect of all the chemicals in our meat. But we do know that vegetarians tend to suffer less from degenerative diseases such as heart disease and cancer as well as intestinal digestive disorders.

Family No. 2: Less Red Meat, More Fish and Poultry

Now let's go next door to the neighbors of the family we have just visited. Family Number Two consists of an older couple, nearing retirement, whose high blood pressure and general aches and pains have led them to become more health conscious. They are concerned about cholesterol and saturated fats, and so they eat very little red meat anymore. When they do, they make sure it is lean, and they cut away any fat that remains. They are especially concerned about nitrites and the other chemicals that are added to frankfurters and luncheon meats, and they have totally eliminated those economically wasteful, additive-laden foods from their diet. Instead, they eat chicken and fish, which they feel are much healthier. And they don't eat too much of these—they know that four or five ounces a day provides them with enough protein.

They have changed nothing else in their diet, except possibly lowering their sugar intake and trying to eat more green vegetables and fresh fruit. They've bought a vegetable steamer, perhaps, to help conserve vitamins lost in boiling vegetables, and they like to nibble and serve nuts and seeds with dried fruit rather than candy, cookies, or potato chips.

They've invited you to Sunday dinner, and are serving roast chicken as the main dish.

If you ask them why they eat chicken now as often as they used to eat beef, they'll tell you an interesting story.

"We used to feel that chicken was pretty much for the poor people," says the husband. "It's less expensive than beef, and we used to get it sometimes, but we thought of beef as the normal American diet —one of the privileges of affluence.

"But you know, we've been doing some interesting reading lately. Did you know that in many societies the poor people eat a healthier diet than the rich? The Oriental aristocracy, for instance, used to eat white rice—that's why most Chinese and Japanese restaurants offer white rice with the food; it's considered more elegant than brown rice. The poor peasants who worked for them, meanwhile, ate brown rice. The aristocracy suffered nutritional deficiencies even in good times. Lack of B vitamins can cause beriberi and pellagra. The peasants, having the benefits of brown rice, only got these diseases when they couldn't get any rice at all.

"So we feel that by eating 'peasant food' we may have taken a step down socially—but it's a step up nutritionally."

This couple is partly right. They have taken a step up nutritionally —but it is only one small step. You can feel better about digging in to dinner with them—but only a little better.

The Real Story of Chicken

They may believe they're eating peasant food, but if they have an image of the chicken being raised in a beautiful, pastoral scene at a farm —of its being fed grains by a woman wearing an apron as it clucks merrily through the day, laying healthy eggs and cooing softly on its roost in the evening—that image is sheer illusion. Their chicken was born and died in a factory—an animal factory, as Jim Mason, leading farm animal rights advocate, calls it.

Today's chicken lives without ever seeing the light of day. In fact, the light in its artificially created environment is controlled so that it will remain subdued. It is packed so tightly together with two to four other birds in a tiny twelve-inch cage that it cannot even flap its wings —it can barely move at all. Its beak is often removed so it won't peck its cage mates to death in frustration. Its environment is temperature-controlled. Its food comes by on conveyor belts.

Naturally, getting no exercise or fresh air and living under such crowded conditions, such a bird is extremely susceptible to disease. By comparison to birds that were once allowed to roam and peck and grow healthy, today's chicken is tasteless. It is usually killed at four or six months of age, or earlier.

Instead of providing fresh air, sunshine, and exercise, the business-men who boast about how good their chickens taste find ways to dis-guise inferior quality. The chemist has replaced the farmer. Artificial dyes are added to chicken feed to give the pasty whiteness of the factory-chicken's flesh a more natural golden color. To give the chick-ens flavor, some are injected with an enzyme called hyaluronidase and a mixture of seasonings such as nutmeg, thyme, and garlic. The en-zymes help dispense the herbs throughout the bird. The fragrant aroma of the herbs and spices will overwhelm the acrid scent the enzymes give off during cooking. The diseases to which the chicken is susceptible, due to its brief, unsanitary existence, include occidosis, a parasitic condition. To help keep down these infections certain breeders use drugs that will kill all bacteria. Antibiotics and nitrofurans made from poisonous arsen-ic could be part of the bird's diet. Arsenic, in the form of arsenalic acid, has been fed poultry since 1950. Still more antibiotics may be added after the chicken is slaughtered: chicken carcasses are sometimes dipped in antibiotic solution to increase their shelf life to up to twenty-one days. That roast chicken may be older than you realize. Antibiotics serve the same purpose in chicken factories as in cattle feedlots. They protect against infection when the conditions are filthy, and they affect growth.

Most people think, when they get sick after eating chicken, that they have ptomaine poisoning or salmonella poisoning. Actually, what might be the cause of severe diarrhea, cramps, and vomiting in some cases is a twenty-four-hour virus whose identity they have mistaken for salmonella. This virus is found in eggs and chicken and is not easily diagnosed. Upward of perhaps 40 million Americans suffer from it each year.

The worst viral disease to which chickens are susceptible is leukosis, a viral cancer specific to chickens. It is estimated that nearly 95 percent of all chickens have leukosis.[3]

Whatever bacteria exists in the chicken when it is killed may be multiplied many times by freezing. It's not the freezing that does it; the problem is, frozen poultry may be thawed and frozen again many times before it is shipped. Once shipped, it may be as long as two years before it is sold. Be glad you are being served fresh and not frozen chicken this evening.

So the Sunday chicken dinner that you are eating with Family Number Two might still contain chemicals, just like the roast beef at the first house. There are probably fewer—chickens are smaller, and since they live a much shorter life than cattle, the chemicals, antibiotics, and pesticides from the feed have less time to build up in their system. But this is a far cry from healthy "peasant fare." And the friendly, thoughtful people with whom you are dining would probably be sickened to realize the cramped, sunless, and wretched conditions under which their chicken was bred.

Eggs from Factory Chickens

The sick state of the chickens is reflected in the eggs they lay. Take a look at your eggs tomorrow morning. Egg yolks are supposed to be firm, round, and yellow. Are yours firm, or are they watery, with a soupy consistency? Whatever their appearance, like the chickens, they probably contain some of the pesticides used on the grains fed to the chickens, along with the antibiotics deliberately added.

Tonight's leftovers will end up as tomorrow's chicken salad. It probably has not occurred to Family Number Two to eliminate store-bought mayonnaise from their diet. One ingredient of mayonnaise is eggs. Now, the eggs that are used to manufacture mayonnaise are not necessarily the ones you buy—they could be the ones that have a hairline crack; the ones no one would buy at the store for fear of salmonella infection. Yet the mayonnaise manufacturers may be glad to buy them at a discount, not knowing if they are cracked.

The eggs that drop on the floor and crack may also be sent to a manufacturing plant where the yolks and whites are separated, flash frozen, and sent to bakers. There they may be incorporated in a wide variety of baked goods. It is fortunate that Family Number Two rarely eats store-bought cake anymore.

Summary

Poultry is not a very good substitute for beef in the diet. While it may be given fewer hormones, tranquilizers, and antibiotics, that is only because its life span is shorter. The miserable, dark, crowded, and stressful conditions under which it is raised require that it be dyed and injected with enzymes and herbs to mask its poor quality. Infections due to unsanitary conditions are suppressed with antibiotics and arsenic-containing nitrofurans. Sometimes the carcasses are dipped in antibiotics to lengthen their shelf life. These may not be effective in preventing bacteria levels in frozen poultry from building up due to repeated thawing and refreezing.

Eggs from factory chickens reflect the sickly conditions of the chickens. Packagers often unknowingly use damaged, cracked eggs in mayonnaise, baked goods, and other processed foods. It is far preferable to eat eggs from free-running hens fed preservative-free feed, obtainable from health food stores, even though these are more expensive.

Family No. 3: Fish as the Main Protein Source

The third household we will visit is that of a young couple with an infant daughter. They are more health conscious than their neighbors, and they believe their diet is healthier and their social consciousness higher. They read consumer publications and listen to nutrition programs. They have given up all meat, including fowl, for a number of reasons, and eat mainly fish and some shellfish as sources of protein. Financially, they feel that meat is too expensive; ounce for ounce, it is the most expensive form of complete protein. (Seven ounces of beef has the same quantity of protein as a cup of skim milk, but it costs many times more—and contains about sixty grams of fat as well.) Nutritionally, they feel they should avoid saturated fats and they are aware that fish is generally less fatty than meat. They know that chicken, while it has less fat than beef, only contains about 20 percent protein, not much different from beef. Besides, as they are aware, cattle, hogs, and chickens are fed numerous hormones, antibiotics, and other chemicals, and they prefer to avoid as many chemicals as possible for themselves and their child.

The Moral Perspective on Meat Eating

They also have moral reasons for preferring fish to meat or fowl. They have read about the conditions under which chickens, hogs, and cattle—especially the young calves raised for veal which are denied iron to keep their flesh white-colored—are raised and slaughtered, and they don't want to be the beneficiaries of the cruel treatment of animals. They figure that fish lead free lives, at least until they are caught, and that anyway, fish and especially shellfish have less sophisticated nervous systems, and therefore a lower degree of consciousness than birds or mammals like us.

This couple has eliminated all refined sugar from their diet, as well as the obvious saturated fat sources. They breast-feed their baby, and wouldn't dream of offering it food containing refined sugar. They eat at least two servings of dark green leafy vegetables and several fruits every day. They've cut out white bread and are only eating whole grain bread. They eat a variety of grains. Some of their protein needs are met by dairy foods: skim milk, yogurt, cheese, and eggs. (They buy their eggs at the health food store, even though that costs them extra, so that they are sure the eggs come from free-running rather than factory chickens.)

Yet, their dinners fall into the same pattern they learned from their parents: an animal food for complete protein; potatoes, rice, or noodles for carbohydrates; a green vegetable and a salad for vitamins and fiber. Since they have eliminated beef, veal, pork, and chicken from their diets, this means that almost every night they eat fish as the centerpiece of their meal.

Fish: Fatty, Perishable, and Painted with Preservatives

Eating fish every night is not as healthy a practice as they have been led to believe. For one thing, they are getting a lot more fat from it than they realize. Like land animals, fish vary enormously in their fat content. Some are upward of 20 percent fat. Albacore, herring, mackerel, salmon, shad, sardines, smelt, and tuna are among the fatty fish. If they want to reduce the fat content of their diet, they should stick to lean fish, with a fat content of under 5 percent, such as bass, halibut, flounder, perch, and sole.

Another problem with fish is that it is highly perishable. Once the fish is dead, digestive enzymes perforate the fish's intestines and attack the entire carcass. Bacterial decomposition and contamination begin immediately and progress right through the entire storage time, even when it is frozen; fish should not be kept more than a week to ten days, even frozen. Extended storage in the freezer will cause the flesh of seafood to become dry, stringy, tough, and tasteless, at best, when it is finally cooked.

Our young couple sometimes buys their fish frozen. This is highly inadvisable. The United States Department of the Interior has discovered some frozen fish on the market over four years old!

By and large, this couple is too nutrition-conscious ever to buy frozen fish sticks. Besides possibly being old, fish sticks are often up to 50 percent bread and, like all but the freshest fish, may have a very high bacteria count.

But even the fresh fish our friends bought at the market to avoid the preservatives they know are found in meats, may have been treated with preservatives. Sodium benzoate, sodium nitrite, hydrogen peroxide, ozone, and chlorine are some of the chemicals which can sometimes be found on fresh fish.

Shellfish Concentrate Bacteria and Pollutants

This couple is very fond of shellfish, and eat it as often as they can afford to. Somehow, they have never been warned not to eat clams, mussels, oysters, crabs, or lobsters that have died before being cooked. (If a clam or oyster shell is not tightly closed, it has died.) They should be roasted or boiled alive. Unpleasant as that sounds, it is better than allowing a moment's extra multiplication for the microorganisms that concentrate in shellfish. Oysters have been known to concentrate polio virus twenty to sixty times greater than in the surrounding water. Shellfish can cause polio, infectious hepatitis, meningitis, typhoid, strep throat, gastroenteritis. Perhaps the Jewish kosher dietary prohibitions against shellfish are sensible health precautions.

Then there is the problem of water pollution. Our highly conscious young couple is well aware that this problem exists, but perhaps they don't realize quite how bad the situation is.

Except for sea clams and sea mussels, shellfish live in estuaries that are filled with the discharge of sewage. Shellfish nourish themselves by pumping up to 300 gallons of water per day through their tiny bodies; if the water contains sewage, then so do the shellfish. Thousands of hairlike cilia paddle water containing suspended particles, microorganisms, sand, and dissolved gases through the organism. The mouth, stomach, and intestines may contain substantial quantities of waste products, which may be one of the sources of the many disease microorganisms they contain.

Shellfish are not the only water creatures to absorb pollutants from the water. Other fish do, too. Family Number Three is certainly aware of the problem. They try to eat mainly freshwater fish, since they feel the ocean areas near the land, where most fish live, are too polluted.

Freshwater Fish and Domestic Water Pollution

What they are not aware of is that thirty-three states have waterways so contaminated with mercury that no fish should be consumed from them; and mercury is only one of many industrial pollutants. Originally, it was believed that inorganic mercury from industrial sources—which is the primary way that mercury gets into the water supply in America—would just settle harmlessly to the bottom and be inactivated.

THE DANGER OF MERCURY POISONING

Regrettably, this is not the case. Bacteria in the water converts inorganic mercury into highly toxic, highly absorbable methyl mercury. Methyl mercury then travels up the food chain—small fish are eaten by large fish which are eaten by still larger fish. Each time one fish is consumed by another fish, the concentration of mercury is increased many times. By the time the young couple eats their fish they are consuming a load of mercury.

Unfortunately, the mercury they are ingesting tonight will be with them for the rest of their life. Mercury poisoning is not uncommon and this young couple and their daughter, if they don't change their eating habits, might suffer in ten years from tremors, irritability, fatigue, headaches, metallic taste in their mouth, kidney damage, even insanity. Do you remember the Mad Hatter in *Alice's Adventures in Wonderland*? He was a figment of Lewis Carroll's imagination. But real hatters did used to go mad from mercury poisoning. It wasn't uncommon for a hatmaker to lose his sanity after a lifetime of breathing fumes from mercury-treated felt. Mercury poisoning is very serious.

THE DANGER OF NUCLEAR POLLUTION

In addition to chemical pollution, perhaps our friends are not aware of all the nuclear pollution that ends up in the world of the fish. The fish are attracted to the warm water near atomic reactors. They may consume plankton and sea vegetation and other fish that have absorbed radioactive waste that has leaked out of these reactors, and become radioactive to some degree.

Family Number Three would be frightened out of consuming all of the fish they eat if they knew how serious the water pollution problem is. They would certainly, at least, limit their intake of fish to the very smallest ones, in which the pollutants would not be so concentrated: sardines, herring, whitebait. They would avoid tuna, swordfish, and other sea giants. And they would begin to investigate how to eliminate fish from their diet altogether, in such a way that they would not cheat themselves of necessary protein.

The best person they might turn to for advice on this subject lives in our Household Number Four.

Summary

Fish has many advantages over meat or poultry as a source of protein, not the least of which is moral: they are not subjected to crowded, tortured living conditions. Fish is often a less expensive form of concentrated protein than meat. Lean fish such as bass, halibut, flounder, perch, and sole are low in fat and high in vitamins. (However, the fatty fish—albacore, herring, mackerel, salmon, shad, sardines, smelt, tuna—may contain upward of 20 percent fat.)

But the pollution of our rivers, streams, and ocean beds has altered fish's chemical composition, and they, too, may be doused with preservatives to inhibit the growth of the bacteria that contaminate fish from the moment it dies and that continue to spread even when the fish is frozen.

Shellfish are particularly dangerous, since they concentrate so much of the industrial pollutants, viruses, and bacteria from the often sewage-laden water with which they nourish themselves. Polio, infectious hepatitis, meningitis, typhoid, strep throat, and gastroenteritis have been linked to shellfish.

"Freshwater" fish are often contaminated with methyl mercury and even radioactive, nuclear wastes, while "ocean" shellfish, with the exception of sea clams and sea mussels, are full of sewage. The smaller fish, at least, contain lower levels of pollutants.

Household No. 4: The Vegetarian Alternative

Household Number Four is a young science teacher and amateur athlete. He is also a vegetarian. His parents regard him as somewhat eccentric, and perhaps he is: he grows a lot of his own vegetables so he is sure to get organically grown foods with as few pollutants in them as possible. At the drop of a hat, he will explain to you that the air and water on this continent are, for the most part, highly polluted, due primarily to industrial wastes. The water washes off crops sprayed with insecticides and forms rivers into which industrial wastes have been dumped. So even his home-grown, unprocessed, natural foods are not completely unspoiled.

If he invited you over for dinner, you'd have to drop by six or seven days in a row before you saw two meals that seemed anything near the same. And yet, he is not eating catch-as-catch-can like some bachelors; as an athlete, he approaches his meals scientifically, and gives food the attention necessary to insure that he gets enough protein. The other three households could profit from taking some science lessons from him. Because with these lessons they could be lengthening and improving the quality of their lives. And they could be avoiding many health problems, from constipation, diverticulitis, and cancer of the colon to high blood pressure and obesity, from infectious diseases and hyperactivity to the daily aches and pains that make so much money for the aspirin manufacturers and their agencies.

What does he eat if not meat or fish accompanied by potatoes, vegetable, and a salad?

The Variety of Foreign Vegetarian Cuisines

Depending on what night you joined him, you might find your main dish was Japanese, Italian, Mexican, Russian, or Middle Eastern fare, and was usually accompanied by at least a small salad. Perhaps it was Japanese brown rice and stir-fried vegetables with tofu (bean curd made from soybeans) on one night; Italian whole wheat spaghetti with mushroom sauce and grated cheese the next; Mexican brown rice and black beans, or corn tortillas with kidney beans and cheese another night; homemade Russian blintzes consisting of thin, whole wheat pancakes wrapped around a delicious cottage cheese and egg filler the next; and houmus or baba ghanoush (mashed chick-peas and eggplant, respectively), combined with sesame paste and served with whole wheat bread, still another night.

Salads, Soups, and Casseroles

His main dish could also be a huge garden salad, liberally sprinkled with sesame seeds and with a delicious yogurt dressing stirred into it; or a steaming, hearty soup accompanied by whole grain bread. In fact, he will tell you his summer specialties are giant, varied salads based on the vegetables from his garden, and his winter favorites are casseroles and soups. He will explain that these mixed-food dishes offer some of the best opportunities for combining various vegetable protein foods, including grains, beans, nuts, and seeds; that no two soups or salads need ever be exactly identical; and that they make leftovers seem like brilliant ideas.

If you ask him why he goes through such elaborate food preparations just to avoid eating meat, he will laugh and tell you it's not necessary for vegetarian eating to be complicated; he just makes a hobby of trying the foods of different nationalities, since he likes to cook. He will point out that the poor people of most nations rarely eat meat, so each culture has evolved various methods of combining staples to provide enough protein and some variety, even without meat.

Then he will grow serious, and outline his reasons for becoming a vegetarian.

Why Stop Eating Meat?

He began to decrease his meat intake in college, when as a science student he started reading about ecology. He learned that many of the chemicals and pollutants that go into meat—from the pesticides the animal eats with feed to the dyes that may be added by the wholesaler —remain in it when we eat the animal. He realized that the same thing holds true of fish and shellfish; our waterways are polluted, and so our fish and shellfish, from the ocean, lakes, and rivers, are all contaminated to one degree or another by sewage, industrial chemicals, pesticides, and sometimes preservatives. He discovered that the animals raised by high technology methods often come down with the diseases of stress such as cancer, and that the carcass of a cancer-ridden animal is considered acceptable if the tumor itself is cut away. Disgusted by what he read about our way of feeding ourselves, he resolved to find alternatives to meat.

Vegetable Protein

What he discovered is that there are many vegetables that contain protein. If they are properly combined with each other, there is no necessity for human beings to feel dependent on meat. Besides, indirect animal sources of complete protein such as eggs, milk, and other dairy products can provide a supplement to vegetables to fully guarantee adequate protein intake. (Technically, his diet is called lacto-ovo-vegetarian, because he eats milk and eggs in addition to vegetables.)

Other Vegetable Nutrients

Not only that, but a diet high in vegetable protein foods—beans, legumes, nuts, seeds, and tubers—offers many health advantages, he learned. Because their diet is low in saturated fat, vegetarians are better protected against arteriosclerosis and heart disease than meat eaters. Better yet, these foods supply a variety of other nutrients along with the protein.

Take one of his favorite lunches. He often carries to school with him a salad containing leftover brown rice, beans, peas, alfalfa sprouts, and tofu (and whatever other leftovers or loose greens he finds in the refrigerator that morning). This provides him with just as much balanced protein as the hamburger he would have eaten a few years earlier. Yet it also offers vitamins such as A, C, and some members of the B group. It contains, too, several minerals and an abundance of fiber, so important for good digestion and protection against gastrointestinal problems. It also provides energy from complex carbohydrates—especially important to an athlete like him.

The hamburger, on the other hand, contained no vitamin C and no fiber. What it may have contained were saturated fats, sodium, antibiotics, tranquilizers, hormones, DES, sodium nitrite, and other dyes, etc. Like most people, he used to eat his hamburgers with ketchup on a bun made from refined white flour. With the ketchup he was consuming liberal quantities of sugar and salt; with the flour, another host of additives. It's not difficult to see which of these two protein-filled meals is nutritionally superior!

The Economics of Meat Consumption

Despite the fact that he sometimes splurges on such relatively expensive treats as imported cheeses, pignolia nuts, and unsulfured, organically grown dried fruits from the health food store, he found his grocery bills declined sharply when he stopped buying meat for every meal.

Soon after that, he stumbled on another fact about the earth's protein resources that helped confirm his commitment to vegetarian cookery. It has to do with the economics of meat consumption. Meat represents an intensive use of the earth's protein resources. Animals are often fed with high-quality grain that could easily be consumed by human beings. If these grains were available to human beings, it could feed many more of us. The land devoted to raising feed for steers produces about a pound of protein (in the form of beef) per acre. The same acre planted with soybeans produces seventeen pounds of protein. Or to look at the figures another way: a pound of beef required eight times its weight in high-protein feed.

In today's world, where one-third of the earth's population faces starvation, he feels that high meat consumption by any one country is needlessly self-indulgent. If Americans ate 10 percent less meat, the savings in grain would be equivalent to the shortfall that produces starvation in India, according to Alex Hershaft, president of the Vegetarian Society and leading animal rights activist, in an interview in October 1982 on "Natural Living" on WBAI.

Summary

Vegetarian foods are as varied as the world's many national cuisines. In every country, people have learned to consume the proteins of grains, legumes tubers, nuts, seeds, and even starchy fruits so that they obtain complete proteins by combining various incomplete sources. This is economically practical both at the individual and global levels: it takes far more acres of land to produce a pound of beef protein than a pound of soy or wheat protein, since a cow must consume eight pounds of high-protein feed to produce a pound of beef protein. Human beings might as well eat that vegetable protein directly.

What Is Protein?

We can see why our science teacher feels his diet is preferable to eating meat. But how does he do it, and why is it possible to substitute other sources of protein for meat?

To understand the answer, we will have to take a look at exactly what protein is.

To a chemist, it's easy to recognize protein. He or she would look under a microscope and would note molecules in the form of long chains. The molecules would all combine the following four elements: carbon, oxygen, hydrogen, and nitrogen. In addition, various particular proteins might also include zinc, sulfur, iron, or potassium. These molecule chains would be formed from shorter chains. These smaller chains are called amino acids. They are the basic building blocks of protein.

You and I cannot look under a microscope to check out the shape of molecules and the carbon, hydrogen, nitrogen, and oxygen content of foods; and amino acids have no particular flavor like sugar or salt. They come combined in food with other nutrients. We can't tell just by tasting a food whether or not it contains amino acids, or which ones; we have to rely on what the food scientists tell us.

And what they say is that those building blocks, the amino acids, are the most important factors in determining the nutritive value of protein foods. Amino acids can be found in all protein-containing foods, in different combinations. A protein food's value lies in the particular combination of amino acids it contains, not in the source from which it is derived. That is why it is possible to get all the protein we need from combining nonmeat sources containing different amino acids. Since proteins in foods are usually found in combination with other nutrients, chemists look at protein foods and divide them into three categories:

Simple proteins contain only amino acids.

Conjugated proteins include another substance such as fat or carbohydrate in addition to amino acids.

Derived proteins are intermediate forms created by the partial breakdown of other proteins.

Most of the foods we eat contain conjugated proteins.

But nutritionists like to classify proteins according to which amino acids they contain, since the amino acids are so important in the problem of getting adequate protein.

The protein we eat contains twenty-three different amino acids in many combinations. Our body needs all of them. But we only have to worry about eight, since the body can manufacture the other fifteen by itself.

The Eight Essential Amino Acids

The eight that concern us we call the *essential amino acids*, because it is essential to our health that we get all of them in our food. In fact, we need each of them every day. When we talk about getting enough protein, we're really talking about consuming these amino acids regularly in the proper proportion and in the proper quantity.

You don't need to remember their names and special qualities. But in case you are interested, the eight essential amino acids are: valine, lysine, leucine, threonine, isoleucine, tryptophan, phenylalanine, and methionine. (Histidine is a ninth that is essential for children because of the role it plays in growth and physical development.[4])

Your body can use them most effectively if your food contains them in these proportions:

> one part tryptophan to
> two parts threonine and phenylalanine to
> three parts methionine, lysine, valine, and isoleucine, to
> three and a half parts leucine.

Egg whites provide these eight essential amino acids in just about these proportions. (That's not surprising—egg white is the protein food nature supplies to the chick embryo; the embryo uses the egg white as raw material for building itself into a ready-to-hatch chick.)

The proper quantity your body needs is .9 gram of protein per kilogram or 2.2 pounds of body weight. We'll discuss this question further later.

Protein Combining

Fortunately, you don't have to learn the amount and proportions of each of these amino acids contained in various foods in order to eat properly. You only have to learn which ones combine best with each other. Luckily, this seems to coincide with which ones taste best together!

What could be more harmonious than a peanut butter sandwich on whole wheat bread (better yet, with a glass of milk, assuming you're not allergic to dairy)? Than the rice and beans, or corn tortillas and refried beans, of Mexican fare? Than the Italians' favorite soup, pasta e fagioli, combining beans and wheat pasta? With the major cuisines of the world as your guide, the right combinations are easy to learn. We'll also discuss them in more detail later.

Nutritionists have divided all protein-containing foods into two groups for our convenience, according to the presence of the eight essential amino acids.

Complete proteins contain all the essential amino acids in approximately the correct proportions, and can therefore (in theory) satisfy all our protein requirements by themselves. This group includes meat, eggs, fish, and milk and other dairy products, as well as soybeans used as tempeh and tofu.

Incomplete proteins have some of the essential amino acids, but not all of them, and not in the necessary proportions. Some incomplete sources are cereal grains, nuts, seeds, legumes, and many vegetables. *Taken individually*, none of these sources would be a fully life-sustaining and building protein source. Taken in combination, they feed millions of people.

You can see now, based on this distinction, why the complete protein foods—especially meat, fish, eggs, and milk—have such a good reputation as sources of protein. They're the rugged individualists of the protein world—they can get the job done all alone. But with a little cooperation, the vegetable sources can do it, too.

The Special Advantages of Vegetable Protein

In fact, perhaps they get the job done even better. Vegetable sources of protein are conjugated proteins: they contain other nutrients. But unlike animal sources, they are usually conjugated together with fiber and carbohydrate (or in the case of nuts and seeds, mostly unsaturated fats), rather than saturated fats. Their extra fiber means extra bulk—you feel full after eating less. Often, you consume fewer calories, and thereby gain less weight. In countries where most protein comes from nonmeat sources, such as legumes (beans and peas) and cereals (wheat, rice, corn, etc.), obesity is much more rare than in the United States. Americans consume, on the average, over 3,000 calories a day—far more than we need. Much of that comes from the "empty" calories in fat and sugar—think of the meat-and-dessert-centered meals most of us still eat. No wonder so many of us are overweight.

The fact that incomplete proteins can be combined with each other to form complete proteins is what makes the science teacher's diet such a nutritious one, one that can sustain his energy for teaching, gardening, cooking, socializing, regular athletic participation, and all his other activities.

Summary

All of the proteins we eat are made up of twenty-three amino acids. These, in turn, are chainlike molecules containing the elements carbon, hydrogen, oxygen, and nitrogen.

There are eight essential amino acids that our bodies require every day, in the right proportions, in order to keep every cell in our bodies functioning properly. These eight (and their proportional relationships) are:

tryptophan	1 part
threonine	2 parts
phenylalanine	2 parts
methionine	3 parts
lysine	3 parts
valine	3 parts
isoleucine	3 parts
leucine	3.5 parts
(plus histidine for children)	

Egg whites contain all these amino acids in just about these ratios. The *complete* protein foods—meat, poultry, fish, eggs, dairy products, and soybeans in the form of tofu or bean curd—contain all eight. *Incomplete* proteins have some of them, in less perfect proportions. But if you combine two or more complementary protein foods, you are completing their proteins.

Although you may not know it, you already do this whenever you eat a peanut butter sandwich on whole wheat bread; sprinkle spaghetti with cheese; serve whole wheat bread with Boston baked beans; or pour milk over your oatmeal.

Vegetable proteins are nutritionally superior in that they come packaged by nature together with vitamins, minerals, complex carbohydrates, and fiber.

The Functions of Protein

Why is protein so important to all our science teacher friend's activities? How does his body use the bowl of whole grain cereal topped with seeds, nuts, and milk that he frequently eats for breakfast? What happens when you eat a breakfast like that? What would happen if you didn't get enough protein? If you got too much?

Let's look at exactly what happens from the moment you start munching such a protein-rich breakfast.

PROTEIN DIGESTION AND ABSORPTION

Chewing is the first step in digestion. Your teeth grind up the solids and mix them with saliva. Your saliva contains an enzyme called ptyalin, which begins to digest the starches with which the proteins are mixed.

Swallowing the food carries it into the stomach, where the protein begins to be digested. The enzyme pepsin, together with gastric juices containing hydrochloric acid, break down the protein into its amino acids—the form in which the body uses protein. (You see why it doesn't matter to the body whether the proteins come from a combination of cereal, seeds, and milk, or from a complete source alone like eggs. Once in the stomach, all protein foods just get broken down into their amino acids, anyway.) This particular breakfast also contains iron, calcium, vitamins, and minerals.

The process of breaking down the proteins into constituent amino acids continues in your small intestine. There pancreatic and intestinal proteases carry out the bulk of this process.[5] It is completed in the lining of the intestine.[6]

How fast is the protein absorbed? This depends, partly, on what else is in your stomach and digestive tract. If you've been eating mostly vegetable protein foods, it won't take long—the fiber in these foods speeds digestion by cleaning out the digestive tract for efficient functioning. It also depends on the amino acids in the protein itself. Apparently, the various amino acids compete with each other for absorption. If you eat them in the right proportion, the egg white ratio, they are all absorbed together. If not, the ones of which there is extra compete to prevent the absorption of those that are lacking, and efficiency is impaired. This may explain why the correct balance of amino acids is so important. Since we are talking about a breakfast of well-balanced, properly combined protein sources, high in fiber, about 92 percent of the protein in it would probably be absorbed.[7]

The capillaries in the walls of your intestines absorb the amino acids from your morning meal, and carry them into the bloodstream. Via the portal vein, they are transported to the liver, which distributes them to the many sites where they are needed.

Where are they needed? All over! Protein is one of the most important nutrients. Your muscles are not the only part of the body that need protein. Every single cell in your body contains protein: hair, nerves, skin, blood, sperm or eggs—all of them. So do almost all the nonliving substances the body produces—enzymes, hormones, blood plasma, even your saliva. In fact, bile, urine, and sweat are the only bodily substances that (in a state of normal health) contain no protein at all.

PROTEIN PROVIDES STRUCTURAL MATERIALS FOR CELLS

About half of the solid substance in our bodies is protein. It gives the cell walls and structures inside the cells their shape—without which they could not survive.

Although it is strong, protein is also unstable. Your cells undergo a constant cycle of breakdown (catabolism) and rebuilding (anabolism). About half the protein that makes up the liver, for example, is broken down every ten days.[8] The amino acids in the cells have to be constantly replaced, and it is the newly digested amino acids from your food that serves this purpose.

Ideally, your diet provides just enough amino acids to replace the proteins that are broken down. This balance is called a "dynamic equilibrium": breakdown and reconstruction proceed at the same pace. If you eat too much protein, your body will still maintain its dynamic equilibrium. But the process may be speeded up: amino acids in your cells may be replaced at a faster rate than normal. There is some evidence that this may make you age faster than otherwise. Some excess protein may also be burned as energy or eliminated as waste. In any event, if you eat more protein than you need, your body will have to dispose of extra urea—the nitrogen-containing waste product of protein metabolism. Urea is formed in the liver and excreted via the kidneys. This extra work for your liver and kidneys can be stressful—it may make you feel fatigued, or as mentioned earlier, it can cause more severe problems, especially if you don't drink lots of water to help the kidneys filter urea out of the bloodstream.

Not only older people, but infants, too, are especially vulnerable. Infants may become severely dehydrated if their bodies use up too much water flushing out excess urea.[9] You may not feed a little baby meat. But don't overfeed your child with cow's milk either—it has a lot more protein than human mother's milk. Giving an infant solid food too young can also dangerously speed up protein metabolism—remember, cereals contain protein, too. Dehydration due to excess protein intake can be deadly to an infant.

If you get too little protein, all the cells of your body will suffer (beginning with the least important ones—your hair and nails). Protein deficiency, however, is very uncommon in the United States. If anything, we usually eat too much of it compared with other foods. In underdeveloped nations, kwashiorkor, the disease associated with protein deficiency, is more common. Kwashiorkor results in low blood levels of the essential amino acids, among other biochemicals, and often occurs between ages one and four. It causes stunted growth, malnutrition, and in severe cases, death. People whose diets are chronically low in protein may suffer nervous disorders, damage to eyes, teeth, and hearing, and baldness.[10]

PROTEIN CAN BE FUEL FOR ENERGY

In an emergency, if you are not getting enough carbohydrates, your most important source of energy, your body may switch over and oxidize protein as fuel instead. When protein is broken down in this way, it is capable of providing the same caloric value as carbohydrates to fuel the cellular functions that maintain life.

However, to use protein as fuel is to mismanage your internal energy policy. A meal of half a fried chicken with no fruit, salad, or vegetables forces the body to use protein from the chicken for energy. This requires more energy than breaking down carbohydrates, and wastes protein that may be needed for cell repair and physical growth.[11] Disposing of the extra nitrogen from the protein can cause fatigue or worse. This is one reason why high-protein, low-carbohydrate reducing diets are not advisable. If you want to eat a healthy diet, it is best for 65 to 70 percent of your food to be complex carbohydrates for energy, 20 to 25 percent protein for the raw materials of your tissues, and 10 percent fat.

This balance among fat, carbohydrate, and protein intake is especially important for pregnant women and children. Children are growing all the time: they need to use all the protein they eat for optimal cellular growth and repair. If they burn their protein for energy, growth may be partially stunted and resistance to some diseases lowered. Similarly, pregnant women need their protein to satisfy the needs of the fast-developing fetus, whose nourishment comes solely from the mother's food. Therefore, both protein and carbohydrates must be eaten in good supply during these periods—protein for growth, carbohydrates for energy. Eggs, milk, and other nonmeat protein sources should be combined with fresh fruits and vegetables to insure an adequate supply of both nutrients. (However, for the best food combining system, fruits should be eaten first.) The proper order for maximum digestion, absorption, utilization, and elimination is as follows. First, eat the foods most quickly digested, such as simple sugars found in fruits, juices, and honey. Then the complex carbohydrates, such as bread, whole grains, cereals, pastas, beans, legumes, and soups. (Vegetables—raw or steamed—can combine easily with these complex carbohydrates.) Last, the longer-digesting proteins and fatty foods, including nuts, cheese, and animal proteins. If you follow this order, you can save yourself a lot of unnecessary indigestion.

PROTEIN IS A REGULATOR

Protein helps to control many of the individual processes that must be carried out throughout the body to maintain life. For example, in osmosis, the mechanism by which vital fluids pass through cell walls, protein helps insure an even balance on both sides. Proteins can adapt themselves to be either base or acid; therefore, they help to protect important body fluids such as blood and gastric juices from pH changes. The biochemistry of our cells is regulated by enzymes. These are made up of proteins, which thus aid thousands of physiological processes. Crucial regulatory hormones such as insulin and adrenaline are mainly protein; so is hemoglobin, the part of the red blood cells that transports oxygen and carbon dioxide. Without hemoglobin, you would suffocate. Without protein, many of these physiological functions lapse into chaos. We cannot afford to live without it.

PROTEIN FORMS PART OF THE BODILY STRUCTURES

Your bodily structures, both hard and soft, contain protein. Your toenails, fingernails, bones, and teeth contain protein; so do your hair and blood vessels. The proteins in these structures are held together by bonds that vary according to whether they are hard or soft tissue. The soft group, for example, get their elasticity from protein. When your hairdresser uses heat to give you a new hairstyle, he or she is breaking down the protein bonds (specifically disulfide bonds) and reforming them in the new style. In muscle, some protein takes the form of the contractile fibers that enable you to move. A huge number of amino acids are found in collagen, the adhesive material that holds individual cells together. Without collagen you would literally fall apart. These amino acids account for about a third of your body's total supply.

It is obvious how essential protein is to life.

It has been found by Dr. Kilmer McCully of Harvard Medical School that the real culprit in heart disease is the protein and not the cholesterol. It seems that homocysteine produced as a result of methionine metabolism is converted to the nontoxic compound cystathionine in the presence of vitamin B_6. If there is no B_6 present homocysteine will damage the artery wall linings which results in arteriosclerosis and finally heart disease. Therefore, the need for vitamin B_6 is much greater when you consume a diet largely of animal fat and protein.[12]

Summary

Protein food is broken up by your teeth, but pepsin and hydrochloric acid in the stomach begin to break it into its component amino acids. Proteases in the small intestine nearly finish this job, which is completed in the lining of the small intestine prior to absorption.

It is believed that competition for absorption explains why you need that proportion of amino acids in your food we call complete.

Once absorbed into the bloodstream, the amino acids of protein are carried to every single cell, where they are used to rebuild the structure of the cell. As structural material, it makes up about half the solid substance in our bodies. Some of these cells produce new protein products, including enzymes, hormones, blood plasma, and saliva.

Protein is unstable: it is constantly breaking down (catabolism) and must be replaced. The structure of your body is always being rebuilt (anabolism). There is a "dynamic equilibrium" balancing the pace of breakdown and reconstruction. If you eat too much protein, that can speed up your metabolism. (The increased height of second-generation immigrants to the United States is probably caused by increased protein intake. But greater height has been correlated with shorter life spans.)

Protein from your food is only oxidized as fuel in an emergency, when your body is not getting enough carbohydrate from your food; under starvation conditions, the body only touches structural protein after consuming stores of starch and fat.

But using protein as fuel is mismanaging energy. It takes more energy to use protein as fuel than carbohydrate, and this wastes protein that might be used for cell repair or physical growth. For pregnant women and children, a diet ratio of 65 to 70 percent carbohydrate for energy, 20 to 25 percent protein for anabolism, and 10 percent fat, is especially important.

Excess protein may also be eliminated as waste. Its waste product, urea, formed in the liver and excreted by the kidneys, can be stressful to these organs, and should be flushed out by drinking plenty of water. For this reason, special care should be taken not to give infants and older people too much protein.

As a regulator, protein is a component of enzymes, hormones, and numerous complex biochemical processes and protective mechanisms. Protein in various body structures may make them elastic (like muscle), or rigid (like bone), bound together tightly (as in nails), or easily bound and unbound (as in hair). Protein in the form of collagen literally holds your body together.

How Much Protein Is Necessary?

Americans are constantly told that protein is important in the diet. But how much do we really need?

Scientists have been working on this question for a long time. The best they can do is to give us a working formula, and warn us that every individual is unique. Your biological individuality must be your guide.

The working formula they have devised is based on your body weight. On the average, they calculate that your body requires .9 gram of protein per kilogram (2.2 pounds) of body weight. A 150-pound woman would need about 61 grams a day, a 200-pound man about 81 grams. However, new evidence shows that because men have more lean muscle tissue and less fat than women, that woman should figure into this calculation of .9 gram the percentage of her lean tissue and fat tissue and the amount of exercise.

This formula is not new: it was proposed in 1935 by a League of Nations commission, and it has been reaffirmed several times since then.[13]

Unfortunately, you are very likely to have been taught now-discredited earlier theories. Were you ever told that people who do hard physical labor need more protein than the rest of us? (This would base the formula on the level of activity rather than on body weight.) They generally don't—they need more calories and a modest increase in protein. The idea that they do goes back to an 1881 study of German laborers who were found to eat an average of 118 grams daily. The researchers assumed that figure to be correct for anyone doing that kind of work.[14, 15]

Several researchers who endorse the .9 gram per kilogram of body weight assume that half the protein comes from complete animal sources.[16] This does not mean they are telling you that you must eat meat to get enough protein. Complete animal sources include eggs, milk, cheese, and other dairy products. It may not be a bad idea to choose a lacto-ovo-vegetarian diet over a pure vegetarian one.

However, if you want to or must eliminate eggs and milk products from your diet, you don't need to go back to meat. You can still get enough protein by increasing the amount of complemented vegetable proteins you eat. The Food and Nutrition Board of the National Research Council goes so far as to say that if you get most of your protein from plants, you should increase your total intake to 1.5 grams. They are asking vegetarians to eat more protein to insure adequate intake.

This is probably unnecessarily overcautious. It doesn't take into account the possibility of combining incomplete proteins to complement each other and add up to complete protein. A handful of mixed nuts and seeds, or a helping of stir-fried tofu flavored with Japanese miso and served over buckwheat noodles, or that breakfast of whole grain cereal topped with seeds, nuts, and milk, certainly supply one meal's worth of high-quality protein. And they do not contain the high levels of fat or chemical residues found in meat.

Any formula, however, is only a starting point. You must modify it to consider your biological individuality. Some of the most important items to consider besides your weight are: your age; the makeup of the amino acids in your body (biochemical tests can be performed to measure your nitrogen balance or the level of urea in your blood plasma); and special circumstances. These include pregnancy, growth, age, illness, and general stress levels. And your diet also should be examined to determine total calorie intake, major sources of protein, etc.

Biological Individuality and Special Protein Needs

Adults normally use their protein resources to maintain a proper balance between the breakdown and buildup of bodily tissues. In certain special circumstances, the protein is needed for other functions as well, and more must be consumed to maintain health.

Infants and children need extra protein for physical growth. Some nutritionists tell us that protein should account for a higher percentage of total calories for children than for adults.[17] The League of Nations commission quoted earlier gave separate formulas for children and adolescents.

Ages 1–3:	3.5 grams of protein per kilogram of body weight
3–5:	3.0 "
5–15:	2.5 "
15–17:	2 "
17–21:	1.5 "

Since these formulas are based on an adult ratio of .9 gram per kilogram of body weight,[18] the recommendations may be slightly too high. They also suggest eating part of this protein in animal form, which is known to be unnecessary.[19] In any case, it is likely that the high-protein diet most Americans eat more than suffices to supply enough protein for the young. You would do better to concentrate on seeing that their protein comes from the right sources.

Pregnant women and lactating mothers are the other major group who need extra protein. High-quality protein intake is required during pregnancy to promote normal development of the fetus and during lactation to guarantee full production of mother's milk. The Food and Nutrition Board of the National Research Council recommends that pregnant women increase their protein intake (based on 1.5 g/kg for normal adults) by 35 percent. Lactating women should increase it even more—by 70 percent. Other authorities recommend simply increasing total protein intake by 10 grams during pregnancy and 20 grams during lactation. This can easily be accomplished with snacks like cheese sandwiches on whole grain bread, handfuls of nuts and seeds, an extra baked potato with sunflower or sesame seeds, etc. You still don't require animal flesh.

Conditions of physical/emotional stress such as illness or a difficult work situation also create temporarily elevated protein needs, and care should be taken to meet them.

One way to achieve the increase is to eat high-quality protein snacks, such as seeds and nuts. If you're working long hours at a stressful job, keep a large bowl of your favorites sitting by your desk. Cashews, walnuts, almonds, peanuts, sunflower seeds, and soybeans can all be used in this way. At meals, be sure to have a protein drink (dozens of formulas are available at your health food store or health section of your supermarket). Also, you can vary grains and legume dishes with different types of cheeses or with eggs.

As you grow older, your body may not use the protein you eat as efficiently, so you may need to eat more from different sources, although older people generally require less protein. Unfortunately, the expense of most high-quality protein foods makes elderly people decrease their intake too much. They buy too many starchy foods and ignore the cheap protein sources such as grains, legumes, seeds, sprouts, tofu products, eggs, and milk. If they reduce their total calories, good protein is often the first thing to go.

Of course, you can't account for variables that change from hour to hour. Not only do your body's needs vary, the content of your diet doesn't remain constant every day. Nor does protein account for a steady percentage of your total calories. You eat at different times; you cook and prepare your food in different ways; you metabolize food at different rates at different times of the day; and the protein content of each food varies depending on how you prepare it. No two slices of cheese are exactly identical. The same slice would be digested and metabolized differently at lunchtime and suppertime, and its nutrition will be affected by whether you toast it, grill it, or use it in an eggplant casserole. All these factors affect the question of how much *usable* protein you get from your food.[20-25]

How Do You Know If You're Getting Enough Protein?

You can obtain biochemical tests measuring nitrogen and urea levels in the urine and blood plasma. However, first take a look at the visible portion of your body yourself. Remember, the structure of all your cells depends on protein. What does your hair look like? Is it healthy and shiny, or limp and dull? What about your fingernails and toenails? Are they hard and smooth, or do they chip and flake? Is your skin healthy looking? Your hair, nails, and skin all rely on protein to maintain their structural soundness and visual appearance. If they look unhealthy, you may not be getting enough protein. Also, minor, superficial injuries such as scrapes and bruises should heal at a prompt, normal rate.[26] If your appearance is below par, you should analyze your diet.

A chart listing the protein content of common foods in grams of usable protein can help you to carry out your own simple nutritional analysis. Give some thought to how you might increase your protein intake. The key to getting adequate protein is to vary and balance your sources. The simplest method (avoiding meat and fish) is to supplement nuts, seeds, grains, legumes, and sprouts with complete proteins such as eggs and dairy products.

As long as you get about one-third of your total protein from complete sources[27] and average about 25 grams per meal,[28] you should be certain of obtaining all you need. If you're ill, or still growing, about one-half to two-thirds of your protein should come from complete sources. Minimal amounts of the right protein are much more important than larger amounts of the wrong ones.

Summary

Your weight is the main factor determining how much protein you need, since protein is so intrinsic to your body's structure. In general, no matter how much or how little exercise they get, adults require .9 gram of protein for every kilogram (2.2 pounds) of body weight. (To find out how many grams of protein you need, divide your weight in pounds by 2.2, then multiply by .9.) Vegans should perhaps get a bit more to compensate for imperfectly complemented incomplete proteins.

Young children need more protein relative to their body weight, but this adds up to less than adults require in total. Children ages 1 to 3 need 3.5 grams per kilogram. (A twenty-five pound, fast-growing toddler would need about 40 grams of protein, compared to the 60 grams needed by his or her 150-pound mother.) Adolescents, again, have increased needs (2 g/kg for 15- to 17-year-olds, 1.5 g/kg for 17- to 21-year-olds).

Pregnant women need 35 percent more protein than usual. People under stress should also increase their protein intake. Although older people generally need less protein, sometimes as you age your body uses protein less efficiently. For this reason, women over fifty-five are advised to increase their intake of high-quality protein foods.

We are each biologically unique, and our need for protein changes at different times and in different circumstances. If your hair is healthy and shiny, your fingernails and toenails hard and smooth, your skin healthy looking, and if bruises heal promptly, you are probably getting enough protein. If not, you should analyze your diet and perhaps consider having your urine and blood plasma analyzed for nitrogen and urea levels.

NPU: Other Factors Affecting Protein Utilization

Let's return again to Household Number Four, the lacto-ovo-vegetarian teacher. As a scientist who weighs 180 pounds, he knows that he cannot just eat any foods that contain 74 grams of protein, the amount recommended for his body weight, and be sure he is getting all he needs. He judiciously matches foods with complementary amino acid profiles: rice with soybeans, wheat with beans, peanuts with milk, sunflower seeds with peanuts, brewer's yeast, wheat germ, etc.

He also takes into consideration other factors that affect what his fellow scientists call net protein utilization (NPU). The NPU of any given food describes its usefulness as a protein source, its quality as a protein. NPU involves two factors: the chemical makeup ("biological value") of the protein—that is, the ratio of amino acids to each other— and digestibility. If you don't eat enough fiber with your meals—like many Americans—you will probably digest considerably less of the protein you consume. And if you don't consume enough of your calories as carbohydrates, some of the protein you eat will just be burned as fuel.

Even more important is how you cook protein. If you cook most protein foods under too high heat, that can interfere with both digestion and absorption. This poses a special problem for people who eat pork. It must be cooked very thoroughly to destroy the trichinosis-causing trichinae organisms. In the process some of the protein content is lost. This dilemma can be avoided by leaving pork out of our diets altogether.

Toasting bread makes some if its lysine content unavailable through binding;[29] this can be compensated for by complementing the toast with another food group such as legumes, which are rich in lysine (try toasted, whole grain black bread with baked beans), or with a complete protein such as cheese (spread your morning toast with cottage cheese), or milk—but make sure it is fresh milk; drying milk also makes the lysine less available.

On the other hand, cooking beans and other legumes makes the protein more available. Heat deactivates chemicals called trypsin inhibitors which are found in uncooked soybeans and some other legumes.[30]

Using these guidelines of chemical makeup and digestibility, nutritionists have determined NPU figures for the major protein sources. On a scale of one hundred, the NPUs for selected foods are:

Eggs: 94   Cheese: 70
Milk: 82   Meat and poultry: 67
Fish: 80   Tofu (soybean curd): 65

Nuts, seeds, grains, and legumes—all foods that play an important part in vegetarian diets—range in NPU from 40 to 60. If you want to get complete protein from the delicious Mexican classic of tortillas with *frijoles refritos* (refried beans), you will probably have to eat more of it than you would eat of a meat dish to get an equivalent quantity of usable protein. But this fact in no way suggests that the tortillas and beans are inferior as a protein source.

Everyone who pays attention to his or her health will have some objection to one or more of the major protein sources. Vegetarians don't eat meat; some of us are allergic to cheese or other foods; others have to avoid milk or eggs because of their fat content. No single food is the answer to everyone's protein needs.

The only solution is to obtain a full spectrum of dietary benefits by eating as many combinations of protein food as possible. Happily, this is the most pleasurable alternative: with care and the right information, you can be sure of getting a balanced protein intake that also provides variety and delicious taste.

How to Increase Your NPU

The most important key to increasing the NPU of the protein you eat is food combining. Eggs are the only food which contain the eight essential amino acids in the ideal mixture. But you couldn't get all your protein by eating eggs, even if you wanted to: they only contain about 6 grams of protein each.

So you must turn to other protein sources, the foods that don't contain the ideal mixture. They, too, provide protein, even though they do it less efficiently.

The NPU of incomplete proteins is determined by what is called the "limiting" amino acid. This is the one present in the lowest proportion relative to the ideal egglike ratio of amino acids. For instance, a slice of bread may contain half the amount of lysine which would be needed for the protein in it to be complete, but relatively correct proportions of the other seven essential amino acids. As a result, your body might be able to use only one quarter of the total protein contained in the bread.

On the other hand, if you eat the bread with a glass of fresh milk, peanut, sesame, or sunflower butters, the low lysine content will be compensated for by that in the milk. As a result, you'll get a complete protein in efficiently usable form.[31]

You could also just eat greater quantities of grains and cereals to compensate for those foods' insufficient levels of lysine. But a far safer way of avoiding lysine deficiency—which may cause nausea and dizziness—would be to complement the grain with a lysine-rich food group such as legumes. Eating whole wheat noodles with a sauce containing eggs and grated cheese would do away with the problem altogether. Adding a mixed salad of lettuce, dandelion greens, carrots, tomatoes, and alfalfa sprouts would give you an almost completely balanced meal.

If you do plan vegetarian meals in a way that compensates for missing amino acids, you can easily eat a nutritionally sound diet. This has been confirmed by a number of studies sponsored by eminent authorities, including the Beth Israel Hospital Committee and the National Academy of Science.[32] Even pregnant mothers and growing children can get sufficient protein from a vegetarian diet according to Dorothy Lane and M. G. Hardinge.[33] Vegans or pure vegetarians (those who eschew eggs and dairy products) may need dietary supplements to supply iron, B vitamins, and other nutrients; but they need not lack protein.

Summary

NPU—net protein utilization—describes the usefulness of any food as a source of protein, in terms of both digestibility and completeness of amino acid makeup. Charts that measure the NPU of various protein sources show *average* NPU. How you cook protein (as slowly and as little as possible is best, except for beans), and how much fiber you consume (fiber in the diet increases protein absorption), affect the actual NPU of the foods you are eating.

The NPU of eggs is 94 percent of the protein in eggs. Milk and fish NPUs are around 80; cheese 70; meat, poultry, and soybean curd about 65. The protein in nuts, seeds, grains, and legumes ranges from 40 to 60 percent usable; but these amounts can be increased by combining these incomplete sources, or adding complete protein foods to them so that the "limiting amino acid"—the one present in the lowest proportion relative to the ideal—is increased. For example, milk (containing extra lysine) can supplement the lysine in short supply even in whole grain bread.

A vegetarian—even a vegan—diet can supply all the protein you need if you are careful about food combining.

Some effective combinations include:

> grains and beans
> grains and seeds
> grains and nuts (or nut butters)
> beans and seeds
> nuts and seeds
> any of these with eggs, milk, cheese,
>   brewer's yeast, wheat germ, or sprouts

Soybeans are particularly effective, since they contain more complete protein than other beans. Sprouting grains, other beans, and seeds also adds to their NPU.

Complete Proteins

Let's take a closer look at the complete protein foods. These foods contain all eight essential amino acids in proportions close to the ideal. Being so well balanced, they provide protein in a highly efficient manner. As a result, they only need to be eaten in small quantities. Six ounces of meat, cheese, fish, or eggs would supply most people's daily needs.

Complete proteins are also blessed with a high "nutrient density," which means they contain high levels of nutrient value relative to their caloric content. Milk, for example, has significant quantities of fat, minerals, and vitamins A and C in addition to protein.

But Americans have been led to think of meat, eggs, fish, and milk as the only suppliers of protein. As you are aware by now, this misinformed view can have serious consequences for individual nutrition. Among other consequences, it can make us believe that *any* meat is a good protein source. Yet cured ham has only 16 percent protein, while the humble lentil has anywhere from 23 to 29 percent. Most hot dogs have about 7 percent protein, far less than dried skim milk (34 to 38 percent) or sunflower seeds (27 percent). Some sprouted seeds and beans are far better supplied with nutrients at a lower caloric level.

MEAT

Most Americans are meat eaters, relying on beef, chicken, pork, etc., to satisfy most of their protein needs. Meat also supplies nutrients such as iron and B vitamins in which many vegetables are deficient. It contains essential fats we need for energy, organ, nerve and heat insulation, and a variety of metabolic functions.

With only six ounces a day of complete protein we could satisfy most of our protein requirements. But meat available in our society has so many other drawbacks that you may prefer to gradually eliminate it from your diet.

FISH

Fish is another excellent protein source that our greed and folly have done much to destroy. Formerly abundant, their number has been decimated by overfishing and by the waste products of modern society. The slow accumulation of industrial wastes has polluted our waters and thus rendered many fish unfit for human consumption. Most fish is now nearly as expensive as the prized cuts of meat.

If you want to keep eating fish in spite of chemical contamination, don't eat more than you need. A six-ounce serving of lean fish supplies much of your protein needs for a single day. Avoid fish that has been deep-fried, especially if the oil has been used previously, and season it only with lemon and pepper or herbs. And stick to the smaller fish, which are lower on the food chain, such as sardines, herring, and whitebait. Larger fish such as the expensive tuna and swordfish are more likely to be contaminated with chemicals.

DAIRY PRODUCTS

Milk is a good protein source and an excellent food generally. In addition to its high protein content (about 8.5 grams per cup), it contains calcium, phosphorus, vitamins A, E, and D, and some of the B vitamins. It is easily digested by most people, and its amino acid content complements that of many plants—making it an ideal accompaniment for nonmeat meals.

Of course, there are problems with milk, as with any animal protein source. Many people are allergic to it—you should avoid it if you are. It, too, may be contaminated with chemicals, including antibiotics, synthetic hormones, and the others found in meat. Penicillin, in particular, fed to milk cows to cure an inflammatory condition called mastitis, finds its way into much of the commercially produced milk on the market today. And some authors observe with alarm the tendency for mothers to give their infants cow's milk instead of breast-feeding them. But even breast milk has been found to contain traces of toxins such as the insecticide DDT.

Still, milk is too good a nutrient source to pass up altogether—especially for vegetarians. Whole grain or whole wheat cereal (even commercial brands such as shredded wheat) supply an excellent complete protein breakfast when served with fresh milk. The frulatti of the Italians—fresh fruit blended with milk to form a sugarless milk shake —makes a delicious dessert or hot-weather drink. Combined with a whole wheat sandwich, milk is an excellent drink, and on its own it makes a good alternative to the tea or coffee break.

Yet the sad fact is that few Americans beyond childhood continue to drink milk. Some of us, worried about our waistlines or arteries, dislike milk because of its fat content. If you're one of those people, you can drink skim milk and get even higher levels of protein—about 36 grams in a single cup. If you want to know how much milk to use to complement grains perfectly in your recipes and meal planning, insuring absolutely maximum protein availability, see *Recipes for a Small Planet*. In this book Ellen Buchman Ewald provides a chart with some figures. She suggests a ratio of one cup of milk to the following quantity of grains (measured dry, before they are cooked): 3/4 cup brown rice; or 1 1/2 cups bulgur wheat; or 2 cups flour; or 1 cup (dry) macaroni; or 5 slices whole wheat bread.

WHAT ABOUT MILK PRODUCTS?

Some of the butter sold in American supermarkets is dyed with chemicals, and adulterated with various ingredients to offset its inferior taste and smell. This low-quality butter has negligible protein, and should not be counted upon as a protein source.[24]

But you can still enjoy and benefit from eating cheese. Low fat cheeses of nearly all types are good protein sources, though some may be as expensive as meat. Cottage cheese contains 15 to 19 percent protein, other cheeses about 25 percent.

One of the best features of cheese is its versatility. Combined with leafy vegetables and/or alfalfa sprouts on whole grain bread, it makes a delicious and nutritionally complete lunch. Grated with cream and served on whole wheat fettuccine, it makes an excellent main course at supper. An all-home made pizza with real mozzarella, fresh tomato sauce, and whole wheat dough can serve six or eight people as a party dish. Cheese soufflés are another good party dish, and cheese omelettes can be whipped up easily if you're eating by yourself. Instead of serving sugar-laden desserts, a bowl of fruit with a good selection of French and Italian cheeses makes an excellent alternative.

Of course, cheese suffers from some of the same contaminants that adulterate milk, but it, too, is too good a protein source to leave out of most people's diet. Cottage cheese is especially attractive to people who want to lose weight, since it's made from skim rather than whole milk. Its protein density is five times greater than that of milk, enabling you to get the same amount of protein with one-fifth the calories. When combined with incomplete vegetable sources, it complements their inadequacies and provides further nutritive value at low cost.

Similar to cottage cheese, but more interesting in flavor, is ricotta, usually made from sheep's milk. This too can be combined with vegetables—it makes a delicious snack when spread on celery—and used as part of dips or vegetable spreads. The Italians mash it up with cooked spinach to make gnocchi and wrap it in dough pockets for ravioli, both excellent high-protein foods.

When buying cheese, avoid the numerous *processed* cheeses available in your supermarket. Processed cheese has had the life taken out of it. It is made from a mixture of different hard cheeses and various chemical agents, all combined to make a relatively bland "convenience" food. Its additive level could be high and the quality of the original cheese used in manufacturing could be low. Processed cheese is also more expensive than many naturally produced cheeses. Even worse are the "cheese products" and "cheese foods" often sold in a way that disguises their true nature. Since they, too, are so expensive, they provide no economic advantage over real cheese.

EGGS

Eggs are another superb protein source. You can utilize 94 percent of the protein in the eggs you eat. Eggs (along with milk and cheese) are superior in protein availability to meat.[34]

Have you been afraid to eat eggs for the last few years because of the great cholesterol scare? It convinced many people that cholesterol (found in egg yolks, among other foods) could almost single-handedly cause heart disease. Few scientists or physicians take this idea seriously, and there is much evidence that undercuts the danger of cholesterol considerably. Unfortunately, many people remain prejudiced against eggs, milk, and other fine nonmeat complete proteins. If you don't eat meats, thereby reducing your intake of saturated fats, get enough exercise, control your stress levels, get enough vitamin E and C and the right proportion of minerals in your diet, the cholesterol in your eggs would not make any great difference. Check with your doctor before eliminating them from your diet.

Like cheese, eggs are astonishingly versatile; the culinary uses to which you can put them are almost endless. They can be eaten in delicious dishes at breakfast, lunch, or dinner, and combined with other foods for both taste and complete nutritive value. The Basque dish *pipérade* and Chinese egg foo young both combine eggs with fresh vegetables and spices; you can do the same in experiments of your own. Omelettes can be made with cheese, vegetables, tofu, and other foods to make a luncheon dish that supplies a full complement of complete protein. A simple but delicious Japanese soup can be made by dribbling a beaten egg into hot miso, thus providing another complete protein package.

Substituting recipes using milk, cheese, and eggs is a nutritionally sound way of cutting down on meat-based meals if you have not yet eliminated meat from your diet. You'll find satisfying recipes in nearly every great cuisine for egg- and dairy-based dishes, and you'll spend less money in preparing them.

Incomplete Protein Foods

You cannot live on incomplete proteins alone. But well-informed vegetarians like our science teacher friend have learned how to use them to make complementary proteins. Complementary proteins—all from plant sources—are complete, and they can supply your protein needs quite adequately. If they couldn't, many more of the world's people would be deprived of their protein than already are. Grains alone supply almost 50 percent of humankind's supply.

SOYBEAN PRODUCTS

The West has discovered soybeans as animal feed and as food for humans in fairly recent times. In the Orient, people have known about soybeans for centuries, and have used them to supply protein at low cost in the absence of cheap meat. Like all legumes, soybeans have low levels of the essential amino acid tryptophan and certain others as well, but are high in lysine. To enhance their biological value you can combine them with complementary proteins such as nuts, grains, and seeds, which are low in lysine and high in tryptophan. And in these countless complementary combinations, they make a variety of delicious dishes.

You have probably become familiar with two of the most common soybean products in Chinese foods: tofu (bean curd), to which the Chinese give the name "meat without bone," and soybean sprouts. Tofu is made by a process similar to that used for making cheese, curdling the soybean milk and packing the solids in layers of cloth. It has an NPU of 65, only slightly lower than animal flesh, and is well complemented by grains such as brown rice. Sprouted soybeans have large quantities of vitamin A, E, and B, and they combine well with any member of the grain family. If you cook Chinese food, stir-frying either bean curd or sprouts with soy sauce, ginger, and garlic and serving the dish with brown rice provides an excellent complete protein and a delicious meal.

Whole soybeans can also be eaten either on their own or in casseroles and soups. You can buy them already roasted in health food shops and some supermarkets, though steaming, boiling, or pressure cooking raw beans is better if you're planning a meal around them. Soybeans cannot be eaten raw because of the trypsin inhibitor they contain that impedes protein digestion; this inhibitor is destroyed by heat.[35, 36] Legumes may contain toxic substances, but these, too, are destroyed by heating or sprouting. In any case, it's far better to deal with these naturally occurring substances than with the man-made additives that adulterate so much of the meat we eat.

If you have stopped eating meat, but miss its texture, you will be glad to discover tempeh. Tempeh is a soybean cake containing anywhere from 14 to 48 percent protein. It is made by cooking the beans and adding a mold to ferment them. It contains vitamin B12 (rare outside the meat family) and can be cooked in a variety of delicious ways. Try sprinkling it with sesame seeds and soy sauce and broiling it, or sautéing it with chopped onions. Serve it with brown rice, green vegetables, and a brightly colored salad for a perfect dinner. You can also make your own tempeh with a starter kit from the U.S. Department of Agriculture.

Soy flour, which contains more protein than meat,[37] can be used in baking. You can find recipes in whole grain cookbooks.

Soy concentrate is the residue created when soybeans are pressed to make soy oil. It contains about 50 percent protein. It is usually used as a feed for animals. But with proper treatment for digestibility and flavor enhancement, it can be turned into a fibrous meat substitute of nearly limitless versatility.

Have you ever eaten a delicious "vegetarian veal cutlet" or "vegetarian drumstick" at a dairy restaurant? They probably contained textured soy protein. Institutions such as hospitals also buy soy concentrate in numerous "disguised" forms, including imitation meats and fish. The flavor is excellent and the texture hardly distinguishable from whatever "original" is being imitated. Other protein-yielding nuts, seeds, and grains can be used in the same way.[28] You can find some of these recipes in older vegetarian cookbooks.

In short, soybeans are one of the most versatile of all our protein sources. One can only hope that their vast potential for feeding mankind will be fully realized, and that the wasteful raising of animals for meat will be realized.

OTHER LEGUMES

Not all members of the legume family are as versatile as soybeans, but they are excellent protein sources nonetheless. And they are numerous: mung beans, chick-peas (garbanzos), black-eyed peas, navy beans, red beans, pink beans, black beans, lentils of all types, split peas, etc. Like soybeans, they tend to be low in certain amino acids (particularly tryptophan) but high in others (such as lysine and isoleucine). And they, too, can be combined with grains, nuts, and seeds to form complementary proteins of high nutritive value. Eaten by themselves, the legumes have an NPU ranging from about 31 (lentils) to 61 (soybeans).

There are countless examples of legume-grain-seed complementation from the cuisine of nations poorer than the United States. The Indians eat dhal, their deliciously fragrant lentil puree, with herbed, nutty pulao rice. Central American and Caribbean nations use beans and rice as a staple food. Middle Eastern countries combine chick-peas with sesame (tahini) paste to make houmus bi tahini and falafel, while the Italians mix lentils, chick-peas, or haricot beans with pasta to make pasta e fagioli and other heartwarming soups. In all these countries, meat is treated as a luxury, rather than a staple. When an Italian family begins its meal with pasta e fagioli, the meat course is likely to provide only a couple of ounces per person. Legumes also provide dietary fiber, which may help you avoid gastrointestinal disorders ranging from constipation to colorectal cancer. The long cooking time of legumes, a disadvantage, can be reduced by using a pressure cooker. The smaller beans—split peas, lentils, aduki, red, and mung beans—cook faster than the larger ones. To minimize digestive distress from beans, make sure they are soaked overnight and thoroughly cooked.

GRAINS AND CEREALS

These make an ideal complement to legumes because they are generally high in tryptophan and low in isoleucine and lysine. Their NPU can range up to 70 (for rice), but is usually in the area of 50 to 60 (for whole wheat, etc.). Grains and cereals supply about half the protein for the earth's people. They are also among the best sources of fiber.

The protein content of grains and cereals varies from about 8 percent for corn to 25 percent for wheat germ. One hundred grams of spaghetti or macaroni will provide about 5 grams of protein. When selecting grains for their protein content, you should also pay attention to their other nutrients. Eat brown rice instead of white for its fiber and vitamin content, and add fiber-rich bran flakes (10 percent protein) to baked goods and casseroles.

Creating complementary protein dishes from grains, seeds, and legumes is easy: we've already mentioned several possibilities in the preceding pages. You can also complement grains and cereals with complete protein from eggs and dairy products, which will raise the NPU of the incomplete sources. Breakfast cereals with milk achieve this very nicely. Macaroni and cheese and Italian risotto (the latter served with generous helpings of Gruyère or Parmesan cheese) also feature the grain/dairy combination. Eggs served with whole grain bread makes an excellent breakfast. With adequate protein supplied, you can count on bulky whole grains, rice, pasta, and bread to prevent overeating.

NUTS AND SEEDS

Nuts and seeds are similar in amino acid composition to grains and cereals. They can be used for cooking in many of the same ways. The residue left over from making peanut, sunflower, and sesame oil is often converted to textured protein and treated in preparation for use as a meat substitute.[38] And the most delicious nuts—almonds, pistachios, walnuts, pine nuts, cashews—have a high protein content. Peanut butter, made from fresh-ground peanuts (actually a legume, not a nut), becomes a complete protein when spread on whole grain bread. Sesame seeds can be toasted, eaten raw, or ground up to make tahini. Slivered almonds make a crunchy and delicious addition to any stir-fried vegetable dish or casserole. Some nuts are very expensive, particularly cashews and pine nuts, and are not economically practical as a protein source; they also have a higher fat content than many people would like to include in their diets. Used in smaller quantities, however, they can play a functional part in many vegetarian menus. Nuts and

seeds complement each other. To make a relatively inexpensive am-
brosia snack—great when you're hiking or coping with stress—combine
3/4 cup of peanuts with 1 cup of sunflower seeds (NPU 64 percent,
according to Ewald) and add some raisins or other dried fruit.

VEGETABLES

Vegetables supply a number of useful nutrients—vitamins, minerals, fiber—but they are generally low in protein. Corn (a grain),
potatoes, and mushrooms have higher NPU levels than most. Corn
combines well with beans, as in Mexican dishes. Try cottage cheese or
yogurt with your baked potato instead of sour cream. Other vegetables
have a high moisture content (and thus low nutrient density) combined
with protein as low as 2 percent or less. They should be valued for their
other nutrients, but not, generally, for protein. Dried mushrooms have
a much higher protein content than the fresh variety.

How to Become a Vegetarian (If You Want To)

From this list it should be obvious that there are numerous excellent protein sources available to us other than meat. If you want to
become a vegetarian, the classic cuisines of the world can provide you
with inspiration.

A word to the wise, however: if you do want to move toward eating
a vegetarian diet, do it in stages rather than all at once. Changing the
basis of one's diet is a major step. It requires an entirely new orientation
toward food and nutrition. Buy a good vegetarian cookbook. (*Diet for
a Small Planet* by Frances Moore Lappé was one of the first books to
explain fully the principles of protein complementarity. *Recipes for a
Small Planet* by Ellen Buchman Ewald applied these principles
through protein-rich recipes.)

Try new food combinations as side dishes at first, rather than the
main course. Eventually, you can let vegetarian dishes take care of all
your nutritional needs. Indeed, essential vitamins and minerals can
more easily be obtained from a vegetarian diet than from one based on
meat. The only exception to this is vitamin B_{12}. But tempeh, various sea
vegetables, miso, and milk can supply all your needs for that vitamin.

Summary

Remember, variety is all important. Mix legumes and grains, and
seeds or nuts and legumes; drink milk and eat eggs in moderation;
concentrate on unrefined carbohydrates (fruit, vegetables, whole grain

bread and brown rice); eat your vegetables raw or very lightly cooked, with the exception of legumes, which should be well cooked.

There are now millions of American vegetarians like our young science teacher who have learned how to utilize grains, nuts, and other protein sources in a balanced, nutritionally unsurpassed diet. Their choice is not necessarily the only way to attain good health, but it sets a standard by which all diets can be measured. It is particularly valuable for those seeking an alternative to the American meat-centered diet.

CARBOHYDRATES: ENERGY AND FIBER FOR HEALTH

It is difficult to think of a more appropriate way to begin this chapter than with a few words from Dr. John Yudkin, M.D., Ph.D., F.R.C.P. Dr. Yudkin, Professor Emeritus of Nutrition at the University of London, may well be the world's most eminent authority on dietary sugar, and especially on the medical/biochemical effects of refined sugar. His numerous articles and books have done an enormous amount to draw world attention—both scientific and lay—to the dangers of that most common food additive. In an interview with Dr. Yudkin, I asked for a general description of some of these dangers.

> Because we have refined sugar, we are able to use it in hosts of ways which we would not have done if we had only unrefined sugars. Much of the confectionery we eat—candies, chocolates—could not be manufactured if we didn't start off with highly refined sugar. Similarly, it is responsible for the sweet taste of all those cola drinks and so-called "fruity" drinks (which may or may not have fruit in them).
>
> The result of all this is that, believe it or not, we go through, on average, something like two pounds of sugar in a week—100 pounds or more every year. In England, two years ago the rate of consumption was up to 240 pounds, though now it's fallen back to about 130 pounds per capita per year. This is an incredible amount of sugar. One possible explanation for this drop is an awakening of the public to the health hazards of overconsumption of simple sugars.
>
> Now, we're led to believe that this doesn't really matter—that sugar is simply *a* form of carbohydrate and it's a good thing to have carbohydrates in our diet. The sugar gives us energy, we are told—which is simply another way of saying that sugar, like all foods, contains calories.
>
> In fact, this view of refined sugar is not true. Irrefutable evidence from experiments has shown that this high amount of sugar in the diet—and remember that many people eat much more than the average because some people (like myself) eat very much less—produces an enormous range of bodily disturbance.
>
> When one talked to people a long time ago and said that they really should be eating this food or that because it's got such and such vitamins,

protein, and so forth, the response was often the same. They would give you a big grin and say, "You know, doctor, my grandparents brought me up because my parents had both died; and I've now brought up five healthy children of my own; and we've managed (like everyone else for thousands of years) without knowing anything about vitamins and protein and nutrition. Why do I need to bother?"

Behind that attitude, I now discover, is the real key to what we should be eating. All animals, including the human animal, managed through millions of years of evolution by choosing from the foods which were roundabout, and eating what they wanted in the quantities they wanted. And they did this without bothering at all about nutrition: you don't find professors of nutrition in the jungle advising giraffes and elephants what to eat. They found the food that was best for them and they ate it in the necessary quantities.

We need to start choosing in the same way ourselves. It's not so much that we ought to be looking for the right things to eat, making certain that we get enough meat and enough high-protein food and enough leafy vegetables. What we ought to be doing is *avoiding* all those miserable foods that have come into our lives in the last couple of centuries. These are the foods you call refined foods. It is because we are eating them— eating a lot of foods that didn't exist when we were hunters and gatherers of food, as all wild animals are—that we run into nutritional trouble.

We run into trouble in two ways. In the first, we do it partly by eating those miserable foods and pushing out the better foods; or, alternatively, we eat the good foods and then on top of that the bad foods, too, getting fat and not eating a good diet. We have distorted our diet by eating certain foods in such large amounts. And the worst of those foods is refined sugar.

So, when people ask me how they can eat a healthier diet, what I would say to them is this: Forget everything you've heard about diet, forget everything you've heard about nutrition. Start to ask the same sort of questions that our grandmothers and grandfathers used to ask about food: Is it wholesome, is it fresh, is it health-giving and unadulterated? We have rather arrogantly pushed those questions aside.

Sugars and Sweeteners

When Dr. Yudkin speaks about our ancestors' dietary habits, he understands full well that sweet foods have always been appreciated. Our love of sweetness is probably instinctive, and for long centuries people found ample satisfaction in fruits, berries, and some vegetables. Eastern Mediterranean peoples in biblical times used honey as an added sweetener, and prized it so highly that Canaan, the promised land of the Israelites, was lauded as "a land flowing with milk and honey." Even today, you can hear honey praised as the finest of tastes in countless popular songs that speak of "kisses like honey" or "lips like honey." Honey has lost none of its appeal. When Asian sugarcane was introduced into Europe in the Middle Ages, it was so rare and costly that druggists sold it—sometimes for medicinal purposes—at prices only the rich could afford.

Unfortunately, modern technology and big business have turned sugar and sugar products from a luxury to a commonplace. In doing so, as Dr. Yudkin says, they have distorted our natural diet and adversely affected the health of whole nations. Americans consume an average of two pounds of sugar per person every week. Taken out of the natural foods in which it exists side by side with vitamins, minerals, and roughage (fiber), most of that sugar comes to us in the form of refined, white table sugar.

Richer nations like America consume more calories than the poorer nations, but most of these calories come from increased (and unhealthy) fat and sugar intake. The people of poorer nations get roughly the same carbohydrate total as we do, but much more of theirs comes in complex, unrefined forms. In this sense, ironically, they are healthier than we are.[1]

The very sugars that, in refined form, help ruin the modern American diet have always been available in natural forms: the fruits, berries, and honey on which our ancestors relied for sweetness. All modern man has done is to purify those sugars, isolate them from their natural forms, and concentrate them in junk foods. We get sucrose from beets (beet sugar) and sugarcane (cane sugar) and glucose from corn. Added into many of the foods we eat, these gradually have taken an even greater part in providing our daily calorie intake. The more refined sugar (and meat) we eat, the less room we have for complex carbohydrates. Of particular importance in this inverse equation is natural fiber, which has been lost in so many of the foods we eat. Western man gets an average of 2 to 5 grams of fiber a day, while primitive cultures get as much as 18 grams.[2] In short, we're rapidly abandoning whole, healthy forms of sugar for precisely the forms that can do most damage to our health.

Why We Eat So Much Sugar

If you are an average American, half of your caloric intake comes from carbohydrate foods. That is, carbohydrates supply half your body's energy needs for keeping each cell going and for all your activities.

Unfortunately, there are good carbohydrates and bad carbohydrates. The kind that nature provides us in the form of fruits, vegetables, and whole grains provide energy in the form your body can best use. But the carbohydrates which the processed food industry offers us in the form of sugary pastries, donuts, cottony white bread, and soft drinks are laden with chemicals and excessive amounts of cheap sugar.

It is these carbohydrates—the refined carbohydrates—that have earned all members of this food group a bad name. Refined carbohydrates can undermine health and, even worse, lay the groundwork for many major diseases, including cardiovascular disease and diabetes. There are many reasons why Americans—perhaps yourself included—have come to willingly accept a diet so high in refined carbohydrates.

Here are a few explanations:

1. *Ignorance.* If you don't read labels, ask questions, and educate yourself, you may be unaware of the low nutritional value processed foods provide.

2. *Advertising.* Processed foods are inexpensive to produce. They generate huge profits. Much of this profit is used to convince the public that processed refined carbohydrates are not only acceptable but healthy.

3. It isn't just the sweet flavor that makes it hard to resist taking a second candy—and a third—and another. Foods containing little more than refined carbohydrates such as sugar or denatured starches are *habit forming.* Sugar creates deficiencies and at the same time it creates a craving for more.

4. *Convenience.* You may be aware that advertisers grossly exaggerate the facts, and that sugar and devitalized starches offer only empty calories that turn into unwanted pounds. You may suspect that you are eating more than you should. But you do it anyway, telling yourself these foods are easy and convenient. After a long, hard day of work or a poor night's sleep, you may not relish the idea of cooking from scratch.

This rationalization can take years off your life by ruining your health.

5. *Hidden carbohydrates.* Surveys based on a sample of 400 members of my radio listening audience turned up evidence that the average American is now willingly and/or unknowingly eating between 4 and 5 ounces of sucrose a day—an amount definitely hazardous to anyone's well-being. And it is not because we are putting too much sugar in our tea or sprinkling it on our morning cereal. No, unfortunately it is because we are eating huge amounts of sugar hidden in a wide variety of popular foods.

An Example of the Effect of Hidden Sugars

This may seen incredible. But let's look at a day in the life of an "average" child.

This child is named Jimmy, and he's ten years old. His parents aren't impoverished or uncaring people, but well-educated middle-class professionals; they pay as close attention to the food their son eats as to the grades he brings home from school.

When Jimmy comes down for breakfast his mother has fixed him a hearty meal, designed (so she thinks) to supply all the nutrients he needs to remain energetic and alert throughout the morning. To start with there is a large glass of orange juice made from pure, unsweetened concentrate; after that a toasted English muffin with a little butter and some "natural" (preservative-free) jam. For his main course Jimmy gets a bowl of cold cereal with milk. The cereal is of the presweetened variety—a concession to Jimmy's sweet tooth—but no further sugar is allowed. And anyway, the cereal (like the English muffin) has been "enriched" with vitamins.

At lunchtime his mother can't control Jimmy's diet, since he eats the school lunch rather than bringing his own. Even so, there's no cause, so she believes, for alarm, because the school dietician always plans a nourishing, balanced meal. Today there's vegetable soup from a can, spaghetti with tomato-and-meat sauce, and canned string beans. Dessert is strawberry Jell-O with nondairy whipped cream.

For dinner, Jimmy gets his favorite meal of all: hamburgers, mashed potatoes, and creamed spinach. The burgers are served on fresh-made buns from a nearby bakery, and Jimmy likes his with plenty of ketchup and relish. The potatoes are made from a mix—Jimmy's mother was too tired to peel, boil, and mash her own—but the package reassures her that they have been enriched with several vitamins and minerals. The creamed spinach is from a frozen commercial preparation, but spinach is spinach—always good for you, she believes, and the freezing process "locks in" so many of the essential nutrients. Jimmy's father is on a diet, so there is no dessert, but when he's finished his homework, Jimmy sits down to watch television with cookies and a big glass of Coca-Cola. The cookies were purchased at the neighborhood bakery, so, like the hamburger buns, they must be okay.

Well, most people would say that Jimmy had only four foods which contain sugar today: the cereal, Jell-O, cookies, and soda pop. They're wrong. He had sugar—common table sugar—in all but a couple of the foods he ate. There was sugar in his muffins, his jam, his orange juice, his vegetable soup, his spaghetti sauce, his ketchup and relish. All of this was added by the companies that manufacture the foods.

Other Refined Carbohydrates

Sugar was not the only carbohydrate Jimmy got in his food today. He also got plenty of steamed, bleached, refined starch—empty calories almost as unhealthy as the table sugar. There was starch in his cereal, his muffins, his spaghetti, his hamburger bun.

What Jimmy missed in this array of bland, processed foods were most of the essential nutrients his mother wanted him to have. He missed out on them because American food production takes naturally nutritious food and strips it of almost everything that makes it worth eating. He got almost no natural fiber, the vital complex carbohydrate (which should have been abundant in his breads and cereals) that enables us to eliminate food wastes efficiently. He got almost none of the complex sugars that exist in plentitude in fresh fruits and vegetables and grains. He got a meager supply of the vitamins, minerals, amino acids, and other essential nutrients that we need to survive. In its natural and original form, his food possessed everything he needed. However, by the time he ate it, its nutrients had been stripped away.

What Jimmy ate instead were a few traces of vitamin additives, a whole storehouse of preservatives and other chemicals, several handfuls of refined starch—and about thirty teaspoons of table sugar. Can you imagine how much worse off he'd have been if his mother didn't care about his diet?

The Psychological Connection

There is good reason to worry about the preservatives and other chemical additives in Jimmy's food. But the worst cause for worry by far is the thirty-teaspoon sugar dose. The consequences of that, along with the nutrients he didn't get, will affect not only his physical health, but his psychological well-being, as well.

To understand how this happens, you have to realize that sugar gives Jimmy an energy boost similar to what adults get from caffeine. As the refined sugar pours into his bloodstream in one swift jolt, he becomes hyperactive and overexcited. He's had a powerful "drug" and the "drug" has a violent effect on the way he feels. But Jimmy doesn't know any of this; he doesn't know why he's feeling the way he does and he doesn't know how to express what's wrong.

As we mentioned earlier, Jimmy is normal in nearly all the areas of his life. However, let's illustrate what could happen when an otherwise balanced, rational child is given a substance which causes a hypersensitive brain reaction.

With that extra, unusable energy propelling him into hyperactivity, Jimmy can only express what he feels through antisocial behavior: anger, moodiness, irritability; he may be unable to concentrate. Since this behavior comes out when he's at school, Jimmy's teacher notices and marks him down as a "problem child" or "slow learner." When the behavior continues, reports start coming home to Jimmy's parents. Conferences are held, psychometric tests are given and therapists consulted, and soon Jimmy becomes an official "problem." And now his problems, initially caused by a simple dietary excess, become part of his family, part of his life. His parents feel guilty and get depressed because they don't know "where they went wrong."

Meanwhile, the cause of the problem goes unnoticed. Jimmy continues eating as much sugar as he always has, and in time he becomes a sugar addict every bit as dependent on his sugar dose as a caffeine addict is on his cups of coffee and cola drinks. (And remember, often Jimmy gets sugar and caffeine in the same overstimulating mouthful, from the cola that he drinks every day.) When he becomes an addict, he needs sugar to cure his "withdrawal symptoms": moodiness, headaches, fatigue, cramps. Unless someone breaks him of the habit, he'll have it for life.

And worst of all, it doesn't take massive doses of sugar to make Jimmy hyperactive all morning; a mere *two teaspoons* are enough. Multiply that dose by ten or fifteen, and you can guess the extent of Jimmy's sugar problem.

How American Adults Eat

Now imagine Jimmy as an adult. With no conscientious mother to look after him, he eats what he wants. Unwilling to take time for breakfast at home, he grabs a Danish pastry on his way to work and washes it down with coffee (two packets of sugar per cup). At midmorning, unable to concentrate because he's improperly nourished, he wolfs down another Danish and more sugary coffee. By lunchtime, he's starved, so after a cocktail (loaded with sugar), it's a king-size hamburger with French fries and lots of ketchup and relish, and then a piece of chocolate cake for dessert—with more coffee to follow. Later that day, if dinner isn't eaten at McDonald's, it will be a few more cocktails, a big steak and some potatoes, salad with dressing, and a piece of pie a la mode. After two cups of coffee (four teaspoons of sugar), he'll settle down to watch television with potato chips and soda.

Jimmy's consumption of table sugar has risen from about thirty teaspoons a day to well over fifty.

If this picture seems "extreme" to you, it may be that you're genuinely better informed about the importance of good diet than Jimmy and his mother. But don't think for a minute that the picture is false.

You might take your own survey about the foods most often eaten by your friends. Then calculate the amount of sugar. You'll be surprised if you were doubtful before.

Later in this section, we'll see how excess refined carbohydrates and lack of complex carbohydrates are implicated in a whole range of diseases and disorders, from constipation to colorectal cancer, from dental caries to heart disease and diabetes.

Changing Carbohydrates in Your Diet

Critics often insist that nothing in our diet is much different than it was three-quarters of a century ago.

But in days gone by, as in areas less affluent than ours, men, women, and children depended on the food they grew or raised, the riches with which nature had blessed them, not the riches they could have shipped in to suit their whims. Thus, until modern times, the diet was rich in complex carbohydrates from grains, legumes, tubers, and fruits in season, combined with dairy products and occasional meat or fish for additional protein.

The kind of sugar we were eating in the last century and that is slipping out of our diets now was the "good kind" that comes from tree-ripened fruits and fresh-from-the-garden vegetables.

The starches then were alive with vitamins, enzymes, and major and trace minerals for radiant health. A cooked, canned potato or carrot is no match for the real thing. It has been subjected to nutrient-killing heat and to the canning process, which may add dangerous contaminants, and it is now hazardously high in sodium and low in fiber. No wonder we reach for one candy bar after another! But that mythical "instant energy" comes from real foods in their natural state.

In America today, it is true that half our diet still consists of carbohydrates, similar to the 56.1 percent level noted from 1909 to 1913. But at that time, carbohydrates came largely from root vegetables and whole grains. Only about 21 percent was eaten in the form of sugary foods. By forty-five years later, fresh potatoes, brown breakfast cereals, and other high-mineral, whole foods had started losing ground. We were eating baked potatoes less often and replacing them with many high sugar convenience snacks. The result is that complex carbohydrates now make up 35.7 percent of our diet.[3-8]

There is no doubt a connection between the fact that one hundred years ago we ate one-fifth as much sugar and that[9] cancer and coronary heart disease were not discussed as "the killer diseases," despite the fact that no one worried about cholesterol. For optimal health, it is important to substitute whole for refined carbohydrates.

Alternatives

Whole foods are the real alternative to a diet of fractionated foods that lead to disease. Here are a few foods that you may have forgotten about lately. Eat them often. You can get all the energizing sugar and starch you need from them.

Whole grains, such as millet and barley, wheat and rye, oats, buckwheat, and corn, are available raw, cracked, or ground from any health food store. They can be turned into breads, side dishes, and hot cereals.

A large variety of peas and beans need only to be soaked overnight and then cooked an hour or so before they're ready to be eaten as soup or stew or as a main dish.

But why cook them at all? To get the maximum benefit from both grains and legumes, sprout them yourself or buy them sprouted and ready to snack on. They provide a starch food that's easier to digest because it's been broken down into simple carbohydrates. And when you sprout, you're carrying on a tradition that dates back as early as 3000 B.C.[10] It's a practice that deserves to be perpetuated.

Fresh corn on the cob is another example of a good carbohydrate starch. The North American Indians knew this. They worshiped corn as the "giver of life." It is available almost year round in many parts of our country and there are a half dozen delicious ways to prepare it—roasted indoors or out in the husk, baked, steamed, or broiled. You can even dry the ear and snack on the kernels. It is low calorie unless you raise the fat content with lots of butter.

How long has it been since you took the trouble to scrub, oil, and bake a nourishing, low-calorie potato? Few foods are so filling and so rich in natural carbohydrate. The skin alone contains almost one-fifth of this vegetable's protein and many nutrients. Many of the world's peoples—especially the Irish and British—still use the potato to great nutritional advantage. It is only slightly less important abroad than wheat. In fact, in 1967, 85 percent of the world's supply of potatoes was eaten by Europeans. And, of course, history books tell the story of how the potato saved so many lives during the eighteenth-century Irish potato famine. After World War I, many Germans escaped death[11] from malnutrition during the economic depression thanks to the availability of this amazing vegetable.

Of course, the ultimate alternative to a no-no like sugar candy is fruit. It has all the instant energy you need, plus all the nutrients that processing has taken out of the high-calorie processed snack. It takes five minutes to juice a pulp-and-bioflavonoid-rich orange, thirty seconds to peel a potassium-rich banana, and no time at all to eat an apple which, along with vitamins, gives you important carbohydrate elements such as fiber and pectin to lower your cholesterol. For fructose, glucose, and cellulose in a safe, natural form, "reach for a peach instead of a sweet."

Summary

All carbohydrates are not alike. Whole, complex carbohydrates are as essential to us as proteins and fats, vitamins and minerals, in maintaining health. They supply us with fuel that energizes every cell in the body. Due to ignorance, advertising, convenience, hidden sugars in our foods, and the fact that sugar is habit forming, we have come to substitute refined carbohydrates for complex. The result is often serious psychological problems: a child may become hyperactive and troubled as a result of his body's inability to process a carbohydrate overload. He or she can become addicted to sugar, as so many of us are: Americans eat about two pounds a week of refined sugar.

Good carbohydrates are abundantly available to all of us as unrefined or "whole" grains in the form of breads, cereals, and sprouts, as fresh fruits and root vegetables, as lettuces and other leafy green vegetables, as fresh or dried peas, and as lentils and beans. This diet, which seems so old-fashioned to us, is what many authorities believe spared our grandparents from such twentieth-century killer diseases as diabetes, cancer, and coronary heart disease. It is worth returning to if a long, healthy life is your goal for yourself and your family.

The Refinement of Breads

Most supermarkets are filled with them, most restaurants serve them, and statistics tell us that they constitute half of the American diet. Refined foods—which are largely refined carbohydrate—have come to replace whole, fresh foods. Bread, which was once known as "the staff of life," is a case in point.

There is a good reason why you no longer see advertisements claiming that white bread can "build strong bodies twelve ways." Bread that has been processed to remove the bran and germ is easy to eat and keeps a long time. But unless you are looking for empty calories, there is little reason to buy it, since most of the minerals, B vitamins, and important trace minerals have been removed. The pure white color certainly doesn't signal innocence—white bread has been refined, denatured, and processed to death. Dead food cannot keep us alive and well, whether it is refined wheat flour in bread, white rice, processed breakfast cereal, or refined sugar.

This does not mean you must avoid bread and starches. It is thanks to such energy foods that 80 percent of the population of less affluent countries survives.[12] But their breads are hearty, whole grain, home-made loaves; their grains are nut-brown, with hulls intact, exactly as nature intended.

What Have They Done to Our Wheat?

The staff of life was not always the same for different social classes. And although the best money can buy wheat that is whole, hearty, chewy, and aromatic, this was not the bread bought and preferred by the affluent. Instead, these privileged classes spent their money on the "clean," snow-white bread we now know is nutritionally inferior. The lower classes could not afford highly processed bread. They baked their own, benefiting from what the rich classes spurned.

Today, the tables have turned. The vast majority of our bread is sold in refined-to-death form, providing nothing more than starchy calories —and the poor and middle classes suffer what used to be the diseases of the rich.

The Changing Loaf

The removal of the life-giving qualities of the bread we eat was a gradual process. Unsurprisingly, convenience and profit were behind the decision to remove the nutritious heart and coating of the wheat kernel before grinding. White flour, it was quickly discovered, was easier to use: bread baked faster, it kept longer, and it looked better in those fancy dessert breads we still crave today because we are conditioned to see them as better than brown bread. Bleaching the flour so that it had even less life but more versatility and even greater shelf life came next.

White Bread for the Millions

The fact that white bread was costly protected the health of many, but not for long. The discovery of a method of removing the vitamin E-rich oil from the germ of the grain was healthy for profits, since this is the factor that contributes most to rancidity. This was discovered in the late 1800s, and steel rolling mills appeared, making inexpensive if unhealthy white bread readily available for the masses, and not just on Sundays.

What's Missing from White Bread

You may think you're economizing when you buy the least expensive, softest, whitest loaf of bread on the supermarket shelf. Unfortunately, convenience and snow-white appearance have a price. When the germ or heart of any grain is removed, you lose precious amounts of protein, fat, and carbohydrates, as well as many minerals and vitamins, especially vitamins B complex and E.

When the bran is ripped away, six entire fiber-rich layers are lost. In fact, according to analysts E. Baker and D. S. Lepkovsky, at *least* half of the mineral content is removed. Manganese may be reduced by 98 percent and iron by 80 percent.[9] In addition, some of the amino acids, the essential building blocks of protein—particularly lysine and tryptophan—are minimized.[13]

Enrichment Isn't What It Seems

So-called "enrichment" has been with us for almost half a century now. But this is largely a deceptive practice, since what is added is only a small part of what's been taken away. According to Beatrice Trum Hunter, the thiamine, riboflavin, niacin, and vitamin D used for enrichment are synthetic, not natural vitamins, and in place of the many minerals lost, only iron and calcium are usually returned. How could this be enough to support health when B vitamins that we know are necessary—such as biotin, pyridoxine, and pantothenic acid—are still missing, as is potassium, manganese, and some amino acids?[14]

Chemicals Worse than the Missing Vitamins

A little robbery here, a little thievery there may not seem so bad, until you realize that over the period of a year you may eat as many as ninety-two loaves of bread. You may try to protect yourself by taking a vitamin supplement to make up for what you're losing. This will rectify some of the loss. But it doesn't cancel out the harmful effects of the chemical preservatives, bleaches, and leavening agents used in the bread.

One of the worst of these is chlorine dioxide, the additive that removes any healthy brown color the wheat still has. This bleach destroys vitamin E, and when it combines with the important growth amino acid methionine it can give rise to a hazardous compound.[15]

It is used, as *Lockwood's Technical Manual: Flour Milling* explains, because "chlorine not only oxidizes the flour pigment but also has a valuable bleaching effect on the coloring matter of the bran, which makes it particularly valuable for bleaching very low-grade flours."[16] This saves the manufacturers money by enabling them to use less expensive flour.

Synthetic, artificially colored acids are also added to the dough. The purpose is ease in handling and smoothness, say manufacturers. Pseudo-butter is also used. No home baker has to use acids and synthetic grease to produce successful bread—nor does she or he worry about an oxidizer to capture air in the dough. Yet the food processors defend the poor value they give. According to *Baker's Weekly* most breads are only 50 percent grain, and a typical cake may be up to 75 percent air and "fillers." Pure profit is the only reason.[17]

A little bit of only *one* chemical can be a dangerous thing. Sodium and calcium propionate, for example, which are two additives the government requires on bread labels, are used in almost all commercial breads as a mold retardant. No one knows what effects combining the assorted bread additives can have on your health in the long run.

The Grain Robbery Goes On

The story of what's happened to all our other grains is similar. The white rice most people prefer because it's fast and foolproof is nothing but nutrient-free starch. Outside of health food stores, the only way you're likely to find rye, corn meal, or buckwheat cereals is cracked, precooked, degerminated, and mixed with additives such as sugar and salt.

As for breakfast, you may be congratulating yourself for passing up the high-sugar pastries, but when you get to the cereal shelf, you don't get much choice.

Rolled oatmeal is virtually the only grain which escapes the horrors of the refining process. According to *Consumer Reports* the ready-to-eat cereal business puts roughly $600 million into the pockets of the cereal corporations.[18] You have fifty, sixty, or more brands to choose from. The inflated prices are comparable and so are the supplementary ingredients—a combination of strange-sounding chemicals that make even the sugars and starches that are also present seem natural.

Few product categories compare with breakfast goods for mass appeal, due to the wonders of modern marketing. The cereal makers bid early for your youngsters' loyalty. According to *Consumer Reports*, together they spend more than $72 million[19] on spreading the word—much of it deceptive—about their products.

What You Can Do

Nothing that is two-thirds sugar is worth having in your house or starting the day with, say many experts who have made their strong feelings known before government committee hearings held by the Senate. For example, you may be familiar with former government advisor Robert B. Choate, Jr.'s widely publicized testimony before the Senate Consumers' Subcommittee.[20] Among the many shocking facts he brought to light was the fact that most of the top cereals "fatten but do little to prevent malnutrition."

If you agree, make your opinion known, too. Write your congressperson. And above all, boycott these junk foods.

Summary

Many of the modern carbohydrate foods upon which we base our daily diets look "pure," are easy to prepare, and last a long time on our shelves. But they are seriously deficient in basic nutrients for building and maintaining everyday health. Bread is perhaps the best example. Once "the staff of life," it has been refined, bleached, and processed to the point where white bread today is nutritionally minimal—at best. It is important to examine slick and deceptive advertising claims closely: cereal manufacturers, in particular, bid early for your children's loyalty to their usually worthless products. It is a good idea to replace any inferior carbohydrate foods in your household, such as white bread or white rice, with real, whole grain foods. Even so-called enriched loaves do *not* deliver all of the B vitamins, minerals, trace minerals, and naturally occurring fiber that is found in the *real* thing. Your bread also should be free of the dangerous, unnecessary additives that adulterate white bread and combine to add an unpredictable health risk to your meal.

Carbohydrates: A Definition

Carbohydrates are not just those substances you worry about in a candy bar, a slice of bread, or a potato if you are on a diet. They are found in every food, and every living plant, animal, or person. Of all the organic chemical families in nature, carbohydrates are most predominant, comprising 75 percent of all plant life on earth. Your house plant and your peanut butter sandwich both contain carbohydrates.

You cannot live without carbohydrates. They are your body's main source of energy: the fundamental fuel that makes every metabolic activity possible, from reproducing a single cell to thinking to lifting a heavy weight.

When carbohydrate levels are adequate, you feel full of vigor. Carbohydrates protect your body's supply of protein from being used for energy, a job it *can* do in an emergency. But when you eat enough carbohydrates, your body does not have to steal from its fat and protein stores to do the job of carbohydrates—giving you energy. The protein can be saved for the important role of manufacturing new cell tissue and maintaining the health of the old.

In your body, carbohydrates are nearly all broken down into glucose, a sugar molecule from which most other carbohydrates are constructed. Glucose is especially essential to cerebral function, since the brain cannot utilize any other energy source: a steady glucose supply to the brain is one of your body's highest priorities. Glucose is in fact the number-one end product of a complex natural process called photosynthesis.

Photosynthesis: The Magic Act by Which Carbohydrates Are Born

All carbohydrates, from the simplest sugars to the most complex starches and fibers, are made up of only three primary chemical elements: carbon, hydrogen, and oxygen.

Photosynthesis is the never-ending process carried on by plants to turn those three elements into carbohydrates. Without photosynthesis, we could not eat. Thanks to photosynthesis, incredible amounts of these elements are turned into edible carbohydrate for human nutrition.[21]

Photosynthesis is a natural form of solar power. Green plants utilize the fleeting energy of a ray of sunlight to create the storable food energy of sugar and starches—at the same time freeing the element oxygen for us to breathe.

It is a wondrous process. The key to it is a substance found only in plants: chlorophyll. Chlorophyll is that restful-looking substance that makes the grass on the ground and the leaves on the trees green. It's found in dozens of foods you probably eat every week—romaine lettuce, spinach, broccoli, kale: all the green leafy vegetables. But that pigment isn't confined just to the leaves and stems of plants; it is found in every one of the plant's countless molecules. Besides its role in photosynthesis, this amazing universal pigment is also responsible for the magnesium content in many of our favorite vegetables and fruits.

Photosynthesis is made possible solely by the fact that, because of the special properties of chlorophyll, all green plants are able to ensnare the rays of the sun, and use their energy to make food.

For photosynthesis to take place, that blade of grass or leaf of romaine must also pull carbon dioxide from the atmosphere and water from the soil. And then, as you would follow a recipe, it uses energy from the sunlight to combine the carbon dioxide (CO_2) of the air with the water (H_2O) it absorbs through its roots. Photosynthesis has been set in motion.

In the process of photosynthesis, oxygen is liberated from the carbon of the carbon dioxide molecule, and released into the atmosphere. (This process makes animal life possible.) The carbon combines with the hydrogen and oxygen of the water to make glucose—energy, in other words, for every activity you will engage in today, tomorrow, and as long as you live.[22]

Glucose is not the only end product of photosynthesis. However, it is the most important one—especially for us, since our brains would starve in minutes without glucose. There are other carbohydrate end products which are responsible for all the rich variety of vegetables, fruits, grains, legumes, nuts, and seeds we enjoy.

Summary

Carbohydrates do more than just contribute to our feeling of fullness after eating a bowl of spaghetti; they are more than just a source of roughage in our diets. Carbohydrates are the fuel cells of life. They do one job that neither fats nor proteins can do as directly: provide energy for every body activity, from cell metabolism to running a marathon. They are found in every living thing.

It is thanks to the miracle of photosynthesis that we have fruits, grains, seeds, nuts, and vegetables to eat—as well as air to breathe. Through photosynthesis, plants transform the energy of sunlight for storage in leaves, stems, roots, and seeds. This miraculous process, constantly taking place, creates the basic sugars from which all other carbohydrates are constructed.

Sugar: Not One, But Three

All sugars and starches are made from the same chemical elements —carbon (C), hydrogen (H), and oxygen (O)—in the same proportions —$C_6H_{12}O_6$.

But the carbohydrates are not all alike.

The simplest are the *monosaccharides*—the most basic of all sugars, consisting of just one sugar molecule ($C_6H_{12}O_6$).

Because they are simple does not mean they are in short supply. Any time you bite into something pleasantly sweet—a ripe fruit or a young ear of corn—you are probably partaking of one of nature's simple monosaccharides.

Nature combines the monosaccharides in chains to form *disaccharides* (double sugar, composed of two simple sugar molecules attached to form a larger one—$C_{12}H_{24}O_{12}$) and *polysaccharides* (complex sugars and starches whose molecules consist of long chains of attached simple sugars).

The two simple sugars whose names you run across in any conversation about carbohydrates are fructose and glucose. The two are *almost* twins to each other chemically—but a very slight structural difference between them causes fructose to be much sweeter than glucose.

Fructose occurs in countless combinations in the foods we eat. It is found in figs, cherries, bananas, and many other fruits—which is why it is called fruit sugar. But the place you encounter it most, unfortunately, is in refined sugar. Ordinary table sugar, whether in cubes or packets or sacks, whether it's white, yellow, or brown, is basically 50 percent fructose and 50 percent glucose bound together.[23]

Glucose, on the other hand, is much less sweet than fructose. Glucose—also known as blood sugar because your body reduces all sugars to this form—is found in most vegetables, including corn. When you read that "corn syrup" or "dextrose" is included in a packaged food, that means glucose—and it also means there's *lots* of it, since glucose isn't as sweet as table sugar.

Why Honey Seems Sweeter than Sugar and Other Mysteries

The reason you can use much less honey than table sugar is that it contains large amounts of naturally sweeter fructose. Here, in contrast to the way it occurs in other foods, fructose is found without its usual companion carbohydrate, glucose.[3] Free-form glucose is a rarity in nature, although you do find fair amounts of glucose in everyone's favorite late summer fruit: grapes.

These two simple sugars are called simple for another reason. They dissolve almost instantly and go directly to your bloodstream to be used for energy. Fruits and vegetables are a good source of simple sugar—something to bear in mind when you crave a juicy fruit or crunchy vegetable. A few good, sweet choices: ripe grapes, berries, apples, plums, and oranges, plus young corn and carrots.

Other Simple Sugars

Two less common simple sugars are *grammin,* a common sugar component in grain foods, and *galactose,* a product of your body's metabolism of milk sugar (lactose).

Double Sugars

If you are a conscientious label reader, then words like *maltose* and *lactose* are familiar to you, because they appear on the labels of hundreds of processed foods. Maltose (made from the breakdown of starch in the malting of barley) is actually a combination of two glucose molecules, while lactose is made up of glucose and galactose. Each is a good example of the double sugar group, the disaccharides.

MALTOSE

Maltose is most commonly found in baby formulas. It is easy to assimilate even by a developing digestive system, since the digestive enzyme diastase breaks it into two molecules of glucose—simple blood sugar.

LACTOSE

If you drink your coffee or tea with milk but no sugar, you're still consuming sugar! Milk contains a natural sugar, the disaccharide called lactose. The digestive enzyme lactase separates it into glucose plus galactose. Then your liver uses the galactose to produce glucose, blood sugar. Cow's milk is roughly 5 percent lactose, which is considerably less sweet than most other sugars in nature. This explains why milk doesn't taste sugary. Breast milk, however, is roughly 3 percent sweeter than dairy milk. (Maybe switching to cow's milk from the sweeter breast milk is the reason children tend to be so partial to chocolate milk, milk shakes, ice cream, and other sweetened-milk concoctions.[24]) Lactase is the enzyme that decomposes lactose into its separate parts. Lactase deficiency is sometimes diagnosed when the trouble, in fact, is more complex and more serious medically. That is, sucrase and mallase may also be in low availability as well.

Your ethnic origins are related to your ability to digest milk. Statistics tell us that while only one-tenth of North American Caucasians are lactase deficient, the figures are considerably higher for other peoples —Asians (90 percent), Israeli Jews (60 percent), Arabs (80 percent), and black Americans (70 percent).[25]

SUCROSE

Sucrose, or table sugar, is the most important and pervasive of the double sugars. Americans consume tons of it every year! It is hidden in thousands of products. Many people are addicted to it.

Sucrose is broken down in your intestines into glucose and fructose by the digestive enzyme sucrase.

Sucrose is generally derived from sugarcane or beets. In their natural state, these vegetables provide B vitamins and lots of fiber to slow the process of absorption and aid in the metabolism of sucrose. Refined, however, it floods your body with immediate, large quantities of glucose and fructose. This can put quite a strain on your endocrine system as the body struggles to keep blood sugar levels normal. If your pancreas overshoots the mark and causes too great a drop in blood sugar, your energy level, thinking ability, and emotional stability can be affected. These are common symptoms of low blood sugar—hypoglycemia. This blood sugar disorder can lead to diabetes—another reason to reduce refined sugar consumption. Sucrose is found, not only in table sugar, but in brown sugar, raw sugar, sorghum, molasses, and maple sugar.[26]

Complex Sugars

This carbohydrate class is found in many of our most-eaten and best-loved foods, such as breads, pasta, rice, cereals, and potatoes. The complex carbohydrates include both the oligosaccharides (a few sugars joined) and the polysaccharides (large multiples). Unlike the simple and double sugars, polysaccharides are not sweet.

Polysaccharides supply your body with energy. They cannot be used for nutritional purposes by your body until converted by a multi-step process into simple sugars, mostly glucose, blood sugar. This does not mean that a polysaccharide-rich yam is no better than a wand of pure sugar cotton candy. You derive no nutrients from the candy, but the yam supplies significant amounts of many nutrients in addition to natural sugar. The polysaccharides include starch; dextrins, which are actually components of starch which have been broken down; and glycogen, a starch which is made by your liver and muscles in order to store the energy of glucose.

The starches are among our most important sources of energy. A banana, a slice of whole wheat bread, or a bowl of oatmeal will help keep you going for hours.

The dextrins are a by-product of the breakdown of starch. They have the advantage of being more highly digestible than starch itself. Remember this: when you cut the crusts off your bread from force of habit, you have just discarded the most digestible part of all, since in baking, the outermost layer of starch in the bread dough was broken down into dextrin more than the rest.

Carbohydrates Increase Your Need for the B-Complex Vitamins

One good reason to bother eating whole grain bread and to take the extra twenty minutes to fix whole brown rice instead of the quick-cooking kind is that complex carbohydrates in their natural state contain all the B vitamins you need to properly digest and use them as nourishment. B-vitamin enriched foods don't provide this. As you may have noticed on labels, "enrichment" usually means that only a few—not *all*—of the B vitamins have been returned to the food.[27] Balance this against the large number removed by extensive refining, and you can see that the food—whether it is white rice, cornflakes, "enriched" flour, or a loaf of white or dyed-brown "whole wheat" bread made from mostly white flour—is still a deficient, unbalanced food.

Without this vitamin complex in its entirety, it is more difficult for your body to digest carbohydrates, to turn them into fuel. How much B complex do you need to accomplish this? That depends on your own individual body chemistry. But you can easily safeguard yourself if you remember that the more sugars and starches in your diet, the more B vitamins you need. If you aren't sure, a B-complex supplement might be in order. Better yet, stop eating refined sugars and starches.

The B_1 deficiency disease is beriberi. This was originally observed in Asia, and it might not have been discovered as a deficiency disease if someone hadn't noted the connection between the substitution of white rice for brown as a dietary staple and the sudden appearance of this "mystery" illness.

The Little-Known Carbohydrates

There are more chain-sugar carbohydrates, the oligosaccharides, which are of lesser importance. But here are a few facts about what they are, where they're found, and how your body uses them:

PENTOSES

You don't have to concern yourself with getting enough of these carbohydrate sugars. Common foods like oatmeal, Cream of Wheat, and brewer's yeast, as well as less common foods such as sea vegetables and fungus-type foods, are all good sources. But your body synthesizes pentoses to meet its needs, so the amount in these foods may be eliminated by the body anyway.

Pentose carbohydrates are the "genetic librarians" in every body cell. They help to store and reproduce information relating to your genetic heritage. One pentose, *ribose*, is necessary for the formation of ribonucleic acid, RNA, the chemical in your cells that holds the codes for protein synthesis. Another pentose is *L-xylose*. "Essential pentosuria" is a disorder that is genetically passed on. When it is present, L-xylose is lost in the urine. This has been the cause of clinical confusion, since this sugar depletion disorder can produce diabeteslike sugary urine even though diabetes is not present.[28]

OTHER OLIGOSACCHARIDES

If you like beans but they don't like you, blame it on the two carbohydrates *raffinose* and *stachyose*, commonly found in legumes. It is suspected that the reason for this incompatibility is that gas is formed when the bacteria in the large intestine acts upon them. This occurs because the enzymes in your small intestine are not equipped to break down these two carbohydrates into usable components.

While raffinose is made up of galactose, glucose, and fructose, and is thus a three-sugar carbohydrate, stachyose has one more saccharide, and thus is known as a tetrasaccharide. Raffinose occurs minimally in legumes, grains, and molasses and in a beet-sugar end product; stachyose occurs only in legumes. Soybeans are the best source.[29] Many people are not aware that cellulose—roughage—is also a carbohydrate. We will discuss fiber in the next section.

Summary

Not all sugars are alike. They are broken down into three classes —simple, double, and complex. The complex carbohydrates include starches, fibers, dextrins, and a few others. Of the simple sugars, fructose contributes the greatest sweetness. Glucose—also called grape sugar, dextrose, corn sugar (made into corn syrup), or blood sugar—is very similar but not as sweet. These two sugars combine to produce the double sugar sucrose, table sugar, that most refined and overconsumed of all food ingredients. The other double sugars, maltose and lactose, are also frequent food additives.

The complex carbohydrates are not sweet but starchy. They are found in grains, root vegetables, nuts, and seeds, and are combined with other nutrients. These are refined to produce white flour, white rice, white bread, pastries, and other products with little food value and lacking most of the B vitamins needed to digest them.

Sugars and starches appear everywhere in nature. They are manufactured by plants, and even by animals, which produce lactose (milk sugar) and glycogen (a starch). It is best to eat carbohydrates in their natural form, in fresh fruits and vegetables and whole grains, rather than in the huge quantities found in refined sugar, flour, and cereal products that your body was not really designed to assimilate.

Other, lesser-known complex carbohydrates include pentoses (found in oats and brewer's yeast) such as ribose, one of the bases of RNA; and raffinose and stachyose, found in legumes. They are another reason why your diet should always be varied enough to assure your body of every food element needed for day-to-day optimum health. No one food group and no one group of carbohydrates provides it all.

The Unavailable Carbohydrates

The sugars and starches described in the previous section are known as the *available* carbohydrates.

But there is another, very important form of complex carbohydrates besides these. They provide no known nutrients; they pass right through the digestive tract and are eliminated, virtually impervious to the barrage of powerful enzymes, acids, and microorganisms that pulverize and digest the rest of your food.

Yet without them, you are subject to such problems as constipation, diverticulitis, appendicitis, and cancer of the colon.

These *unavailable carbohydrates*, the indigestible polysaccharides, are, of course, the fibers found in fruits, vegetables, and grains. Fiber is so prevalent in plants that it is absurd that Americans rarely get enough of it. Cellulose is more abundant than any other organic compound in the world. The name "unavailable carbohydrates" refers to the fact that these carbohydrates are not metabolized in the body—not to lack of abundance!

The members of the fiber family include cellulose, hemicellulose, ligrin, pectin, agar, alginates, and vegetable gums such as carrageen (Irish moss).

CELLULOSE

When you eat an apple you are getting a little fructose, a bit more glucose, and a lot of cellulose. These carbohydrates don't compete with one another. The sugars provide sweetness, and cellulose lends strength. If you looked at cellulose under the microscope, you would see a strong fibrous substance that does not dissolve in water. These properties make it desirable for many commercial purposes; for example, natural clothing fibers such as cotton are made of cellulose. Considering its physical qualities, it should come as no surprise that cellulose occurs largely in the cell walls of plants, shaping and supporting each cell and the plant as a whole.

Despite the fact that cellulose is indigestible and yields no vitamins, minerals, or nourishment for your system, it is indispensable. Fiber keeps your intestines swept out. The microflora in your large bowel degrades cellulose only slightly, but this unavailable carbohydrate *is* available to prevent clogged bowels and colon. Along with absorbing water to make your stool soft, and adding bulk and weight so it can pass easily, cellulose absorbs toxins and helps eliminate them from your system.

Fiber is crucial to digestion. One of its most important roles is to stimulate the intestinal movements, peristalsis, which push the food masses through the digestive tract. Thus, fiber is a natural laxative—far healthier than the artificial, chemical laxatives to which so many Americans are addicted, and which actually end up preventing peristalsis from proceeding normally. Unlike chemical laxatives, fiber gives the muscles along the walls of your intestines the exercise they need to keep functioning properly for you.

Many staple foods are rich in valuable roughage. Cellulose is found in the outer or bran layer of grains, such as whole rye, brown rice, and wheat kernels. There is no need to sprinkle bran on your food if you eat the whole grains in the first place. Bran is just one of the layers discarded when the grain is refined. Why pay extra to the manufacturers to buy again what they shouldn't have separated from your grain in the first place?

Cellulose is also found in the "stringy" section of common fruits and vegetables, especially the ones that call for lots of chewing—apples, celery, and carrots, for example.[30]

Should you eat your vegetables cooked or raw? A good cellulose source may in some cases be a poor nutrient source if you don't break down at least some of the cellulose of the cell walls by chewing, cooking, or steaming. A high-fiber root vegetable such as a carrot is one example of a food whose nutrients are available *if* you chew it well or cook it. Grinding or sprouting are other ways to treat whole grains so that the nutrients they contain will be available to your body cells.

Though fiber is easily available in nature, there are foods which contain virtually *no* fiber. Any food that has been highly processed by the manufacturer, fruit juices without any pulp or sediment, honey so clear you can see through it, Minute Rice and most white breads have negligible amounts. Some relatively natural foods like meat and fowl are nearly fiber free, too.

PECTIN

Cellulose is often found with pectin, another "roughage" carbohydrate derived mostly from fruits such as grapes, apples, peaches, plums, and berries. This complex sugar may help keep your cholesterol levels low and healthy. Pectin absorbs and holds water. If you are a home jam and jelly maker, you have probably used pectin to turn fruit juice into fruit spread. But pectin is more than a gelling agent. It is a polysaccharide that is beneficial, especially when used as it occurs naturally with large amounts of cholesterol-lowering fiber. Although vegetables supply this complex sugar, too, the richest fruit pectin sources are plums, real apple juice (79 percent), and blackberries (53 percent).[31, 32]

AGAR

Agar, like pectin, is used as a gelling agent. Agar comes not from fruits but from seaweed.

VEGETABLE GUM AND ALGINATES

The vegetable gum carrageen (Irish moss) and the alginates (from seaweed) are often added to packaged foods like ice cream. They smooth out the texture of mixed ingredients. They are harmless food additives, although they may be added to foods whose texture wouldn't seem of such high quality without them.

A Riddle About Carbohydrates

If both vegetables like carrots and snacks like caramels contain carbohydrates from which glucose is derived for energy, why does one supply quick energy while the other doesn't?

Part of the answer concerns the slow pace of digestion of complex carbohydrates. The candy is composed largely of refined sugar, so your body converts it rapidly into its two main carbohydrate components—fructose and glucose—and within minutes[33] you feel a lift as it is picked up by your bloodstream.[34]

By comparison, nature had something else in mind with a vegetable, with its more nourishing but complicated combination of carbohydrates. The various polysaccharides are broken down at a slower pace than table sugar. The energy from sunlight that photosynthesis has locked into the carrot's starches and sugars takes longer to become available, but also lasts longer.

Another part of the answer concerns the role of fiber in digestion. The carrot has fiber, but the empty calorie snack has none. The indigestible fiber helps lubricate the gastrointestinal tract and assures normal digestion and elimination; however, it also locks some of the starches and sugars inside the carrot's cells.

There is a way to get a "quick energy" lift from a carrot, though. Put it through a juicer! (If you don't own one, many health food stores, snack bars, and restaurants now do, and sell fresh carrot juice.) This will pulverize the cell walls and make the sugars (and starches) inside more quickly available for digestion and absorption.

This is a much healthier dose of sugar than that from the caramel. Since it is less concentrated and smaller in quantity, it does not contribute to stress by causing blood sugar levels to fluctuate, as does the candy. Drinking small quantities of carrot juice won't give you hypoglycemia. Too much candy may.

Summary

The unavailable carbohydrates are among the most important. They provide no energy—yet without them we are liable to suffer the loss of energy that comes from poor digestion.

Cellulose, from the cell walls of plants, is also known as dietary fiber or roughage. It stimulates peristalsis and keeps the intestines clear of residue and toxic wastes. It absorbs water from the intestines, adding bulk and weight to the stool and making it smooth and easy to eliminate. It is found in whole grains, fruits, and vegetables. It beats chemical laxatives hands down, since it prevents the intestines and colon from getting lazy and out-of-practice.

Other unavailable carbohydrates are used in home and industrial food processing. They include pectin, agar, alginates, and vegetable gums.

Sugar as a Food Additive

Repeated daily doses of refined sugar—especially when packaged with other health-hazardous food components such as saturated fats and chemical additives—can lead to serious health problems. These include coronary heart disease, cholesterol buildup, and other disorders arising from veins, arteries, and a heart muscle weakened by a high-sugar diet.

Yet our diet is rife with sugar. We add it to our coffee, cereal, and desserts, and our food producers throw it into nearly everything they package—canned vegetables, processed meats, condiments, not to mention canned syrupy fruits and other desserts.

An educated consumer learns to read labels, to recognize sugar in all forms, and to avoid it wherever possible, since most people can get all they need from fruits, (nature's main source) and vegetables, and from the breakdown of starch in digestion.

Let's look at some of the sugars used as food additives.

Sucrose. This is the most common. It is usually listed on packages as "sugar," but sometimes, in foods with so much sugar that sugar *should* be the first word on the ingredients list, "sucrose" is listed separately near the end of the list along with several other kinds of sugar, to pacify the unwary. Don't be fooled. "Sucrose" is really plain old table sugar, the same stuff that makes dessert such a mine field for dieters.

Corn syrup. Strange as it sounds, it's possible that most of the sugar you eat comes in the form of corn syrup. This cheap, almost 100 percent glucose sugar is extracted from corn starch. It is inexpensive, liquid, and easy to use. It is therefore the one most manufacturers of processed foods prefer, and the one they use the most, in everything from soup to nuts. The term "corn syrup" on a label is a tip-off that the product —anything from coffee lightener to candy bars—contains glucose in an uncombined form.

"Glucose" or "corn syrup" is also a tip-off that you are getting more sugar than you would be getting if you made the product yourself using table sugar. This is because glucose is less sweet than table sugar. It is also very cheap, and thus profitable for manufacturers to use in large amounts.

Sugar growers and processors have effectively blocked any legislation requiring label declarations of the amount of glucose used in a product. Since the sweeter a product is, the more appealing, it is easy to understand how much sugar a high-sugar diet of store-bought foods may be yielding you.[35, 36]

Don't forget that glucose may also be referred to as grape sugar, fruit sugar, or blood sugar. (It won't be called blood sugar on a label, though.)

When you're tempted to choose a can of glucose-loaded soda over a piece of naturally energizing fruit, remember the description one glucose critic—Dr. Harvey Wiley, the person primarily responsible for passage of the important Pure Food and Drug Act of 1906—used for this unhealthiest of all the sweeteners. He called it "the champion adulterant."[37]

Fructose. There are foods being sold with the label "no sugar added" that plainly include fructose on the ingredients list. This is false. Make no mistake—fructose *is* a sugar.

If you read magazines for dieters or athletes, then you've read the ballyhoo on behalf of the supposedly "new, improved" sugar, fructose. Fructose sales benefit agribusiness, because when used commercially, this sweetener is derived from corn. Income from sales also accrues to the pockets of food marketing corporations, since fructose is widely used in fast foods in its liquid form.

Could this be the explanation for the sudden interest in this high-priced sugar substitute? It seems likely, since defenders of the consumers' best interests and respectable medical authorities seem to be conspicuous by their absence on the fructose bandwagon.

Human beings have been consuming fructose in its natural, unrefined state as long as we have walked the earth. Real fruit sugar is found in cherries, bananas, apples, and grapes (5–8 percent) and is also found in smaller quantities in strawberries, grapefruit, oranges, blackberries, and blueberries (2–3 percent).[38] Fructose also accounts for almost half of the sweeteners you get in honey. And of course, your body breaks down cane or beet sugar—sucrose—into fructose and glucose. Certainly, our bodies are adapted to use fructose. But it is questionable whether refined, pure fructose is better for you than any other refined sugar.

There are those who claim that fructose does not cause the sharp changes in blood sugar levels that sucrose does, and therefore must be beneficial for diabetics and hypoglycemics as a sucrose substitute. They argue that it is digested at a very slow pace, and thus, unlike sucrose or glucose, does not flood the bloodstream with sugar. Such flooding can overstimulate insulin production, causing wide fluctuations in blood sugar levels.

Then, in the liver, fructose is metabolized twice as fast as glucose, where it is rapidly transformed into glucose and then glycogen for storage.

The proponents of fructose conclude that, even if you do eat too much, it enters the bloodstream slowly and leaves it fast (due to the rapid conversion by the liver), bypassing the whole insulin-producing mechanism so fraught with peril to hypoglycemics and diabetics.

In addition, they point out that, since fructose is sweeter than glucose, you are likely to eat less at one time.

These arguments might be persuasive, were it not for the fact that most fructose is converted to glucose in the body—and is then indistinguishable from the glucose that comes from sucrose or corn syrup.

Furthermore, experiments with animals indicate that the theory that fructose does not stimulate insulin production is probably wrong. Animals fed pure fructose show higher levels of both insulin and triglycerides than animals fed starch. (High triglyceride levels have been implicated in coronary heart disease.) Researchers have demonstrated that fructose raises glycerol levels. (Glycerol is a part of the lipid-fat family.) They concluded that fructose raises lipid levels more than other refined sugars do. Lipids are fats: you do not need extra fats circulating in your bloodstream.

And fructose has other disadvantages. The liver doesn't convert all of the excess fructose in the system to glucose. What escapes conversion and is not used by the cells (which use it far less efficiently than glucose)[39, 40] may be thrown out via the urine. This can cause confusion about test results for diabetes mellitus, whose diagnostic indication is sugar in the urine.

Fructose has also been shown to raise uric acid levels (though this is not considered a threat to normally healthy individuals).

Too much sugar of any kind isn't good for you. Fructose, in particular, can cause diarrhea if you eat too much.

Finally—and this has to be a consideration for most of us—fructose is expensive to produce and costly to buy. Since many medical authorities feel it offers no special advantages in diseased states, i.e. dental caries or diabetes, you should not be too anxious to switch.[41]

Sorbitol. This is another sweetener often used as a food additive. If you are avoiding sugary chewing gums, you may have switched to a sugarless brand compounded with this carbohydratelike substance. Chemically, it is a monosaccharide-derived alcohol, sweet like sugar, but not really a sugar. Sorbitol can be extracted from fruits; however, when we encounter it in chewing gums, diabetic foods, and commercial bakery foods, it is usually synthetic. Manufacturers like it because it not only makes food sweet but keeps it moist.[42]

Which Form of Sugar Should You Use on the Table?

We have already discussed the pros and cons of the sweetest sugar, fructose. Now let's look at the many forms in which people eat the most common one, sucrose. Are there advantages to eating it as brown sugar or raw sugar, or to using maple syrup, molasses, or honey instead?

Brown sugar. Unfortunately, according to sugar researchers, both light- and dark-brown sugar may be even more dangerous than white sugar, since brown sugar usually gets its healthy looking "tan" not from nature, but by way of a colorizing process involving charcoal and other factors that are suspected presently of being carcinogens.[43] Otherwise, brown sugar is just like white sugar: highly refined, nutrient-depleted, too-rapidly-absorbed sucrose.

Raw sugar. When you buy raw sugar, if you think you're purchasing a more natural, less refined product that will do your body less harm than refined, white sugar, you'll have to revise your thinking. Raw "turbinado" sugar has been through almost the whole refining process white sugar undergoes. Dr. John Yudkin, the eminent sugar authority quoted at the beginning of this chapter, uses this humorous analogy to describe the similarity:

> Imagine me walking out into the street wearing nothing but my tie, and then stating that I am dressed; but if I take my tie off, I might say that I am now undressed. It's the same way with raw and refined sugar. Those who imagine raw sugar as nearly natural material are like people who would think me wonderfully dressed if I walked into the street wearing only my tie.

Maple syrup. Does the quality and the unusual flavor of maple syrup justify the price? How much nutrition are you getting for your dollar?

Even when it's the real thing, maple syrup is still largely sugar.

And when it's *not* pure maple syrup—as most waffle and pancake syrups are not—it may be worse than sugar.

Consider this warning from Beatrice Trum Hunter, the author of *Consumer Beware:* what you are blissfully dribbling over your morning waffles may be rich in *paraformaldehyde* as well as sugar. In some maple-tree-producing states, this chemical is used in the tree to eliminate certain bacterial factors. The sap flows faster and, of course, this benefits the producer—if not the consumer.

You can avoid contaminated syrups by buying only those from Canada, Vermont, or other states that do not permit this practice.[44]

Of course, real Vermont or Canadian maple syrup is scarce and expensive. Many waffle syrups do not even contain maple syrup. You can only read the labels to decide whether it's worth buying these concoctions of corn syrup, sugar and, often, artificial flavors. As an alternative, try switching to honey, perhaps combined with a more nutritious, rarely contaminated sweetener such as unsulfured molasses, if you appreciate a more robust, pronounced flavor in your syrup.

Light cane molasses. If you have a sweet tooth you've decided to try to live with in a healthy way, here's a sweetener to consider. Molasses is produced during the process of refining sugar from sugarcane. But this product is the fraction that manufacturers are least interested in—the small portion bearing the mineral and B-vitamin content.[45] However, even *this* sweetener borders on being an empty calorie food, too. So use it in moderation.

Honey. If you are at all health conscious, you probably put honey instead of jam on your toast. A few drops of Orange Blossom honey have replaced the sugar in your tea; you dribble it over your breakfast fruit and flakes, and use it as an afternoon energizer.

Your honey may not be the pure natural food it's reputed to be. But if you can answer the following questions yes, then you have purchased a true health food, superior in many ways to sugar, reminiscent of the food famous since the days of the Israelites.

• Did it come from a reputable health food store?
• Does the label use one or more of these descriptive terms: "raw," "unfiltered," "unpasteurized," "unheated," "no heat used"? This label declaration, which is not required by law, is your assurance that you have not purchased just a "liquid sugar,"[46] a product that has been so heat-treated and refined that it offers no advantages over sugar.

Honey is a naturally occurring sugar requiring no refinement. It supplies more nutrients than white sugar or maple syrup. Honey consists of minerals such as potassium and calcium, important trace minerals, and small amounts of essential B vitamins. The darker your honey is, the truer this is.

Honey is free of pesticide poisons, thanks to the fact that bees will usually avoid blossoms that have been sprayed, or will perish after exposure because of their intolerance to such toxins.[47]

You cannot automatically replace white sugar with honey unless you realize that honey, like all sugars, can produce dental caries and add appreciable amounts of calories to the diet.

Additionally, honey will digest at approximately the same rate as the other simple sugars, and is therefore not recommended for hypo-glycemics or diabetics. It is a common allergen.

On the more positive side, unlike its overly refined counterparts, honey does have a full complement of vitamins, minerals, amino acids, and enzymes, which allow it to be digested without robbing the body of B vitamins that are necessary for the digestion and absorption of other simple carbohydrate foods.

Also, honey has antibacterial and antiseptic qualities.

Saccharin

Saccharin is not a sugar and it is not a food. It is a nonnutritive, artificial sweetener made from coal tar. However, it is important to discuss it in a chapter on sweeteners because so many people use it as a sugar substitute, and very few are aware of how extremely serious the risk of consuming saccharin is—especially to their children.

While it has been around since 1879,[48] it is only since the 1960s, when dieting became a national obsession (remember Twiggy?) and diet soft drinks and other snacks became big business, that Americans began consuming it in large quantities. Saccharin is three to four hundred times sweeter than sugar. By now a whole industry has grown up based on it—an industry that is fighting to protect its investments, even if serious health disorders occur over the years.

Although Food and Drug Administration pathologists had raised the question of whether saccharin might cause cancer as early as 1951, it was not until the late 1970s that saccharin was decisively shown to cause cancer in laboratory animals, as the result of a carefully designed study by the Canadian Health Department of the effects of both saccha-rin and OTF (ortho-toluensul formide), a common impurity found in saccharin, on rats. Three out of one hundred rats fed a diet of 5 percent saccharin from birth developed bladder cancers. Still more frightening, a whopping fourteen out of one hundred of their offspring tested did, too. The normal rate for bladder cancer in rats is less than 2 percent. (Rats fed OTF showed no such ill effects.)

This means, according to the FDA, that at the highest level of risk for humans, 4 persons out of 10,000 would develop bladder cancer if they drank just one twelve-ounce can of diet soda a day for a lifetime. That's 90,400 out of 226 million Americans.

U.S. law requires that the FDA immediately ban the use of any food additive shown to cause cancer when fed either to animals or to human beings. There is good reason for this clause, called the Delaney amendment (after New York Congressman James D. Delaney) in the Federal Food, Drug and Cosmetic Act of 1938. There is wide agreement among authorities in the study of cancer worldwide that there is *no safe amount* of a carcinogen: if something causes cancer in large doses, it will do so in small doses also, though the cancer may take longer to appear.

Thus, the aggressively asserted and widely publicized argument of the powerful agribusiness and food industry interests, that the Canadian study was irrelevant because the rats were fed such a large quantity of saccharin (they equated it with 800 cans of diet soda a day), is so much hot air. Should industry really have the right to sell you a carcinogenic soda just because you or your children are likelier to come down with bladder cancer at the age of fifty rather than seventeen if you drink it habitually today?

No two people have the same tolerance level for any nutrient or nonnutrient. And the effects of saccharin tend to be cumulative. Therefore a person having a diet containing a high saccharine content—in foods such as diet soda and chewing gum, diabetic candies, bread or other items—would, over a period of years, increase their cancer risk rate far above that of a person not consuming these as regularly. Additionally, the person's state of health when consuming the saccharin could make the saccharin more potent in its effects. For example, a person recuperating from a major disease that has lowered his immune response, especially a child or elderly individual, could have a greater likelihood of having an adverse reaction to the saccharin than an otherwise healthy individual.

Therefore no one, no scientist anywhere, can claim that saccharin is an innocuous substance, as our reactions to it are so specific.

It is tragic that so many people were taken in by the food industry's media blitz. Now that the Delaney amendment has been weakened by the precedent of Congress's allowing saccharin to remain on the market, you are less likely to be protected from other carcinogenic food additives that will be discovered in the future. Caveat emptor, let the buyer beware, has again become the watchword of the food industry. For your health's sake and that of your children, you'd be well advised to take it very seriously, and beware of saccharin.[49]

Summary

Know your sweeteners. Glucose is the "champion food additive," and is present in any food whose label mentions corn sugar, corn syrup, dextrose, grape sugar, or fruit sugar. It is not very sweet, so there is probably a lot present if it is there at all. Table sugar may also be listed by its chemical name, sucrose. Supersweet fructose, or fruit sugar, is usually derived from corn for commercial purposes at considerable expense; its advantages over other forms of refined sugar are probably greater to manufacturers in the form of large profit margins than to consumers in the form of any of the much-ballyhooed health benefits. Sorbitol, while sweet, is not actually a sugar, but is metabolized in the body like sugar.

A quarter of the sugar you eat is probably added by food processors. If you must use sugar on your table and for baking, raw, unrefined honey is probably the healthiest form in which to use it. (But have you tried including dried fruit in baked goods instead even of honey?) Real maple syrup, uncontaminated by paraformaldehyde, is delicious, but awfully expensive—and it is still mostly sugar. Unsulfured molasses supplies some B vitamins and minerals that table sugar does not. But *all* sugary sweeteners can be habit forming and should be used with great moderation.

Table sugar, turbinado sugar, brown sugar, and raw sugar are so similar that it makes no difference which you choose—except that brown sugar has added chemicals that may be harmful.

Saccharin has been shown to cause cancer in test animals and their offspring, and using it doesn't reduce your caloric intake all that much. It is a carcinogen that should not have been allowed to remain on the market.

The healthy alternative is to wean yourself away from all added sugars as much as possible. Switch from gooey desserts to chewy, naturally sweet fruits. And use dried fruits only in moderation, too: the natural sugar in them is extremely concentrated, and may cause cavities just like refined sugar. Rice syrup, barley syrup, and other grain syrups are less processed, have more vitamins and minerals, and are preferable over all other sugars mentioned.

Eight Facts About Sugar

1. You could be eating a high-sugar diet even if you don't own a sugar bowl. Half of our carbohydrate intake is in the form of sugar, experts tell us; between 20 and 25 percent of our calories come from sucrose. Most of it is already in the foods we buy.[50]

2. If your family includes an average teenager or preteen, he or she

consumes even more sugar directly and indirectly than you do—150 pounds a year, compared to the typical adult intake of 130 pounds a year.

3. If you eat processed foods, it's easy to take as much as one-fourth of your food energy in the form of empty calories, because sugar is "hidden" in many of our favorite everyday store-bought foods. Some are alarmingly high in sucrose: ketchup, coffee lighteners, and salad dressings are a few examples.

4. Part of the blame for sugar dependency in our society belongs to food processors. It is easier and more profitable to turn out devitalized foods than to take the care that the production of real food requires. Examples of companies who offer cash "rebates" to schools in exchange for proof of purchase from their sugary, empty-calorie offerings brought in by pupils are unfortunately growing.[51]

5. In its natural state, before the processors get to it, raw cane sugar juice actually contains unsaturated fatty acids, almost half of the B complex, vitamins A and D, protein substances we call enzymes, plus some minerals. All but a trace of the minerals, however, are destroyed by refining.[52]

6. You may be a "sucroholic," if you can't leave those sweets alone. Many investigators, such as Dr. Abraham Nizel of Tufts University, tell us that a dependency on sugar is similar to drug addiction. Look closely at your diet. If it is so high in refined sugary foods that you are forced to rely on three-quarters of it to supply the nutrients your body needs for growth and cellular repair, then your diet is in need of reform.[53]

7. Sugar plays a determining role in the development of many diseases. Problems of fluid retention which may be caused by sugar can lead to hypertension. Sugar is just as suspect as dietary fats in promoting cardiovascular disease, say experts such as Dr. John Yudkin.[54]

8. Dietary imbalance and malnutrition occur when the sugar and other negative foods in your diet outweigh the positive foods you eat. Millions of Americans are not much different from the animals described by a report in *Nutrition Reviews* revealing that when both high-sugar and high-nutrient foods were available, the animals made the worst choice.[55] Abnormal body fat deposits, often a result of sugar intake, are frequently linked to a diet low in protein and thiamine, the B vitamin needed for activating the glucose that gives you energy.[56]

The ABCs of Carbohydrate Digestion

Understanding how your body digests carbohydrates will help you see why unrefined, whole carbohydrates are healthier than refined sugars and starches. The process begins before you even put the food in your mouth.

1. Aroma. A sharp sense of smell is the first step in digestion, strange as it sounds, because the nerves that act as aroma perceptors in your nose help to stimulate the production of saliva in your mouth and the gastric juice in your stomach. Good-smelling foods "make your mouth water." These savory aromas help insure good digestion.

2. Saliva acts fast. As soon as the parotid glands behind each ear receive the signal, saliva is produced and the enzymes it contains go to work digesting your morning toast or lunchtime cole slaw—right in your mouth.

3. Chew your food thoroughly. You may have heard this many times since you were a kid. There's a reason for such advice. The more the food is masticated, the more completely it is digested and assimilated. And the longer that raw carrot remains in your mouth, the more amylase or ptyalin enzyme will be secreted. This in turn converts the polysaccharides—glycogen, starch, and dextrin—into the double sugar maltose.[57] One thing these oral enzymes can't do is turn disaccharides into monosaccharides. Sucrose remains undigested in the mouth.

4. Half a minute after you swallow, everything changes. Any ptyalin that finds its way to your stomach meets its end there, because among its many activities, the powerful hydrochloric acid in the stomach destroys this enzyme, and carbohydrate digestion is slowed somewhat.[58] Hydrochloric acid also liquefies the carbohydrate components as a blender might, so they can be passed along to be further digested as they progress along your body's digestive tract.

5. The upper section of your small intestine is called the duodenum, and the sugar-digesting enzyme found there is similar to ptyalin. This enzyme is called pancreatic amylase. Once more the tempo of carbohydrate digestion is picked up, as this enzyme attacks the starches and sugars that food contains.

6. Double sugars are decomposed by enzymes secreted from the wall of the small intestine. The enzyme lactase attacks lactose (milk sugar); sucrase splits sucrose (table sugar), dextrin, and the other products of the breakdown of starch. Your intestinal wall also secretes enzymes that turn fructose into glucose. Total breakdown of complex carbohydrates will take roughly two hours. Simple sugars can take as little as fifteen minutes. But carbohydrate food can remain in the stomach for as long as ninety minutes. How the food was cooked, how you feel, how much available glucose was present, and how much you eat are factors that speed up or slow down that transit time. Carbohydrates and simple sugars usually move through your system faster than all other foods. Honey may require more time than sucrose, fructose, or glucose to travel from your stomach to your small intestine to be assimilated.[59]

You Are What You Assimilate: How Absorption Works

Digestion is only part of the process that turns food into nourishment. If it's true you are what you eat, there's even more truth in the observation that you are what you absorb. Here's how that postdigestive process works.

Since foods cannot be taken up by your bloodstream until they have been turned into simple sugars, let us observe what happens to the carbohydrate fragments of that carob brownie you ate, in their simplest, single-sugar form. Absorption takes place so quickly following conversion of starches and sugars into monosaccharides that the largest percentage of carbohydrate has been taken up and utilized by the time the food reaches the midpoint of the small intestine. Conversion and absorption seem like one and the same process, so rapidly does your system do both jobs. Your system acts like a kitchen food processor, turning large food molecules into minute ones. Your digestive tract is equipped with meshlike material that is in actuality a colony of enzymes that are capable of miniaturizing molecules as needed.[60]

The different kinds of carbohydrates are assimilated at different speeds. Sucrose, for example, is so simple it requires little effort to be assimilated: as soon as it hits the small intestine, sucrase breaks it into glucose and fructose. That's why you feel its effect so rapidly; it is literally in your bloodstream in no time.[22] A stalk of celery, in contrast, cannot readily be broken down. The cellulose-type carbohydrates that predominate in this vegetable are so complex, they don't go into your bloodstream at all.

In the middle are the complex carbohydrates represented by starch, the kind found in potatoes, corn, and bread. Conversion here is slower than that for sugar, but not as slow as that required by high-roughage foods. For this reason, digesting and assimilating such a good food is easy on your very active gastrointestinal system.

If you know what factors are at play in food absorption, you can sometimes do a thing or two to facilitate matters yourself at mealtime.

• The fewer different foods fight for the attention of your enzymes, the smoother the whole operation is bound to be.

• If you're hungry and distraught because your blood sugar is low, the breakdown and absorption of food will be less efficient than if you are experiencing true hunger at a normally appointed time.[61] It's important to space your meals intelligently, not waiting until you're famished to eat.

• Try to eat at least one fiber food with each meal. Your fat- and protein-rich foods will be better digested because roughage smooths the way through the entire gastrointestinal tract.

Summary

Carbohydrate digestion begins before you even bite into your foods. The savory aroma of good food stimulates saliva production; your saliva contains enzymes which break starches and sugars into double sugars. It is important to chew your food well to facilitate this process. In your stomach, hydrochloric acid liquefies your foods; but it is in the small intestine that most carbohydrate digestion takes place. There is a meshlike net of enzymes in your intestine to break down all the starches and sugars that your body is going to use into single sugars, because only these tiny molecules can be absorbed through the walls of the small intestine and into the bloodstream. To help your intestines along, you can eat only a few different foods at each meal; chew your food well; and be sure that each meal includes some roughage from the skins of fruit, the hulls of seeds, the bran from grains, or from legumes or raw vegetables.

The Role of Your Liver in Carbohydrate Metabolism

No other organ is as important as the liver in the processing of your body's fuels. All sugars are routed through the liver before they are used by the rest of the body.

Let's take a step-by-step look at what happens to the sugars and starches you have eaten after they are digested.

You've had your salad and sandwich lunch. Once it has been digested, your body begins the work of absorbing the components of the sugars and starches in their simplest, single-sugar form.

From the intestinal wall, after absorption into the blood, these sugars make the journey to your liver by way of the portal vein.

Your liver then "decides" what to do with all these simple sugars. The liver may send glucose right back into your bloodstream so your cells can use it for energy. Or the glucose "juice" may be turned into glycogen, a complex carbohydrate. The glycogen may then be sent to the muscles, for use as fuel or for storage, or this potential fuel may be stashed away for emergencies in the liver itself.

Carbohydrates such as glucose may also be transformed into fat. This triglyceride substance will then find lodging somewhere in your body's adipose (fat) tissue.

The liver takes numerous factors into account in making these complex decisions. How much glucose you have stored, how much your brain, muscles, and nerves have available at the moment, and how much fat, protein, and cholesterol have also been taken in along with the carbohydrate in your meal will all influence the decisions your liver makes.

Your liver has been called the body's most amazing organ. This title is well deserved. It is the body's carbohydrate "traffic cop"—keeping the flow of ingoing and outgoing glucose normal. It will store sugars until they are needed. Then, when it receives chemical messages that more monosaccharides are needed somewhere, that more glucose is needed by your brain, adrenal glands, or muscles, the liver—with some help in certain cases from other hardworking organs such as the glands and kidneys—frees the glucose from where it is stored (or takes new glycogen being freshly absorbed from your food) and ships it to where it is needed.

For example, you need a reserve of 350 grams of carbohydrate in your body. Since 1 gram of carbohydrate supplies 4 calories of heat energy, this means your ever-busy liver has to assure that you have 1,400 calories available to carry you through a dozen or more hours of fatigue-free work or play.[62]

How Carbohydrates Affect Your Liver

Just as you would not survive long without your lungs, since they supply oxygen for every cell in your body, you could not live without your liver either. Not only does it process carbohydrates for storage or use, it also helps you cope with the chemical stresses to which our bodies are subjected day in and day out. These include air and water pollution, food contaminants and poisons from hundreds of assorted sources. For example, suppose you take a vacation trip by car with a clothing bag filled with suits and coats, fresh from the dry cleaner. Every mile of the way you are inhaling potentially deadly amounts of trichloroethane. Exhaust fumes from the cars along the road add to the chemical stress on your body. Your liver extracts these chemicals from the blood before they can poison large numbers of body cells.[12]

Your liver detoxifies your blood of more than deadly fumes. When you make contact with arsenic in a household cleaner; when you have one too many cocktails; when potentially disease-promoting microorganisms enter your body with your food, or when you take steroid-containing drugs that may include carcinogenic substances,[12] the liver is on the job. By way of the bowel, kidneys, and bladder, the liver does its best to rid the body of all the toxins it finds.

Carbohydrates enter into all the liver's housekeeping activities. Glycogen—produced as a by-product of dietary carbohydrates—is the fuel that makes the completion of these crucial jobs possible. Eat adequate carbohydrates and your liver will always have a healthy supply of this fuel.[12] Normally, starches and sugars from the foods you eat supply glucose to produce the glycogen.

The liver makes every effort to normalize your metabolism. Suppose your diet is less than adequate; suppose it is much too high in protein and much too low in carbohydrate. In such a case, the extra protein you are eating will be used in place of glucose to manufacture glycogen. Your liver must produce glycogen; if it can't produce it from glucose, it will produce it from protein or fat. It needs glycogen, not only to supply fuel to your muscles and for general metabolism; not only for housecleaning and toxic waste disposal; but also to help manufacture and police the movement of hormones throughout your glandular system. It also uses this glycogen as a help in processing fats in your metabolism.[63]

It is stressful to your liver to convert other foods than glucose into glycogen. If you want to protect your liver from this stress, you must be careful to get sufficient carbohydrate, and perhaps be less concerned with high protein. If you do this, your body will naturally do what it was designed to do: use carbohydrate for energy and protein as a building block for tissues. (Note: One gram per each kilogram of body weight is the amount of protein recommended.) When you violate this practice, protein is diverted into a fuel, but not very well.

Likewise, when too much fat and too little carbohydrate are consumed, your liver must work extra hard to turn a slight amount of fat into glycogen. It is an effort that you can and should spare your liver.[64]

The reward for eating a sufficient amount of unrefined carbohydrate will be generally improved health. The resulting adequate glycogen stores in your liver will give you immunity against many conditions induced by toxins, at the cost of minimal diet-induced stress to your liver.

Summary

The liver is the most crucial organ in the metabolism of carbohydrates. It is an energy "traffic cop," routing glucose to where it is needed in the body or changing it to glycogen for storage until it is needed. If you don't supply that energy as carbohydrates, the protein you eat may be used inefficiently, converted to glycogen and eventually burned as fuel instead of being broken into amino acids, the building material for your cells and tissues. Forcing the liver to use the wrong fuels in supplying energy to your brain, nerves, muscles, and other organs causes unneeded stress. Eating enough complex carbohydrates is also one of the best ways to help your liver carry out its other major task, ridding the body of toxins. A carefully balanced diet should supply you with a reserve of 350 grams of carbohydrate—enough to carry you through the ups and downs of an average day.

Carbohydrate Digestive Disorders

When the course of digestion does not run smoothly, the culprit may be a defect in your metabolism. Here are a few of the conditions that lead to malfunctioning:

1. Gout medications. Are you being treated with atropine, digitoxin, phenformin, or ethnacrynic acid for gout? It's best to discuss with your doctor the potentials these drugs seem to have for adversely affecting your body's intake of starches and sugars. A fifth offender in the gout-drug category is colchicine, which has been reported to have a damaging effect on the delicate membranes that line your intestines.[65]

2. Other drugs. Not all drugs can interfere with your ability to process carbohydrates properly. Common drugs such as aspirin, as far as we know, have no pronounced effect. But some antibiotics such as neomycin, for example, have a short-term damaging effect on mucous secretions in the digestive tract. And if you already have a condition that impairs carbohydrate metabolism, drugs will be an added stress.[66]

3. Protein deficiency. If this condition is sustained long enough due to a poor diet caused by poverty, by lack of available food, or by a "fad" reducing diet, the body cells will begin to change. The rate at which carbohydrate digestion proceeds declines dramatically, even though in the initial stages of such a decline a step-up in glucose absorption may occur.[67] The subsequent addition of protein to the diet may put the system back on track, but the result of sustained protein deficiency may be continued difficulty in handling the sugars in milk products, say researchers.[68]

4. Galactosemia. This is a disorder in which there is too little galactase enzyme to permit the sugar galactose to be turned into glucose.

5. Any flaw in your intestines can result in malabsorption syndrome with symptoms similar to mono- and disaccharide intolerance.

6. Your glands regulate your metabolism. Since the proper utilization of fuel—mainly glucose (stored as glycogen)—is so crucial an aspect of maintaining a balanced metabolism, improperly functioning glands can affect the digestion, absorption, or utilization of carbohydrates. The pituitary gland controls the others. The thyroid regulates the pace of metabolism. The adrenal cortex directly regulates blood sugar levels, by producing a hormone, cortisol, which increases blood sugar levels when you are under stress.

Sugar Metabolism and Your Glands

If your life-style is such that you are constantly subject to stress—whether from a stressful job; air, food, water, or noise pollution; depression or other psychological problems; or cold, hunger, or other depriva-tion—your adrenal glands may become depleted and less able to se-crete the hormones like cortisol that raise blood sugar levels so you can cope with emergencies.

The pancreas is even more directly involved in the regulation of blood sugar levels. We shall discuss it further below.

The malfunctioning of any of these glands may affect your sugar metabolism.

THE ADRENALS AND SUGAR METABOLISM

A primary cause of immune system destruction is adrenal exhaus-tion from overstimulation of the adrenal glands. There are a multiplic-ity of factors that can be responsible, including environmental stressors as well as emotional distress—such as anger, fear, anxiety, depression. But of primary concern is the environmental stressor of refined carbo-hydrate—i.e., sugar. This causes the adrenal glands to secrete more adrenaline than would be normal to its function. The hypoglycemic and diabetic are even more susceptible, due to radical fluctuations of the blood sugar level.

THE PANCREAS AND SUGAR METABOLISM

Your pancreas controls the delicate balance between two hor-mones—insulin and glucagon. These hormones keep you feeling pooped or peppy or somewhere in between. They do this by regulating the amount of energy in the form of glucose circulating in your blood-stream.

It behooves you to keep your pancreas healthy through a low-sugar, well-balanced diet. Your mood from hour to hour and day to day, and your ability to work efficiently and play energetically, depend on a pancreas that is healthy enough to issue forth these two hormones. These secretions come from a colony of special cells in the pancreas called the islets of Langerhans.

Insulin and Glucagon

Suppose you have just indulged in a sugary donut; your blood sugar level is much too high. Insulin will bring it back down into the normal range of 1 mg/ml. If it then drops too low, glucagon will elevate it to normal.

Insulin flushes unneeded glucose from the blood. When insulin levels increase, the excess glucose is drawn from the blood by the activation of metabolic processes that control blood threshold levels of glucose. Excess glucose is rerouted so that tissues that need it, have it. The muscles use it to produce glycogen for energy storage.

The liver converts glucose into glycogen in even larger quantities.

Adipose tissue converts glucose into fatty acids. The energy from the glucose is thus kept handy so when you're ready for your morning run or swim, it's there.

Glucagon triggers the reserve processes. If not enough blood sugar is circulating to keep you in high spirits—say you've taken your usual swim at the Y and postponed breakfast until a more convenient hour —to compensate, your pancreas will produce a flood of glucagon. The glucagon forces your liver to send surplus glycogen into the blood-stream to provide energy for all the body's cells.

We know that insulin and glucagon balance and counterbalance one another, but we don't fully understand how the whole, complex process works.

There are many other factors that trigger the increase or decrease of production of both insulin and glucagon than just blood sugar levels. For example, there are certain amino acids and hormones whose presence stimulates glucagon production, increasing blood sugar levels. Other amino acids and hormones—including glucagon itself—stimulate the production of insulin. (However, in states of severe caloric restriction, glucagon, which gives its orders primarily to the liver, seems to adjust insulin production levels downward.) Still other hormones (including insulin itself), and certain minerals, chemicals, and states (such as starvation), decrease insulin production.

When the islets of Langerhans of the pancreas don't supply enough insulin, we call the disease state that results diabetes. The supply of insulin to a diabetic is a matter of life and death. The diabetic's insulin shortage causes an inability to utilize glucose; diabetics cannot move glucose through the cell walls as you and I do countless times a day with no voluntary effort. This is a serious condition. In juvenile diabetes, because the urine washes away the glucose that would normally be used for energy and life, severe sugar starvation can result in death if insulin replacement does not intervene.[69]

Summary

If you have trouble digesting and utilizing carbohydrates, and your diet is good—high in complex carbohydrates and other nutritious foods, and very low in refined and junk foods—then it's possible that medical conditions are complicating the process of digestion. Antibiotics and gout medications can disrupt digestion. Victims of drought, war-related food shortages, and fad low-protein diets, whose diets lack protein for extended periods, digest carbohydrates poorly—sometimes even after the shortage of protein ends. Occasionally, a person is born without all the enzymes needed for sugar digestion. If your intestines are infected or otherwise malfunctioning, this can affect carbohydrate absorption.

Several glands regulate blood sugar levels, in part by affecting sugar absorption and storage. The two most directly involved are the adrenal glands and pancreas. Your adrenals flood the bloodstream with extra glucose in emergencies, when you are under stress. The pancreas normally produces insulin to lower the blood sugar level, and glucagon to raise it. Diabetics have trouble producing enough insulin.

Feeling Your Oats: Where Does Real Go Power Come From?

Normal blood sugar or blood glucose levels are crucial to every activity you perform. When you are tired, your blood may be circulating too little glucose. A momentary boost in energy usually accompanies the ingestion of any type of sugar, which raises the blood sugar level, usually in no more than five to ten minutes. However, this rise is temporary. If you've ingested too much sugar, your blood sugar levels will then fall precipitously. This then puts you on a metabolic roller coaster, causing a new craving for sugar to overcome the effects of fatigue. Don't give in to the craving for quick-energy, high-sugar foods that add calories and little else. To maintain proper sugar levels, consume a complex carbohydrate food, such as brown rice, grains, nuts, and seeds, or a complete protein. This will allow your blood sugar—hence, your energy level—to be maintained at normal.

If you feel fine—able to focus your energy on the task at hand, whether it's reading a newspaper or swimming forty laps—your glucose levels are probably near normal, which means between 90 and 110 milligrams per each milliliter of blood. Unless you are planning something as stressful as a tennis tournament, you have the fuel you need.

If your blood sugar level drops due to a stressful event, there is no need to rush out for a candy bar. Your body will automatically normalize blood sugar levels by calling up the glycogen it has in storage in your liver. This it transforms by freeing glucagon hormones in your pancreas —and what results is a flood of new glucose. Fat or protein from your diet or from body stores can also be converted into fuel in a crisis.

If no source of glucose supply were available, this would be grave, indeed, since all the cells in your body—which make up your bones, skin, liver, brain, heart, muscle, etc.—need this glucose to carry out their activities.[70] A long-term condition in which not enough fuel is consumed is called starvation.

Because of the risk human beings (like other animals) face of not always having food available—whether due to natural causes or man-made disasters—we have evolved the ability to store fuel at many sites in the body. When there is a shortage, this fuel comes into play. Your body knows which supplies to use and in what order. First your circulating blood sugar is drawn upon. Next your muscle supplies are used. Then glucose is made from storage fat. And last to go are those precious proteins, because these are the least efficient raw materials for energy and the most valuable building materials.

If you are the athlete in the family, then, like a workhorse, you have generous amounts of glycogen stored in your muscles. That concentrated, caloric glycogen has to be at the ready when you run, swim, or pole vault. Your body energy bank holds about 245 grams of glycogen in your muscles plus slightly more than 100 extra grams in your liver. The availability of glycogen right in your muscles means there's no low-energy delay while you wait for glucose to be carried from your liver to your hardworking heart or legs, for example. It's already there in the glycogen chains.

There is one organ that uses glucose differently than the others, and that organ is your brain. One-quarter of your total fuel supply is used to meet the needs of ongoing cerebral activity. In other words, even though your brain constitutes only 2 to 3 percent of your total weight, it is greedier than any other organ as far as fuel is concerned. Furthermore, this organ hoards the fuel it has and will not release it in a crisis. This is another reason to obtain adequate carbohydrate in your diet. Unlike other body organs, your brain cannot turn fat into glucose.[71]

Of course, the brain, like the rest of your body, needs oxygen as well as glucose, in order to transform the blood sugar into energy. Just as heat and light are released when you burn wood in a fireplace, so energy is provided for all your activities by the oxidation of fuel in your cells. If the supply of either fuel or oxygen is cut off to the brain, this can spell disaster; this is why a stroke can cause brain damage.

Taking a run will frequently make you feel a little brighter, a little more energetic. But taking a refined carbohydrate snack while you watch somebody else exercise may or may not have that effect, because you may already have enough glucose for your energy and glycogen storage needs. If that's the case, triglycerides and other fats are manufactured and stored up in your adipose, or fatty, tissues. You need generous amounts of thiamine, B_1, to digest carbohydrates—and that's one of the vitamins of which a junk food diet is unlikely to give you very much.[72]

So why satisfy a snack attack with empty calorie food? It is better to ignore the urge and exercise, or to have an intelligent snack that builds health rather than boosting fat stores.

While it is important to have some potential energy stored for an energy-low day, you don't need much unless you are faced with a true crisis such as starvation or an extended fast. When you must break down the extra stored fuels in your body—the fats and amino acids your body uses after exhausting its glycogen supply—you don't even get all the caloric energy contained in those stored supplies. And, besides, there is a certain threat of sodium depletion when you use up the carbohydrates that you have readily available.

Although carbohydrates are the first choice for energy, don't forget there is more to well-being than energy. You must take in balanced amounts of protein, fats, vitamins, minerals, and water so that your dietary carbohydrates are able to function as they should.

Too Little Carbohydrate: Are There Consequences?

The most frequently discussed people likely to use up all their stored carbohydrates are victims of a mysterious disorder, both mental and physical in nature, which has been termed the "dietary teenager disease," or anorexia nervosa. But this disorder is only one way to run short of carbohydrates. Those high-protein diets whose effectiveness is dependent on deliberately, sharply reduced carbohydrate levels can produce the same effect. This effect is usually not dire. But there are some disadvantages:

• A no-carbohydrate diet is stressful. Fats and proteins, says Rachmiel Levine, can pinch-hit for carbohydrate for short periods: when you eat very little carbohydrate, your liver is alerted that carbohydrate is running out, so it mobilizes your stored fat to produce energy. It also releases free fatty acids to keep the hundreds of muscles throughout your body doing their energy-intensive jobs. Ketone bodies are also produced to fuel cerebral cells. In other words, the excess fat you may have in your liver and tissues is being used up to keep you alive and functioning. However, this is a stressful deviation from the usual metabolic process.[73] It puts a strain on the liver, which already has an estimated 500 major and minor jobs to perform, and on the kidneys, too.

• It is hazardous if you are diabetic. Ketones can build up to a threatening level in such a sufferer. If you live with a diabetic who must follow many restrictions in diet and life-style, you may know some of the warning signals that insulin levels are dangerously low because of carbohydrate depletion, and that a state of diabetic ketosis has been created. A common one is the smell of acetone, the most primary of all the ketonic substances, on the breath. To counteract this condition, which has been known to lead to unconsciousness and can even be fatal, insulin must be administered without delay. This measure enables the cells to recover and resume their uptake of life-sustaining glucose again.[74]

• It is a threat to seriously underweight individuals. Anorexia victims, as well as any person of any age threatened with starvation, are doubly threatened if they have low or no carbohydrate reserves, because at this stage they will have depleted stored body fat, too. The only source of energy that's left is protein. Protein is the wrong source of energy. The transformation of protein into energy is called gluconeogenesis and it is something to be avoided if you wish your kidneys and liver to last you a lifetime. Protein depletion can lead to death, and it's easy to understand why. With protein as a raw material, new body cells are manufactured and old ones are kept in good repair. Protein is also the only way, in many cases, that important hormones, enzymes, and nerve-impulse transmitting chemicals that allow one organ to communicate with another in the body are produced.

The moral of all this is: get enough unrefined carbohydrates each day and protect your supplies.

Enough Is Enough: What Happens When You Get Too Many Carbohydrates

You know what happens when you follow a careless diet heavy in bread, cookies, and French fries, or even too much stir-fried rice, beans, and homemade corn fritters. You get too many carbohydrates, and with them many more calories than you need, so the extra energy is stashed away at various fat depots in your body. In other words, glucose you don't need is turned by your fatty adipose cells or your kidneys into that problematic padding on your thighs, buttocks, and elsewhere.[75]

Carbohydrates only seem to cause the pounds to pile up faster than any other food group. Actually, they don't. You just eat more of them because it's easier to overindulge on carbohydrates like bread or cake than it is on fatty foods like butter, nuts, or fatty meats, for example. Another reason you may indulge more in this area is that carbohydrate foods, especially those from the shelves in any lower-income neighborhood supermarket, tend to be cheaper than foods that provide chiefly fat or protein. In addition, they are often prepared with a lot of fats or oils, which add even more calories.

Apparently, however, carbohydrates may also lead to extra poundage because they cause insulin to collect in the bloodstream, and this can affect fat metabolism.

Too much refined carbohydrates can lead to B-vitamin deficiencies, since this vitamin complex has usually been removed from unrefined carbohydrates. Adequate amounts of B vitamins must be available so that your liver can produce glycogen. Glycogen is fuel; but it also aids in metabolizing fats, and in the proper use of protein. Glycogen, its presence made possible by adequate carbohydrate intake, will improve your immunity to disease as well.

Summary

Eating too few carbohydrates can have serious health consequences—especially if you are diabetic. Fad diets, starvation, and fasting can all create carbohydrate shortages. To compensate, your liver must work overtime to turn fats and protein into energy. This can also strain your kidneys.

But a diet too high in carbohydrates, especially the kind that have been overprocessed, the kind found in fast foods and empty calorie junk snacks, can result in excess calorie intake and fat deposits throughout the body. These extra pounds place a stress on your major organs. Also, high levels of serum insulin may occur.

Refined carbohydrates deplete your body of B vitamins, needed for the production of glycogen. Glycogen is not only a fuel, it aids in metabolizing fats and transforming the proteins you eat into the proteins of your body. Getting enough carbohydrates helps you use proteins and fats properly, and can help you ward off disease.

Weight Control and Carbohydrates: Seven Facts

1. If you know anyone who is very overweight, even obese, you probably know someone who has a sweet tooth. But their obesity may also be a sign of alcoholism. It is easy to eat sweets or drink alcoholic beverages to excess and still keep coming back for more.

Unfortunately, that's why we get so fat so easily. Sugary foods are always low in nutrition; eating them often triggers bingeing. And they give you almost nothing but calories you don't need. As Dr. Yudkin summed it up, "Sugar and alcoholic spirits share the distinction of being the only dietary items that supply nothing but calories."

2. Another side effect of low-nutrition, refined carbohydrates is that as you stuff yourself with caramels and bubbly soda, you lose interest in real foods such as raw vegetables. To a sugarholic, a tossed salad seems unexciting, even though it's what he or she really needs.

3. If you are fat, not fit, join the crowd. One in four Americans is overweight. And millions of Americans are suffering from undernourishment, according to Dr. Richard Passwater, author of *Supernutrition* (Dial Press, New York, 1975). It is obvious that these two facts are not unrelated.

4. Were you born with fully functioning endocrine glands, and are your major organs in good health? When you are not blessed with such health, obesity may develop despite good eating habits. But, says Dr. T. L. Cleave, in his outstanding book, *The Saccharine Disease*, this is rare. Ordinarily it is not a faulty body but a faulty diet that causes the overeat-

ing that leads in turn to extra pounds. And most often it is the worthless foods that "go down the hatch" so easily that are to blame. If you are already tipping the scales, don't substitute three or four sweet or salty snacks for one balanced meal which includes needed fiber to make you feel an honest fullness.[76]

5. One good way to avoid high blood pressure and obesity is to ban junk food carbohydrates. People who respond to pressure by frequent snacking pay a stiff price, since the payoff for indulging in sodas and donuts is excess weight along with the risk of heart disease and diabetes, as well. Obesity turns up far more often among those who settle for the quick-bite meals we associate with big city life-styles.

Weight loss can be less painful if you concentrate on more complex carbohydrates, especially the crunchy, chewy, fibrous kinds instead of sweet desserts and snacks. Contrast our traditional diet, say Dr. C. Slome et al. in the *South African Medical Journal*, with that of those members of an African Zulu tribe who still adhere to their native high-fiber foods, and stay both slim and healthy.

6. You probably derive more good from starch-based carbohydrates than you do from carbohydrates in the form of sugar. Both fat and protein are assimilated more efficiently in the presence of starch rather than sugar. These were the results in an experiment in which rats were fed a low-protein diet. Cornstarch was the carbohydrate used, but the principle would probably hold true for other starches. When sugar is the carbohydrate used, your body is encouraged to manufacture fat, it appears, at least when the diet contains normal or high amounts of protein.[77] Furthermore, if research with animals by A. R. MacRae et al. from the University of Guelph in Ontario is valid for humans as well, you'd be better off using either rice syrup, barley syrup, or date sugar, rather than refined sugar if you are fending off those extra pounds.[78] Even so, all sugars add extra calories, even the "unprocessed" ones.

7. You *can* lose weight without dieting, but it takes a lot of work. The evidence is an experiment by A. S. Leon, M.S., M.D. and his research team. He put a group of young men, all overweight, on a special program to lose weight by walking one and a half hours daily for four months. They showed a typical loss of a dozen or more pounds. Wouldn't you be happy to note such a change without any major diet modification? What was even more gratifying was the fact that there was an increase of more than 25 percent in high-density lipoproteins. (These are good for your heart.[79]) Exercise is more important than diet for weight control. Dieting should not be undertaken without exercise.

The Dangers of Dieting: How a Change in Life-Style Can Help

This chapter on carbohydrates seems like an appropriate place to propose some general rules for weight loss and fitness, as long as we are discussing particular diet plans.

Weight loss is not just a matter of losing pounds. You want to optimize your health by losing only excess pounds that represent unneeded fat, fat that has accumulated—most noticeably on hips, thighs, buttocks and abdomen—by eating too much too often. The presence of this excess fat represents a loss of muscle tissue. If you don't want fat to infiltrate and undermine your muscles, you'll eat wisely and moderately, and exercise all your body's muscles.

What does it mean internally when you get fat externally?

- Useless fat is actually being deposited inside your muscles.
- Lack of exercise is causing reduced, weakened muscles in your arms, legs, back, and elsewhere.
- The body's fat-to-muscle ratio is being distorted. A reduction in caloric intake and increase in exercise will prevent further deterioration. Your body should be about 15 percent fat if you are a man, or 22 percent if you are female; most men have about 23 percent, most women 36 percent, according to Covert Bailey, in his book *Fit or Fat*. People who carry fat at higher levels are not just overweight, but at risk of developing numerous degenerative diseases.

What Physical Fitness Means

Extra fat and excess pounds are not synonymous. Losing weight only to wind up looking thinner but ten years older should hardly be your goal. Yet, this is often the result when you fail to augment your diet with an aerobic exercise plan. Here are a few facts:

- Your muscles are heavier than your fatty tissue. There's no need to feel glum when the scales say you've added a pound. If you're making the dietary reforms you should and working out, too, this may be a vital sign.
- Would you like to smile with pleasure when you look at yourself in the mirror, when you see smooth, lean, well-contoured muscles? It's inevitable, say experts like Covert Bailey in his book *Fit or Fat*, if you exercise with the emphasis on aerobic activities.[80]
- The best way to slim down and achieve fitness is by an easy aerobic program you can stick to, do easily, and adapt to the rest of your daily activities plan; one that you can enjoy every day no matter how fat, discouraged, or unfit you are to start with.
- Dieting is easier, in fact, if you use aerobics to "recondition" your body first, because this is the only type of training that truly improves

muscle tone, according to Covert Bailey. This is accomplished when you persist at a slow pace.[81]

BENEFITS OF AEROBIC EXERCISE

Aerobic exercise has special benefits for your body:

• Enzymes, which use up calories, are built up in muscle tissues.
• Your metabolism becomes less sluggish because it has an improved ability to get and use oxygen.

Using this additional oxygen, your body will burn more stored fat more efficiently.

EXERCISING AT MAXIMUM EFFICIENCY

When you do put on your running shoes or swim suit, or get out the jump rope to do your aerobic workout, it should be done in a way that makes your heart beat at 80 percent of its maximum capability. You should continue the exercise for a minimum of twelve minutes, resisting the urge to stop and start. The specified time allotment is important if you wish to receive the benefits just enumerated. Exercising too enthusiastically at the beginning—for example, running vigorously for sixty minutes rather than twelve—may even defeat your self-improvement purposes.[82]

The concept of working at 80 percent of your heart's capacity has been scientifically determined. At that pace, your heart and lungs fall into the kind of healthy, invigorating, balanced relationship that benefits your total health. This "training ratio," as it's called, changes according to your age (see chart below). Discuss your exercise plans with your physician if you are over forty.[83] Be sure to work up to the maximum rate gradually if you are out of shape.

If you wish to be certain that those precious exercise moments aren't wasted, then don't guess. Get a stopwatch or one with a second hand and do it right. After a few minutes of exercise, listen to your pulse for a full sixty seconds. If you haven't reached your goal, pick up your pace. If you've overshot your goal, simply reduce your effort a bit.

WHAT YOU CAN EXPECT

• Be patient. If you have more than a few pounds to lose, you can't expect a new you in a week. But you can console yourself with the thought that this method is one of the few that not only produces weight loss results but also improves your sense of well-being. Once you do arrive at the weight you want, you'll find yourself enjoying your healthier new life-style. So keep it up, and you'll never have to worry about that "old you" making an unwelcome comeback.

• If you find after a month or two of aerobics that you can only get your heart beating hard enough if you bicycle, run, or swim a little longer, that's normal, say experts. It means your body has become accustomed to the workout; you're using oxygen more efficiently, so it takes longer before your heart and lungs have to exert themselves to the same degree.

Which Exercise Is Best?

Which exercise is for you? Should you tackle jogging, buy a bike, or join the Y to swim? Remember, you are looking for a sport that starts your heart beating hard and keeps it going. That rules out racquet sports, golf, gardening, and handyman jobs, even if they are exhausting, says Bailey.

Recommended Heart Rates During Exercise*

Age	Maximum Heart Rate	80% of Max. (Recommended Training Rate)	75% of Max. (Heart Disease History)
			Not to exceed
20	200	160	150
22	198	158	148
24	196	157	147
26	194	155	145
28	192	154	144
30	190	152	143
32	189	151	142
34	187	150	140
36	186	149	140
38	184	147	138
40	182	146	137
45	179	143	134
50	175	140	131
55	171	137	128
60	160	128	120
65+	150	120	113

Based on resting heart rates of 72 for males and 80 for females. Men over forty and people with any heart problem should have a stress electrocardiogram before starting an exercise program.

Here are a number of choices to consider, in order of increasing physical exertion:

*From Fit or Fat by Covert Bailey (New York: Houghton Mifflin, 1977)

1. Walking, outdoor and stationary bicycling, ice skating and roller skating, and swimming. You can choose one of these or alternate two —for example, you could walk three days a week and roller skate the remaining four. In any case, the minimum time is twenty minutes.

2. Jogging or running, cross-country skiing, rowing, aerobic dancing. These exercises are a bit more strenuous, and some of them call for special clothes or gear of some sort, but it's worth the investment. In the case of skiing, essentials are easily rented. Whichever you choose, you need only do twelve minutes a day at your 80 percent maximum heart rate. But add an extra three minutes to warm up and achieve your plateau pulse rate.[84]

3. Jumping rope, stationary jogging, jumping jacks, or jumping on a Rebounder (a miniature, indoor trampoline). You need just twelve minutes for any of these. To make it easier and enhance your enjoyment, try exercising to music, since all of these keep you indoors, anyway. There's a variation that belongs in this group, too, which your doctor may have suggested if he or you feel you are out of shape: it's called chair stepping. And that's just what you do. Use a common kitchen chair and alternating right and left feet simply step up and down on the seat. You may stop between steps or increase your speed if it is not uncomfortable to do so.[85]

Summary

When fat has accumulated on your waist, hips, and thighs, it undermines the strength of your muscles. One of the best ways to regain your strength and to lose weight, no matter what diet you choose, is to set up and stick to an aerobic exercise regimen. Whether you walk, jog, skate, jump rope, dance, ski, swim, or ride a bicycle— or even just run up and down stairs—aerobic exercise will tone up your muscles, especially your most important muscle, your heart. It will make you feel good, and help inspire you to stick to your diet.

There are three keys to success with aerobic exercises. The first is to find a kind of exercise that you enjoy (or two or three: try alternating swimming with jogging or jumping on a Rebounder; or ski when you can and jump rope the rest of the time). The second is to make time for your exercising every day and carry out the program in a disciplined way. If you should miss a day, though, don't get demoralized and stop: just go on and continue the next day. You have to juggle your schedule and make sure to find the time; no one ever really has time without making it.

The third key is to exercise a minimum of twelve minutes a day (after working up to this level) at your optimum "training ratio," taking your pulse with a watch to make sure you are giving your heart and lungs the thorough workout they need.

Be sure to discuss your diet and exercise program with your physician before you start.

Sugar and Your Teeth

One of the few aspects of refined-sugar consumption about which many medical authorities have agreed for years is that sugar, if allowed to remain in the mouth, causes cavities.

OBESITY AND DENTAL CARIES

Because a little bit of sugar usually leads to a little bit more, in the form of high-calorie food or extra sugar in beverages, excess weight is a common reflection of a sugar-laden eating pattern. But your mouth as well as your waistline can be a sign of a high-sucrose diet. Dental caries are not a fact of life, just a reflection of how damaging refined carbohydrate in general and sugar in particular can be for your oral health.

REFINED SUGAR AND CAVITIES: THE WORST COMBINATION

Preventing cavities? Before you spoon any more sugar on your cereal, consider these facts:

1. If a well-meaning friend or teacher told you that all sugars—sucrose, maltose, glucose, fructose, dextrose, whatever—are alike, when it comes to cavities, don't believe it. This information came from studies with rodents that are now discredited. These tests and others suggested that only the uncooked carbohydrate in wheat caused little or no danger of decay.[86]

2. If you had your choice among fructose, glucose, or the Finnish sugar substitute xylitol, which should you choose? According to Drs. Arje Scheinen, Professor of Cardiology and Kavko K. Makinen, Associate Professor of Oral Biochemistry, at the University of Turku in Finland, with xylitol you run the least risk of winding up with a mouthful of silver fillings. Using human subjects, this medical team clearly illustrated that no sugar does a better, faster job of destroying dental health than sucrose.[87] Although all sugars have negative aspects, as discussed elsewhere in this text, fructose and xylitol both appear capable of causing an actual decrease in cavity count—by one-quarter in the case of fruit sugar and as much as 90 percent in the case of the Finnish sugar replacement.[88]

3. If it causes plaque, it causes cavities. They found that two indisputable plaque precursors (which biochemists identify as fructans and extracellular fructose polymers) are natural components of table sugar. In these studies, although glucose, a starch/lactose combination, maltose, lactose, fructose, and sucrose were pitted fairly against one another, table sugar—sucrose—in each case emerged the champion cavity-causing carbohydrate.

4. What would happen if you ate a pound of candy over a long weekend and never brushed your teeth once? A test like this with school children was actually conducted in London by an oral health team at Guy's Hospital.[89] A hard-to-remove layer of plaque, with a high bacteria count, built up on their teeth. If unchecked, this could lead to substantially increased caries.

If you ate bread rather than candy and neglected to brush, the results wouldn't be quite as bad. A second control group used in the cited study was fed on a wheat-starch confection, with far less plaque buildup after the trial period. This is not an isolated example, but a common outcome, as Dr. L.E.A. Folke et al.[90] of the School of Dentistry at the University of Minnesota discovered. When these experts ran a similar test to see if sugar was the culprit in stimulating bacteria to multiply on the teeth, they reached the same conclusion—namely that a complex sugar called dextran, associated with sucrose, is the worst dental health vandal of all the carbohydrates, so powerful that even when subjects eat sucrose diluted 40 to 50 percent with glucose, dental damage may be just as extensive.[91]

5. Is it wise then to switch to sugar-free gum, or use fructose or xylitol-sweetened snacks? It seems not.[92] Dental researchers make these points:

• Oral organisms adapt to changes, too. This means that over a period of regular use, any sugar substitute begins to nourish your oral bacteria just as happily as sucrose did and with the same undesirable effect.

• Although sucrose does it more efficiently and faster than other food, remember that an acid environment inviting decay can, in fact, be set up in your mouth easily no matter what carbohydrate source is used. The key to prevention is immediate removal of all food residue after meals.[93]

PREVENTING COMMON DENTAL DISEASES

Cavities are *not* inevitable. They are not just a part of growing up that's bound to cause you pain, trouble, time and expense. To a considerable extent, dental disease, especially cavities, can be prevented, because to a large extent caries come from a high-carbohydrate diet, especially when accompanied by poor hygiene.

CAUSES OF DECAY

Plaque is a second skin that "grows" on your teeth and it is due to poor eating and cleaning habits. It is very much alive. It would have to be, since it is composed of cells called leukocytes (white blood cells), complex carbohydrates, and various bacteria plus water. This unhealthy coating becomes acid after only a short period of time. If it is not removed by you, through brushing and flossing your teeth, you know what happens next. The acid causes fissures in the surface of the teeth and decay sets in.[94] If you want to know whether you are flossing and brushing properly, ask your dentist for plaque disclosure tablets. When you chew these after flossing and brushing, they temporarily stain any remaining plaque on your teeth a garish pink. Scrape it off with floss before rinsing it off and practice your dental hygiene technique until you are certain you always remove all the plaque from your teeth. Besides regular trips to a dentist, proper cleaning and a diet that eliminates or sharply reduces refined sugars and starches are a must.

Carbohydrates from low-nutrient foods like candy bars, donuts, and white bread provide fuel for the proliferation of the microorganisms (heptocaucus metans) that live in your mouth. And this builds plaque, which literally attaches itself to your teeth like a sticky film.

Drinking and rinsing are inadequate to flush bacteria, sugars, and starches out of your mouth, because once the process of plaque formation begins, these elements become stubbornly bonded together.

Sugary pies and chocolate bars aren't the only carbohydrates to avoid if you're fighting decay. Even naturally sweet foods from nature —sun-dried raisins, for example—can lead to a mouth full of fillings if you eat too many too often and don't remove the plaque with a brush. The stickier the food, the greater its decay-causing potential, even if eaten only now and then.[95]

If you must have a carbohydrate snack, have some whole grain bread or a plate of raw carrots and celery with bean sprouts. The roughness of these nonsweet foods actually gives your teeth a healthy scrubbing while you chew.[96] A diet that minimizes intake of the simple sugars and is high in fibrous complex carbohydrate foods is the one most effective in preventing decay. Clinical tests indicate that foods composed largely of dextrose or starches provide greater dental health than those including sugars.

If your oral environment isn't all it should be despite good eating habits, blame it on your genes. Genetics plays a role in how immune you and your children will be to the effects of various carbohydrates on your teeth. Stick-to-your-teeth, high-in-refined-sugar snacks should be the best way to ruin your teeth in short order—but some people escape this comeuppance. On the other hand, you may have inherited saliva that puts any sugar you eat to work producing dental lesions 30 percent faster than normal.[96]

Keep your toothbrush handy. Even a raw apple or a baked sweet potato may leave some sugar behind in your saliva to contribute to caries-causing plaque. So brush and floss after eating any snack, no matter how healthy or natural.

Summary

Two reasons to skip the sugar that every expert, including your own dentist, will agree on: sugar is a quick way to gain weight and a fast way to ruin your teeth with cavities. Sucrose, common table sugar, works faster than other sugars in creating caries, especially if it is eaten in the form of anything sticky like candy or sugar-coated dried fruit.

On the other hand, switching to sugar substitutes will not save you from decay either, since it appears that sugar substitutes used regularly develop the same caries potential as sugar. In addition to proper dental hygiene, remember that the foods that keep your mouth and teeth healthy are the same foods that build a healthy heart or a healthy head of hair. Substitute naturally sweet fruits for sugary snacks, choose foods that are raw, high in nutrients and crunchy and chewy, not gooey.

Sugar and Heart Disease

Few physicians or scientists have done more to warn us of the dangers created by our excessive consumption of refined carbohydrates than Surgeon-Captain T. L. Cleave, M.D., F.R.C.P. Dr. Cleave, a British physician, first became aware of one type of refined-carbohydrate danger—fiber-depletion—when serving on the battleship *King George V* during World War II. Learning that most of the crew suffered from constipation, he started adding unprocessed bran to their diets. Within days the problem had passed, and some of the ship's crew even credited Dr. Cleave with having aided their efficiency and more relaxed state of mind. The sailors knew from long experience that chronic constipation often creates irritable moody behavior.

After the war, Dr. Cleave returned to more peaceful pursuits, and he concentrated much of his attention as a researcher on refined carbohydrates and their effect on Western health. In addition to numerous articles, he has published a major book on the subject: *The Saccharine Disease*. Because of his distinguished position, I thought that it would be appropriate to share a few comments Dr. Cleave made to me when I talked with him in the English countryside in 1979.

Take, for example, the relation between the saccharine disease and arteriosclerosis. I think this is more crucial for people than anything else. In diabetes, for example, coronary thrombosis is the commonest cause of death.

It's not for me to go into the chemistry of the matter, but it is absolutely certain that the American figures—and the British too, for that matter—are incontestable. Coronary disease is now killing millions of people in these islands each year—and, of course, even more in America—because of the dangerous sugar habit.

I think it's most important to realize that what I say and what others say is utterly inconsequential compared to what nature says herself. . . . Unfortunately, with the rapid progress of civilization, especially of civilized foods, we are too likely to be distorted by fabricated products sold in supermarkets instead of relying on our own natural instincts for natural foods. What we get in supermarkets is so much simpler and easier to get hold of, and easier and more delightful to eat. . . . But I think there can be nothing more dangerous than eating a lot of foods manufactured for the supermarket—foods that do not exist in natural form to activate and satisfy the natural appetite.

Therefore any overconsumption of sugar—above all other things—is very likely to precipitate not only diabetes in the first place, but the still more dreadful coronary thrombosis in the second. . . .

Carbohydrates and Two Killer Diseases: Is There a Connection?

If you indulge in sweets often, if you eat a lot of sugar of any kind, and come from a family with a predilection for diabetes or heart disease, you could be headed for trouble. This, basically, is the warning issued by Dr. John Yudkin, M.D., Ph.D., F.R.C.P., Professor Emeritus of Nutrition at the University of London, who is considered by some medical authorities to be one of the most knowledgeable of sugar's opponents in the world today.

Here are some of the questions any health-minded person might like answered—followed by Dr. Yudkin's feelings and findings.

Question: Has the link between refined sugar in the diet and diabetes and heart disease been proven?

Answer: Sugar alone does not cause either disease, but there are many provocative findings that indict sugar as a contributing factor in both disorders. If you have seen this idea dismissed in print, don't be surprised. The sugar cartel and all segments of the food business that are dependent on the continued use of sucrose actively oppose disclosure of any "bad" news about this substance.

Also bear in mind that both of these disorders are less simple and more serious than adding too many pounds or developing a few bad spots in your teeth. Sugar is one factor, along with such other influences on your health as air pollution, smoking, drinking, mental health, etc. Even what part of the country you live in and your ethnic background are determinants of your health. Your genetic heritage is higher on the list of considerations, for example, for diabetes than it is for coronary disorders.

Question: Why does Dr. Yudkin believe that sugar is an important causative factor in coronary heart disease and high blood sugar disorders?

Answer: Any substance that can do the bodily harm that sugar can do is obviously capable of contributing to the progress of major degenerative diseases, too. For example, sugar alters both the blood sugar levels and the body's normal response to insulin. These two changes are commonly observed in victims of maturity onset diabetes.

Question: How does sugar affect the body's major organs?

Answer: Yudkin tells us that the kidney is damaged identically by either a high sugar intake or by inducing a diabetic state. We know this because laboratory experiments using rodents have accomplished that astonishing result. These alterations were actually seen by routine biopsy as well as by microscopic and electron-microscopic methods.

Question: The eyes are commonly affected by diabetes and this often leads to cataracts. Does sugar duplicate this effect?

Answer: Yes. If you wish to bring about degeneration of the retina, you can do one of two things, feed a rat sugar or make it diabetic.

Question: Is it true that diabetes sufferers often have coronary heart disease as well?

Answer: Yes. These diseases are often found together. In fact, when diabetics succumb, the cause is often a coronary disorder.

Question: How does sugar affect the blood and the heart muscle?

Answer: It has been repeatedly observed that the greater the sugar intake, the greater the increase of fats in the blood—including triglycerides and cholesterol. Just as grave is the observation that more cholesterol plaques may be observed in the body's vascular system after heavy sucrose fueling. This accumulation dangerously accelerates the rate at which the blood platelets clump together. This is one of the characteristics in most types of heart dysfunctions.

Epidemiology: A Tool to Explore the Sugar–Heart Disorders Link

The medical community does not seem to be in agreement in regard to the connection between coronary heart disease and refined carbohydrates, especially sugar. It is difficult to prove in any one individual case that a heart attack, for example, was brought on by refined sugar overindulgence. However, the case against sucrose is a strong one if you look at the right epidemiology studies. This refers to scientific observations of large groups, perhaps all the men in one town, or all of the members of one ethnic group in an urban or rural area. F. Grande of the University of Minnesota has done such a study, feeding groups like this sugar at high dose levels. There have been other studies, as well, and we learn from this special method of investigation the following:

• The more dietary sugar, the greater the likelihood that coronary disorder will appear.[97]

• If you are a male and have a myocardial infarction to worry about, plus an uncontrolled sweet tooth, you should know that sugar may well be a factor contributing to your state. Such sufferers often have 50 percent more sugar in their diets than nonsufferers.[98]

• High-sugar diets and peripheral artery disease also seem to be linked, says Dr. Yudkin.

• If you are one of the small group of individuals unfortunate enough to have acquired or inherited a weakness of your heart or circulation, sugar may pose a special threat to you.

• Population studies of this type also build the case against sugar by revealing that when high levels of fiber are present in the diet, coronary heart disease is comparatively low. (Diets high in refined carbohydrates are usually low in fiber, since it is the fiber that is refined out.)

The Usefulness of Animal Studies

It is obvious that a human—although he or she might be the most desirable subject for testing the hazardous effects of food ingredients—cannot be used. Thus we have many of our fellow creatures—guinea pigs, rats, mice, dogs, cats—to thank for saving countless lives. Their metabolisms often are so similar to ours that they become very useful as substitutes.

Here are some examples of animal studies linking sugar to coronary heart disease:

• Employing common barnyard chickens, Dr. Richard A. Ahrens, reporting in the *American Journal of Clinical Nutrition*, showed that when fed quantities of sucrose and little else, these fowl led lives that were short, even if they were also sweet. Autopsy revealed arteries clogged with fatty deposits not unlike those seen in human cases of atheromas of the aorta. Dr. Ahrens blamed sucrose, especially the fructose portion. Also observed were such risk factors as the increased platelet stickiness, which often signals arterial disorders, a frantic proliferation of the liver cells, called hyperplasia, kidney disease, and gallbladder stones.[99]

• Or consider this experiment with rats reported by Drs. A. E. Bender and K. B. Damji in their article, "Some Effects of Dietary Sucrose." Empty-nutrient sugar and starch fed to these creatures, the kind that constitutes most of our junk foods, literally filled them full of life-threatening poisons. This resulted from the fact that sugar reduces the potency of the enzymes in the liver. And your liver, remember, is what filters out incoming toxins and thus protects you from infection, disease, and death.[100]

To further prove the point, another group of rats was also fed the sugar-starch combo, but as it occurs in natural foods such as fruit and grain foods. The result was remarkably reduced incidence of cellular tissue damage.[101]

In yet another study it was concluded that it is unrefined, fiber-rich carbohydrate administration that makes all the difference. "Processed-to-death" carbohydrates produced a degenerative disorder of the kidney called Bright's Disease, reported Drs. L. M. Dalerup and N. Visser, in the rat colony fed generous amounts of sugary dietary items. As for a control group that was allowed to eat a more moderate, less adulterated fare, it outlived the first group by a wide margin.[102]

Summary

Does sugar contribute to diabetes and coronary heart disease? Dr. John Yudkin, considered one of the world's leading authorities on sugar in the diet, concludes that the trouble sugar causes goes considerably beyond tooth decay and extra pounds.[103] For example, sugar causes irregularities in the insulin response; sugar causes diabeteslike damage to the kidneys; it contributes to degeneration of the retina; it raises blood fat levels; and it increases the stickiness of the blood platelets, a common precursor of heart trouble.

The medical community may prefer to look the other way, but even so-called "conventional" epidemiology studies have produced evidence that the more sugar in the diet, the greater the likelihood of cardiac trouble starting, and the greater the likelihood of it worsening if you are already afflicted.

Animal studies, too, indicate that fatty degeneration of the inner coat of the arteries can be caused in part by high-sugar diets. Fiber and unrefined carbohydrates are not only safer than processed carbohydrates, but offer protective benefits as well for the heart, the liver, and all the body's vital organs.

In some cases, there are respected professional people who have refused to take a stand against sugar largely because they are simply being extra cautious until the link between sugar and many degenerative diseases in humans is firmly established. This does not mean that sugar is safe to consume in the meantime.

Unhealthy Sugar vs. a Healthy Heart

You've heard all about dietary cholesterol's role in heart disease, but chances are you aren't aware of how equally bad for a healthy heart sugar may be.

You may be eating more sugar than you realize. Sugar on your cereal, then in your coffee, a sugary yogurt for dessert, and suddenly you've had a quarter cup of refined sugar and the day isn't even done. If you have diabetes and you are also a heavy smoker, you face even greater risk of danger from sugar.

No one factor or "bad habit" can be singled out as the sole promoter of heart disease. There is a domino sort of effect, suggests Dr. Yudkin. High sugar intake leads to excess weight, and excess weight leads to inactivity, which may figure eventually in heart disease, since so many major organs have been overstressed. But large quantities of sugar each day (six teaspoons or more) can make the risk of heart disease five times greater, says Dr. John Yudkin, who views sugar as the primary cause of cardiovascular disorders such as atherosclerosis.[104]

In Yudkin's view, saturated fat intake and high cholesterol are secondary to sugar as heart disorder factors. Professor Richard A. Ahrens of the University of Maryland, in an article in the *American Journal of Clinical Nutrition*, confirms this view. He says there's nothing more efficient than sugar in raising those triglyceride and cholesterol levels. As a consequence, Ahrens continues, your circulation suffers and high blood pressure may result.[105]

How Do Diabetes and Refined Carbohydrates Affect Your Cardiovascular Profile?

Perhaps no two experts agree on what risk factors are most serious where the etiology of cardiovascular and coronary disease is concerned. But the chief factors cited usually include diabetes, as well as the following:

- overweight
- cigarette smoking
- inactivity
- excessive low-density lipoproteins
- poor adaptation to stress
- high blood sugar
- inherited susceptibility

A diet high in complex carbohydrates, like whole grains and raw fruits, is healthier for your heart because, as Dr. Ahrens tells us, blood fat levels often rise in response, not just to sugar alone, but to the excess calories they contain. Here are a few of the theories offered to explain this fact:

1. Such foods are more filling, unlike sugary snacks and beverages. You eat less and the calories don't lead to the state of obesity that so often is a step in the direction of heart disease.

2. Complex carbohydrates seem to cause your gallbladder to eliminate more cholesterol-rich bile salts, thus lowering the amount of cholesterol in your bloodstream. An example is provided by Dr. Yudkin. A diet which includes a lot of brown rice has been shown to be a potent agent for reducing cholesterol levels for individuals with certain dietary intolerances.[106]

3. Some individuals profit by getting their carbohydrate from fibrous food and starches rather than sucrose because this sugar, above all others, causes the greatest variation in insulin response, along with elevated blood lipids, increased weight, and a reduced ability to prevent harmful blood coagulation. These reactions are recognized as conditions conducive to coronary heart disease.[107]

Complex Carbohydrate: An Anticholesterol Factor

If you have a cholesterol problem, you know how many drugs modern medicine markets, supposedly designed to bring blood fat levels down. But if you are wary of "miracles" created by drugs, you may be interested in how natural complex carbohydrates can aid in cholesterol control. Here's how fiber affects blood fats:

- Because of the rapid rate at which fiber moves through the intestines, there is reduced opportunity for cholesterol in the food you've eaten to be assimilated through cell walls and absorbed into the blood. Still, it is estimated that only about 10 percent of the cholesterol in your body comes from your diet. The balance is synthesized by the cells.
- If your cholesterol is bordering on high, your doctor may have discussed bile salts with you. If he hasn't, you should know that bile salts

are a by-product of cholesterol synthesis. Too much of this substance is not healthy. Neither is a diet high in fat, because it encourages bile salts to be absorbed twice. Yes, the first cycle is important, because fat in the diet cannot be properly metabolized unless bile is there to break it down and disperse it. Unfortunately, when your diet tends to be deficient in raw, crunchy, natural foods, you wind up with reabsorbed bile salts in your system. This can create a situation of too much stagnated fat in your vascular network. The solution? More fiber, such as raw bran, at each meal, because fiber, with its spongelike capacity, "mops" up excess bile, sterols, and cholesterol and helps to excrete them, thereby lowering fats circulating in your serum.

A good breakfast can help reduce cholesterol levels, too. If it's been ages since you've filled your bowl with rolled oats or old-fashioned barley, why not get off to a good start tomorrow? And since the two carbohydrates pectin and guar do this as well, add some chopped apples and bananas to double the benefit. But don't get samples of every whole grain on your grocer's shelf: unrefined wheat kernels, as good as they are for you and as rich in fiber, have not demonstrated the same cholesterol-lowering effect. The ingestion of carbohydrates prior to exercise results in hypoglycemia due to a rise in blood glucose level and a rise in carbohydrate utilization by those muscles being exercised. "Fructose ingestion is associated with a modest rise in plasma insulin and does not result in hypoglycemia during exercise."[108]

Summary

It isn't just too much saturated fat that elevates cholesterol and other blood fat levels. Sugar alone may be an even more important causative factor. And when eaten together with such fats, sugar can compound the problem considerably. Two bad dietary habits, in other words, are worse than one—especially if you have any susceptibility to diabetes or heart disease.

Keep active, keep your weight normal, and don't smoke. These good habits will protect you from the killer diseases. For even greater protection, switch from sugary pick-me-ups and desserts to complex carbohydrates, rich in fiber: snacks like whole grain crackers, popcorn, and raw fruits reduce cholesterol, keep all blood fats within normal range, and help keep your entire vascular system healthy.

Sugar and Coronary Health: Yesterday and Today

The news that sugar is bad for your cardiovascular health is more than eighty years old. One of the first attempts to determine whether a high-sugar, high-starch diet might be harmful—at least to rodents—indicated that rats became fatter in response to the extra carbohydrates. In some cases, where it was the sugar that did the most harm, the fructose component of sucrose received most of the blame. Other studies since the turn of the century have corroborated these findings.

• A drop in sugar availability, leading to a decline in consumption, is usually associated with a decline in heart and blood fat disorders—especially when fat in the diet is also omitted or restricted. Wartime sugar and butter rationing in Great Britain was better for people than they realized at the time.

• Large amounts of fat in the diet seem less productive of cardiovascular complications when sugar is absent. This has been observed in so-called "less advanced" societies following natural diets.

• Over the last two "sugar centuries," as sugar intake increased twenty times, both Americans and Europeans have suffered far greater levels of heart trouble than ever before.

• Approximately one-half of our calories are derived from carbohydrates like sugar today. Authorities such as Dr. Yudkin note that diabetes, as well as heart disease, has been on the rise.[109] Diseases that involve changes in glucose levels in the blood and major organ damage do not occur in a vacuum. And they do not occur without dietary provocation.

• Researchers are now suggesting that "the reason people develop adult-onset diabetes may be because they eat the wrong kind of carbohydrates, meaning those that give rapid rises in blood sugar, rather than simply too many carbohydrates." Ms. Kolata cites the work of Dr. Jerrold Olefsky, who points out that "diabetics may want to know that some foods that they frequently avoid, such as ice cream, are fine as far as blood glucose is concerned." It is suggested that diabetics may start to question the starch exchange lists of their diet.[110]

• Ms. Kolata and Toni Goldfarb give further information about "slow-release" carbohydrates mentioned in Kolata's other article above. Dr. David Jenkins of the University of Toronto has done tests to see how different foods affect blood sugar and has devised along with Dr. Thomas Wolever of Oxford a "glycemic index" This measures the intensity and duration of the glucose response in the blood.[111]

Sucrose Elevates Blood Fats

Blood lipid levels—cholesterol and triglycerides—are usually high in people with heart and circulatory problems. Scientists and researchers who have uncovered the relationship between sugar consumption and blood lipid (fat) levels have made an important contribution to our understanding of the current epidemic of heart disease.

They say that fructose in sugar is the main lipogenic (fat-causing) agent, whether it is fructose administered to test animals, or fructose as found in refined sugar. (This is another reason not to hop on the fructose bandwagon.) Lipid levels seem to escalate sharply when sugar is ingested in large quantities and taken up rapidly by the bloodstream.

Sugar, either as fructose or sucrose, seems to cause a speed-up of function of the liver, prompting it to make too many fats and pour them into the blood. Such overproduction is checked by other mechanisms in the body, which flush out excessive blood fats. The normal metabolism can adjust to such temporary ups and downs; if overburdened, however, the normal mechanisms may not be able to control blood lipid levels, and cardiovascular disease may result.

A single candy bar (or three big baked potatoes, which are the same thing in terms of carbohydrate totals) may cause too many blood fats to accumulate in your bloodstream. After eating large amounts even of natural foods such as potatoes or rice, your blood fats can rise, too, even if you are in good health.

Many other studies have produced similar results, using various starches and sugars. Sometimes different sugars are pitted against one another. For example, when starch and glucose were studied side by side with sugar and fructose, refined sugar was shown to raise serum triglyceride levels consistently. Lowering sugar also lowered lipid levels. Serum triglyceride levels stay lower when a low-sugar diet is followed—so watch your intake.[112]

Fatty acid production increases when a diet of 12 percent sugar is fed to rats, says S. Mukherjee et al. at the Laboratories of Lipid Research at the University of Calcutta. In this third study utilizing fructose and sucrose, both caused neutral fat levels to go up, but sugar caused the manufacture of more cholesterol in the liver. This means, undoubtedly, that cholesterol breakdown products are proliferating as well. Glucose and fructose intake also stimulated production of triglycerides.[113]

Fructose vs. Sugar

Even if your diet is adequate or better, adding fructose may add a greater risk factor for heart disease than sugar, since it can stimulate, even more rapidly than sugar, production of undesirable glycerol and fatty acids. Glucose appears to be third in terms of provoking such chemical changes, according to a study by J. L. Kelsay, which reported results with a group of females consuming a high-sugar diet.[114]

These results with sucrose may stem from the fact that this sugar is speedily absorbed because it stimulates excess synthesis of sucrase enzymes. Its rapid absorption may encourage a buildup of lipids in the liver cells as well.

If you have high blood fat levels, it is a good idea to avoid sugar and fat to prevent the situation from getting worse. According to M. A.

Antar et al. in *Atherosclerosis,* saturated fats and sucrose are a danger-ous combination. Elements contributing to the rise of blood lipid levels include:

1. The percentage of total calories as sucrose and starch. (Do you eat too many sweet snacks?)
2. The amount of saturated vs. polyunsaturated fat. (Salad oil is far preferable to the saturated fats used to make commercial French fries, buttered popcorn, etc.)
3. The amount of cholesterol in the diet.[115] (Have you cut down on red, "marbled" meat?)

Sugar may not alter your blood fat levels if your metabolism is relatively normal. Even when you eat a diet abnormally high in sugar, your lipid levels may or may not change dramatically, since other fac-tors are involved.

• If you follow a low-cholesterol diet rich in the PUFA (polyun-saturated fatty acid) foods, then starch and sugar, even in sizable doses, may not change your fat serum levels. For example, according to Dr. I. MacDonald, as reported in the *American Journal of Clinical Nutri-tion,* although triglyceride levels rose when animal subjects ate a com-bination of cream and table sugar, this did not happen when they were fed either cream and glucose or sunflower seed oil and glucose. How-ever, cholesterol and triglycerides do rise if sucrose *is* added to either of those combinations, according to Dr. Yudkin.[116]

• If your blood fat levels are already abnormally high, large amounts of carbohydrate foods may cause elevation.

Based on these and other findings, many researchers have con-cluded that the riskiest path is to add large amounts of sugar to a diet when it is already unbalanced by such undesirable elements as satu-rated fats, salt, and overprocessed foods that contain these negative factors. Also, the risk is greater when, for whatever reason, the blood fat levels are already above normal.

A further fact to bear in mind is your own biochemical individual-ity, which will determine your degree of susceptibility. For example, a man beyond the middle years is at much greater risk, *generally speak-ing,* of worsening the health of his heart with a sugary diet than a teenage girl.[117]

What We Know About Sugar and CHD from Animal Experiments

Sugar is the food most of us love the most and the ingredient we use the most. And heart disease is the most common of our killer dis-eases.

One way to explore the connection that may exist between these two facts is to study animals who have been experimentally fed sugar. Here are a few more findings that have resulted from such inquiries.

• If you are a female, you may have a built-in ability to protect yourself from the sugar diseases and their blood-fat-elevating effect. This "sexist" immunity, seen in both humans and animals, is no doubt due to hormone factors.

• Animals react with major organ damage and with damage to veins and arteries as well, reports Dr. M. Murakami in the *Japanese Circulation Journal*, when sugar is fed at high dose levels. Their blood showed high glucose levels and high fat and serum cholesterol levels.[118]

• If you would do anything to protect yourself from buildup of dangerous fatty plaques, the warning signal for coronary heart disease, then avoid sugar. Reports by K. R. Bruckdorfer, I. H. Khan, and John Yudkin at the Department of Nutrition of Queen Elizabeth College in London, tell us that both cholesterol and atheromas became more serious as more sugar was added to the diet.[119]

• Sugar is not kid stuff, according to two studies with rats, the first conducted by Phyllis H. Moser and Carolyn D. Berdanier of the College of Human Ecology, University of Maryland, and the second by Dr. Berdanier and two colleagues from the University of Nebraska College of Medicine. In one study, sugar in large amounts quickly clogged the blood with fats, and either caused rodent life expectancy to be greatly curtailed or resulted in out and out death.[120]

Summary

You need carbohydrate for energy, especially to fuel your brain. But you don't need sugar. Too much glucose in your bloodstream—an after-effect of a typical coffee-donut break, actually worsens fatigue and overburdens your vital organs rather than waking you up. If you are keeping your metabolism healthy with a well-balanced diet, your liver will send forth new energy from its reserves, if it is not already there as you need it in your working muscles. Remember, carbohydrates alone—in a candy bar, for example—do not provide healthy energy.

Relying on sugar for energy and a lift has a particularly serious impact for cardiovascular well-being. For example:

• The harm that fat intake does is worsened when you eat sugar, too.

• As our sugar intake has risen dramatically, so has the incidence of heart disease.

• Eating sugar probably causes your liver to produce excess fats which are sent into circulation in your blood.

• Sugar may cause such disorders as ulcers or the Type IV hyperlipidemia syndrome, which in turn may lead to diabetes and other serious problems.

Studies using animals have furthered our understanding of sugar's effects on the body. Females seem to be less vulnerable than males to cardiovascular symptoms. But sugar—especially sucrose—has been shown to damage major organs, veins, and arteries; to increase plaque buildups in the arteries; and to shorten rodents' lives, especially when fed to them when young.

For a healthy heart, it is a good idea to:

• Stick to a low-sugar diet that does not cause unhealthy blood fats to rise in your blood. Such a diet may even lower your blood fat levels.

• Watch your carbohydrate intake. Remember, a small candy bar is the carbohydrate equivalent of three baked potatoes. Of course, there are nutrients and fiber in the potatoes which make them less stressful to assimilate.

• Concentrate on a diet that eliminates sugar and refined foods as much as possible and you may never have to worry about your energy levels, your cholesterol, or an ailing heart.

The Sugar/Hypertension Connection

Salt is not the only food implicated in high blood pressure. Another factor that worsens it is sucrose, the worst carbohydrate of them all. Clinical casework at Louisiana State University Medical School tells us, for example, that this killer disease was produced in monkeys fed a diet high in both sodium chloride and sucrose.[121]

• A healthy kidney is important in preventing hypertension. But a high concentration of blood solids may undo your kidneys by causing edema and hypertension. Sugar, like salt, may play a role in this process.

• Your kidneys must cope not only with the burdens of ingested sugar, but appear to manufacture some of their own, reported researchers at Louisiana State University Medical School in New Orleans.

• In the opinion of Dr. Ahrens, the presence of hypertension could lead to glucose intolerance, a state that accompanies or precedes sugar disorder diseases like diabetes. Hypertension, then, may be caused in part by the sugar you eat. And it may result, in turn, in the lessening of your ability to process the sugar you eat.[122]

• Ulcers may be a "sugar sickness." Like disorders affecting the heart, ulcers usually are accompanied by a variety of problems that might be grouped as blood dysfunctions. Another suggestive sign is that withdrawal of refined sugar frequently results in healing. If you are suffering from ulcers, try eliminating sugar from your diet.

• A woman's menstrual cycle is related to her glucose tolerance level (the cells' ability to use glucose properly). Experiments by Dr. I. MacDonald have shown higher blood sugar levels between the thirteenth and eighteenth day. And experiments also indicate that mature female baboons retain intravenously injected fructose longer than male animals.[123]

• Men in general are at a health disadvantage to women in that they have higher serum triglyceride levels. Women's advantage narrow as they age, however. Women enter this risk group as they enter the middle years, often around the critical period of menopause.

• If you're going to continue eating sugar, consider adding chromium-rich foods. According to H. A. Schroeder of Dartmouth Medical School, raw sugar, which is naturally rich in this trace mineral, did not show the cholesterol-escalating potential of white table sugar, which is stripped of most of its trace mineral content during the refining process. Further evidence of this link is an experiment in which participants treated with chromium showed lowered glucose and blood fat levels.[124]

MEDICAL OPINION AROUND THE WORLD

What do they think about the sugar–heart disease connection in other countries? A sixteen-nation study, reports F. Grande in *World Review of Nutrition and Dietetics* (1975), revealed that the physicians do not consider the link clearly enough established to counsel their patients against sugar use.

Two typical examples are noted from the studies of the Medical Research Council of England, which denied any connection after doing its own research. But perhaps the methods employed by this group bear investigation, suggests Dr. Yudkin.

Dr. Grande, the author of the survey, states that atherosclerosis has many causes, but in his opinion sugar cannot be included. He adds that he feels the studies using large populations as a base do not support the antisugar case. He cites those nations—many in Latin America—where sugar intake is high and coronary trouble is low. And Dr. Ancel Keys argues that there is an ever-increasing disparity between coronary heart disease and sugar use here in the United States. The rebuttal? Can you really forecast results for each individual, who may, indeed, provide faulty information on his dietary habits? In any case epidemiological results are very difficult to interpret since so many elements are involved, of which food patterns are but one.[125]

In addition, medical opinion frequently lags behind the findings of researchers—what doctors think is not always based on up-to-date information.

Less Sugar for a Healthy Heart: Evidence Is Clear

Healthy or not, male or female, less sugar may be a factor in assuring a healthy heart. Here are three more provocative studies.

• If approximately three-quarters of your total caloric intake comes from the natural "good" carbohydrates, you can expect added protection from coronary heart disease. Grains and root vegetables seem to be the most protective foods in the group. A well-balanced diet rich in such foods keeps fats in the blood from building up and helps bring levels into normal ranges; important finding for hyperlipidemia (elevated blood fats) sufferers.[126]

• Diet alone may have a significant reversal effect in the case of myocardial infarction. A. M. Roberts in the *American Heart Journal* reports on one group of men studied who had suffered this disorder of the heart muscle; they reduced their sugar intake and their serum triglycerides were reduced as a result.

• Eliminating some of the sugar in your diet can lower blood triglyceride levels. These are the fats that are found at high levels in most incidences of coronary heart disease. One study proving this involved pre-middle-aged men who had ischemic heart disease, which blocks the blood flow to the heart.[127] Their serum triglycerides were significantly reduced by following a reduced sugar diet, even though cholesterol only dipped slightly.

• Also, it has been observed that if you exercise regularly you may be spared the ill effects of sugar on your lipid levels; they stay low for longer periods.

To Keep Your Insulin Levels Down—Reduce Sugar

Lowering dietary sugar can safeguard you from elevated hormone levels in the blood. This finding was reported in two studies by Dr. I. MacDonald of Guy's Medical School in London.

Several pre-middle-aged males suffering from peripheral vascular disease were examined for physical condition and diet. Their diets were high in sugar and, as a consequence, so was the amount of insulin hormone circulating in their blood. And also, a poor sign for anyone afflicted with a disease that causes reduced flow of blood to the extremities, clumping of blood platelets was noted as a consequence of the high sugar intake.[128]

However, in nutrition research not all studies show comparable results. For example, in contrast, another group of young men free of disease was examined. Although large amounts of sugar were also part of their diet, these neither heightened hormone levels nor caused the platelet problem to appear.[129]

A second study also indicated that sugar has a hazardous insulin-raising ability. If you already have a problem with abnormal blood fats, sugar may be more dangerous for you than for the average individual. But remember, sugar affects insulin secretion in all of us. So if you are healthy, you should still watch your intake.[130]

• Should you concern yourself about lactose or the sugar in the milk you drink? No. This has no elevating effect on insulin output or on blood fat levels.[131]

Blood Fats Rise and Fall: All It Takes Is Sugar

You may be inviting a heart attack if you eat a sugary diet day in and day out. Dr. Yudkin feels that your biochemical susceptibility is the determining factor. So it appears from other studies. Victims of the disorder called hyperlipoproteinemia, for example, have been test-fed sugar, nonsugar carbohydrates, and meat-derived fats. Various amounts have produced various results, but when sugar was coupled with large amounts of animal foods or other high-cholesterol food, sugar consistently demonstrated its ability to promote accumulated fats in the blood serum.[132]

These same hospitalized sufferers fared better on a diet composed of the more desirable carbohydrates—such as raw fruits, fresh vegetables, dried beans. Cholesterol declined for them; perhaps you could expect similar good results. Don't exclude whole grain cereal products either. These are blood fat-reducing foods, too, although they may not be as dramatic in this respect as the foods just cited. Complex carbohydrates should be used for the wide variety of nutritional benefits they bestow.

Summary

If you have hypertension, you should avoid salt, as you well know. But you should avoid sugar as well, for the health of your kidneys as well as your heart. Animal studies suggest that high blood pressure may in turn lead to blood sugar disorders. If you have this disease, you have greater reason to eliminate sugar from your diet.

When you do, you are eliminating a factor that may figure in the development of ulcers, elevated triglyceride and cholesterol levels (especially in men of middle age and menopausal women), hyperlipidemia, high blood pressure, myocardial infarction, and ischemic heart disease, to name a few ills complicated and/or caused by sugar according to recent research.

In sharp contrast to sugar is the whole world of "good" complex carbohydrates available for building and maintaining energy and health. Substituting complex carbohydrates for sugars may offer a simple, drug-free way to prevent the biggest killer disease of them all.

While doctors in the United States and other countries are not generally in agreement with this advice, they may not be aware of the growing body of evidence, much of it cited in this chapter, linking heart disease with sugar consumptions, or they may be influenced by the "scientists" who work, directly or indirectly, on behalf of the sugar industry.

Preventing Diabetes

Check yourself for two life-style factors common to many diabetics:

1. Are you a sitter? Lack of exercise makes you susceptible to many degenerative diseases, especially diabetes. The risk of diabetes is greater as you advance in years. When it strikes older individuals, it is called maturity onset diabetes.

2. Do you eat a lazy man's diet? High-fat, high-sugar, high-calorie meals, low in fiber and fresh foods, are the common fare of diabetics, whether in this country or in Europe. Such a diet raises insulin levels in the blood and lowers insulin in the cells.

All refined carbohydrates, but especially refined sugar, produce these two chemical reactions. Eating such a diet places you at high risk for diabetes, a disease in which abnormal insulin production causes a glucose imbalance.

Defining Diabetes

Diabetes is a complex disorder. But here are a few of the distinguishing characteristics:

When your pancreas synthesizes abnormal amounts of insulin hormone—usually too little—the blood sugar becomes unstable.

The diabetic metabolism cannot perform one of these two essential jobs that your body normally does readily: send glucose for energy across membrane walls, and convert glucose fuel in the liver into glycogen.

As a result, a hazardous form of hyperglycemia—high blood sugar —ensues, a faulty supply-and-demand situation where the fuel concentrated in the blood cannot be relayed to the millions of cells in the body crying out for nourishment.[133]

Diabetes can do considerable damage to your pancreas, but it also causes you to produce more cortisol, and damage to both the kidneys and the retinas of the eyes is common as well.

Some diabetics suffer from hyperinsulinism; that is, their blood contains too much, rather than too little insulin hormone.[134]

The common types of hypoinsulinism (too little insulin) are considered to have reached epidemic proportions, affecting up to 6 percent of U.S. residents. "In the U.S.A., diabetes is now the fifth leading cause of death by disease, and the sixth of all causes."[135] As many as 5 to 12 million Americans may be diabetic.

The Diabetes-Carbohydrate Link

You can do much to prevent diabetes if you begin your infants on no-sugar diets. This is the conclusion of a diabetes researcher, Dr. A. M. Cohen. Avoiding sugar may not be the only way to avoid diabetes, but it is one of the best ways. In rat studies conducted by Dr. Cohen, animals fed refined sugar throughout the day, much as we feed sugar to ourselves, quickly manifested the damaged kidneys and deterioration of the retina that are characteristic of diabetes.[136] These results mirror the human studies he has conducted, which are discussed here. Starch feeding produced nothing comparable.

While we don't have enough tests of long enough duration with large numbers of subjects to define the perfect diet to help control diabetes, the evidence suggests that high-fiber, low-sugar diets are the best.

Diabetes statistics fell during both world wars when sucrose was a rationed staple.

Refined sugar, because so many nutrients are removed from it, is believed to be more likely to produce diabetes than unrefined sugar-cane, which is rich in the glucose tolerance factor, chromium.[137] Investigators tell us that even though the South African diet is rich in raw sugarcane, diabetes is rare among the workers who cut and eat it daily.[138] This may also be due to the fact that the sugar is eaten in its high-fiber natural state, or that these workers are exercising strenuously each day.

Ethnic groups whose diets have not been adulterated with refined sugar suffer less diabetes than we do.

Starch is a carbohydratelike sugar, but people consuming large amounts of starchy food do not suffer diseases like diabetes. The more of these "good" complex carbohydrates are eaten, the less often diabetes is seen.[139]

Are You a Special Risk?

Do you stress your system every time you eat sugar? Some of us do, some don't. For example, in an experiment on adult diabetic men eating plenty of this sweet and dangerous stuff, Dr. Yudkin reports that both insulin and cortisol levels rose. But when this diet was repeated on a group apparently not so susceptible, this response did not occur.[140]

At present we do not have large numbers of studies that echo this one; we cannot make an airtight case against sugar as a cause of diabetes. However, a few more findings of significance include these:

1. Glucose intolerance turns up most often when sugar is ingested in quantity. The average person probably does not show abnormalities at low or moderate levels of sugar intake, says the research team of Dr. B. M. Rifkind, Senior Registrar in Medicine at the Royal Infirmary at Glasgow. Two factors of importance include inherited immunities and individual biochemistry.[141] Dr. Rifkind determined this by studying animal subjects.

2. Eliminate sugar, say some authorities, and you will see diabetes levels drop as they did between the world wars. Other authorities interpret this historical, epidemiological data less conclusively. The low interwar figure, they claim, is an indication of the good that can be done by a diet low in fat and high in fiber as well as low in sugar. Sugar alone, they say, was not the reason.

3. If you are an adult male with a sweet tooth, your diet bears watching, especially if you are middle-aged. Individuals with special sensitivity to sugar are at risk of succumbing to hyperinsulinism, suggests research by Drs. Stephen Szanto, M.D., M.R.C.P.I., and Dr. John Yudkin that compared high and low sucrose intake in a small group of healthy men. After only fourteen days, not one or two but all of the subjects with high intake had unhealthy levels of triglyceride fat in their blood. Along with higher serum immunoreactive insulin, clumping of platelets is often a prelude to diseased arteries, and added pounds. We know that sugar produced these devastating changes because removing it caused a return to normal health.[142]

4. If you have a family background of coronary disorders and/or diabetes, too much sugar can be especially hazardous to your health.

Exercise and Diabetes

Exercise more and you'll have less cause for worry about coronary heart disease, excess weight, or diabetes. They all go together, suggests Lionel H. Opie, M.D., of the Ischemic Heart Disease Laboratory of the University of Capetown, South Africa, writing in the *American Heart*

Journal. A diet that can make you diabetic can also make you fat.[143]

Diabetes or the propensity for it may be prevented by exercise.

Running, cycling, or even vigorous walking have the following health-giving, diabetes-preventive effects:

- They will lower your blood lipid levels.
- They will improve your ability to use glucose and decrease the amount of immunoreactive insulin you synthesize.
- They will improve your cell's ability to get maximum good out of whatever glucose is present, however minimal.
- They will minimize adverse reactions to a heavy carbohydrate load.[144]

Summary

Diabetes is a complex disorder in which genetic inheritance, obesity, sedentary habits, and poor diet all play a part.

Experts are not in total agreement on what the ideal diet for preventing or controlling this disorder ought to be. But one thing is clear: sugar makes it worse, and causes many of the symptoms typical of prediabetic and diabetic states.

Blood hormone levels escalate and insulin levels in the cells plummet when diabetics follow the type of high-sugar, high-fat, low-fiber, high-calorie eating pattern that is typically American.

If you are diabetic, your system is not able to transport glucose normally across membrane walls or convert it into fuel in your liver. Eliminate sugar, follow a well-planned, balanced diet that meets with your doctor's approval, and exercise regularly. These three steps virtually always produce improvement in the hyperglycemic state.

Can Dietary Supplements Help Prevent Diabetes?

If you get adequate chromium, zinc, and B_6 in your diet, you may be able to prevent or lessen the likelihood of diabetes. If any nutrients stand out above the others as a help in controlling diabetes, they are probably these.

According to Dr. J. B. Bennett, in a talk before the Academy of Orthomolecular Psychiatry, animals developed what appeared to be diabetes when chromium was removed from their food supply, but returned to full health when this element was added back to the diet.

We know that chromium normalizes glucose utilization for humans, too. There are two studies of interest in this regard. The first involved young people, all residents of Israel; the second involved a number of American older people. As dissimilar in eating and life-styles as these two groups were, they shared a common deficiency of chromium. Reliable sources conclude we get only 10 percent of what we need for health from a typical American diet.[145] This is one of the reasons nutritionists urge you to eat brewer's yeast daily.

Zinc plays numerous roles in maintaining the integrity of all your body's cells. It helps assure proper growth, partially protects you from prostate problems and many degenerative disorders, and it is indispensable in helping your metabolism handle the carbohydrates you eat daily.[146]

These nutritional "additives" work best when supported by a balanced diet that supplies plenty of fiber.

• Using bran from any grain as a supplement, as a food, or both is beneficial, too, according to Dr. A.M. Cohen, who cited fiber as one of the reasons for lowered glucose levels in the Yemenite subjects he studied, as discussed in the next section.

• Healthy individuals who followed a diet based on quantities of fibrous bread each day while eliminating sugar showed positive results, says Dr. Cohen.

• And an eating style concentrating on more fiber than is found in the usual Western-style diet showed this response as well in Israeli Yemenites.

A Case History: Could This Happen to You?

Here's how choosing the right carbohydrates can make a difference where diabetes is concerned. It also illustrates the crucial difference between a high-starch and a high-sugar intake.

One researcher in Israel compared the diets of 5,000 individuals newly immigrated to a second group of nonimmigrant old-timers. Both groups were similar in that both were Yemenite Jews. Their level of health, however, was dissimilar. The established Yemenites took their coffee with as much as six tablespoons of sugar, and the rest of their diet was nearly as sugar-saturated. Among the established sugar-loving Yemenites, almost 145 out of every 5,000 were diabetic. However, among the newly arrived Yemenites, accustomed to a high-starch diet, only 3 out of 5,000 suffered this disease. This controlled study was conducted over ten years ago by Dr. Aaron M. Cohen of the Rothschild Hadassah University Hospital in Jerusalem, in response to the dramatic rise in cardiovascular and diabetic fatalities.

Heart Disease: How Is It Linked to Diabetes?

Diabetics die of heart disease more often than other people. Why?

• Your artery walls are very sensitive to many chemicals, among them the hormone chemical insulin which your pancreas produces. And a diabetic's system tends to produce and circulate more insulin through the arteries than a nondiabetic's.[147] This particular risk factor is also seen in obese nondiabetic individuals who have dangerous levels of fat in the blood.

• Now, consider this finding by Dr. H. Keen, of Guy's Hospital Medical School in London: When insulin levels rise high enough, your system may respond by manufacturing more lipids and putting them into your blood to circulate. Unfortunately, accompanying this unhealthy action, your artery walls respond by slowing down the rate at which they normally break down the fats that can endanger the health of your vascular system. The result is often atherosclerosis.[148] More fats are being pumped into your bloodstream and fewer are being taken out.

There are variations of this chain of events for different groups.

• If you are a female who hasn't yet reached middle age, you have a slight margin of protection.

• The typical American diet that is high in fatty foods and calories, too, adversely affects your tolerance for glucose. In some studies, raising blood fat levels alone did not produce escalation of hormone levels.[149]

• Like humans, animals have biochemical individuality. Rats who do not respond well to refined carbohydrates are more prone to develop vascular illness when force-fed glucose, especially as they age.[150]

It appears that when insulin levels are raised high enough, obesity, heart trouble, diabetes, or a combination of these ills is the danger.[151]

Three more studies that bear out the bad effects of high fat, high sugar, and low fiber have been produced by Dr. S. Reiser, in his definitive article, "Metabolic Effects of Dietary Carbohydrate." Fed large amounts of sucrose, animals all showed high blood levels of insulin and glucose, and grew obese.[152] A similar study with high sucrose feedings produced disorders of the eye (retina) resembling the ocular tragedy that afflicts so many human diabetics.

But we do know what helps keep diabetics and potential sufferers healthier: less fat, moderate amounts of protein, plus exercise on a daily basis to aid in normalizing glucose use by the body's cells.

Summary

Many reliable studies indicate that diabetes is nutritionally treatable. Especially important are zinc, B6, chromium, fiber, and the foods in which they are found, such as whole grains and brewer's yeast.

A comprehensive epidemiological study of Yemenite immigrants to Israel show that replacing a high-starch diet with a high-sugar diet may cause high increases in cardiovascular problems and diabetes.

Remember, if you are diabetic, that fat, sugar, and high-calorie processed foods increase body fat and circulate blood fat. This, in turn, may raise insulin levels and artery wall structure may be damaged, and a disease such as atherosclerosis could result. As you age, the likelihood that such changes will occur is greater, calling for even more careful attention to life-style habits, especially diet and regular exercise.

Troubleshooting Your Other Sugar Troubles

If your body is troubled these days, somebody's bound to point an accusing finger at something you're eating. Among the foods that most deserve criticism are refined carbohydrates, above all refined sugar. Every week, new research turns up new facts concerning the role of this adulterated food group in promoting or worsening everything from simple hypoglycemia or occasional headache to full-blown coronary heart disease.[153] Some of the bad news has not been proven to the satisfaction of every physician or scientist or researcher; still, the studies are too disturbing for us to simply ignore.

Malabsorption

If dairy products give you gas, or if milk doesn't always agree with you, your problem may not be the milk but the sugar it contains, lactose. Some people suffer ill effects from this "good" food because their digestive tracts lack the enzyme lactase, which breaks milk sugar into its simplest form for your nutritional needs.[154]

Milk may be a "natural," but if you're getting older you may be forced to limit or avoid it because you suffer from primary malabsorption. This is not as crippling as it sounds. But there's no question that the diarrhea and stomach gas it causes are an annoyance.

Failure to digest milk properly can cause runny stool. The reason is a buildup of pressure in your bowels caused by a chemical reaction between the undigested sugars and organisms in your colon that act upon and ferment the sugars. As a by-product, usable sugars may even be dumped into your stools for elimination.

If you experience discomfort after milk drinking only occasionally, this may be a side effect of an illness from which you are recovering. Doctors call this variation secondary malabsorption.

Another explanation for the experience of cramps or nausea from a healthy tumbler of fresh, cold milk is temporary malabsorption. This is caused when the mono- or disaccharides you've just eaten have difficulty passing through the intestinal walls because of some impediment in the system, which normally provides passage for simple sugars.

But you need the calcium and the oil-soluble vitamins A and D that milk provides, so what should you do? In all cases of malabsorption, you should avoid milk, and milk products containing milk or cream. Refined carbohydrate foods are best avoided, too, in the case of temporary malabsorption, until you are back to normal. A good nutritious alternative, however, is available to you in all cultured dairy products such as yogurt, kefir, buttermilk, and acidophilus drinks. These are safe and nonstressful on your digestion because the offending milk sugar in them has been converted into usable glucose and galactose by specialized "lactic acid" microorganisms.[155]

Sugar Trouble and the Pill

If you take birth control pills, your ability to metabolize glucose may be below par, says Dr. George A. Bray in *The Western Journal of Medicine*,[156] at least while you are on the medication. If there is an alternative contraceptive method you might consider, it's worth a thought. After taking one of these powerful pills, your blood sugar levels begin to rise; in an hour they may be 10 to 100 milligrams higher. The agent behind this unfavorable response, which may be responsible for metabolic side effects that last much longer than sixty minutes, is probably one of the growth hormones or female sex hormones.

Sugar and the Pathogenic Bacteria

If you've ever suspected that going off on an eating binge prompted your cold, stomach flu, or a more serious infection, you could be right. Perhaps a vacation spot rich in good restaurants, or perhaps a bout of the blues prompted that urge to indulge in elaborate desserts or in cookies, colas, and cakes. The resulting illness may have been a result, in part, of the fact that refined sugar has an adverse effect on your ability to fight infections. Dr. Yudkin and other researchers agree that you are interfering with the ability of your white blood cells to protect you whenever you flood your body with sugary foods.

The result is that your immunity is lowered or, as medical professional Winston Murdock, writing in *Bestways* (July 1976) put it, your phagocyte activity is impaired. While carbohydrate in the form of starch does not produce this effect, another study by yet another researcher, Dr. Albert Sanchez of Loma Linda University, demonstrated that adding only a little more than three ounces of glucose, fructose, honey, or citrus juice to a meal caused a depression in the protective functions of the cells that work as scavengers of alien particles that invade your body regularly.[157]

Skin Changes and Stomach Woes

A cause to celebrate in our culture—whether it's a birthday, a homecoming, a reward for a job well done—usually involves sugary, starchy devitalized foods. Pastry shop frosted cakes are a perfect example. As a result of all that sugar, you may suffer visible or invisible adverse changes.

One survey of patients with a common dermatitis disorder showed a 100 percent return to normal when sucrose was omitted from their diets. Acne sufferers, also, are well advised to take a "sugar vacation" and see what results.

Refined sugar is a big factor in the proliferation of *E. coli* bacteria. You've heard about these microorganisms before in connection with appendicitis, urinary-tract infections, cholecystitis, and diverticular disease. It appears that a potent "chemical cocktail" can result in your intestines when large amounts of fats or meats high in this strain of disease-causing bacteria are eaten.

If you are an overweight victim of a disease such as hiatus hernia or dyspepsia, thought to result from emotional stress, you know it is important to keep the pepsin levels in your stomach high, and your pH levels low (i.e., less acidic). The best way to do this may be to skip sugar and switch to a valuable natural starch food, suggests one reputable study in *Nature*.[158] This also helps keep adrenal hormone release normal.

Sugar in the Life Cycle: Children or Their Grandparents?

Sugar offers both long- and short-term hazards for children, toddlers, even babes in arm. If eating sugar is begun shortly after birth and continued, it increases the chance of tooth decay, and worse, of heart disease later in life.

Do you use "gourmet-type" prepared baby foods such as fruit puddings, custards, and parfait desserts? Don't, says Dr. John Yudkin. This habit can lead to obesity and even diabetes.[159]

If a few ounces of sugar is a health hazard for a mature adult, what dangers does it present where babies less than a year old are concerned? One expert who has answered this question is Dr. I. Tamir. In an experiment that I would not have wanted my child to be part of, Dr. Tamir had a group of infants on a diet almost three-quarters of whose calories came from either glucose or sugar. Unlike a more typical diet, which might be slightly less than half glucose, this very saccharine experiment had dramatic effects: blood fat readings rose sharply. Only after the excessive sugar was withdrawn did blood fat levels return to normal.

Children beyond the bassinet years fare even worse, especially if given considerable exposure to the media. Manufacturers of processed food continue to sugar their products heavily, and the worst are advertised directly to children. Sixty-six percent of all TV commercials for children's foods were high-sugar products in 1970, while less than 10 percent of commercials aired were for anything nutritious. The average number of advertisements for high-sugar foods in 1972 per each viewing hour was ten. Do you agree that this is an area where some government regulation is in order?

Nor do older family members escape the ills our offspring suffer. According to one expert, Dr. P. A. Crapo, as we age, the body changes the way it processes carbohydrates. The body slows down, and too much insulin is usually synthesized. This lowers our blood sugar—and energy —levels. Obviously this, plus a predominance of sugary convenience foods (which also stimulate insulin production) and poor living habits such as lack of exercise, take their toll.[160]

Especially important is the fact that the older you are, the less able you are to degrade the sugars you take in, because your body is less capable of producing or processing normal amounts of glycolytic enzymes. When you are younger, enzyme production rises to meet your needs as you ingest extra sugar. But when you reach a more advanced age, it appears that this important function declines, too, report Dr. Julio Espinoza and Norton S. Rosenzweig.[161]

Summary

Refined sugar is a problem for all of us. Even naturally occurring sugars pose problems for some of us. Your gastrointestinal complaints, for example, could be caused by a sensitivity to the lactose or milk sugar in these products. People may suffer from primary, secondary, or temporary malabsorption of lactose.

Cultured dairy products, which are more easily digested, including yogurt, can provide relief for some people as well as vitamins and minerals you would miss if you avoided milk.

As for refined sugar, another bonus you receive when you avoid it is improved resistance to infections. The protective functions of your cells is depressed by all forms of sugar, but especially sucrose. Also, sugar seems to provoke and worsen skin conditions such as acne; withdrawing it often results in visible healing. Omitting refined sugar from your meals will also keep the acid and pepsin levels in your stomach normal.

If you are older or younger, the risks that sugar poses are intensified. This is because the immature metabolism, just like the very mature metabolism, works less efficiently at assimilating sugar. Enzymes necessary to sugar digestion or absorption may be in dramatically reduced supply. Sugar should not be fed to small children because it is addictive and sets the stage for early obesity and tooth decay.

Hypoglycemia: Another Carbohydrate-Caused Disorder

Hypoglycemia is another carbohydrate disorder. If you have decided low blood sugar is the reason you feel so tired, so cranky or half crazy sometimes, you're probably right.

Less than a decade ago, the average doctor would have sent you away with a prescription or two, but now when you describe this syndrome, he will probably understand. The symptoms of this disorder are many and they often mimic those of other diseases. Hypoglycemic symptoms can include schizophrenia, alcoholism, migraine headaches, hyperactivity, lack of sex drive in women, impotency in men, obesity, fatigue, trembling, irritability, nervousness, depression, anxiety, destructive outbursts, allergies, cold sweats, dizziness, fainting spells, mental confusion, inability to concentrate, and forgetfulness.

When you feel as if you can't survive another minute without something sweet or stimulating, the energy-giving sugars in your blood are probably at a low ebb. Other common signs include feelings of unsteadiness or faintness, an uncontrollable urge to nap or to eat. But eating a sweet at such a time is the worst step.

It's not nice to fool your pancreas. In fact, it rarely works. When you have a high-sugar snack, the refined carbohydrate goes from your intestines right into your bloodstream. You feel good, but not for long, because now your overworked pancreas must compensate for this unnatural act by producing more insulin hormone. Your blood sugar "high" evaporates and you soon feel worse than before, because the excess insulin reduces your blood glucose to a level even lower than before. Your liver also enters into this juggling act by manufacturing glucose for the blood supply, but it must steal glycogen from its stored supply to do this. Imagine how stressed this poor organ becomes when you have a heavy candy bar habit.

Chronic hypoglycemia is dangerous. The brain and nervous system cannot survive without a reliable supply of glucose. It is possible to lapse into a coma without it. You can damage your central nervous system. And in any case, you are endangering the health of your supersensitive hypothalamus. This control center of the brain regulates many functions having to do with your appetite for both food and sex. If you feel both urges are always unsatisfied, take a look at what your diet is doing to your glucose levels. All areas of the brain, remember, are affected by low blood sugar. This is often the mysterious causative factor in depression, fatigue, and hyperkinetic behavior, as well as in mood swings.

Unfortunately, it does not take long to develop low blood sugar. If you feel you can't get enough candy, if you indulge in several colas or coffees a day and perhaps even snack on pastries at the same time, you are inviting a hypoglycemia attack each time you do. A few big doses of any sugary food can do it. If you are serious about avoiding or coping with this disorder, which may lead to serious diseases such as diabetes and to great unhappiness, you must also eliminate cigarettes, caffeinated teas, and all stimulant-containing food and drink. These and sugar can be highly addictive. For relief and improved well-being, substitute foods that will stabilize the blood sugar—specifically, protein and the high-fiber carbohydrates. In other words, a whole grain cracker with cheese, or a baked potato and some lean fish are perfect.

Summary

If you suspect you are one of America's millions of hypoglycemia victims, don't take this blood sugar disorder lightly. Consult your doctor; he can order the necessary lab tests. Hypoglycemia not only may lead you to snack too often or nap too often because of the fatigue and hunger it causes; but it could also lead to diseases as serious as diabetes or schizophrenia. Remember, if you follow a poor diet high in refined carbohydrates—especially sugar—you are inviting hypoglycemia's damage to your brain and nervous system. Neither can survive if you don't maintain a constant supply of glucose in your bloodstream.

If you eliminate or sharply reduce sugar, cigarettes, caffeine, and stimulants in all forms including colas, and concentrate on healthy food and drink with an emphasis on protein, you will see improvement. A nutritionist can recommend a helpful supplementation program as well.

Sugar and Hyperactivity

If your son or daughter has been diagnosed as hyperactive, you not only have a hard-to-manage child on your hands; you have to face conflicts among doctors about the cause and cure.

The most popular prescription with doctors, teachers, and school administrators today is for amphetamine-containing drugs like Ritalin. These are powerful drugs, and work to calm down some children. But more holistically oriented doctors and researchers have hoped to find the cause of hyperactivity. (They reason that it is surely not a lack of amphetamine, which no one claims is a nutrient, and which can have serious side effects.)

In 1973, Dr. Benjamin Feingold published his theory of one possible cause of hyperactivity. He felt that some children might be allergic to food additives or combinations of food additives. (There are literally thousands of artificial chemicals in the typical American supermarket diet.) He reported considerable success in treating hyperactive children by modifying their diet to exclude these chemicals. The "Feingold diet," which prohibits all foods containing artificial ingredients, became a lifesaver to thousands of parents of hyperactive children, some of whom could be taken off amphetamines as a result of the diet.

However, the Feingold diet is not easy to enforce for young children, when so many social influences entice them to eat brightly colored and gaily-wrapped treats. Even more important, the Feingold diet helps only a small minority of hyperactive children. Dr. Feingold may have found *one* cause of hyperactivity in *some* children—but apparently not the main one.

Several researchers since then have investigated other possible causes. Sugar is one of the substances they have tested. If you have hyperactive children in your family or deal with them in your work, you will be very excited about some of their results, reported by Ronald J. Prinz, William A. Roberts, and Elaine Hantman of the University of South Carolina.[162]

The sugar-related disorder hypoglycemia can cause erratic behavior and emotional outbursts in adults. Could hypoglycemia be a factor in hyperactivity in children?

One study in 1978 indicated that in five-hour glucose tolerance tests, the accepted method for measuring hypoglycemia, 74 percent of the hyperactive children studied showed abnormal patterns in their fasting blood sugar responses to glucose, with half of those possibly indicating hypoglycemia.

When this clue was followed up by Prinz, Roberts, and Hantman, with a much more detailed, double-blind controlled study of the relationship between the amount of sugar in the diet of hyperkinetic children and subsequent behavior, it was found that hyperactive behavior was much worse following high-sugar snacks or meals.

In particular, this well-designed study analyzed the food intake over a one-week period (as reported in detail by their mothers) of children who had been diagnosed as hyperkinetic, against that of a control group. Then independent, trained observers analyzed each child's behavior based on videotapes taken through a one-way mirror. The foods eaten were categorized and quantified; so was the behavior.

High-sugar foods (as well as other refined carbohydrate foods like white bread) increased hyperactive behavior (especially destructive-aggressive behavior and restlessness, two of the categories analyzed). Nutritious foods by and large decreased such behavior. The effects of foods included on Feingold's not-permissible list were also analyzed. Those that didn't contain sugar or refined starch didn't seem to have much effect one way or the other. The researchers wondered whether Feingold's good results might have been at least partially due to the fact that three-quarters of the foods on his forbidden list are junk foods with large amounts of sugar in them.

These studies imply that your children's social and academic success may well depend on your controlling the amount of refined sugar and starch in their diets: hyperactive children are rarely able to participate well in constructive group activities.

When you think about the amount of sugar children in the United States consume and the discipline problems teachers complain of across the country, these studies raise serious questions about what the sugar and processed food industries are doing to our children and their future.

Sugar, Learning Disability, and Criminal Behavior

Most doctors today would still pooh-pooh the idea that learning disabilities might be caused by hypoglycemia. But in 1979, J. Kershner and W. Hawke studied the results of giving a high-protein, low-carbohydrate, sugar-free diet to a group of carefully screened and diagnosed learning-disabled and hyperactive students. Improvements in learning ability, and in behavior, were so dramatic that the experimenters, who had intended to test the efficacy of vitamins in bringing about the same results, could hardly measure any significant changes attributable to vitamin supplements.[163]

This experiment is especially important because learning-disabled children are one group who seem so often to get into trouble with their schools and with the police. Most teachers and psychologists assume that learning-disabled students misbehave because they are frustrated about their inability to succeed at school, striking back at an institution which they perceive as rejecting them. But in 1975 J. A. Wacker came up with a new idea. He suggested that the same perceptual distortions and lack of reasoning ability that lead to learning disabilities might also cause extremely poor judgment and lack of foresight in coping with the social world.[164] In other words, inability to learn to read and inability to foresee the consequences of breaking a window might be caused by the exact same perceptual problem.

Hypoglycemia, often a result of eating too much sugar, is one of the factors that can cause these perceptual distortions and learning disabilities, as Kershner and Hawke's experiment demonstrated. Does Wacker's concept imply that eating sugar can cause juvenile delinquency, too?

It looks as if much of the suffering inflicted on others, on their families, and on themselves by young lawbreakers and other problem youths could, indeed, be avoided if young people were taught not to eat so much sugary food.

In 1978, A. G. Schauss studied the dietary habits of delinquents and behaviorally disordered youths.[165] Delinquent youths, on the average, consumed forty-six teaspoons of refined sugar per day, ten more than the control group of nondelinquents. Some were found to ingest over four hundred pounds of sugar per year.

Schools, police, and prison officials cannot afford to ignore these discoveries. A few are testing them themselves.

The San Luis Obispo County (California) Probation Department, in a major year-long experiment with teenagers with behavioral problems, found that persuading the teenagers and their families to give up refined sugar and flour products, as part of a clinical-ecological approach to behavioral change, was very successful in preventing the teens from getting into trouble again.

The Los Angeles County Probation Department has stopped buying all sugar and refined-flour products for their juvenile facilities; so have the Los Angeles and New York City schools. You should do the same in your home or classroom if you want the children for whom you care to be socially responsible young people.

It Works in Rehabilitating Adult Criminals, Too

A number of adult correctional facilities around the country are also finding that their probationers', prisoners', and parolees' moods, judgment, and social behavior have been improved by cutting out sugar, refined flour, and junk foods.

Barbara Reed and Alexander Schauss are two of the people whom we have to thank for introducing these ideas to court and prison officials. Barbara Reed is chief probation officer in Cuyahoga Falls, Ohio. Looking for tools with which to help the young adults she was trying to keep out of jail, she began investigating nutrition. She persuaded some of her charges to avoid junk foods, refined sugar, and refined flour (as well as high-fat foods and foods to which they were allergic), and to eat nutritious foods and plenty of complex carbohydrates. As a result of her experiment, Cuyahoga Falls gradually came to have what is probably the highest nonrecidivism rate for probationers in the country. Barbara Reed testified before the Senate Select Committee on Nutrition and Human Needs in 1977, which helped bring her methods nationwide attention.

Alexander Schauss, a criminologist and director of the Institute for Biosocial Research, Tacoma, Washington, has written extensively about his success as a probation officer, and that of others, in using diet to rehabilitate criminal offenders. His popular book on the subject is *Diet, Crime and Delinquency* (Berkeley, California: Parker House, 1980).

These two concerned professionals have opened the doors. Now it is up to our politicians, police, and correction officials to put to use this major breakthrough in the rehabilitation of criminals. A few are doing so. Their successful and encouraging experiments in institutional settings have confirmed Reed's and Schauss's positive experiences. On November 1, 1978, white flour was removed from the diet of inmates at the Naval Correctional Center in Seattle, and on February 3, 1979, refined sugar products were also eliminated. Not only did patients' physical health improve; not only did the number of disciplinary reports against prisoners decline by 12 percent in the first year; but two years later the correction officers in charge of the facility reported that "the attitude of tension, frustration, and anxiety that ordinarily pervades correctional facilities is greatly reduced at the Seattle facility. Visitors . . . often comment on the positive demeanor of the containees."[166]

Diana Fishbein, Ph.D., was allowed to set up a controlled experiment at the Lantana Correctional Institution in Florida involving analysis of the inmates' prior diets, and reported mental and physical symptoms to categorize them as hypoglycemic or nonhypoglycemic. The inmates also answered questions aimed at pinpointing maladaptive behavior. That is, they were given the Hoffer Osmond Diagnostic Test, originally designed to quantify symptoms of mental illness. (Not surprisingly, the hypoglycemics tended to be less well adapted than the others.)

Then the inmates' diet was changed. Their new diet was designed for the treatment of hypoglycemia. It featured a reduction in refined carbohydrate to less than 5 percent of their diet, and an increase in complex carbohydrates.

After only two weeks of adjustment to the new diet, the results were obvious. *All* the prisoners in the study were helped by the improved diet; the hypoglycemics' scores on the tests improved by an average of 44 percent.

As demonstrated by Reed, Schauss, and Fishbein, the study of the effects on criminal behavior of sugar in the diet offers a fresh, scientific, and humane approach to crime prevention—one that has already been proven to work.

Summary

The human brain has been likened to a "soggy computer." Like a computer, it has millions of circuits for transmission of information. Unlike a computer, the circuits are not hard metal, but soft, wet nerve tissue, and communication between "circuits" takes place in a liquid medium. When the chemistry of the liquid changes, communication among the circuits can be broken or distorted.

Your brain must have a constant supply of glucose, blood sugar, in order for the "circuits" to communicate properly. Hypoglycemia—low blood sugar, often caused by overconsumption of refined sugar and flour—can distort perception, emotions, and behavior. Too much refined sugar could be a contributing factor in causing children to become hyperkinetic or learning-disabled, young people to be learning-disabled or delinquent, and adults to behave criminally. This is not merely a hypothesis: it is an observation that has been verified by both controlled experiments and clinical experience involving parents, educators, psychologists, and probation and prison officials. Among the institutions that now refuse to order refined sugar and flour products, as a result of these discoveries, are the Los Angeles County Probation Department; the Los Angeles and New York City school systems; and the Naval Correctional Center in Seattle, Washington.

The results of persuading delinquent youth (as did the San Luis Obispo County Probation Department), adult probationers (as did Barbara Reed, Cuyahoga Falls, Ohio), parolees (see Alexander Schauss's work), or prison inmates (Lantana Correctional Institution) not to consume sugar or white flour have been dramatic improvements in learning ability, emotional stability, and/or socially acceptable behavior.

If these findings were to be applied nationwide, it might well prove possible to reverse spiraling crime rates.

Fiber and Your Health

Fiber is so important for our health, and its effects on the body are so different from those of other carbohydrates, which primarily supply energy, that I have reserved detailed discussion of fiber for this later section of our chapter on carbohydrates.

A Carbohydrate Bonus: Roughage

There's nothing new about fiber, except to manufacturers who are now charging us extra to add it to our breads and cereals after decades of removing it from all the staple foods in our diet. But you don't have to pay the price. There's a better way to get that essential roughage.

Most fibers are indigestible, but that does not mean they serve no useful purpose. Nature had a reason when she made cellulose, hemicellulose, pectin, lignin, and several gums a part of the cell walls of all fruits, vegetables, seeds, nuts, and grains. All these substances, complex polysaccharides known collectively as fiber, give the plants the power to grow up structurally strong. And this special carbohydrate group called fiber does a great deal for us, too.

Crunchy apples, stringy okra, chewy dried dates chopped into a bowl of oatmeal all give us not just vitamins, minerals, and oral gratification; these foods, unlike refined carbohydrates or milk, cheese, ground beef, and similar protein items, also provide a kind of janitorial service for our intestines, keeping them free of hazardous substances, including even powerful carcinogens. Except for lignin, most of the fibers can be partially fragmented by the actions of friendly bacteria in the body's colon. Such microorganisms are in generous supply throughout your gut if you eat a diet rich in good, natural carbohydrate fiber. But when your diet is a typically American one—high in fatty meats, no-fiber breads, and sugary desserts—there are fewer of the disease-preventing organisms in your intestinal tract; they are not needed, because their normal food supply is absent when your diet is so low in fiber. So concludes *JAMA*, (*Journal of the American Medical Association*) October 17, 1977, Vol. 238, No. 16, p. 1715.

How Fiber Keeps Your Whole System Clean

Fiber's effects begin right in your mouth. You probably know that a sure way to invite stomach cramps is to gulp down a quickly eaten, poorly-chewed apple for breakfast, or to wolf down a huge salad on a short lunch break. But you may not realize that, besides being necessary for good digestion, chewing is important for the health of your teeth, gums, and the membranes that line your oral cavity; and of course, chewing represents a kind of calisthenic for the many facial muscles.

The next good cleansing deed fiber performs is on your gut. One medical observer, Dr. Martin A. Eastwood of the Western General Hospital in Edinburgh, Scotland, says that fiber "passes through the gut somewhat like a sponge." This is significant because the unique ability of fiber to absorb fluids such as saliva and gastric secretions enables it to enlarge its volume considerably as it goes along, and thereby scrub clear cell walls. Your whole digestive system is thus being swept and scrubbed, lessening the potential harm of foreign agents. This may well explain why a high-fiber diet can both help and prevent colonic disorders. It has been observed by Dr. Eastwood, for example, to change the environment of the intestinal pouch (called the cecum) from unhealthy to healthy.

Another benefit of adding more fiber is that fiber helps you feel full, and thus better able to resist temptation between meals. This, in turn, should help you to eat nourishing, well-balanced meals when you do get to the table. Fiber also produces its "fill-you-up" effect sooner than junk foods. Fiber may not be magic, but without it, it may well be impossible to lose weight or maintain it at normal levels or to make any claims to real health.

One of fiber's publicized benefits is as a natural laxative. Believe it or not, you can throw away your Ex-Lax. Just add apples, cherries, spinach, and whole grains to your diet if constipation is your problem, or try a tablespoon of sugar-free, raw bran with each meal. In no time at all, those painful, hard, dry stools you've been plagued with will change to large, smooth, water-laden, well-formed ones that are readily passed.

Fiber may help you fight those extra pounds. If you're a die-hard between-meal snacker, take an honest look at your eating patterns. Do they include lots of empty calories—candy bars, sugar, starchy, refined convenience foods? These don't satisfy the appetite as well as unrefined carbohydrates. In fact, they stimulate you to eat even more.

Fiber can help you feel full without taking in extra calories to do it. You are forced to take more time when eating high-fiber foods like corn on the cob, whole rye cereal, and raw pineapple, so you may eat half the usual amount. Also, fiber naturally slows down your uptake of the nutrients, including sugar, in food. The energy is available to you in a steady supply rather than a spurt, so you won't be tempted to keep snacking to fill yourself up.

Although it may seem to be your stomach that makes you overeat, the blame really belongs elsewhere. When you can't seem to put down that fork, blame it on your brain. It should be receiving the red light signal when nerve endings along your gut walls become aware that satiety levels have been reached. That's another reason high-fiber apples are better than high-calorie candy. Fiber stimulates these countless receivers to flash the "no more eating" sign to your brain. Fats and proteins seem not to have this characteristic to such an extent.

Remember, too, that fiber, for the most part, does not contribute calories. Also, that it helps you feel full and encourages appetite control because it absorbs fluid, expanding and creating the satisfied feeling the dieter craves.

Summary

Fiber cannot be digested and used nutritionally, but it is essential to your intestinal health, since fiber keeps your whole digestive tract free of a wide variety of poisonous substances. Fiber is not found in meats, cheeses, or highly processed foods.

Fibrous foods stimulate and exercise your mouth and gums, oral membranes, and facial muscles. Fiber also scrubs the cell walls of your colon and bowels, cleaning and hastening transit time through the digestive system for the foods you eat, thus reducing the possibility that your body will harbor toxins longer than it should.

Fiber also provides satiety value, so you aren't tempted to snack too much.

Fiber in Disease Prevention: Comments from Dr. Burkitt

Dr. Denis Burkitt, discoverer of a rare form of cancer, Burkitt's lymphoma, is a surgeon who worked for a number of years with East African natives and a major proponent of high-fiber intake. He has granted an interview for this book, which is an appropriate introduction to our section on the diseases caused by low-fiber diets.

"When I came back from Africa, I was involved in cancer epidemiology full-time, studying the distribution of different forms of cancer to try to find causes. Shortly thereafter, I was introduced to Surgeon-Captain Cleave, who had written a book connecting many of the characteristically Western diseases to Western diets, in particular to fiber-depleted carbohydrates.

"I thought his concept was brilliant. At the time I was getting regular information from about 140 hospitals in rural areas, mostly throughout Africa, partly throughout Asia, and I realized that what Cleave was saying was actually right . . . that is, common diseases such as coronary heart disease, gallstones, appendicitis, varicose veins, obesity, diabetes, bowel cancer—to mention a few—were very, very much commoner in sophisticated, affluent societies than in the third world (undeveloped or emerging countries—especially in Africa and Asia). I felt that Cleave was the first man to propose a hypothesis which might explain these contrasts on epidemiological grounds, so I decided to test this hypothesis throughout the world.

"The study aimed to try to ascertain approximately how often certain diseases occurred. Appendicitis, for example, is the most common abdominal emergency in Western countries, but a friend of mine, who has spent forty-three years in northwest Uganda, has yet to see his first case of appendicitis at his mission hospital. Hugh Trowell, who coedited a book on this subject, reported the first case of coronary heart disease in East Africa. This, of course, is the commonest cause of death in Western countries.

"Our efforts, then, were to determine how rare some of our commonest diseases are in less affluent societies, and then to try to find out what the reason for this might be. Not only did we find that these diseases were rare in third world communities, but also that they were relatively rare even in Western countries before this century.

"One is faced with the totally inescapable conclusion that many of the diseases filling our hospital beds and doctors' offices are, to a large extent, preventable diseases. We must eliminate or modify at least some of the causative factors.

"There are many life-style differences between, say, East Africa and New York, but there is no reason to believe that any one difference is the cause of those diseases, because all of them are in some way related to our alimentary tract.

"We looked into changes in diet, examining the major changes in diets which always preceded the rise in these diseases in Africa, Asia, and other countries, or in Western countries in the last half century. Our results showed that:

1. The protein intake has stayed static. We haven't changed our protein intake significantly, so that can be left out.

2. The fiber in carbohydrates is always reduced with Westernization, particularly in cereals. Not only do we reduce the total amount of carbohydrate we eat, but half our carbohydrate comes from sugar, which is totally refined carbohydrate.

3. We also always increased our fat intake. We eat almost three times as much fat as people in the third world countries.

"Now, the package we would offer for increased health would inevitably be eating more complex carbohydrate, retaining the fiber, but consuming less fat and sugar. Recently, in the escalated work on fiber, it has developed that the most important fiber is cereal fiber, and this is what we have largely jettisoned from our diets. While salads may be good food, from a fiber point of view they are almost useless. Cereal fiber is what we've really got to get back into our diets.

"Briefly, then, the package we offer means eating far more bread (our ancestors used to eat about a pound and a half per person per day), preferably whole grain bread; less sugar; less fat; more potatoes, not cooked in or eaten with fat (potatoes are slimming so long as they are not cooked or eaten in fat); more legumes such as peas and beans, with relatively little emphasis on fruits and vegetables. They are all right, but they don't give you a lot of fiber.

"It is important to get a whole grain bread, which is different from whole wheat. 'Whole wheat' means nothing. 'Whole wheat' flour is about as heavily processed as bleached white flour, and some brown breads are just white bread with molasses coloring added. Bread should contain at least an 85 percent extraction of flour, rather than the 72 percent found in white bread. Bread should be required to be labeled as to what we are eating.

"When I said there was less effect on bowel behavior on the part of salads, I was quoting the work done in Cambridge, which found that cellulose and pectins were not among the foods that alter bowel behavior. Cellulose is one of the least important elements of fiber, although it used to be looked on as almost synonymous with it. The importance of cellulose has been overemphasized, in my opinion. The work done in Cambridge shows that about four or five slices of whole meal bread or a couple of ounces of bran have the same effect in increasing bowel weight as seven and a half pounds of apples a day. There are various elements of fiber that are important for bowel behavior, the most important of which are the pentoses, which are eight times richer in whole meal flour than in white flour; but either flour is richer than fruits and vegetables.

"So to prevent diseases related to constipation—and we are a totally constipated nation—if we could get the pentoses found in cereals we could practically eliminate the laxative industry.

"When it comes to diseases like diabetes, there is a different aspect of fiber involved, guar gum; the pectins are also slightly involved.

"However, I am talking primarily about the type of fiber that is going to get rid of our national constipation, which is responsible, at least in part, for diseases like bowel cancer, hemorrhoids, diverticular disease, appendicitis, varicose veins, and hiatus hernia.

"I am not saying that fruits and vegetables and the like are not good —only that relative to the diseases to which I was referring, they do not contain as much of the necessary fiber as whole grains. A balanced meal program is most important, and one should consume fruits and vegetables along with the grains. A disproportionate amount of grain in the diet often adds up to a diet high in calories, while fruits and vegetables contain many nutrients needed by the body but not found in the grains.

My work is looking at communities that have a minimal incidence of these diseases and comparing their foods with ours, or comparing the food of England or the United States a hundred years ago to what we eat now.

"You see, the average African does not eat a lot of fruits and vegetables, and in this country—until we could store food to keep it fresh—we had to live on what could be put on the floor of the barn for most of the year. That meant cereals, pulses, legumes. You ate fruits during the period they were on the trees in summer, but you didn't live with them during the rest of the year. The same applies, of course, to third world countries.

"While it is possible to be a vegetarian and yet have a low-fiber diet, vegetarians are better off than nonvegetarians on the average. Recent studies have shown that the increase in cereal fiber in the vegetarian diet has given vegetarians about one-third the risk of diverticular disease of nonvegetarians. I think a lot can be said for a vegetarian diet.

"With regard to the role of meat in the occurrence of these diseases, I believe we ought to eat more fiber-containing carbohydrate and less fat. A high-fat diet is always a low-fiber diet; a high-fiber diet is always a low-fat diet. I'm not saying the key is fiber alone, but plenty of carbohydrate with this fiber. Meats certainly contribute to fat—40 percent of even lean meat in this country is fat. So to have a diet lower in fat and higher in carbohydrate essentially means reducing meat.

"Of the diseases I have mentioned, fat may play a role in diabetes and does play a role in coronary heart disease. There is no evidence whatsoever that fat plays a role in appendicitis, hemorrhoids, or diverticular diseases; however, fiber plays a role in all these diseases, fat only in some.

"For example, the evidence that food additives play a role in bowel cancer is very weak; the evidence that fiber and fat play a role is very strong.

"When it comes to diseases like diverticular diseases, appendicitis, or hiatus hernia, the most important factor is related to the bulk, consistency and, to some extent, the transit time of bowel behavior.

"There is no subject about which so little is known as bowel behavior. People in America only pass about 80 to 120 grams of stool a day, while people in Africa or Asia pass about a pound and a half. Whereas it takes thirty hours for food to go through the intestinal tract in third world countries, it takes three days in young, healthy adults in the West, and often over two weeks in elderly people.

"The fibers of the diet, particularly the pentosans, enormously increase the bulk of stool and keep it soft, although it is not quite known how they do it. It is to a large extent due to water in the gut. If you hold water, the contents remain soft. The pentosans also beneficially increase and modify the bacteria. Whatever the process, we do know that the pentosans insure the passage of a large, soft stool.

"Hemorrhoids are primarily a result of constipation. Diverticular disease is almost exclusively due to constipation. Bowel cancer is probably due to diet—fat being the most important factor. Fiber in the diet is protective in insuring that whatever the poisonous substances are, they are diluted in large volume and swept away every day. There is a great deal of evidence to suggest that one factor of the causation of gallstones is the lack of cereal fiber, because fiber modifies the metabolism of cholesterol and bile acids, both of which are implicated in the causation of gallstones and coronary heart disease—although there would be many other factors as well.

"People on fiber-rich diets tend to have lower serum cholesterol levels. You can't, I think, lower serum cholesterol levels by adding fiber to the diet, but you can alter bowel behavior by adding fiber to the diet. The cheapest and most effective way is to have one or two heaping tablespoons of bran in your diet daily, which will eliminate constipation. From the point of view of diabetes, coronary heart disease, gallstones, and obesity, it is better to eat a diet from which the fiber has not been removed than to take it out and put it back again.

"I must not give the false impression that Africans are fitter than we are because they do not get our characteristic diseases. They still get most of the diseases that killed us in the last century. But the diseases that kill us now are not the same diseases that killed us in the last century. We've managed to conquer infectious diseases. Africans are relatively free of our characteristic diseases, although they do get many other diseases.

"Now, most nations of the world before industrialization got their energy from starchy, staple foods—cereals, tubers, potatoes, yams, legumes, and beans, flavored and supplemented by an occasional fruit or vegetable. These foods do vary enormously in various parts of the world.

"In all cases, people consumed primarily starchy staples—their diet was 88 percent carbohydrate, with fat content at about 10 or 15 percent of the food. The protein intake in many of the countries who eat this way today is even higher than what it is in North America, but in the form of vegetable protein rather than animal protein.

"We thought that we would improve our carbohydrate by removing the fiber because we didn't understand what fiber did. We thought that it was inert, that it didn't provide energy. The big mistake in nutrition has been removing the part of food that doesn't provide nutrients but is enormously valuable as a protection against disease.

"I am not convinced that there is any significant difference from a health point of view between brown and white sugar. Both are 99 percent refined. But there is all the difference in the world between white and whole meal bread. If I resolved to make only two recommendations for improving the health of North America and Britain, one would be outside the realm of food and that would be the elimination of cigarettes, because cigarettes are probably the single most common cause of death. Second would be to have far more of our energy come from bread—to multiply our whole meal intake by two or three times.

"The major change we have made in our homes since I became interested in diet (which was only five years ago) is never to eat white bread. If we could enormously increase our intake of high-extraction bread, I think it would revolutionize our health.

"It is not a secret that England's Royal College of Physicians—who some years ago sponsored a major commission on smoking—have another major committee sitting at this very moment on the whole question of the importance of fiber in food to maintain health, and I hope their report will come out this year. I think then people in the industry will have to prick up their ears and listen.

"People were talking about fiber in the last century way before their time. But until about ten years ago, a lot of the medical profession looked upon fiber as a fad promoted by health food stores and food cranks. That option is no longer open. There's too much good scientific work going on: about 400 papers a year are being published on fiber. A professor of nutrition at London University opened a conference recently by stating that fiber was the fastest moving subject in medical science today.

"If you take a cell, the contents are the 'nutrients' and the wall is the 'carton.' We've discarded the carton and put the emphasis on nutrients. If you take a grain of cereal, the outside—the bran—is the carton and the inside is the starch; we've discarded the carton, and we've emphasized only what is inside. On the other hand, there is a danger in today's overscientific world in dealing with patients—and I say it as a doctor. The biological framework of a patient is the carton, and the man, woman, or child is the content. We are fundamentally and essentially—spiritually, if you like—resident in a biological framework. There is an awful tendency to put all the emphasis on the plumbing and looking after the carton, and forgetting the content. I think we have to bear that in mind."[167]

Preventing Diseases of Affluence: Pressure Disorders

Your life-style can be the death of you! This is clearly the message where gastrointestinal diseases are concerned.

A pressure disease is one brought on through external stressors—i.e., noise pollution, environmental contaminants, life-style, and attitudinal responses to one's environment—causing internal distress manifested in shortness of breath, tension throughout the body, and a disruption of biochemical processes, resulting in conditions as far-ranging as migraine headache and constipation.

Colorectal cancer, constipation, appendicitis, hiatus hernia, hemorrhoids, and varicose veins are all "pressure diseases." They are connected with defects in life-style that can literally kill you if a "comfortable" life pattern has led you far from nutritious foods, healthy exercise, and clean, simple living.

Colon Disease and Colorectal Cancer

If you are young, healthy, and happy on your fast food diet, you don't think about fiber or colon disorders. Why should you?

Unfortunately, lack of fiber catches up with most Americans sooner or later. It is closely associated with cancer of the colon or the rectal area. This tumorous disorder is frequently fatal, but the good news is that it needn't be if you control your diet.

DR. BURKITT'S FINDINGS

The scientific work of Dr. Denis Burkitt, consisting of studies of East African tribes still following high-carbohydrate natural food diets, was the first to provide an answer to the question of what is causing a near epidemic of colon cancers in America, and why this situation is not replicated elsewhere. There is no better alternative explanation for the almost total absence of colonic cancer in Japan, Africa, India, and other areas where only minimal amounts of animal protein are eaten and fast foods are virtually nonexistent.

The inhabitants of these countries who do have access to a nonnutritious diet, and who succumb to its low-fiber temptations, find that tumors begin to appear as a consequence. People with a low disease incidence seem to lose that immunity once the native diet is exchanged for an unnatural one that is high in fat and low in fiber.

The fact that bodily predisposition plays a part makes these studies all the more important. A good diet or a bad one, in other words, appears to be the factor that is most decisive in determining whether you develop a colorectal cancer or not. Low fiber intake can tip the balance in or out of your favor. If anyone in your family has had colorectal disease, or if you tend to be constipated, it is especially important for you to eat enough whole grain cereals and breads for healthy bowel function.

Too little fiber is even more serious a deficiency when accompanied by excessive animal fats. If you don't like (or are allergic to) whole grain foods, it's especially important for you to eat only the leanest fish and meat—and as little as possible of that. (Try soy foods like tofu and tempeh for protein—or cultivate healthier tastes and learn to enjoy whole grain foods. If you can't eat wheat, there are oats, rye, millet, buckwheat, and hybrid grains like triticale.)

Bowel tumors turn up more often in that segment of the intestines where fecal matter stagnates in individuals eating a low-fiber diet. The longer the waste matter spends "in transit" in your system the higher your chance of becoming a colorectal victim.

Furthermore, the longer fecal matter spends in contact with the sensitive walls of your intestinal system, the greater the likelihood that potentially noxious materials will be absorbed. Eat high-fiber foods to speed passage of the toxic by-products of digestion through your intestines. You don't want them circulating in your blood to every cell!

Another reason slower transit time of waste matter becomes a factor in colorectal cancer is that bile salts are routed into your intestine and degraded into possible carcinogens. Here's where fiber helps in the diet. Bran has been shown to slow this conversion process down.

HIGH-FAT DIETS AND COLONIC TUMORS

• Vegetarians or those who eat very little meat, such as the Seventh-Day Adventists, automatically eliminate most animal fats. Such groups show less large-bowel cancer than normal meat eaters.[168, 169] Research tells us there is a link. Meat—especially beef—and colon cancer seem to go together.[170]

• You are safer with fish on your table, according to these same studies.

• Remind yourself before you have a double helping of greasy hamburger that several studies have concluded that high intake of fatty animal protein is one of the reasons our death rate from colorectal cancer is so shamefully high.[171]

Summary

When adequate amounts of fiber are missing from your diet, you are at risk of developing constipation, colorectal cancer, or one of the other common diseases that attack the gastrointestinal system. This risk becomes greater when your diet is low in fresh, nutritious whole foods and high in fat and sugar. An added stress factor is inactivity. If you have any sign of colorectal cancer, you should report it to your doctor right away. And in any case, an annual checkup is in order.

By contrast, a diet emphasizing moderate amounts of protein, high intake of natural fiber foods, and low fat intake results in better health of the bowels and the whole body and provides protection against certain types of cancer. Vegetarians, because of their high-fiber, low-fat diet, run the least risk of developing these diseases.

HIGH FIBER CONTRIBUTES TO THE FIGHT AGAINST LARGE BOWEL CANCER

When the choice is a slice of whole rye toast or a white roll, consider what fiber does to build carcinogenic immunity:

• Reduces the likelihood of poisons accumulating in the gastrointestinal tract because high fiber helps to move all foods—good and potentially bad—through your system at a faster rate.[177]

• Reduces the time that the bile acids, sterols, and other substances being eliminated spend in contact with the very absorbent intestinal walls. Cancer experts tell us that this appears to be one of the factors influencing the development of large bowel cancers. You can see how it might stress your bowels to be subjected constantly to an acidic environment.

• According to one researcher, Dr. V. Aries, and his associates[178] a natural high-fiber diet seems to provide a special protective effect by assuring that your intestines are not overwhelmed by large amounts of the type of harmful bacteria that may be a factor in the genesis of colorectal cancers. Dr. Aries tells us that when his group studied microflora of men and women in a certain geographical area of England noted for a high incidence of colon cancer and compared these flora with those in the intestines of rural Africans where this disease did not prevail, the result was a great difference in both the kinds of bacteria present and the tendency of bacteria to break down bile salts. The British group had more decomposed bile salts in their bowel matter, and had more of a type of bacteria called bacteroids, which can turn bile salts into potential carcinogens. Vitamin C, however, has been shown to neutralize a substantial number of the potentially cancer-causing bacteria in the colon.

HELP YOURSELF

What can you do if you think you may have cancer of the colon? The American Cancer Society tells us that you should report any sign of blood in your stool to your doctor without delay. A certain percentage of the cases of colorectal cancer can often be reversed if diagnosed and treated soon enough. An annual checkup is in order. This physical should include a proctoscopic rectal, a sigmoidal colon examination, or a colonoscopic examination of the whole colon.

This will be momentarily unpleasant, but you will have the peace of mind of knowing that you are not developing cancer. Even if you do have it, if caught at this stage it may be reversible.

Irritable Colon Syndrome

You eat good high-fiber food, you have cured your sweet tooth, and so far as you know, you have inherited no genetic predisposition to gastrointestinal trouble. Why then do you have so much trouble with your colon? One day you may have cramps or spasms, another day mucus in the stool, other times just general instability in this area, perhaps diarrhea alternating with very infrequent movements. Sometimes your stomach may become swollen. Your physician may be less surprised by all these symptoms than you are, because he's seen them so often. Irritable colon syndrome, as this dysfunction is usually known —it is also called gastric neurosis, colonic neurosis, common enteritis, hypertonic constipation, enterocolitis, colitis mucosa, and even "unhappy colon"—is second among the illnesses that account for days lost at work in America.[179]

If you aren't truly physically sick, why do you have "spastic colitis," as your doctors may also call this problem, or "awful nervous indigestion" as you may put it?

A KIND OF COLITIS THAT'S ALL IN YOUR HEAD

You don't have to be mentally disturbed, just moderately stressed to make yourself highly susceptible to this disorder. That is one of the theories that currently carries considerable weight with physicians. It has been about thirty years since Dr. Frank Slaughter suggested that like ulcer victims, irritable-colon sufferers often are highly emotional people and their illness is psychosomatic, a reflection of how well or how poorly they are responding to the pressures of daily life.[180]

Dr. Slaughter points out that if you suffer from irritable colon syndrome, chances are you expect everything in life to be in apple-pie order. You may be a true workaholic. What causes your illness most likely is your abhorrence of conflicts. Your body uses this illness to complain that it feels repressed.

Drs. J. W. Wilson and N. S. Painter tell us that there is one common thread that runs through observations of this disease—most people with such poorly functioning colons appear to be in low spirits.[181] In other words, where other people can roll with the punches, the person who suffers from irritable colon syndrome often has trouble coping, and perhaps punishes herself or himself by getting sick. These doctors believe that therapy that treats both mind and body will probably be the most successful. Medical science does not yet bear out this theory, and it seems to leave many questions unanswered, but it is provocative.

ARE YOU HYPODYNAMIC?

If you simply suffer from constipation, you are likely to be a rather different psychosomatic type, say many researchers. You may be hypo-dynamic, that is, an underachiever, easily defeated and given to darker moods and negative emotions. Your intestines may reflect this attitude. They too may literally give up their peristaltic reflex, causing such a slowdown in your organs that constipation results.[182]

If you have a spastic colon, a close inner look not at what you're eating but rather at what it is that's eating you may be in order. Changes in your moods and resultant emotions may be the number-one factor causing or worsening this disorder, explaining why this disease comes and goes so mysteriously.[183]

WHEN ONLY A PSYCHIATRIST CAN CURE YOUR COLITIS

Occasionally, a more than mild emotional disturbance lurks behind irritable colon syndrome. In a study at Washington University, this connection was illustrated. A double-blind study was used—employing a Group A composed of healthy individuals, and a Group B composed of victims of this colonic syndrome. When the individuals were closely examined, interviewers found that almost three-quarters of the sick group manifested signs of mental illness such as depression and hyste-ria. By contrast, less than 20 percent of the disease-free group showed any mental imbalance. It seemed clear, the medical team said, that psychiatric support would be needed to return the members of Group B to health.[184] For optimal results, both dietary and emotional modifica-tion would be required.

GETTING BETTER

Beware of self-medication. Laxative abuse has a harsh and abrasive effect on membranes that are already scarred and rippled. Hemorrhag-ing could result.

Does this pressure disease seem baffling to you? This is the way doctors feel, too. It is frustrating to treat because there is no clear-cut cause. But that does not mean it is incurable. Many modalities are helpful. For example:

• Reduce stress.
• Have suspected allergies investigated and treated. Especially look into your tolerance for seasonal patterns, dairy products, eggs, and foods of the nightshade family such as eggplant, tomatoes, green pep-pers.

Beyond Irritable Colon Syndrome: Ulcerative Colitis

If you answer yes to one or more of the following questions, you may be a victim of ulcerative colitis:

- Do you often have a blood-streaked diarrhea?
- Would you rate your response to stress as poor?
- Do you have a dozen or more bowel movements a day?
- Are you between twenty and forty, and have you ever had a moderate-to-serious case of an irritable colon syndrome, one that perhaps was never properly cured?
- Do you have any of the above symptoms in a come-and-go fashion, so that you seem to recover, then lapse again? M.V. Krause and M. A. Hunscher, in *Food, Nutrition and Diet Therapy*,[172] have noted that this is characteristic of ulcerative colitis.

DEFINING THE DANGERS

According to the *Merck Manual of Diagnosis and Therapy*, ulcerative colitis is one that a practicing specialist should treat immediately, because when it has advanced to its final stages, your colon may actually tear or burst because of extensive damage. Death is a possibility. When your colon becomes chronically inflamed due to food, drink, and stress, the tissues that line it begin to degrade, and hemorrhaging is common. Ulcers appear and usually bloody sores as well.[173]

POSSIBLE CAUSES OF ULCERATIVE COLITIS

1. Kenneth Lamott, in his book *Escape from Stress*,[174] reports that there are doctors who believe that ulcerative colitis may be an infectious disease.

2. Other theorists, say Krause and Hunscher,[175] suspect allergic tendencies and chemical intolerances as culprits. Discuss this with a qualified specialist. Meanwhile, eliminating any foods or chemicals to which you are exposed that may be a problem is a step in the right direction.

3. Do you get enough protein and B-complex vitamins in your foods? Long-term deficiency of protein or B complex may be a source of ulcerative colitis as well. If you combine whole grains with beans, nuts, seeds, and green vegetables, this should be no problem.

4. Emotions that get the best of you may be making matters worse for you. Do you mope when you should cope? Do you often experience helpless feelings? Another characteristic turned up by researchers who believe there may be an identifiable ulcerative colitis personality type is that of dependence or attachment, often to someone your senior,

perhaps a parent.[176] If you are excessively neat and dutiful on the surface, but seething underneath with feelings of repressed violence, this and frequent bouts of the blues may make you a candidate for ulcerative colitis.

Don't Confuse Ulcerative Colitis with Regional Enteritis

Regional enteritis is a pressure disease that has several long Latin names, and yet, while it is often mistaken for ulcerative colitis, it is actually very uncommon. If you hear the terms Crohn's disease, granulomatous ileo colitis, jejunoileitis, and terminal ileitis, the speaker is discussing regional enteritis.

Although one name for regional enteritis is jejunoileitis, this term refers to a section located midway in the small intestine, while the disorder itself is actually a disease of the last (and lowest) segment of your small intestine, known medically as the ileum. The ileum leads to the large intestine or colon.

Summary

Ulcerative colitis strikes many men and women, particularly between twenty and forty. Symptoms include episodes of blood-streaked diarrhea. Your first step if you have or suspect you have this disorder is to have a complete physical and rule out the possibility of allergy, infection, or a serious disease such as cancer as the cause.

Then consider what you can do for yourself. This includes avoidance of laxatives, which can worsen the condition, and adding fiber with the approval of your doctor to restore bowel health. Also, since this disorder is often caused by stress or poor emotional well-being, consider what a therapy such as meditation and yoga, biofeedback, and regular physical exercise might do to help you recover.

Because poor emotional health and a poorly functioning colon, rectum, bowels, or intestines seem to go together, this advice applies to victims of ulcers, chronic constipation or diarrhea, regional enteritis and ileitis, and related ills.

WHAT'S DIFFERENT ABOUT REGIONAL ENTERITIS?

Sufferers from this disease are more likely to come from a Jewish background than any other.[185] Your chances of being a victim are less if you are over thirty; people from sixteen to thirty are the most frequently afflicted.

There is one certain way to distinguish between ulcerative colitis and regional enteritis, says the *Merck Manual*. You need X rays. In the case of regional enteritis, the X rays will show that the ileum is red and irritated. This irritation may even have crept into the colon. The intestines in general may be deformed by masses of "pocks." The X rays will look like a close-up of a cobbled street.[186]

Regional enteritis gives its victims much misery—including abdominal pain, fever, and diarrhea with loss of appetite, weight loss, anemia, and sometimes fatty stools, called steatorrhea.[187]

At least five more conditions often accompany this disorder.

1. Water retention or edema caused by a faulty blood supply. (Your blood transports fluid around the body.)
2. Deterioration and thickening of the entire intestine, which loses its flexibility and may develop abscesses and sores.
3. A gradual closing up of the intestinal aperture, called the lumen, due to impaction—that is, the feces clogs the passageway between the small and large intestines.
4. The lymph system, which helps keep you healthy by preventing infections, is affected too. Extra cells collect, and there occurs a stoppage in the passage of nutrient-rich blood to the diseased intestine.
5. As it does in all the pressure diseases, diarrhea inevitably causes serious undernourishment. Anemia is also a possibility. It may even be life threatening, since it may lead to a diseased liver, or to total damage of the intestine by perforation.[188]

WHAT CAN BE DONE?

Hospitalization or home rest is essential to clear up this disease. A very carefully controlled diet concentrating on good protein, adequate calorie intake, and low levels of roughage is also important. Fat in minimal amounts and juices are preferred to harder-to-assimilate whole fruits and vegetables while the system is recovering.[189]

Good news for victims is that recovery rates are good when the disorder is identified and treated early.[190]

The Unnatural Natural Disease

Appendicitis is both commonplace and puzzling to us. Does removal of your body's appendix seem normal to you? The answer is probably yes—but that is purely because it has become an acceptable custom. Here are a few surprising facts:

• According to Dr. Denis Burkitt, if you had what your doctor may have described as a "vestigial abdominal organ" removed this year, you had lots of company. This operation is so common that 5,000 men, women, and children are operated on each week. Ten percent of us have already had our appendix removed and probably think little of it.

• Did you ever wonder whether this disease is indeed a necessity? You should, because many responsible nutritionally-oriented physicians consider an unhealthy appendix to be another of the pressure diseases under discussion in this section. Like diverticulosis, appendicitis is frequently caused in large part by too little fiber in the diet.[191-193]

• If your family doctor was planning to perform an appendectomy on you, you may have read up on this operation. If so, you are aware that no other type of emergency operation involving the stomach is done as often. This is true both here and in western Europe. That doesn't, of course, mean that the appendectomy is universally accepted as standard practice.

Dr. Burkitt's information became available about ten years ago. Only a few other doctors early in this century had previously considered that diet and appendicitis might be related.

DO YOU UNDERSTAND YOUR APPENDIX?

The appendix is small, perhaps no more than three to six inches long and under a half-inch in diameter. It is attached to the cecum, which is the lower-right corner of your large intestine. There it forms a narrow, tubular pocket just at the point where the large intestine turns upward. Its location and shape make it vulnerable to the collection of waste matter. Appendicitis often begins as an infection caused by an invading organism. The resulting organ inflammation produces pain, even intense pain, in the area of the navel and lower-right abdomen. Moving quickly, or almost any involuntary jerking movement, may worsen matters. At an advanced stage, you may have an urge to regurgitate. Surgery is usually the next step, since the organ is dangerously diseased.

Again, Dr. Burkitt's statistics tell us that this operation is not at all common where a high-fiber diet is the rule, even considering all other variables—ethnic differences, heredity, climate, etc. But if you take the same people who are resistant to pressure diseases and expose them to our Western diet, appendicitis begins to show up. The connection between diet and disease seems devastatingly clear.[194]

THE REAL CAUSE OF APPENDICITIS

Your appendix may be in a virtual state of blockage due to the presence of abnormally forced fecal balls, says Drs. Burkitt and Painter.[195-197] This causes unhealthy amounts of pressure to be exerted on the delicate lining of the intestine.

• Weakened intestines, like a weak lung or heart muscle, is likelier to become diseased and irritated.

• The average American diet, low in fiber and high in refined carbohydrates and protein, is an almost certain prelude to appendicitis. We know this by studying the ills of immigrant Japanese Americans and Afro-Americans, who are more susceptible to appendicitis than native Japanese or Africans, just as other Americans have an increased incidence in contrast to the reduced incidence in their country of origin. Similarly, Indians from big cities have more appendicitis than Indians in nonurban areas.[198]

Diverticular Disease

Americans get diverticulosis fifty times more frequently than natives of so-called underdeveloped countries, where corn, peas, beans, and the bananalike plantain appear at most meals. Drs. Burkitt and Painter call this one of the "deficiency diseases of Western civilization."[199]

A low-fiber diet seems to be the culprit, just as high fiber seems the most effective treatment. How things have changed! Years ago your physician would have insisted you eat practically fiber-free meals if you were diagnosed as having diverticular disease.

EXPLAINING DIVERTICULAR DISEASE

You should know what your colon looks like if you are to cope with this disease that can only be controlled, not cured, say experts. It is a long, segmented, but continous tube, surrounded by groups of muscles that can squeeze food through the segments, working in harmony. They contract, then relax, and this peristalsis is what keeps fecal matter containing foods not assimilated on a steady course to your rectum for elimination. When that matter contains enough indigestible, absorbent fiber, the stool will be easier to pass, because roughage increases peristalsis.

When you consume too little roughage, that mass stagnates in the large section of the colon and your feces fragment, resembling just the opposite of the long, moist, thick, soft, compact stool you should pass if you are healthy.

The hard little balls of fecal matter can push pocketlike fissures into the walls of your intestines. These little herniations may vary in dimension from the size of a small blueberry to that of a large cherry. They appear because your colon has been stressed so much that the tissues of the walls are breaking down. You may develop as many as one hundred, as few as a half dozen.[197]

I'm not in any discomfort, so I'm not a candidate for *this* disease, you say? Not so. Diverticular pockets can exist where no pain is present. But naturally, once infection sets in, as it does in time, so does pain. The worse you feel, the likelier it is your infection has progressed beyond the milder stages.

WHAT TO DO ABOUT DIVERTICULOSIS

If you know how it occurs, you should be able to help yourself avoid it, with the guidance of your doctor. If you are beginning to show signs of it, they will probably recommend:

• Infection-fighting antibiotics plus a stool softener that absorbs water and makes stool bulkier (just like fiber). You should experience less irritation as a result.

• Also, they may suggest raw wheat bran, probably three teaspoons after meals. When the feces are normal in all respects, you can cut back on bran intake if movements are now occurring every twelve to twenty-four hours. If your doctor hasn't specified how much bran, you could try two teaspoonfuls or so per day.

• Less milk seems to help some people. Also try eating fewer spices, since these promote flatulence. Your physical condition and biochemical type will dictate the course to follow.

• The treatment for diverticulitis is bran in unprocessed form. Foods that contain it help increase the bulk of the feces. Bran can absorb large amounts of fluid and move fecal matter quickly through your intestinal tract, says the report by J. N. Finlay et al. in *The Lancet*. As a result, your disease is reduced to a discomfort you can at least live with.[200]

Doctors used to prescribe a low-fiber diet for diverticulitis. Now, thanks to studies such as those conducted by Drs. Burkitt and Painter, we know that this is the opposite of what is indicated for a high cure rate for diverticulitis.[201]

You are what you eat. The high-sugar, high-fat diet in the United States, Europe, and other "rich" nations has produced a high rate of stomach, intestinal, and rectal disorders. Adding fiber, especially bran, to the diet commonly results in a total reduction of symptoms. Only 20 percent of patients treated don't respond with reduced discomfort. Adding whole grain crackers can produce excellent results.[202]

Constipation: Scourge of the Twentieth Century

If you're "normal," you have trouble with your regularity. Half of all Americans over twenty-one do, says the research team of Painter and Wilson.[203] That this problem is widespread is obvious just from watching TV and reading magazine and newspaper ads.

There is little agreement as to exactly how long it should take for undigested food to be evacuated, but probably the sooner it is the better for your overall health, since feces retained too long can cause a proliferation of harmful toxins and bacteria. Still, we are all different in regard to how we function in this respect. Twelve hours may be normal for you, but for other family members the time may be two or three days. Of course, if you lived in a relatively unspoiled area of a place such as Africa and followed their local customs, you'd never have this problem.

Here is how a fiber-rich diet can affect dramatically the time it takes for food to move through your system and be eliminated.

In one country of Africa, the food transit time for members of the black community was only 35.7 hours, while in contrast, the typical time for food passage in the Westernized diet was as long as three and a half days. The age of the subjects mattered little; for students from England on a typical school diet that included snacks and sugary dessert, the transition was only seven hours shorter than that for the British naval subjects. A further significant difference: fecal matter for the natives on the local diet was healthier—averaging more than a pound and having greater bulk as well. By contrast again, the stools of the English males and the students was approximately 360 grams lighter.[204]

A QUICK WAY TO CREATE CONSTIPATION

Does fiber really make a difference? Ask the director of our government's space program how they make certain that astronauts will have bowel movements no more often than once every fifty hours. This trick is accomplished by deliberately restricting our astronauts to the kind of diet most Americans follow every day—one that is low in fiber and thus constipation producing. It isn't healthy, but it is a quick way of producing constipation if toilet accommodations are poor.[205]

DEFICIENCY CONSTIPATION

It may be a minor disorder, but because constipation involves stress and strain, it can and does lead to problems worth worrying about, such as ulcers, hernia, or any other of the many dysfunctions of the colon region.

Most examples of constipation are classified as "functional": just because you are constipated doesn't mean you have stomach cancer. Your constipation is probably discomfort that you have brought upon yourself through a faulty, low-fiber diet. You may be underhydrated as well: many people experience bowel problems when they drink less than eight to ten glasses of water daily. But sometimes, as a result perhaps of diet or genetic weakness, constipation may be more serious. It can result from structural degeneration of either the lining of the walls of the intestine or a breakdown in the supply or activity of nerves or glandular secretions found there.[206]

Most authorities agree that you should seek medical help, if you have not had a bowel movement in a week, say M. V. Krause and M. A. Hunscher in *Food, Nutrition and Diet Therapy.*[207] Anywhere from half a day to three days is considered normal transit time for food to make the journey to your colon and be expelled.

If you are not in pain and in good spirits, even though you feel you are late in having a movement you probably needn't worry, says Leslie C. Thompson in *Intestinal Fitness: New Light on Constipation.*[208] Just ignore the urging of those drug makers who'd love to have you buy their wares whether you need them or not.

If your movements are painful and infrequent, on the other hand, you probably are genuinely constipated. But there's still no need to reach for laxatives. Reform your diet; allow plenty of quiet time to perform this function privately and properly. Also, set aside a time each day for this ritual. Having a regular routine often prevents or remedies constipation.

HELP FOR CONSTIPATED BOWELS

• Because there are so many factors to consider in constipation, suggests Leslie C. Thompson, you may have to effect changes not only in the way you eat but also in how you operate emotionally.[209] Anything less may not work. Bowel actions, as Thompson says, are connected to your feelings. Fear in any form tends to dry up natural secretions. But exercise is important, too. It can reduce emotional stress and improve muscle strength.

• Eating regularly spaced meals and choosing food of high nutritional value is a safeguard. So is slow, purposeful eating and proper chewing. All these habits encourage normal digestion.

• Have you ruled out any serious bodily disease as a possible cause? If changes in your habits don't seem to help, consult your doctor—and don't use any medication unless your doctor finds that nothing else will work. Diseases of the nervous system, a tumor, diverticulitis, or appendicitis can be the cause of irritation and inflamed tissues that in turn produce sluggish bowels.

• However, if you suffer from functional constipation, it is highly likely that this is a by-product of some physical disturbance.

• Try bran and high-fiber foods. Cereal fiber can be helpful in many of the recognized types of blocked bowel syndromes.

• Stop abusing laxatives! This is the only sure cure for what doctors call "atonic constipation" or "lazy bowels," say Krause and Hunscher. In this condition, even though pressure is applied to the fecal matter, your intestines are too weak to move waste at a normal pace through the bowels. Even feces in the rectum move literally at a snail's pace.[210] As might be guessed, this condition is most often found among obese individuals, pregnant women, and senior citizens, especially those who have used laxative drugs for many years.

Diarrhea: Do You Ever Have to Have It Again?

You may never have had an ulcer or a hernia, but no doubt you are no stranger to diarrhea. Like constipation, even the healthiest person seems to get it sooner or later.

Here are some of the reasons diarrhea is so common:

1. If you love fast foods and can't get through a night in front of the TV without half a dozen sugary or greasy snacks, you are a good target for this gastronintestinal ill. Taking in too much food at one sitting or over the course of a single day is one way to provoke "the runs." Eating food that carries any foreign matter capable of causing mild poisoning is another way, says Drs. Painter and Wilson.[211] And junk foods, such as potato chips, corn curls, salted nuts, and candy, are likeliest to answer this description. If you want to avoid ingesting trouble-making ptomaines, fungus, and "bad" bacteria, then reduce your intake of processed foods.

2. Are you suffering any kind of nutritional deficiency? Both low levels of essential vitamins and a high intake in over-the-counter bowel-regulating medications can eventually lead to diarrhea.[212]

3. Constipated? If you are doctoring yourself for this condition while continuing to eat a poor diet, you may well find that you aren't constipated, you are having runny bowel problems. They go together if you do not get to the root of the trouble.[213]

4. If you are overtaxing your sphincter and abdominal muscles to overcome constipation, such straining may also be perpetuating this cycle, so that you produce a watery discharge and your bowels frequently seem to move without warning. Attendant problems of soreness and inflammation are familiar.

5. When your bowels are out of control, your body is really making a violent attempt to expel materials that it regards as potential poisons. Contaminated water may be one provocative factor. Strange food that has been improperly stored or served in restaurants where no hygienic standards are enforced is a common cause.

Several diseases are characterized by diarrhea. Dysentery may occur when your fecal matter contracts harmful bacteria and transmits it through your gastrointestinal tract. Unsanitary foods handled by persons carrying such organisms may be the cause. Dysentery is usually accompanied by symptoms more severe than just diarrhea. Lumpy, "potatoey" stools may startle you with traces of mucus and blood. One form of this upset is amoebic dysentery. This is caused by an amoeba, and is often accompanied by nausea, high temperatures, and cramping.

Intestinal flu is a term you hear often. This is a disease that begins when your intestinal organs are attacked by a virus. If your system cannot defend itself, an intense internal irritation flares up along with the characteristic runny stool. Other unpleasant symptoms include the urge to vomit and painful stomach muscles.

Ptomaines and assorted poisonous organisms that are always present around us are not the only contaminants to cause this disorder. According to Dr. J. H. Pollack in *Gaseous Digestive Conditions*, if you experience sudden mysterious attacks, you may have ingested salmonella, or one or more of a lot of toxins including lead, arsenic, cadmium, strychnine, and nitrates or nitrites. Obviously, if you suspect that this has occurred, see a doctor or visit an emergency ward without delay, or you may suffer convulsive seizures.[214]

Diarrhea may also be caused by nonphysical factors such as stress, or mental disorders such as hysteria, say Krause and Hunscher. These cases, advise experts, may be the most intractable forms of this disorder.[215]

If you are certain that there is no good organic reason why your colon, bowels, or rectal area are so often in poor health, consider this: medicine tells us that how we feel about the quality of our lives and our jobs, or our family, or especially, our selves, is reflected in our physical health. Diarrhea, according to clinical findings, is found in people who tend to have exaggerated reactions to situations where others better adjusted might respond with only a moment of anger or chagrin. When these emotions are vented and forgotten, life goes on. But when they are blown out of all proportion, you pay a price.[216]

DIARRHEA: HOW SHOULD YOU TREAT IT?

Although usually diarrhea does not persist for more than forty-eight to seventy-two hours, it can be debilitating because so much weight is lost due to fluid loss, say Painter and Wilson.[217]

• So increase your liquid intake: drink consommé-type soups and herb tea, for example.
• Foods such as grains and legumes that encourage the formation of bulk in your intestines can be purchased from your health food store. These foods help you absorb excess fluid in the intestines and firms up the bowel matter.

• If you eat anything, it should be something that is easily digestible—cooked, gruellike, soft cereals (Wheatena, Cream of Wheat, oatmeal), steamed rice, or unsweetened applesauce.

• To quell a queasy stomach, try sucking a chunk of ice like a cough drop. Abdominal pain may be relieved by use of a heating pad.

• If the condition has been prompted by something other than food or drink, you should consider counseling or self-help methods in the form of meditation, exercise or other therapies widely available today.[218]

WHEN DIARRHEA IS CHRONIC

If you have been troubled gastrointestinally for more than five days, your problem may be chronic diarrhea. Researchers tell us there are many possible causes.

• Personal worries can tie your stomach up in knots. This is a major cause of gastrointestinal trouble. According to some research, your basic personality may hold the key to your problem. Researchers say chronic diarrhea sufferers are often nonextroverted types who have excessive self-control, which often indicates that strong, unpleasant feelings are just being repressed.[219]

• You may have colitis accompanied by ulcers, gastric dysfunction, amoebic infection, gallbladder problems, or a poorly functioning pancreas. Even tuberculosis may be the reason for your runny bowels. So may a diseased intestinal tract or a vitamin deficiency. Cancer, too, can cause diarrhea.

But most people do not suffer from anything grave. They are like a case discussed by researchers Painter and Wilson, too embarrassed to admit that they can't even recall when their bowels functioned normally.[220] This woman may be your twin. Are you plagued by what she termed "explosive movements" numerous times a day? Have you used practically everything on your druggist's shelf without relief? Are you wondering what this poor woman finally did that you can do?

It is amazingly simple. Raw bran—available at any health food store —turned the trick. Within twelve months of supplementing your diet faithfully with this natural food, you should be rewarded with regularity at last. You can take it safely as you need it—up to four teaspoons a day, always accompanied by fluids. When you reach this stage, you can reduce your intake by half, if that is sufficient.

This may sound like impossible folk medicine; but it is much safer and more effective than most of the products your druggist can offer you. But it is also wise to have a complete physical to rule out any serious organic disease or a food allergy. In the latter case, eliminating a food you eat in excessive amounts or have frequent cravings for may be the answer. Shellfish, strawberries, milk products, and fatty foods are frequent causes of allergic diarrhea.

Brown rice and other cooked, whole grains can also be helpful for diarrhea. We do not want to give the impression that bran is a miracle food. It is not. But it is indicated in more conditions than had previously been thought.

Summary

As common and widely accepted as this operation is, removal of your appendix may be something you can prevent by adding more fiber to your diet. Many knowledgeable nutritionists today classify appendicitis, like ulcers, as a pressure disease. In communities where the foods eaten are still largely natural, unprocessed, and high in fibrous grains, there is little incidence of this disease, because the bowels move naturally and often. When the reverse is true, constant pressure exerted on the lower abdominal organs because of unnaturally hard stools weakens those organs and makes them susceptible to diseases, including appendicitis.

Likewise, you can probably avoid diverticular disease if you eat a high-fiber diet and maintain good health habits in other respects. The cause of this colonic dysfunction is often faulty peristaltic action, and fiber can return the function to normal.

Another pressure disease produced by a diet high in fat and sugar and low in fiber is constipation. If your bowel movements are less frequent than once every two days, adding bran to your meals daily and including fresh raw fruits and vegetables and grain in your regular eating plan should easily and safely end this uncomfortable condition. And don't forget to drink at least eight to ten glasses of water a day. You should, of course, get a complete physical checkup to rule out a deficiency and make sure no other debilitating diseases are present. Discuss your diet with your physician or nutritionist. Under no circumstances should you resort to over-the-counter laxatives if they can be avoided. These are easy to abuse and can be counterproductive.

Diarrhea, too, is a pressure disease. And though it can be brought on by many factors, when it is of long standing, you could definitely benefit from a dietary reform that includes bran or whole grains and legumes each day. Examine your life-style—are you eating at unsanitary restaurants? Consuming excess amounts of fast food? Following an unbalanced diet that is making you vulnerable to intestinal infections and irritations? Exposing yourself to stress of various kinds? Coping with these problems is a must and, as in the case of the other pressure diseases, it is also important that any steps you take to remedy your condition be preceded by a good physical examination.

How to Save Yourself from Hiatus Hernia

Getting older can make you vulnerable to another pressure disease physicians call hiatus hernia. Doctors usually treat this disorder as they would ulcers. A low-fiber diet, which they consider "non-irritating", is prescribed, along with drugs to counteract stomach acidity.

The *Merck Manual,* an indispensable doctors' reference book, gives more details on this diet. A conventional physician will also advise that you lose weight and avoid clothes that prevent you from moving freely. When these measures fail, surgery will probably be suggested. The fact is, you *do* have to age, but you *don't* have to have hiatus hernia.[221]

There are natural ways both to prevent this disorder and, should you be unfortunate enough to develop it, to deal with hernia and improve your general health as a bonus.

1. A diet rich in nutritionally poor foods does not really make sense, despite the fact that this is just the kind of diet most doctors recommend for this disease. Hiatus hernia has much in common with all of the other pressure disorders that commonly affect the colon, anus, and rectum. Yet many physicians point out that these diseases are prevalent as a direct result of such a diet, low in natural bowel-cleansing fiber. It wouldn't be wise to discuss this question with your medical advisor if he has recommended a nutritionally hazardous eating plan.[222]

2. As your brain and your skin age, so does your whole intestinal system. It should be no surprise, then, that the reason you are straining more to eliminate waste matter is partly due to the fact that all the muscles in the lower body are not as powerful as they once were. Be careful not to overstrain the muscles around the colon and rectum, as this can lead to hemorrhoids.

If you eat right, drink plenty of water, get enough exercise, and set aside an unhurried time to move your bowels, you should be able to relax and let nature take its course.

• Twenty per cent of the cases of hiatus hernia doctors diagnose are discovered by accident.[223] Often, a person has gone in to have a laboratory test performed because he or his doctor may have suspected the presence of an ulcer or malabsorption syndrome, to name but two possibilities. Instead, the doctor may have found this disorder. A hernia of the stomach is caused when a portion of this organ is actually pushed through your diaphragm. Or the hernia may occur at the junction of stomach and esophagus. In this version, which may be inherited or developed in later life, the sphincter muscle between these two organs is prevented from doing its job. As a result, masticated food that should remain in your stomach backs up into the esophagus.

• You can prevent hiatus hernia, according to Burkitt and Painter.[224] By now, you can predict how to prevent any pressure disease: increase the amount of whole grain bread and cereal you eat, along with fibrous vegetables and fruits, and you may be amazed to find this disorder reversing itself, even if it has already appeared.

• Hiatus hernia may be present without your knowing it; you may be painfully aware it's there, because you find yourself regurgitating food and drink, or you find you have little or no appetite at mealtime.

Two other unusual conditions—one healthy, one not so healthy—that may contribute to this pressure disease are pregnancy and excessive weight.

Hemorrhoids

Hemorrhoids are uncomfortable, and if you are over fifty, the chances are twice as good as when you were twenty or thirty that you have them. Hemorrhoids, sometimes called "piles" when they are external only, are described by Drs. Burkitt and Painter as the most widespread of all the five pressure diseases.[225, 226] Maybe you have them, maybe you don't. Either way, chances are that much of what you believe about hemorrhoids is false.

Myth: No matter what your age, it is crucial to have one or more bowel movements a day.

Truth: Laxative manufacturers would love to have you think this is so. That is why their annual ad budgets equal $30 million or more. But no two persons have the same toilet habits, nor should they, say reliable physicians. Biochemical individuality may dictate that one movement every other day is unhealthy for your husband but normal for you. Try to avoid laxative medication unless absolutely necessary. It can get to be a daily habit and cause considerable ill health, especially since the taking of laxatives is often coupled with self-medication of other kinds. Consult a doctor if you are experiencing bowel disorders or pain and adding fiber to your diet doesn't help.

Myth: Hemorrhoids are just the manifestation of an internal infection or irritation. They are a simple annoyance that usually passes.

Truth: This condition is not only a true disease worthy of your attention, but it is actually two diseases, one occurring externally, the other internally. Let's consider internal hemorrhoids first. The mechanism in this disorder involves an enlargement of the vascular network in your rectum near the sphincter muscle of the anus. If this valve cannot open and close normally due to the hemorrhoid veins, the aperture may become blocked. This is the point at which you probably run to the pharmacist begging for a pill to make your movements less painful. But by now the pain may be complicated by the bursting of those engorged and inflamed veins.[227]

Myth: External hemorrhoids (piles) must be accepted as a consequence of aging.

Truth: Not so. Piles can be serious. They can even lead to varicose veins if you allow them to persist. When you suffer piles, your anal sphincter muscles may swell up to such an extent that a palpable fissure is visible and painful to touch And, of course, you must exert much force to eliminate waste material. In turn, this expulsion effort puts great stress on all the tissues in the rectum and anal area. Your stomach may even be sore as a result of the unnatural effort. As this stress spreads, the veins and their valves lose flexibility. Blood may pool in the veins and remain stationary in these byways. It becomes increasingly more difficult for the veins to transport blood smoothly and efficiently. And here, after months or years of eating thoughtlessly and rarely bothering with any fresh or fibrous foods, you face the consequences in the unpleasant form of varicose veins.[228]

The consequences may be less dire than varicose veins. You may only develop mild inflammation, some itching, perhaps a low-grade infection. Or the consequences may be much more dire: researchers tell us of cases where thrombosis has resulted.[229] This often fatal malady is basically a major clotting of blood platelets.

Myth: If you have pain while moving your bowels, the most effective remedy is a prescription laxative.

Truth: This is the last resort only. The best way of both coping with hemorrhoids and preventing them in the first place is to follow a high-fiber diet.

Myth: Basically, if you are healthy there's nothing wrong with taking medications for hemorrhoids, as long as the problem is not too advanced.

Truth: This is not a solution. In fact, it adds new problems for the sufferer. The constipation which makes you grunt and groan causes the blood-engorged hemorrhoidal tissues to swell; but the opposite is true, too. If your colon has become sluggish because you are using laxatives, this may initiate the first stages of hemorrhoids. Diarrhea can also be a price you pay for using "regularity-promoting" drugs too often.

Summary

Hiatus hernia is often treated by prescribing drugs and a number of low-fiber foods. Unfortunately, such a combination may, in fact, pave the way for constipation, which in turn weakens lower-body musculature.

A tendency to develop this disease can be inherited, but a faulty life-style can also bring on the condition. In either case, increasing the natural fiber in your diet is a good idea. So is the addition of bran to at least one of your daily meals.

Hemorrhoids, which may develop at any age, usually occur in the later years after a lifetime of poor dietary habits. But they don't have to occur at all if you are careful to keep sufficient fiber in your meals. Although this may not seem like a disorder of great consequence, it can lead to varicose veins and more serious forms of the pressure disease syndrome or even thrombosis.

Laxatives and all bowel medicines may worsen the condition by causing a sluggish colon or, at the least, diarrhea. All drugs should be avoided if at all possible, especially potent prescription drugs of the psychoactive variety. Whether you are young or old, food—honest, full-value food rich in natural fiber and nutrients—is your best medicine.

Questions About the Treatment of Pressure Diseases

Question: If so-called psychoactive drugs work, why not use them to relieve the adverse body conditions that are bringing on a pressure disease?

Answer: All drugs—but especially potent medications that cause dependencies such as barbiturates and antidepressants of all kinds—can do more than give a brief respite from symptoms. They may cause further bodily damage. Foods that are also "medicines" such as bran are a far better choice, since they promote health while relieving symptoms. Of course, they require more patience on the part of the patient. The ideal combination is psychological support plus a healthier diet.

Question: Why do older people usually succumb to these diseases?

Answer: Long years of poor eating and less than positive living habits spell trouble. Besides, your bowels go through a functional decline like all other organs. You have been exposed millions of times to poisonous substances stagnating in your bowels by the time you are sixty or seventy. This takes its toll.

Questions and Answers About Fiber

Question: I'm allergic to wheat bran. Can I use nuts for fiber instead?

Answer: Yes, you can. Fiber that is derived from grains is best, but you can use nuts. Consult a chart to how much you are getting. Also, remember nuts lose many of their nutrients when they are roasted, dry roasted, or processed in any way. Eat them raw and chew them well to make sure they are properly digested.

Question: Does everyone have the same fiber requirement?

Answer: If you are in fairly good health, 10 to 12 grams of fiber from natural sources should be adequate. You will profit by extra amounts if you are suffering from any of the pressure diseases already discussed. If occasional periods of irregularity are a problem, a few extra tablespoons of untreated, unheated wheat germ, wheat bran, or even a tasty variation—such as rice or corn bran—can be sprinkled over your morning cereal or evening salad.

If you prefer to use fruits and salad foods to meet your roughage requirements, a raw salad for lunch and a partially cooked grain salad such as tabouli for dinner, plus a big puree of fresh fruit in season, would fill the bill nicely. However, try to consume some whole grains in your diet, since some researchers believe these absorb the most water in your intestines.

Question: Is there a great difference between the fiber in processed foods like ready-to-eat supermarket cereals and natural foods such as millers bran?

Answer: Yes. Fiber should be eaten in its natural form. Our bodies have evolved based on the foods our ancestors ate, and are adapted to derive the total value from a food—vitamins, minerals, trace minerals, and enzymes, along with the bulk necessary for good bowel movements. The processing of most supermarket cereals is based on several factors. Profit is one. Another is the erroneous belief that fiber serves no useful purpose. Now that we know better, processing methods are slowly changing. Recently a few whole-fiber breakfast cereals have begun to be distributed through supermarkets. Read the labels of "natural" cereals carefully to avoid sugar, though: some are genuine whole foods; others contain large quantities of sugar in various forms, or are packaged with preservatives.

Question: If I don't like fruits and forget to eat vegetables regularly, is bran enough?

Answer: Certainly a little bran every day will improve your health and regularity, but there's no substitute for a well-balanced diet. That means you should aim for a variety of foods that are rich in many nutrients, including fiber. All fiber is not the same. The fiber in fruits and vegetables provides different values than that in grains. Include them all.

Also, don't forget that bran is only one of the good parts of any grain. Unrefined whole grains are triple-layered foods, and each of these layers is nutrient rich. The first layer is bran. The center component is the endosperm which is rich in starch and protein. And finally, the heart of the grain, containing protein, essential fats, and vitamins B and E, is the germ. Most store-bought breads and cereals have the germ and bran removed, at least initially. Later this deficit may be made up by fortification, but this isn't quite the same thing. Be sure to look for some descriptive phrase on the box that assures you that the product is from whole grains and is minimally processed. When in doubt, stick with the old-fashioned favorites—noninstant oatmeal, cracked wheat, undegerminated corn meal, brown rice, and buckwheat groats (kasha).

Question: Are products fortified with bran as acceptable as natural bran or wheat germ itself?

Answer: Why pay more for devitalized foods that have been processed an extra step to return what has been taken out? The more food is treated, heated, and handled by food processors, the more the overall value of the food declines. Take a few extra minutes to cook whole grains from scratch. Make a stop at your local natural foods store to buy whole wheat bread and unprocessed cereals that are the real thing. And become an ingredient-reader to maximize your health and protect yourself from harmful sugars, salt, and unnecessary additives.

Question: How should I eat fruits and vegetables to get the most fiber?

Answer: Buy your produce in season, buy it fresh, and eat it raw when possible. Vegetables can be grated for uncooked salads. When you do cook carrots, peas, corn, and other fresh vegetables, prepare them with as little water as possible to save nutrients. This is done easily if you use so-called waterless cookware or an inexpensive collapsible steamer, which can be inserted into any saucepan. If you must occasionally choose between frozen vegetables or canned, frozen foods retain more nutrients and fiber and contain less sodium, although they are a poor second to fresh in terms of palatability.

All vegetables weren't created equal in terms of fiber. Many of the root vegetables, as you might suspect, are at the top of any list: their crunchy quality and hardness indicate a high fiber yield. They also require beneficial exercise of your jaws and teeth. In fact, your whole mouth must be used.

Don't neglect the less common tubers: yams, kohlrabi, parsnips, even eggplants can be eaten whole. Never peel away any vegetable skin if it isn't essential to your recipe to do so, since in and near the skin is stored much of plant's roughage and nutrients.

The whole legume family deserves your attention, too. A good way to eat these and profit by the skins is to sprout your peas, chick-peas, mung beans, and lentils rather than cook them even minimally. Thus you are rewarded with the full value of the live food, including minerals, amino acids, and carbohydrate energy.

Question: Do bananas and apples and grapes have as much fiber as root vegetables and sprouted legumes?

Answer: Here's one way to tell whether the fruit you've selected is a high-fiber food: is it filled with seeds and/or does it have a tough or thick skin? Thus, berries of all kinds make good choices; they are rich in pectin and cellulose carbohydrate, too. Equally good are tasty tropical fruits such as mangoes and papayas. Bananas constitute an excellent fiber-rich source of carbohydrate.

Question: What is protopectin and why is it so important?

Answer: If you've had a grapefruit or orange for breakfast, you've had this beneficial two-carbohydrate food factor that is exciting considerable interest in biochemistry circles. The pulp of all citrus fruit contains this combination of cellulose plus pectin. Even vegetables are an occasional secondary source.

Here's how you benefit: after you've enjoyed your citrus fruit cocktail, the cellulose absorbs fluid from your intestines, and as it enlarges it quickly pushes along any contents of that tract. Meanwhile, the pectin becomes gelatinous, and in counterpoint to the cellulose, it provides lubrication and smooth passage for the food.

Two more plus factors are:

1. Protopectin helps you get maximum value out of the other nutritious foods you eat.

2. Protopectin helps your system use the dietary fats in an improved fashion. This, in turn, protects you from the cardiovascular dangers high cholesterol levels pose.

Question: What is the best kind of fiber for reducing blood fats?

Answer: It is usually agreed that grain is best. Two more types of fiber are:

• Guar, a gelatinlike fiber that combines with the fluids in the intestines, increases the bulk, and helps to depress unfavorable glucose-insulin reactions.

• Pectin, commonly found in apples, berries, and other fruit, works much like guar.

Fiber Deficiency in Special Conditions

DIABETES

What kind of diet would produce the ideal inner body climate to help those who suffer from this blood sugar disorder? One that is easy on a stressed pancreas, and one that improves the absorption of sugar by cells to keep the "insulin response" at near-normal levels after each meal, keeping the processing of glucose for energy on an even keel.

The ideal diet for this is one that is rich in natural carbohydrates and low in refined sugar products, like lots of salad, raw fruit in season, and homemade bread. There's nothing better for keeping you extra healthy.

ELIMINATING AN EMBARRASSING PROBLEM

Some people have maintained an aversion to beans due to digestive distress—i.e., bloating and flatulence. However, this can be substantially reduced by soaking the beans overnight, thoroughly cooking them, and most important, not consuming fruits or simple sugars at the same meal. Also, eliminate fatty or deep-fried foods. Though we place little importance on it, our emotional state when we eat plays an important part in how thoroughly our foods are digested, absorbed, utilized, and eliminated. A brisk walk prior to eating, relaxing music and conversation during the meal, and an unhurried pace, soft lights, and a comfortable environment provide the optimal benefit from a meal.

PREGNANCY

For most women who are in good health, pregnancy runs its course smoothly, interrupted only by endurable discomforts such as occasional nausea, food cravings, and sleep disorders. But one out of 4,000 pregnant women suffers a serious complication. It may be a serious case of water retention or edema. It may be hypertension. Or both of these toxic conditions may be present along with even worse symptoms. In this case—when coma or convulsions occur—eclampsia is usually the diagnosis. The literal meaning is sudden flash, but this is actually a condition so serious it can lead to death.

Eclampsia is a form of toxemia. Toxins in the body and the retention of too much sodium produce edema and high blood pressure, as well as a serious whole-body state endangering both mother and fetus.

Fiber can help by flushing more of these stagnant toxins from the system. Thus, this condition can be prevented in part or made less life-threatening.

Summary

You need 10 to 12 grams of fiber a day. Bran is one of the best natural sources, working most effectively as a blood fat reducer. But if you cannot tolerate this wheat product, consider fiber from other natural foods such as rice, corn, millet, soy, buckwheat, barley, oats, nuts, and seeds—such as poppyseeds, chia, sunflower, sesame, pumpkin, and flax-seed—or raw vegetables and fruits. Processed foods offer poor quality fiber and poor nutritional value. Also, different foods provide different fibers: a little of each is a good idea. Root vegetables and foods that require some healthy, vigorous chewing are excellent sources of fiber. The fresher they are, the more nutrients you receive.

Citrus fruit provides a type of fiber called protopectin which helps you get maximum value out of the other nutritious foods you eat, and helps your system use dietary fats more efficiently. This, in turn, provides protection from cardiovascular disorders.

Even fiber-rich beans can be eaten and digested without flatulence if they are soaked overnight, cooked long enough, and not eaten with fruits or simple sugars.

In the pregnancy disorder known as eclampsia, fiber may help to flush some toxins out of the system, making it less life-threatening.

LIPIDS:
HOW FATS AND OILS
AFFECT YOUR HEALTH

Fats

It is not necessarily true, as most people today believe, that you must avoid fats or that vegetable oil builds healthier hearts. Saturated fats have gotten a lot of negative publicity recently. Some of it is well deserved, but considerable confusion persists. There is a place in the human diet for all types of fat. It is important to know how much of which to include, and to maintain a *balanced* dietary fat intake.

Our knowledge of the connection between fats in our diet and fat in our body is not very new. Sixty years ago, researchers overfed hogs, first on unsaturated fats from legumes. As a result, the hog's adipose tissues were 28 percent higher in linoleic acid (an essential component of dietary fat) than usual. Similar results were achieved when dogs were used as subjects and linseed was the fat food. Excessive amounts of unsaturated fats generally produced out of shape, too easily malleable torsos. Saturated fats resulted in excessively firm flesh, indicating cause and effect between the type of fat consumed and the state of the body. It does matter what kind of fats you eat—but the consequences of the different kinds may surprise you.

Lipids, a Large Family

Lipids are one group of macronutrients indispensable to your health. Like carbohydrates, they are as important to your overall well-being as protein.

You ingest lipids every time you have a meal. Lipids are all the fatty or oily nutrients you consume or which your body manufactures, including fats, butters, and oils; vitamins E, K, A, and D (the fat-soluble vitamins); the essential fatty acids (EFA); sterols such as cholesterol and the sex hormones estrogen and androgen; wax compounds; and such tongue twisters as the lipoproteins and the phospholipids. (This last group includes an ingredient that may already be a part of your daily diet: lecithin.[1])

All these compounds have a similar chemical makeup. They are like carbohydrates, your body's other main energy source, in that they contain carbon, hydrogen, and oxygen; however, they have much less oxygen. They are soluble in alcohol and chemicals of the chloroform type—that is, organic solvents—but they do not mix with water. Dietary lipids are crucial for optimal physical and mental health.

Simple Fats and Compound Lipids

There are two basic kinds of lipids: the *simple fats* you usually think of when you hear the word fat (but which includes oils, also); and *compound lipids*, which are particles of fat that are combined with phosphate, protein, carbohydrate, or other substances to make such lipids as phospholipids, lipoproteins, cholesterol, etc.

The simple fats (or "fat") are much more abundant in the body than the compound lipids. The simple fats are *triglycerides*. When the doctor measures your triglyceride levels, he or she is trying to find out how many fats are circulating in your blood.

The simple or *neutral* fats are called *tri*glycerides because they consist of three long chain molecules of fatty acids.

Compound lipids are derived from the neutral fats. In compound lipids, one of the three fatty acids of the triglyceride is replaced by a different substance. In a phospholipid like lecithin, for example, that substance is a phosphate. In a lipoprotein, it is a protein. Lipid derivatives like sterols are more complex chemically.[2]

Simple Lipids: Saturated vs. Unsaturated

Lipids are derived from both animal and vegetable foods. Are you avoiding animal fats and using nothing but vegetable oils? In fact, fats and oils are close chemical cousins, since they are formed from the same base material. They are both simple fats. Here is how they differ:

Unsaturated fats have a low melting point, so low that they are liquids at room temperature. Your favorite vegetable oil, such as corn or safflower oil, is an example.

Saturated fats, however, have a high melting point. That's why butter is solid at room temperature and why the fat drippings from a cooked roast solidify if allowed to cool on the kitchen counter.[3] Foods of both plant and animal origin usually contain *both* these types of fatty acids, but in different quantities.

All Fats Were Not Created Equal: A More Technical Explanation of the Differences

Simple lipids consist of fatty acid molecules that are attached to a glycerol molecule. All fatty acids are composed of short-chain or long-chain carbon atoms linked to hydrogen atoms.

But here's how the acids differ from one another.

Fats are unsaturated (polyunsaturated) when:

• they can be poured and cannot be spread at room temperatures.

• their molecular makeup depends largely on short-chain fatty acids.

• two or more carbon atoms in the fatty acid chain are double-bonded together.

• there are fewer hydrogen atoms attached to the carbons than in saturated fats.

• the ratio of unsaturated to saturated fats in the food being described is high. A good example of this is the fat found in all fish, from lean types such as sole to fatty varieties such as mackerel.

Fats are saturated when:

• they are relatively solid at room temperature.

• their molecular makeup depends largely on long-chain carbon atoms (there are usually fourteen or more). These carbon chains are saturated with hydrogen atoms. This means that the carbons are connected to each other by single bonds, and each carbon is also bonded to as many hydrogen atoms as it can hold.

• they are derived from any nonaquatic animal. In order of hardness (or saturation), chicken is the lowest, followed by pork, while beef and lamb are at the top of the scale. Whole milk also contains saturated fat. There are only a few plant sources of saturated fats, such as coconut and palm nuts.

Vegetable oils can also be saturated by a process called hydrogenation, that is, by the addition of hydrogen atoms. This step hardens or saturates the oils and prevents them from separating when they are combined with other ingredients in high-fat processed foods like peanut butter or candy bars. This process is widely used by manufacturers, as a scrutiny of food labels will reveal. Vegetable shortening and margarine are examples of hydrogenated fats.

Another way to remember this distinction between the two types of fats is that fat is saturated when its molecule holds as many hydrogen atoms as the carbon chain can support. The reverse is true of unsaturated fatty acids: in their case, double bonds are present rather than the extra hydrogen atoms.

Summary

Fats, or lipids, as biochemists call them, are indispensable to your health. Lipids include not only simple fats and oils, but also oil-soluble micronutrients; components of fat like the essential fatty acids; and compound lipids derived from fats or composed partly of fats. Some lipids (like the essential fatty acids), must come from foods; others can also be manufactured by your body for its own use (such as saturated fats). Fat derivatives like cholesterol, vitamin D, a few hormones, and parts of liver bile are also manufactured in the body from the fats you eat.

Simple fats and oils consist of a glycerol molecule with three fatty acid chains attached to it. The fatty acid chains can be short or long, and there are many different fatty acids, and thus many different fats and lipid compounds made from them.

There has been much controversy about saturated vs. unsaturated fats. In general, it is preferable to obtain more unsaturated than saturated fats in the diet, but neither should be avoided completely. They are usually found together in nature: oils are said to be *poly*unsaturated when they include many more unsaturated than saturated fats. Fats are said to be saturated when virtually all carbon atoms in the fatty acid chains are saturated with hydrogen atoms. Unsaturated oils contain short fatty acid chains with the carbons double-bonded together. These double bonds are made of electrons. This makes them vulnerable to oxidation, so it is necessary to take vitamin E, an antioxidant, along with unsaturated fats.

Sources of Fat

In their natural state, the fats in unrefined oils and plants are for the most part beneficial, since they are accompanied by vitamin E. This vitamin is always found naturally in plant sources containing fat. This is fortunate, because vitamin E has a big role to play as an antioxidant. It protects the liquid fats or oils, full of polyunsaturated fatty acid, from being damaged by oxidation. These oils are highly susceptible to such damage.

Here are some common sources of fats in your diets:

1. All animal products, including cheese, yogurt, and other milk products.

2. Poultry and eggs.

3. Fish and shellfish.

4. Nuts (pecans are 73 percent fat, walnuts 64 percent, peanuts 45 percent).

5. Plant foods such as legumes and grains. Wheat germ, for example, is a good nonanimal source of fats and vitamin E.

The exact percentage of fat a food contains depends largely on its origin. When the leaves, roots, or stalks of a plant are the source, the food is usually much less oily or fatty than seeds or nuts. Some cuts of meat and fish are also fattier than others. Your doctor or nutritionist or a knowledgeable butcher or fishman can tell you which is which. (A partial list of fatty and lean fish appears in the chapter on protein.) As a general rule, darker meat on both chicken and fish contains more fat than lighter.

Fats in the Diet: More Essential than You Think

The word "fat" probably makes you think of spareribs and fast-food burgers. But practically *all* foods contain some form of fat, and nature has a reason. The lipids contribute in various ways to the health of every cell and organ in your body, but above all to the well-being of your heart and nerves.

If you have ever discussed diet with a health professional, or perhaps read a nutrition book, then you know that foods like nuts, cheese, and peanut butter are often recommended as "pick-me-ups," instead of popular but fattening candy bars or donuts. These natural foods really are energizers. They all supply natural fats, and fats offer lots of calories for energy.

If you've been on more than one diet, you probably know a lot about the calories in all kinds of foods. You may have tried a weight-loss plan discouraging fats and emphasizing natural carbohydrates, for example. If so, you know that ounce for ounce, unprocessed carbohydrate foods such as apples and carrots supply only half the calories of fatty foods such as steaks and ice cream.

But calories aren't everything. Your diet must supply fats and oils on a regular basis for a number of very important reasons.

Your Need for Dietary Fats: Twelve Facts

1. Fat protects you. If you have ever taken a belly flop in the local pool or received a punch in the abdomen, you were no doubt grateful for any extra body fat you have. Nature has done a good job of seeing

to it that organs like your spleen, pancreas, bladder, and liver are protected from injury by making the abdomen a fat depot. Fat accounts for almost half of the makeup of this cavity.

2. Fat helps keep you warm. Are you underweight and often colder than your companions? You may not have sufficient body fat to guard against excessive loss of body heat when the winter winds blow.

3. Fat provides you with energy. Gram for gram, fats give you twice as many calories as the same quantity of carbohydrates or protein. That's why you think of fats as fattening. But low-calorie reducing diets should, nonetheless, include some fats. (For this reason Weight Watchers, Inc., for example, several years ago added salad oil to even their strictest meal plans.) This is because energy production in your body is dependent on a regular supply of fatty acids. (There are unusual circumstances, such as starvation, in which ketones can substitute for fats. But even ketones are products of fats in the body).

4. Fat is needed for digestion and absorption of many oil-soluble nutrients. For example, you must consume fats (including oils) in order to properly absorb vitamins A, D, E, and K, and the essential fatty acids. Fats are also needed for calcium absorption.[4] Fats help to move these nutrients through your body and deposit them where they are needed. A very low-fat diet followed for too long can be harmful for this reason as well.

5. Fats are a major ingredient in the makeup of the myelin sheaths, the protective coating on some nerves that insulates your brain and helps nerve impulses travel quickly the whole length of your body.

6. Fats supply your body with the essential fatty acids—EFA. The presence of these three essential acids—linoleic, linolenic, and arachidonic—are one of the major reasons you use vegetable oils and nut butters. These three essential fatty acids are so important in your diet because they are the only ones your body can't manufacture from the others.

7. Our cell membranes protect us, but not unless they are healthy. A good supply of fatty acids keeps them in shape. And, in turn, cellular tissue requires these fats to be produced and reproduced.[6]

8. If you are over forty, your doctor may have told you about the importance of an adequate hormone supply at this midlife period. If your adrenal, pituitary, and pancreas glands are operating normally, then you have sufficient hormones. Although the fatty acids in your blood come from the fatty or adipose tissues of the body, their release depends on hormones. Insulin depresses their release, while adrenaline, ACTH, glucagon, and growth hormone cause an increase in their release.[7]

9. Prostaglandins, lipids associated with various membranes in your body, are crucial hormonelike substances. Without them, your blood pressure would be abnormal, your heart might develop erratic

rhythms, your entire central nervous system—and that includes your brain—could develop dysfunctions, and your muscles, too, might be affected.[5] Unsaturated fatty acids keep those prostaglandins in healthy production.

10. If your weight is normal and you exercise regularly, go ahead and indulge yourself in those extra few nuts or that hard-boiled egg. A little extra fat is useful, because when you take in a little more fat than you need right away, proteins don't have to be diverted for use as fuel. They can do what they are primarily intended to do—build and repair body cells. You may wonder why, if it's true that both proteins and carbohydrates can be burned for energy, we eat fats at all. The ability of proteins to act as fuel is only a secondary purpose: it takes extra energy for the body to convert protein into fuel, so it is not as efficient to use as fatty acids. And carbohydrates simply do not supply as much energy per gram as fats.

11. Biochemically speaking, fats are the best type of molecular transporter for calories, because they are quite dense and they do not dissolve readily.

12. Fats are used in the production of many crucial body substances. For example, hemoglobin, the pigment that enables your red blood cells to carry oxygen to all parts of your body, is a lipid. And your hair is shiny and your skin soft because of an oily secretion called sebum made by oil glands in the skin.

Summary

Fats are indispensable nutrients. They are a highly concentrated source of energy; they insulate your internal organs from the cold and from physical shock; and they must be present for you to absorb oil-soluble vitamins, the essential fatty acids, and calcium. They also help in transporting these nutrients through the bloodstream to where they are needed. Fat compounds and fat derivatives are found everywhere in your body. The membranes of each cell are made of phospholipids, which are also highly concentrated in nerves and brain tissue. Steroids are also important: cholesterol is always found in the blood and nervous tissue and other cells (don't forget that you *need* cholesterol so much your body manufactures it itself; it's only when there's *too much* in your bloodstream that the risk of heart disease is increased for some people). There are lipid portions of your red blood cells (the hemoglobin), of your liver bile, and of each cell. The fatlike vitamins A, E, and K are crucial for vision, and blood clotting, respectively.[8]

So don't neglect fatty foods in your diet. Not that it would be easy to do so! You can choose from nuts, seeds, and even whole grains and legumes, and the germs, oils, and butters derived from them. Lean fish, eggs, and animals and their milk also contain fats. (The latter, of course, includes human milk: your infant needs fat along with all the other nutrients in mother's milk.)

Fatty Acids

As we have seen, there are many different kinds of lipids: simple and compound, saturated and unsaturated, triglycerides (there are also diglycerides and monoglycerides) and lipid derivatives as complex as hemoglobin and prostaglandin. But all of them involve various combinations of different fatty acids with other molecules.

Our foods contain dozens of different fatty acids. Meats and other animal protein contain saturated fatty acids like palmitic and stearic acid, found especially in lard, beef, eggs, chicken, butter, and milk. In fats from vegetable sources, unsaturated fatty acids tend to predominate. These include linoleic, oleic, linolenic, and arachidonic acids.

In nature, none of these fatty acids is isolated. Plant sources will contain saturated fatty acids like palmitic acid; animal sources will contain unsaturated fatty acids like oleic acid.

No matter what sources of fats you include in your diet, your body can manufacture *almost* all the fatty acids and other components needed to produce the long (but not exhaustive) list of lipid substances mentioned in the previous section. Like a skilled chemist in the laboratory, it combines and separates various elements to obtain the precise substance it needs. It can take one fatty acid from the fat stored over your belly, perhaps, and turn it into another needed to replenish lipoprotein cell membranes of your skin, or to produce the oily sebum secreted at your hair follicles. It can even turn carbohydrates into fats (as those with a sweet tooth are only too aware). But there are three fatty acids that the body cannot manufacture from others or from carbohydrates. For these, it must turn directly to the food you eat.

These three essential fatty acids are linoleic acid, linolenic acid, and arachidonic acid. You should be sure to include foods containing these in your diet every day.

Essential Fatty Acids: Some Essential Facts

If you had a salad with grains, nuts, beans, sprouts, and unrefined oil, then you've satisfied your daily requirement for the essential fatty acids (EFA). Another type of meal rich in EFAs would be soybeans with a thick slice of millet toast or nut bread, or oatmeal sprinkled with sunflower seeds and lecithin.

Including the EFAs in your diet might do all of the following for you:

- Improve the contractibility of your muscle fiber—this will make you feel stronger.
- Reduce your blood pressure, making life easier (and probably longer) for your heart.
- Normalize blood clotting time throughout your body.
- Help prevent reproductive diseases.[9, 10]

These bonuses are only a few that you can expect when you increase the EFA in your diet. Researchers have also discovered that glands and nerves function more efficiently as a consequence of good prostaglandin levels. Essential fatty acids are *prostaglandin precursors:* without them, your body can't manufacture prostaglandins. If you increase the amount of EFA-rich foods you eat—especially the linoleic acid-rich foods: walnuts, millet, wheat germ, and soybean foods such as tofu—you will be doing your nerves and glands a favor. And they should repay you by helping your whole metabolism function more smoothly. Adequate levels of vitamin E and B_6 are also a must. A varied natural food diet should provide these.

(Don't forget your daily brewer's yeast. It will give you more prostaglandins indirectly by improving your selenium levels. This trace mineral, so abundant in yeast, is needed for prostaglandin metabolism.)

You also need prostaglandins if you expect your kidneys to do their job. What better reason to enjoy EFA-rich foods such as lecithin, safflower oil, and crunchy snacks like sunflower seeds? These B_6-rich nuts give you a big helping of linoleic acid, and the composition of the oil extracted from them is 94 percent EFA. Use it on your salads.[6]

Arachidonic acid has some special properties beyond those of its companion fatty acids, linoleic and linolenic. For example, tests with humans indicated that this fatty acid could decrease the threat of atherosclerosis by normalizing the clotting of red blood platelets in less than a month's time. Prostaglandin levels also rose. In an emergency, this EFA, found in what's probably one of your favorite foods—peanuts —can be manufactured in the body from linoleic acid if a requisite quantity of B_6 is also available.[11]

Are you tired all the time? Is your complexion poor? You could be EFA-deficient.

If you are over forty, do yourself a favor: hold back some of those dreaded symptoms of aging by getting more EFA foods each day. As you age, the tissues do not retain these particular fatty acids well. Some researchers have speculated that a shortage of EFAs might explain why cystic fibrosis develops in certain individuals. Victims of cystic fibrosis suffer low levels of this fat group, have cellular secretion problems, and are often helped by treatment with EFA-rich supplements and the prostaglandin precursors via varied nuts.[12]

Summary

Fatty acids of different kinds are found in all fats and oils. The body has mechanisms for transforming one fatty acid into another as needed. However, the three essential fatty acids (EFA) cannot be manufactured from the others. Linoleic acid, linolenic acid, and arachidonic acid should be obtained directly from food.

The essential fatty acids are indispensable to the health of your circulatory system. They (particularly arachidonic acid) decrease the threat of atherosclerosis by normalizing the clotting of blood, helping to keep blood pressure low. Your strength and energy levels may be boosted by them, since they increase the ability of your muscles to contract. If your complexion is fine, it's a good bet you're getting enough EFA: they aid in the healing of certain skin problems. As prostaglandin precursors, they help keep your glands, nerves, and kidneys healthy. (Vitamins E, B_6, and selenium are also important in prostaglandin production.)

In general, nuts, beans, and seeds are the best sources of the essential fatty acids. Soybeans, soy lecithin, and soy oil all contain EFA. Almost any unrefined seed oils are good sources—another reason to use sunflower or safflower oil on your salads. Peanuts supply arachidonic acid—which, in a pinch, can be made in your body from linoleic acid if you get enough B_6 in your diet.

Fats: Which Ones Are You Really Getting?

If you care deeply about your internal environment, your weight, and your physical and mental health, you want to know what ingredients are contained in everything you eat. Until 1976, this would not have been possible. But people with health problems such as allergies have lobbied to change that. Now, Federal Department of Agriculture requires:

- that all processed foods list the common name of the fats that are used.
- that the name be specified, such as "soybean oil," not "vegetable oil."[13]

Fats in Your Diet

You obtain some fats for good health every time you eat—whether a plate of lentils or a slice of whole grain bread. That is not to say, however, that adequate amounts of all types of fat essential for health will be supplied by your diet, unless you know the facts and you plan accordingly. For example, here are a few findings on the subject of fats in foods from a report by USDA scientists in the *Journal of the American Dietetic Association*, based upon reports from the Department of Agriculture.

Fats in Peas, Beans, Nuts, and Seeds

Legumes such as peas and lentils yield only very small amounts of fats: the younger the plant, the better the quality. They contain polyunsaturated fatty acids (PUFAs), such as the essential fatty acid, linoleic acid. It is better to snack on mixed nuts rather than only one nut, because you derive a better variety of fats that way. While pecans and walnuts give you one type of PUFA, if you add a few Brazil nuts and toss in some exotic pine nuts, you boost your linoleic acid intake. And linoleic acid is good for your heart, your skin, and your nerves. Variety, along with moderation, is the key to a healthy diet, don't forget.

All seeds and nuts are rich in polyunsaturates. Almost 100 percent of their fat content may be in the form of those beneficial, shorter, unhydrogenated fatty acids. One exception is an oil that should never be sold for the home—cottonseed—though it is. It is unlike most vegetable foods in that it has a high level of saturated palmitic acid. This fat is usually associated with animal foods. Cottonseed oil has the added disadvantage of being derived from cotton plants which, because they are textile rather than food-producing plants, may have been sprayed with more insecticide than other seed-bearing plants. But, in general, even a tablespoon of seeds or nuts crumbled or slivered on your luncheon salad or supper casserole gives you the fats that you need in the highest quantities. Peanuts or walnuts, for instance, supply lots of unsaturated oleic acid. These fats contain less hydrogen than saturated fats, but not as little as PUFAs.[14] Palm nuts and coconut contain largely long-chain (saturated) fat.

Fats in Seafoods

It's no surprise to learn that seafood is a good source of healthy fats, or that lipid levels in fish may run as high as 25 percent. But here are a few facts you may *not* know:

• The chemical structure of the oil found in fish is actually closer to that found in plants. The predominant fats in fish are short-chain fatty acids.[15]

• What's your favorite part of the fish? If you're hoping to benefit by the nutrients in the fat, there are more of them in the head than in the tail. Pick a fish with more fat—such as mackerel, bluefish, or sardines —for healthy phosphorus-loaded lipids.

• The amount of triglycerides fish yield is variable. Fish caught in the summer may be more nutritionally fatty than those caught at other times of the year.

• You don't find tuna fish or flounder oil sold next to safflower oil in your market because oil from ocean fish is used as food only in Canada and abroad. There, these oils are sometimes put into margarines, but since they are unsaturated, unstable, and bad tasting, the United States does not use them. If hydrogenated, they have a flavor similar to vegetable oils but sweeter.

Fats in Dairy Foods

Weight watchers know that whole milk contains fats—mostly saturated. This is also true of whole milk yogurt. If you like natural cheeses, they are a good source of the same fats you get from meat. Cheese also contains a bit of EFA, with 2 percent linoleic and 1 percent linolenic acid. This is true, too, of eggs, often called nature's most perfect food because of the quality of its protein. Cheese also contains complete protein.

Fats in Meats

Have you had your saturated palmitic and your unsaturated oleic acids today? You've had both if you had meat. These are the two fats in greatest concentration in most meat. But they are also found in plants in small amounts.

If you must avoid saturated fats, it is important to realize the meat you cook at home is not the only source of these fats. There are numerous others. To avoid unhealthy amounts of saturated animal fats:

• Avoid restaurant foods that have been prepared with fried batters or processed in tallow. This hard fat is widely used. It is derived from beef drippings. It is easy to use in a cooking fat blend, so restaurants and food processors may prepare their donuts or French fries in various mixtures of unhealthy hydrogenated oils with beef tallow added.

• Lard is the secret ingredient in a flaky pie crust. But it's no secret that this solid fat is not an ingredient for good arterial health. Use very small amounts of unhydrogenated, cold-pressed vegetable oils instead if you care about living well for a long time.

Also, beware of fats used for frying that spatter or have an off taste. If you need smooth, easy-to-handle fat, butter or soy margarine should be your first choice.

Don't Cook Fats or Oils Too Long

Avoid overheated, overused oils. Ask how long the same oil has been used without being changed before you order French fries at a restaurant, for example. Overcooking and overheating cause the glycerin which fat contains to be transformed into a potential poison called acrolein. In addition, oxygen attacks the lipids present in the fried food and speeds up their degradation. Then when the food is eaten you may experience belching, flatulence, heartburn, or other related complaints. The lining of your stomach has been attacked by oxygen just like the lipids of the ingested food. Eating overcooked fats may also predispose you to cancer.

Cooking for extreme times at excessive temperatures is not the only factor that can affect the digestibility of fats. Middle age is another. All your body's processes gradually slow down after forty. This means a high-fat shake and a greasy fast-food burger may irritate your intestines, bowels, and stomach hours after you eat them, while the same meal doesn't give your teenager a moment of indigestion. The younger you are, the better you absorb fats of all types.

Good advice if you're getting along in years is to avoid *all* greasy foods, especially those offered by restaurants. Also, it is desirable to emphasize the easier-on-your digestion, high-in-polyunsaturate foods. But don't neglect fats. Overeating is discouraged if adequate fat is consumed, since it promotes satiety.

Notes on Fat Digestion

While fats do not dissolve in water, they are not difficult for your intestinal tract to break down. Your body manufactures some superefficient acids and emulsifying agents that help you metabolize and assimilate all but 5 percent of the fats you eat. Foods with a high content of long-chain saturated fats probably are the only edibles that may go through your system without being broken down.[16]

If you eat lean fish while your husband has chopped sirloin, you will probably digest your meal more quickly, because the fat in fish is primarily polyunsaturated, not as dense or as satiating as beef fat, and more quickly digested. This means it does not linger in your stomach so long. This is true of the fats in vegetables, too, as compared to animal fats. (That's why Americans used to fatty beef and pork meals often com-

plain that they're hungry an hour after eating at a Chinese restaurant
—at least if they choose chow mein rather than spare ribs.) Saturated
fats, like that from beef, lamb, and pork, require more time for digestion
and are generally harder for the body to assimilate.

French fries are hard to digest! You may know that raw food is
usually preferable to cooked because heat and excessive handling destroys nutrients. But heat does more than destroy vitamins, minerals,
and enzymes in those fries. Cooking at the 400° plus temperatures
required for French fries also makes the fat treated this way less digestible. A steak that broils five to ten minutes has been only minimally
damaged. But how about chicken that spends forty-eight minutes in the
broiler? This extended exposure to heat has the same effect on the fats.

Summary

We need a wide variety of fats in our diets. The essential fatty acids
are prevalent in vegetable sources (though cheese contains small
amounts also). Linoleic acid, necessary to your heart, skin, and nerves,
is abundant in nuts like Brazil and pine nuts; there is also a small amount
in legumes. Pecans, walnuts, and peanuts supply other EFAs.

You can count on seeds and nuts and their oils (except for cottonseed oil) for polyunsaturated fats. Fish, too, supply a lot of fat—much of
it unsaturated, depending on the type of fish.

Dairy foods like milk, natural cheeses, and eggs are also excellent
sources of lipids in the diet.

Meat is another source, tending to be much more highly saturated.
If you are trying to avoid saturated fats, you should avoid animal proteins and restaurants that cook with tallow (a hard fat made from beef
drippings) and lard. Another danger of restaurant fats is that they may
be overcooked, transforming their glycerin into harmful acrolein, adding a cancer risk, and making the fat less digestible, especially for older
people. Of course, you know enough to avoid rancid fats, which can also
spoil your digestion.

Fats are usually not hard for your body to digest, and they are
filling, especially saturated fats. It is only when they are overheated that
they become difficult to digest.

Oils: How Much Do You Know About Them?

You use salad oils and cooking oils every day, probably without thinking about whether they are good or bad, or how they might have been processed before they got to your pantry shelf. How much do you actually know about these foods? Here's a test.

1. True or false: If an oil is not labeled "hydrogenated," you can be pretty sure it's in its natural state.

False. Hydrogenation, which is done to improve the "keeping" quality of oils and raise their melting point, is only one of the ways vegetable oils and fats are changed from a natural to an unnatural food. When you toss your next salad with that innocent-looking, mild-tasting commercial oil, remind yourself of all it's been through. For example:

• Lye, caustic soda, or a strong bleaching agent is added to the oil. This step reduces the vitamin E that is available to you. It also means less protein, less vitamin-A-rich coloring material, less of all the phospholipids, including lecithin, so essential for the health of your nerve tissue.

• Next, your cooking oil is cleaned. To remove material that may contribute to faster spoilage, the oil is "steam-cleaned," or mixed with water and then filtered.

• Then your oil is bleached. Food processors use bleaching agents like clay or Fuller's earth to further "clean up" the oil that will soon have a place on your grocer's shelf and yours. This step removes more vitamins, plus much of the health-promoting chlorophyll found in all plant foods.

• To make certain the oil taste is acceptable, is odorless, and has minimal aroma, it is further treated with high heat and distilled steam. Result? An oil that can resist rancidity much longer than nature intended.

• Lastly, to improve shelf life even more, this devitalized oil may be adulterated before packaging with an undesirable preservative such as citric acid or phosphoric acid.

2. Each oil has some characteristic peculiarity you should know about. Can you name a few?

Peanut oil is excellent for pan frying and deep frying, but have you noticed how it solidifies when it cools down? This is natural, but makes it less useful as a salad oil.

As tasty as some oils are, many of us don't like their odor. Do your children reject corn oil because it occasionally smells like wine? Or maybe you don't like soybean oil when it's been heated because it is vaguely reminiscent of codfish oil?

Safflower oil has a pleasant, delicate flavor for salads, but if you've tried to cook with it, you've noticed it's less aromatic than oils like corn and peanut for such processes.

3. True or false: Corn oil is produced in this country for commercial use more than any other type of oil, which is good, because corn oil is very high in beneficial linoleic acid.

It is true that corn oil is high in linoleic acid, but false that it is the most commonly used oil. If you read labels you know how often soy oil turns up as an ingredient in foods like spreads and dressings. Actually, soybean oil accounts for all but 27 percent of the oils processed in the United States these days. And cottonseed—not corn oil—is second in use.

As for benefits, soybean oil is 54.5 percent linoleic acid, while corn oil is 58.7 percent. But soy oil has this advantage: it is a source of lecithin. It is a good idea to include it in your diet if you are not already using lecithin granules or pure lecithin oil on your daily salads.

4. True or false: It doesn't matter which oil you use. They are all essentially alike.

False. If you are concerned about using polyunsaturates to reduce your blood fat levels, it is important to use an oil in which the level of PUFA is high and the saturated fats are low.

Here are the ratios of unsaturated to saturated fats in commonly used oils: safflower has a ration of 7.8/1, corn oil 4.6/1, and sunflower oil 4.6/1 or 6.2/1. Sunflower oil has two figures because the place of origin makes a difference in nutritional content. Plants that come from the north have the higher PUFA content, those from the south have the lower.

5. True or false: Polyunsaturated fats are found in many foods besides sunflower seeds, soybeans, corn, and fish livers.

True. These liquid fats are also extracted from walnuts, sesame seeds, fruits such as avocado, and vegetables and plants such as the safflower. They are ingredients in many margarines.[17]

6. True or false: Olive oil is the most highly processed of all oils. Therefore, it spoils easily and this is why it's called a more saturated oil.

False. Overall, olive oil is less processed. In this sense it is superior. If it originates from a country like Greece, it probably has not been heat-treated, for example, although once it is exported and shipped to us, it must be pasteurized before being sold. This is true of Spanish and Italian types, too. If you enjoy your olive oil in the country where it was pressed, you are enjoying a truly natural food. This virgin oil has not been "cleaned up" to remove natural aroma, nor has it been adulterated with cottonseed oil. This practice occurs in the United States when it is prepared for use as a salad dressing, and when a general cooking oil is being prepared by manufacturers. It is also false that olive oil spoils readily. Actually, it keeps better at room temperature than most oils (still, all oils should be refrigerated after being opened). But olive oil contains only 15 percent linoleic acid and the acids it is highest in, monounsaturates, are less beneficial than PUFA.[18]

7. True or false: Heat-treated oils present a risk of cancer.

True. When excessive heat is used in producing an oil, residues of the chemicals sprayed on the plants during the growing period or used during storage may be released. Researchers tell us these chemicals have carcinogenic potential for humans. Furthermore, the extraction process itself may leave behind substances that are unhealthy at least, and potentially carcinogenic at worst. This is because once the original material is crushed and heated, it is exposed to a harsh petrochemical. Chemical analysis often reveals undesirable traces of this solvent, which is an ingredient of gasoline, in commercial food oils.[19]

8. True or false: Sunflower and safflower oils are equally beneficial.

True to an extent: Their linoleic acid content is similar—sunflower oil contains 75 percent and the safflower 78 percent. Also, both are stable oils with good keeping qualities.

9. True or false: Sunflower seeds are called that because they grow in sunny climates, like the southern United States.

False. You'll find them growing in wintry climates like Canada and the USSR.

10. True or false: Cottonseed oil has as much linoleic acid as soybean oil. Therefore, you can safely use any processed foods in which it is an ingredient.

False. Cottonseed oil is not even sold for home-cooking use to the general public, because although it does contain 33 percent linoleic acid, it also contains coloring material that is hazardous to human health, and because cotton plants are often sprayed with excessive pesticides. Cottonseed oil is not as widely produced as it was formerly, but it is still popular with snack food processors and manufacturers of oils for use in restaurants, catering concerns, and similar volume businesses. Concerns such as these value the fact that because some of its saturated fat content is removed to facilitate storage, it has a somewhat better "keeping quality" than mass-produced soybean oil. Health-wise consumers, however, avoid it.

11. True or false: Coconut oil is as beneficial as safflower.

Not true. The oil from coconut is saturated, just like beef fat. It is often used for frying and in novelty foods like candy bars because, as you might guess, it is ideal for high-heat cooking. And it usually resists spoilage longer than other fats, which is why it is used sometimes in a nonhydrogenated form in sweet snack foods, although it can eventually spoil and go bad.

12. True or false: Mayonnaise is nutritionally similar to butter.

False. This product is very much "doctored" by processors. Besides being heated and neutralized to remove sediment and coloring, it is often altered to give it stability on the shelf by repeated cooking and filtering out of fatty solids. In this state it stays creamy when refrigerated—but its nutritional value is minimal. But did you know that it's easy to make your own mayonnaise?

13. True or false: Natural oils contain natural preservatives so they do not spoil.

Both true and false. It is true, for example, that vitamins E and B_6 and the phospholipids are present in all natural oils. These vitamins work as antioxidant factors for a short time. Unfortunately, they cannot keep oil fresh as long as food processors would like. This explains the popularity of hydrogenation, which allows products containing oil to remain on shelves a year or more at almost any temperature.

To avoid spoilage of unsaturated oils, buy small bottles of cold-pressed oils or unrefined "crude" oils. They will keep for short periods of time, refrigerated in glass containers that keep out the light. What you get in return for your precautions are all the valuable nutrients that processing has destroyed in supermarket salad oils. You can also add some vitamin E to your oil to protect its PUFA and improve its keeping quality.

14. True or false: It is impossible to tell if a natural oil is unsafe to use.

False. A natural oil that has been kept on a warm shelf in a container that is not resistant to strong sunlight will go bad, perhaps in only a few weeks. You will know because bad oil develops an off taste, and an unpleasant smell. Discard it! Spoiled oil can upset the digestive process, and spoilage bacteria destroy many nutrients as well. This does not mean it is safer to buy oils to which stabilizers and preservatives have been added. These oils are totally devitalized; a food that is so unnatural that it cannot "go bad" is definitely not good for your health.[20]

Summary

Commercial oils and fats may be processed to death. Not only are they often hydrogenated to make their shelf life longer; but even simple salad oils may be treated with lye, bleach, heat, steam, and various petrochemicals and preservatives. It's not easy to find natural, unrefined oils. "Polyunsaturated" or "unhydrogenated" is not an adequate guarantee.

You may want to use different oils for different purposes. Safflower and sunflower seed oil make light salad oils; or try soy oil if you want to add lecithin to your diet. For pan or deep frying, peanut oil is ideal, but it solidifies when it cools. And of course, olive oil, the only oil you can keep for long outside the refrigerator, is a classic in Mediterranean cooking, and is generally relatively unprocessed, even when mass marketed. Its fatty acids are monounsaturated.

For polyunsaturates, choose safflower oil, sunflower oil, corn oil, or soy oil. They also contain vitamins E and B₆, and phospholipids. (You can add vitamin E to them to retard spoilage.) Unlike these, coconut oil contains saturated fats. And you should avoid cottonseed oil, which is highly adulterated and widely used commercially. (Look for it on potato chip ingredients lists, for example, and if you must eat potato chips, make your own.)

Mayonnaise and margarine are two other highly processed foods. Fresh butter is far preferable from a health point of view.

Never eat rancid oil—or oil that "keeps well" because of preservatives.

Hydrogenation: Dispelling Some Myths

If you read labels when you shop, you've seen the word "hydrogenated" again and again—on everything from peanut butter to candy bars. Bakery goods, such as commercial donuts, coffee cakes, muffins, and all related products, are probably the heaviest users of hydrogenated fats, but there are many others as well. Treating fats can prevent such foods from picking up the odor of other foods and ingredients. It also improves creaminess, since hydrogenated fats have qualities similar to animal shortening.

If hydrogenated foods are so much a part of the American food supply, they *must* be safe. Right? Unfortunately, this may not be a safe, logical conclusion to draw.

There is something unnatural about a food that can sit for months, maybe years, on a shelf without spoiling, and that's what hydrogenated foods are: unnatural. Those processed quick-and-easy toaster tarts, peanut butters, and pizzas may taste good, but they have lost large amounts of nutrients that were originally present in the oils. Those oils are either obliterated by extensive processing or transformed into forms that may threaten your health.

Is butter appearing on your menu less these days? Have you switched to margarine because of the advertisers' claims regarding the healthy qualities these unsaturated spreads provide for your heart?

Well, here is another example of laxity on the part of the FDA, an agency supposedly guarding us from deceptive practices by manufacturers and advertisers.

These advertisers have been allowed to give you the impression that margarine is a little bit better for your health than butter, because butter contains saturated fats while margarine's oils are supposedly "pure." The fact is that the polyunsaturated oil found in those supermarket spreads has been hydrogenated. Therefore, their nutritional composition has been altered, as previously explained. In addition to some sort of hydrogenated oil derived from corn, safflower, soybeans, or other plants like cottonseed, you get several other ingredients, some of which are not so desirable. Water and milk may be acceptable along with pulverized soybeans, and the lecithin that makes margarine taste deceptively like butter. But do you really want chemical flavors, synthetic preservatives, and emulsifying agents? None of this has to be listed on the label. Think twice when the choice is between margarine and butter.[21] And read the label. Some margarines sold in health food stores are made with nutritionally acceptable ingredients.

A good start on weaning yourself from foods containing hydrogenated oils is to understand a little more about the way these oils are produced.

• These "new" fats are more resistant to rancidity because they are dead, thanks to high temperatures and extreme pressures used to turn the beneficial unsaturated fats into less beneficial saturated fats.

• Do you fancy a bit of heavy metal in your food? You may be getting traces of nickel or platinum in your next "quick-bite" donut. These potentially toxic metals are commonly used as catalysts in the hydrogenation process. Now, catalysts are supposed to trigger a chemical process, but not be used up in it. Theoretically, none of the platinum or nickel stays in the oil. But, in practice, some may.

The oil subjected to a process to make it clear, colorless, and odorless is then turned into animal or vegetable shortening or one of the many popular "margarines."[22]

When you eat these foods, you miss out on many vitamins, minerals, and essential fatty acids. Often, according to Dr. Bicknell and Dr. Keys, the EFAs are converted into forms that are antithetical to unprocessed fatty acids in your diet and your body, and of course, this creates further metabolic disharmony.

The food industry now uses many saturated fats that formerly were sold to soapmakers. When fortified with additives and preservatives, they are added to a wide variety of hydrogenated foods. This information does not always appear clearly on food labels.

Summary

Hydrogenation offers fat manufacturers and distributors numerous advantages. When oils are saturated with hydrogen, they turn into odorless, creamy, solid fats which resist rancidity. However, they are usually so adulterated with chemical preservatives, coloring agents, and flavors that they are unpredictably harmful to your health. Besides, the heat used in hydrogenation alone makes them dead foods.

Don't be fooled by margarine. Even those advertised as high in polyunsaturates have to be at least partially hydrogenated just to make them solid. You might as well enjoy butter, which is far less processed.

Some fats once considered fit only for soap are now chemically treated and added to foods.

Polyunsaturated Fatty Acids: Some Bad Things About Those Good Fats

The discoveries that the consumption of saturated fats seemed to correlate with high blood cholesterol, and that high blood cholesterol levels seemed to correlate with heart disease, led inevitably to an obvious solution: Less cholesterol! Less saturated fats!

That's the prescription for health in the opinion of all but two of nineteen countries recently surveyed. No one seems to doubt that diets low in highly saturated, cholesterol-containing foods—such as that generally followed in Japan—result in a low incidence of coronary fatalities,[13, 14] at least when accompanied by other healthy life-style habits. By contrast, atherosclerosis and all blood fat levels are dangerously high in the meat-eating United States. Our diet affects even animal subjects adversely.[23]

More polyunsaturates seems to be the most popular prescription for preventing and curing our number one killer—but polyunsaturates should not be regarded as a panacea.

1. Polyunsaturates can be dangerous enough to injure cells and even cause tumors. PUFAs can be harmful in ways that saturated animal fats are not. The very molecular nature of animal fats makes them less reactive, more predictable. By contrast, PUFAs have a molecular structure characterized by electron-rich double bonds. They easily interact and are prone to attack by electron-poor or electron-seeking compounds or elements such as oxygen. If you take polyunsaturated oils, be sure to get enough antioxidant vitamin E. And if you must eat French fries, bake them instead of frying them, for health's sake. Dr. David Kritchevesky of the Wistar Institute warns us about heating cooking oils—even polyunsaturated oils—to very high temperatures, as in deep frying. It promotes atheroma formation. And the higher the heat, the greater the risk.

High heat causes a chemical reaction that turns PUFAs into dangerous *polymers*. Does this word ring a bell? No wonder. It's an ingredient often found in hardware stores; it's found in painting products. Certainly it doesn't belong on your dinner table.[27, 28]

2. If you follow one current popular suggestion, you could cause toxicity that might actually lead to heart problems! This suggestion is to consume 75 percent of the fats in your diet in the form of PUFAs. This is fine if you consume very little fat. But if you are considering doubling or tripling your intake of PUFA-foods such as fish, fish oils, and nuts, think twice. There is evidence that by so doing you will find yourself eating an unbalanced diet that causes elevated levels of uric acid in the blood. When uric acid is high, cells and tissues may be dying and a heart disorder may be in the making. Fats and oils together should constitute only 10 percent of the calories you consume.[24] *Of those*, it's best if 75 percent are PUFAs.

3. When you increase your PUFAs, you may be eating fewer eggs, no meat, and fewer foods rich in amino acids. This may be one of the reasons why you are looking and feeling older than you should. In one study, almost 89 percent of the individuals on a diet similar to that recommended by the American Heart Association suffered this hardly beneficial side effect.

4. Most people who switch over to a diet high in PUFA foods, especially corn, safflower, and soy oils and who also reduce their intake of healthy foods such as eggs, butter, and milk, make this change only because of advertisements provided in magazines, TV, etc. But advertisers of most popular polyunsaturated oils are violating government regulations when they carry unfounded, exaggerated statements on labels or elsewhere announcing the advantage of their oils over products such as butter, eggs, and meat. The country's largest medical association endorses these products silently by accepting their ads. Let the buyer beware: remember that those butter imitations are largely composed of cholesterol-elevating hydrogenated fats!

5. If you are sensitive to contact with pesticide residues, then stay away from supermarket oils and margarines.

6. Do you take all four tablespoons of polyunsaturated oil that the American Heart Association recommends you do each day? Maybe you won't once you learn that PUFA intake, without adequate vitamin E intake, destroys the cells.

7. If you are trying to lower your cholesterol by eating lots of low-calorie, protein-rich fish instead of red meat, moderation is the key. There may be a link between the mammary tumors and cancer of the stomach that has been found in men and women on diets high in this source of PUFA. However, eating fish occasionally does not seem to be a problem.

8. Is it a coincidence that breast cancer also, rose more than 100 percent when female rats were nourished on a diet high in cooked polyunsaturated oil?

• When PUFA levels are high in breast tissue, cancer in this part of the body is also likelier to be observed.[25]

• The University of Western Ontario adds that this cause and effect is seen in other parts of the body and in animal subjects. The researchers there found "a high correlation between intake of dietary fat and incidence of breast cancer."

9. If you have suffered a stroke or have angina, you no doubt have curtailed your dietary intake of cholesterol. But this step often *increases* the incidence of a future attack! And if you increased your PUFAs too much you run the risk of depleting vitamin E, which you need.[26]

10. So many disease-causing factors surround us that the elimination of just one risk can be significant. Consider then that in various test situations, steady diets too high in PUFA-rich foods have caused:

• Amyloidosis, in which a gelatinous substance is stored in large amounts. This state sometimes leads to old age disorders such as arthritis and mental illness.

• Hepatitis (perhaps due to a shortage of vitamin E to protect PUFAs from degrading).

• Cardiac disease.

• Dermatological disorders.

• Poor growth.

• Hearing loss.

11. Polyunsaturated fatty acids may have a potential for cellular damage. On a purified PUFA diet, say researchers at both Tulane and Duke universities, the liver's ability to keep you safe from poisoning is altered.

12. If you have asthma or emphysema, note that a high PUFA intake has a damaging effect on lung tissue. Red blood cells clump up in the vessels. This impedes blood flow and reduces oxygen delivery. These changes occur in a number of animals, and scientists suspect that man is no exception. If you have a special need for more oxygen and you also live in a high pollution area, this combination puts you at a double risk.

Summary

Polyunsaturated fatty acids (PUFAs) are necessary to provide your daily quota of the essential fatty acids. And decreasing saturated fats in the diet does seem to reduce the risk of heart disease (especially for people who get plenty of aerobic exercise, enough rest, etc.). But there are certain drawbacks to PUFAs, especially when they are practically the sole source of fat in your diet.

If you've fallen for the advertising implying that you should give up all saturated fat foods, including butter, eggs, milk, and cheese, and substitute margarine, ersatz eggs, etc., consider that a low-protein, high-polyunsaturate diet can lead to old-looking skin and a less-than healthy body. Too-high levels of PUFA in the diet have been correlated with cancer of the breast in animals; arthritis or mental illness; hearing problems; poor growth; cell damage; worsening of the condition of the lungs in cases of emphysema and asthma; and even heart disease, the problem to which PUFA is supposed to be the solution. Furthermore, cooking with polyunsaturates can lead to a chemical reaction usually limited to paint factories: the creation of extremely long carbon-chain compounds called polymers which your body is simply unequipped to metabolize. Polymerization, oxidation, and other unpredictable transformations are due to the presence of the electron-rich double bonds which characterize unsaturated fats. They are easy prey to any electron-seeking compound that may happen to be present in their vicinity.

Step by Step: Here's How Fats Get Digested

You may experience hunger pangs soon after lunching on only salad and dry toast, and there's good reason. Carbohydrates are digested fast; fats much more slowly. If you'd had a fat-rich steak and an oil-rich sliced avocado with high-fat cream dip, you might not feel like eating again for four or five hours, because that's how long such a rich meal must wait in your stomach.

Protein agents called enzymes break food down into its various components. There are no enzymes for fat digestion in the mouth or esophagus. Fat begins its digestion in the stomach. The processed protein and carbohydrate and the partially digested fat from your meal is moved from your stomach to your small intestine by the peristaltic action of your digestive tract.

Your small intestine has the job of breaking down and promoting assimilation of the fats in food. The fatty food remains in your system longer because the fat must wait for digestion until it reaches the duodenum, the first part of the small intestines. When it arrives there:

- The walls of the intestine release a hormonal substance that slows down the rate of elimination.
- This hormone also instructs your gallbladder to pump bile into the intestine. (Bile is produced by your liver but stored in your gallbladder.)
- Bile sets the process of fat emulsion into motion. Bile salts, present in the bile, emulsify the fat you have eaten. That is, they break the fat into tiny globules so fat-digesting enzymes can get at the individual fat molecules.

• A special fat-digesting enzyme enters the duodenum from the pancreas, where it is manufactured. It is called pancreatic lipase. Lipase breaks lipids into their components, fatty acids and glycerol. However, the lipase often can't separate all the fatty acids from the glycerol to which they are attached. Thus, the products of fat digestion are fatty acids, glycerol, and *glycerides*—that is, glycerol molecules to which one or two fatty acid chains are still attached. *Mono*glycerides have one fatty acid chain. *Di*glycerides have two.

• The bile salts surround small amounts of digested fats. In this form the fats are absorbed into the cells of the skin that line the small intestine.

• Fats are actually absorbed in the duodenum and the jejunum (the rest of the small intestine).

• Finally, peristalsis, contractions of the muscles lining your digestive tract, continues and any food that remains unabsorbed is transported through its final stages.

Summary

Fat digestion, which takes place in the stomach and small intestine, accomplishes the following:

1. Fats are transformed into water-soluble form.

2. A hormonal substance is released to slow down the rate of elimination.

3. Bile salts emulsify the fat into tiny globules so that fat-digesting enzymes can act on them.

4. Fats are then broken into their chemical components, glycerol, fatty acids, and some remaining mono- or diglycerides, and absorbed into special cells lining the duodenum and jejunum.

Fat Absorption

Digested fats (fatty acids, glycerol, and mono- and diglycerides) are absorbed into the system through the lining of the small intestine. Special mucosal cells there separate the bile salts from the fat components, and then distinguish between short-chain fatty acids (usually unsaturated) and long-chain fatty acids (usually saturated). The mucosal cells make a decision based on the distinction: the smaller, short-chain fatty acids pass right through the cell lining into the portal vein, which delivers them to your liver. Your liver will release them into the bloodstream as needed.

An interesting thing happens to the long-chain (usually saturated) fatty acids in the mucosal cells. They are recombined with the glycerol and glycerides which have accompanied them into the cell. In effect, the digestion process is reversed, and triglycerides are reformed. The process of breaking down and recombining fats will continue throughout the metabolism of the fats.

These long-chain fatty acids stay in the membranes of your gastrointestinal tract for some time. The mucosal cells coat them with protein to form little buds called *chylomicrons*. A chylomicron is a package designed for transportation of fats. From the intestinal lining, the chylomicrons enter the lymph system and thereby the general blood circulation directly, bypassing the liver.[29]

Malabsorption of Fats

This is a disorder someone in your own family may have. When it exists, bile production or flow is seriously slowed, or too few pancreatic enzymes may be available to handle dietary fats. This condition may be genetic or inherited, or it may appear as the result of some other metabolic defect. In any case, once established it may lead to deficiencies in vitamins A, D, E, and K, since they require fats for utilization.[30] Eating foods rich in the more easily absorbed short-chain fatty acids— milk and freshwater fish are two examples—in preference to marine fish, for example, may help. These fats are not transformed into fats a second time around like the fats containing more carbon. In other words, their absorption is less complex.[31]

Summary

Fat absorption takes place through the lining of the small intestine. However, special cells in the lining first perform a sorting and packaging function. They send short-chain fatty acids (usually unsaturated) to the liver. Then, they combine long-chain fatty acids with glycerol, or monoglycerides, or diglycerides (whichever remain from the digestion process). They package the resulting triglycerides (along with a bit of phospholipids and cholesterol) in a protein-encased bud called a chylomicron.

The chylomicrons then enter the general circulation via the lymph.

The sorting function of the mucosal cells may be helpful to people with problems absorbing fats, since short-chain fatty acids are shipped straight to the liver.

Bile: A Few Important Facts

If you wish to understand how your digestive system works, and how you can improve its efficiency, it's essential to know about bile.

What Is It and What Does It Do?

You can't digest fatty food without bile. Your liver manufactures bile as an end product of cholesterol metabolism. Bile often takes the form of "salts." The body's repository for bile is the gallbladder. It is released only when fat is present in the gastrointestinal tract.

How Bile Keeps You Healthy

Bile normalizes your absorption by emulsifying and hydrolysing lipids. It makes sure you absorb monoglycerides, triglycerides, and all fatty acids. And it transforms hydrogenated fats from your diet into a soluble form.[32] This is accomplished as bile, in the company of a small quantity of cholesterol (which is sent through the blood circuit that begins with your intestines), proceeds to and through your liver and returns to the liver, its starting point.[33] Only 2 to 5 percent of all of the bile secreted is not absorbed again. After this takes place in the small intestine, bile circulates, then establishes itself in the liver.[34] Any abnormality in bile production, transport, storage, or absorption will inhibit fat absorption.

WHAT OTHER PURPOSE DO THE BILE SALTS SERVE?

Bile salts serve one more very important purpose. Without them, you would not fully metabolize cholesterol and the fat-soluble vitamins such as A, D, E, and K.

Adipose Tissue

Right after eating a fatty meal, your blood fat levels rise considerably as the chylomicrons (along with some other lipids, including phospholipids and cholesterol) circulate through the bloodstream. Most of the fat from the chylomicrons, however, is soon deposited.

Your body saves fats just the way you save money. In the case of your metabolism, the "bank" is your adipose or fat tissue. It has "branches" all over your body. These little (or large) depots have a threefold purpose: fat stored can be drawn on for energy; it also serves, as you know, as a layer of padding or insulation, under the skin; and if you are thin, bruises show up in a flash, while on a fatter person they may be barely noticeable.

Just as money circulates constantly through a bank, fat is always moving through the bloodstream from one depot to another, even though it may not be needed yet for energy. Perhaps this is why overweight people tend to have high blood fat levels. Some researchers have estimated that every day as much as half the fat in your adipose tissue stores may change places![35]

All this fat is stored to make sure you always have enough energy to carry on with your life. A state of severe malnutrition may reduce body fat stores to 4 percent of body weight or less. By contrast, the figure may soar to 60 percent or more of total body weight in extreme overweight.[36] You can prevent this in yourself and your children by making sure you eat moderately at all times. This is most important when there is a genetic tendency to gain weight readily. Many experts speculate that when you overeat as an adult you cause your fat cells to increase in size, not number. Another possibility, according to this theory, is that when a pattern of gluttony gets started in childhood, fat cells become more numerous and remain that way through adulthood.[37]

If you want to keep your liver as healthy as possible, then avoid depositing too much fat in your fatty tissues. Your liver may respond by becoming too large to carry out its normal jobs. On a diet that reduces carbohydrates unfavorably, for example, your liver is forced to produce larger than usual amounts of fat to supply you with energy to get through the day. Fat is deposited in the liver when this happens. Deposits may also result from a junk food diet, one that is too high in calories, or one that is inadequate in more than one essential food group.

You can also keep your liver healthy by avoiding a diet high in saturated fats. Take this step and you will never have to worry about a disease such as hyperlipidemia in which adipose tissues degenerate because of excessive amounts of cholesterol or other fats.

Summary

Fat as we normally think of it—those layers of poundage under our skin, however thick or thin—is an integral, necessary part of the metabolism of dietary lipids: they almost all end up there sooner or later. It is wrong to attempt to make all the fat on your body disappear: you need fat as stored energy. Fat also provides insulation and padding to protect your internal organs, among its other functions.

However, too much fat in your adipose tissue, as the cells designed to store fat are called, can lead to liver disorders and other health problems.

Fats are always entering and leaving the adipose cells; that's one reason we can gain and lose weight so fast, depending on the number of calories we consume in relation to the number we expend. (Fats in the diet are not the only source of padding for your adipose tissue: excess carbohydrate and even protein are also converted to fat for energy storage.) In order to enter or leave, they have to be first broken up into their components, fatty acid and glycerol.

Oxidation of Fatty Acids and Glycerol

Your adipose tissues work closely with your liver and your glands. When you need energy, your endocrine glands signal the adipose cells where fat is stored to break the triglycerides in the cell back down into glycerol and fatty acids. This frees them for release into circulation. The fatty acid portion may be picked up and oxidized by virtually any cell in your body. Your liver usually then picks up the glycerol portion. Your versatile liver can oxidize glycerol for energy or use it to synthesize glucose, the fuel your body prefers to burn rather than fat. (It can do the same with a combination of glycerol and fatty acids, or even protein and carbohydrate.[38]) Your liver can also turn one type of fatty acid into another by increasing the length of the carbon chain.

Ketone bodies are a normal intermediate product of the oxidation of fatty acids in many tissues, particularly when you are consuming a lot of fatty acids at one time. Most cells can then use the ketone bodies themselves for energy. Liver cells, however, cannot, so when it metabolizes fatty acids, the liver releases ketone bodies into the bloodstream for use by other cells. Ketosis is the condition in which blood ketone levels rise above normal. It can lead to abnormally acidic blood (acidosis). Ketosis can be caused by starvation, low-carbohydrate diets, or problems with metabolism such as diabetes, in which insufficient insulin is produced. Insulin, as you know, is required for the cells to consume more than minimal glucose. When they can't consume glucose, they turn to fatty acids.[39] You can tell when a diabetic is insulin-deficient by the sweetish smell of one ketone body, acetone, on the breath.

Insulin and Fat Metabolism

You probably don't think of your pancreas when you look at a puffy egg-rich omelette, or a sugar-rich sundae, but you'd be right if you made that association. When your secretion of the pancreatic hormone insulin is normal, so is your fat metabolism. And the opposite, of course, is also true.

Have you been doing a great deal of strenuous exercise? Have you been on a strict fast? These are two conditions that lower your levels of insulin. And if your blood were to be analyzed, it would then appear rich in free fatty acids.

If you are diabetic, here are some things you should know. Doctors may report that your triglyceride levels are abnormally high. But do not make the assumption that any treatment designed to lower these levels is suitable for you. The reason for faulty fat metabolism in the nondiabetic is somewhat different than it is for you.[40] Elevated blood fat levels usually decline in response to insulin supplementation.

In a medical condition characterized by overproduction of insulin (such as hypoglycemia), blood lipid levels rise as insulin prods your liver to make more fat. It also triggers fat synthesis throughout the body, including cell membrane tissue. Some of these excess fats, as you may imagine, are diverted into the bloodstream. Excessive insulin production may also precipitate a step-up in triglyceride levels as well, especially if insulin levels stay high. No wonder hypoglycemics are often overweight.

When you change your diet or improve your health habits in such a way that insulin levels normalize, blood lipid levels decline and triglycerides are flushed from the blood.

Summary

While your cells oxidize glucose for most of their energy, they also use fatty acids for this purpose. At a hormone signal, your fat cells release fatty acids and glycerol into the blood. Any cell that needs them may pick up the fatty acids and oxidize them. Only the liver consumes the glycerol: it can oxidize it for energy, or use it to synthesize glucose for the other cells. However, it does pick up fatty acids, too: it can take one fatty acid and turn it into another, usually by lengthening the fatty acid chains. (It can't synthesize the short-chain essential fatty acids, though.)

Ketosis is a symptom that an unusually large number of fatty acids are being oxidized. This can occur in starvation, when the body is consuming its own fat reserves; on low carbohydrate diets, when virtually nothing is available to burn but fat or protein; or when the metabolism is inhibiting normal glucose metabolism, as in diabetes.

It's a Chemical Reaction: A Few Definitions

Before we go on to discuss compound lipids, it's worth reviewing their chemistry. When an alcohol compound called glycerol combines with essential or nonessential fatty acids, *simple fats* or *lipids* are formed.

When three of the essential fatty acids—linoleic, linolenic, and arachidonic acid—or three nonessential fatty acids join forces with glycerol, *triglycerides* are formed.

When one or more of the fatty acid chains of the triglyceride is missing, and some other substance is substituted in its place, you have a *compound lipid.*

When such a cluster includes phosphoric acid, choline, and two of the essential fatty acids, it is known as a *phospholipid.* (You may use one of these every day. It's lecithin.)

And finally, when two substances that lack the characteristic structures of simple lipids and the phosphorus of compound lipids are combined, as in a sterol such as cholesterol or vitamin D, for example, this is called a *derived lipid,* since it is derived from simple and compound lipids.

When either linoleic acid or linolenic acid is joined with as few as two or as many as five other lipids and a fat-soluble vitamin like vitamin E or A, you have produced a *compound lipid,* too.[41]

B_6 (pyridoxine) teams up with linoleic acid. Consequently, another essential fatty acid—arachidonic acid, the one found in large amounts in peanut butter—can be formed.

Lecithin: That Fabulous Phosphatide

One of the phospholipids provides a reason for including soy granules in your diet occasionally. It's called lecithin.

If you've ever sought out supplemental nutrients to help you lose weight, you may know about one function of lecithin. But this nutrient does dozens of other jobs, from lowering blood pressure to improving digestion.

According to Dr. Lester Morrison, whose lecithin-based diet, *The Low-Fat Way to Health and Longer Life,* has been widely praised, lecithin is one of the most significant nutrients to emerge in decades, considering the wide range of health benefits it bestows.[42]

What It Is

Lecithin is so important to your everyday health it's found in every cell.

Lecithin is manufactured in the liver. The ingredients are hard to picture, but you already know two—the fatty acids and an alcohollike (and sugarlike) substance called glycerol. These perform various nourishing functions throughout your system. The third, a derivative of the mineral phosphorus, which works with calcium, is a phosphate ester (this is a combination of phosphorus, oxygen, carbon, and nitrogen).

How It Works

Lecithin has a few unusual characteristics. For example:

1. Although small amounts of lecithin can be taken up by your system without transformation, this is usually not the case. Your body does not assimilate lecithin as it is. Instead, it goes into your digestive system, and there it is changed by the lecithinase enzymes. Later, after combining with fatty acids such as linoleic acid in the liver, it is reconstructed from its constituents, choline, inositol, phosphorus, and fatty acids. There are good biochemical reasons for this. Lecithin is improved by the addition of the EFA. And in this new, improved, reconstructed form, lecithin assists in disposing of blood clots that may collect in the arteries.

2. Authorities on atherosclerosis disease speculate that by emulsifying cholesterol, lecithin is able to reduce atheromas (fat buildup in the arteries) in animals and aid in its destruction.[43, 44]

3. How to improve your whole immune system: make sure you add high-potency lecithin granules to every salad, and sprinkle them into your health beverage. Experts theorize that this remarkable phosphatide improves globulin levels in your blood, and these must be in proper supply for proper immune function.[45] This means better resistance to all types of infection and disease.

What Lecithin Does for You

Preserves fats. Lecithin acts as a kind of natural preservative in your body. Without it, the fats in your body and those found in the foods you eat would be denatured by exposure to oxygen.

Improves digestion. This phosphatide changes fats into easily digested, water-soluble form. This chemical change allows you to absorb more of the fats you take in at each meal.[46]

Transports fats. You can't name an organ in the body that doesn't use fatty acids. But some systems, such as your nervous system, need more than others for a steady supply of energy and for protection. And some organs, such as the liver, need more fats for a variety of purposes. It is lecithin that regulates storage in all the body's fat depots,[47] and delivers fat wherever it is needed in the right amount.

If your brain or liver, for example, needs more cholesterol, lecithin gives this blood fat the required solubility, then carries it to the organ in need.

Benefits the bloodstream. If you know anyone who suffers from phlebitis, then you are probably aware of heparin. It is a natural blood factor that has an anticoagulation effect. If you are concerned about the health of your body's most important muscle, the heart, you ought to know about this substance. But when your lecithin is inadequately supplied, you miss out on this benefit, and run the risk of blood coagulating, particularly in the plaque areas of your arteries.

Similarly, lipoproteins are involved in favoring normal blood clotting. And lecithin is a lipoprotein booster of great importance.

Provides important nutrients. Lecithin is not just a crutch for dieters who must be concerned with emulsifying fats in the body. Nor is it merely a sort of protective medicine for those of us who may be susceptible to cardiac problems. Lecithin is food we cannot do without. It is a superior source of the mineral phosphorus, needed for a healthy skeleton; the B vitamin inositol; the essential fatty acids (EFAs); and a substance called choline.

Because it is a "food within a food" (especially when fortified with extra calcium to balance lecithin's high phosphorus content), it is possible that lecithin may be the reason people who switch to a diet that includes such protein foods as soybeans, eggs, and whole grains feel such an improved sense of well-being.[48]

Prevents vitamin deficiencies. Without lecithin, your body's efficiency in utilizing all of the fat-soluble vitamins would be seriously disturbed; you would actually derive 50 percent less vitamin A from foods such as eggs than you should. A similar type of reduction would occur in the case of vitamins E, D, and K[49] and carotene, since they are oil-soluble, too.

Improves brain function. Can't remember where you put your glasses? Can't seem to remember names and phone numbers the way you used to? Massachusetts Institute of Technology researcher Dr. Richard Wurtman has suggested that you may be able to give your brain a memory boost with more choline. Why not sprinkle some lecithin on your yogurt, salads, or soups at each mealtime. Choline is a precursor of a nerve messenger called acetylcholine, which is essential for a sound mind and a good memory. Lecithin is one of the best sources of choline available.[50]

And if you feel blue, note that the National Institute of Health reports success using lecithin-derived choline in addition to lithium to help patients suffering from depression.[51]

Contributes to normal cardiac function. If you have a family history of heart disease, or if you are predisposed for any other reason to developing hypertension or angina pectoris or arterial blockage in the limbs or neck, there *is* something nutritional that you can do for yourself every morning. And it not only tastes good, it has helped prevent or lessen the severity of the conditions just cited.

If you've been eating just a quick bowl of cornflakes for breakfast, here's something a little bit better to spoon into that bowl. Start the night before, if time is at a premium in the morning.

Step one: Combine the following in equal parts: soy lecithin, debittered brewer's yeast, untoasted wheat germ, and powdered calcium.

Step two: Mix two tablespoons of this combo with one tablespoon barley malt, one teaspoon cold-pressed safflower or soybean oil, and milk or soy milk or juice as needed to dissolve the sweetener. You might consider adding plain yogurt for creamier texture, or fruit, or even a tablespoon of granola or cooked whole grain cereal.

Where did the formula come from? It's called "The Lecithin Breakfast," and because it was invented by Dr. Jacobus Rinse, it is also known as the "Rinse Breakfast."

There are impressive studies from Europe that indicate that such a meal, enjoyed daily, lowers the incidence of heart disorders. But don't leave any of the essential ingredients out. These include vitamin C, E, and the linoleate from the lecithin, oil, and wheat germ.

Manufactures new cell material. Lecithin is an essential ingredient of all your living cells. It is on most druggists' counters and in every health food store in tablets, grains, liquid, and capsules, and for good reason. By interacting with proteins and cholesterol, lecithin is able to manufacture the living membrane material for every cell that keeps you alive. Enough lecithin means you will have healthy cells that do not lose their shape or degenerate. This is important because the accelerated death of cells leads eventually to earlier death for the entire body.

Sources: Important Facts

Organ meats, otherwise known as variety meats, are high as a source of lecithin. For example, almost one-third of the fat in the brains of all animals is lecithin. And nearly one-tenth of the contents of the other organs may be composed of phosphatide fats.[53] If the fact that lecithin from animal foods is also a source of saturated fat bothers you, or if you are a vegetarian, then concentrate on sources of this supernutrient from plants and dairy products. These include eggs, soybeans, cereals, and flours derived from whole grains, salad oils that are minimally processed (soybean oil is 0.3 percent lecithin), as well as all natural seeds and nuts.

Many commercial food products contain lecithin. If it is in a natural form, it may have a remedial effect on high blood pressure.

But, remember, refined foods are not a good source of lecithin compared with natural foods. Suppose you buy a commercial dessert made with milk, soy oil, and whole wheat flour. It sounds as if you should be getting lecithin from three sources. But are you? When fat is hydrogenated, the lecithin is destroyed.[54]

Before you consider how and where to fill your lecithin needs on a daily and weekly basis, there are a few points to consider. Studies suggest that the lecithin you get from unsaturated fatty acids in plant foods, for example, may do a better job of lessening the harmful effects of cholesterol than the lecithin you derive from meats and other sources of saturated fats. Buildup of cholesterol plaques may be better controlled by non-meat-based lecithin, too.

How to Use Lecithin as a Supplement

You can get more lecithin into your system with less trouble if you take lecithin itself rather than by eating several cholesterol-rich eggs or a pound of gassy soybeans. But lecithin wasn't always available in this convenient form. It was purely for practical reasons that lecithin was extracted from the soybean oil that is such a rich source of this substance. Transporting barrels of soy oil caused vessels to slow down considerably. The lecithin in the oil was absorbing extra water, adding extra weight. Converting soy oil into the concentrated forms we use today—without much lecithin—solved this problem.

When you buy lecithin in your health food store, it contains 30 to 40 percent oil, while 60 to 70 percent of the content is phosphatides. In addition, 1.3 mg/gm of vitamin E and 0.42 mcg/gm biotin is standard, but varies with the source.[52]

WHICH FORM OF LECITHIN TO BUY

Lecithin comes in a confusing variety of forms—liquid, grains, powder, capsules—and they are not all the same. Before you buy, here are a few things to look for:

1. *Phosphatidyl choline content.* If you are buying lecithin, look for its phosphatidyl choline content. (This is another way of describing how much lecithin it contains.) Encapsulated liquid lecithin should have a phosphatidyl choline content of at least 35 percent. It should also deliver a potency of at least 61.5 percent phosphatides. This is not the same as phosphatidyl choline. Ask if you are in doubt.[55]

Granule lecithin, however, should be labeled "25 percent phosphatidyl choline" (this applies to the oil-free powder as well). Most lecithin products on the market contain about 10 to 15 percent phosphatidyl choline. Granule lecithin or powder should deliver a potency of at least 35 percent phosphatides.

2. Is the product all lecithin with nothing added? There are "purity standards" that apply to lecithin. If you are curious, you will find them in the food chemical codex. Soy flour is sometimes added to granular products, producing a product with more protein but less potency—usually 40 percent less. Read labels to spot this practice.[56] Powdered dolomite (a source of calcium and magnesium) may also be added. Manufacturers explain this practice as "fortification," to balance the phosphorus present in the lecithin.

3. Are you buying *pure* lecithin? How can you be sure? "Food" grade lecithin suggests that soy flour may be an ingredient—not unhealthy but unnecessary. Oil-free powder is potent and does not have this fault.[57]

4. How much more do you want to pay for the convenience of taking your lecithin in capsule form? One tablespoon of the regular granular product of 10 to 15 percent phosphatidyl choline gives you as much lecithin as you'd get from nine 1200 milligram capsules containing 10 to 15 percent phosphatidyl choline.[58]

Summary

Lecithin is present in every single cell in your body, because each cell has a boundary called the cell membrane. Lecithin helps hold together the protein and lipid portions of this lipoprotein cell membrane.

Lecithin itself is a phospholipid. That is, it consists of a glycerol molecule to which are attached two fatty acid chains and a phosphatide.

Lecithin is indispensable to normal fat metabolism—and therefore, you should consume it to assure good arterial health. (Your liver does manufacture it if you don't eat it, though.) Having trouble with fat digestion? Try taking more lecithin. In the intestines, it helps improve digestibility of fats. It also acts as a natural preservative in the body of the particularly vulnerable essential fatty acids. It has been credited as a weight loss aid because it regulates the storage of fatty acids by helping dissolve them and carry them through the bloodstream. In addition, it is important to nerve function, and may improve memory. It also is one of the fatty components of the skin.

You can obtain lecithin by eating organ meats, bone marrow, eggs, soybeans (or refined soy oil), or whole grain cereals. (The vegetable sources may be used more efficiently by the body.) If you take a lecithin supplement, be sure, if it's liquid, that its phosphatidyl choline content is at least 35 percent, or if granular, that it is 25 percent phosphatidyl choline—and there's no need for added soy flour.[59]

The Secret Ingredient in Lecithin: Choline

There are seven big jobs that choline, one of the two little-known components of lecithin, performs for you around the clock:

• Regulates cerebral function.
• Normalizes operation of the autonomic nervous system.
• Aids in general growth.
• Assures adequate supply of milk for the breast-feeding mother.
• Prevents degeneration of the liver due to fatty deposits.
• Improves your ability to absorb and properly use fat soluble vitamins A and D.[60]
• May lessen the miseries of hypertension and kidney dysfunctions, two diseases that choline-deficient rats develop.[61]

How Important Is Choline?

Choline is no longer considered a vitamin, but it is still classed as an important lipotropic agent. That is, it promotes good fat metabolism.

Without choline, your body could not manufacture acetylcholine, which makes the transmission of nerve impulses possible.

Without the choline in your blood—derived from the food you eat —your brain and nerves would be deprived of food and could suffer deficiency that could wreck your mental stability.

HOW CHOLINE WORKS

You don't have to wait for illness to strike before you use choline. Choline can improve your memory, your sleep patterns, and your nerve responses. And there are no "roadblocks" to keep choline from passing from your bloodstream to your brain, such as occurs in your body's utilization of other elements.[62]

The following findings were reported at a conference at the Massachusetts Institute of Technology.[63]

1. If you get approximately 0.9 gram of choline a day, you are getting an average intake.

2. However, more choline is needed when your diet is high in fats and carbohydrates.

3. Less choline is needed when your diet is high in two of the amino acids, betaine and methionine. These amino acids make the choline in your diet go farther. If you are taking amino acid supplements, this may apply to you. However, the reverse is also true. More cholesterol, especially with more cystine, another amino acid, creates an increased need for choline.[64]

4. More choline is needed if you have any arterial disorder. When the diet of animals contains too much fat, choline is lowered and cholesterol deposits appear in the blood vessels and all the major organs.[65]

Choline as a Healing Factor

Egg yolks and legumes are also good sources of choline. Choline is essential for the proper functioning of your brain and adrenal glands. When you eat choline-rich foods like wheat germ, you increase the acetylcholine needed throughout your body to help in the transmittal of nerve impulses.

You get 20 to 30 percent phosphatidyl choline (250 milligrams of phosphatides) in each teaspoon of soy lecithin granules. This is plenty of choline, the healing factor in many hopeless and near-hopeless ills. Here are a few facts that highlight its usefulness.

Tardive dyskinesia is an iatrogenic illness caused by prescription medications used in treating various types of psychological problems. According to studies by researchers at Stanford University and MIT, almost half the TD patients receiving choline or lecithin showed signs of recovery.[66] Almost all ten of the TD sufferers seen by Dr. John Growdon of MIT likewise showed healthier levels of choline in their serum after this healing nutrient was administered.

When this neurotransmittal nutrient is used for other neural disorders, such as Friedrich's ataxia or Huntington's chorea (Woody Guthrie's disease), it has been shown to improve the metabolism. In fact, in Dr. Growdon's study, choline in chloride form caused serum levels to improve slightly less than 100 percent only half an hour after administration. An hour after ingestion, blood levels of choline reached an apex —actually more than two and a half times higher than that achieved using this ACH (acetylcholine) precursor in pure choline form. Moreover, this increase could be observed for a total of twelve hours. Choline is administered in lecithin to guard against a possible degradation of choline by flora in the intestines.

Any nutrient that shows potential for curing disorders so serious they disrupt the brain's functioning should be tested widely. This is true of lecithin, says MIT's Dr. Wurtman.[67, 68]

Inositol: Another Factor Hidden in Lecithin

You are getting inositol every day through your diet—in lecithin-rich foods like eggs and beans. And no doubt you take a B vitamin which contains inositol, too.

Inositol is one of the four basic categories of compounds essential for fat metabolism. The other three are choline, phosphatides, and fatty acids. For the best effects, get your inositol in your daily dose of soybean-derived lecithin.

Inositol is needed for proper growth and healthy musculature of the intestinal tract. It may prevent fat deposits in the liver and excessive loss of hair, as well.[69]

Summary

Choline and inositol are the two substances of which lecithin is composed. Both are important in fat metabolism. Choline, in addition, seems to be especially important in nerve function. In fact, it is a precursor of the neurotransmitter acetylcholine, a chemical that carries messages across nerve synapses. It is therefore not surprising that it can improve memory, sleep patterns, and nerve response, and has been shown to be useful in such neural diseases as tardive dyskinesia, Friedrich's ataxia, and Huntington's chorea. In addition, it is used by your adrenal glands.

Inositol is involved in the growth of the intestinal tract, particularly the smooth muscles lining it. It may also prevent too much fat from being deposited in the liver and excessive loss of hair.

Both of these components are found, of course, in lecithin sources such as egg yolks, beans, and wheat germ. Chicken and fish are also mentioned as sources of choline.

Healing Aspects of Lecithin

MENTAL ILLNESS

When your reserves of lecithin are low, your nerves are deprived of an important food. You are also shortchanging your brain, since lecithin, you recall, is the raw material for the brain's outer layer of insulation called myelin. It should come as no surprise, then, that lecithin is helpful in treating mental disorders, including retardation, in children.[70] And if lecithin, which is a totally natural food and not a drug, can reduce irritability, tension, and fatigue, and improve your thinking powers, why turn to tranquilizers? Drugs only worsen the condition when your nerve tissues, especially the brain's protective lining, are already low on lecithin.

Another serious mental disorder that many doctors call "hopeless" is Alzheimer's disease. Yet, two physicians, Dr. Pierre Etienne of Quebec and Dr. Janice Christie of Edinburgh, used lecithin and reported healing results.[71, 72]

Or consider the spinal cord disorder known as multiple sclerosis, MS. Usually considered incurable, MS has been helped by use of lecithin, a low-fat diet, and special nutrient intake. When you consider that proper nerve function depends on the fat supplied by lecithin for healthy nerves throughout the body, it is not surprising that it has proven helpful to MS patients.

Friedrich's ataxia is a nerve disease that often causes an inability to speak and difficulty in balance and coordination. A number of patients recovered these faculties on a regimen of 24 grams daily of lecithin over a sixty-day period, says Dr. Barbeau of the University of Montreal.[73]

SKIN DISORDERS

Many prominent nutritionists and health-oriented physicians have commented on dermatological problems being improved by lecithin. Are you troubled by eczema, acne, or painful and embarrassing disfigurements such as scleroderma? Ask your doctor about the advisability of using lecithin as an adjunct to the treatment he prescribes. This healthy way of handling skin disruptions is certainly nothing new. Your physician may even recall reading in the medical literature about California's Dr. F. Pottenger and his success in clearing the disorders mentioned as long ago as 1944. Perhaps old-fashioned lecithin can safely work some of the same benefits as today's cortisone does, without the harmful side effects of the latter.

ATHEROSCLEROSIS

If you suffer from atherosclerosis and must reduce your cholesterol levels by 40 percent or more, you might consider adding lecithin to your nutritional regimen. In an experiment conducted by Dr. Lester M. Morrison, two tablespoons taken before meals three times a day caused a remarkable lowering of serum cholesterol levels.

Lecithin can also be administered with good results in other ways. According to the Simon Stevin Research Institute in Bruges, Belgium, intravenous injections of soy lecithin once a day for two weeks resulted in a 40 percent reduction in cholesterol. It even reduced other lipids.[74]

Here are some of the reasons patients with infarcts may respond to natural therapy using lecithin:

1. Such patients show a higher body ratio of cholesterol to phosphatide than others. Experts speculate that a deficiency of phosphatide factors such as lecithin in the body sets the stage for the formation of atheromatous plaques. After all, as cholesterol fats rise and plaque formation proceeds, phosphatide levels fall.

2. Infarct sufferers also show poor reserves of catalysts called choles-

terol esterases. Such a person is unable to assimilate fats properly. Lecithin helps in such conditions, says Dr. Lester Morrison, president of Granshaw and Santa Ana Doctor's Hospital in Los Angeles. In fact, lecithin can help you even if the possibility of developing any type of arterial disease seems remote. To guard against such trouble, Dr. Morrison suggests, making a habit of having at least one tablespoon of supplemental lecithin each day, and up to four tablespoons if you prefer. Another reason not to forget to sprinkle these nutty-flavored grains on your morning cereal or evening salad: they may help you lose weight and improve your energy levels.[75]

3. Many victims of atherosclerosis must take medications that do something their systems can no longer do properly—clot the blood normally. Lecithin can help in a drugless way, says Dr. Armand J. Quick of the Medical College of Wisconsin, since it can reduce bleeding time in patients.[76]

GALLSTONES

Gallstones often yield to extra lecithin. No surprise, since a major ingredient in these stones is cholesterol, and lecithin is the number-one phospholipid in bile salts.[77]

A Few Final Facts About Lecithin

So vitally important is this cell-making nutrient that your body has the ability to make more phospholipids, including lecithin, in an emergency—if your body has enough B_6 to assist in the manufacturing process. Every cell is invested with this ability. But do not put the burden of supplying your lecithin needs on your body. Eat phospholipid-rich foods daily.

Phospholipids, like glucose, contribute to your energy levels, but unlike glucose, they can be assimilated without extra insulin. In addition, the more phospholipids in your digestive system, the better you will absorb those beneficial fats in the foods you eat. If you are diabetic, you will be interested to learn about one study in which individuals like you had a reduced need for the usual medication when given phospholipids such as lecithin.[78]

• Why is lecithin extracted from soy instead of egg yolk? Because soy oil is less saturated and has an improved ability to protect the organism from the risk of atherosclerosis.[79]

• Lecithin truly lives up to its reputation as an anticholesterol aid. Consider this study: in slightly more than one month, several individuals with hypercholesteremia who took the equivalent of 100 teaspoons of this pleasant-tasting, powerful phosphatide were rewarded with a drop in lipid levels of almost 80 percent. Further proof that lecithin lives up to its reputation: in six weeks' time, cholesterol levels rose 14 percent when participants ceased supplementation.[80]

• Take vitamin C when you have your daily lecithin "sprinkles." This combination helps to speed up the process by which cholesterol is made soluble and flushed from the system.

• Ascorbic acid and this soy-based antioxidant have in common the fact that both agents render cholesterol less harmful. Both help to keep cholesterol at normal levels in the body. We have research dating from 1942 illustrating these findings in the case of lecithin, and similar supportive material on the subject of vitamin C is on medical record.[81]

• Boost your vitamin E with a spoonful of lecithin.

• Some authorities consider soy lecithin more effective than vitamin E in preventing free radical peroxide formation. If you take a generous helping of wheat germ, nature gives you these nutrients already packaged together for your good health.[82]

Summary

Your nerves, your skin, your heart, and your gallbladder may be helped by adding lecithin to your diet. While it can be manufactured in your body (if you get enough B_6 in your diet), you really need it from your diet, too.

The fact that lecithin is one of the raw materials for myelin, the nerve sheath, may be of benefit in cases of multiple sclerosis, which involves myelin breakdown. It also helps explain its usefulness in treating mental retardation in children, and tension, irritability, and fatigue in adults. And some positive results have been reported in treating Alzheimer's disease with lecithin.

As an anticholesterol agent, lecithin works best with vitamin C in cutting blood lipid levels and also arterial plaque. This ability may also explain its value in dissolving gallstones without surgery.

As an antioxidant, lecithin helps prevent free radical peroxide formation.

Lecithin can give you more energy. Unlike carbohydrates, it does not require insulin to metabolize, and it aids in the metabolism of other fats.

Finally, if you suffer from psoriasis, eczema, acne, or other skin disorders, you may want to ask your physician about lecithin.

Lipoproteins and Your Health

Hyperlipoproteinemia. It's not a word you hear every day. But it does occur every day. If you are suffering from this disorder (or are concerned about cholesterol), it means your bloodstream has an abnormally high level of a substance that circulates fats in the blood. This substance is actually a compound containing both protein and lipids. Biochemists call it lipoprotein.

When we used the word bloodstream we meant that your blood really is like a stream. Like a brook running through fertile fields and nourishing the crops, it consists largely of water. And just as the brook can only bring to the crops planted in the fields minerals and other nutrients that are dissolved in it, so your blood can only carry to your cells those nutrients that it can dissolve.

Fat is an indispensable source of energy. Yet it's not compatible with water. What can your body do to carry fat downstream—build a raft?

Well, yes. The "raft" is made of materials like protein (and phosphate) that *will* dissolve. The vehicle for transportation of lipids down the bloodstream is lipoprotein.

By studying the lipoproteins, science is developing an understanding not only of nutrient transportation, but of heart disease as well.

The lipoproteins are described by their density—that is, by their weight relative to their volume. There are four kinds of lipoproteins (some scientists say five).

You are already familiar with the least dense of the lipoproteins, the chylomicrons. As you know, these are the first transporters of newly digested fats. Chylomicrons are made up almost completely of triglycerides: they are 90 percent triglycerides and only 10 percent protein, phosphate, and cholesterol. Chylomicrons don't figure into the picture when we worry about lipoproteins and the health of your heart, since they appear and disappear quickly after you eat any fats.

The three most important lipoproteins are very low density lipoproteins (VLDLs), low density lipoproteins (LDLs), and high density lipoproteins (HDLs). Their levels in your blood are more constant than that of chylomicrons. (The most prevalent fatty element in your blood, the free fatty acid/albumin complex, is also sometimes considered a lipoprotein.)

The high density lipoproteins are considered by heart specialists to be the "good guys," a delightfully colloquial and apt expression that has been widely adopted. The high density lipoproteins are mostly phospholipids—and you know how good one phospholipid, lecithin, is for your circulation.

It is very low density lipoproteins (VLDLs), and especially low density lipoproteins (LDLs) that are dangerous when too many of them are found in your blood. These are the main carriers of triglycerides and cholesterol between adipose and other tissues. The VLDLs are over 50 percent triglycerides and 20 percent cholesterol. The LDLs are nearly 50 percent cholesterol and about 10 percent triglycerides.

If you picture a piece of marbled beef as the fat is trimmed off, you will notice that a half-inch cube of fat (mostly, of course, saturated triglycerides) is much lighter in weight than a half-inch cube of meat. Triglycerides are not dense at all. Cholesterol is denser than triglycerides. And phospholipids, which contain the mineral phosphorus (adding to their weight) are denser still. That is why chylomicrons (90 percent triglycerides) are the *least dense* lipoproteins; those containing over 50 percent triglycerides and 20 percent cholesterol are *very low density;* those containing only 10 percent triglycerides but nearly 50 percent cholesterol are *low density;* and those containing mostly phospholipid and 20 percent cholesterol and very little triglyceride are *high density.*

Of all the lipoproteins in the blood, the LDLs (50 percent cholesterol) seem to be the worst for your heart. They have a tendency to stick to the walls of arteries and build up as plaque, narrowing the passageway and thereby causing an increase in blood pressure. Generally, the higher your LDL levels, the greater your risk of heart disease.

The higher your level of HDLs (mostly phospholipid), however, the better. You can have a high blood cholesterol reading, yet if your HDL levels are high, your risk of heart disease may still be low.

How can you raise the level of HDL in your blood and lower LDL?

The best thing to do is to get enough exercise. We don't know why, but HDL levels are raised by exercise. Other good health measures of the kind we have discussed throughout this book are also helpful: keep your weight down, eat a healthy diet, and get enough of all the vitamins and minerals you need. Another factor that can affect blood lipid levels is medication. Doctors have found that women with too low a level of HDLs can often be helped by switching from contraceptive pills containing estrogen to another form of birth control.

It can take months for blood cholesterol levels to change, even after you have adopted good health measures. Cutting animal fats out of your diet is probably not enough, in any event. Cholesterol is made by your body, not only from dietary fats, but from carbohydrates and even protein, as well. All of these make acetyl coenzyme A, which can be converted to cholesterol. A too-high cholesterol reading is usually a symptom of poor nutrition in general. Or it can be your body's normal response to certain stress situations. It has been noticed, for example, that people recovering from typhoid and certain other diseases have extremely high blood cholesterol levels.

Normally, blood cholesterol levels vary between 200 and 250 mg.

A reading of 300 would be abnormally high and of great concern. Unless HDL levels are also correspondingly high, high blood cholesterol levels indicate an increased risk of atherosclerosis.

Summary

Lipoproteins carry fat through your bloodstream to adipose tissue or any cell that needs it for energy, or to help manufacture hormones, vitamin D, and other substances made from fat. Lipoproteins contain varying amounts of triglyceride, cholesterol, protein, and phosphorus. The "good guys" among the lipoproteins are HDLs—high density lipoproteins, containing mostly phospholipids, and also carrying needed cholesterol and triglycerides. To raise your HDL levels, be sure to get enough exercise regularly.

LDLs—low density lipoproteins—are almost half cholesterol and about 10 percent triglycerides. These are the "bad guys" among the lipoproteins, the ones that can get caught on your artery walls. If your LDL blood cholesterol readings are high, your risk of heart disease is increased. Blood cholesterol levels do not change rapidly: cutting out dietary cholesterol is not enough, since your body manufactures cholesterol from carbohydrates and even proteins.

VLDLs are over 50 percent triglycerides and 20 percent cholesterol. They're really bad guys, too, since too many triglycerides in the blood are another factor in coronary heart disease. Alcohol, sugar, and refined starches are the dietary factors to watch if you want to keep your blood triglyceride levels down.

Chylomicrons and the free fatty acid/albumin complex are also sometimes considered as lipoproteins.

How Cholesterol Keeps You Healthy

Cholesterol cannot and should not be eliminated from the diet and the body. It's hard to imagine how you would stay healthy without this vital substance. You probably think of cholesterol as a kind of fat, since it is found in fatty foods. Chemically speaking, it is not a true fat at all but an alcohol. However, it is a special kind of alcohol, a steroid alcohol, or "sterol." In partnership with protein and lecithin, a combination that makes cholesterol water soluble, it aids the transport and metabolism of fats throughout the body.

You could not thrive without a supply of sex hormones or adrenal cortical hormones such as cortisone and aldosterone, vital regulators of your metabolism. Cholesterol is just as important as these. In fact, this complicated, waxy, but fluid traveler in your bloodstream makes the synthesis of the hormones possible, since hormones are derived from cholesterol.

Cholesterol is a constituent of the membrane structure of all the cells in your body. It works to keep each of the cells structurally strong. Cholesterol is also required for proper nervous system responses.

As for your hardworking liver, this organ uses up 80 percent of the body's supply of cholesterol. Cholesterol is used in manufacturing bile salts, which aid in the fat digestion process once they have been relayed to your small intestine.

You may not think of boiled eggs as the best things for a radiant complexion. But the cholesterol in those eggs keeps your skin from drying out and prevents it from blotting up water-soluble environmental matter that may be harmful.[83]

Cholesterol is so essential that your body makes its own cholesterol if you neglect to eat any. If you are healthy, it simply excretes any excess you eat by means of your bile salts. This is one of the remarkable feats of the liver. And even if there is some abnormality in the ducts of the bile, the liver responds by creating a new bile salt supply.[84]

The Cholesterol Scare

High cholesterol is not the only factor influencing heart disease risk. Even individuals with normal or low cholesterol levels can develop heart disease. Atherosclerotic buildup has been observed in nonsmoking athletes and seemingly healthy teenagers. Furthermore, there are ethnic groups where the staple foods are dairy products and meats (high in saturated fat and cholesterol, just like the American diet), yet no trend toward atherosclerosis is observed. Good health—even of the heart and vascular system—is a rule rather than an exception in these ethnic groups. The Masai tribes of Africa and the Eskimos are two peoples whose well-being contradicts the so-called cholesterol theory of heart disease.

Are you avoiding cholesterol-containing foods because radio, TV, magazine articles, and advertising have convinced you that cholesterol is a killer?

Have you cut your consumption of most dairy products in half like the majority of Americans?

If so, you may wish to reconsider your fear-ridden eating pattern. Here are a few more facts:

• Reputable researchers who are unaffiliated with the food industry or with food-industry-financed study groups tell us that cholesterol may not even be the number-one factor in the development of heart disease.

• It is true that cholesterol is present in large amounts in arterial plaque, which is characteristic of atherosclerosis. However, no hard evidence exists to prove that such a condition is the inevitable result of a high-cholesterol diet. Nor is there convincing proof that such buildup is even caused by dietary cholesterol.[85]

• Did you know that dairy products are very big business? Have you ever wondered why the multimillion dollar margarine business has gotten the polyunsaturates-for-your-heart message across so effectively with the blessing of the FTC and the AMA, while the less affluent egg industry has been ordered to stop pleading the cause of eggs as a valuable nutritional element? The almighty dollar could be a clue.

Scientists are not sure that it is good for your heart to substitute the so-called heart savers, the polyunsaturates, for cholesterol-rich foods. E. R. Pinckney and C. Pinckney are concerned that our nationwide fear of cholesterol may be raising our expectation of how much heart protection PUFAs can provide. Even the American Heart Association has delivered a report to the federal government citing the hazards of polyunsaturates. They say, in effect, that *no* conclusive evidence exists to justify a change in the type of fat people eat, and that polyunsaturates have not been shown to prevent heart trouble! It's possible they may even be implicated in cancer, says the American Heart Association.

Other authorities make the following points. Big profits are being made on "ersatz" eggs, butter, imitation bacon products, nondairy cream, etc., and millions are spent promoting these profit makers not only to you but to your family doctor at big medical conventions. The advertisers base their conclusions on tests results that are not universally accepted. There is *no real proof* that dietary cholesterol reduction will prevent hypercholesterolemia. Salad oil may also speed up the aging process. If food is at fault, why is it that over the last two decades there has been less saturated fat intake but more heart trouble? Other factors are obviously involved in this multidimensional, number-one human killer.

Cholesterol in Your Diet

Does yogurt lower your blood fats? Yes, and don't avoid other milk-based products if you're concerned about cholesterol. In one recent test comparing two types of yogurt and a low-fat milk, all three caused a lowering of up to 10 percent of blood fats.[86] Even low-fat milk caused a small reduction. And though triglyceride levels in the blood did not change, the result is impressive. And it is not the only research on record supporting the essential all-around role milk foods play in human nutrition.[91]

Before you restrict the increase of cholesterol in your diet, here are a few important points:

• Which protein to have—meat or fish—if your doctor has suggested cutting back? Dark-fleshed fish such as bluefish is lower in cholesterol than lobster or shrimp. Among meats, organ meats, especially brain, and variety meats from the glands are big cholesterol builders.

• If you automatically reject that steak with the streaks of fat, remember this, that cholesterol is found in all the cells of an animal raised for food. The visible fat may not be the best clue as to how much cholesterol you are getting.

• If your doctor insists you restrict dietary cholesterol, be aware that eating plenty of fiber with your meals can also help keep blood cholesterol levels low. And show the doctor the evidence reported here, that you may not have to eliminate all cholesterol-rich foods.

• Depending on the type, fiber-containing foods, taken with cholesterol may help keep blood cholesterol levels from excessive increases. This is because this roughage increases the speed at which your body gets rid of bile salts, thereby increasing cholesterol elimination.[87] Pectin from high-fiber natural foods may be the best type of fiber for this purpose. So don't pass up that fresh apple cake with the eggs and whole grains!

• Or how about keeping those high-nutrient proteins such as eggs and yogurt in your diet and compensating for the cholesterol content by putting more PUFAs in your diet, too?[88]

• Polyunsaturates such as those found in fish may produce a lowering of cholesterol levels of between 5 and 10 percent, with reduced triglycerides, too. In one study on record, in which two groups of religious professionals participated, a high fish diet produced these results. Also noted as a result of ingesting high levels of beneficial fish oils were higher HDLs and a mild rise of LDLs in the male volunteers.[89]

• To know how much cholesterol you are actually getting from your meals, you should consult a guide such as the following compiled by the USDA.[90]

Cholesterol Content of Common Foods

Beef, lamb, veal	70 mg	Chol/100 g	
Butter	250 "	"	"
Buttermilk	2 "	"	"
Cheese	100 "	"	"
Chicken	80 "	"	"
Chicken fat	65 "	"	"
Fish	50 "	"	"
Crab	100 "	"	"

Egg	500 mg Chol/100 g
Egg yolk	1700 " " "
Ice cream	50 " " "
Liver	400 " " "

Summary

Many Americans—doctors included—have been the victims of a massive scare campaign against cholesterol. The fact is, this substance is so vital to the health of every cell in your body that your liver manufactures it if you don't supply it in the diet.

Cholesterol is a complex compound lipid, a sterol. It is part of the membrane of every cell. It helps the liver manufacture bile salts used to digest fats, and it is one ingredient in the chylomicrons that transport fat. It is the most important chemical component of your brain by weight.

Not only that, but cholesterol is vital for your sex life! Important sex hormones are made from cholesterol, as are certain adrenal cortical hormones. Finally, it helps keep your skin moist.

Furthermore, while high blood levels of cholesterol are *one* factor predicting high risk for heart disease, they are by no means the only one. Diet, general nutritional level, stress levels, exercise, age, blood lipoprotein levels, genetic predisposition, and many other factors are involved. Finally, high cholesterol levels in the blood may not be due to dietary cholesterol, but cholesterol metabolism within the body.

Moreover, polyunsaturated fatty acid oils usually substituted for cholesterol-laden saturated fats have disadvantages, discussed earlier, especially when consumed in large quantities.

Cholesterol in Your Blood and Cholesterol in Your Tissues: There's a Difference

Cholesterol is found everywhere in all animal bodies. In human beings, more than 93 *percent* of the cholesterol in your body is inside the cells. But these days most doctors and heart specialists are concerned largely about *the other 7 percent,* the blood cholesterol, since it is the cholesterol circulated in your bloodstream, not that in your tissues, that is likely to end up clogging your arteries and thereby putting a strain on your heart.

1. Taking medication may increase your serum cholesterol more than eating eggs. Steroids, for example, can cause an increase of 50 percent in your blood cholesterol levels. Similarly, long-term medica-

tion with cortisone-derivative steroids has been cited as a factor in such cardiac conditions as atherosclerosis. Researchers at the Stanford University Medical School suspect that steroids may cause LDLs to multiply and thus cause cholesterol to rise; or that these drugs result in an increase in the production of VLDL.[91] This makes sense, since cholesterol is a type of steroid. If you are taking steroids, your doctor should be carefully monitoring your serum cholesterol levels.

2. Stress may raise serum cholesterol levels through a similar mechanism, because it elevates your body's corticoids. Being ill has an effect on serum triglyceride levels. In addition, an infectious disease state decreases the activity of lipoproteins, with possibly a small increase in serum cholesterol.

3. Severe hypercholesterolemia may also be caused by a rare genetic disorder. People with the severest forms of this defect have high blood cholesterol levels from birth, and are at great risk of atherosclerosis by their teens. This danger may prove to be controllable by a blood cholesterol lowering drug.

4. You can have normal blood levels of cholesterol but still have an excess of cholesterol in your body, it seems. The reason is that cholesterol is not a constant. It is part of an ester-bearing compound in the blood when it is attached to polyunsaturated fatty acids. It also moves back and forth replacing the free or unesterified cholesterol in your tissues.

5. If the word cholesterol makes you think of whipped cream and T-bone steaks, you are only partly correct. This substance is also produced in the liver, muscles, heart, sex organs, intestines, and even the body's largest organ, which is your skin. You cannot be certain that your cholesterol reading will pass the test, even though you may have become a vegetarian. Here's why.

• Your body can make as much as 1,500 milligrams of cholesterol a day, more than six times the amount you normally eat in a twenty-four-hour period.

• Your body responds to sharp reductions in dietary cholesterol by making its own supplies.

• The bile and bile salts from your liver and gallbladder can speed up or slow down storage of cholesterol in the gallbladder. They can also affect the rate of expulsion.

6. There are some surprising reasons why your cholesterol may be low or normal. Polyunsaturated fats in the blood lipoproteins can force out cholesterol concentrations. Polyunsaturated fatty acids may have a flushing-out effect on cholesterol deposits, either transforming them into bile salts or forcing the cholesterol out of the bloodstream and into cellular tissues.[92, 93]

7. If you live in Georgia, it's just possible your cholesterol profile is

totally different from someone living, say, in New Guinea or at the North Pole. Diet *may* be the chief explanation, but we are still exploring other factors—geographic variation, climate, exercise, life-style, etc.—that may be involved.

8. Something else you should know about the polyunsaturated fatty acids that probably appear regularly in your diet in the form of salad oils: they don't work miracles, but they may help ward off coronary heart disease by causing the cholesterol in the body to be used, circulated, or expelled.[94]

9. Cholesterol is assimilated from your diet by the same process as the other fats you eat. The cholesterol in that forbidden hot fudge sundae is taken up first by your intestines and transported to the body cells, then eventually is sent to the liver via the lymphatic system.

10. If cholesterol, whatever its source, isn't unnaturally building up on arteries in the form of plaque or circulating in your tissues, you might wonder what else it is doing. Actually, as much as one to two grains may be reprocessed and rerouted each day. Your gallbladder accounts for 50 percent of this turnover.

11. Has your doctor warned you about how saturated fats affect the health of your *liver,* as well as your heart? A diet rich in animal fats makes this organ work overtime. But it is the fat, and not that cholesterol, that deserves the blame. Your liver responds to a fatty meal by processing more fats and sending them into the blood pool.

12. Linoleic acid is a factor of importance. You should get 15 percent of your calories from salad oils, from linoleic acid-rich foods like cold-pressed oils, nuts, seeds, and nut butters. If you do, then high-cholesterol foods won't elevate your blood cholesterol levels as greatly as they might someone on a diet with limited linoleic acid. If your diet is a bit more praiseworthy than that of the typical American—who gets almost 40 percent of his calories from fats—you will probably escape the 25 percent elevation in blood cholesterol levels that occur to such individuals as a result of their eating patterns.[95] But even if you obtain most of your fats from PUFAs, you should still get only 15 percent of your calories from fats and oils.

Did your doctor confuse you when he said that even though heart disease runs in your family, you could keep eating that egg each morning? It's not as contradictory as it sounds.

A Cholesterol Quiz

1. What would happen if 40 percent of your calories were eaten in the form of hard fats such as lard, and in addition you took in 500 milligrams of cholesterol from egg yolk?

Answer: You would be consuming the typical American diet, which is one of the major factors that keeps heart trouble at the top of the list as a killer disease.

Significant increases in arterial plaque and bloodstream levels of beta-VLDL were observed in different kinds of test animals who were fed a diet containing only slightly more cholesterol, and fat, than the above unhealthy, fatty diet. It was reported that the risk of heart disease increases when we take in excess cholesterol, even though our bodies produce their own cholesterol.

2. True or false: Low cholesterol means good health.

Answer: False. If you have low cholesterol, it isn't necessarily an indication of good health; it may be a side effect of anemia. A below normal reading is sometimes the consequence of hepatitis as well. Or it may be a clue that your body is storing up excessive amounts of toxins such as mercury, lead, or cadmium.

3. True or false:

(A) If your doctor takes your cholesterol reading once, that's enough to decide on your blood lipid status.

(B) Elevated blood fats always mean disease of the heart muscle.

(C) Neither stress nor racial background are significant factors in heart disease or cholesterol levels.

Answer: Actually, all of these myths are false:

(A) Your cholesterol can go up and down even in the course of one hour. It should be assayed several times before any conclusion is reached.

(B) High cholesterol in the blood may indicate heart disease. But it can also mean that you have a kidney disorder, pancreatitis, hyperglycemia, protein deficiency, an underactive thyroid (hypothyroidism), even bone cancer. Are you in bed with a viral disease or are you a mother-to-be? Surprisingly enough, even these conditions can be responsible for an apparently worrisome cholesterol report.

(C) Stress can be a significant factor in cholesterol levels; and your racial background or family genetic inheritance may also affect your cardiovascular health.

4. Can vitamin deficiency cause atherosclerosis?

Yes. If you are deficient in vitamins C and E and/or nicotinic acid, you are at special risk. For example, when the body's cells are saturated with ascorbic acid, cholesterol levels tend to decline. Also, sufficient vitamin E can help prevent heart disease by improving blood circulation and blood oxygen efficiency. Nicotinic acid, also known as B_3, is the third nutrient commonly missing in the American diet, which so often is implicated in the development of heart disease. These findings have been noted in *Supernutrition* by Dr. Richard Passwater.

5. What about mineral deficiency? What minerals are important to the health of your heart?

Calcium, magnesium, and zinc are essential for the health of your heart. Do you *over*indulge in whole grains, love all those high-fiber carbohydrates like granola cereal? Beware! *No* food should be taken beyond your actual needs. The phytic acid in grains can bind up zinc and calcium, keeping them from being absorbed by your intestine. And do you cook with chemically softened water and drink it throughout the day? Beware again! This water is not only fairly high in sodium, but has too little calcium, too little zinc, and too much copper.

6. True or false: There is no one "normal" serum cholesterol level for an individual.

True, your level is changing constantly. A few, but not all, of the factors that contribute to fluctuations include:

- Stress
- Strenuous exercise
- Sleeping disorders
- Undernutrition/malnutrition
- Pregnancy
- Many drugs

A poor diet is probably a more important contributor to hypercholesterolemia than nondietary factors.

If your serum level falls between 125 and 200 milligrams of cholesterol per 100 milliliters of blood, this means you have probably adopted a reasonably healthy life-style. What's high? Some experts say 175, others say 275 milligrams. It's best to discuss this with your own trusted and qualified physician.

Summary

High cholesterol in your bloodstream does not necessarily mean you have too much in your tissues. In fact, it may mean the opposite.

There are numerous factors besides diet that can affect blood cholesterol levels. Medications such as cortisone-derived steroids can increase them significantly, causing harmful low density lipoproteins to multiply as well. Stress, including illness, can have the same effect. And levels may fluctuate from moment to moment. Deficiencies of vitamins B$_3$ (nicotinic acid), C, and E can also cause increases in blood cholesterol levels. Nor will your heart be healthy without proper levels of necessary minerals such as zinc, magnesium, and calcium.

Blood Triglycerides and Very Low Density Lipoproteins (VLDLs)

Blood triglyceride levels are another factor in cardiovascular disease. To be accurately measured, they must be tested after fasting. Suppose your breakfast consisted of two greasy, sugary donuts, sweetened fruit juice, and coffee with sugar. After such a meal, your triglyceride blood level can increase by 50 percent, especially if your blood fat levels are already up.[96] Following such a meal, not only are dietary fats circulating as chylomicrons, but dietary sugar is also transformed into fat in the liver. The fat is then transported through the bloodstream by the lipoproteins—mostly VLDLs.[97]

When blood triglyceride levels are measured, the readings are determined mostly by the levels of VLDLs in the blood, since these carry the bulk of the triglycerides present.

Blood triglyceride levels respond to changes in diet much faster than cholesterol levels. (Some believe that high triglyceride levels cause high cholesterol levels.) It is still controversial which dietary changes are the most effective. The conventional wisdom is to cut dietary fats in order to reduce both cholesterol and triglycerides. But, as Dr. Robert Atkins points out, most people who begin to become diet-conscious by reducing dietary fats also make other beneficial dietary changes—such as cutting down on refined carbohydrates—as well. In his experience, the most important foods to eliminate or cut down on to reduce blood triglyceride levels are alcohol, sugar, and starch, in that order.

Also if you are an adult male, a diet high in sugary foods may cause a significant rise in blood triglycerides.

There is also evidence that a high sugar intake causes a rise in the fats found in epithelial tissue. Triglycerides are also metabolized in your skin cells. This is one reason why counting calories is not enough when you diet; you need to cut out sugar in order to look and feel slim.

Remember when you are tempted by junk food that refined sugar leads to unhealthy buildup of fats in your liver and fat-storage tissues. So if you love to eat, drink, and be merry, try eating whole, unprocessed foods, and drinking fresh vegetable juices, or fruit juices mixed with bubbly spring water, instead of bourbon or beer. You'll enjoy better health, look better, and have more years in which to be merry.

If your doctor warned you that you are "carbohydrate intolerant," this means you should not eat sugary or starchy foods, especially when highly refined. You are at greater risk of incurring high triglycerides than other individuals. It may also mean that you have greater difficulty ridding your blood of the fats that occur after a high-carbohydrate meal.[98] Your diet should therefore include *complex* carbohydrates, instead of refined foods high in sugar and starch. Fruits, vegetables, whole grains in their natural state, and other natural carbohydrate foods such as potatoes and even whole grain pasta will not raise your triglyceride levels the way refined sugar may.

Diet is not the only factor that can raise blood triglyceride levels. Your genetic predisposition can make a difference. So does the health of the glands that regulate fat metabolism, including the adrenals, thyroid, and pancreas. Your thyroid gland helps regulate the breakdown of fats and the rate at which they are consumed for energy. In a condition of hypothyroidism, blood lipoproteins are elevated—especially those of the low density type.

But the pancreas is the most important. It is the pancreas that produces insulin, the hormone that lowers your body's blood sugar. Diabetes raises blood triglyceride levels, as does any insulin disorder. Any stress or other influence which causes your pancreas to over-produce insulin will also raise triglyceride levels. This is why alcohol, refined sugar, and refined starch (which the body rapidly converts to sugar) affect triglyceride levels: your body produces extra insulin to cope with the flood of sugar (alcohol functions like refined sugar, but even faster), and the insulin instructs your liver to produce VLDLs quickly to use up this flood of sugar by turning it to fat. When insulin levels are lowered, generally blood triglyceride levels are, too.

If you're hungry, remember that high-sucrose, high-starch pastry will increase the triglyceride-laden VLDLs in your body while lowering not only the LDLs, but also the more beneficial phospholipid-rich HDLs.[99]

If you are diagnosed as having triglyceridemia—or any other high-blood-fat disorder, for that matter—don't try to treat it yourself. You must consult a specialist. But you should be aware that there are many measures you can take, starting today, to improve your condition. In general, losing weight if you are overweight should be your first objective, along with careful attention to a balanced, healthy, low-sugar diet.[100]

Specifically, when both LDLs and triglycerides are up, you must sharply reduce dietary fats and calories from all sources and eliminate all alcohol consumption and cigarettes. Complex carbohydrate foods such as fruits, vegetables, bran muffins, and dried fruits should replace refined, store-bought snacks high in sugar, salt, and starch.

If triglycerides are increased in relation to cholesterol, this is a distortion of the ratio of cholesterol to triglyceride. Usually, if it is under 0.3, external symptoms such as changes in the tendons and wrinkling of the palms may be noted. The dietary recommendations listed above are applicable in this case, also. In addition, you will be helped by avoiding creamy dishes, sauces, gravies, and any dish that has been fried or heavily buttered. Consider fruit for dessert, and save low-fat cheese for no more than an occasional treat.

When hyperlipidemia has arrived at an advanced stage, a variety of symptoms may appear. The most serious is an increased risk of coronary atherosclerosis. Imbalance in the nerves and muscles, and severe discomfort in the abdomen may also emerge. There may be no "cure" at this stage, but fasting under supervision may help, followed by adoption of a sensible diet. You may have to exercise many cautions for years, suggests Dr. Tzagournis of Ohio State University, but this should not be seen as an inconvenience in view of the health benefits.

If these "natural" remedies don't work, vitamins such as nicotinic acid may be prescribed, although excessive amounts may produce undesirable side effects.[101] Nicotinic acid, which you may know as vitamin B_3 or niacin, can reduce cholesterol and triglyceride levels in the blood. Side effects are also a danger with frequently prescribed VLDL blood-fat-inhibiting medications such as clofibrate. At a meeting of the Federation of American Societies for Experimental Biology, Dr. Nina Mercer of the University of Western Ontario reported that in a study where soy protein drink was substituted for milk, cholesterol levels were lowered.[102]

Summary

Blood fat levels—specifically, the levels of simple fats, triglycerides—are one of many factors implicated in increased risk of heart disease. Right after a heavy meal, chylomicrons flood into the bloodstream carrying triglycerides. But there are always some VLDLs, along with the other lipoproteins, circulating triglycerides. Triglycerides are formed from both dietary fats and sugars. Fasting blood triglyceride levels are the ones measured as a predictor of coronary heart disease risk.

Factors that can increase blood triglyceride levels include diet, genetic inheritance, diabetes, exercise and life-style, stress levels, and carbohydrate intolerance. The most important is probably the amount of refined carbohydrates, especially sugar, in the diet. If you have high triglyceride readings—especially if accompanied by high LDL levels—your doctor will no doubt insist that you cut down, not only on sugar, but on fats and total calories as well.

High blood triglyceride levels not only increase your risk of coronary heart disease, atherosclerosis, etc. They can also cause extra fat deposits in your liver and under your skin, unbalance your nervous or muscular systems, and cause abdominal discomfort.

What Causes Atherosclerosis? A Few of the Theories

DIETARY CHOLESTEROL

If you were keeping abreast of health news in the early 1920s, you would have witnessed the birth of the theory that too much cholesterol causes heart disease. It was a result of feeding a diet high in cholesterol, especially eggs, to a group of nonhuman subjects. When the vascular systems of the animals were examined, the considerable erosion, in the form of plaques in the vascular system, was attributed to the rabbits' diet. This theory has not been totally proved yet, although it is given great credence in conventional medical circles.[103]

ARE YOU GETTING SUFFICIENT B₆ AND METHIONINE?

It is interesting to note that several factors within your control will assure you of heart-protective amounts of both B₆ and methionine.

- High-fiber fruits and vegetables eaten raw have fair amounts of B₆, but only when consumed uncooked and unprocessed. B₆ is water soluble and may also be destroyed by heat.
- Avoid unnecessary medications which destroy B₆. Contraceptive pills are one example.
- Take a B₆ supplement if you are in your middle or later years. B₆ reserves decline with age. (It's okay to take it as part of your regular B-complex or multivitamin tablet.)
- Keep protein intake moderate. Excessive protein elevates your B₆ requirements.[104]

THE WEAKENED BLOOD VESSEL CONCEPT

In this theory, dietary fats play a role, but a less important one, says Dr. W. E. Stehsens. Primary in this concept, which may be referred to as "the vibration injury to vessel" theory, is that the blood vessel walls are in a state of deterioration, probably in response to high blood pressure. There are a number of explanations, as we know, for blood pressure irregularities—including smoking, inactivity, stress, and poor diet, to name a few.[105]

EXCESS SUGAR THEORY

According to Dr. John Yudkin, it is overeating of refined carbohydrates—sugar above all, in all its forms—that is a major factor in the formation of those patches in the arteries that shorten so many lives. Sugar gives you nothing of nutritional value but empty calories. Meanwhile, to process sugar, your adrenal glands must work overtime, and eventually the delicate hormonal balance in the body is destroyed.[106]

XANTHINE OXIDASE THEORY

Start eating those folate-rich leafy greens if you're a big milk drinker. According to Dr. Kurt Oster of Connecticut, an enzyme substance called xanthine oxidase in milk is what starts arterial plaque formation by manufacturing the first lesion. Fortunately, folic acid—a B vitamin—can help to cancel this effect.

Vitamins That Help Prevent Heart and Vascular Diseases

VITAMIN E

You need vitamin E to protect the fats in your diet and in your body. Vitamin E is oil soluble, and thus the body can store supplies of it. If you conclude that you don't have to worry about having enough, though, realize that all the vitamin E you take is not assimilated. Also, the fact that vitamin E works in partnership with the fats may render your levels lower than they ought to be. Vitamin E and cholesterol, for instance, are relayed by the lipid proteins in your blood. And if these are in short supply, your vitamin E may be low, too.[107]

Tocopherol the active ingredient of vitamin E, can be decreased if you are taking too much cod liver oil, or if you are using excessive amounts of fish oil in your meals. And tocopherol may be decreased in adults who consume too much PUFA over an extended period—without vitamin E supplementation.[108]

Your red blood cell membrane is rich in PUFAs, but if your body levels of vitamin E get too low, these membranes can literally burst. Low levels spell other trouble besides. Hemolysis—resulting in low levels of all fats in your blood and symptoms of aging—usually goes hand in hand with vitamin E deficiency.

If you had to pick the most important nutritional weapon there is in the fight against old age, it would be vitamin E, which performs its antiaging role by preventing the damage of cell tissues by oxidation. Dangerous substances called *free radicals* are released in your system when polyunsaturates are broken down in certain ways. Also, both cell tissue and body stores of protein are adversely affected.

The damage done when free radicals are released is serious, according to experts who observe the consequences that occur as a response to various types of intended or accidental radiation exposure.

Aging symptoms such as altered pigmentation arise as a result of the process just described. But vitamin E can prevent the process from starting, especially if you take it along with extra amounts of ascorbic acid.

VITAMIN C

Not only does vitamin C fight colds and other infections, it also has been linked to the health of your heart. Here are some of the findings.

• The cells of all your muscles—and that includes your heart and all the vascular passageways, which are lined with tiny muscles—require specified amounts of stored ascorbic acid to keep your cholesterol normal. Therefore, unless you supplement your diet with extra vitamin

C, you are likely to be more susceptible to heart trouble when your vitamin C intake is low during the colder months of the year. Studies by Drs. Ginter and Onizer of the Institute of Human Nutrition Research in Czechoslovakia, pursued for a twelve-month period with adults and children, support this theory.

• Rejoice if you are a vegetarian. Your chances of having a healthy heart are greater, because you automatically ingest more vitamin C. British pathologist Dr. Constance Spittle says ascorbic acid can lower your cholesterol levels by 10 percent.

• And, in this country, experiments bear out Dr. Spittle's findings —that atheroma formation (the process of fatty degeneration of the inner coating of the arteries) is lessened when the diet is high in vitamin C.

• Another animal experiment found that this amazing vitamin lowered the cholesterol levels in rats that had been raised on a high-fat diet.

Contraceptives and Heart Disease

Use of birth control pills may undo some of the good you're doing your heart with vitamins and a proper diet. Here's why.

1. Contraceptives elevate triglycerides, often to abnormal levels. Large amounts of contraceptives, taken regularly, also increase your chances of stroke or heart attack, because they raise all of the other lipids almost as much. The rise may be in the vicinity of 30 percent or more.[109]

2. Some combinations of progesterone and estrogen are worse than others. Here are a few findings reported by *Fertility and Sterility*, Vol. 26, No. 1, January 1975: While negestrol acetate had no effect on serum lipids, norethirdrone ethynodiol diacetate and nestrarol elevated triglycerides. In general, estrogens have the effect of raising both phospholipids and triglycerides, and of lowering cholesterol. How concentrated are the estrogen and progesterone in your pill? This, it appears, is the factor that determines the extent of the danger.[110]

If you have high cholesterol, or if any other elevated lipid is already a problem, you should beware of contraceptive use. Age is a factor, too, in body chemistry. Women not yet at the menopausal stage have lower blood fat levels, generally, than older women.

If your blood pressure is already over the normal limit, birth control medication may raise it even higher. If the amount of estrogen you are getting from your medication is too high, you may also be creating abnormally high vitamin A levels in your blood.[111]

Atherosclerosis: Fact and Fiction

Fiction: A few glasses of milk each day probably increase your risk of heart disease. So do eggs.

Fact: Dairy products eaten in moderate amounts do not raise blood cholesterol levels dramatically in the healthy individual.[112]

If the dietary cholesterol theory were sound, what would be the explanation for low serum cholesterol levels and low level of atherosclerosis among population groups such as the New Guinea tribes, Bedouins, and Eskimos?

Fiction: Medication is the best way of altering an unfavorable blood cholesterol reading.

Fact: It is always best to try natural methods first, and there are many drugless ways to influence blood fat levels. An exercise program, especially vigorous walking, running, or swimming, is often effective. Also, switching from the customary three big meals a day to smaller, more frequent meals has proven remedial for some sufferers, as has eliminating refined sugar from the diet.

Do vitamins work? One, in particular, is worth investigating. Nicotinic acid, a nutrient we know better as B_3, niacin, or niacinamide, reduces blood lipid levels. Although it may not change your HDL levels, many individuals have been rewarded by lower VLDL and LDL levels when taking nicotinic acid regularly.

It is probably effective because of its ability to keep the bloodstream from accumulating free fatty acids. When these substances leave fat-storing tissue, they may migrate into the bloodstream.[113] Calcium in doses of 2,000 milligrams daily has also been helpful for some patients, while doses of silicon in a water solution has produced a blood fat reduction for others.[114] Ask your doctor, too, about the possibility that you may have a deficiency of the B vitamin biotin, if you are a victim of the blood fat disorder hypercholesterolemia.[115]

Drugs, in fact, often have highly unfavorable effects on cholesterol metabolism. A drug such as alcohol, for example, may increase triglycerides by 50 percent, even though it does not effect cholesterol and VLDLs as much.[116] And there is medical evidence indicating that lipid levels may shoot up in some individuals in response to treatment with hormonal agents such as steroids and estrogens, as well as the phenothiazines, major tranquilizers.

Besides vitamins, certain foods may have cholesterol-lowering properties. Research tells us that protein from soybean-based foods may be effective, since they are almost fat free and high in many nutrients and B vitamins. It is worth incorporating soy oil, soy milk, cheeselike tofu, or soy sprouts in your weekly meal plans.

Fiction: Protein-deficient diets are another cause of hypercholesterolemia.

Fact: In reality, cholesterol levels will most often be below normal as regards LDL and VLDL content, with HDLs in normal supply,[117] when you follow a low-protein diet.

Fiction: To prevent atherosclerosis you should abstain completely from the foods that are richest in cholesterol.

Fact: Not so. Here's why.

1. You may actually be inviting heart disease when you eliminate all cholesterol-containing foods from your diet, because you could be eliminating some of the best dietary sources of important minerals essential to body processes not yet completely understood. Eggs and dairy foods are rich sources of these nutrients.

2. Furthermore, research indicates that it may be healthier to follow a diet in which lipids represent approximately 15 percent of your caloric intake, and in which there are balanced amounts of saturated and unsaturated fats.

3. You cannot fully metabolize certain nutrients, such as the oil-soluble vitamins A, D, E, and K, without fats in your diet. Indeed, many foods that are good sources of these vitamins are foods in which fats are normally present.

Fiction: Records indicate that the cholesterol-controlled diets recommended by most physicians have had the greatest success in halting heart disease.

Fact: Actually, some experts feel that these diets may have caused increased mortality, only creating the illusion of success because the conventional cholesterol-control diets are usually accompanied by an increase in vigorous exercise, weight reduction, and a closer monitoring of blood pressure levels. Alcohol and cigarette use may also be terminated at this time.

Fiction: Vitamin E plays no role in cardiac disease control.

Fact: In the opinion of Dr. Wilfrid Shute, a pioneer in the clinical use of vitamin E, plaque may actually be the result of deficiency of vitamin E and other antioxidants. When the unsaturated fats present in your tissues and in your foods are exposed to free radicals, plaque may form. Growth of the dangerous plaque may be prompted further when the individual exposes himself to polluted air, contaminated water, and other environmental ills.

You can best protect yourself from this chain of events by improving your antioxidant status. This calls for increased amounts of vitamins

E and C and selenium. All three will stand guard over the highly vulnerable fatty acids in your system so that free radicals do not arise. In addition, ascorbic acid also acts to dislodge cholesterol deposits. To make certain these vitamins operate at maximum efficiency, a well-balanced, low-sodium diet should be followed, negative health habits should be examined, and a program of exercise to eliminate stress should be started.

Sir John McMichael believes "the time has come to avoid making any substantial change towards polyunsaturated fats in the diet, as this change will not prevent coronary disease but could possibly have other damaging effects on the heart and circulation." Vegetable oils, in his opinion, may cause more damage than the animal and dairy fats.[118]

Summary

No one knows for certain why any particular individual develops heart disease. There are many theories as to its causes, and each points to a different factor that is no doubt important.

High dietary cholesterol has received the most publicity. Though it may well be a contributing factor, high dietary fat levels are probably really more like the culprit. Dr. Kilmer McCully has noticed that B_6 deficiency leads to a buildup of the substance homocysteine, which may increase plaque formation.

Weakened blood vessels due to high blood pressure may be the cause, or may lead to the buildup of LDLs at weak points.

Excessive sugar in the diet and its influence on blood triglyceride levels is another possibility.

Milk contains xanthine oxidase. Could this enzyme trigger plaque formation?

Hormone contraceptive use also alters blood fat levels, and has been shown to increase women's risk of heart and artery disease.

Finally, deficiencies in one of two vitamins, C and E, can be harmful to your heart. Vitamin C helps keep cholesterol levels normal. Vitamin E, the antioxidant, is extremely important, as it prevents the formation of free radicals from PUFA breakdown; these are as dangerous as radioactive contamination.

Gallstones

How's your diet? If it's rich in sauces, gravies, fried foods, and butter, you may be headed for gallstones. Eating patterns like this raise the body's cholesterol and phospholipid levels and reduce the amount of lecithin in your body. This is undesirable because a certain amount of lecithin is essential to prevent your bile from becoming cholesterol-logged.

Although there are cases of individuals following low-fat diets for weight loss who nevertheless developed gallstones, in general, gallstones occur when too much bile salt is secreted, due to unhealthy levels of cholesterol and other lipids in the body.[119]

If you want to avoid gallstones—as everyone should, since they can be quite painful—avoid rich fatty foods. This is the factor that caused gallbladder problems for monkeys in laboratory tests. And we are, after all, biochemically speaking, not all that different from the simian family.

Overweight: The Health Consequences

It is estimated that nearly half of adults over forty in this country are more than 20 percent overweight. If you or any member of your family are quite a few pounds overweight, don't consider it just a nuisance. Obesity can be hazardous to your health in numerous ways.

• Excess calories are transformed into fat which is stored in the fatty tissues throughout the body. But that's not all.

• Overweight can cause cellular hypertrophy or hyperplasia. If you are seriously overweight, it's more than possible that you are affected by both disorders. In cellular hypertrophy, cells designed to store fat become abnormally swollen. In cellular hyperplasia, your body may produce a surplus of fat cells.

• Hyperplasia victims have trouble losing weight once the fat cell process has gotten a good hold.

• Protect your children from a lifetime of unhappiness over their appearance by controlling their weight. Extra fat cells acquired in youth may become permanently established in the body. Although serum triglyceride levels may not rise as they do in grownups, children who overeat usually complicate their misery by leading sedentary lives.

• If you are sedentary, then expect any calories over the average of 2,500 daily (depending on your weight and metabolism) to go into storage, contributing to extra fat, and burdening the kidney, liver, heart, and all other major organs.

Losing Weight: A Few Tips on Different Methods

1. *Fasting.* On 600 to 1,000 calories a day, you will lose slightly less than a quarter to half a pound per day. At first, it will be water; later

you can expect that fat and some lean protein, rather than water, will disappear. A bonus for the obese is that unhealthy fat deposited in the liver is often reduced as well. But *fasting should not be done except under medical supervision*. Side effects of diets that border on starvation can include reduced blood pressure, dehydration, and protein deficiency.

2. *Avoid nutrient deficiencies.* You can create these more rapidly than usual while on a diet. You must supplement your new eating plan with the whole range of essential vitamins, minerals, and even trace minerals. One missing link can spell health problems.

3. *Low-calorie diet.* You can achieve weight loss sensibly simply by taking in fewer calories than you burn, or burning more than you consume. If you eat a lot of fatty or sugary junk foods, just cutting them out of your diet should enable you to lose weight gradually.

4. *Walk off your pounds.* Many people have done this while reducing calories and increasing their intake of whole-fruit juices and fresh vegetable drinks. Walking is frequently prescribed for exercise during the first two months of a fast before solid foods are reintroduced.

5. *Eat often during the day.* Reducing your food intake to one meal daily may not reduce your weight the way you expect. Studies show that numerous small snacks may be preferable. A single meal raises cholesterol levels and activates the fat-cell manufacturing process. Also, note that evidence from animal studies tell us that the food in a nibbler's diet is turned to less fat, less rapidly, than the food in a one-meal-a-day plan. And people, it seems, follow the same pattern.[120]

6. *Avoid radical surgery or hormone treatments.* Intestinal bypass operations have been shown to be quite dangerous and are no longer recommended even in cases of severe overweight.

For improved well-being and especially for the health of your heart:

1. Include moderate amounts of fat—particularly polyunsaturated fats in your meals. A balanced diet is important. Avoid extremes and make no changes in diet without consulting a doctor first.

2. If you have any medical problems, eat less saturated fats—especially solid animal fats.

3. Eat less high-cholesterol foods (i.e., eggs, shellfish, organ meats, cheese).

4. Substitute polyunsaturated fats (largely liquid vegetable oils) for saturated fats in the diet where possible, but make certain you are getting sufficient vitamin E to protect these PUFAs from oxidating.

5. Watch your calorie intake to prevent overweight.

6. Eliminate as much processed, refined foods as possible, especially those containing hydrogenated fats or sugar.

7. Examine your life-style. Do you smoke, drink excessively, get too little exercise? Remember, no change in diet will compensate for the harm such habits can do. The key, as in all things, is enough information to make the right choices, and the exercise of moderation.

VITAMINS

Introduction

What sounds like the alphabet but has the power to keep you healthy, radiant, and beautiful? What comes deliciously packaged in a broad range of whole, unprocessed foods for everyday consumption, or in tablets and capsules for emergency situations or just extra health insurance? What keeps every organ, every bone, indeed every cell in your body doing their jobs with optimum efficiency? The answer is vitamins!

In this chapter, we will meet the members of the vitamin family one by one to learn just how they serve you in sickness and in health, how much of each you need for great health, where the best places to find them are, and how to tell if you need more.

There's vitamin A, so necessary to an abundance of all-over health.

And B, who isn't just one vitamin but a whole family that works to let you be at your best.

And C, a veritable army of protection for your cells, and the major constituent of collagen—your cellular cement.

Vitamin D, "Mr. Sunshine," who has a literally delightful effect on your bones and teeth.

There's energizing E, enormously effective for the enjoyment of life.

And K, a little-known but vital nutrient.

And last but not least, vitamin P, a group of elements called bioflavonoids with names like rutin, citrin, hesperidin, and quercetin.

Let's meet the vitamins.

Vitamin A:
Nutrient for Total Health

What Is Vitamin A?

Vitamin A plays an astounding number of roles in maintaining your day-to-day health. Important in keeping skin and teeth healthy, vitamin A is also a watchdog against infections of the respiratory and urinary tracts. It plays an important part in keeping your reproductive system reproducing, your ears hearing, and your eyes seeing. It even helps to build your genetic material.

Vitamin A is fat soluble, like its brothers D, E, and K. What does "fat soluble" mean? A fat-soluble vitamin depends on the presence of certain nutrients—fats and minerals and the other fat-soluble vitamins —for your body to use it properly. In other words, you need fat and/or protein in adequate amounts in your diet to fully absorb fat-soluble vitamins into your bloodstream. Also, the bile must be released from your liver in normal amounts for you to absorb the fat-soluble vitamins you need to maintain optimum health.

Fat soluble means something else, too—something very important to keep in mind, especially if you are treating yourself for any ailment with vitamins. In contrast to the water-soluble vitamins (like B and C), fat-soluble vitamins like A are *not* excreted through the perspiration or urine. Therefore, an overdose over a period of time can be toxic.

What about vitamin A? Even before its official discovery in 1913, the medical profession was aware of the myriad powers of this vitamin. Heard about eating carrots to prevent night blindness? The Egyptian physicians in 1500 B.C. recognized this best-known manifestation of vitamin A deficiency. Their prescription wasn't carrots, but liver of ox (easier to come by in those days, we suspect), a rich source of vitamin A. Why? Because the livers of all living creatures hold up to 90 percent of their bodies' vitamin A store.

How Does Vitamin A Work?

Vitamin A plays a key role in maintaining the health of the membranes of all the cells in your body. How? It helps your cells secrete the mucus that coats and protects the membranes. Thus, the membranes remain strong and healthy and able to resist attack and/or infiltration by viruses and bacteria.[1] What this activity means is that vitamin A is absolutely necessary to the broad spectrum of cellular functions throughout your body.

Where Does Vitamin A Work?

Obviously, vitamin A works everywhere. One of its all-encompassing functions is to maintain healthy epithelial (skin cell) tissues throughout your body. In addition, vitamin A protects you against common infections of the throat and sinuses, the nose, ear, and eyes. Vitamin A also keeps your gum tissue healthy, and your teeth and reproductive organs working properly. Let's pinpoint the places where vitamin A is most important.

• *Immunological system.* Vitamin A's membrane-strengthening action means fewer infections in the places we mentioned above, in addition to the kidneys. Vitamin A can also protect your stomach, bladder, kidneys, lungs, and uterus against cancerous tumors, by keeping the cellular membranes strong.

• *Eyes.* Vitamin A helps your vision. In fact, there are cases documented in which inadequate A has resulted in irreversible damage to the eye tissues. Conversely, A has been used in curing night blindness, cloudy vision, and retinitis pigmentosa.

• *Ears.* Your ears depend on adequate vitamin A, too. It has been used in treating otosclerosis (abnormal hardening of the ear canal tissue).

• *Teeth and mouth.* Did you know that jawbone and tooth formation, healthy mouth membranes, and gums all depend on an adequate amount of vitamin A? It's a mouthful to say, but it's true.

• *Skin.* Acne and plantar warts both respond to vitamin A therapy.

• *Reproductive system.* The overall health of your reproductive system—including your fertility or sperm production—depends on vitamin A. It also helps to build RNA, the nucleic acid that determines the genetic code.

Who Needs Vitamin A?

The above list proves without a doubt that we all need vitamin A. Let's expound on it to learn just how vitamin A can help when you are under stress, exposed to a lot of pollutants in the environment, dieting, or actually suffering from a disease in one of the above "target areas."

VITAMIN A FOR STRESS

Like its partner, vitamin E, vitamin A is used up by pollutants or stress. You should be especially aware of this fact if you work outdoors in a large city. You may be exposing yourself to more than one ton of pollutants—including heavy metals, carbon monoxide, and ozone—every year. Astounding? Consider Manhattan, for instance, where eighty tons of chemically polluted particulate matter falls on every square mile each *day*!

We don't quote these statistics to frighten you, but to make you aware that living in a metropolitan environment, particularly if you spend a great deal of time outdoors, may leave you without the vitamin A you need to protect your eyes, lungs, and the oxygen-carrying capacity of your bloodstream. Without the protection of vitamin A, you may be especially vulnerable to the cancer-causing capabilities of pollutants like dioxydenitrates or ozone, which are converted into nitrite in the digestive system, drastically affecting thyroid activity. Some chemicals like DDT "deplete the liver of vitamin A so that a vitamin A deficient diet would increase the possibility of damage from this insecticide," authorities tell us.[2]

After a day in the city, do you feel weak? Confused? Perhaps you need more vitamin A. Taking more of the other protective vitamins like C and E might also be a good idea. Incorporate more foods containing these vitamins into your diet, or take supplements.

And speaking of diet, let's talk about the physical stress caused by eating foods processed with chemical additives. Did you know that both processing foods and adding chemicals to them—and the two often go hand in hand—destroy vitamin A? You may not be getting the vitamin A in foods that you think you are. Two examples of chemical additives that zap the vitamin A content of food are benzoate of soda and citral (a lemon flavor substitute).

Anywhere from 15 to 35 percent of both plant-derived vitamin A (beta-carotene) and animal-derived vitamin A may be destroyed by food preparation and processing, nutritionists tell us.[3] So be aware of how your food is processed, and furthermore, how you cook it!

What polluted air and polluted food add up to is physical stress. Add that to the emotional stress that all of us experience and you have a good case for taking more vitamin A to supply the strength your cellular membranes need to keep every tissue healthy. It's a good idea to take extra vitamins and to eat especially well if you are under chronic or acute physical or emotional stress.

VITAMIN A AND DIETERS

These days it seems that almost everyone is on some kind of diet, whether to reduce their cholesterol levels or to lose weight. Two popular diets that may affect how your body uses vitamin A are the vegetarian diet and the low-fat diet. We're not saying there is anything wrong with either of these regimens, but the reduction of total fat in your diet can limit the availability of vitamin A. You may be cutting out vitamin A when you reduce your intake of fat: nuts, seeds, avocados, olives, dairy products, egg yolks, and fish tend to be high in both vitamin A *and* fat (with the exception of many varieties of fish), and are often eliminated in an effort to lose weight or lower cholesterol counts. So be careful what you cut when you diet!

In this connection, you should know that serum cholesterol levels have been lowered in people who took vitamins A and D together. The dosages were only slightly more than the recommended daily figures. Vitamin D was helpful, but it looks as if vitamin A is the more active ingredient in normalizing the metabolism of cholesterol.[4]

VITAMIN A FOR DISEASE

When you are ill, your body may be depleted of its store of vitamin A. In turn, some diseases are the direct result of a vitamin A deficiency; it's a vicious circle. Luckily, it can be reversed. Vitamin A therapy can help in conditions like anemia, poor vision, or faulty hearing; ulcers, bone, teeth, and skin problems; reproductive ailments; and cancer.

If you suffer from anemia, you will be interested to know that vitamin A plays a big part in producing a good supply of healthy red blood cells. Bet you thought iron deficiency was the problem! That could be part of it, but researchers such as Robert E. Hodges, M.D., of the University of California at Davis would tell you that vitamin A is of equal importance in treating anemia.[5]

Hodges discovered, and reported in the *American Journal of Clinical Nutrition,* that giving test animals who were deficient in vitamin A small amounts of the vitamin resulted in both gained weight and improved blood quality. He noted that if the animal had been anemic for a long time, then it took a long time to make its blood healthy again. He also discovered an interesting connection between vitamin A and iron: iron levels in the liver could be normal or even high, but if there was not enough vitamin A in the diet, iron concentrations in the blood were low.[6]

We all know about the connection between inadequate vitamin A and night blindness; it's one of the facts our mothers used to make us eat our carrots. But did you know that both moderate and heavy drinkers are particularly susceptible to vision problems? There's a biochemical reason: drinking damages the liver, and when the liver is damaged, its vitamin A stores are drastically depleted. The logic is obvious: without vitamin A, proper vision is impossible.

Robert M. Russell, M.D., head of a team of nutritional researchers from the University of Maryland School of Medicine and Columbia University College of Physicians and Surgeons in New York, studied the connection between vitamin A, vision, and cirrhosis of the liver.

He and his colleagues found that when test subjects stopped drinking and took 30,000 I.U. of vitamin A daily for a number of days, both the low levels of vitamin A and the vision damage were gone.[7]

Cloudy vision or retinitis pigmentosa (a debilitating visual disorder that may be hereditary) has also been improved with vitamin A therapy. Patients at the National Institute of Arthritis and Metabolic Diseases in Washington, D.C., who were suffering from clouded vision took up to 200,000 units of vitamin A—under medical supervision, of course. In some cases, the patients found their vision more clear within *hours* of a single megadosage.[8]

In fact, reported *Medical World News*, some patients who had actually been going blind were able to see clearly for up to three months on a single dose of 200,000 units of vitamin A. For others, clear vision lasted for up to seven years![9]

Vitamin A is also vital to good hearing. If you are deficient in this vitamin, an overgrowth of the internal auditory canal and resultant hearing loss could be the unfortunate result. The University of California's Richard A. Chole, M.D., found that such ear damage was the result of a test diet free of vitamin A for as little as fifteen months.[10]

Otosclerosis is another kind of hearing problem that can result in part from low levels of vitamin A. Particularly common among the elderly, the presence of this condition indicates that the bones that surround the middle and inner ear have hardened and enlarged. Otosclerosis interferes with the transmission of sound waves that we interpret as words and noises. Often, surgery is the only way to help.

But vitamin A also offers hope to victims of otosclerosis. Oswald A. Roels, M.D., of Columbia University, used the vitamin to restore flexibility in the bones of the ear. Furthermore, he discovered that vitamin A therapy could actually prevent the cell membrane damage that causes hardening in the first place!

VITAMIN A FOR ULCERS

Now that we know how vitamin A works, it isn't too surprising that it would also be effective in the treatment of ulcers, which are lesions of the stomach membranes. A healthy diet, stress management, and exercise, in combination with generous amounts of vitamins A and E, can prevent and control, even put an end to painful gastrointestinal ulcers. We know what healing powers these two vitamins contain by themselves; put them together and they really pack a punch.

For example, let's look at the results of an experiment that T. L. Harris, M.D., conducted and reported in the *Proceedings of the Society for Experimental Biology and Medicine*. He used two groups of test animals. The first group was given vitamin A, but not vitamin E; there were one or more stomach ulcers after the test within the animals of the group. The second group was supplied with plenty of both vitamins. Not a single animal showed a sign of ulcers.[11]

Why are A and E together so powerful? Vitamin A prompts secretion of the mucus that keeps the cellular membranes well lubricated. When that mucus is present, the cells are protected from strong acids that can cause erosion.

Simultaneously, vitamin E protects your cells by preventing a process called oxidation. (See the section on vitamin E for a detailed explanation.) Vitamin E also prevents the destruction of vitamin A in your gastrointestinal tract. You can see how these two powerful nutrients in combination could protect your gastrointestinal tract from ulcers and promote healing when ulcers do occur.[12]

Some ulcers erupt suddenly; for example, under the physiological stress of a serious accident. Vitamin A can help in these cases, too, says Merrill S. Chermov, M.D. Chermov and his team of physicians are specialists in treating patients hospitalized with major injuries, including burns.

Here are the results of one of their experiments: thirty-six patients hospitalized with injuries were also low in vitamin A. Chermov gave fourteen of them 10,000 to 400,000 units of a special water-soluble variety of vitamin A every day. Of this group, twelve showed no signs of developing ulcers. Two developed some lesions.

The other twenty-two patients were given drugs, but no vitamin A supplements. Fifteen developed stress ulcers. Of these fifteen, fourteen showed serious upper gastrointestinal bleeding in addition to the ulcers.[13]

VITAMIN A FOR BONES AND TEETH

Do you, like most of us, think of calcium as the vital ingredient in the growth and maintenance of healthy bones and teeth? Bet you didn't know that vitamin A is in the recipe, too, especially for women in the postmenopausal stage, who often show signs of osteoporosis (fragile bones) due to calcium loss.

According to the book *Understanding Nutrition* by Whitney and Hamilton, "Some of the cells involved in bone formation are packed with sacs of degradative enzymes which can take apart the structures from which bone is made. With the help of vitamin A, in a carefully controlled process, these cells release their enzymes, which gradually eat away at selected sites in the bone, removing the parts of its structure that are not needed as the bone grows longer."[14]

Low levels of vitamin A can result in impaired or decreased bone formation rates. Why? When the body is deficient in vitamin A, the uptake of phosphate and sulfate, two bone mass components, falls below normal. You also need vitamin A for your body to use ash, calcium, and hydroxyproline—a constituent of the intercellular cement collagen—efficiently.

If vitamin A is essential to healthy bones, you can bet that your teeth need it, too. Vitamin A protects against malocclusion (poor bite), strengthens the jawbones, and promotes the health of the teeth. In addition, it helps create healthy gums that are resistant to infections, especially an inflammation of the gums called gingivitis.[15]

Karl Rinne, a dentist in Germany, tried treating patients who were suffering from gingivitis with vitamin A. Those who took large amounts of vitamin A daily for six days, together with 30 milligrams of intravaneous vitamin E, were cured. To insure that the condition would not recur, the patients then took 50,000 units of vitamin A three times daily and 200 milligrams of vitamin E twice daily, for the next three weeks. It worked. However, this was under strict medical supervision. You could easily develop acute toxicity trying this on your own, so don't do it.

VITAMIN A FOR SKIN

Have you ever suffered from acne? If so, you know just how psychologically debilitating it can be, and how difficult and stubborn to treat.

But you may not know what a remarkable healing power vitamin A has for acne sufferers. Doctors using nutritional therapy on this disfiguring disease have seen positive results in six months or less.

Jon D. Straumfjord, M.D., of Astoria, Oregon, was a pioneer in the use of vitamin A for treating acne. Working in the 1940s, Straumfjord produced impressive results on acne victims, preparing the ground for the nutrition-minded skin specialists who now treat acne with A as a matter of course.

Taking large doses of vitamin A (halibut oil), one hundred of Straumfjord's patients were treated. In just three months, over one-third were free from acne. Of the others taking part in the "A-for-acne" test, forty-three also found their acne responsive to the fish-oil treatment, except for "an occasional acne papule or pustule."

And no matter what the time it took the acne to heal—three months, six months, a year—the positive effect of vitamin A treatment was noteworthy, reports Dr. Straumfjord. Even the most stubborn cases responded, and few recurred.[16]

Similar success was reported by Drs. Leonard E. Savitt of Los Angeles and K. D. Lahari of India. Dr. Savitt treated thirty-five acne-plagued college students with 100,000 units of vitamin A daily. He noted marked improvement in the conditions of twenty of them.[17]

Using the same daily dosage of 100,000 units, Dr. Lahari treated seventy-five patients. "All had previously resisted other forms of treatment, some for several years," he says. "The lesions disappeared in two and a half months in thirty cases, in three months in another thirty cases, and in five and a half months in ten cases." To put it plainly, in only six months most of the patients were free of acne![18]

In its water-soluble form, vitamin A palmitate has shown remarkable success—to the tune of a 50 to 100 percent success rate—in treating stubborn plantar warts. How? By creating an antiviral action that stops the condition. The statistics tell all: in one experiment with 228 victims of plantar warts, the warts disappeared with vitamin A therapy in 208 of the cases.[19]

VITAMIN A AND SEX

Vitamin A is vital to the proper functioning of the male and female reproductive organs. Here's how.

• *Synthesis of sex hormones.* According to research undertaken at the Howard University Medical School, "Vitamin A actively participates in the synthesis of sex hormones and there is a direct relationship between vitamin A and sexual maturation and reproduction." Experiments with laboratory animals showed that the reproductive disorders that occur as a result of vitamin A deficiency happen because the skin cells that line the reproductive organs weaken. Without adequate vitamin A, the cells dry and harden and stop producing the mucus essential to the workings of the whole system.[20]

• *Formation of reproductive organs.* By the same token, reproductive organs may actually atrophy or shrink when vitamin A is under-supplied. Why? With inadequate vitamin A, vital hormone production diminishes. For example, a study quoted in the *Journal of Animal Science* reported that bulls fed diets low in vitamin A suffered degeneration of the tubules that transport semen. When their diets once again included adequate A, the bulls showed full sexual potency.[21]

• *Potency.* Sufficient sperm count levels depend on A. The above-mentioned experiment shows that A is a prime factor in maintaining potency. Why? Because vitamin A participates in a series of biochemical reactions in which cholesterol is converted to sex hormones—androgens for males, estrogens for females. For example, *Rivista di Ostetricia a Ginecologia* (May 1954) reported that when men who were deficient in vitamins A and E took supplementary doses of these nutrients, their sperm counts returned to normal levels.[22]

• *Fertility.* The female reproductive organs also need vitamin A. Dr. Thomas Moore of Cambridge, England, reports that vitamin A helps create fertility, produces sexual desire, reduces problems in delivering children, and helps prevent both fetal fatalities and birth defects of the eyes and heart, as well as cleft palate.[23]

What do all these findings prove? That a sound nutritional program that provides plenty of vitamin A through whole foods is not only healthy, but sexy as well.

VITAMIN A AND CANCER

Vitamin A may be one of the more promising nutritional agents around as far as cancer control and prevention are concerned.

For example, the more vitamin A your body absorbs and utilizes, says E. Bjelke of Norway's Cancer Registry, the lower your risk of lung cancer may be. In Bjelke's studies, even heavy smokers demonstrated a greater resistance to cancer when their intake of vitamin A was abundant.[24]

He says, "The present findings do suggest that vitamin A active compounds or some closely associated dietary factors may modify the expression of pulmonary carcinogens or cocarcinogens in man." He suggests that those people who simply cannot stop smoking take vitamin A supplements, as they may "be potent prophylactics against the effects of smoking."[25]

Other doctors agree that making sure your intake of A is adequate may be a good insurance policy against developing cancer. David Smith and his colleagues at MIT have long "speculated that cancer was the result of a local vitamin imbalance produced by factors that removed vitamin A in the body." Their experiments showed that low levels of vitamin A may be a common denominator among people who develop tumors. As a cancer preventative, making sure your intake of vitamin A is adequate is one factor over which you *do* have control.[26]

A Practical Guide to Using Vitamin A

Now that we've seen how important vitamin A is to our senses and organs, where do we get it? How much do we need? Is it possible to take too much? What other nutrients does vitamin A work especially well with? How do you know if you are deficient?

The best place to get any of the nutrients your body needs is through fresh, unprocessed food. Vitamin A is found in animal foods like liver, butter, whole milk, cheese, and egg yolk. In plants, vitamin A occurs in carotene. Eat yellow vegetables, spinach, beet greens, carrots, and turnips for your daily A.

A note: The carotene in plants is not as immediately accessible to your body as is the vitamin A in animal foods. In fact, your body must convert the carotene into vitamin A before you can use it. That's why the vitamin A in plants is sometimes called *pro*vitamin A. In raw carrots, for example, the carotene is not readily available because it is found inside the indigestible cell walls. To get the most vitamin A per carrot, juice them!

And by the way, the human digestive system is not particularly well equipped for converting carotene into vitamin A. Studies show that only one-sixth of the carotene you eat may be converted to vitamin A. Beyond that, only a third of that amount may actually be digested.

How much vitamin A should you take? Since each of us is biochemically different, the suggested intake varies. A lot of it depends on factors such as how much fat and other nutrients you eat. But if you are in good health, these amounts of vitamin A should be enough to keep you that way:

Male and female adults	4,000 units daily
Pregnant women	6,000 units daily
Nursing mothers	8,000 units daily

Such are the recommendations of the Food and Nutrition Board of the National Research Council. But "reports in the literature suggest that total vitamin A requirements may possibly be increased by fever, infection, reduced environmental temperature, hyperthyroidism, chemical substances, and excessive exposure to ultraviolet rays," advise Mildred S. Rodriguez and M. Isabel Irwin, nutrition researchers from the USDA.[27]

Can you take too much vitamin A? If you get all of your vitamin A as it occurs naturally in the foods you eat, most likely not. But if you undertake to treat yourself with megadose supplements, you do run the risk of creating a toxicity.

The American Academy of Pediatrics warns: "Excessive intake of preformed vitamin A may result in serious and potentially toxic effects. The easy availability of vitamin A in large doses without prescription exposes individuals to the danger of severe clinical toxicity."[28]

Vitamin A is a fat-soluble vitamin, remember? What that means is that your body does not excrete excess amounts; it stores them. Be aware of the dangers of consuming more vitamin A than you need. Toxicity symptoms include fatigue, restlessness, nausea, vomiting, headaches, skin rashes, dry scaly lips, hair loss, brittle nails, weight loss, and liver and spleen enlargement.[29]

It seems that huge doses—approximately 100,000 units taken daily over a period of three years—produce toxicity. In fact, only twelve cases of vitamin A poisoning have ever been reported in the United States, according to the USDA.[30] In one such case, a doctor who had used himself as a test subject treated himself with a million units daily for three weeks.[31]

Can you get too much vitamin A from plant foods? Probably not. Although there is a condition known as carotemia, it is generally not serious. Just for the record, though, its symptom is a slight yellowing of the skin caused, for example, by eating enormous amounts of carrots or the juice of carrots.

In one experiment, physician-scientist Robert A. Peterman found, "Fifteen human subjects received daily oral dosages of beta-carotene equivalent to 100,000 units daily of vitamin A for three months. Serum carotene values rose from an initial 128 to 308 after one month, but did not rise above this level during the remainder of the observation period." Dr. Peterman reported these test results in the *Journal of the American Medical Association.*[32]

What the report says is that vitamin A, as it is found naturally in foods, rarely presents any cause for alarm over possible toxicity. To consume even the minimum daily requirement of 4,000 units from vegetable sources in your diet, you would need to eat a dozen carrots for example.

An interesting footnote: taking oral contraceptives may raise vitamin A levels abnormally. The *British Medical Journal* reported that in one study researchers discovered that oral contraceptives taken until shortly before conception can raise blood levels of vitamin A in a woman who then becomes pregnant. High vitamin A levels can cause toxicity in the developing fetus, resulting in a damaged central nervous system in the newborn child.

Isabel Gal, of the Institute of Obstetrics at Queen Charlotte's Hospital in London, cautions: "Further work is necessary to determine whether this excess may affect the fetus in patients who become pregnant shortly after discontinuing oral contraception."[33]

In commenting on Gal's study and warning, nutritionists in the *Journal of the American Dietetic Association* said, "The question is raised as to whether women taking oral contraceptives raise their plasma vitamin A to such an extent as to run the risk of inducing malformations in their offspring once they discontinue the medication and conceive." They concluded with the view that the risk is "insignificantly small," but does possibly warrant caution.[34]

The use of oral contraceptives holds another danger as far as vitamin A levels go: it depletes your liver supply of the vitamin, diminishing your ability to use and absorb A.

With all these confusing and seemingly contradictory reports of the pill's affect on vitamin A levels, perhaps the best advice is to simply find a safer form of contraception!

VITAMIN A'S PARTNERS

Who are vitamin A's partners? We've already seen how closely it works with vitamin E. In addition, taking additional amounts of the essential mineral zinc will help your body absorb its vitamin A.

John R. Duncan and Lucille S. Hurley, researchers at the University of California at Davis, report: "There is increasing evidence that zinc may be necessary for the metabolism of vitamin A. Several reports have suggested that adequate amounts of zinc are required for the maintenance of normal concentrations of vitamin A in plasma." The two doctors found that a deficiency in zinc can create a deficiency in vitamin A.[35]

The moral of the story is to eat foods that give you a broad range of all the nutrients your body needs, from A to Z!

SPOTTING VITAMIN A DEFICIENCY

How can you tell if you are deficient in vitamin A? Look at your fingernails. Are they in bad shape—even though you're eating plenty of protein and calcium-rich dairy foods and leafy green vegetables?

If you don't see a glowing pink underneath your nails, if they break easily or don't grow very fast, check the foods in your diet to see if you are getting enough vitamin A.

Other signs of vitamin A deficiency at its early stages are easy to see. They include frequent infections, night blindness, cloudy vision, itchy dry eyes, and ulcers of the cornea. (Under these circumstances, they may *not* be so "easy to see"!) Other symptoms of low levels of A are dry and brittle hair, dry skin, and skin rashes. If your child shows poor growth, slow weight gain, and loss of appetite, he or she may need more vitamin A. If you notice signs of a deficiency, see your doctor. He will determine your vitamin A levels and direct you in supplementing your diet.

In citing an article in *Nutrition Week*, the *Natural Foods Merchandiser* reports that the Center for Science in the Public Interest has proposed that Vitamin A in large doses for extended periods of time may be hazardous. "Taking more than 25,000 I.U. of vitamin A a day for several weeks or more can be harmful to adults and teenagers. Consumption of more than 10,000 I.U. can be harmful to children and infants." They would like warning labels on high potency vitamin A. However, this warning applies only to those vitamin A pills with dosages of over 10,000 I.U., the most common dosage.[36]

Summary

Vitamin A is more than just another vitamin. It is a nutritional weapon against cell atrophy and infection. In addition, it is a guardian of your eyesight, hearing, and the health of your skin. In short, it is a powerful healer and protector.

Used with other nutrients—especially zinc and vitamin E—in a balanced diet, sufficient vitamin A can be your best bet for an abundance of "A"-one health.

Vitamin B: Rejuvenator of Body and Mind

What Is Vitamin B?

Would you like to enjoy radiant good health, sustained energy throughout the day, feel less stress, and enjoy an overall vitality of body and mind? Who among us wouldn't? Vitamin B is part of the key to these riches and more.

Actually, there is no such thing as simple "vitamin B." What the term denotes is a whole family of vitamins that together form the vitamin B complex. There's B_1, B_2, B_3, B_5, B_6 (all of which have other names, as we'll see later), B_{12}, biotin, pantothenic acid, choline, folic acid, inositol, and PABA. This family is a harmonious crew who work together as building blocks that make beaming and beautiful good health for you.

Chemically speaking, the vitamin B complex is a group of water-soluble vitamins found especially in nutritional yeast, seed germs, eggs, liver, meat, and vegetables. They have varied metabolic functions and include coenzymes and growth factors. (A coenzyme forms the active portion of an enzyme system. Enzymes are produced by living cells and catalyze specific biochemical reactions at body temperatures.) There are substances—specifically carbon, hydrogen, oxygen, and electron-linked atoms—in the B vitamins that cause vital chemical reactions within your body, providing fuel for important biological processes.

How Does the Vitamin B Complex Work?

The members of the B-complex family literally unlock the nutrients in fats, carbohydrates, and proteins, making them available to you as energy. They release all the fuel you need to be at your very best.

Obviously, fuel is important in making your body work. In conjunction with enzymes, the B vitamins act as catalysts to transform what you eat into the energy you need to function.

As E. Whitney and M. Hamilton, two noted nutritionists, put it, "Without B vitamins, you would certainly feel tired. You would lack energy. Why is this? Some of the B vitamins serve as helpers to the enzymes which release energy from the three energy nutrients—carbohydrate, fat, and protein . . . Some of them help to manufacture the red blood cells which carry oxygen to the body's tissues; the oxygen must be present for oxidation and energy release to occur."[11]

Where Do the B Vitamins Work?

Like many families, the vitamin B complex maximizes its strengths and minimizes its weaknesses when all members are present and working together. When each member of the B-complex family is present in the proper ratio, you can find the whole gang working harmoniously in every cell of your body. Here are a few of the places where the crew is on the job, twenty-four hours a day:

• *Enzymatic system.* B vitamins help the body's enzymes to release energy from the food you eat and the dietary supplements you take.

• *Metabolism.* Because of its important role in the enzymatic system, the B complex promotes proper metabolism of carbohydrates, fats, and proteins throughout the body, normalizing your appetite and digestion.

• *Cells.* Vitamin B complex helps keep the body supplied with plenty of oxygen and helps form red blood cells. In this way, it is a depression- and fatigue-fighter par excellence. It helps build your cells' immunity to infection, too.

• *Organs.* The vitamin B family helps detoxify organs such as the liver. In addition, it helps protect the heart against serious cardiovascular disease.

• *Nervous system.* The B complex is a great stabilizer of your nervous system functions.

• *Hair and skin.* B vitamins are a wonderful tonic for keeping hair and skin healthy and beautiful.

• *Eyes.* The B vitamins also help prevent defective vision.

In addition to these specific functions, the B complex has been used with success to treat a wide range of debilitating conditions. Nutritionally oriented physician Henry Borsook lists them in his book *Vitamins:* nerve damage connected with chronic alcoholism; the stress of pregnancy; the nausea and sickness accompanying massive exposure to radiation; constipation; intestinal discomfort; persistent arthritis; and cardiovascular disease.[1]

The vitamin B complex also occupies the center of a controversy surrounding its use in the treatment of mental illness. But more on that later.

Where do the B vitamins work? In the enzymatic system, the metabolic system, the cells, the organs, the nervous system, and the hair, skin, and eyes. And remember, they work as a family. Although single B vitamins are often helpful in treating and preventing certain specific conditions—as we shall see in our discussion of them individually— the B vitamins are most effective when they work in harmony. Also, any B vitamin taken in large doses by itself, without the supplementation of the remaining complex, may create a dangerous state of imbalance.

Who Needs B Vitamins?

We all need B vitamins—all of them—every day. But there are circumstances under which we need the vitamin B family even more. For example, if you drink a lot of coffee, tea, or alcohol, perspire heavily, are under any sort of stress up to the point of being emotionally disturbed or even mentally ill, your needs for the B-vitamin complex may be greatly increased.

The B vitamins are water soluble. What this means is that your body does not store up a reserve of B vitamins as it stores a reserve of the fat-soluble vitamins like A, D, and E. You need B vitamins every day, and if you should wash them out of your body by drinking a lot of coffee and tea or alcohol or perspiring heavily, you need them even more. Stress—physical, psychological, emotional—is another reason to increase your intake.

As you can see, there are times when you would need more B vitamins than normal. A business convention or a visit home for the holidays are good examples. In those highly sociable atmospheres, you find yourselves drinking loads of coffee or tea (often accompanied by sugary, nutrient-poor "treats") with your friends, families, or colleagues. You keep up a breakneck pace all day, scurrying from one activity to the next, with no time for a nap or for exercise out-of-doors. Then in the evening you might eat a rich, meaty dinner sandwiched between cocktails and after-dinner drinks. You stay up talking and drinking late into the night. The next morning you need even more coffee or tea to get yourself going. Sound familiar? Unfortunately, it's the perfect scenario for a partial wipeout of your B vitamins.

If you find yourself coming down with a cold or flu or requiring a few days off for "R&R" on the heels of such an occasion, perhaps you could save yourself the time and trouble of being ill by taking along a good hearty B-complex supplement on your next trip. Or if the above example describes your life-style in general, you might find yourself much less worn out if you incorporate B-rich foods into your daily regimen.

And incidentally, once you start giving yourself more vitamin B, you may notice that you aren't so interested in sugary, processed food or alcohol anymore. Or if you are beyond the point where the word "interest" would describe your relationship to alcohol, B vitamins could deter you from a life of alcohol abuse.

B VITAMINS FOR THE ALCOHOLIC

A tremendous number of lives are affected by alcoholism. To a majority of Americans, reported a Gallup Poll in November 1982, alcohol abuse constitutes a major national problem. In the opinion of many authorities, alcoholism is not so much a "disease" as a biochemical derangement that both causes alcohol addiction and exacerbates it as well.

The drinker drinks to satisfy a craving to lift his depression. It works temporarily, but a vicious cycle ensues in which the more the body takes, the more it wants. More drinking is the result. The ravages of this process do not show up overnight. Gradual cell-tissue damage and general deterioration of the entire body lead slowly to emotional and physiological breakdown, manifesting in various mental symptoms—such as the very depression the drinker is trying to escape—and acute malnutrition. The irony of alcoholism is that while it is sucking the life out of its victim, it is also anesthetizing his ability to see what is happening, much less to do anything about it.

Authorities such as Carroll M. Leevy, M.D., of Seton Hall College of Medicine in New Jersey, feel that the physical changes that occur in the drinker are related not simply to the toxic effects of alcohol, but also to the serious nutritional deficiencies that alcohol abuse creates. Sometimes these deficiencies are present long before the addictive cycle begins, heightening the problem to a critical stage all the more rapidly, perhaps even causing it, according to Roger Williams, award-winning biochemist at the University of Texas at Austin.[2] Before we talk about how B-vitamin supplementation can help the drinker, let's look at the specific kinds of nutritional damage brought about by alcohol abuse.

• *Protein starvation.* Protein, among many other nutrients, cannot be absorbed properly when alcohol consumption is excessive. Why? To digest protein properly, your body needs the enzyme trypsin. To make trypsin, you need trypsinogen, which is produced by the pancreas. The pancreas cannot produce enough trypsinogen to make trypsin when there is excess alcohol in the bloodstream.

Other vital enzyme precursors are inhibited by the presence of alcohol. Hydrochloric acid and pepsinogen, precursor of pepsin, are among them. Both are important to the digestion of protein.

It seems obvious that if your body cannot secrete hydrochloric acid and these two important proenzymes, you cannot digest protein properly.

If you cannot digest protein properly, your body is unable to manufacture and maintain hormones, enzymes, and neurotransmitters. Neurotransmitters are vital messengers between the brain and the body.

• *Liver damage.* Cirrhosis of the liver is a well-known side effect of heavy drinking, caused by a dangerous increase in fatty deposits. To put it very simply, when someone drinks alcohol instead of eating—a common pattern among heavy drinkers—the liver simply cannot keep up with its work. Two areas in which it fails are the production of glucose from the nutrients containing carbohydrate and fat, and glycogen production. Without glucose and glycogen, the heavy drinker has no energy reserves upon which to draw.

• *Stomach and intestinal damage.* Excessive amounts of alcohol on a regular basis severely damage the lining of the stomach. The result: the intestinal system can no longer absorb nutrients properly.

Drinking heavily, even if one is eating well, uses whatever stores of vitamins one might have to help digestive processes. But most drinkers don't eat well. The sugary, salty, low-fiber foods that they do eat serve to disrupt their digestive and eliminative systems even further.

Combined with simple drugs like aspirin, alcohol in excessive quantities has the power to produce ulcers.

So the addicted drinker must not only deal with the toxic effects of alcohol, but also the devastating effects of alcohol abuse on his intake of protein and other nutrients, his liver, pancreas, and general digestive system.

The nutritional approach to reducing the alcoholic's craving for a drink, or to preventing the biochemical derangement (discussed above) that may lead to alcoholism, has been successful. Dr. Roger Williams, who pioneered this approach, and is the author of *Nutrition Against Disease,* says, "It has long been my opinion that good nutrition is a key to the prevention of alcoholism and that biochemical individuality plays a tremendous role in that some individuals have unusual needs which make them highly vulnerable . . ."[3]

Dr. Williams also asserts that you are less likely to become an alcoholic if you follow good nutritional practices. "If 90 percent of the calories one consumes are in the form of wholesome food," he says, "malnutrition will not become a part of life; individuals will never pass through a period of preparation for drinking which is the *sine qua non* or prerequisite of becoming an alcoholic."[4]

Dr. Williams also suggests that one way you can prevent a drinking problem from developing is to allow no more than 10 percent of your calories to come from foods that are salty, sugary, high in fat, or low in body-building materials.[5]

In addition, Dr. Frank S. Butler, writing in the *Journal of the American Geriatrics Society*, said that "alcoholism can be controlled with a diet high in protein and rich in vitamins, especially the B vitamins. Since the alcoholic cannot be expected to accept a change in diet, he must be fed involuntarily."[6]

All of the vitamin B family is desperately needed to help the alcoholic. But as we shall see when we meet them individually, vitamins B_2, B_3, and B_{12} have special functions when it comes to treatment and prevention of alcoholism.

VITAMIN B FOR MENTAL ILLNESS

Enzymes are vital to every biochemical process. Our genetic potential, carried by the nucleic acid DNA, depends upon enzymes for realization. For the production of molecules, too, enzymes are essential. Your brain is as dependent on enzymes as is the rest of your body.

As we have seen before, the B vitamins have a very special relationship to enzymes. In many cases, they actually catalyze an enzyme so that a vital biochemical function can take place. The vitamin B complex has a special relationship to the functions of your brain because of its role in the manufacture of neurotransmitters such as serotonin, as we saw in our discussion of alcoholism.

The B-vitamin complex can be essential for those suffering from emotional stress or mental illness. We're going to hear more specifics later when we talk about the individual members of the vitamin B family, so let's just get a general overview for now.

There is impressive evidence that mental conditions such as schizophrenia and chronic depression are in many persons expressions of a biochemical imbalance. Although the exact nature of the imbalance is not clear, here are a few findings in the field of nutritional approach to mental illness.

• Vitamin and mineral deficiencies may be a significant factor in the development of some mental disorders, in particular, schizophrenia.

• Some individuals suffering from mental illness may have nutrient needs far above the government-set RDAs because of their genetic makeup or as a result of years of nutritional deficiency.

• Psychosis and depression may stem in part from low levels of vitamins B_1, B_6, and B_{12}.

• Did you know that vitamin deficiencies may cause nerve impulses to malfunction? As a result, the brain's ability to perform its normal functions may be impaired. The consequence? Psychosis.

• In numerous experiments and clinical practice, mental illness or emotional imbalance has been effectively treated with megadoses of vitamins C, E, B_3, and B_6.

In light of these discoveries, one sad irony in the current conventional approach to mental illness is that the very chemicals that are used to treat the symptoms of mental disorders may alter the way in which the body uses nutrients, thus altering the patient's nutritional status and perhaps sharpening the biochemical imbalance that is at the heart of the disorder.

Can vitamins really help the victims of mental illness? Yes, according to two noted nutritionists, Drs. George Watson and W. D. Currier. Their work in this field reveals that "some states which are psychologically diagnosed as functional mental illness and at the same time are not accompanied by clinical evidence of nutritional deficit, apparently involve unsuspected nutritional deficiencies and may be helped by appropriate nutritional therapy."[7]

To prove that it is no illusion that vitamins work when biochemical deficiencies are involved, these doctors conducted an experiment with thirty individuals, all of whom exhibited emotional dysfunctions. Half of the patients were given large daily doses of vitamin B_3 along with a supplement containing the other B vitamins plus additional vitamins and minerals. The other patients received placebos.

Here's what Watson and Currier found: on the placebo, seven patients improved, six got worse, and seventeen showed no change. Among the patients taking the vitamins, twenty-two patients showed substantial improvement, two became worse, and six remained the same. With the passing weeks and months of continuing supplementation, the success rate climbed even higher.

Here's another example: Gregory Stefan, in his book *In Search of Sanity,* recalls being confined to a hospital bed for four years, diagnosed as a hopelessly ill schizophrenic. After being subjected to continuous electroshock therapy and mentally and physically numbing drugs day after day, Stefan had the good fortune to encounter a psychiatrist who used B_3 and other nutrients to restore him to a normal, healthy mental state.[8]

In *How to Live with Schizophrenia,* nutritionally oriented physicians Abram Hoffer and Humphrey Osmond recount dozens of similar recoveries from mental illness, attributable in part to the B-complex family.[9]

Even if you don't suffer from acute mental illness, you may find additional vitamin B helpful to your state of mind. Like a big black thundercloud, chronic depression hangs over the lives of millions of people in our country today. Could this plague possibly be connected to our heavy consumption of white flour, which has been robbed of its B vitamins in the refining process; white sugar, which had no vitamins to begin with; and nutrient-poor "fast" foods? Could be. If you suffer from chronic depression, why not try eating more foods rich in B vitamins, perhaps even adding a supplement to your routine? It's cheaper than a psychiatrist, and may be more effective in the long run. If your mental condition is due to a biochemical imbalance or a nutritional deficiency, the addition of vitamin B to your diet may contribute to a healthy state of mind and body in which you can be your naturally cheerful, sunny self.

VITAMIN B FOR VISION

People with visual problems are another group who may be helped by increased amounts of the B-complex vitamins. There is a definite link between improved eyesight and increased amounts of the B complex, according to M. Damodaran and his colleagues of the National Institute of Nutrition of the Indian Council of Medical Research. Their studies concluded that "supplementation with vitamin B complex was found to have a beneficial effect in improving the visual-acuity status of defective children and in preventing visual defects from developing."[10]

Vitamin B Complex for Health

The vitamin B family has a direct relationship to how effectively you use the nutrients your body takes in through food or supplements —so isn't it obvious that an adequate supply of this harmonious group is one of the best insurance policies around?

And even if you are in the best of health, additional help from the B-complex family may supply that extra boost of day-long energy that seems a vague childhood memory to most of us. Indeed, you will find the benefits of getting plenty of this vitamin family showing up in your hair, your eyes, and your skin. In short, your whole body will get a big boost from beefing up your intake of the B-vitamin complex.[11]

A Practical Guide to Using Vitamin B

Even though you haven't yet met the individual members of the vitamin B family, you now know how necessary to your whole well-being a healthy supply of the entire complex is. So what are the best food sources of vitamin B? How much of the B complex should you take, if a supplement is in order? Does the vitamin B family have any special nutritional "partners," the way some of the other vitamins do? How do you know if you need more vitamin B than you are getting?

The answer to the first question lies in this one: what's for dinner? Sautéed liver, spinach salad, brown rice, whole grain crackers or bread with peanut butter? Besides being delicious, these are all high-quality B-vitamin foods. So are whole grain cereals, dried beans, eggs, and fresh leafy green vegetables like turnip greens, broccoli, collards, dandelion greens, kale, mustard greens, cabbage, and cauliflower.[2] Salmon, heart, and kidney are other good sources. And for some real B-boosters, try adding wheat germ, rice bran, and brewer's or nutritional yeast to your diet!

Two things to remember about these B-rich foods: first, if you cook them improperly, you may unwittingly be tossing those valuable B vitamins down the drain. For example, boiling your fresh vegetables will leach out their rich supply of B vitamins. Try steaming your vegetables, or use the cooking waters to make a sauce for your whole grains or a delicious, vitamin-rich soup.

Second, even if you think you are eating a hearty quantity of B-rich foods, you may not be if you depend heavily on processed or canned foods. B-vitamin values are readily destroyed by extremes of temperature and other methods used to process food, as well as nutrient-robbing handling and storage techniques.

Even though you eat well and know the value of getting your nutrients through whole, unprocessed foods, you may wish to invest in the insurance policy of a supplement. According to the Food and Nutrition Board, of the National Academy of Sciences, and the National Research Council, your minimum needs for some of the members of the B-complex group are:

	Adult Males (23–50)	*Adult Females* (23–50)
B_1	1.4 milligrams daily	1.0 milligrams daily
B_2	1.6 milligrams daily	1.2 milligrams daily
B_3	18 milligrams daily	13 milligrams daily
Folic acid	400 micrograms daily	400 micrograms daily
B_6	2.0 milligrams daily	2.0 milligrams daily
B_{12}	3.0 milligrams daily	3.0 milligrams daily

VITAMIN B'S PARTNERS

The members of the vitamin B family work best with each other, as we've said before. Deficiencies in one member of the family may drastically reduce the effectiveness of the others, or even lead to other deficiencies. Too little B_3, for example, will cause a reduction in the body's supply of B_1 and B_2.[11]

It's worth repeating: always make sure that you are getting all the members of the vitamin B family in the proper ratios. In most of the low dosage B-complex supplements on the market, these amounts are properly predetermined. Not so with the megadosage levels. But if you are taking one of the particular members of the B-complex family for some specific condition, you may want to consult your doctor or nutritionist as to what amounts of the other B vitamins you should be taking as well.

How do you know if you are deficient in the vitamin B complex? Some telltale symptoms include skin rash, sores in the mouth, loss of appetite, poor muscle tone, chronic fatigue, depression and other nervous disorders, premature graying of the hair, and lowered resistance to colds and other common infections.

Unnoticed symptoms include changes in the chemistry of the blood and the brain.[12]

A simple way to check your daily vitamin B status, advises Paul Jay Friedman, M.D., of Blodgett Memorial Medical Center in Grand Rapids, Michigan and Robert E. Hodges of the University of California, Davis, is to look at your tongue in a mirror each morning. If it is pink and clean, you are getting enough B vitamins. If it looks very dark with unhealthy ridges, you could be deficient. Dr. Friedman considers an abnormally blue (cyanotic) tongue color to be symptomatic of deficiency, generally speaking. He cautions that in certain situations the tongue could look normal, but there could still be a vitamin B deficiency.[13]

If you *are* deficient in the B vitamins, your doctor may order laboratory tests that will reveal the concentration of nutrients, and the degree to which the particular deficiency has advanced.

It is important to remember that certain very ordinary conditions may lead to a chronic deficiency of the B vitamins. These include drinking too much coffee and tea, perspiring heavily, drinking alcohol in excess, and psychological or physical stress. Interestingly enough, each of these conditions can affect how and what we eat as well. If any of these circumstances apply to you (as they do to most of us at one time or another), a good vitamin supplement may be necessary.

Now that we know how the vitamin B family functions as a unit, let's meet them individually and learn how they work in times of illness and in times of health.

B₁ (Thiamine)

If your get-up-and-go has got up and gone, if you need antacids too often, if you suffer from a poor appetite, if you're chronically tired, you may need more B_1 (which also goes by the name thiamine) than you are getting through your daily fare.

WHAT IS B_1?

Vitamin B_1 was the first of the eleven known B vitamins to be discovered, and it is still the best known. It is essential to normal metabolism and nerve function. Your body stores it for only short periods of time, primarily in the heart, liver, kidneys, and brain.

Thiamine is found in a variety of foods, including whole grains, legumes, poultry, and fish. Relatively cheap to manufacture commercially, it is one of the food processor's favorite additives for stimulating sales of cereals, snack items, and low-quality baked goods. By law, it is added to bleached white flour to "enrich" the vitamin-poor product from which it was earlier removed through refinement.[14]

HOW DOES IT WORK?

When absorbed by the small intestine, thiamine is circulated throughout the body to nourish the basic organs and countless body cells. B_1 converts carbohydrates into glucose, which is the sole source of energy for the brain and nervous system. It also helps in the formation of ribose, a sugar vital to the manufacture of the nucleic acid RNA, which contains our genetic information. B_1 helps your heart by keeping it firm and resilient.

WHERE DOES IT WORK?

B_1 performs its vital activity in every cell of your body. However, there are a few special places where B_1 works especially hard.

• *Nervous system.* B_1 is necessary for the optimal functioning of the nervous system and for good mental health, because your nervous system and brain depend almost wholly on carbohydrates (glucose) for energy. Deficiency of thiamine causes a 50 to 60 percent reduction in glucose utilization by your nervous tissues because nerve cells become enlarged and communication between different segments of the central nervous system breaks down.

A thiamine deficiency may result in the degeneration of the insulating and protective sheath—myelin—that covers certain nerve fibers. Your nerves then become hypersensitive, so you are irritable, sluggish, forgetful, and apathetic. If such nerve destruction continues, nerves in the legs may become weakened, and pain—that "pins and needles" sensation—may develop in the legs and feet. Paralysis may be the end result.[15]

Thiamine supplies the only energy source for the nervous system and brain by converting the carbohydrates you eat into glucose. An adequate amount of vitamin B_1 may mean steady nerves for you.

• *Digestive system.* Thiamine promotes a healthy appetite, good digestion, and good elimination. It helps maintain firm muscle tone in the digestive tract to stimulate the elimination process. When B_1 is inadequate, severe constipation can be a problem, in addition to indigestion and anorexia.

• *Metabolism.* A healthy intake of vitamin B_1 is absolutely necessary to metabolic health and efficiency, as it is essential in releasing energy from the foods you eat.

• *Heart.* B_1's function in helping maintain muscle resiliency extends to the most important muscle in your body, the heart. B_1 deficiency may increase the normal circulation of the blood to organs and place an extra burden on the heart. The ability of the heart's lower chambers to deal with such prolonged stress may be inhibited, with a direct adverse effect on cardiac tissues. In addition, the diminished elasticity and tension of the heart muscle caused by low levels of B_1 may result in an abnormal heartbeat.

Although the link has not been fully substantiated, a diet high in refined foods that are low in B_1 and that use up the available B_1 for their conversion in the body may contribute to cardiac trouble.

In this regard, researchers Ruth Adams and Frank Murray tell us about a Dr. E. Cheraskin who has "discovered a significant relationship between the amount of thiamine in one's meals and the frequency of complaints related to heart disease and the possibility of heart attacks."[16]

B_1 deficiency may result in edema, a condition in which tissues in the ankles and elsewhere swell.[17] In some cases, injections of thiamine relieved the problem where diuretics failed.

In its advanced stages, B_1 deficiency affects the heart muscle dramatically, increasing its oxygen needs to a level you may not be able to meet. In addition, debilitation of the heart may occur due to enlargement of the right side.[18] Expansion of blood vessels can cause an increase in the volume of blood that must be pumped by your heart, putting a further strain on the entire cardiovascular system.

WHO NEEDS B₁?

Obviously, we all need thiamine to keep ourselves working not just efficiently, but energetically as well. Anyone who has beriberi or who runs the risk of developing beriberi has a special need for thiamine.

There are two types of beriberi—dry beriberi and wet beriberi— and both are related to low levels of B_1. With an even slightly inadequate intake of B_1, dry beriberi, characterized by all the symptoms of severe thiamine deficiency, can occur. If you follow a crash diet or use drugs like amphetamines (two situations that often go hand in hand), you run the risk of developing dry beriberi.

Wet beriberi occurs when B_1 is vastly undersupplied (under .2 milligram per 1,000 calories). The symptoms are severe swelling of the tissues, neurological changes, an enlarged heart accompanied by painful palpitations,[19] weight loss, sore and weak muscles, limb paralysis, an enlarged liver, gastrointestinal problems, and breathing difficulties. The severity of the symptoms depends on the severity of the thiamine deficiency, and on the patient's age and health.

The elderly may also have special needs for thiamine. Burning feet, bad circulation, and depression are all common symptoms that can be alleviated with the addition of foods rich in vitamin B_1 and/or a good supplement.

After a hard day's work that may have included several cups of coffee or tea, do you arrive home dead-tired, feeling almost as if your brain were wearing out? Don't ignore your symptoms! According to Dr. M. K. Gaitonde and his British colleagues reporting in the *Journal of Neurochemistry,* "Thiamine deficiency in the rat leads to a depletion of thiamine in the brain by about 70 percent." Such a deficiency can also cause a reduction in essential amino acids, glutamate, and threonine, Gaitonde discovered.[20] So if you feel mentally drained, it may well be due to simple thiamine deficiency, which may be easily corrected by proper attention to diet, reduction of coffee or tea, and the addition of a quality dietary supplement.

Besides the obvious washout effect that the caffeine and tannic acid in coffee and tea have on water-soluble vitamins like B_1, tea in itself may contain "anti-thiamine substances," according to Dr. T. Kositawattanakul and his colleagues of Mahidol University in Thailand, reporting in the *American Journal of Clinical Nutrition.* Dr. Kositawattanakul states that "thiamine deficiency is one of the nutritional problems in Thailand. One cause is tea drinking and chewing fermented tea leaves. The major component having anti-thiamine activity is believed to be the tannins,"[21] or tannic acid, in black tea.

Worthwhile substitutes for the tea or coffee habit are herb teas and grain coffees. They are healthy, harmless, and high in minerals. You'll find a large selection at most health foods stores and herbal pharmacies. Even supermarkets sometimes carry them.

Mild thiamine deficiencies do reduce stamina, cause depression, and decrease your capacity to work. A deficiency will cause you irritability, insomnia, headaches, and indigestion, reports Michael Lesser, M.D., in *Nutrition and Vitamin Therapy*.[22]

If you notice any of these chronic symptoms, you may be one of those who *really* needs B_1—more than your current diet is supplying. Especially if you drink loads of tea or coffee, perspire a great deal, are under heavy stress, are taking antibiotics, or have a fever, your intake of thiamine should be increased.

Another situation in which additional thiamine would be helpful is if you are suffering from diarrhea or any other intestinal problem "that would adversely affect the absorption and/or utilization of nutrients," suggests nutritional scientist Dr. Myron Brin.[23] Taking additional B_1 during an intestinal illness will help your body make the most efficient use of the nutrients it does absorb. You could get well quicker and be less susceptible to a secondary ailment.

A PRACTICAL GUIDE TO USING VITAMIN B_1

What foods can you eat to make sure you are getting enough vitamin B_1, so essential for your nerves, heart, and digestive system? Try increasing your consumption of whole grains like wheat and brown rice, dried beans (especially soybeans), poultry, liver, and fish, seeds and nuts, and supplementary items like brewer's yeast (a powerhouse of B vitamins), bran, and wheat germ. Remember when you enjoy that B_1-boosting breakfast of whole grain waffles, or oatmeal sprinkled with sunflower seeds, wheat germ, and bran, that scientific studies show that the higher your B_1 intake, the healthier you'll be (up to a certain limit, of course, and in conjunction with all the other nutrients your body needs).

Also remember that the way you cook your food has a great deal to do with your actual vitamin intake from it, particularly in the case of B_1. As an Australian medical team reported in the *Medical Journal of Australia*, "Thiamine is thermolabile [heat-altered], and some is likely to be destroyed when food for human consumption is cooked; the percentage destroyed depends on a number of factors, including the temperature reached. . . . The diets of most Western countries are based on cooked meats and vegetables, highly refined cereals, and large quantities of fat and sugar, both of which are devoid of thiamine."[24]

How do you know if you are deficient in thiamine? If you suffer from any of the chronic symptoms we talked about above, you have a good clue. You may want to see your doctor, who can tell, through a urine sample, whether you are getting enough thiamine.

Blood samples, too, give considerable data on your nutritional status. In fact, they are considered the most reliable and accurate indicator of thiamine status, for a reduction of activity in red blood cell enzymes indicates a definite B_1 deficiency state.

So how much thiamine should you take? Emanuel Cheraskin, M.D., and his colleagues at the University of Alabama, report in the *Journal of Oral Medicine* that "there is no claim that the dosage of vitamin B_1 recommended by the Food and Nutrition Board is intended as the 'ideal' daily intake for optimal general health." You may need much more thiamine than the government recommends. He tells of an experiment he conducted involving the nine doctors who noted that when their daily intake of thiamine was adequate, deficiency symptoms almost vanished. Cheraskin concluded that a daily dosage of 9 milligrams of thiamine—about eight times the RDA—might be a better "ideal" allowance for many of us, although we must still consider "biochemical individuality."[25]

Vitamin B₂ (Riboflavin)

WHAT IS IT?

Vitamin B_2, or riboflavin, is a yellow crystalline compound that is a growth-promoting member of the vitamin B complex and occurs both free (as in milk) and combined (as in liver). Needed by every organ, every tissue, and every cell of your body every day, B_2 helps promote proper growth and repair of tissues, and cell respiration. It helps release energy from the carbohydrates, protein, and fat in the foods you eat. It is essential for good digestion, steady nerves, assimilation of iron, and as a partner with vitamin A in providing normal vision.

HOW DOES B₂ WORK?

Much of riboflavin's activity takes place in conjunction with two enzymes to whom riboflavin is vital. These protein substances oxidize so-called "intermediates" when your body is processing glucose and fatty acids, transporting hydrogen ions that release energy. If riboflavin is not available, the enzymes cannot perform the necessary chemical reactions to release energy, thus the body's energy cycle is interrupted or slowed.

For your body to get the most energy out of the food you provide, it must have an adequate supply of riboflavin.

WHERE DOES IT WORK?

B_2 is found throughout the body as an active substance. The liver and kidneys have greater stores than other body tissues, but even these reserves are minimal, so you need to get plenty of B_2 in your diet and supplements every day. B_2 is especially vital to the operation of the enzymatic system and the glandular system.

• *Enzymatic system.* As we saw above, riboflavin is an essential constituent of the activity of two important enzymes that convert glucose and fatty acids into energy. Without B_2, you simply cannot be at your best.

• *Glandular system.* Riboflavin is vital to the health of your entire glandular system, most particularly to the adrenal glands. If you've ever heard or read anything about stress control, you know that these two glands, weighing only a quarter ounce each and located against the upper portions of your kidneys, come in for a big share of attention.

The adrenals help control how and where fat is deposited in the body; help regulate the body's sodium/potassium balance, in turn influencing all of your muscles; release hormones that have an important influence on the functioning of the nervous system; and raise and lower the blood pressure and exert a stimulating effect upon the action of the heart muscles. So you can see just how important their well-being is to your overall health.

So where does riboflavin come into the picture? It plays a big part in making your adrenal glands function properly, because it is needed to release the hormone that stimulates the adrenal glands to send forth their own hormones. For example, B. R. Forker and A. F. Morgan of the University of California, Berkeley,[26] found that a deficiency of riboflavin caused an upset of the glandular hormones and increased sensitivity to tension. When adequate amounts of riboflavin are in the diet, the adrenal glands produce necessary antistress hormones. Why? "in the absence of riboflavin, the stimulus for production of corticotropin may be lacking or ineffective." Riboflavin is needed to stimulate the adrenal glands to do their very important work in your body.[27]

• *Eyes.* As we'll see below, riboflavin is as important to your optimal vision as is vitamin A.

• *Blood cells.* B_2 works in your red blood cells to keep them healthy and normal. Inadequate B_2 can cause disorders in blood cell formation and abnormalities in the bone marrow where the cells are synthesized.[10] This condition may lead to anemia.

It is obvious that we all need B_2's activity in every cell of our bodies, every day of the year. For the enzymatic and glandular systems, the eyes, and the blood cells, B_2 is a vital ingredient in your recipe for good health.

WHO NEEDS B₂?

Under certain conditions, your needs for B_2 may be greatly increased. For example, if you are a vegetarian or on a diet, if you eat a lot of processed foods or drink alcohol to excess regularly, you need more vitamin B_2 than you otherwise would. If you are taking antibiotics, oral contraceptives, or are pregnant, if you suffer from stress, anemia, or cataracts, you might also consider improving your health by boosting your intake of B_2.

Being a vegetarian is a special situation that requires unflagging attention to your diet in order to meet all your nutritional needs, especially if you do not drink milk or eat dairy products—rich sources of riboflavin. In such a case—"calcium, riboflavin, and B_{12} needs must be met in other ways," note researchers Whitney and Hamilton in *Understanding Nutrition*.[28] Make friends with the nutrient-rich soybean to guarantee that you get plenty of the vitamins and minerals that animal products supply in a nonvegetarian diet. For example, sixteen ounces of soybean milk daily can provide the necessary calcium and B_2, while a B_{12} supplement will do the rest. Or explore other versatile soy foods like tofu, tempeh, and miso. It's also a good idea for you to snack on vitamin-rich grains, nuts, beans, and seeds as well.

Dieters need to pay attention to their B_2 intake, too. If you are on a very strict diet, be careful not to overdo the undereating. Starvation can cause what nutritionists call "negative nitrogen balance." That means that more tissue is being broken down than is being made or repaired. Thus, you lose a serious amount of the limited store of B_2 your body has to begin with.

It's the same story as with vegetarianism: if you are dieting to lose weight or lower your cholesterol levels, you may be excluding the very food groups that supply the most riboflavin. Whitney and Hamilton remind us, "About half of the riboflavin in the American diet comes from milk and dairy products and another 25 percent from the meat group (meat, poultry, and fish). Milk drinkers have little trouble meeting their needs."[29]

Even on a balanced diet, you may not be getting a sufficient supply of B_2 if you do not eat fresh, unrefined food. Riboflavin may have been present when a food was grown and harvested, but it is easily destroyed by processing, cooking, and storage. Even riboflavin-rich milk loses considerable amounts of the vitamin when it is pasteurized and exposed to ultraviolet rays, then irradiated to add vitamin D. Robinson and Lawler state that "pasteurization, irradiation for vitamin D, evaporation, or drying of milk accounts for loss of not more than 10 to 20 percent of the initial riboflavin content of milk. On the other hand, milk that is bottled in clear glass loses up to 75 percent with 3½ hours exposure in direct sunlight."[30] As a consumer, you can buy your milk in a dark container to guarantee minimal destruction of riboflavin.

So even if your diet is well balanced, if you depend largely on processed food, you may wish to include more raw and unrefined foods, such as whole fruits and vegetables and unheated nuts to insure yourself of a plentiful supply of B_2.

Here's another helpful hint for preserving the riboflavin content of foods you cook: never cook with the pinch of bicarbonate of soda (baking soda) some recipes call for. It destroys B_2.[31] If you must use the soda, compensate for the loss by adding a bit of brewer's yeast or bran to your recipe.

Another dietary consideration that raises your need for riboflavin is the consumption of moderate to large amounts of alcohol (or tea or coffee) on a regular basis. You should look back at the section on the B-complex family for the details; the fact is that alcohol in particular knocks the B vitamins right out of your system. So if you drink, you may want to take some brewer's yeast or a supplement to replace the vitamins you are losing in the process.

If you are taking antibiotics or oral contraceptives, you need more B_2. Use of oral contraceptives can lead to B_2 depletion by interfering with riboflavin absorption. N. Sanpitake and L. Chayutimonkul of the Human Genetics Research Laboratory at Chiang Mai University in Thailand suggest that as oral contraceptives interfere with the absorption of riboflavin and thiamine "supplementary administration [of riboflavin] may be indicated [for women taking oral contraceptives] . . ."[32]

Leonard J. Newman, M.D., of New York University Medical College and his colleagues also found a definite riboflavin deficiency among women taking birth control pills. Dr. Newman postulates that "the effect of oral contraceptive agents on riboflavin metabolism may be an interference with gastrointestinal absorption, and metabolic conversion to active coenzyme forms."[33]

If you are pregnant, need you be told that the health and development of your unborn baby depends in great part on your eating the right foods? And the right foods include those heavy in riboflavin. The health of your baby's nervous system is particularly dependent on adequate amounts of riboflavin. Here's what the experts say:

"Recent studies indicate that the process of structural growth, differentiation, and development of the brain can be influenced by the nutrient supply available during gestation and lactation. . . . The vitamin [riboflavin] is a fundamental constituent of animal tissues, new tissues cannot be formed unless a minimal amount of riboflavin is available. . . . Riboflavin deficiency has been shown to depress weight gain and to cause degeneration of nerve tissue," report Marianna K. Fordyce and Judy A. Driskell from Florida State University.[34]

In addition to disrupting brain development, a low level of B_2 in your prenatal diet may result in poor DNA-RNA metabolism. DNA and RNA are the nucleic acids that contain the human genetic code, so it is easy to see how important their strength is to your newborn's health.[35]

What we're saying is that ample amounts of B_2 in your diet during pregnancy help to prevent birth defects. Such was the conclusion of Dr. Bruce Mackler of the University of Washington School of Medicine, discussed in his Borden Award Address published in *Pediatrics*.

Mackler deprived pregnant animals of riboflavin. A high incidence of gross malformation of the skeleton and split lip anomaly (cleft palate) was the result.[36]

Riboflavin levels during the time in which the embryo is developing, it seems, can tip the balance in favor of a normal birth or a problematic one. The reason lies in the enzymes necessary for growth that depend on B_2 to be activated, which we discussed above. Without adequate B_2 supplied by the supplements you take and the foods you eat—including dairy products, whole grains, and nutritional yeast—the enzymes will not be activated. Growth deformities may be the unfortunate result.[37]

We've already discussed how vital riboflavin is to the proper functioning of your adrenal glands. It literally enables them to secrete the antistress hormones so important in helping you cope with the ups and downs of everyday life. Too little B_2 can cause an increased sensitivity to tension and have a profound influence over the way you react to stress. So if you are under a lot of pressure in the first place, as so many of us are, remember that assuring yourself of plenty of riboflavin may be your way to smoothing out the rocky road of emotional and physical stress.

A PRACTICAL GUIDE TO USING RIBOFLAVIN

The importance of B_2 in your daily diet simply cannot be overstated. What foods should you eat for an ample supply? Be sure to include plenty of dairy products, meat, poultry, fish, nutritional yeast, whole grains and whole grain flour products, and leafy, green vegetables. And remember, if you are a strict vegetarian, pay special attention to meeting your B_2 needs through soy foods. (Even if you are not a vegetarian, soy foods are an economical and nutritious occasional alternative to meat.)

How do you pinpoint a deficiency of riboflavin? Lack of vitamin B_2 is one deficiency you can see. Stick out your tongue. If it is purplish red and inflamed, or if it is shiny (a condition called glossitis), you may need more B_2. Other deficiency symptoms to be on the alert for are cracking of the corners of the lips (cheilosis); greasy skin; occular problems such as blurred vision, hypersensitivity to light, water itchiness, and blood-shot eyes; or headaches, depression, absentmindedness, dizziness, trembling, insomnia, and loss of mental alertness.

If one or more of the above symptoms lead you to suspect a riboflavin deficiency, see your doctor. A good indicator of B_2 deficiency is the relative activity of an enzyme called glutathione reductase found in your red blood cells. It depends on B_2, so when it shows low activity, you are below par as far as B_2 is concerned. Your doctor will be able to discover what your B_2 status is through a simple blood test.

On the other end of the spectrum, can you take in too much B_2? Unlikely. B_2 is water soluble, which means that you are excreting it through perspiration and urine all the time. Large amounts of riboflavin seem to be safe; B_2 toxicity has not been observed in man or animals.[38]

B_3 (Niacin)

WHAT IS B_3?

Niacin, or B_3, or nicotinic acid, as it is sometimes called, is the B vitamin with a difference. How does it differ from its fellow B-complex brothers? It is one of the few B vitamins that the body can manufacture. It is different in another way, as well—although it is a water-soluble vitamin, it is not destroyed as quickly as the others by the cooking and storing methods that are the natural enemies of vitamin potency.

Don't be deceived by B_3's differences, though. Although your body can manufacture it, it can do so only when there are adequate supplies of B_2, B_6, and B_1.[39] And unfortunately, this manufacturing process doesn't provide enough niacin to meet your everyday needs. Furthermore, as much as sixty milligrams of tryptophan, an essential amino acid, is needed to yield one gram of niacin.[40] So you can see how necessary it is that you include niacin-rich food and supplements in your daily fare, rather than merely expecting your body to make all you need.

Even though niacin is not so easily destroyed by cooking methods as are some of the other water-soluble vitamins, if you boil, poach, or blanch your food, a substantial quantity of niacin may evaporate.

HOW DOES B_3 WORK?

Niacin is essential to every cell in your body. Indeed, many vital metabolic functions would cease without an adequate supply of it. The fundamental material of two molecular networks (enzyme systems), niacin helps you transform sugar and fat into energy.

WHO NEEDS B₃?

It is quite obvious that all of us need B_3 to function properly. But B_3 in even greater quantities is needed if you suffer from pellagra (a B_3 deficiency disease), mental illness, arthritis, alcoholism, high cholesterol levels, cardiovascular troubles, or chronic migraine headaches.

Pellagra, like so many diseases once believed to be the result of infection or unsanitary conditions, is actually a nutritional disease. Around the turn of the century, it was taking about 10,000 lives a year, largely from less-educated, lower-income families.

Dr. Joseph Goldberger, a bacteriologist, devoted his life to the study of pellagra, trying to discover just what was causing the terrifying variety of symptoms the disease produces: disorders of the skin, diarrhea and other problems due to the faulty functioning of the intestinal tract, extreme mental unbalance, and death.[41]

Dr. Goldberger's studies revealed a curious correlation between the incidence of pellagra and dietary habits. He found the disease most frequently where the diet was unbalanced, and sometimes when the cornerstone of the diet was cornmeal, accompanied by meat and molasses and very little else.

Although Goldberger uncovered the root cause of the disease—malnutrition—it was not until 1937 that Conrad Elvehjem at the University of Wisconsin identified nicotinic acid as the antipellagra factor.[42]

But the healing effect of supplementing the diet of the pellagra victim with niacin was only partial. Years passed before further studies revealed that pellagra is actually due to a deficiency of other B vitamins as well as niacin. Since then, the cumulative effect of the antipellagra research has saved many lives.

But pellagra is by no means a disease of the past. Wherever diets are seriously unbalanced, doctors and nutritionists tell us, pellagra is certain to turn up. Making sure you take a balanced supplement of the vitamin B complex, as well as getting plenty of the B vitamins in your food, is a sure way to avoid the "three D's" of pellagra: dermatitis, dementia, and diarrhea.[43]

Mental illness is another condition that sometimes seems due to dietary deficiencies. Low levels of niacin, especially when coupled with inadequate amounts of ascorbic acid, have been linked to mental illness, including the dementia of pellagra, obviously, and also schizophrenia.[44]

And it certainly seems that niacin may be capable of reversing some of the symptoms of mental illness. One nutritionally oriented physician, R. Glen Green, has found that patients with severe types of psychosis, as well as other mentally disturbed individuals with subclinical pellagra, respond favorably when niacin treatment is begun at the earliest sign of a disturbance.[45] Dr. E. Cheraskin and his colleagues at the University of Alabama agree. They even go so far as to recommend that you ingest at least 115 milligrams of niacin a day, six to seven times more than the government guidelines currently recommend, as an insurance policy against mental imbalance.[46]

Can pellagra and related symptoms of full-blown schizophrenia be helped by vitamin therapy? Possibly. Here is a convincing example from Norman Cousins, former *Saturday Review* editor.

Joan, a college student, was suffering from a mental disorder in which her thoughts were disconnected from external reality, even the reality of her own body. She hallucinated, compulsively wiping away nonexistent spots on mirrors. Hospitalized as a schizophrenic, she was given electroshock therapy along with large doses of sedative drugs.

As you might suspect, the best treatment medicine had to offer did nothing for Joan. Indeed, she became catatonic. After five years and seven hospitals, plus medical bills of $230,000, Joan remained seriously psychotic. What finally saved her life?

"Systematic examination revealed that Joan's mental symptoms were the result of chronic pellagra," Cousins reports, "a disease caused by malnutrition."[47]

Joan was especially deficient in niacin. No surprise, since disorders in the way the body metabolizes this B vitamin are believed to be one of the most important causes of central nervous system disease.

With the addition of megadoses of niacin as well as ascorbic acid, Joan's pellagra eventually vanished. Nutritional therapy providing all the vitamins and nutrients needed for whole body health returned her to normal mental health and a new life.

Your general state of health may even be improved by increasing the amount of niacin in your daily fare. The Cheraskin-Ringsdorf team of nutritional researchers, for example, tells us that in reviewing the results of numerous tests designed to reveal the relationship between food intake and clinical symptoms, time and again fewer symptoms went hand in hand with a diet high in B_3.[48]

If you suffer from arthritis, you too may benefit from additional amounts of niacin. One of B_3's first uses as a curative vitamin was in treating arthritis.[49]

We've talked a lot about alcoholism and the B vitamins, and by now you should know how important this vitamin is in the treatment—and some say prevention—of this destructive condition. If you have a drinking problem, you will be interested to hear that niacin may help you. Safe and effective, niacin's action is totally different from that of drugs. More and more members of the medical community are using it to control alcohol addiction.

Do you suffer from high cholesterol levels? You will be delighted to hear that vitamin C and lecithin aren't the only nutritional elements that can help you. Niacin, too, can lower elevated blood fats including cholesterol and free fatty acids.[50]

Do you take any kind of heart medication? Then here's more good news: niacin may soon prove useful. Niacin was one of four substances scrutinized recently by the National Institute of Health's Coronary Drug Project Research Group using over 1,000 cardiovascular patients. Researchers noted that the five-year survival rate in the patients treated with niacin and those who took placebos was about the same. But niacin "may be slightly beneficial in protecting persons to some degree against recurrent myocardial infarction."[52]

And if you are one of the millions of Americans who suffer from occasional or chronic migraine, you will be interested to know that niacin may help there, too.

Niacin's therapeutic effect on migraines is probably due to its ability to dilate the veins and stimulate a freer flow of blood, says Dr. Miles Atkinson, formerly of New York University, retired.[51] You may have noticed such a "niacin rush" if you've ever taken a tablespoon of brewer's yeast in water or juice. It is a perceptible effect.

Studies have also shown a link between the disability of the ear canals called Ménière's syndrome and niacin deficiency, particularly when the sufferer's diet is unbalanced and high in processed food.

It may not be a panacea, but niacin works efficiently in treating and controlling a number of ills. It's an established fact. And yet it is still widely rejected by the segment of the medical community that treats disease by simply matching drugs with symptoms.

Don't be deceived by antivitamin-therapy propaganda that may be rooted in medical "scrutiny," but is actually emanating from a large drug industry that feels threatened by the potential of a nondrug like niacin, or any other vitamin, for that matter. After all, niacin could someday represent a safe alternative to popular tranquilizers like Valium and other psychoactive drugs. If so, it would mean increased health benefits, since it does not disrupt the normal metabolism as drugs do.

We refer specifically to the report of an American Psychiatric Association task force that investigated the effect of megadoses of niacin on mentally disordered patients. The general result was an overall condemnation of niacin as mental illness therapy. The task force reported these side effects in conjunction with niacin therapy:

• Liver damage (through jaundice).
• Unfavorable changes in cholesterol levels noted over an extended treatment period.
• Dermatological changes.
• Ulcers.
• High levels of uric acid, abnormal lipid readings, and erratic glucose metabolism

The one positive point the task force found in favor of niacin therapy was that all these effects were temporary and could be eliminated or controlled by manipulating the niacin dosage. In fact, niacin therapy produced no irreversible problems of any kind, in contrast to prolonged treatment with conventional psychoactive drugs, which may have debilitating long-term effects.

Nutritionists feel that the task force's conclusions were somewhat misleading. For example, niacin was used in conjunction with electroshock treatment and chemotherapy, which could easily have been responsible for many if not all of the side effects noted. Furthermore, to produce these adverse effects, doses thirty or more times larger than the conventional "megadoses" used in therapy were employed.

So nutritionists question whether or not the task force test was appropriately conducted, whether the information was accurately interpreted, and if the results were reviewed fairly. It seems to many nutritional researchers who have seen the positive effects of niacin on any number of ailments that the task force was not objective and the test model grossly flawed.

A PRACTICAL GUIDE TO USING NIACIN

Next time you go out to dinner, if you eat animal protein don't pass up that liver or kidney on the menu in favor of steak. All organ meats are first-rate sources of B_3.

But what if you are a "partial" vegetarian? What if you eat no meat, just fish on occasion? Niacin is also found in salmon and tuna. You can also get a reasonable amount by eating wheat germ, brewer's yeast, green leafy vegetables, beans, peas, dried figs, prunes, and dates.

Although not all of these foods are *great* sources of B_3, you'll find that by eating plenty of them in combination you'll be doing yourself a big B_3 favor.

But remember, when any of these foods has been processed or refined, it has suffered a loss in niacin content. Eat foods as fresh and close to their natural state as possible for the full B_3 value—and for the full value of all the other vitamins and minerals as well.

How much niacin do you need? The RDA is 20 milligrams, depending on your age and sex. If you eat a mixed balanced diet, you can easily receive 16 to 33 milligrams of niacin daily from food. But there is something else to remember.

You can eat niacin-rich foods and still not get enough niacin because B_3 is sometimes chemically "bound up" in the food. Remember Dr. Goldberger's observation that the cornerstone of the diet of many pellagra patients was corn? Corn contains B_3, but it lacks adequate tryptophan, the essential amino acid without which niacin cannot properly be synthesized. That is why a balanced diet is so important.

(Also, there are certain ways to prepare corn that release the B_3. Ever wonder why maize in Central America and Mexico is traditionally prepared with lime? Or why certain Indian tribes bother to roast their corn, sun-dry it, then boil it? These methods release some of the niacin that would otherwise have remained dormant.)

Many experts feel that a daily supplement of niacin (preferably in a ratio-determined balance with the other members of the vitamin B family) is in order. Especially if you are getting along in years, suggests Dr. Hoffer, a niacin supplement may mean extra protection against arthritis, premature senility, and abnormal cholesterol levels that may be partially due to B_3 deficiency.[53]

There are cases on record of niacin sensitivity, especially with mega-megadoses. Also, as we mentioned before, this "vasodilator" vitamin may produce a "flush,"—a burning, itching sensation that spreads gradually through the whole body, producing a "hot all over" feeling.[54]

B_5 (Pantothenic Acid)

WHAT IS PANTOTHENIC ACID?

The root of B_5's name, "panthos," means "everywhere." "Everywhere" is a good clue to B_5's presence in foods, and to its activity throughout your body. B_5 is found in foods as diverse as organ meats, egg yolks, peanuts, whole grains, brewer's yeast, and beans.[55] And it works in virtually every cell of your body. Like the other B vitamins, B_5 is water soluble. That means that it is easily excreted and destroyed by such factors as heavy coffee drinking.

HOW DOES IT WORK?

What are the primary functions of pantothenic acid?

- It converts carbohydrates and fats and proteins to energy.
- It acts as an antistress agent by helping calm tension.
- It manufactures antibodies that fight infectious compounds in the bloodstream.

WHO NEEDS IT?

We can all benefit from the presence of B_5 in our foods and in supplements. But if you are under a lot of pressure, suffer from chronic fatigue, eat processed food, suffer from mental illness, or grind your teeth, additional pantothenic acid may be especially helpful. For the elderly and arthritic, pantothenic acid requirements are also higher.

If you suffer from hypoglycemia or allergies, the stress your adrenal glands are under also increases your need for pantothenic acid.

Pantothenic acid has been described by Dr. Roger Williams as "one more link in the chain which is required to prevent mental disease."[56]

He found that low B_5 levels produce "profound mental depression. . . . The fact that both animals and humans are reported to stand stress better when they are administered large doses of pantothenic acid is pertinent to this problem."[57]

If you grind your teeth during your sleep, your nerves are under-nourished. In addition, nocturnal teeth gnashing, or bruxism, may be hazardous to your health. It grinds down your teeth, causing gum disease and improper bite.[58]

But you need not resort to tranquilizers to stop gnashing your teeth, nor must you turn to barbiturates to get a good night's sleep. Nutrients like calcium, vitamins A and C, iodine, vitamin E, plus healthy doses of pantothenic acid helped curb bruxism in patients treated with them. Other patients treated with the same formula, minus pantothenic acid and calcium, continued to be troubled by the condition.[59]

So if you grind your teeth during sleep, or if you suffer from insomnia, try this combination of nutrients, emphasizing calcium and pantothenic acid.

A PRACTICAL GUIDE TO USING B_5

We already know that B_5 is found in many common foods: organ meats, eggs, peanuts, whole grains, and beans. How much pantothenic acid do you need?

Although the requirement for pantothenic acid is not yet known, the Food and Nutrition Board suggests 5 to 10 milligrams daily for adults. The only side effect ever reported at high dose levels has been diarrhea.

What are the signs of deficiency? They include high susceptibility to illnesses and infections; digestive malfunctions like abdominal soreness, pain, and vomiting; muscular and nerve disturbances like leg cramps, weakness, "pins and needles" sensation; skin rashes and disorders; insomnia; and mental depression. If you suffer chronically from any of these symptoms, it is worth your while to pay more attention to giving yourself plenty of B_5-rich foods in a carefully planned, well-balanced diet. You may also wish to try a supplement.

B_6 (Pyridoxine)

WHAT IS B_6?

What is B_6? Composed of three chemical compounds—pyridoxal, an aldehyde; pyridoxine, an alcohol; and pyridoxamine, an amine compound—B_6 is necessary for the biochemical production of several enzymes that catalyze amino acid increase and/or decrease.

HOW DOES B₆ WORK?

Pyridoxine nourishes the central nervous system, controls sodium/-potassium levels in your blood, and assists in the production of red blood cells and hemoglobin. It is an important protector against infection, too.

Like all the other members of the vitamin B family, B_6 has a profound effect on your central nervous system. Most likely these effects are due to the role of pyridoxine in protein and nucleic acid synthesis. The important fact to remember is that if your diet does not contain enough B_6, you could be starving your central nervous system and setting the stage for symptoms ranging from mild depression to convulsions.

B_6 is one of the factors that controls the sodium/potassium levels in your body fluids. The correct ratio of these two elements has a direct influence on how smoothly your nervous system and muscles function. If your sodium/potassium ratio is thrown out of balance by a B_6 deficiency, you may suffer swelling of the tissues in your legs, face, and hands (edema).

Like so many of the B vitamins, B_6 also assists in manufacturing DNA-RNA, the nucleic acids that contain your genetic code for growth, repair, and multiplication of all the cells and tissues in your body.

Along with B_{12}, folic acid, iron, and protein, B_6 is responsible for the production of red blood cells and hemoglobin. Along the same lines, B_6 protects your body from anemia. How? Iron needs B_6 to make the hemoglobin your body requires. If B_6 is not available in adequate amounts, iron will not be fully utilized and granular deposits will build up in your blood cells. In other words, B_6 helps prevent anemia by keeping iron available to your bloodstream.

B_6 is important in protecting you from infections, especially genitourinary infections. It helps produce antibodies that fight tetanus and typhoid as well.

WHO NEEDS PYRIDOXINE?

Anyone who wants to enjoy the best of health needs plenty of all the B vitamins, as we've seen over and over. But the pregnant, the dieting, and the elderly may have a special need for B_6. In addition, those who eat processed foods or take drugs—especially oral contraceptives—may have increased need for B_6. And if you suffer from chronic liver disease, malabsorption of nutrients or any other form of malnutrition, acne, dental cavities, renal disorders, rheumatism, hyperactivity, or asthma, pyridoxine may have a special place in your life. If you, like everybody else, would like to reduce to some degree your chances of developing cancer or atherosclerosis, B_6 may help.

Remember how important B_6 is to your nervous system? If you are pregnant, keep in mind that B_6 is vital to the healthy development of your baby's nervous system, too. A deficiency can be harmful for your newborn. Dorothy M. Morre and her colleagues at Purdue University, who conducted tests on experimental animals, discovered that "maternal vitamin B_6 deficiency during a critical period of brain development interferes with this orderly process [of brain development] in the young." Her team also noted lower brain and body weights as a result of B_6 deficiency.[60]

According to Michael H. Brophy, M.D. and Pentti K. Silteri, Ph.D., "The importance of B_6 to the development of the fetus is indicated by the fact that the active form of the vitamin pyridoxal phosphate is concentrated across the placenta in greater amounts than is iron at term of normal pregnancy . . . Normal brain maturation is dependent upon adequate levels of B_6. . . ."[61]

They refer to other researchers who have discovered that witholding just B_6 from the mother and child caused a reduction of 30 to 50 percent in what experts call cerebral myelinating lipids, plus lowered fetal brain weights.[62] Today I feel these types of human experiments would not be allowed. Depriving any mother or infant of any essential nutrient seems thoughtlessly cruel and inhumane.

If you are pregnant, it is important that you get plenty of B_6 in foods and supplements. But if you are pregnant and considered at high risk of developing hypertensive disorders of pregnancy, says Dr. Brophy, your doctor-should actually supervise the amount of pyridoxine in your diet to assure the normal brain development of your baby.[63]

John M. Ellis, M.D., found B_6 along with magnesium, to be indicated as a factor in the "prevention of convulsions in patients with toxemia of pregnancy and treatment of convulsions of eclampsia." Dr. Ellis has found B_6 useful in easing various distressful side effects of pregnancy, such as nausea and vomiting, cramps and pain in the limbs.[34] He states that "all pregnant women should have at least 50 milligrams of B_6 as a supplement throughout their pregnancies and many of them will require considerably more than that." While your needs for pyridoxine may be small, the slightest deficiency can cause big discomforts when you are pregnant. Protect your own health and that of your unborn child by paying careful attention to your intake of B_6.

If you are on a diet, be aware that you may need more B_6. Perhaps your diet emphasizes high protein and natural fats like those found in nuts, avocados, and dairy products. In the beginning, you lose a lot of weight and feel greatly energized. But then you notice these symptoms: irritability, edema of the face and ankles, and a skin rash.

What is wrong? Could be you're suffering from a vitamin B_6 deficiency. "Diets rich in fat or protein, or both, contribute to the exhaustion of vitamin B_6 in the plasma because of the many pyridoxine-dependent biochemical reactions involved in the breakdown and conversion of these substances," says Donald A. Mitchell, a biochemist at Florida's Nova University. In addition, he cautions that a "pyridoxine deficiency produces a pronounced impairment of the immune response." What he's saying is that if you are deficient in vitamin B_6 because you've gone on a diet or for any other reason, there is a chance you may get sick due to the depression of protein metabolism.

A B_6 deficiency results in a poor antibody response and your body becomes more vulnerable to many illnesses. If you are on a diet, you may need to cut down on high fat and/or protein intake. It is quite possible to eat plenty of whole grains and vegetables, with some meat and dairy products, and still lose weight. But if you stick to the fat/-protein method, you need to fortify yourself with B_6 to avoid its being "leached" out of your body.

If you are elderly, your need for B_6 is higher than it was when you were younger. But you need fewer calories—therefore it is especially important that you eat nutrient-dense foods and take supplements if necessary. B_6 deficiency may contribute further to such age-related ills as stiff joints, depression, and poor muscle function. According to Drs. Sheila C. Vir and A.H.G. Love, at Queen's University of Belfast, "Vitamin B_6 deficiency in the aged may be more prevalent than appreciated . . . recent dietary surveys have also revealed a low intake of vitamin B_6 among the aged." They recommend a daily dietary allowance higher than 2.5 milligrams per day.[64]

And if you eat refined and processed food, a supplement of pyridoxine and all the rest of the vitamin B complex may be in order. We'll repeat: the refinement process is very hard on vitamins; it's better to eat whole, unprocessed foods for full vitamin value.

Are you taking drugs? High drug intake, whether through recreational, over-the-counter, or prescribed means, can interfere with B_6 utilization. A few B_6 antagonists are isoniazid, penicillamine, and semicarbazide, as well as oral contraceptives.[65]

Your need for B_6 is also increased if you suffer from chronic liver disease or malabsorption—the inability to extract all the nutrients from food that a well-nourished body can. Obviously, any other form of malnutrition could be improved not just with the addition of B_6, but the whole range of vitamins and minerals.

Other healing benefits of B_6 include the ability to reduce acne disfiguration, improve resistance to cancer and atherosclerosis, and diminish the incidence of dental cavities.

For anyone suffering from renal disorders, the vitamin-mineral combination of B_6 and magnesium appears to prevent or help decrease recurrence of kidney stones in particular, report Harvard University researchers.[66]

Why do B_6 and magnesium have such an influence on renal disorders? By altering its pH, magnesium makes the urine more solvent to the substances called oxalates that form kidney stones. The urine is able to maintain the kidney stone precursors in soluble crystal form. The risk of these crystals forming stones again is greatly reduced.

On the other hand, vitamin B_6 does not particularly alter the oxalate substances. But it does regulate the amount of oxalic acid that is actually delivered to your kidneys.

As Dr. Stanley Gershoff puts it, "It would appear that for many, if not all, individuals, the dietary level of vitamin B_6 needed to insure minimal oxalate excretion is greater than the amount needed to protect against most other known manifestations of vitamin B_6 deficiency."[67]

To lessen the potential of formation of stones in the urine and kidney, make sure your diet contains ample amounts of B_6.

Have you resigned yourself to years of medication to relieve the pain of arthritis? B_6 might spare you some of this agony. The work of Dr. John Ellis should be of interest to any arthritis patient on a heavy regimen of cortisone or aspirin. Taking 100 milligrams of this vitamin daily produced healing, he reports, in one victim whose hands and feet were so swollen he could barely move. B_6 suppressed the pain as well as reduced the swelling, and the patient returned to normal health.

Even 50 milligrams of B_6 daily sometimes works wonders for those suffering from arthritis. Ellis used this dosage to improve patients' coordination, tactile ability, and even the rate and degree with which they could flex their afflicted limbs. "Some patients experienced a return to health after a week or two; some, in six weeks; others, usually the elderly, had gradual improvement, up to six and eight months," he reports.[68]

Does your child suffer from hyperactivity or asthma? B_6 can be a boon to alleviating either of these conditions.

The noted Canadian physician Abram Hoffer, the *Journal of the Canadian Medical Association* reports, successfully treats hyperactive children with a combination of B_6 and niacin. He is amazed at the personality and behavioral changes produced by this vitamin combination. Hoffer suggests "that physicians try treating hyperkinetic children with these vitamins which seem to be so effective."[69]

Asthma is another common problem in children that responds to B_6 treatment. Platon J. Collipp, M.D., chief of the Nassau County Medical Center's Department of Pediatrics, and his colleagues have found B_6 both safe and effective when it comes to relieving this respiratory stress.

Collipp and his team observed notable improvement in asthma victims who were treated with 50 milligrams of B_6 daily for three months, followed by 100 milligrams of B_6 daily for six months. In fact, children taking 200 milligrams daily were relieved of their wheezing, difficult breathing and tightness in the chest even more quickly than those who took only 100 milligrams.

Collipp's conclusion: "The data from these patients suggest that pyridoxine therapy may be a useful medication which reduces the severity of asthma in many, but not all, asthmatic children."[71]

A PRACTICAL GUIDE TO USING B$_6$

The best food sources of B$_6$ are brewer's yeast, beef, and pork liver, fish such as salmon and herring, brown rice, bananas, and pears. It is so common that if you eat whole grain cereals, beans, and all fresh vegetables and meats in general, you will have plenty.

But remember, when B$_6$-rich foods are processed into frozen dinners and B$_6$-rich vegetables and fruits are turned into canned goods and convenience foods, considerable nutrition may be lost. Although somewhat heat and acid resistant, B$_6$ *is* water soluble, so be sure to use a minimum of water when cooking to preserve pyridoxine.

How much B$_6$ do you need? The official RDA is 2 milligrams. Storage of B$_6$ is short term and no overdose symptoms have been recorded. But B$_6$ *deficiency* can cause you serious problems.

How can you tell if you are deficient in B$_6$? Deficiency signs are similar to those of niacin or B$_2$: irritability, nervousness, and personality changes; weakness, dermatitis, and other skin changes including lesions, particularly around the eyes, eyebrows, and peripheral regions of the mouth; and insomnia.

Another commonly observed side effect is edema—swelling of the tissues.

Not visible, but vital, is the fact that a deficiency of niacin may result when B$_6$ is inadequate. Why? Because niacin cannot be properly produced from tryptophan when levels of B$_6$ are low.

If you suspect a B$_6$ deficiency, your doctor can give you precise information through a simple urine test. On the other hand, Dr. Herbert Schaumberg of Albert Einstein College of Medicine reported that an overdose of vitamin B$_6$ can cause nerve damage. He suggested that "flooding the system with it is probably killing nerve cells." Many women in the hope of alleviating their menstrual cramps might be consuming excessive amounts of B$_6$.

When we asked Dr. Robert Atkins what he thought of Dr. Schaumberg's statement he said that "if you take B$_6$ in combination with the other B-Complex members you can avoid any symptoms of nerve damage." Excessive amounts, in Dr. Atkins's opinion begin at 1600 mg.[70]

B_{12}

WHAT IS IT?

B_{12} has an almost legendary connection with energy. A B_{12} shot is practically a synonym for an injection of pep. Why? What mysterious power does B_{12} have over fatigue?

It's no mystery. B_{12} is the most complex of the B vitamins, having at its center an atom of cobalt. Your small intestine absorbs B_{12} when something called "the intrinsic factor" is produced in your stomach. The whole process depends, incidentally, on the presence of calcium.

WHERE DOES B_{12} WORK?

Like other vital nutrients, B_{12} works its wonders in every cell of your body. Here are some of its key territories:

• *Energy.* For normal energy levels, B_{12} is a prerequisite.

• *Cells.* Every cell in your body depends on B_{12} to function properly. It is especially vital to the cells in your bone marrow, gastrointestinal tract, and nervous system.

• *Metabolic system.* Like all the B vitamins, B_{12} plays a key role in transmuting protein, fats, and carbohydrates to energy. Metabolically, B_{12} helps you maintain a normal weight.

• *Blood.* To form new red blood cells, you need B_{12}. It also helps regenerate nucleic acid and bone marrow. Without B_{12}, the synthesis of normal red blood cells in the bone marrow cannot take place.

B_{12} keeps enlarged red blood cells from forming. What does this mean? It means that oxygen can be freely transported in the blood, without interference from malformed cells, a condition called macrocytic megaloblastic anemia.[72]

• *Liver.* B_{12} helps prevent fatty deposits from accumulating in your liver. It plays a key role in the manufacture of methionine and choline, two substances that help move fats.

• *Nervous system.* B_{12} offers you protection against spinal cord lesions, mental disturbances, and visual problems. How? It protects nerve fibers in the central and peripheral nervous system.

WHO NEEDS B_{12}?

The foregoing list is the answer to that question: we all do. But if you are a vegetarian, an alcoholic, or suffer from mental illness, B_{12} is superimportant.

Vegetarians owe it to themselves to be extra careful about their diets. As Richard W. Vilter, M.D., of the University of Cincinnati College of Medicine, warns, "Persons who eat absolutely no animal protein (called vegans) or extreme vegetarians have no source of vitamin B_{12}, but much folic acid in their diets. Frequently in such subjects, neurologic abnormalities develop of the posterolateral column degeneration type. This is a situation analogous to a patient with pernicious anemia who is treated inadequately with a mixed vitamin capsule containing folic acid."[73]

There is another danger for those who abstain from animal foods, including dairy products: dietary deficiencies don't show up for five to ten years because the body is able to hold some B_{12} in reserve. Nerve damage may exist without signs of deficiency until it is too late. The result of degeneration of the nervous system and the spinal cord is so irreparable that death may be the result.

A daily supplement of B_{12} is a must to prevent such a deficiency. If you are wise, you will take B_{12} and folic acid together, because folic acid cannot be activated if B_{12} is not present.[74]

A complication of the B_{12}-folic acid partnership of which all vegans should be aware is that if folic acid is present in the diet that lacks B_{12}, it may disguise the B_{12} deficiency. For example, if folic acid is adequate in the diet, no anemia will result from B_{12} deficiency. "The anemia caused by vitamin B_{12} deficiency can be mistaken for that caused by folacin [folic acid] deficiency," report nutritionists Whitney and Hamilton in *Understanding Nutrition*, "because both are characterized by large red blood cells that are indistinguishable under the microscope. As a result, the B_{12} deficiency anemia can be misdiagnosed as folacin [folic acid] deficiency anemia, and the wrong vitamin administered to correct the disorder.

"Intact folacin [folic acid] does clear up the blood symptoms of B_{12} deficiency, but if fails to correct the neurological damage, which may persist and advance while the obvious symptoms are masked."[11]

Heavy drinkers should note that even if they are eating a properly balanced diet—which most heavy drinkers aren't—alcohol is interfering with the B_{12} present in their food, so that it does not reach the places that need it.

Those on a heavy regimen of any kind of drugs should also be aware that they may not be absorbing the B_{12} in their food.

Since B_{12} is safe and easy to add to your diet, why wait until you exhibit symptoms indicating you are deficient?

What sort of symptoms? The *British Medical Journal* (March 26, 1966) tells us that many "mental disturbances may be the first manifestations of B_{12} deficiency."[9] These range from severe psychosis to less serious but still abnormal mood swings to mental slowness and short-term memory problems.

A PRACTICAL GUIDE TO USING B_{12}

All B_{12} in its natural state is manufactured by microorganisms, so it is not normally found in the fruits and vegetables you eat. That is why vegans have so much difficulty obtaining the proper amounts of B_{12}.

If you eat meat, poultry, nonfat dry milk, or fermented soybean products such as tempeh, you should be getting sufficient B_{12} in your diet.

Common symptoms of B_{12} deficiency are motor and mental abnormalities; rapid heartbeat or cardiac pain; facial swellings; jaundice, weakness, and fatigue; loss of weight or hair; hallucinations; depression; and impaired memory.

If you suffer from any of these symptoms, see your doctor. If he diagnoses B_{12} or B_{12}–folic acid deficiency, B_{12} injections will be used to restore your health.

Folic Acid

WHAT IS IT?

Even though your body needs only comparatively minuscule amounts of folic acid, it is a vital nutrient. Folic acid—along with all the other nutrients, of course—is your guarantee of optimum physical and mental health. Your levels of folic acid are dependent on outside sources; your body does not make it on its own. Furthermore, it needs vitamin C to work properly.[7] It works in partnership with B_{12} and B_6, as well as the other B vitamins.

Folic acid is essential to the production of norepinephrine and serotonin, chemical go-betweens of the nervous system.

WHERE DOES FOLIC ACID WORK?

Folic acid works mostly in the brain and nervous system. A vital component of spinal fluid and extracellular fluids, is an important factor in normalizing the functions of your brain. So the places where folic acid is most active are your brain and your nervous system.

WHO NEEDS FOLIC ACID?

If you are pregnant, elderly, or suffer from any sort of nervous disorder, you may benefit from additional amounts of folic acid in your diet.

Pregnant women, for instance, must be wary of folic acid deficiency. Folic acid supplementation has been helpful in preventing abortion and miscarriage.

The elderly need additional folic acid, too. If you are over sixty and depressed, withdrawn, and chronically tired, you may be deficient in this vital element.

Let's look at the results of a study in which folic acid was added to the diets of elderly individuals: three groups of patients were used, all with varying degrees of circulation problems. The first group, those with the least degree of difficulty, experienced improved vision less than an hour after receiving folic acid. (Among those with circulatory problems, vision is often impaired because of poor circulation to the optical tissues.)

The second group, individuals who had been suffering from peripheral vascular disorder for up to ten years, reported feeling warmth and comfort in their faces, heads, and hands within only ten minutes after supplementation.

The third group, the most severely affected, with diabetes, reduced vision, and almost total blockage of their arteries, also enjoyed visual improvement and increased skin temperature in affected limbs, with no side effects from the treatment at all.

Results of the study were reported in the *Journal of the American Geriatrics Society:* "The study's findings indicated that the younger patients with the longer duration of vascular disease showed the best response to folic acid therapy, probably because of the development of a larger number of blood vessels and a better collateral circulation."[75]

Nerves on edge? Folic acid can help. *The Lancet,* Britain's prestigious medical journal, reports, "In the past decade [however] there has been increasing interest in the role of folate [folic acid] in neuronal metabolism, in neuropsychiatric illness, and in antiepileptic and convulsant mechanisms."

When a folic acid deficiency occurs, your nervous system suffers, because there is normally such a high folate concentration in your cerebrospinal fluid. In many psychiatric and geriatric patients with mental dysfunctions, deficiency is common. "This is a promising area for future research," *The Lancet* adds.[76]

Meanwhile, if you are emotionally upset or just "on edge," consider reaching for some folic acid instead of a potentially harmful drug.

A PRACTICAL GUIDE TO USING FOLIC ACID

Eat plenty of these foods to avoid folic acid deficiency: brewer's yeast, liver, kidney, and green leafy vegetables like spinach, parsley, watercress, and kale.

And remember, folic acid can be destroyed by exposure to heat and strong light.

When we talked about vitamin B_{12}, we discussed its important partnership with folic acid. Take these two together. B_{12} alone may increase the utilization of folate and lead to folate deficiency. Folate taken alone may eliminate the symptoms of anemia, but B_{12} is needed to eliminate the neurological effects of the deficiency. Folic acid supplementation can then mask these nerve-related disorders, and the resulting spinal cord degeneration can be fatal. So take them together, and if you are a vegetarian, reread the scoop on B_{12} for special cautions concerning that vitamin.

Another way the B_{12}–folic acid partnership operates is that folic acid cannot be mobilized without B_{12}. And methionine, a sulfur amino acid essential for the manufacture of new protein, cannot be produced unless both B_{12} and folic acid are adequately supplied.

Para-aminobenzoic Acid (PABA)

WHAT IS IT?

A component of folic acid, PABA acts as a coenzyme in the body's metabolism of proteins and helps in the manufacture of healthy blood cells. It teams up with folic acid and pantothenic acid to create all-around good health.

WHO NEEDS IT?

PABA has some special functions that may interest you if you have prematurely gray hair or suffer from hair loss or skin disorders. In addition, it's a great skin protector when you want to guard against sunburn.

If you suffer from hair loss, PABA may help. Dr. Frank A. Evans author of *Diseases of Metabolism* had success in controlling hair loss among a group of dieting women with PABA. "Results have been satisfactory and its continued use is recommended," he reports.[77]

PABA has also been helpful in healing skin disorders. If your doctor diagnoses lymphoblastoma cutis, lupus erythematosus, scleroderma, pemphigus, or dermatitis herpetiformis, consider the use of PABA in combination with zinc, B_6, manganese, and pantothenic acid, suggests Dr. Carl Pfeiffer.[78]

Dr. Pfeiffer also reports that added to certain medically approved skin lotions, PABA is one of the best sunscreens.[79] PABA performs its protective role by absorbing the portions of the ultraviolet spectrum that are known to cause serious sunburn and even skin cancer. PABA clings to the skin, protecting it from the sun's harmful rays by reacting biologically with substances in the stratum corneum.[7]

Be advised, however, that PABA sunscreen products are not a guarantee against sunburn. The only guarantees against sunburn lie in caution and avoidance of extended exposure to the sun. Taking PABA internally may also provide some protection against sunburn in susceptible sun-seekers, but Dr. Pfeiffer says that B[6] may be a better nutrient to take for this purpose.[80] PABA's benefits lie largely in its external use.

A PRACTICAL GUIDE TO USING PABA

For plenty of PABA, eat eggs, brewer's yeast, molasses, wheat germ, and whole grains every day.

Deficiency signs are digestive trouble, nervous tension, emotional instability, and blotchy skin.

Choline

WHAT IS IT?

Choline is present in all your cellular membranes as a lipotropic agent, or fat mover. It is actually part of a group of fats itself, called phospholipids. This fat family also contains phosphoric acid and polyunsaturated fatty acid.

Choline is produced in the liver, from which it helps regulate your cholesterol levels. You can also find choline in a variety of foods: wheat germ and bran, beans, egg yolks, brewer's yeast, whole grains, nuts, lecithin, meat, and fish.

WHERE DOES CHOLINE WORK?

Choline's core activity happens in your liver, heart, and nervous system:

• *Liver.* Since choline is a fat mover, it keeps fats from accumulating in your liver. This is important because fatty deposits in the liver interfere with its normal filtering order. Says Sailen Mookerfea, University of Toronto: "It is known from histological and biochemical evidence that withdrawal of choline from the diet in one single *meal* causes accumulation of lipid in the liver . . ."[39]

Choline is vital to the liver's functions. It helps your liver change fats into phospholipid substances so they can be flushed out. If choline is not present, the liver is unable to process any sort of fat—either those fatty acids in the bloodstream from foods, or those broken down within the body's tissues and released.[40]

Choline also helps prevent buildup of liver toxins. It aids in lipoprotein secretion, the system by which dangerous amounts of the blood fats known as triglycerides are transported from your liver by the blood. If the triglycerides remain in the liver, its ability to detoxify unhealthy substances that invade your bloodstream is greatly hampered. When you have enough choline, poisons are eliminated from the body through your liver.

• *Nervous system.* As the precursor for the neurotransmitter acetylcholine, choline aids in building and maintaining steady nerves and a healthy nervous system.

• *Cardiovascular system.* Both choline and inositol have been called effective agents in protecting your heart muscle from disease. A study conducted by Los Angeles physicians Lester M. Morrison and William F. Gonzales administered choline to patients recovering from coronary thrombosis and myocardial infarction. Some of the patients received choline for only twelve months; the others were treated for two to three years. The doctors found that "the subsequent mortality rate of patients was significantly reduced under the choline treatment."[81]

So if you or someone you love suffers from cardiovascular disease, choline-rich foods may be nature's very best medicine.

It's hard to avoid choline if you concentrate on a variety of natural foods, especially wheat germ, wheat bran, brewer's yeast, whole grains, green leafy vegetables, seeds, nuts, meats, fish, eggs, lecithin, and soybeans. (You may have noticed by now that all these foods are great sources of nearly all the B-complex vitamins!)

Inositol: The Big Little Vitamin

Why do you so rarely hear about inositol when the B complex is discussed? Some scientists feel that inositol should *not* be considered a vitamin since the need for it in human nutrition has not been established. It is naturally stored in your body—especially in the brain, kidney, liver, heart, thyroid, and even the hair. Your body manufactures considerable amounts of inositol through the bacteria in the intestine. So, in a sense, inositol is similar to choline, that other little-known member of the B complex.

And like choline, inositol is a lipotropic agent that occurs as a major portion of the phospholipid molecules in your body. It performs the big job of emulsifying fats, thus playing a role in preventing cholesterol buildup and in normalizing the metabolism of fats.[82]

WHO NEEDS INOSITOL?

Well, we all do. But if you suffer from insomnia, hair loss, high cholesterol levels, or cirrhosis of the liver, inositol may be an especially good friend.

Can't sleep? If you hate the idea of being one of America's medicated millions, meet inositol. Carl C. Pfeiffer, M.D., has done studies at the Brain Bio Center that indicate that inositol has an anxiety-reducing effect similar to tranquilizers like Valium.[83]

He notes too that when used in combination with vitamin C and vitamin B6, inositol helps induce sleep. He suggests that you experiment to discover the dose that is most effective for you.

If you suffer from high cholesterol levels, you will be interested to know that, in one study, cholesterol levels were lowered by the use of inositol supplements.[84]

And in another experiment, reported in the *American Heart Journal*, inositol supplements lowered cholesterol levels in a group of patients suffering from both high blood sugar and atherosclerosis.[85]

In yet another study, in the *Proceedings of the Society for Experimental Biological Medicine* 54 (1943), doctors broke up the deposit of fats in individuals with liver damage due to cirrhosis with supplements of fat-emulsifying inositol.[86]

A PRACTICAL GUIDE TO USING INOSITOL

Keeping a healthy intestinal tract may be the best way to make sure you are getting enough inositol. The bacteria or intestinal "flora" found there are indispensable to the process by which inositol is made in the body. Conversely, the inositol and biotin present in your intestines help keep the flora healthy.[7]

Will a good diet supply enough inositol? If by good you mean one that includes generous amounts of all those B-rich foods—wheat germ, brewer's yeast, calves' liver, and whole grains—the answer is yes. Inositol is also present in oranges, nuts, and molasses.

Biotin

Even though you may not have heard of biotin, your hair, skin, bone marrow, and glands know that it exists. It keeps them all healthy and growing.

Here's how—and where—it works.

• *Metabolic system.* Biotin helps produce and transmute fatty acids, carbohydrates, and amino acids into energy. It is vital in the production of glycogen, the energy elixir—distilled from carbohydrates —stored in your liver and muscles.

• *Genetic system.* Biotin is also a vital ingredient in making purines. What are purines? Essential nitrogen compounds of nucleic acids, in which our genetic material is contained.

• *Nutrient synthesis.* Biotin works with folic acid to transform it into a coenzyme.

Your body manufactures biotin in the intestinal tract with the hard labor of thousands of microorganisms. They are stimulated by another B vitamin, inositol. You can also obtain biotin by eating eggs, cheese, nuts, and many other common foods.

Large doses of sulfa drugs and antibiotics destroy biotin-producing microbes, but ordinary doses such as most of us would take, over a short period of time, appear to have little effect on biosynthesis,

How do you know if you need more biotin? Deficiency is rare, luckily. Its symptoms are fatigue, depression, skin disorders, slow healing of wounds, muscular pain, anorexia, sensitivity to cold temperatures, and elevated blood cholesterol levels.[87]

A cautionary note: to get the full potential biotin in egg whites, eat them cooked. A protein called avidin, present in raw egg white and rendered harmless by cooking, prevents your absorbing biotin.

Summary

Now that you've met the whole family of B vitamins, isn't it nice to know that you've got such an active and harmonious crew of helpers to unlock all the nutrients in the food you eat, providing all the energy you need to be at your very best, both mentally and physically?

And isn't it good to know that they are hard at work within your enzymatic system, your metabolic and nervous systems, your cells, your organs, your hair, skin, and eyes, to bring you beautiful and bounteous good health?

Why not enjoy all their benefits by eating plenty of organ meats, greens, whole grains, beans, eggs, and fish? And add a B-complex supplement as well? Or supplement your diet with B-dense foods like nutritional yeast and wheat germ?

Remember, all the B vitamins work together, so be sure to take them in their proper ratios, if possible. And don't throw them out in your cooking water!

Be sensible. Enrich your entire being by giving yourself plenty of B vitamins for radiant good health, high energy levels, less wear-and-tear from stress, and an overall state of vitality that only a well-nourished body can have.

Vitamin C for Holistic Health

What Is Vitamin C?

The "C" of vitamin C represents well a number of its properties. Vitamin C is the center of controversy in the cold-preventive claims that scientists have made for it. C is a complicated catalyst that continually contributes to the construction of your "cellular cement"—collagen, the chief constituent of connective tissue fibrils. C plays a central role in controlling, preventing, and improving common conditions from colds to cardiovascular disease to cancer. C can even help keep you calm.

Vitamin C is a water-soluble vitamin occurring naturally in citrus fruits and green vegetables. Involved in practically every biochemical reaction that takes place in the trillions of cells in your body, vitamin C is especially associated with your protective mechanisms. Chemically, vitamin C is an organic acid.

Another name for vitamin C is ascorbic acid, and in this name we find the real story of vitamin C. "Ascorbic" comes from Latin *a-scorbutus*, *a-* meaning "not" or "without"; *scorbutus* meaning "scurvy." Realization of the power of this simple substance was the solution to one of the great mysteries of the eighteenth century.

Most of us have heard about how British sailors often died mysteriously in the midst of the long ocean voyages of two centuries ago. Those sailors who didn't die often showed symptoms of scurvy, a disease marked by spongy gums, loose teeth, and bleeding into the skin and mucous membranes. Dr. James Lind deduced from this condition that something was missing from the sailors' diet at sea, which consisted mainly of dried meat and other preserved foods. It was easy to see that the sailors were lacking fresh fruits and vegetables. Obviously most fruits and vegetables could not survive a long ocean voyage; hence lemons and limes were added to the food cargo of the British ships. The condition called scurvy disappeared. Some substance supplied by a lemon or lime could actually save lives.

In 1928, Dr. Albert Szent-Györgyi, a biochemist, isolated a substance from citrus fruits and cabbages that looked like ordinary granulated sugar. "Hexuronic acid," as he first called it, demonstrated remarkable therapeutic and curative properties. Not until several years later did "hexuronic acid" become "ascorbic acid" and subsequently, "vitamin C." In 1937, Dr. Szent-Györgyi, who devoted his life to vitamin research, prophesied that "vitamins, if properly understood and applied, will help us to reduce human suffering to an extent which the most fantastic mind would fail to imagine."[1]

Today, vitamin C is helping to fulfill that prophecy, sparing innumerable lives from needless suffering. On a more everyday level, it is saving us days of misery and convalescence in bed with colds, flus, and allergies. Overall, in its ability to build up natural bodily defenses, protect our cell tissues from disintegration, and boost our bodies' natural healing powers, this simple nutrient is one of the wonder-workers of our times.

How Does Vitamin C Work?

Now that we know what a wonder-worker vitamin C is, let's explore just how it works its wonders.

Vitamin C plays its main role in the production and protection of connective tissue, which is found throughout your body. How does it accomplish such a large and all-pervasive job? By helping to manufacture collagen, the chief constituent of connective tissue, and by protecting it against breakdown. Collagen is itself composed of protein fibrils, or chains, and this is where vitamin C enters the picture. Vitamin C encourages the growth of the protein chains, thus strengthening the collagen, which is like a glue that "cements" the cells together to form tissue.

As Michael C. Alfano, D.D.S., of the MIT Department of Nutrition and Food Science, along with his colleagues, found, vitamin C creates an "effective epithelial ["epithelial" means "relating to the epithelium," or membranous cellular tissue] barrier which minimizes the penetration of bacteria and toxic bacterial by-products into the underlying connective tissue." He adds that a vitamin C deficiency "has been qualitatively related to an altered mucosal barrier function, decreased resistance to infectious disease, increased incidence of periodontal disease, and altered synthesis of basement membrane collagen."[2]

To understand this most important function of vitamin C, let's imagine that we are building a house of stones that are somewhat variable in shape and size. To make the foundation and walls perform their functions properly and resist the wind and rain, we must join the stones together with a quality cement that will keep the stones from falling out of order. It must also be strong enough to keep plants and insects from growing between the stones, or burrowing in the cement and weakening the whole structure. If we wanted the house to last a long time, with few repairs, we would find the strongest, best cement available.

Our bodies are that house, and our cells are the stones from which the house is built. Collagen is the cement that holds the stones together, and vitamin C is one of the active ingredients in making the cement strong enough that insects and plants (which we might see as infectious diseases and cellular disorders like cancer) do not find a home within the stones of our house—the cells of our bodies.

But unlike cement and stones, collagen and cells are alive. Vitamin C is a truly active ingredient in the manufacture of "cellular cement." Not only does it aid in production, it also keeps the protein fibrils in collagen healthy and growing.

Vitamin C also acts as an antioxidant, like vitamins E and A and the trace mineral selenium. Antioxidants protect the cellular membrane from free radical oxidation, which results in membrane destruction, or cell "blowout."

Another way vitamin C works is that it has "a sparing effect on several other vitamins, including those of the B-complex group, vitamin A, and vitamin E," according to a report by Dr. Roberto J. Moran of Vanderbilt University. Dr. Moran also found that vitamin C "enhances absorption of iron and inhibits absorption of copper from the digestive tract."[3] Thus, by making certain that your daily intake of vitamin C is sufficient, you are insuring protection and maximum efficiency of other vital nutrients as well.

Vitamin C, then, acts as a producer and a protector of vital cellular functions. It helps *produce* collagen, the protein-based compound that holds cells together, thus making connective tissue stronger. It *protects* cellular membranes against viral invasion and free radical oxidation. It also protects other key vitamins and minerals from inefficient use within your body.

An easy way to remember vitamin C's most important function is to keep in mind that stone house we are building, and the "C"-ment so important in making the structure strong.

Where Does Vitamin C Work?

Since vitamin C's work is mainly in and around the cells, of which our entire bodies are composed, it is easy to see that the answer to the question posed above is "everywhere." But there are some places throughout our bodies where C is an especially active ingredient in making things work.

• *Cells:* As we already know, vitamin C is a wonder-worker of the cells, cooperating with the enzymes proline and lysine to manufacture collagen and insure its strength and optimum condition.[4] In addition, vitamin C protects your cells from disintegration in its role as an antioxidant, keeping just the right amount of oxygen available to cellular tissues. It also protects the other antioxidant vitamins A and E.

• *Blood.* Vitamin C helps maintain the normal healthy composition of your blood. Pretty important, eh? It works with a number of elements important to blood, like folic acid, vitamin B_{12}, and iron. Iron and vitamin C are especially good friends, since vitamin C changes iron from transferrin (the iron carrier in blood plasma) to the more accessible ferritin, an iron-protein complex.

• *The nervous system.* Vitamin C keeps your nerves on an even keel by insuring that you keep making two amino acids—phenylalanine and tyrosine—which are essential to the smooth activity of the central nervous system. Vitamin C also works to convert the amino acid tryptophan into the neurotransmitter compound called serotonin.

• *Skin.* Because of its activity in making collagen, vitamin C plays a big part in healing cuts, lesions, or more serious topical or internal injuries.

• *Teeth and bones.* Wait a minute, it's *calcium* for teeth and bones, right? Calcium and more. Vitamin C is essential in making sure that calcium reaches the places that need it.

• *Glands.* A gland is a group of cells that selectively removes materials from the blood, concentrates or alters them, and secretes them for further use in the body or for elimination. Hormones are one of the secretions of glands. Vitamin C has a direct relationship to the health of your glands—particularly the thyroid gland and the adrenal cortex, which is the outer portion of the adrenal gland. Certain amounts of vitamin C are necessary in helping these glands produce hormones.

In both cases, the hormones produced—thyroxine from the thyroid gland; adrenaline and noradrenaline from the adrenal cortex—are vital in helping you cope with stress. When you are under physical or emotional stress, you use a lot of C simply to produce these hormones, which increases your need for vitamin C. It's a bit of a vicious circle: if you are low on vitamin C due to stress or other reasons, these glands cannot produce enough of their stress-coping hormones. It is easy to see how stress can cause you anguish—even illness—if you are low on C.

Where can we find vitamin C hard at work, seven days a week, twenty-four hours a day? In our cells, blood, nerves, teeth, bones, skin, and glands. That just about covers it. And yet, what about the controversy that surrounds our hardworking friend as a part of the treatment for colds, for cardiovascular disease, even for cancer? The controversy is undeserved, for study after study has shown that vitamin C can affect these conditions and many others. Vitamin C is vital in preventing illness and in treating it.

Who Needs Vitamin C?

Everybody needs vitamin C, and most of us probably need more than we get. In times of health, you need vitamin C to insure the proper functioning of the very building blocks of your body, the cells, as well as other essential components like nerves and glands. Every body needs vitamin C, and all the time, simply to look and feel good.

But if you have a cold, or just feel one coming on—and the same goes for flu and hay fever attacks—vitamin C can make the difference between misery and comfort. If you suffer from chronic conditions like diabetes, cataracts, gallstones or kidney stones, backache, or simple stress, vitamin C can help. If you have an acute condition like meningitis, heat rash or other skin conditions, viral infection, or impending miscarriage, vitamin C can be part of the answer. If you are plagued by emotional disturbances, drug addiction, alcoholism, or are a heavy smoker, vitamin C can make the road less rocky. If you suffer from cardiovascular disease or cancer, vitamin C could be a lifesaver.

VITAMIN C FOR COLDS, FLU, AND ALLERGIES (OR, WHO IS LINUS PAULING?)

Okay, who *is* Linus Pauling? We've all heard of him in connection with the claims made for vitamin C versus the common cold, which were first made public in 1970 with his surprising book, *Vitamin C, the Common Cold, and the Flu.* Newspapers and magazines quickly spread Dr. Pauling's gospel to the general public, and doctors sat up and took notice. Pauling's story was worth the hullabaloo, for in it he related how vitamin C could build immunity to colds and other common ailments. He went on to tell how these illnesses could be prevented—as well as cured—with vitamin C. Dr. Pauling's discoveries met with considerable opposition from the medical establishment, as they still do.[5]

Dr. Pauling's claims were based on years of scholarly research as well as impeccable academic credentials. Linus Pauling, Ph.D., became a full professor at the California Institute of Technology, from which he had graduated in 1925, in 1931. The same year, he was granted the Langmuir Prize of the American Chemical Society in recognition of his scientific work.[6]

Twenty-three years later, Dr. Pauling received the Nobel prize in his field, chemistry. Since then he has garnered a second Nobel prize, seventeen medals, and twenty-eight honorary degrees. After becoming Professor of Chemistry at Stanford University, he even received a Presidential Medal for Merit in recognition of his work on rocket propellants. At the same time, Dr. Pauling was honored as the creator of a substitute for human serum in medical treatment.[7]

Dr. Pauling explains his work on vitamin C: "My conclusions about the value of vitamin C in providing protection against the common cold and related infections are based upon . . . careful double-blind studies, which involved many hundreds of subjects, and which were carried out over a considerable period of time," he says.[8]

Dr. Pauling worked with a noted Scottish researcher and surgeon, Ewan Cameron, M.D. Together they determined that megadoses of vitamin C made most individuals immune to colds and, beyond that, helped to promote overall good health. (The same research uncovered the value of vitamin C in the treatment of cancer, but we'll discuss that later.)

Just how does vitamin C work to prevent and cure an illness that occurs more often than any other on earth—the common cold? One of vitamin C's many functions is to protect white blood cells from various bacteria. How? Vitamin C activates interferon, the infection-fighting protein our cells produce to prevent viral invasion throughout the body. Vitamin C helps prevent the spread of germs by activating this substance. In turn, your natural immunity to colds and related illnesses is heightened.[9]

Another of vitamin C's functions is to keep mucous membranes throughout your body strong and healthy, and to repair damage when it occurs. Together, these functions act as your greatest armor against the ravages of colds and related viral or bacterial infections.

Here's how. If you are low in vitamin C, the white blood cells are more open to an attack from various bacteria, and your immunity level is low. This may result in a cold, which, as we all know, is extremely irritating to the mucous membranes of the nose and throat. Once these membranes are irritated, they are weakened and therefore you are even more susceptible to a secondary viral or bacterial infection. If a bacterial infection sets in, it may spread to the tonsils, pharynx, trachea, bronchi, or lungs.

Taking vitamin C as a protective measure against colds works because with adequate vitamin C the white blood cells are strong enough to resist cold-carrying bacteria and viruses. Taking vitamin C as soon as you feel a cold coming on helps to prevent continuation of the illness and possible secondary infection, because the vitamin works right away to strengthen the white blood cells by activating interferon and to repair any damage already sustained by the mucous membrane linings of your nose and throat.

Get the picture? Vitamin C is like an army, and your body is the castle it protects. When you have a cold and take vitamin C for it, part of the army fights the enemy while the rest repairs the battlements that have already been damaged. And of course, if the army is strong enough to begin with—that is, if you take enough vitamin C *before* the onset of a cold—the enemy will not be tempted to attack at all.

An ordinary cold shouldn't kill you, but it can certainly make you miserable. Here's where megadoses of vitamin C can help. Not only can they influence the number of colds you get and how long each lasts, but these large doses also act to destroy other disease-producing agents that are always present in your body.

How much vitamin C should you take to prevent catching cold? Since you are different from everyone else on earth, so is your personal daily requirement for vitamin C. The range necessary for cold prevention can vary from 250 milligrams to 10,000 milligrams per day.[10]

Different doctors and researchers into vitamin C's effect on the common cold have different ideas. Dr. Robert Cathcart of Incline, Nevada, for example, suggests 250 to 4,000 milligrams daily as a maintenance dose for anyone wishing to boost his resistance to respiratory ills.[11] Dr. Michael H. M. Dykes of the University of Chicago, reports, "[One] study suggests that 1 gm of ascorbic acid daily may increase the proportion of individuals who remain free of illness from 18 percent to 26 percent."[12]

Even though the recommended dosage may vary from doctor to doctor and is dependent on your individual body chemistry, the evidence conclusively points at vitamin C's effectiveness in reducing the incidence of colds and related illnesses. For example, in one large-scale double-blind test run by T. W. Anderson, Ph.D., of the University of Toronto, those who took vitamin C "experienced approximately 30 percent fewer total days of disability (confined to the house or off work) . . . The reduction in disability appeared to be due to a lower incidence of constitutional symptoms such as chills and severe malaise."[13] In another study conducted by Dr. John E. Coulehan of Stanford University, reported in the *New England Journal of Medicine,* 34 percent of the 641 Navajo children administered vitamin C in a double-blind test over a fourteen-week period reported no sick days at all, versus a lower 28 percent of the children who took a placebo.[14]

So vitamin C can help keep you from ever "catching cold." But what if you already have a cold, or suddenly feel as if you're coming down with one? Good news! Taking vitamin C can cut your time with a cold significantly, or can even stave it off. How much should you use?

Dr. Linus Pauling, one of the world's most knowledgeable authorities on the subject, says, "It is wise to carry some 1,000 mg [1 gram] tablets of ascorbic acid with you at all times. At the first sign that a cold is developing, the first feeling of scratchiness of the throat, or presence of mucus in the nose, or muscle pain or general malaise, begin the treatment by swallowing one or two 1,000 mg tablets. Continue the treatment for several hours by taking an additional tablet or two tablets every hour. . . . If, however, the symptoms are present on the second day, the regimen should be continued, with the ingestion of 5 g to 20 g of ascorbic acid per day."[15]

The key, according to Dr. Pauling, is in the size of the dose. If the dose is too low, the cold will come on anyway. It is also important to keep the dosage high for several days thereafter. Edme Regnier, M.D., advises that "the viral infection does not disappear entirely. It remains subdued, almost camouflaged. For that reason, it is essential that the vitamin C regimen be continued for a longer period of time to effectively destroy the germ."[16] In other words, don't stop taking vitamin C if you think you have averted catching cold, or if your cold is nearly over!

Vitamin C works. Dr. Michael Dykes reported, ". . . 4,000 milligrams of vitamin C daily taken during a cold may reduce the number of days confined to the house per individual by approximately half a day during the three winter months."[17]

Remember, a little more is always better than a little less, in the case of vitamin C. Since the vitamin is water soluble and not stored in the body, there is no danger of being poisoned by it. Just because your virus infection seems to have gone, doesn't mean it is. Take a protective amount of vitamin C each day to prevent relapse.[18]

Dr. Regnier suggests this regimen: 4 grams of ascorbic acid in divided doses for the first three to four days, then 3 grams for the next three to four days, then 2 grams a day, tapering down to 1 gram daily. The dose might be higher or lower, depending on the amount you normally take.[19] Note your physical reactions when you take large doses of vitamin C; that way you can adjust your dosage to an amount that is right for you.

One way of knowing you've had too much vitamin C is if you get diarrhea. Dr. Cathcart has observed that diarrhea is the only side effect you'll encounter from taking megadoses of vitamin C. He reports that the appearance of diarrhea is your body's way of saying, "That's enough vitamin C. Don't send down any more."[20]

If vitamin C is so effective against the common cold, why isn't it prescribed by doctors in place of aspirin, cough syrups, and antibiotics? After all, these drugs do not actually cure a cold, nor do they shorten it. What they do is provide temporary relief (which is sometimes quite nice), while vitamin C combats and cures.

One report published in *Fact* magazine speculates that the principle reason vitamin C is not commonly prescribed is that it is not as profitable as those syrups and pills your doctor dispenses. Drug companies, which are politically and economically quite powerful in this country, would suffer a considerable setback if 90 percent of the population suddenly stopped blowing their noses.[21]

VITAMIN C FOR ALLERGIES

And speaking of blowing your nose, are you one of those unfortunates who suffer from allergic reactions to the various pollens that flood the air during the spring, summer, and autumn months? If you are the typical hay fever victim, you've probably stocked up on patent medicines to dry up your runny nose and watery eyes, eliminate your coughing, and help ease your itching. Not only are these drugs costly, they only suppress your symptoms. And most drugs' benefits are accompanied by one or more side effects.

Is there a better, safer, cheaper way? Yes. You guessed it—vitamin C. According to Arend Bouhuys, M.D., of the Yale University School of Medicine, vitamin C in doses of 1,000 to 2,000 milligrams daily can save you respiratory miseries. When researchers followed such a regimen, they reported less discomfort in nasal passages and throat during hay fever season.[22]

Vitamin C has the properties of a natural antihistamine. Biochemist I. B. Chatterjee of the University College of Science in Calcutta, India, reports, "We have indicated that the beneficial effect of large doses of ascorbic acid may be due to its ability to detoxify the excess histamine produced or released in stress conditions."[23] In experiments in which guinea pigs were given a daily dose of 50 milligrams of C per kilogram of body weight, Chatterjee found that the animals were rapidly detoxified of the excess histamines.[24]

Dr. Bouhuys agrees that vitamin C is effective because it reduces the severity with which the histamines in your body can attack and eventually cause hay fever, the respiratory condition typified by severely inflamed mucous membranes of the nose and throat. You should have fewer symptoms of hay fever and shorter periods of incapacity if you add vitamin C to your diet during high pollen seasons.[25]

VITAMIN C FOR OTHER CHRONIC CONDITIONS

Vitamin C is good for more than scurvy and respiratory ailments. It can also be helpful in the treatment of chronic conditions like diabetes, cataracts, gallstones and kidney stones, backaches, and simple stress. Let's take a look at these conditions one by one and see how C can help.

Are you a diabetic? Although you cannot replace the drugs your doctor has prescribed with vitamin C, extra amounts of C can protect you in the long- and short-run against possible side effects of those substances. In fact, Dr. Irwin Stone, author of *Vitamin C: The Healing Factor,* feels that diabetics could use more vitamin C and would thus require less insulin.

Dr. Stone also tells us that mega-ascorbic acid therapy has been used to successfully treat cataracts. Stone reports that when one scientist administered 500 milligrams of vitamin C twice daily to glaucoma sufferers, the patients' intraocular pressure (pressure within the eye) dropped. A subsequent report suggested that oral intake of 2,000 milligrams gave the same results.[26]

How could vitamin C accomplish on painful cataracts the results that often come only with drugs and surgery? Researchers observed that vitamin C clears the optic components; exerts a beneficial effect on the blood vessels in the retina and in the eye's nerve; nourishes the eyes; and helps prevent visual disorders, especially those that are stress related. Its overall effect is to improve your eyesight, whether or not cataracts are a problem.

More good news: vitamin C can help reverse gallstone and kidney stone formation. In fact, if either of these conditions is in your family medical history, you have one good reason to increase your intake of vitamin C, before symptoms appear.

According to Emil Ginter, M.D., of the Institute of Human Nutrition in Bratislava, Czechoslovakia, gallstones may form because of impairment of the "formation of the bile-salt (substances), which keep cholesterol dissolved in the bile." It is suggested that the formation of gallstones may be stimulated by a deficiency in vitamin C.[27]

Here's how: in a laboratory test, Dr. Ginter observed that animals with a chronic deficiency of vitamin C had a metabolic problem that caused cholesterol to collect in their livers. As a result, cholesterol was not being converted to bile acids at the normal rate. Thus, the formation of gallstones.[28]

Kidney stones, too, often form as the direct result of a vitamin C deficiency. In dramatic tests, W. J. McCormick, M.D., cleared up kidney stone conditions in a short period without using drugs. Dr. McCormick says his clinical tests demonstrated that using amounts of 500 to 2,000 milligrams of vitamin C produced a urine clear of organic sediment symptomatic of kidney stones "in a matter of hours."[29] Pretty remarkable!

Vitamin C also strengthens the intervertebral discs of the spine, thus forestalling chronic backache. For those who already suffer from this miserable condition, here's a helpful three-point program that will help most "back, neck, or leg pain due to spinal disc injuries,"[30] according to James Greenwood, Jr., M.D., of Baylor University College of Medicine. The program combines optimum amounts of vitamin C with daily exercise and a sound nutritional program, which result in increased freedom from back pain. In many cases, patients in Dr. Greenwood's program completely avoided resorting to back surgery for their chronic pain.

Dr. Greenwood's program is based in part on vitamin C. He suggests starting with 250 milligrams daily, divided into three doses. The dose is then increased to 1,000 milligrams or 1,500 milligrams if the pain persists. When the injury is severe, a larger dose of 2,000 milligrams can be taken safely, advises Dr. Greenwood.[31]

Dr. McCormick, who pioneered the use of vitamin C as treatment for kidney stones, also found it to work wonders with "repairs and relief" for aching backs. One of the most necessary nutrients for strong ligaments, joints, and spinal discs, vitamin C eases pain, speeds healing, and banishes tenderness caused by improper use of muscles, Dr. McCormick discovered. It also prevents deterioration of the spinal disc that may occur when nutrition is inadequate, he adds.

We already discussed vitamin C's importance in dealing with stress. Remember? It works by helping the adrenal cortex and thyroid glands produce the hormones that are so vital to you when you are under physical or emotional stress. Here's an interesting footnote: the bio-chemist I. B. Chatterjee, whose work is discussed in the section on hay fever, discovered that through the process of evolution, "the biosynthetic capacity [to make vitamin C] has been lost . . . in man."[32] Thus, we can't expect our bodies to naturally synthesize the vitamin C they need in times of stress. And many of us are under extraordinary amounts of stress these days. Even if our life-styles are relatively quiet —even if we live in the country, for that matter—the sheer physical stress of breathing polluted air, drinking polluted water, and eating processed and refined foods is enormous. You can help your body along in such stressful conditions by supplying plenty of vitamin C at all times. And if you are under special stress, increase your intake of vitamin C to avoid becoming ill. Your body simply cannot supply the amount of C to make the important hormones you need to deal with this chronic condition.

VITAMIN C FOR ACUTE CONDITIONS

Vitamin C may also help alleviate acute conditions like heat rash and other skin problems, viral infections, and impending miscarriage in pregnant women.

If you have ever suffered from prickly heat rash, skin lesions, burns, or shingles, you know just how uncomfortable they can be. And if you are one of the many unfortunate victims of the herpes epidemic currently raging, you will be relieved to hear that C can help.

Many drugs are available to treat prickly heat rashes, but all of them have one or more side effects. Did you know there is a better way than drugs? Right again! It's our wonder-working friend, vitamin C. Dermatologists tried using a dose of 1,000 milligrams of vitamin C daily as the sole treatment for prickly heat rash. T. C. Hindson, M.D., of the British Military Hospital in Singapore, where the experiments took place, reports that the rashes were completely cleared in less than two weeks. How and why did vitamin C work? Dr. Hindson explains that when your sweat glands are overworked, as in high heat, you quickly use up your supply of vitamin C. This is dangerous, as vitamin C is a "hydrogen ion carrier for certain enzyme systems which relate to the sweat glands,"[33] and thus is crucial to normal sweat gland operation.

A rash is a deficiency symptom. Your body is telling you that one portion of the enzyme system has been weakened and cannot do its job. When you take large doses of vitamin C, your exhausted system is reenergized and the rash, as a result, may lessen or disappear.

Vitamin C can treat more than just heat rash. For simple cuts, blemishes, and bruises, vitamin C speeds healing and alleviates pain. Vitamin C can also help relieve the symptoms and misery of skin lesions, a common condition in elderly people, whose diets are so often lacking in fresh fruits, vegetables, and juices. Mark Vrana, M.D., of Cornell University Medical College, reports that one of his patients, a sixty-one-year-old man suffering from bleeding skin lesions as a result of vitamin C deficiency, was completely healed within two weeks under a rigorous regimen which included vitamin therapy.

His report suggests that even if you are not elderly, vitamin C can be the key in treating bleeding under the skin, around the gums, or even in cases of bruises that take some time to disappear.[34]

Vitamin C has also been used in treatment of badly burned patients. One such patient was treated with a 1 percent solution of vitamin C, and experienced almost instant pain relief. According to David H. Klasson, M.D., of Greenpoint Hospital in Brooklyn, New York, even though heavy painkilling drugs were discontinued, with vitamin C the patient's agony did not resurface. Klasson reports similar successes with vitamin C, achieving faster healing in patients suffering from wounds and burns than with other methods. In addition to bathing the injuries with a vitamin solution, the doctor administers vitamin C internally in doses of 200 to 500 milligrams, four times daily.[35]

Dr. Klasson's research led to these conclusions about vitamin C's activity in the treatment of skin injuries and burns:

- Vitamin C combats pooling of poisonous substances.
- It reduces pain and the need for potentially dangerous painkilling drugs like morphine.
- C promotes healing free of side effects, as opposed to other treatments such as sulfa drugs, which sometimes result in complications.
- It may lessen dependence on antibiotic drugs.
- In burn victims, vitamin C reduces accumulation of fluid under the skin so that a graft may be done sooner. Being able to graft sooner lowers the risk of infection and shortens recovery time.[30]

Do you, like so many others, suffer from herpes or shingles (which is a form of herpes)? If you do, you know that these are miserable diseases, characterized by pronounced fatigue and widespread painful blisters. During an acute attack, your doctor may prescribe bed rest for several days.

But did you know that you can shorten your suffering with vitamin C?

Fred Klenner, M.D., of North Carolina, found that vitamin C in 2 to 3 gram doses applied in twelve-hour intervals, with the addition of 1,000 grams taken orally every two hours, can lessen the effects of herpes.[36]

When Dr. Klenner tested this program on herpes victims, the majority reported feeling no more pain after the inital two hours. So complete was recovery that drugs and sedatives could be terminated. The remaining subjects responded to treatment favorably within hours.

How could a simple nutrient like vitamin C create such dramatic results? Dr. Klenner explains that shingles, in particular, is actually an infection at the site where sensory nerve cells meet the spinal cord. Blisters on the skin are simply a message from your body saying that all is not well with the affected nerves in the area. Vitamin C raises your cells' immunity and virus-fighting capabilities (just as in its battle against the common cold), and speeds your healing and detoxification processes as well. An unbeatable combination.

Vitamin C appears to be a hard worker in dealing with almost any type of injury or infection. It safeguards the mucous membrane linings from attack by harmful substances. This function is important in strengthening and repairing damaged tissues, as is vitamin C's role in the manufacture of collagen.

Biochemist Winston Whei-Yang Kao of Rutgers Medical School reports that the use of vitamin C can speed recovery of infectious disease. He notes that adding vitamin C to your diet can actually produce collagen that is triple helical—three-stranded—in form, a much stronger compound than ordinary collagen, which is two-stranded (or less).[37]

Yet another condition that vitamin C and bioflavonoids can help alleviate is spontaneous abortion, or miscarriage. "If capillary fragility is present," says Robert B. Greenblatt, M.D., of the Medical College of Georgia, "the use of bioflavonoids [described in a later chapter] may correct the capillary defect by modifying capillary permeability and vascular disturbance, whether in the skin, liver. . . or placenta, and, consequently, influence the efficacy of established therapeutic procedures. . . . The use of bioflavonoids and hormonal therapy, in the hands of this investigator, has considerably improved the salvage rate in his own cases of habitual abortion."[38]

Whew! What Dr. Greenblatt is saying is, if you have a tendency to miscarry, vitamin C and bioflavonoids can help by strengthening the capillary and vascular system of the placenta. Pregnant women should be especially certain to take their vitamin C with iron.

VITAMIN C FOR MENTAL ILLNESS AND DRUG ADDICTION

Since we've already seen vitamin C to be such a wonder-worker, it shouldn't surprise you to hear that vitamin C has been used effectively as part of the treatment for emotional disturbances, mental illness, drug addiction, and alcoholism. This is not to imply that it is curative but rather the body's chemistry benefits from additional vitamin C when placed under chronic or acute stress such as the conditions mentioned above.

A team of doctors at a medical school in Virginia decided to use vitamin C as an alternative to the usual psychiatric drugs. Why vitamin C? Because it was believed that since the psychiatric patient is under high stress, very large doses of vitamin C might be needed.

One important aspect of the study was that patients were tested periodically to see how much vitamin C was being excreted. In this way the doctors could verify whether or not the patients were actually using the vitamin C. At first, thirty-one subjects were excreting vitamin C through their urine; sixty were not. This means that two-thirds of the patients were in desperate need of large doses of vitamin C, and that their bodies were using it as fast as it was supplied.

After sixteen weeks, the doctors conducted tests again. Fewer of the psychiatric patients were excreting the vitamin C. The evidence suggests that emotionally disturbed patients need—and use—large amounts of vitamin C. The doctors concluded that supplementation with vitamin C in a long-term treatment of psychiatric patients appeared to be a low-risk program.[39]

Vitamin C has also been used to treat such extreme anxiety states as schizophrenia. And with thiamine, it has been found to have a sedative effect.[40]

The use of drugs in this country—prescribed, over-the-counter, and illegal—has reached astounding proportions. During the 1982 "Extra-Strength Tylenol" scare, we realized just how many of us reach for a bottle of *something*—Valium, codeine, diuretics, laxatives, or aspirin —each day in an attempt to make some sort of problem disappear. Millions more of us reach for a bottle of alcohol, a cigarette, or an illegal "fix" of one drug or another. Here are the facts about vitamin C and drugs.

• If you use one or more of the above substances, you are losing considerable amounts of vitamin C.

• You should be sure to take larger than usual amounts of vitamin C to make up for this loss.

• All drugs—even aspirin, over-the-counter drugs, and your daily cup of coffee—cause a buildup of toxins within your body, which increases your need for vitamin C.

These facts point once again to the answer to our question, "Who needs vitamin C?" The answer is, of course, "Just about everybody."

Heavy drug users and addicts can especially benefit from large doses of this meganutrient. Vitamin C is perhaps one of the most important of all natural agents in preventing, controlling, and eliminating drug habits. Dr. Irwin Stone, a trailblazer in research on the rejuvenating properties of vitamin C, suggests that supplementation with very large doses of vitamin C may allow long-term drug addicts to refrain from narcotics without experiencing withdrawal symptoms.[41]

Dr. Stone's research led him to discover that in an addict's body, the sodium element found in ascorbic acid is metabolized in such a way that it actually carries away the elements of the drug from opiate (pain) receptors of the brain. These molecules of the drug are replaced by vitamin C molecules instead.

The doctor has watched the health of addicts improve during just one week of his vitamin C program. When the craving for the addictive substance disappears, often after only six days, Dr. Stone reduces the dose of vitamin C to a maintenance level of 10 grams daily.[42] This dose seems to prevent the addictive cravings from returning.

Another eminent researcher, who has been treating drug addicts with 25 to 85 grams of vitamin C daily, is Dr. Alfred F. Libby. Dr. Libby has found that vitamin C is especially effective in rehabilitation if the dose is accompanied by adequate supplements of other vitamins and minerals, as well as protein.[43]

A twenty-two-year-old ex-addict who was cured by the program of supervised daily doses of vitamin C reports, "I began feeling good for the first time in a long while." He says he doesn't need or want drugs any longer and continues to "cure" himself with 10,000 milligrams a day.[44]

Alcoholism is another common addiction in our nation. A Gallup poll conducted in November 1982 revealed that over 80 percent of Americans surveyed regard alcohol abuse as a major problem nationwide. In addition, the poll revealed that alcohol abuse has affected one in every three American families—a stunning statistic.

Are you dying for a drink? What works better than willpower when you have the urge to overindulge in alcohol? Dr. Pauling finds that you can lessen such cravings with 6,000 milligram doses of vitamin C. Take it *before* you have that first cocktail, and you may not want the second.[45]

If you are a moderate drinker, vitamin C can provide some protection to your liver, responsible for ridding your body of toxic substances. Remember, alcohol *is* a poison, connected to a compound called acetaldehyde. Vitamin C protects your liver by minimizing the chemical reaction that produces that toxic compound.

If you are a heavy drinker, you may greatly benefit from megadoses of vitamin C, because you are greatly deficient in ascorbic acid. In fact, when used by a trained physician, megavitamin therapy emphasizing vitamin C has been a most effective tool in reversing the effects of alcohol abuse.[46]

VITAMIN C AND SMOKING

Nicotine is another substance to which many of us are addicted. If you smoke, you should be aware of the following facts:

• Smoking uses up about 25 milligrams of vitamin C *per cigarette.*
• Smokers may be 40 percent lower in vitamin C than nonsmokers.
• Smokers are ill more often, with more types of illness, than non-smokers. Many of these illnesses are directly related to low vitamin C levels.
• Each cigarette you smoke emits extremely high levels of gaseous pollutants.[47]
• Smoker's scurvy (chronic vitamin C deficiency) can afflict anyone who smokes or who is around concentrated amounts of smoke. Poisons released by cigarettes are deposited on oral cavities and tissues in your throat and lungs. The irritation they cause *further* lowers your body's vitamin C supplies.

By far the best way to cope with the physical complications of smoking cigarettes is simply to stop. But if you can't give up the cigarette habit, extra vitamin C can help you by neutralizing the toxins—including heavy metals such as cadmium—in cigarette smoke. In addition, vitamin C "will provide some protection against cancers, emphysema, coronaries, and other diseases which afflict smokers," according to Dr. Stone, one of the world's foremost ascorbic acid authorities.[48]

THREE C'S: VITAMIN C, CARDIOVASCULAR DISEASE, AND CANCER

Let's explore Dr. Stone's statement about vitamin C in connection with two other "C's"—cardiovascular disease and cancer, two of our nation's biggest killers. If you have one of these conditions yourself, know someone who does, or, like all of us, wish to prevent either of these conditions from occurring in your body, read on.

Cholesterol buildup within the cardiovascular system is one of the major contributing causes to cardiovascular diseases such as arteriosclerosis. Plaques of cholesterol can collect anywhere in your cardiovascular system, resulting in a particular form of arteriosclerosis known as atherosclerosis, characterized by the deposit of fatty substances in and fibrosis of the inner layers of the arteries. In turn, this condition can lead to a heart attack.

Within the last decade, most of us have become more aware of the possible consequences of eating high-cholesterol animal fats and dairy products, which can contribute to the formation of cholesterol plaque. Many of us have cut down on eating meat, and have switched from using hydrogenated fats to polyunsaturated vegetable oils. (See the chapter on vitamin E.) But did you know that keeping the levels of vitamin C in your body high can also help prevent cholesterol buildup, or reduce symptoms if buildup does occur?[49]

Carl F. Shaffer, M.D., of San Antonio, Texas, reports that when vitamin C levels are high, the production of all important intercellular substances called fibroblasts—cells involved with making connective tissue—improves. As a result, collagen manufacture is facilitated. These factors lead to a condition in which the cells can be more resistive to cholesterol buildup.[50]

Although cancer runs a close second to cardiovascular disease as the nation's most prevalent killer disease, striking all ages, both sexes, and all organs of the body, it is certainly the number-one concern of most of the medical profession. Consider the facts about this dreaded disease:

• Of the 1.9 million Americans who will die this year, one-fifth will die as a result of an uncontrollable malignant tumor somewhere in the body.[51]

• Cancer is the second major plague in America.

• Despite the fact that millions of dollars are spent each year in research and treatment of cancer victims, progress toward finding a cure for the disease—or even an effective treatment—has been slow.

• Chemotherapy? Radiation therapy? Drugs? They may slow the destruction and ease the pain, but they do not cure cancer.

• The nutritional approach, utilizing a wide variety of natural therapies, is the avenue being explored by today's leading visionary physicians. And vitamin C is one of the key ingredients in that approach.

How can something as simple as vitamin C be effective against a complex and deadly disease like cancer? In a group of laboratory tests conducted by the National Cancer Institute by Dean Burk and his colleagues, vitamin C demonstrated the ability to destroy cancer cells, while leaving healthy cells functioning and intact, unlike conventional cancer therapies—radiation treatment and surgery. The NCI research team found that "the great advantage that ascorbates . . . possess as potential anticancer agents is that they are, like penicillin, remarkably nontoxic to body tissues, and they may be administered to animals in extremely large doses (up to 5 or more grams per kilogram) without notable harmful pharmacological effects."[52]

The NCI research reinforced the findings of Dr. W. G. Deucher, a German physician who as early as 1940 had found up to 4,000 milligrams of vitamin C daily effective in improving his cancer patients' overall condition. Dr. Deucher also discovered that high levels of C helped his patients withstand X-ray treatment for the disease.[53]

Dr. Irwin Stone explains that it often happens that patients treated for "neoplastic [tumor-growing] disease are also suffering from severe chronic subclinical scurvy. . . . Unless they are ingesting many grams of ascorbate each day, they have had it since birth and it may have been a factor in [their] carcinogenesis. If they have been depending upon their diet for their sole source of ascorbate, their bodies are practically depleted of this vital substance," he says.[54]

As a result, he continues, "their enzyme systems are not working efficiently, they have low resistance to bacterial and viral infections," and the ability to excrete poisons and carcinogens from the body is poor or nonexistent, because of the poor quality of the collagen in their bodies. Cells and organs in this weak condition "permit fragments of cancer tissue to break away . . . and metastasize [spread] to other parts of the body."[55]

Dr. Linus Pauling further explains just how vitamin C works in rebuilding the diseased cells and tissues of cancer patients. He calls vitamin C "a natural, essential substance that may participate in almost all of the chemical reactions that take place in our bodies and is required for many of them. Our bodies can fight disease effectively only when we have in our organs and body fluids enough vitamin C to enable our natural protective mechanisms to operate effectively."[56]

These statements are fairly general; let's look at just how, *specifically,* vitamin C can help those who suffer from cancer:

• A cancerous cell makes more of two deadly enzymes—hyaluronidase and collagenase—than a normal cell. Both of these enzymes attack and destroy collagen. An increased level of vitamin C may not only prevent tumorous cells from manufacturing these dangerous substances, but also prevent weakening of the intercellular "glue" by causing collagen bonds to flourish. Thus, vitamin C restricts the cancer's growth in two ways.

• Vitamin C also encourages your body to produce protective amounts of special antibody molecules, which strengthen your entire immunological system. Along the same lines, vitamin C heightens the level of "complement," a protein substance found in normal blood serum and plasma, that combines with the antibodies to destroy malignant and invading cells,

• Vitamin C also increases the number of lymphocyte cells your body has available to fight off alien cells that attack components of your immune system. These cells seem to be the most important members of a group that medicine calls the phagocytes—literally "cell-eaters"— cells that consume unhealthy cells and toxic cellular debris.

• As we saw in the section about vitamin C and the common cold (above), vitamin C activates interferon, the infection-fighting protein our cells produce to prevent viral invasion throughout the body. One current view of cancer, supported by many studies, is that the condition is caused by a virus.

Since vitamin C is one of the best ways to promote buildup of larger supplies of interferon (one researcher discovered that C produced a hundredfold increase in the amount of interferon that test animals were able to produce in their bodies), it follows that if cancer is indeed a virus, C may be one of the best cancer-fighters.

Benjamin V. Siegel, M.D., professor of pathology at the University of Oregon, says that "any agent that stimulates interferon might thus in turn eradicate viruses or cancer cells. We've inferred that vitamin C may be the agent in this case. . . . the interferon then gets into neighboring cells, producing more interferon by a sort of cascade effect and thus preventing replication of the virus."[57]

In Dr. Siegel's view, there is "solid evidence" in the medical literature that interferon production is improved when the body's supply of vitamin C is improved. Once activated this way, it seems that interferon has a favorable effect on the macrophages, "those 'angry' cells that selectively but nonspecifically contain and destroy virus and cancer cells [and which] are enhanced by interferon."[58]

Dr. Siegel explains that interferon's ability to prevent tumors from proliferating may be due to its neutralizing action on these out-of-control cells.

If you or someone you love is suffering from cancer and you can find a physician who will consider treatment with a nutritional approach, consider yourself extremely lucky. Forward-looking physicians and scientists such as Dr. Pauling and Dr. Cameron, have discovered just how much vitamin C treatment can benefit the cancer patient.[59]

• Megadoses of vitamin C—10 or more grams daily—are definitely useful, especially in conjunction with conventional radiation therapy and surgery.

• This combination of the nutritional approach with conventional treatment seemed to prolong the lives of cancer patients, compared to those who were treated by conventional means only.

• In some cases, vitamin C relieved the pain associated with cancer to the extent that sedative drugs were no longer necessary.

• On megadoses of vitamin C, patients exhibited improved appetites and reported feeling less ill.

Dr. Pauling's work is a pioneering step in the field of nutritional alternative cancer therapies. But there are also simple ways in which we can lessen the risk of developing cancer in the first place. Dr. Pauling tells us, "The practical prevention of cancer requires a two-pronged approach, namely, the reduction of carcinogens in the human environment and the adoption of measures to render our human population more resistant to cancer."[60]

There actually are some very simple steps you can take to minimize your risk of cancer. The following suggestions are based on the results of research conducted by Dr. Pauling and other highly respected doctors and nutritionists. No matter what your life-style, they are measures that you can incorporate easily:

• Become aware of and rid your environment of known carcinogens. For example, drink purified water, stop smoking, cut back on foods containing harmful preservatives and additives.

• For best results, eliminate sugar from your diet, or at least reduce your intake of sugar sharply. At the same time, eat more vegetables. Both these steps reduce your chances of developing tumors in your gastrointestinal tract. Studies indicate that the vegetables and fruits high in vitamin C are particularly effective in this regard. (See "A Practical Guide to Using Vitamin C," below, to find out which fruits and vegetables fall into this category.)

• Eat regularly timed meals, in moderate amounts. Don't skip meals—especially breakfast.

• Exercise. Walk, run, swim—whatever you most enjoy—regularly.

• Do not smoke.

• If you drink alcoholic beverages, drink only a small to moderate amount.

• Increase your intake of vitamin C to levels up to five times higher than the 45 milligram minimum figure set by government guidelines. According to Dr. Pauling, at least "250 milligrams, and for most people a daily intake between 1 and 10 grams may lead to the best of health."[61]

• In addition, be sure to get plenty of the other nutrients—vitamins A and E as well as all the minerals—that work with vitamin C to maintain healthy cellular function within your body.

These suggestions add up to one answer for cancer prevention: good common sense, with a capital C!

VITAMIN C AND LEUKEMIA

Surprisingly enough, many of the symptoms of scurvy are identical to the symptoms of that cancerlike infection of the white blood cells, leukemia.

Is this just a coincidence?

No, says one expert, Solomon Garb, M.D., of the University of Missouri. Leukemia victims, he tells us, just like those who suffer from scurvy, may show signs of bleeding, skeletal changes, and increased susceptibility to infections. He suggests that "there is a possibility that some of the more distressing and dangerous symptoms of leukemia may be due to a relative deficiency of ascorbic acid."[62]

Dr. Garb is not suggesting that vitamin C deficiency is the cause of leukemia. What his work and the work of other researchers has demonstrated is that leukemia is a condition under which the body's supplies of vitamin C are quickly depleted, and which continues to use enormous amounts of the vitamin—more than even a healthy person's body could supply. As a result, scurvylike symptoms often appear.

Leukemia is an acute or chronic disease characterized by an abnormal increase in the number of leukocytes (white blood cells) in the tissues and often in the blood. In its beginning stages, the bone marrow and tissues that compose the blood become infected. The white blood cells weaken, and fail to reach their potential as healthy, disease-resistant units. At that point, abnormal cells begin to proliferate; at later stages of the disease, they may actually displace normal white cells. Like an unquenchable fire raging out of control, the diseased leukocytes may consume everything in their path until the leukemia victim dies.

Dr. Garb and others believe that vitamin C can and should be used in treating leukemia victims to effectively reduce their symptoms. Their belief rests on the discovery that when the white blood cells of leukemia victims are saturated with vitamin C, the rampant proliferation process may be interrupted. Their research has also shown that with megadoses of C, patients can even eliminate the abnormal cells from their bodies.

Because leukemia causes such an unusual deficiency of vitamin C, the leukemia patient must have more than the 4 grams required by a normal body to saturate white blood cells with the vitamin. In fact, up to 9 grams daily may be required to offset the deficiency. "Thus, the daily requirement . . . would probably be several times the normal requirement, even if the initial deficit were made up," speculates Dr. Garb.[63]

He further suggests that the reason the leukemia victim requires so much vitamin C is that the leukocyte cells may be absorbing it. Furthermore, it appears that the diseased cells do not release the vitamin when they are routed out of the body.

According to Dr. Garb, 5 to 15 grams of vitamin C daily, administered in 500 milligram doses at two-hour intervals, produces a beneficial saturation effect that insures the total cell nourishment of the leukemia victim. He has found that smaller doses at frequent intervals are particularly necessary for the victim who is already suffering from hemorrhages, one of the scurvylike symptoms of gross vitamin C deficiency. After tissue saturation is reached, a remission of these symptoms is often noted.

VITAMIN C FOR HEALTH

Fortunately, the positive effects that vitamin C can work on the healthy human body are of more immediate interest to most of us than its activity in treating chronic and acute disease. If vitamin C can show such results in the treatment of illness, just think what it can do for you when you are in a state of health!

Vitamin C helps us maintain our healthfulness. It contributes to the strength and disease-resistance of every cell in our bodies, and it also has special wonder-working capabilities in certain very important areas. It is at least as effective in helping prevent disease as it is in treating it.

One very important area that keeps vitamin C hard at work is your skeletal structure—your bones and teeth. If you are making more trips to the dentist than seem necessary, or are breaking bones frequently, a contributing factor could be that you are low on C. Vitamin C? Isn't it calcium that makes bones and teeth strong, and resistant to decay and disease?

Like many people, you may not realize that your bones and teeth are very much alive and that calcium is being moved in and out of them daily. But the movement of calcium is maximized by the activity of vitamin C. Remember, vitamin C helps manufacture the connective tissue—collagen—that is so very important in skin, tendons, cartilage, and yes, bones and teeth. So be sure you take plenty of calcium for maximum durability, but add extra vitamin C to your diet as well.

Another important place where vitamin C has a special function to keep you healthy is your thyroid gland. We've already seen how vitamin C keeps the thyroid gland producing enough of the hormone thyroxine to help you cope with emotional, physical, or psychological stress. It is important that the gland secretes enough thyroxine, because thyroxine is responsible for speeding up your metabolic rate when you confront an everyday crisis. Without sufficient vitamin C, it may have difficulty responding.

And you pay the price. A thyroid that is overactive or underactive cannot properly regulate the metabolism and other bodily functions, even when you are *not* under any particular type of stress. If your thyroid gland is not operating properly, you open yourself up to all sorts of other unhealthy conditions, such as obesity. You also lose one very valuable safeguard against illness.

Did you know that vitamin C has both antiseptic and diuretic properties? One of its qualities as an antiseptic manifests in keeping you free of urinary tract infections, or in helping one if you've already got it. This type of infection occurs when certain microbes that break down urine into ammonia are present in your system. Ammonia can increase the pH of your urine, thereby inducing a type of kidney stone production that results in an infection. The quality of the pH of your urine can be neutralized by ascorbic acid. Vitamin C to the rescue![64]

Vitamin C also has the qualities of a diuretic, and can save you the danger of side effects from diuretic drugs. Dr. Irwin Stone reports that vitamin C's nontoxic diuretic activity is well documented. It stimulates the body to release urine when your tissues are saturated with fluid, making it particularly important in cases of edema. Swelling of the tissues can be particularly stressful to important organs like your heart and kidneys, and high blood pressure is often one painful consequence.

DETOXIFY WITH C

Another important function of vitamin C, already briefly noted, is as a detoxifier. We all accumulate small but hazardous amounts of carbon monoxide, sulfur dioxide, arsenic, mercury, lead, copper, and other poisons in our bodies, simply by virtue of being alive in the twentieth century. We eat, drink, touch, and breathe poisons every day. If our bodies were not the miraculous organisms that they are, we wouldn't have a chance of survival. But vitamin C, for one, keeps our bodies clear of these toxins by "complexing" them so that our kidneys and bowels are able to excrete them.

According to Dr. Stone, "Ascorbic acid detoxifies carbon monoxide, sulfur dioxide, and carcinogens," making it the only "immediate protection we have against the harmful consequences of air pollution and smoking."[65] By "complexing" the toxins, vitamin C renders them into less toxic compounds. It also safeguards an enzyme called glutathione peroxidase, vital in the protection of all of your cellular membranes.

A further note to smokers: one of the risks you face is heavy metal poisoning from the cadmium in cigarette smoke. Two pharmacological researchers, Drs. H. S. Loh and C.W.M. Wilson of the University of Dublin, Ireland, discovered that supplementary intake of vitamin C (which you as a smoker need anyway, as we've seen already) can minimize the risk. "The accumulation of cadmium in organs [caused by smoking] and the severe anemia associated with cadmium toxicity are prevented by dietary ascorbic acid [vitamin C] supplements. The accumulation of cadmium increases with age and cigarette smoking," they found.[66]

Even if you are not a smoker, you should be aware that unfortunately, cadmium is in the air for all of us to breathe. It is widely used in the construction industry, for example. FDA researcher M. R. Spivey Fox has found that cadmium poisoning in laboratory animals produces:

• disorders in the sexual organs.
• irregularities of the blood in the duodenum as well as in the bone marrow and in both the adrenal and esophageal glands.
• anemia and a reduction in growth.[67]

Fortunately, in the same tests the subjects were found to respond positively to treatment with vitamin C. In all cases, vitamin C appeared to relieve the symptoms of cadmium poisoning. Spivey Fox speculates that because ascorbic acid increases the body's absorption of iron, it helps your body protect itself from the perils of heavy metal poisoning.[68]

Lead is another heavy metal that is, regrettably, a staple item in our daily diet, through auto pollution, toothpaste containers, and glazed earthenware pottery. We also take some in when we eat canned foods, because lead is used as a sealant during processing. In some cities, it may be in the pipes that transport municipal drinking water.

Lead poisoning is always serious. When high levels of lead accumulate, says E. D. Hobart, M.D., of Chicago's Rush Medical College:

• The connective tissue surrounding the muscle fibers is damaged.
• Thus, this tissue cannot perform its fiber-protective functions.
• Undesirable deposits of calcium around injured cell tissue may build up.

Researchers found that since vitamin C is involved in the production and protection of connective tissue, taking a good healthy dose every day appears to be one of the very best ways to prevent damage to connective tissue through lead poisoning.

Researchers in Yugoslavia came to a similar conclusion. Their experiments revealed that ascorbic acid helps to alleviate symptoms of lead poisoning and also makes potentially harmful effects less severe.[69]

LIVE LONGER WITH VITAMIN C

Another very positive effect vitamin C can have on your health is that it can actually lengthen your life. It can also keep you looking younger and feeling more energetic during your older years.

According to R. M. Drake and his fellow researchers, reporting to a meeting of the American Public Health Association, people with lower intakes of vitamin C actually run the risk of a higher mortality rate than those on a higher vitamin C regimen. In Drake's studies, those with low levels of vitamin C showed a mortality rate two and a half times greater than those with higher levels.

But don't think that the simple solution to extending your life span is to triple your vitamin C intake. Nothing is *that* easy, especially since no nutritional element works in a vacuum. Remember, you need all the known (and unknown!) nutrients simultaneously, because they all interact to maintain and promote optimum physical and mental well-being.

However, a careful analysis of all the available data reveals that vitamin C intake—above all other variables taken into consideration, including cigarette smoking—was the element that correlated most closely with what the epidemiologists call age-corrected mortality rates.

Just how does vitamin C keep you living longer? And looking younger? By literally remaking your body from within. Remember vitamin C's important function in keeping connective tissue strong and healthy, and in heightening the immunity levels of your very cells.

If you are a woman, you may have noticed the ingredient "collagen" in many of the "rejuvenating" skin creams on the market these days. Does that tell you anything? Because of vitamin C's part in the manufacture of strong, healthy collagen, it may be your best bet for rejuvenation—from inside out.

Dr. Irwin Stone calls vitamin C "the healing factor." After years of research on this vitamin, he is convinced of its function as a rejuvenator, thanks to its ability to promote regenerating cells. Abundant daily amounts of vitamin C—along with an ample supply of other vital nutrients, of course—can guarantee you good health and youthfulness, he claims. He adds a qualifier: "Anyone who depends solely on foodstuffs for vitamin C cannot expect 'full correction' of hypoascorbemia."[70]

Here's how vitamin C can affect you, no matter how old you look or feel right now:

• Large amounts of vitamin C can protect youthful health by providing a good supply of collagen and healthy connective tissue, the foundation of all the body's organs. M. L. Riccitelli M.D., of the Yale University School of Medicine, found vitamin C deficiency may contribute to the "irreparable tissue damage" he has seen in elderly individuals.[71]

• A large supply of vitamin C allows your body to make repairs whenever there is a breakdown anywhere in your body's enormous cellular network.[72] Its healing power helps you "snap back" fast after illness or injury, two primary factors in the aging process.

• Vitamin C rejuvenates your enzyme processes, contributing to the smoother functioning of your entire body.[73]

• It promotes good digestion and helps you properly utilize all of the proteins, fats, and carbohydrates you consume.[74]

• C has a favorable influence on insulin, the hormone secreted by the pancreas.[75] When insulin levels are normal, there is less chance of diabetes or low blood sugar, two conditions on the upswing in this country.

• Says Dietrich Hornig, a Swiss nutritionist, "A distinct relationship has been established . . . between ascorbic acid tissue concentration and aging in the brain, adrenal and pituitary glands, pancreas, kidneys, and heart muscles, indicating a significant decline with age."[76] The older you get, the more these vital bodily components need vitamin C.

• Vitamin C is an antisenility nutrient. Because it is involved in nerve transmission, it assures the proper operation of your nervous system, as well as your brain's metabolism.

• Vitamin C is a detoxifier. And together with vitamin E, it works to clean up your whole system. This function is crucial because the delicate membranes of your cells remain alive and well only if toxic or foreign bodies are kept out of the bloodstream. While vitamin E works to protect cells from destruction by "free radical oxidation" (explained in the chapter on vitamin E), vitamin C breaks down the toxins that *do* collect and flushes them out of your system.[77]

Even if you are still young—*especially* if you are still young!—now's the time to institute a program of prevention with vitamin C. If you don't get enough vitamin C now, chances are your body will produce a collagen of poor quality. As Dr. Stone reminds us, collagen makes up almost "one-third of [your] body's total weight of protein and is the [body's] most extensive tissue system. It is the substance that strengthens the arteries and veins, supports the muscles, toughens the ligaments and bones, supplies the scar tissue for healing wounds and keeps the youthful skin tissues soft, firm, supple, and wrinkle-free."[78]

For those who are not so young, or who are injured, animal studies reveal that calcium and ascorbic acid together can lead to the rapid healing associated with youth. However, you should note that calcium salts and vitamin C together have demonstrated the tendency to promote calcium oxalate kidney stones in the urine for some individuals. If you suspect you may be at risk, consult your family doctor.

Remember, no matter what your age or physical condition, taking vitamin C now may mean protection later against arthritis and joint diseases, broken hips, and the cardiovascular conditions that so often cause tragic sudden death or the strokes that bring on senility. Protect yourself now by helping your body produce a generous supply of that cement that holds the stones of our houses together for a long, healthy time.

VITAMIN C HELPS PROTECT YOU FROM CANCER

In our discussion of vitamin C and disease, we spent a long time demonstrating just how vitamin C can help fight—and help prevent—cancer. Here are some more ways in which vitamin C keeps your body strong enough to resist the plague of our times:

• Prostaglandin is an essential hormonelike compound that performs a variety of actions from controlling blood pressure to maintaining smooth muscle contractions. Researchers such as D. Horrobin, M.D., and his colleagues have discovered that if you are able to manufacture a sufficient supply of prostaglandins, your body may become more cancer-resistant. To make more prostaglandins, you will need an adequate amount of these ingredients: linoleic acid (an essential fatty acid found especially in safflower oil); gamma linolenic acid, zinc, B_6, and vitamin C. When your diet is low is any of these dietary elements, inadequate prostaglandin formation is the result.[79]

• Vitamin C offers some protection against nitrosamines, which are "among the most powerful chemical carcinogens known. They are effective [in producing cancer] in all animals in which they have been tested,"[80] according to John H. Weisburger, M.D., of the Naylor Dana Institute of the American Health Foundation in Valhalla, New York.

Nitrosamines are formed when we consume foods that have been processed with sodium nitrite or sodium nitrate, such as frankfurters, sausages, and bacon. Sodium nitrite is added to these particular foods to fix the red-pink color, inhibit bacterial growth, and enhance flavor. According to the 1979 review of food safety policy conducted by the U.S. National Academy of Sciences, it is converted into nitrosamine compounds in our digestive systems.

Don't think that just because you don't eat meat, you don't consume nitrites or nitrates, and therefore don't produce the carcinogenic nitrosamines. Large amounts of nitrates can be found in a vegetarian diet, too. Nitrate fertilizers are used to grow all vegetables except organic produce. In addition, beets, celery, radishes, spinach, and broccoli all contain quantities of naturally occurring nitrates.

Gastric cancer may be one consequence of ingesting substances that cause nitrosamines to form, and there is substantial evidence that the consumption of vitamin C-rich foods reduces its incidence. There are fewer cases of gastric cancer reported in areas where people consume lettuce, green vegetables, and other sources of vitamin C on a regular basis. This evidence suggests that a year-round diet rich in vitamin C may guard against the development of nitrosamines.

According to Sidney S. Mirvish, M.D., of the Eppley Institute for Research in Cancer at Nebraska, and Jerome J. Kamm, M.D., of the Roche Research Center of Nutley, New Jersey, ascorbic acid can actually block the formation of these cancer-causing compounds. Their research notes that "ascorbate has also been . . . of potential value in preventing nitrosamine formation in food products such as frankfurters and bacon."[81]

Further research written up in the January 1980 issue of *The Sciences* suggest that nitrites themselves (not compounds like nitrosamine alone) can kick off the carcinogenic process. It is still not entirely understood how what we eat affects our whole intestinal system. In this case, it is possible that the nitrite produced in our bodies could be of even greater concern than what we ingest. The same study suggests that if you take in more vitamin C and alpha-tocopherol (vitamin E) than the normal dietary intake, you can minimize the risk of cancer by exerting a "blocking effect" on the production of nitrosamines, especially if you are careful to take enough C and E when you eat foods that may contain nitrates.

It is sadly true that you increase your risk of developing all forms of cancer just by living in an environment that contains many carcinogenic agents. This fact seems painfully obvious.

What most of us may not realize is that exposure to several so-called weak carcinogens may be more dangerous than exposure to one very strong carcinogen.

For example, let's say that each day you eat bacon or luncheon meats preserved and colored with sodium nitrite, a possible carcinogenic agent. And you also have several cups of coffee throughout the day, all sweetened with an artificial sweetener containing saccharin, another known carcinogen. At the same time, you are taking a prescription drug twice daily that is on the government's list of "suspected" carcinogens.

This chemical burden may be more dangerous, in terms of the possibility of developing cancer, than if you were smoking one pack of cigarettes a day.

There are unknown risks as well, as suggested by Drs. Pauling and Cameron.[96] How much risk are you taking each time you are forced to remain in a smoke-filled meeting room? What kinds of risks do you take by constantly eating refined foods heavy in chemical additives?

Remember, all these factors add up. And they may add up to a grim total. For the protection of your health, follow the suggestions detailed earlier for changing your life-style to minimize your risk of developing cancer. Take extra vitamin C to increase your overall immunity as well as increase your body's ability to dilute or delete the poisons you breathe, eat, and otherwise encounter every day.

VITAMIN C KEEPS YOUR CARDIOVASCULAR SYSTEM CLEAR AND HEALTHY

Here's some more good news about vitamin C's effect on your health. Along with a sane and healthy diet, vitamin C can be one of your best insurance policies against cardiovascular disease, the nation's number-one cause of death. Vitamin C can actually protect your heart and arteries against cholesterol buildup that leads to this debilitating and deadly condition.

In the section on vitamin C and disease, we touched briefly on how vitamin C can help victims of cardiovascular disease. *Before* you become a victim, you should know that nutrition alone plays a very large part in whether or not you develop heart disease.

Atherosclerosis is a form of hardening of the arteries characterized by a change in the artery walls, which causes a blockage of the blood flow in the vessels. The change takes place in several different stages: first, the inner lining of the walls thickens and becomes abnormal due to deposits of fatty streaks; then a plaque, whose principle ingredient is cholesterol, builds up on the walls; the last stage includes the appearance of lesions and ulcers on the wall, sometimes accompanied by undesirable deposits of calcium.

This is a condition that none of us would choose to have. And yet, if you smoke, eat loads of fatty foods and refined foods, or have high blood pressure and let it go untreated, you are in some way choosing to cultivate cardiovascular disease. Atherosclerosis is both serious and frequently irreversible. When your arteries are clogged, both the brain and the heart receive less blood. Cells and tissues die from lack of oxygen and nutrients. There may be cerebral infarction or myocardial infarction as a result. You may even develop gangrene, if the blood flow to your hands and feet is seriously disrupted.

How can diet help? A good diet can protect you from this disease by lowering cholesterol levels, especially if it includes plenty of foods that are rich in polyunsaturated fatty acids and the antioxidant vitamins C and E.

Here are some basic suggestions for changing your diet to minimize your risk of developing cardiovascular disease:

• Eat fewer foods high in refined sugars and starches, including all the notorious "empty calorie" foods like candy bars, manufactured desserts, and snacks.

• Reduce your intake of foods such as butter, shortening, and fatty meats. Include more fish, whole grains, and vegetables.

• Increase your intake of polyunsaturated fatty acids and take extra amounts of vitamin E to protect them (see the chapter on vitamin E).

• Take more vitamin C daily.

For years, people have been regulating their consumption of eggs in an attempt to keep their cholesterol levels low. But did you know that sugar and refined foods pose far more danger to your heart and arteries than do eggs? Eggs represent an important source of high-quality protein. On the other hand, a high intake of refined carbohydrates has been closely linked to high serum cholesterol levels. In particular, it appears that the fructose element in the sugar molecule causes this elevation. Dr. John Yudkin, internationally renowned authority on sugar and the author of several books, including *Sweet and Dangerous,* has concluded that coronary heart disease is closely related to a high sugar intake.

How does reducing your intake of foods like heavily marbled meats, butter, and shortening lower your risk of developing cardiovascular problems? The saturated fats contained in these foods raise serum cholesterol levels, a major factor in raising your level of risk. Hold it, isn't cholesterol necessary for certain functions in the body? Yes, but the body synthesizes it regardless of what you eat. And despite your diet, the addition of vitamin E and vitamin C will affect your body's synthesis of cholesterol.

When you increase the amount of unsaturated fats in your diet— by switching from butter to vegetable oils, for instance—your cellular membranes will benefit, but they will also be more vulnerable to "free radical oxidation." When free radical oxidation occurs regularly, the results can be atherosclerosis and premature aging.

The switch from saturated fats to polyunsaturated fats makes sense only when you increase your vitamin E intake at the same time. Vitamin E, as an antioxidant, protects oxygen from being destroyed, thus preventing damaging "cellular blowout." All this information is thoroughly discussed in the chapter on vitamin E.

Taking more vitamin C every day is another step in our program to reduce your chances of developing heart disease, and a vital step at that. Why C? Ascorbic acid not only "spares" your important vitamin E supply, it also lowers your serum cholesterol levels.

One British physician described how she could dramatically manipulate her own serum cholesterol levels between 140 and 230 milligrams per hundred simply by taking varying amounts of vitamin C. The amount of cholesterol-containing food she ate seemed to have no effect, as long as she was taking vitamin C.[82]

Constance Spittle, M.D., of Pinderfields General Hospital in Wakefield, England, said, "I suggest that atherosclerosis is a long-term deficiency [or negative balance] of vitamin C, which permits cholesterol levels to build up in the arterial system, and results in changes in other fractions of the fats."[83]

Norman M. Sulkin, M.D., of Wake Forest University, has seen similar results in his vitamin C research. He notes that a long-term deficiency of ascorbic acid may have the effect of altering cholesterol metabolism. How? Too little vitamin C causes changes in the liver, which in turn responds by manufacturing more cholesterol than your body needs. This excess is then deposited in unhealthy plaque deposits throughout the body.[84]

In Czechoslovakia, another researcher, Emil Ginter, M.D., reports success in slowing the conversion of cholesterol into bile acids in animals by creating a vitamin C deficiency. When he reversed this state by including adequate vitamin C in the diet, the vitamin C seemed to melt the extra cholesterol away. "Cholesterol is catabolized into bile acids in the liver and the rate of this process is evidently a function of ascorbic-acid concentration in this organ," he says.[85]

Another study by Dr. Ginter indicates that vitamin C turns a portion of cholesterol into bile salts. These salts help normalize your digestion and prevent gallstones.[86]

Vitamin C is a chemical trigger that can improve your body's metabolism of fat and prevent fatty buildup in your organs. Dr. G. C. Welles emphasizes its importance by noting that if you are deficient in vitamin C it would be only three weeks before fatty degeneration occurs.

One physician tells us that he recorded a profound drop in cholesterol in his cardiovascular patient after the first 500 milligram dose of vitamin C. The drop occurred in a matter of hours. In some atherosclerotic patients, vitamin C doses of 1 gram per day caused serum cholesterol levels to *increase*. Researchers speculate that the increases were due to the mobilization of arterial cholesterol, or that a longstanding vitamin C deficiency may account for the increase. They observe that under normal conditions healthy individuals show depressed serum cholesterol levels with vitamin C supplementation.[87]

Another way ascorbic acid prevents the development of atherosclerosis—and this seems almost obvious—is by building strong, healthy collagen. Collagen is absolutely essential in keeping our arteries, veins, and capillaries healthy. Without a good supply of vitamin C, collagen cannot be manufactured at all.

Dr. Spittle reports that vitamin C also helps in preventing blood clots in the veins and arteries. In a double-blind trial on patients vulnerable to deep-vein thrombosis, Dr. Spittle gave one of the groups 1,000 milligrams of vitamin C daily. The others received none. The thrombosis observed in the no-vitamin C group was 60 percent; in the group that took vitamin C daily, it was only 33 percent. The latter group also reported fewer "physical signs," such as swelling of the calves, tenderness of the muscles, and irregularities of temperature.[88]

Dr. Spittle concluded, "I have been able to demonstrate that vitamin C has a powerful protective action against thrombosis (blood clot in artery or vein). It has been known for many years that this substance was responsible for the health of the capillaries. I am now entirely convinced that it is responsible for the health of the arteries. It would therefore be logical for it to be responsible for the veins also."[89]

In other words, we can count on vitamin C to help guard our cardiovascular system against painful, debilitating, and often fatal cardiovascular disease.

VITAMIN C FOR HEAT TOLERANCE

You may have noticed that one of the observations that Dr. Spittle made in her tests was that vitamin C seemed to account for fewer irregularities of temperature among her patients. You can carry this benefit of vitamin C with you all around the world.

An exhausting game of tennis under a hot sun calls for a cool drink. But for real rejuvenation, try a 500 milligram tablet of vitamin C. A healthy body store of ascorbic acid improves your tolerance for hot temperatures, both inside your body and out.

Going on a South American cruise? Pack vitamin C, and you'll find yourself adjusting to those steamy nights and torrid days a lot better than your friends who take salt tablets and drink rum punch.

Vitamin C will also help lessen the effects of heat exhaustion. How? Sweating is your body's attempt to keep cool. But perspiration floats away large amounts of all the water-soluble vitamins—and that means that you may be sweating away the vitamin C your body needs to protect you from other stresses.

Consider this telling case history; two groups of male volunteers were subjected to a stressful period of labor under extreme heat. Only group A received vitamin C supplementation. Both groups alternated periods of rest with long hours of labor. According to A. Henschel, M.D., who conducted the test, group A had slightly cooler body temperatures and suffered fewer heat-related problems overall, compared to the group who took no vitamin C.[90]

VITAMIN C AND WOMEN

If you are a woman, additional vitamin C can be a special boost to your health. Vitamin C has been used to help conceive babies and to ease menstrual pain, as well as to prevent spontaneous abortion, which we mentioned before.

Some doctors have found 200 to 1,000 milligrams daily of vitamin C a very effective measure against the severe menstrual pains experienced by some of their patients. Why was more C needed? Because the metabolism of ascorbic acid increases considerably as the menstrual cycle progresses, and can possibly culminate in a real deficiency. By the same token, testing for vitamin C levels is one way medical researchers can determine fertility periods, helping childless couples conceive in some instances.

If you are pregnant, your need for vitamin C—along with all other nutritional elements—increases. Your baby is growing, using much of the ascorbic acid that passes through the placenta. As a result, your own blood supplies of vitamin C drop, a process that continues through lactation. Poor growth in the baby and overall poor health in both mother and child can be the unfortunate result of a vitamin C deficiency in the mother.

Making sure you are getting plenty of vitamin C—and taking it with iron—is one way of guarding your unborn or nursing child against hemorrhagic disease, which may also be related to a maternal vitamin C deficiency.

There are so many ways in which vitamin C helps you maintain your health, no matter who or where you are, that there seems no good reason why we all don't take plenty.

A Practical Guide to Using Vitamin C

Now that we know how necessary and useful vitamin C is, let's be practical about it. In what foods can it be found? Should we take it in supplements as well? How much should we take to get maximum protection against colds and more serious illnesses? Is there a difference between natural and synthetic vitamin C? Is it best to take vitamin C with certain other vitamins or minerals to maximize its efficiency? Should any substances be avoided while we're taking supplementary vitamin C? Can vitamin C *cause* problems, as well as cure or prevent them? What are the symptoms of vitamin C deficiency?

The foregoing questions are all loaded—loaded, that is, with information about the "what, how, when, why, in what form, who, and where" of vitamin C.

Let's start with this one: what are the official recommendations for vitamin C? According to the Food and Nutrition Board, of the National Academy of Sciences from figures released in 1974:

Infants 0 to 1 year of age	35 milligrams daily
Children 1 to 10 years of age	40 milligrams daily
Males 11 to 51+ years of age	45 milligrams daily
Females 11 to 51+ years of age	45 milligrams daily
Pregnant or lactating females	60 milligrams daily

VITAMIN C IN FOODS

What foods can we eat to satisfy these minimum daily requirements? If you enjoy eating oranges, grapefruits, tangerines, lemons, limes, papaya, strawberries, cantaloupe, tomatoes, broccoli, bell peppers (red and green), raw lettuce, and other leafy greens every day, you're lucky. You are able to take in a substantial amount of your vitamin C requirement through foods you like eating. Let's look at the precise vitamin C content of some of these and other high-C foods.[91]

Food	Amount	Vitamin C (milligrams)
Broccoli, cooked	1 whole stalk	162
Brussels sprouts, cooked	3 to 4	68
Peppers, sweet, green	1 medium	94
Collards, cooked	1/2 cup	44
Cauliflower, cooked	1/2 cup	33
Cabbage, coarsely shredded	1 cup	33
Potato, baked w/o peel	1 medium	22
Tomato	1 medium	42
Orange	1 medium	66
Cantaloupe	1/2 medium	63
Strawberries	1/2 cup	44
Grapefruit	1/2 medium	40
Lemon juice	1 T.	7
Lime juice	1 T.	5
Tangerine	1 medium	27
Banana	1 medium	12

Something to keep in mind is that the way you store and cook your food has a great deal to do with whether it will or won't be a good source of vitamin C by the time it enters your mouth. For instance, Mary S. Eheart of the University of Maryland discovered that broccoli and green beans lost between 10 and 40 percent of their vitamin C when stored at a temperature of 46 to 50°F for four days.[92]

If you boil your vegetables or fruits and then discard the cooking water, you are tossing out the vitamins, and perhaps your health as well! Canning, freezing, and dehydrating foods also destroy vitamin C through washing, blanching, conveying, and grading.

Do you depend on processed orange juice and canned vegetables for your daily vitamin C? If so, you can bet that heat and oxidation have sapped the amounts of C these foods normally supply. The canning process leaches out nutrients such as vitamin C. And the heat used by food processors to sterilize, as well as the hot warehouses in which canned and dried foods are stored, cause large amounts of vitamin C to evaporate.

Do you depend on fresh foods shipped in from other states to fulfill your daily needs for vitamin C? If so, you may be surprised to learn that much vitamin C is lost in their trip from tree to thee. Excessive exposure to sunlight, or to the artificial light used during sorting, as well as grading, inspecting, and packaging of such raw foods are great vitamin C sappers.

Which foods contain the most vitamin C? The ones in the tables above. How can we get the most vitamin C out of those foods? Here are some suggestions.

Raw foods eaten in season, preferably grown in your own garden, contain more vitamin C than foods that have been subjected to cooking, processing, or dehydration. And of course, fresh foods contain many other factors essential for building good health, too. But it may be their simple freshness that explains how some foods high in vitamin C do a good job in lowering cholesterol levels and protecting your heart.

Dr. Constance Spittle, whom we met in the last section, says, "The reason why there is a seasonal variation in the incidence of heart attack is that the consumption of vitamin C is greater in the summer than in the winter. Not only does vitamin C keep down the cholesterol level, (but) it enhances the activity of (the enzyme) lipoprotein lipase, thus bringing down the triglycerides, and it also reduces the B-lipoproteins. In other words, (vitamin C) is essential for the proper metabolism of fats."[93]

Could we extrapolate that there would be fewer fatal coronary thrombosis victims if we all ate more raw oranges, broccoli, cabbage, papaya, and so forth?

My answer is yes, since there is every indication that nature intended us to eat of her bounty "as is." And it is true that the lowest rate of heart disease deaths occurs at the end of the summer—the period during which most of us eat the most fresh food in season.

If you are hard put to find a fresh green vegetable in winter, are on a tight budget, or simply like the little critters, you might try growing sprouts. There is no better or cheaper way to improve your overall health or to supply a steady, reliable supply of vitamin C. The sprouting of seeds develops the ascorbic acid that is latent in most foods, and develops the farmer in all of us! Wheat berries, alfalfa, lentils, mung beans, and sunflower seeds all become good sources of vitamin C when germinated.

Some foods deserve to be on the charts as hefty suppliers of vitamin C; others don't. Apples, for instance, may indeed "keep the doctor away" because of the fiber and pectin they contain for the good health of your teeth, gums, and digestive tract. Another good reason to eat them is that they retain many of their nutrients longer than other fruits, even when shipped, stored, and handled. Yet an apple gives you less than 5 milligrams of vitamin C, so you would have to eat at least nine a day to satisfy the minimum needs of your body!

THE ORANGE JUICE STORY

Orange juice has long been touted as an excellent source of vitamin C. Is it? Yes and no. If your orange juice is fresh-squeezed, you are probably getting a fair amount of vitamin C as well as three natural carbohydrates—sucrose, fructose, and glucose—and plenty of pick-me-up potassium. Three ounces supplies at least 60 milligrams of vitamin C. Valencia oranges (which are sweeter than other varieties) and oranges harvested later in the season are lower in vitamin C, so try to get the most C by being aware of these facts when you buy.

If you drink reconstituted frozen juice instead of fresh, have a second glass. According to Consumers Union, "Few of the frozen juices could be relied on to deliver enough vitamin C to meet the recommendation for adults if served in the common 3½ ounce portion. . . . You can't rely on a small glass of frozen orange juice to meet your daily needs."[94]

One reason frozen juice supplies less vitamin C is that the heating and evaporation processes used to turn the fruit juice into concentrate destroy the vitamin. Then, when you prepare the concentrate at home by adding water, more vitamin C is lost by exposure to light and air.

Canned and bottled juice also run a poor second (or third) to the real thing. According to Consumers Union, these juices have less body than fresh-squeezed, which means less healthy fiber. And although they are not prepared in exactly the same manner as frozen juices, they are subjected to the same C-sapping processes, including heating, cooling, and warehouse storage.[95]

As for juice in a carton, you never really know how much vitamin C you are getting. Prepared from concentrate and then thinned by the manufacturer to the consistency he desires, the vitamin C content is dependent on many factors, from the type of fruit used to the amount of water added to the length of time the juice was stored.[96]

So what is the wisest choice? To insure that you get an adequate supply of vitamin C, try to drink fresh juices, and consider taking a supplement of ascorbic acid as extra security.

Here's an interesting footnote to the orange juice story: combining eggs and juice at a meal is a good way to maximize your intake of vitamin C and iron (though not necessarily proper food combining). USDA research found that drinking fresh orange juice when eating eggs improves the body's absorption of iron from the eggs. Without the vitamin C from the orange juice, in fact, the iron in which the egg yolk is rich is bound in a form which the body cannot fully utilize.

There is a wide range of delicious food to choose from in fulfilling your daily vitamin C requirement. But keep this in mind: even though the government has set 45 milligrams as the minimum daily requirement of vitamin C for an adult, most nutrition specialists advise that you take in at least 500 to 1000 milligrams daily for optimum health. So we repeat, it's wisest to depend on a supplement, as well as on a balanced diet that provides plenty of C-rich foods. A supplement can insure that you are getting all the C you need, but only foods can give you ascorbic acid in its natural state, along with minerals, other vitamins, enzymes, and the fiber that is found in complex carbohydrates for the smooth functioning of the entire digestive tract.

VITAMIN C IN SUPPLEMENTS

You are convinced that you and your family could benefit from taking more vitamin C. You have even determined the amount that should be helpful. Now all you have to do is go to the health food store to buy your supply, right?

Wrong. When you arrive at the health food store, you will be overwhelmed by the bewildering array of vitamin C supplements. What's best for you? Ascorbic acid? Rosehips vitamin C? "Natural" vitamin C? Vitamin C with bioflavonoids? And is there a difference between natural and synthetic vitamin C?

The following list can help you in deciding which form of the vitamin is your best bet.

• *Pure rosehip tablets or powder.* Says Dr. Carl Pfeiffer, "Oranges provide calcium, trace elements, bioflavonoids, and pectin while synthetic vitamin C tablets are only pure vitamin C. Rosehips eaten from the rosebush undoubtedly provide similar advantages. However, pure rosehip vitamin C, when available, is five to ten times as expensive as synthetic vitamin C. When large daily doses are needed . . . then rosehip vitamin C is too expensive for the family with an average income."[97]

If you decide to pay the price for rosehips, be sure that's what you get. The FDA requires manufacturers to disclose only the *proper amount* of vitamin C used. That means that it is not mandatory for the manufacturer to tell you whether the product was derived from rosehips or corn sugar—the material from which synthetic vitamin C is manufactured[98]— or both. Furthermore, the product may be diluted with fillers that are not listed.

So if you decide to go the rosehip route, be sure to ask for *pure* rosehips powder or tablets at your health food store.

• *Ascorbic acid tablets.* You pay for the convenience when you buy ascorbic acid tablets, because they do not retain their potency or quality as long as do nontableted forms like powder or crystals.

Dr. S. H. Rubin and his research team found that the potency of vitamin C is minimized when stored at home, which means that the consumer might not be really getting the dosage he thinks he is taking.[99]

Because of the manufacturing steps involved in making ascorbic acid tablets, you pay for the convenience in another way as well: they cost more. But if your work and life-style necessitates using tablets or capsules, they can be an excellent form of supplementary vitamin C, especially if you store them in a vial or box that keeps out nutrient-destructive heat and light. And remember, tablets of higher potency (such as 1,000 milligrams) are usually cheaper than those of lower potency, and often contain less filler material as well.

• *Vitamin C in crystals (crystalline ascorbic acid).* Crystals are the least expensive and most concentrated form of ascorbic acid available. In terms of cost and potency, they compare to oranges and other citrus fruits. And they're no more difficult to prepare and use than squeezing an orange. For the highest concentration of vitamin C, mix any amount of these quick-dissolving crystals in any amount of fruit juice and drink immediately.

• *Vitamin C in powdered form.* High potency and purity? If these are the most important considerations for you, buy your vitamin C in this filler-free, loose form. Powdered form is preferred by purists who also desire as much of vitamin C's magic in as small a dose as possible. Generally, a teaspoon will give 4,000 milligrams (4 grams), but you should take no more than 500 milligrams at one time, otherwise you will simply be wasting it. Use it just as you would vitamin C crystals. If you have no access to fresh citrus juice, you can stir it into broth, another kind of juice, or just plain lukewarm water, and sip slowly.

Note: Both powdered and crystalline vitamin C lose some of their potency when exposed to air, light, or heat. They should be carefully stored in amber bottles or containers that exclude as much heat and light as possible. A cap with a tight closure is also essential.

HOW MUCH VITAMIN C?

As we said above, most nutritionists agree on 500 to 1,000 milligrams of vitamin C daily as the dose that will:

• manufacture and repair the collagen in the connective tissue in your skin, tendons, cartilage, and bones most effectively and quickly.
• promote healing by boosting the formation of scar tissue.
• strengthen the intervertebral discs and forestall trouble with your back.
• offer some protection, if you are a cigarette smoker, against formation of tumors.
• help protect you against the common cold.

Remember, government guidelines for vitamin C were intended to cover just the minimum needs of a hypothetical individual. Many nutritionists have drawn the conclusion that to enjoy your very best state of health, you need much more than the government recommends, for these reasons:

• The vitamin C found in C-rich foods is not the same from one portion to the next, or from one day to the next. For example, this morning's fresh-squeezed orange juice may contain twice as much vitamin C as yesterday's. And the broccoli that you grow and pick yourself will usually supply greater amounts of ascorbic acid than will vegetables shipped to you from another part of the country.

• Vitamin C is water soluble, so your body cannot store large amounts.

• Vitamin C is rapidly utilized by the stress of everyday living.

• Vitamin C is lost in sweat and washed away through the kidneys and bowels.

The difference between the government RDA of 45 milligrams of vitamin C and higher doses may spell the difference between just average health and superior health. Some of us, says Alfred E. Harper, M.D., of the University of Wisconsin in Madison, have exaggerated requirements for all nutrients, including vitamin C. It may be that we have been ill, or perhaps we suffer some metabolic defect, or perhaps we are simply especially sensitive to twentieth-century stress. Or perhaps just for simple, everyday reasons, we need extra vitamin C.[100]

"It is important to emphasize that RDAs do not take into consideration losses of nutrients during the processing and preparation of foods, nor are the RDAs designed to cover increased needs resulting from severe stress, disease, or trauma above the usual minor infections and stresses of everyday life. The first of these must be allowed for separately in planning a food supply, and the second represents clinical problems that must be given individual consideration," says Dr. Harper.

Another proponent of vitamin C in large doses is orthomolecular physician Abram Hoffer of Saskatchewan, whose specialty is psychiatry.

Does he see frequent side effects when he uses high doses of from 3 to 30 grams daily of vitamin C? In his eighteen years of practice, says Dr. Hoffer, "I have not seen one case of kidney stone formation, of miscarriage, of excessive dehydration, or of any other serious toxicity."[101] At the same time, he *has* seen success in reducing the frequency of respiratory ills and in treating various aspects of mental illness, including schizophrenia.

Dr. Hoffer has used megadoses of ascorbic acid on more than a thousand patients. In fact, he believes that "ascorbic acid is less toxic even in megadoses than any other currently recommended treatment for cough or cold."[102] He does see occasional diarrhea, but finds that it can often be reversed by lowering the dosage by 1 or 2 grams.[103]

Two more staunch advocates of vitamin C in levels above what the government recommends are Dr. Man-Li S. Yew, of the University of Texas Biochemical Institute in Austin, and Lewis A. Barness, M.D., of the University of South Florida.

According to Dr. Yew, "It is apparent not only that the [vitamin C] needs of normal, healthy human subjects may differ distinctively from individual to individual, but also that the range of variation in ascorbic acid needs may be extremely wide. The level of ascorbic acid need of an individual may further vary due to changes in the rate of metabolism, hormonal activities, and stages of development."[104]

Dr. Barness has administered up to 8 grams daily to individuals in good health and observed little effect on the acid-alkaline levels of the blood. His experiments led him to conclude that "many of the toxic effects of large amounts of vitamin C are insignificant, or rare, or troublesome [such as diarrhea] but of little consequence."[105] His findings:

• High doses of vitamin C might be responsible for stomach cramps, diarrhea, and a tendency to vomit. These effects can be avoided by taking buffered vitamin C, taking vitamin C after a meal, and never taking vitamin C on an empty stomach. Remember, vitamin C is an acid substance.[105]

• Dr. Barness found "no evidence of renal [kidney] stone formation, except in a few instances."[106] Individuals who did develop kidney stones were susceptible to them in the first place. The doctor adds that no incidence of gout was reported with an increased intake of vitamin C.

• Dr. Barness's tests did not reveal any significant hyperglycemic reaction. In other words, very high vitamin C levels did not cause a diabetic reaction.[107]

The question is, what is a healthy maintenance dose of vitamin C for *you*? The answer is, you are different from everyone else, and so will be your vitamin C requirement. We all have different needs, and different metabolisms. Here are some pointers to help you establish your requirements:

• Have a thorough physical to help you determine if you have an acquired or inherited error in your metabolism that raises your need for vitamin C.[108]

• Don't rule out the possibility that you may be that occasional person who has an out-of-the-ordinary reaction to vitamin C, or a condition that contraindicates its use. That is what Terence W. Anderson, M.D., of the University of Toronto means when he says, "It may be noted that although we have seen no symptomatic evidence of toxicity resulting from doses of up to 2,000 milligrams daily over three or four months in healthy persons, this does not mean that this dose level is necessarily safe for longer periods . . ."[109]

• Add C-rich foods to your diet. Include the widest possible variety of whole, fresh fruits and vegetables in your diet as you can.[110] Experiment with C-rich teas like rosehips, too.

• Discuss your supplement needs with a qualified physician or nutritionist to discover how much you need to remedy any longstanding deficiency. At the same time, find out how much you need to keep running smoothly—free of colds and coping efficiently with stress—on a daily basis. Notice how different daily dosages of vitamin C make you *feel*. Do you feel good every day? That may well mean you've chosen the right potency.

• Increase your intake whenever you and your physician see that your recovery rate from an illness or injury is slow, or when your overall health is not optimum.

While you're experimenting with discovering what your own individual daily requirement of vitamin C is, you might keep Dr. Linus Pauling's message in mind: "Orthomolecular medicine is the preservation of good health and the treatment of disease by varying the concentrations in the human body of substances that are normally present in the body and required for health."[111] Disease, Dr. Pauling believes, can be prevented or lessened in many cases when ascorbic acid is used in preference to drugs that are alien to the human body. Orthomolecular medicine, he tells us, is based on the following facts:

• A disease can be cured by large doses of vitamins because they function as coenzymes. When these coenzymes join forces with pure protein enzymes, to varying degrees, special beneficial changes can take place within the body. These changes can include the healing of infections, improvement of a cancerous condition, the reversal of aging effects, and so on.[112]

• If your genetic code is a little weak, you may have inherited a greater need for certain vitamins—such as vitamin C—in order to make sure that an effective union of coenzymes and enzymes takes place. Your enzymes may need more nourishment to function as the catalysts they are meant to be.

• Enzyme kinetics, a specialty of orthomolecular doctors, may seem difficult to fully understand. But that doesn't mean we can't benefit from its findings!

VITAMIN C'S PARTNERS

Vitamin C and iron are partners. Together they can protect you against anemia, a disease that afflicts millions of women of all ages, perhaps without their knowledge.

You know what good deeds vitamin C and iron perform by themselves. But did you know that vitamin C is essential for the body to absorb the iron it needs from a supplement.

As Emil Schleicher, Ph.D., hematologist at Minneapolis's St. Barnabas Hospital, explains, "While clinicians may be aware that iron salts such as ferrous sulfate and ferrous gluconate are effective hematinics [blood builders], they may not fully appreciate the reason for compounding ferrous salts with vitamin C."[113]

Drs. H. S. Loh and C.W.M. Wilson of the University of Dublin agree that taking iron alone to build the blood necessitates an increase in the level of vitamin C. They found that "the desirable ratio of vitamin C to iron for optimum hematopoiesis [blood building] is 5 to 1." In other words, they recommend that you take five times more vitamin C than iron for optimum blood cell formation.[114]

In a third study, reported by Dr. Roberto J. Moran, we learn that vitamin C "enhances absorption of iron and inhibits absorption of copper from the digestive tract. It facilitates the transfer of iron from transferrin [original form] to ferritin [usable form] and enhances iron mobilization and chelation in iron overload."[115]

And while we're on the topic of vitamin C's partners, Dr. Moran also found that vitamin C "has a sparing effect on several other vitamins, including those of the B-complex group, vitamin A, and vitamin E."[116]

BIOFLAVONOIDS

While not exactly vitamin C's partners, bioflavonoids have a very close relationship to our friend C. Let's say they're like rich relatives.

Why do some people insist on taking only natural vitamin C? Why do these same people insist on eating the white inner skin of citrus fruit that most of us throw away?

In both cases, they've probably heard about the health benefits of the bioflavonoids (vitamin P), natural substances that belong to the flavonoid compound group. The best-known member of the bioflavonoid family is rutin, found in buckwheat and eucalyptus. Rutin helps build resistance to cerebral vascular disease and promotes the healing of broken cells and tissues, just like its cousin vitamin C.

Other bioflavonoids include citrin, hesperidin, and quercetin. Together they improve the resiliency of your capillaries, mend needy cells, prevent bleeding, and stop it quickly when you are injured.

Doctors began using bioflavonoids in treating specific conditions about fifty years ago, when they noticed that something other than vitamin C in a compound extracted from red peppers and lemon juice was helping to heal patients with vascular problems. Dr. Albert Szent-Györgyi identified the substance as citrin. Then as now, it was used to help patients whose capillary walls cannot withstand normal biochemical stress. Vascular permeability can be improved by treatment with bioflavonoids, even though the flavonoids are not officially considered a dietary element.[117]

Citrin is rated as an excellent deterrent in cases of vascular hemorrhaging, and the bioflavonoid family in general has proved useful as an alternative to anticoagulant drugs.

Of all the bioflavonoids, rutin works best to normalize capillary strength. Studies on record indicate that it even helps to prevent strokes. And when given rutin, hypertensive test animals showed a lowering of their high blood pressure levels.[118]

Why do bioflavonoids have such a profound effect on the capillaries and red blood cells in your body? Possibly, they play some special role —since their nutritional role has not been established—that nature has designed for them but that we have not yet discovered. Or it may be that they combine chemically with minerals and make them more readily available to the body in addition to improving the vitamin C supply.

So even though we don't know exactly *how*, we know that bioflavonoids do perform a valuable job in the cardiovascular system. What is your best bet for making sure you have enough of vitamin C's rich relatives in your diet? When you eat a whole orange for breakfast, include the white membrane; you'll get around 1 gram of bioflavonoids along with your 60 milligrams of vitamin C. You can also eat grapes, plums, grapefruits, apricots, cherries, currants, and blackberries for optimum bioflavonoid intake. But remember, they are located in the skins, peels, and outer layers, so don't throw them away!

Less easy to find but also excellent sources of these compounds are acerola cherries and rosehips, the pods that develop when your roses stop blooming. Fortunately, all health food stores carry bioflavonoids in supplement form, some even in combination with their wonder-working cousin vitamin C.

VITAMIN C AND B$_{12}$, ANTIBIOTICS, AND ASPIRIN

Here are some facts you should know about vitamin C's "partnerships" with vitamin B$_{12}$, antibiotics, and aspirin.

• There is a rumor that large doses of vitamin C destroy your body's supply of vitamin B$_{12}$. If this were true, those who take large doses of vitamin C would develop serious pernicious anemia and nerve damage.

There was in fact a study made in 1974, upon which this rumor is founded. However, the study was invalidated as a result of poor chemical analysis for B$_{12}$, and new research tells us that moderately large doses of vitamin C (half a gram daily or more) pose no threat whatsoever to our vitamin B$_{12}$ status.[119]

• Tetracycline and possibly other antibiotics cause a drop in the vitamin C level in your blood. B-complex vitamins are also depleted when you are being treated with tetracycline. Knowing this, some hospitals routinely administer vitamins C and B complex to their patients. But if you face a hospital stay, you may want to take your own vitamins along, just to make sure. Geoffrey Taylor, M.D., recommends that during hospitalization or illness "all [patients should] have the recommended daily allowance of vitamin C and the B group of vitamins."[120] At least!

• Aspirin can be taken more safely when large amounts of vitamin C are taken at the same time. Why? Because vitamin C promotes the painkilling effects of aspirin while reducing the possibility of aspirin poisoning.[121]

However, you should not take vitamin C's partnership with aspirin as an excuse to use more aspirin. Studies have also revealed that aspirin greatly reduces vitamin C absorption, and may be conducive to stomach ulcers and perhaps even cancer, because of its anticlotting effect on the blood.

PROBLEMS WITH TAKING VITAMIN C

Most of us are able to take large doses of vitamin C with no side effects at all. But for some, there are problems connected with intake of vitamin C, particularly in supplements.

Does vitamin C upset your stomach? The reason may be that you took it on an empty stomach. We remind you again that ascorbic acid is just that—an acid—and can irritate the stomach lining unless taken with a meal or directly after one to assure smooth assimilation.

Are you puzzled that you can tolerate vitamin C powder or crystals, but are bothered by both tablets and capsules, even when you take them with meals? It's not the dose, and it's not your imagination, either. Most likely you are bothered by a flavoring or coloring agent or some chemical necessary in the processing of ascorbic acid into the convenient tablet form.

Fortunately for anyone with a sensitive stomach or with an allergy to vitamin C's acidity, there is a solution. It's called calcium ascorbate, a mild calcium compound containing all the benefits of vitamin C and one more: it also supplies calcium.

If for some reason calcium ascorbate doesn't work for you, or you are unable to take it because of a family medical history of kidney stones, for example, you might try taking your supplementary vitamin C in the following way:

• Stir one-sixth teaspoon of pure vitamin C powder into a glass of fruit or vegetable juice at room temperature. When dissolved, drink slowly, a tablespoon or two at a time, so that your system can adjust to the acid content. Refill your glass and repeat after each meal and before bedtime. As you become more accustomed to the vitamin C dosage, you can increase your intake if desired. This formula will assure you of a daily total of 1,500 to 2,000 milligrams.

This method is particularly good for ulcer patients or people with other stomach problems. Consult your physician.

There are a few individuals who cannot tolerate any type of supplementary vitamin C taken orally. And yet, the vitamin could prove extremely helpful to them under particular conditions. If you are one of these people, you should ask your physician about the possibility of his or her giving you vitamin C by injection, usually with other vitamins.[122]

Does vitamin C give you diarrhea? That's its most commonly observed side effect. If diarrhea is a problem, experiment with the dosage and form of vitamin C you are using. After you experiment with different potencies and forms, perhaps you will discover that you thrive on one particular type of supplementary C.

On the other side of the coin, if you suffer from constipation, you may find that vitamin C is a gentle, safe laxative that can replace other drugs you may have been using.

One more precaution: if you take more than 3 to 4 grams of vitamin C daily as calcium ascorbate or with a calcium supplement, you may run a slight risk of developing oxalate kidney stones, especially if your family has a medical history of such a condition.[123]

To prevent this possibility, make sure that you are also taking plenty of magnesium (as in dolomite, a supplement that contains both calcium and magnesium). The magnesium will expel any excess vitamin C. The calcium-magnesium-C combination may also increase vitamin C's power to lower your cholesterol level, absorb more dietary iron, and excrete any hazardous heavy metals your body has stored.[124]

Remember, your metabolic system is unique, just like your fingerprints. And nearly everyone has some weaknesses. Yours may well be a hypersensitivity to vitamin C. See your physician before you begin any self-therapy with megadoses to ascertain if you are one of the few sensitive to vitamin C.[125]

How can you tell if you are deficient in vitamin C? The symptoms of scurvy are the symptoms of vitamin C deficiency. Do you ever notice bleeding under your skin? Large bruises that appear suddenly—out of the blue—on your legs, arms, almost anywhere? Do you frequently suffer from bloodshot eyes? Do your gums bleed?

Moreover, according to Charles D. Gerson, M.D., of the Mt. Sinai School of Medicine in New York City, "Patients with peptic ulcer disease, with prior gastric surgery, and with malabsorption syndromes were noted to have significantly reduced [vitamin C] levels when compared with a normal population."[126]

Other ailments of the intestine related to low vitamin C stores include regional enteritis or ileitis, a chronic inflammatory disease of the bowels; and fistulas, a type of penetrating wounds or ulcers.[127]

If you are being treated for duodenal ulcers, you may need additional ascorbic acid. There are reports of ulcer patients developing scurvy, as their condition creates such high demand for vitamin C.[128]

Hopefully, you will not notice any of these symptoms of vitamin C deficiency in yourself or in someone you love. But if you do, see your doctor immediately and institute a sensible program of a vitamin C-rich diet combined with supplementation in whatever form he or she finds best for you.

According to Dr. Emanuel Cheraskin of the University of Alabama Medical School in Birmingham, the study by Dr. Earl Dawson of the University of Texas Medical Branch in Galveston shows "a direct connection between vitamin C and reproductive dysfunction." According to Dr. Dawson, sometimes the sperm tends to "clump together" and the woman is unable to become pregnant. Dr. Cheraskin believes that vitamin C plays a vital part in treating infertility.[129]

Dr. Weisburger concluded "that a regular intake of vitamin C-containing foods from childhood onwards may prevent the development of stomach cancer."[130]

Summary

Controversial C, relief and prevention for the common cold and to an extent cancer, cholesterol-lowering preventative for cardiovascular conditions, plays a central role in the construction of collagen, that intercellular cement whose strength or weakness can make the difference between sickness and health.

Chemically, vitamin C is a water-soluble substance known as ascorbic acid that occurs naturally in many citrus fruits and green vegetables. It is involved in almost every biochemical reaction that occurs in almost every cell of the body. More vitamin C or less vitamin C can make the difference in how you look, how you feel, how you live, how you age, and how you die.

In every infectious disease, a high level of vitamin C will act like an army divided into two battalions. The first battalion will fight off the viral or bacterial invaders who are trying to take over your body. The second battalion will simultaneously repair the cellular damage that the attackers have already caused. And remember, if your army is on alert at all times—that is, if you maintain a high level of vitamin C in your body whether you are sick or well—the invaders may never have a chance.

Remember, a deficiency of this vitamin can endanger your health. So be sensible and use the form of supplementation best for you. Then observe the results in improved health and additional security against disease.

The Sunshine Vitamin D

What is Vitamin D?

An essential nutrient, vitamin D comes to us through sunshine. It is formed as a result of the chemical reaction that occurs when ergosterol, an oily substance on the skin, is irradiated to form calciferol[1] or melanin (that's a suntan).[2] Sunlight-generated vitamin D enters the skin through the pores and then enters the bloodstream.

Vitamin D is also found in foods as a fat-soluble vitamin. Either way you get it, you need vitamin D for your body to perform an endless variety of essential functions, as we shall see.

How Does Vitamin D Work?

Vitamin D helps your body utilize calcium and phosphorus, which help form strong bones and teeth and healthy skin. How? Vitamin D boosts your blood levels of calcium and phosphorus, speeding them to the cartilage and bone matrix. Its metabolic action with minerals is vital to your nervous system as well.[3]

Where Does Vitamin D Work?

Since vitamin D is a fat-soluble nutrient, excess amounts are stored, not excreted. The liver, skin, lungs, brain, spleen, and kidneys are its main repositories.[4] From these essential sources, your body uses it in the following ways.

• *Bones.* Since vitamin D is required for bone mineralization, an adequate amount is necessary to prevent all sorts of bone diseases, principally rickets. The result of a lack of calcium and phosphorus available to bones, rickets causes bone material to weaken in the young. Its adult counterpart is osteoporosis (brittle and fragile bones), the most common of bone diseases.

The University of Arizona's Mark R. Haussler, Ph.D., explains: "Vitamin D promotes intestinal calcium and phosphate absorption and also mediates the mobilization of calcium from bone. In this fashion, the vitamin maintains blood calcium and phosphorus levels to permit normal calcification in bone matrix and cartilage."[5]

• *Teeth.* Your teeth are composed of dentine, which is in turn made up of crystals that are quite like but much more dense than bone crystals. Your logical guess is correct if you are thinking that you need vitamin D for your teeth for the same reasons you need it for your bones. Calcium and phosphorus are vital to the strength and well-being of the calcium salts in the dentine and the collagen network of the teeth and gums. Adequate mineralization of the teeth depends on adequate vitamin D.

If your levels of vitamin D are low, your calcium and phosphorus levels are bound to be low, too. The result may be softening of the teeth, irregular tooth formation, rough tooth surface, and thin and inadequately calcified enamel, since even the outer surface of the tooth is composed of crystals that are made from minerals.

• *Kidneys.* Kidney health depends on vitamin D. Vitamin D is particularly helpful if you already have a kidney disorder, as one of the side effects you may experience is a weakening of the bones.

Jack W. Coburn, M.D., of the Wadsworth Hospital Center in Los Angeles, reports: "Many clinical similarities between renal osteodystrophy and nutritional rickets have suggested that a defect in either the metabolism or action of vitamin D exists in chronic renal failure. The discovery of the kidney as the organ that manufactures the active metabolite of vitamin D has provided direct evidence for a relationship between renal failure and altered vitamin D metabolism."[6]

Coburn points to the possibility that an abnormality in the function of vitamin D metabolism could result in the osteomalacia and osteitis fibrosa that plagues so many victims of serious kidney disorders.

Vitamin D is vital to the health of your bones and teeth, and may even prevent some disturbing side effects of kidney failure. Let's look at some diseases that paradoxically can become just plain eases when vitamin D is adequate.

Who Needs Vitamin D?

As usual, the answer is "*You* do!"—particularly if you suffer from a bone disease or renal disorder, as we discussed above. If you are an expectant or nursing mother, your condition may increase your need for vitamin D.

For years, vitamin D has enjoyed the reputation as the antirickets nutrient. And with good reason: it is able to protect the bones from rickets, and also to heal them from it. Vitamin D was added to commercially processed milk to control rickets. Surely the desired result has come to pass: rickets is more and more rare in our country.

Human milk also offers some protection against rickets, even with its comparatively low vitamin D content. Most breast-fed children do not develop rickets. D. R. Lakdawala, M.D., of Addenbrooke's Hospital in Cambridge, England, finds human milk underrated as a child's insurance policy against rickets. His research found vitamin D levels in mother's milk low, yet he concluded that "there must be something other than vitamin D in breast milk that protects infants from rickets," and in his research he found it to be "clear that most of the vitamin D in human milk is present as a water-soluble conjugate of vitamin D with sulphate."[7]

And what about the adult bone disease, osteoporosis, which is so extremely common among women? It is especially prevalent among postmenopausal women, in whom there are fewer estrogens. There may also be too little calcium and too much phosphorus in their diets, which in combination with a lack of adequate vitamins C and D, could create this condition involving a depressed rate of bone mineralization. Sedentary living also contributes to osteoporosis.

Doctors now know that if their female patients start a regimen of calcium and vitamin D supplements at the age of thirty, there is a far slimmer chance of their developing osteoporosis. An adequate diet in every respect and sufficient exercise can also greatly decrease the risk of developing this disease.

The simple fact is, your chances of getting bone disease in any form are "decreased by having an adequate supply of vitamin D. Everything we have discussed so far points to the reality that adequate vitamin D is necessary for maintaining strong, healthy bones." So reports Steven L. Teitelbaum, M.D., of Washington University in St. Louis. "Recently reported successes in treating metabolic bone diseases with analogs (supplements) of vitamin D have generated interest in further clinical application of these compounds," he says. Vitamin D strengthens the bones because it influences "extraskeletal mineral metabolism."[8]

Expectant and nursing mothers have a greater need for all the vitamins and minerals, and vitamin D is no exception. During pregnancy, vitamin D helps the fetal system metabolize calcium and phosphorus for healthy bones and teeth. And meanwhile, it helps the mother keep her own bones and teeth healthy while her baby is developing.

Nursing mothers need vitamin D, too. D in the diet or from the sun helps the body utilize calcium and phosphate, which can then be passed along to the infant through the breast milk. Nutritionally deficient milk can be a result of inadequate vitamin D in the mother's diet.

Vitamin D supplementation can help the kidney patient. But if you suffer from chronic renal disorder, there are certain facts you should know about the dangers of vitamin D poisoning. As we shall see, the treatment of renal disorder with vitamin D is a very tricky business, and should be left up to a nutritionally oriented physician, not to yourself.

As we saw earlier, one side effect of kidney malfunction or failure can be serious bone disease. Wadsworth Hospital's Dr. Coburn has found that vitamin D supplementation can actually help reverse these symptoms. Using vitamin D, he reports, "may provide the clinician the means to correct or even prevent the serious bone disease that frequently complicates the course of chronic renal failure."[9]

But, and this is a very big "but," vitamin D supplementation to kidney patients must be undertaken with great care. Why? As a fatsoluble vitamin, excess quantities of vitamin D are not excreted, but stored in the fatty tissues of the body. In turn, an excess quantity of vitamin D can lead to an excess quantity of calcium in the blood. This extra calcium may be deposited in the kidneys, thereby complicating the problems of a victim of renal disorder rather than easing them.

According to a report of the National Academy of Sciences: "An excess intake of vitamin D can result in serious toxicity. Vitamin D is stored in fatty tissues of the body and is present in the circulating plasma. Because vitamin D promotes absorption of calcium from the intestine, a large excess of vitamin D can cause excessive quantities of calcium in the blood (hypercalcemia), persisting for months after intake of vitamin D has been discontinued."[10]

In using vitamin D supplements to counteract the bone disease that may accompany renal disorder, a great deal of precision and medical observation is in order. In fact, a doctor must determine if a kidney patient should take extra vitamin D—and if so, how much—on a patient-by-patient basis. Some kidney disorder victims should *not* "self-medicate" with vitamin supplements that contain vitamin D, advises W. H. Taylor, M.D., United Liverpool (England) Hospital.[11]

A Practical Guide to Using Vitamin D

A prime source of vitamin D is plain old healthy sunshine. Just a brief twenty-minute exposure to sunlight will catalyze the synthesis of vitamin D that is a result of the biochemical reaction of certain oil glands beneath the skin and ultraviolet light.

Sounds simple, doesn't it? And yet any number of things can come between you and sunlight: clouds, smog, clothing, even ordinary window glass. And with skin cancer so much in the news these days, we are more and more aware that too much sunlight can be unhealthy. So you should consider getting your vitamin D from food as well as sun. These sources are good: fish liver oils, fortified foods like butter and milk, egg yolk, and seafoods like sardines, salmon, tuna, and herring.

Should you take a supplement? It may be a healthy habit to develop, especially for youngsters and older people, or those who live in a sunshine-poor climate. Reported physicians writing in *The Lancet*, Britain's well-respected medical journal: "Vitamin D supplements should be given to the elderly, particularly the housebound, who are at high risk."[12]

Supplements are important to nursing mothers, also, as we noted above. And when the winter comes and our daily intake of sunshine is decreased by clouds or cold weather, a supplement may be a good idea for everyone. Why? Even though excess vitamin D is stored in the body, if you aren't getting enough on a daily basis, that store may be gone in a matter of weeks. Your bones and body could begin to feel the ravages of a deficiency, characterized by localized back pain or easy bone breakage in the beginning, but eventually resulting in osteomalacia (soft skeletal structure, often misshapen), osteoporosis, or the kind of rheumatism or arthritis that manifests when the bones aren't getting enough minerals.[13]

Don't take a chance. Instead of waiting for your bones to ache in cold weather, why not plan ahead? Here's an idea: throughout the year, follow a simple regimen of supplementing your diet with D by taking fish liver oil or a capsule. As winter comes on, increase your intake. That way you will actually be strengthening your bones against cold weather discomfort.

Older people are especially hard hit by bone disease. Statistics tell us that bone structure begins to weaken as we pass the age of thirty-five. In fact, the total bone mass decreases as much as 10 percent in women and 5 percent in men for every decade past that age. So the elderly— or just the older—may especially need vitamin D supplements for the proper mineralization of their bones and teeth.

Children, too, may need extra vitamin D in supplements. Their bones are rapidly developing, so there is a special need for plenty of calcium and phosphorus to be absorbed via adequate vitamin D. Says Sara B. Arnaud, M.D., Mayo Clinic: "Children less than three years of age are the most vulnerable to vitamin D deficiency disease and consequently are the ones for whom supplementation is most common."[14]

Like their parents and grandparents, children may need more vitamin D during the winter months, when sunshine is scant. Dr. Arnaud suggests a supplement that contains 100 units a day—enough to protect your child from rickets.[15]

How much vitamin D should you take? The Food and Nutrition Board of the National Research Council suggests at least 400 I.U. daily.[16] Nutritionists advise that this minimum amount should be considered "survival" potency; more may be needed to build strong resistance against bone disease.

Researchers have found that people should not take more than 2,370 I.U. daily of vitamin D to avoid toxicity. In other words, megadoses of this fat-soluble vitamin are *not* recommended.

And why not? As you may remember from our discussion of vitamin D and kidney disorders, too much vitamin D can be extremely hazardous to your health. One reason is that it causes excessive quantities of calcium to be absorbed. Calcification of your body's soft tissues can be the unfortunate result. There may be serious damage to the kidneys, liver, and other organs.

There are certain circumstances under which megadoses of vitamin D have been used: in the treatment of rheumatoid arthritis, psoriasis, and tuberculosis, for example. But even under these conditions, toxicity symptoms were observed when adults took more than 10,000 I.U. daily, and children more than 4,000 I.U.[17] The symptoms? Anorexia, nausea, vomiting, headaches, excessive urination and thirst, diarrhea, and fatigue. Calcium and phosphorus levels in the blood increase to dangerously high levels. The lungs, kidneys, large blood vessels, heart, and other soft tissues of the body become calcified.

You can imagine how dangerous such calcification would be for an organ like the heart. The process would also contribute to the plaque formation that leads to advanced atherosclerosis.

If you suffer from any kind of liver or kidney disease, or from any intestinal malabsorption problem, check with your doctor about your vitamin D needs. Because the liver is involved with the metabolism of vitamin D before it becomes a mineralizing agent, you may need more vitamin D—or less—if your liver is diseased. Says a National Academy of Sciences report: "The vitamin D requirements of patients with liver diseases and kidney disease must be separately determined and such patients may require greater amounts of this vitamin than is normally given."[18]

It continues, "Because of poor absorption of vitamin D by patients with intestinal malabsorption, increased amounts of dietary vitamin D are needed in their treatment."[19]

Certain cosmetic companies have jumped on the vitamin bandwagon by adding vitamin D to their soaps and other preparations.[20] It's hard to say if it will be helpful but it's doubtful that vitamin D in an external preparation could awaken the "reservoirs" beneath the skin that release ergosterol. Your best sources of vitamin D are sunlight and food.

How do you know if you are deficient in vitamin D? Brittle and fragile bones are a dead giveaway. Other deficiency signs are pale skin, some forms of arthritis, sensitivity to pain, insomnia, irregular heartbeat, injuries that take a long time to heal, soft bones and teeth, and low blood calcium.

If you should observe any of these deficiency symptoms in yourself or in someone you love, see a doctor and follow his instructions for supplementing your diet. The result may be a significant improvement in your health!

Some doctors believe that children who have been nursed and weaned may not be getting all of the vitamin D they need. The 15 to 40 I.U. per liter of mother's milk is not nearly enough to satisfy the child's requirements, especially when you consider the RDA for infants is 400 I.U.[21]

Summary

Vitamin D, "the sunshine vitamin," has a direct metabolic relationship with the minerals calcium and phosphorus. It helps your body utilize these minerals in making strong, healthy bones and teeth.

Yet, since vitamin D is a fat-soluble vitamin, excess amounts can be stored in your body. Therefore, there is a real danger of toxicity if you take very large amounts. Any self-supplementation program should be undertaken with the greatest of care, and better yet, under a doctor's supervision.

Vitamin D-rich foods include fish liver oil, butter and milk to which vitamin D has been added, egg yolk, and sardines, salmon, tuna, and herring. Include these in your diet along with other whole foods and you will find yourself enjoying the good health you and your family deserve.

Vitamin E: The Super Nutrition Factor

What Is Vitamin E?

Vitamin E performs many important functions. It is effective in maintaining optimum physical and mental health. In illness or injury, its healing properties are extensive. Making sure you get plenty of it is an effortless way to look younger than your years. And it is an excellent protector against the stresses of our modern way of life.

Chemically, vitamin E is known as tocopherol. Tocopherol is a Greek word meaning "ability to reproduce." It is an apt description for vitamin E, as we shall see, for in study after study E has demonstrated the ability to reproduce muscular, cellular, and circulatory health. Its topical healing power can reduce scarring and maintain skin quality after serious injury. And it is a great aid to the reproductive system.

There are seven tocopherols that make up vitamin E: alpha, which is the most biologically active (more on that later); beta, gamma, delta, epsilon, eta, and zeta.

Basically, vitamin E is an antioxidant. What's that? Webster describes it as "a substance that opposes oxidation or inhibits reactions promoted by oxygen or peroxides." In its role as an antioxidant, vitamin E has properties that protect the vital fatty acids of your body from destruction, and can keep your nerves and cells normal and more disease resistant. Quite a feat!

How Does Vitamin E Work?

Medical authorities such as Dr. Jeffrey Bland,[1] Associate Professor of Chemistry at the University of Puget Sound in Tacoma, Washington, and Cindy Eisenmeyer, nutrition researcher at MIT, have described the simple way in which Vitamin E performs its basic function as an antioxidant:

• The lipid portion of the membranes that line the countless cells of your body is composed of fatty acids that are polyunsaturated. (Polyunsaturated means rich in chemical bonds that are capable of absorbing or dissolving more of something. These fatty acids have two or more double bonds.) Being polyunsaturated, the fatty acids in the cellular membranes are susceptible to free radical oxidation.

• Oxidation of the polyunsaturated fatty acids (PUFAs for short) causes damage or destruction of the cell membranes and can infringe on your health or even contribute to a state of disease. Vitamin E, as an antioxidant, helps keep the PUFAs from oxidizing.

• When PUFAs from your diet are added to the lipid portion of the cellular membranes, the overall amount of these special fatty acids is increased. In addition, PUFAs influence the fluidity of the membranes and serve as the substance from which local hormones are formed. Thus, through diet you can alter the quality of the lipid content of the membranes of your cells.

Get the picture? A cell is like an automobile tire. When the cholesterol in the cellular walls—the rubber of the tire—has been oxidized, it is transformed into a harmful hydroperoxide compound that can cause a "blowout." Vitamin E to the cellular membrane is like the steel belting on a radial tire: it adds strength and endurance that enables the cell to meet the stress of daily wear and tear without blowing out.

The word "blowout" as a description for what happens to your cells under stress is not just a convenient analogy. A study by Dr. Bland showed that cells that have been exposed to stress can oxidize and literally explode their walls, which can cause a disintegration of the actual cell structure. This "blown-out tire" look is not one for which any of us would strive. In fact, it's known as premature aging! And once the cells have been so drastically weakened, the body is increasingly susceptible to a number of illnesses.

We can look at the same study to see just how effective our "steel belting"—vitamin E—is against cellular damage. Two groups of twenty-four people each participated. One group took 600 unit doses of vitamin E; the other took nothing. Then, for sixteen hours the groups were bombarded by superstressful elements such as harsh sunlight, smoke, and impure air, all ever-present in our modern environment and known to cause the degeneration of the cellular membranes that appears to us as aging.[2]

The results? Blood samples showed that the "steel-belted" group showed just a slight degree of internal cell damage. On the other hand, the unsupplemented group suffered many total cellular "blowouts," reported Dr. Bland. His study suggests that vitamin E may be an indispensable buffer on the bumpy, stressful road of everyday life. It could even keep you from looking old before your time!

Let's look at another way E performs its antioxidant role. Vitamin E can actually eliminate some of those corroding materials called free radicals from your cell tissues. Chemically, free radicals are poisonous by-products of various enzymatic processes that go on all the time. Unchecked, they pose a constant threat of membrane destruction to your cells. They can wipe out your supply of PUFA through oxidation and simultaneously destroy the cellular membranes. A sufficient supply of vitamin E, however, can eliminate these free radicals before they begin their destructive action. Vitamin E is particularly important in keeping the walls of your arteries and heart clear.[3] But more on that later.

Where Does Vitamin E Work?

Now that we know how this veritable white knight of the cells works, let's take a quick look at some of the functions of this nutrient throughout your body.

• *Oxygen.* When the body's vitamin E supply is adequate, all the organs and vascular passageways are guaranteed the oxygen they need to function properly. In fact, more-than-adequate vitamin E may reduce the amount of oxygen the organs and muscles need, because the vitamin "spaces" the oxygen your bloodstream carries.[4]

• *Blood.* Vitamin E rejuvenates the blood and strengthens capillary walls. It is nature's own antithrombotic agent, which means it dissolves blood clots without interfering with the normal clotting activity of the blood. Adequate vitamin E insures that enough blood platelets will be produced for normal clotting to take place. Thus, the healing process is quickened. In addition, the capillaries dilate, which strengthens your circulation.[5] A strong circulatory system means that your heart, brain, and other vital organs receive all the blood they need. On a microscopic level, red blood cell walls are strengthened by vitamin E. Thus, vitamin E brings round-the-clock nutrition—via the blood—to every cell in your body.

• *Skin.* Vitamin E heals skin lesions and scar tissue, both internally and on the surface. "It will even act favorably on old scar tissue, reducing scars even to the point of near disappearance."[6] Its effects on burned skin can be dramatic.

Beyond these specific functions, vitamin E has a considerable reputation. Nearly everyone has heard tales of near miracles attributed to large doses or applications of vitamin E. Much of what you've heard is based on fact—it does appear to aid in fertility, and to promote a youthful appearance, for example. But some of vitamin E's noted effects are still controversial. Is it an aphrodisiac? Can it improve athletic performance by providing that "second wind"? Is it the solution to heart disease?

Yes, no, and maybe.

Dr. Evan Shute, a founder of Ontario's Shute Institute, reports that thousands of persons have been spared from heart disease and premature aging at his clinics through the use of vitamin E.[7]

He notes that vitamin E often hastens recovery from a variety of bodily ills and can promise something "extra" that drugs, with their often harmful as well as helpful effects, cannot give us.

Where does vitamin E work? The muscles, the blood, the cells, the skin. That's everywhere.

Like a good marriage partner, vitamin E is your ally in sickness and in health.

Who Needs Vitamin E?

Every body needs it, and that means you! We all need vitamin E. Some of us need it more than others. But every body needs it.

If you are under stress, breathe polluted air,[8] drink impure water, and/or eat processed food,[9] your need for vitamin E is increased. If you suffer from fatigue—even occasionally—have leg cramps sometimes,[10] are a superathlete or even just a weekend athlete,[11] your need for vitamin E is increased.

If you, like millions of others, suffer from any of these chronic conditions—diabetes,[12] its associated eyesight disorders,[13] shingles,[14] anemia,[15] sterility or infertility[16]—increasing your intake of vitamin E could improve your life. If you have been seriously burned, vitamin E could help.

In these modern times, simply being alive increases your need for vitamin E. Destruction of cells throughout your body occurs naturally, twenty-four hours a day, but certain factors inherent in the twentieth-century way of life increase the process of cellular damage by depleting your body of vitamin E. Stress and tension are among the chief offenders. When you think how common stress and tension are, it is easy to see why most of us need more vitamin E than our food supplies us.

Indeed, stress and tension are as endemic to our century as polluted air, polluted food supplies, and impure water, three of their primary causes.

• *Polluted air.* Even if you live in the country, you are probably breathing polluted air. Even without the obvious polluter—automobile exhaust fumes—there are cigarette smoke and chemicals emitted by industry, as well as ozones. (Ozone is a form of oxygen that is a bluish irritating gas of pungent odor and it is a major agent in the formation of smogs.) Many pollutants can be airborne over long distances, and all can enter your system.[17]

According to the study with rats done by Dr. D. Warshauer, and his colleagues at the Department of Internal Medicine at the University of California at Davis, "respiratory infections are a major complication of exposure to ozone." Dr. Warshauer notes that ozone actually generates two more dangerous elements within the cells—free radicals and lipid peroxides. Free radicals we know about; lipid peroxides are the compounds that are formed when the free radicals cause oxidation, which leads to cellular destruction. Dr. Warshauer calls these compounds "highly injurious," suggesting that they must be inactivated for your good health.[18]

Dr. Warshauer and his team also discovered that being deficient in vitamin E, with its cell-saving antioxidant qualities, puts you at an even greater risk not simply of respiratory infections, but also of heart injury. Why? Because vitamin E protects your lungs from many types of oxidants.[19] And the lungs are connected by the pulmonary artery to the heart.

If a vitamin E deficiency can *heighten* problems caused by air pollution, it follows that making sure you are getting enough E is a good defense against respiratory problems. Dr. A. L. Tappel states that some air pollution can produce damage to the lungs in the form of oxidation. Vitamin E and the related protective systems now appear to be among the most important defense systems . . . With regard to animal studies on this subject, Tappel commented that "since so many of the basic features of these animal tests are similar to conditions affecting some humans, it does not seem unwarranted to speculate about the application of these results to the human."[20]

Vitamin E plus a sound nutritional plan will give you a hedge against the pulmonary problems associated with varying degrees of polluted air. In other words, anyone breathing polluted air can help themselves before respiratory problems begin, by helping themselves to nature's own antipollution device, vitamin E.

• *Polluted food supplies.* Today, much of the food most Americans eat is processed. We are eating devitalized foods that are not fresh, with fewer nutrients. We are also eating lots of chemicals like coloring agents, artificial flavors, and preservatives that all make the food appear more attractive and taste fresher. (In some cases, the processed "foods" we eat are not foods at all, but mere empty calories and chemicals, packaged to appeal to our eyes.) Even nonprocessed foods like fresh fruits and vegetables, dairy products, whole grains, and meats often contain chemical residues from pesticides, herbicides, hormones, and other products used to make them grow. All of these substances may reduce the amount of vitamin E you have available for biochemical and physiological processes.

• *Impure water.* What is your drinking water like? Is it free of toxic metals like lead? Is its mineral content well balanced? Any mineral in excess, sodium for example, can cause illness when ingested over long periods of time. Impure water is an environmental stress of which you are often not even aware. Such a stress can deplete your store of vitamin E.

Stress depletes your store of vitamin E. Polluted air, polluted food, polluted water—all are everyday environmental stresses to which most of us are exposed. Vitamin E is a "must" nutrient for twentieth-century human beings (in combination with a sound nutritional program, of course).

Okay, so now we've discovered that anyone alive in the twentieth century, which means you, needs an increased supply of vitamin E simply to replace what is being depleted by environmental stress. But who *especially* needs vitamin E?

VITAMIN E FOR MUSCLES

Do you ever suffer from leg cramps for no apparent reason? This common affliction, known as "restless leg syndrome," may actually be your body's way of telling you that you are running low on some essential nutrient such as a vitamin or mineral. Sometimes the painful tightening of leg muscles can even keep you awake at night. During the day the aching may mean you take lots of aspirin.

Vitamin E might help end those cramps. Samuel Ayres, Jr., M.D., Clinical Professor Emeritus of Medicine at UCLA, and Richard Mihan, M.D., Associate Clinical Professor of Medicine at the University of Southern California, in an article in *California Medicine* report that vitamin E often relieves muscles in spasm. How? It rushes a supply of "sugar" to the deficient site, where it can be used or stored as glycogen. In other words, just as your stomach may growl when it's empty, when your leg muscles are low on glucose, they also "talk" to you. You should listen, then respond, by sending vitamin E to the rescue. And remember, vitamin E is just as essential to the proper functioning of all your muscles. The legs may be "speaking" for your whole body.[21]

VITAMIN E FOR ENERGY

Tired? When it's impossible to take a nap, or even a break, do you find yourself reaching for the nearest coffee, candy, soda, or other caffeine-and-sugar fix? Did you know that vitamin E can pick you up without letting you down hard, the way sugar, caffeine, and other drugs do?

Vitamin E naturally peps you up because it supplies more oxygen to your cells. Hey, hold on! Weren't we just saying that vitamin E is an antioxidant? That's right. So how can it also bring more oxygen to your cells? It doesn't seem logical, but it is. Because vitamin E is an antioxidant, keeping the oxygen from going into the process called "oxidation" with the free radicals, *more* oxygen is available to your tissues. In other words, vitamin E allows your cells to better use the oxygen that they have.[22]

Here's a good way to test the notion that vitamin E can pep you up, and it happens to involve another group that needs increased vitamin E: athletes, whose level of activity demands a steady level of energy. Let's look at the results of three studies that show vitamin E's role in physical activity.

• In Czechoslovakia, Z. Jirka, M.D., head of the Institute of Sports Medicine of the Medical Faculty of the Palacky Institute, administered vitamin E to a group of athletes and noted that the vitamin produced higher levels of stamina and helped discourage fatigue.[23] "Vitamin E, and especially its most active form alpha-tocopherol, has a widespread activity taking part in a great number of biological processes," he said.[9]

• In Russia, researchers at the Soviet Academy of Medical Sciences

Nutrition Institute and the Central Institute of Physical Culture tested the idea that intense physical activity increases the need for vitamin E.[24] Three groups of athletes were used in a test that involved a double-blind method. While all the athletes ate a diet high in food energy calories and performed similar types of exhaustive exercises, two groups took vitamin E in different dosages. The third group received no vitamin E supplements at all. The athletes who took no vitamin E supplements or very little were the first to tire. The tocopherol in their blood serum was simply used up by the physical activity.

• In the United States, Dr. Wilfrid Shute, reported that he saw very gratifying results while working with a championship swimming team that took large supplementary doses of vitamin E.[25] In fact, his own daughter brought home top honors in her swimming age group, he believes, thanks to vitamin E.

Here's how the test worked.

The swimmers were kept in steady competition and workouts. Vitamin E was given or withheld at various levels. Careful monitoring of the swimmers made it easy to see that vitamin E contributed to the improvement in the times turned in by the first four swimmers in each event. Other swimmers also demonstrated remarkably improved performances by taking vitamin E—E for energy, in this case.

How *much* "E" for energy? Sixteen hundred units a day worked for two top skaters, also supervised by Dr. Shute. However, this is not the amount needed for daily supplementation. One hundred to two hundred units, obtained from our food intake or supplements, would be more than adequate under most conditions. These champions "were the only athletes in the rarefied air of Squaw Valley who did not need supplemental oxygen, although prior to their taking vitamin E they had actually suffered from shortness of breath," said Dr. Shute.[26]

These three studies show that vitamin E can contribute to energy in a big way. All of us can learn from their results.

• You *do* need more vitamin E if you work hard or train hard. For a training period of one and a half to two hours daily, the supplementary dosage could be 20 to 100 units. A three-to-four-hour strenuous training period might require 250 to 300 units.[27]

• You can benefit from additional vitamin E even if you are not an athlete. By allowing your blood to use oxygen more effectively, it improves your alertness. And it's remarkable vitalizing effort doesn't let you down with a bang, the way drugs do.

• The average diet is so processed that vitamin E is not in ample quantity; therefore it becomes difficult to rely on food alone to meet your vitamin E for energy needs. For a good concentrated amount of this nutrient, supplements may be necessary.

VITAMIN E FOR CHRONIC DISEASE

Who needs vitamin E? The list goes on and on. Those with chronic conditions such as diabetes, shingles, anemia, sterility or infertility, or chronic miscarriage, could find their health improved by adding a vitamin E supplement to their daily fare.

If you suffer from diabetes, you will be interested to hear that vitamin E favorably influences the release of insulin from the pancreas. Vitamin E has also been successful in dealing with the severe hardening of the arteries which results from diabetes, as well as the retinal problems that frequently develop.

In one case on record, supplementary doses of vitamin E were able to reduce the pain in a victim of the eyesight disorder. It also shortened the time spent in the worst stages of the disease, notes Dr. Shute.[28]

In other cases of patients with arteriosclerotic changes in the retina, reported by Dr. Morgan Raiford of the Atlanta Eye Hospital at the 1974 meeting of the International Academy of Preventive Medicine, a combination of vitamins E and C not only seemed to stop the ocular disorder from advancing, but actually reversed some of the symptoms.[29]

How does vitamin E help victims of this disease? The arteries are usually damaged by either diabetes, high blood pressure, or simply degeneration as a result of aging.

With its ability to reduce the possibility of cellular membrane damage as well as to clear vascular passageways, vitamin E has the potential to help victims of many visual disorders, Dr. Shute reports. In fact, he himself used vitamin E to cure the reading disabilities of diabetics. He recognizes that many ocular problems require a much broader therapeutic approach, using a variety of nutrients. Obviously, the more careful attention paid to obtaining every nutrient necessary for optimum health, the more complete the healing process.[30]

Shingles is an extremely painful skin disorder, caused by a common virus that infects the sensory nerves. Vitamin E, applied to the surface condition and taken internally, can relieve the numerous symptoms and side effects of shingles. In one study by Drs. Ayres and Mihan, vitamin E ointment was found to remedy the nerve pain, while the cramps and angina of this painful condition were relieved by a daily 1,200-unit dose of tocopherol.[31]

If you suffer from anemia, you should be taking vitamin E. Because of its role in rejuvenating the blood and keeping cells strong, vitamin E can be useful both in relieving anemia and in preventing it.

Patrick J. Leonard, Ph.D., Director of Clinical Chemistry at St. James' Hospital of England, reported that he and Monty S. Losowsky, M.D., have shown that "alpha-tocopherol therapy has a beneficial effect on malnourished, anemic children living in tropical areas."[32] The

effect of vitamin E in the treatment of anemia, which involves hemo-
globin-poor red blood cells, stems from its promotion of the integrity
of the red blood cell membranes by protecting the PUFA contained
therein. Vitamin E's antioxidant action could give you a new zest for
life if you are one of the many who suffer the joyless experience of
anemia.

VITAMIN E FOR BURNS

Vitamin E is somewhat of a miracle worker as far as burns are
concerned. Here's a true story.

Scott N., an orchard manager, was seriously burned while burning
a pile of limbs and branches with gasoline. The skin was completely
burned away from his face, upper arms, and chest. The infirmary in the
small Louisiana town near the orchard applied a fairly routine approach
to his second degree burns: a mercury compound that eats away the
dead skin, which must then be very painfully scrubbed away in a daily
shower. From the first hour of his accident, Scott's wife, based on her
readings about vitamin E, gave him massive doses internally—about
500 units every three hours or so for the four days he was in the infirmary. When he left, the doctors told him to expect to be badly scarred
for at least two years. At home, he continued the large internal doses
and his wife applied vitamin E mixed with aloe vera juice directly to
his burns while they continued to heal.

The result? In two months, healthy new skin had fully grown where
there should have been scars. There was little indication that Scott had
had major burns. Now, three years later, those who know Scott find it
incredible that so much of his skin was ever burned away. He is a
walking testament to the healing power of vitamin E.

Where does vitamin E's almost miraculous power to heal come
from? Vitamin E has a bacteriostatic response that makes it an excellent
first aid tonic for burns. It actually limits the production of infectious
bacteria, helping your cells defend themselves against potentially
harmful invading substances, as well as lessening the pain that accompanies burns.[33]

You don't have to be traumatically burned to take advantage of
vitamin E's remarkable properties. It can help heal even the slightest
burn.

VITAMIN E FOR MUSCLE DISEASE

Vitamin E can also help in a condition called polymyositis. You may
know an elderly person who suffers from this dangerous inflammation
of muscle cell tissues, which can be doubly threatening because it invites serious infection.

Polymyositis is serious, particularly for the elderly, whom it most affects. They may require hospitalization. Worse, they may be so ill that even drugs have a limited effectiveness, or only make them sicker. They may even lose a major bodily function, such as urination, which can cause even more serious problems. The condition may last for months.

Raymond Killeen, a physician at the Hospital of the Good Samaritan Medical Center in Los Angeles, tried the alternative therapy of vitamin E on a polymyositis patient who was too ill to respond to the usual drugs. Most of the symptoms connected with the condition were alleviated. Dr. Killeen found that:

• Blood levels of aldolase, an important muscle enzyme, were restored to normal.
• Vitamin E caused the cell membranes to be stabilized.
• Further release of destructive enzyme proteins was blocked by the availability of adequate vitamin E.

Dr. Killeen concluded from these dramatic results that vitamin E may represent, in part, a valuable alternative to drugs that simply suppress the symptoms of polymyositis.[34]

Another chronic disease that may be alleviated by increased E is cystic fibrosis. According to a medical researcher at the National Institute of Health, cystic fibrosis may even arise in part due to low levels of tocopherol in the body. He found that cystic fibrosis sufferers are usually deficient in vitamin E.[35]

In conjunction with this research, a scientist gave large daily doses of vitamin E to the patients he was studying. The results? Four patients in the study reported varying degrees of pain reduction with vitamin E therapy. As for the other patients? Their conditions were completely reversed with vitamin E.[36]

VITAMIN E FOR REPRODUCTIVE DISORDERS

Another special group that may benefit from an increased supply of E are those with reproductive disorders that may result in infertility or sterility.

How did vitamin E earn its reputation as a sex potion or fertility drug? The facts are these. Vitamin E and the sex hormones are chemically related and therefore vitamin E's relationship to fertility is chemically plausible. How does that relate to us? Scientists in the 1920s, noticing this chemical plausibility, used vitamin E in an experiment to enhance fertility in animals. It worked!

In later "reverse" experiments, rats deficient in vitamin E were seen to change color and diminish in size. One result observed in the male rats was a failure to produce sperm. Drs. C. Raychaudhuri and

I. D. Desai of the University of British Columbia, who monitored the animals, also noted considerable tissue damage in the sex organs. The damage was caused by the process of lipid peroxidation—in part the result of a low level of vitamin E.[37]

In the female rats, the uterus and Fallopian tubes showed the pattern of discolored pigments, more evidence that the process of destruction of the fats in the cells may have occurred because of insufficient vitamin E.

While experiments like this have not been recorded for human subjects, researchers believe that they may draw some connection between E-deficiency-related reproductive disorders in animals and similar conditions in humans. However, at this time we cannot say that vitamin E will repair or prevent reproductive disorders in humans, or cure sterility.

While we're on the subject of vitamin E and sex, you might be interested to know that women have a special need for vitamin E. One particular need for E stems from production of the female hormone estrogen. According to Dr. Shute, estrogen is a vitamin E antagonist and minimizes blood circulation. He thinks that because women have greater concentrations of estrogen within their systems, they may have a much higher vitamin E requirement than men.[38] In addition, if you are pregnant or lactating, you may require even higher supplies of vitamin E, since your estrogen levels are elevated.

Vitamin E may also reduce your chances of having a miscarriage. Henry Borsook, M.D., a well-known vitamin specialist, has found that vitamin E is able to promote the growth of a normal placenta, essential to the process by which the embryo attaches itself firmly to the wall of the uterus. If the placenta does not allow the fetus to embed in the uterus, a miscarriage may be the result.

How does vitamin E promote the growth of a normal, healthy placenta? Dr. Borsook says that it neutralizes a counteracting substance sufficiently to let the digestive ferments of the placenta eat their way deeply enough into the uterine wall so that the placenta will not become loose or separate from the wall prematurely. In this way, vitamin E may help prevent miscarriage.[39]

If you have had a miscarriage before, or fear having one, you may want to take sensible precautions against it. It would be wise to seriously consider extra vitamin E supplementation. Ask your doctor.

Vitamin E for Health

Now that we've seen how vitamin E can help you during stress and illness, let's see how vitamin E can help keep you radiantly, youthfully healthy.

VITAMIN E FOR A HEALTHY HEART

The heart is, well, the heart of the matter when it comes to a healthy body. And the heart is actually a muscle that is hard at work, twenty-four hours a day, pumping blood. As we have seen, vitamin E is the number-one nutrient for optimum muscular health. Vitamin E, in a word, is vital to the vitality of your heart.

If you have already suffered a heart attack or other cardiovascular disease, vitamin E can help keep the cell membranes that line the walls of your arteries and heart from degenerating further. And unlike drugs, vitamin E works without the possibilities of harmful side effects.[7]

Vitamin E can also help protect you or someone you love against the possibility of a stroke, or even of a second stroke if you have already had one. You have probably been advised by your doctor to use more of the liquid unsaturated oils and fewer of the hard fats. Did you know that you should also be using more vitamin E if you are serious about controlling your blood fats?[40] According to Dr. Tappel, this is why:

• Butter or fats and polyunsaturated oils are chemically different. Dangerous free radicals attack the PUFA of oils readily, making them highly susceptible to oxidation. Vitamin E is needed to protect them.[4]
• Margarine, for example, may be more dangerous to your cardiovascular system than butter if you have not supplemented with vitamin E to prevent possible peroxidation.
• Butter has very little PUFA, so the danger of peroxidation is lower. But no, this does not mean that it is safer to use butter, since it is high in the saturated fats that increase your vulnerability to developing formation of plaques and eventually mineralized lesions in the arteries. These can lead to impeded blood flow, and sometimes to a stroke or cardiac arrest.

The solution? Use polyunsaturated oils for cardiovascular health. Protect their integrity—and thus the integrity of your cells—by increasing your intake of vitamin E. Vitamin E is PUFA's partner. It keeps PUFA from being oxidized or destroyed by free radicals. To keep your cardiovascular system healthy and your blood fats low, you must maintain a healthy balance between the PUFA content of your diet and the vitamin E that protects it. Dr. Philip L. Harris and his colleagues have suggested a ratio of 0.6 unit of vitamin E per each gram of PUFA as the balance for a healthy heart.[41]

VITAMIN E: MINIMIZING THE RISK?

Cancer is the scare word of our century. Most of us live with a quiet dread of this killer disease. What we don't realize is that we could be taking positive action in order to minimize our own risk of developing cancer. How?

By making sure you get plenty of vitamin E, both in foods and in supplements. And if you are serious about making your body more resistant to cancer, here are some further measures you might consider for increased protection. They come from Douglas Rotman, M.D., of Hartford, Connecticut, whose findings were published in *The Lancet*.

• Foods like butter, fatty meats, and other animal foods, and saturated fats like lard, are not good sources of vitamin E. Try to include vegetables that contain PUFA in your diet on a regular basis such as sunflower seeds, soybeans and small quantities of unheated oil, such as in salad dressings.

• Get plenty of vitamin E in your diet or through supplements. Dr. Rotman refers to Dr. Ewan Cameron's theory that adequate vitamin E insures that your body will not manufacture hazardous levels of hyaluronidase, an enzyme that may actually set off carcinogen formation within the cells.[42]

• Another good reason for eating a diet sufficient in vitamin E is that E keeps the PUFA you eat from being oxidized and destroyed. Cell destruction invites tumor formation.

• Try not to eat fried foods. Why? When polyunsaturated oils like safflower and sunflower seed are heated, toxins may form. These toxins, which contain peroxides, destroy vitamin E.

Dr. Rotman's[15] findings are that an adequate supply of vitamin E can make your body more resistant to developing cancer. Again, the reason lies in vitamin E's basic role as an antioxidant in keeping cellular membranes normal and healthy.

VITAMIN E FOR YOUTHFULNESS

Vitamin E contributes to your health in yet another important way. It fights cellular aging.

Have you ever known an older person who was not old? Sure, perhaps his or her hair was gray, but at the same time there was something about him or her that radiated vitality, beauty, energy—all qualities we usually associate with youth. If there were a pill that could help you look like that in your "old age," wouldn't you take it?

There is a pill that can help you look and feel vital and beautiful right through your later years. It's called vitamin E. If you could peer inside the body of one of those glowing "elderly" persons who looks like forty at the age of sixty, you would see this supernutritious antioxidant, says Dr. Bland,[43] sitting in the fatty bilayer of the cellular membrane doing its job as protector against the consequences of so-called aging.

Let's take a look at how the aging process works to understand vitamin E's part in slowing it down.

• First, cells are degraded and devitalized as they are exposed to peroxides (the result of oxidation) in the human system.

• Then, pigments manifesting these changes appear.

• Next, enzymes capable of dissolving cells arise. These in turn activate the widespread collapse of the metabolism.

How does vitamin E slow this process down? It combines with three cholesterol and two other groups of fats—phospholipids and triglycerides—to prevent them from oxidizing. In other words, vitamin E can keep your cells from suffering premature "blowouts" at the hands of those dangerous free radicals that cause oxidation. According to Dr. Bland, it assists "particular 'ports' on the cell membrane which are programmed to recognize various substances—kind of like 'molecular doormen' to protect your cellular membranes from invasion by these health vandals that can cause you to look old before your time."[44]

Vitamin E also protects you from the consequences of what biochemists call lysosomal leakage, another cause of premature aging. Lysosomes are organelles (a specialized part of a cell analogous to an organ of the body) that reside in the membranes of cells. They secrete enzymes with hydrolytic power that can be hazardous to your inner body health when they are released into the cell cytoplasm (fluid).

When these self-destructive cellular bodies spill over due to inadequate levels of vitamin E and other protective factors in your system, the result is that you age prematurely. Aging prematurely is a sign that there is something amiss in the various structures within the cell, which is the basic unit of life itself. Vitamin E, as the guardian of the health and life of your cells, can slow down premature aging and, in combination with other nutritional factors, actually extend your youthfulness.

Extend your youthfulness? Yes, indeed. An important experiment undertaken by Drs. Lester Packer and James R. Smith[45] at the University of California demonstrated that vitamin E performs a supernutritional feat as far as the life of the cell goes. It extends it as far as it will go, literally! You see, within the course of your life, each cell in your body may generate itself fifty times. Packer and Smith found that a boost in the vitamin E intake resulted in more robust cells capable of reproducing themselves a greater number of times, and thus living longer than usual.

Vitamin E can not only keep you from looking older than your years, it can actually keep you looking younger!

A Practical Guide to Using Vitamin E

Now that we know how necessary and useful vitamin E is, let's find out more about the vitamin itself. Where in the body is it found? What foods can you eat to make certain you are getting a good daily supply of the supernutrient? Should you take supplements? Natural or synthetic? What other vitamins and minerals are especially necessary to insure that the vitamin E your body has will work most effectively? How do you determine how much vitamin E your body needs?

Where in the body is vitamin E found? In the healthy body, obviously, vitamin E is found in all of the cells and tissues, especially those that store fats (adipose tissue). Like the other oil-soluble vitamins, E is concentrated chiefly in the major internal organs such as the liver, and in muscles such as the heart. Relatively high concentrations of E are also found in the pituitary and adrenal glands,[17] and in the testes.

VITAMIN E IN FOODS

What foods can you eat to make sure you are getting a good daily supply of this supernutrient? Ideal foods are wheat germ and wheat germ oil. Not only are they superior sources of vitamin E, they also contain polyunsaturated fat. (Being fat soluble, vitamin E requires fat and bile salts for absorption in the intestinal wall.) Leafy plant foods are a minor source of vitamin E; eaten with salad oil (safflower, soy, etc.), the E in the greens is readily absorbed. All whole grains, unrefined cereals, whole grain baked goods, seeds, nuts, bran, and fertile, organic eggs are excellent sources of vitamin E.

Remember, refined foods high in PUFA may contain vitamin E before processing. But methods used to lengthen the shelf life of such foods destroy large amounts of it. Long storage of foods has the same effect on E, as do cooking methods.

Vitamin E is also found in polyunsaturated oils—such as safflower oil and other vegetable oils—from which it can be readily absorbed. Here are a few facts about buying such oils that will help you get the most vitamin E for your money.

• The amount of natural vitamin E or alpha-tocopherol found in vegetable and nut oils varies. Some contain more of a beneficial and essential polyunsaturated acid called linoleic acid. For example, is corn oil your favorite? It is composed of 50 percent linoleic acid and 90 percent gamma-tocopherol. While gamma is natural vitamin E, experts such as Dr. Carl Pfeiffer say that the alpha form is more potent.[29] Now compare corn oil with safflower. Safflower has more alpha-tocopherol than any other vegetable oil. This is reflected in the fact that the linoleic acid level is 80 percent. So if you are depending on oil in your diet to supply your vitamin E, safflower is a better buy than corn.

• Almost as important as the *type* of oil you purchase is *where* you buy it. If you buy your oil at a conventional supermarket, it is quite likely a poor source of vitamin E. Why? Because processing removes much of the vitamin E that nature puts into our oils. Like many perishable foods, oils can be offered for sale much longer if there is no possibility of their becoming rancid. And in removing the possibility of rancidity by heating, pasteurizing, filtering, and deodorizing the oils, the processors also remove much of the vitamin E.

Such oils do provide polyunsaturated fatty acids but not vitamin E. Ironically, you may become vitamin E *deficient* by consuming commercially processed polyunsaturated oils, because increasing your intake of PUFAs increases your need for vitamin E.

• Buy cold-pressed oils that have been only minimally refined so that the natural vitamin E is there to prevent oxidation of the fatty acids. Such oil is full of those tongue-twisting but terrific nutrients, PUFA and alpha-tocopherol. The best source for it is a natural foods store, or the "health food" section of your supermarket.

VITAMIN E IN SUPPLEMENTS

If nature has already supplied vitamin E in so many readily available foods, do we also need to take vitamin E supplements? Probably so. Most of us have an increased need for vitamin E simply from the many environmental stresses inherent in our way of life. And think how fattening it would be to add a cup of high-calorie salad oil or a dozen bowls of wheat germ to your diet each day in order to increase your intake of vitamin E accordingly!

Each of us is biochemically different. Just as our needs for amounts of food vary greatly, so do our needs for vitamins. Many physicians feel, however, that just about everyone needs more vitamin E. Lloyd A. Witting, Ph.D., an associate professor of nutrition and food sciences at Texas Women's University, cites several reasons why we all need more vitamin E:[46]

• Our needs for vitamin E increase whenever we add more foods high in PUFA in our diets, as most of us in the past few years have done in response to advice on avoiding cardiovascular difficulties.

• Most of us eat a lot of refined foods, which give us only marginal amounts of vitamin E. M. K. Horwitt, Ph.D., a biochemistry professor at the St. Louis University School of Medicine, agrees with Dr. Witting that many of our foods have been depleted of their tocopherol in the refining process. He feels that supplementation is necessary to protect ourselves against a vitamin E deficiency. In fact, Dr. Horwitt has discovered through his research that "it is relatively difficult to incorporate much more than 20 I.U. of alpha-tocopherol into some diets using normal foods that are compatible with our cultural patterns."[10] Even the intelligently planned diet, says Dr. Witting, may not contain enough vitamin E.[11]

• Are you a "malabsorber"? Frequently, an inability to metabolize or absorb dietary fats effectively is inherited. You are thus at risk of developing deficiencies in any of the fat-soluble vitamins A, D, and E. You may need to protect yourself by taking more of these vitamins.

• If you are deficient in iron or suffer from anemia, if your blood is less rich in red blood cells than it should be, you probably have a vitamin E deficiency as well. Takaaki Fujii, M.D., of the school of medicine of Keio University in Tokyo, Japan, reports a definite correlation between iron-poor anemic blood and vitamin E deficiency.[47] A boost in the form of a vitamin E supplement may help not just your blood supply but also your overall well-being.

• If you take estrogen, mineral oil, or laxatives, you especially need supplementary E. Such drugs leach fat-soluble vitamins out of the gastrointestinal tract, creating a deficiency. Ultraviolet light, rancid fats, and lead are also vitamin E antagonists.

Taking capsules that supply vitamin E in just the right amount is a wise thing to do for yourself. And don't forget to double your health benefits by eating foods rich in vitamin E, too.

NATURAL OR SYNTHETIC VITAMIN E?

But which supplement should you take? There are so many. Natural or synthetic E? And how much? Here are five facts you should know about taking vitamin E supplements.

• Read the labels. Try to choose a supplement that lists "pure alpha-tocopherol," which should be easy in a good pharmacy or health food store. Why? Because alpha-tocopherol is the most active biologically and is better than mixed tocopherols. Also, the effectiveness of the vitamin E in a mixed tocopherol preparation may be diluted,

• Some people have trouble digesting fats. If you suffer from this problem, buy vitamin E in its water-soluble form.

• Natural vitamin E can help you heal more quickly than a synthetic version. More on that to come.

• Talk to your doctor about how much vitamin E you need. If you suffer from any special problem that may increase your need for E, bring it up with him or her. Under your physician's guidance, decide how much vitamin E you should take and stick with the prescription.

• Remember, taking a vitamin before or with a meal increases its effectiveness because it is better absorbed.

Why is natural vitamin E preferable to the synthetic E? Defenders of synthetic forms of vitamins tell us that biochemically a vitamin has only one molecular structure, and that is the same whether it is extracted from a natural product or synthesized by the manufacturer.[48]

However, California practitioner Samuel Ayers, Jr., M.D., has made some strong points in the case for natural vitamin E.

• Vitamin E in its natural form reacts differently than synthetic forms when it comes into contact with polarized light.
• Synthetic vitamin E has been shown to be 80 percent *less* active and thus less effective compared to natural vitamin E. Clinical tests with nonhuman subjects produced this discovery.
• Natural vitamin E may be up to 36 percent more beneficial in its activity than synthetic.

If you still believe that natural and synthetic vitamin E are the same creature, try comparing the two under a microscope. Both are composed of the same hydrogen, carbon, and oxygen atoms. But the molecules of natural vitamin E are of different shapes, while those of synthetic vitamin E are of exactly the same shape and dimension.

The difference is this: nature's own vitamin E contains *variety*, like nature itself. Synthetic vitamin E looks machine-made, which it is. Nature's design, as in so many other cases, is a hard one on which to improve. If you had to choose between a vegetable grown in earth and one grown in a factory, which would you choose? The answer is obvious. Why cheat yourself when choosing a vitamin supplement?

When reading the labels on a bottle of vitamin E supplements, how can you tell the natural form from the synthetic?

• Vitamin E is natural if it begins with a "d." Examples: d'alpha-tocopherol, d'alpha. Other natural forms are beta, gamma-tocopherol, mixed tocopherol, or mixed tocopherol concentrate.
• If the description of what is in the bottle begins with "dl," such as "dl'alpha," or ends with a "yl" as in tocopher*yl*, the product is synthetic.

HOW MUCH VITAMIN E?

How much vitamin E should you take as a daily supplement? Since deficiency may be present but not obvious, Dr. Myron Winick, a nutritionist at Columbia University, suggests that "short-term, high-dose supplementation (e.g., 300 units daily for several months) is entirely safe."[49] Nutritionists and doctors suggest that 30 to 400 units a day may be appropriate, unless you suffer from a specific illness or condition requiring higher amounts, at which time you should consult your physician.

However, there are special cases that do call for caution. If you have high blood pressure, or are taking cardiovascular medication such as digitalis, you should consult your physician before embarking on a vitamin E supplementation program by yourself. With high blood pressure, beginning with a smaller dosage and building up to a higher one is often recommended. Vitamin E can interfere with the activity of some cardiovascular medications. So ask your doctor.

How can you tell if are deficient in vitamin E? Some common symptoms of low vitamin E levels are edema (swelling) in the face, ankles, or legs; poor skin condition; cold fingers and toes even in warm weather; muscle cramps; an abnormal heartbeat, and respiratory difficulties. These symptoms may be recognizable without medical diagnosis.

"Blown-out" red blood cells, the result of free radical oxidation, can be detected by medical technicians and is another telltale sign of vitamin E deficiency. There are other symptoms that may also be noted by a doctor or other trained specialist.

ANTIOXIDANT PARTNERSHIPS

Are there other vitamins and minerals that are necessary to insure that vitamin E will work effectively? Yes and yes again. Vitamin E works best in partnership with a balanced diet containing *all* the nutritional elements your body needs. But there are three elements that are especially important for their interrelationships with vitamin E.

• *Vitamin A.* If you've wondered why nutrition books stress simultaneous consumptions of vitamin A with vitamin E, it's because vitamin E acts to protect vitamin A from oxidation. Vitamin E in amounts of 110 I.U. daily has been found to actually double the health-building affects of vitamin A. Good sources of vitamin A include yellow fruits and vegetables.

• *Selenium and sulfur amino acids.* Vitamin E can keep your cells alive, well, and functioning, but it needs a little help to do a thorough job. You must supply sufficient amounts of the trace mineral selenium and the sulfur amino acids, particularly cysteine and methionine, by eating foods or taking supplements rich in these elements. Good food sources include complete proteins such as meat, seafood, milk, and eggs. In addition, nuts and seeds and brewer's yeast also supply sulfur amino acids.

What do vitamin E, selenium, and sulfur amino acids have in common? Their chemical structures differ, but together they function as a team to protect the PUFAs from destruction, and to maintain the integrity of the membranes in which the PUFAs reside. Selenium works with the enzyme glutathione peroxidase, whose principal job is to neutralize the harmful substances called peroxides into neutral water and alcohol compounds. Thus, the vitality of the cellular membranes is safeguarded because the formation of free radicals is blocked. Sulfur amino acids are essential to the production of glutathione peroxidase.

Vitamin A, selenium, and the sulfur amino acids are indispensable helpers in keeping vitamin E at the peak of its antioxidant efficiency.

While we're on the subject of other vitamins and minerals, let's talk about iron. Iron is an important element in the diet and therapeutically invaluable in the treatment of anemia, as is vitamin E. But vitamin E and iron should never be taken simultaneously, as iron can interfere with your absorption of vitamin E. So be sure to let eight to twelve hours elapse between the time you take vitamin E and iron. Even to get the most value from your iron-rich foods like spinach, raisins, and meat, and those rich in vitamin E (or the supplement itself), eat them separately.

Dr. M. K. Horwitt believes that although vitamin E deficiency is uncommon in man there is much evidence in support of its pharmacologic benefits, and sees "therapeutic roles for vitamin E in treating certain encephalopathies, myopathies, eruthrocyte abnormalities, certain hereditary deficiencies, responses to toxic agents, retrolental fibroplasia and cardiovascular disease."[50]

Summary

Vitamin E, the "E" of which could stand for so many of its energetic, effective, and enormously powerful properties, has been the center of attention and the center of controversy among nutritionists, scientists, physicians, and the general public as well. Basically, vitamin E is an antioxidant. It protects your fatty acids from destruction and maintains the health and integrity of every cell in your body.

Vitamin E is especially important in promoting the health of your muscles, cells, blood, and skin. In other words, it is vital for the health of your entire body. We all need it, especially in these modern days of heavy environmental stress that can deplete our supply quickly.

In addition, vitamin E can be of special value to athletes, diabetics, those who suffer from certain skin disorders, anemia, muscle disease, burns, cystic fibrosis, sterility, and infertility. It may help prevent miscarriages.

Vitamin E is important in preventing disease as well as treating it. It can help those suffering from heart disease, as well as those who want protection against cardiovascular difficulties. It may be able to minimize your risk of developing cancer. And it is the number-one defense against respiratory infection and disease.

Eating foods rich in vitamin E can form the foundation of your program to supply plenty of the supernutritious vitamin to your cells. But for most of us, a daily supplement is a "must" for total protection.

Don't wait for a deficiency to appear. Make sure that you are getting plenty of vitamin E in your diet and through supplements. In

Dr. Tappel's words, "Vitamin E inadequacy is manifested in subtle and more diffuse ways, the most serious being the increased destruction [of cells] by lipid peroxidation."[51]

Vitamin E can help keep you looking younger longer and feeling healthier and more energetic through all your years. Remember "E" for excellence in the quality of your muscles, blood, and skin; "E" for enjoyment of life in a state of glowing good health; "E" for the extra-special qualities of this extraordinarily nourishing element.

Vitamin K

What Is Vitamin K?

A little-known but nonetheless essential nutrient, vitamin K is a fat-soluble substance that helps your blood clot properly. The microflora that live in your large intestine produce vitamin K. You can help them in their work by eating plenty of yogurt and other fermented dairy and soy products, as such foods promote the growth of these bacteria.

How Does Vitamin K Work?

Prothrombin, a blood-clotting protein necessary to prevent hemorrhages, is formed by vitamin K. So are three other protein substances vital to the clotting ability of your blood. Vitamin K helps you recover more rapidly and effectively from wounds and injuries by giving your blood the ability to coagulate.

Vitamin K is useful to your bones as well as your blood. It helps form a protein called osteocalcin,[1] which binds calcium. Osteocalcin is like an interior designer who is constantly remodeling your bones. Thus, if you are low in this particular protein due to a vitamin K deficiency, your bones may not be able to utilize minerals to develop and function properly.

Who Needs Vitamin K?

Obviously, we all need vitamin K on a day-to-day basis for the good health of our blood and bones. But there are certain situations in which your need for vitamin K may be increased. If you suffer from cancer, take chemical laxatives, or have ulcerative colitis or diarrhea, your needs for vitamin K are altered. If you are to undergo surgery, you will also need more vitamin K.

If you are a cancer victim, you may need more vitamin K than others, or you may need less. Vitamin K plays an ambiguous role in the formation and inhibition of the growth of tumors. If you don't metabolize vitamin K properly, some nutritionists say, "certain surface properties of tumor cells"[2] may change, resulting in malignancy. On the other hand, in other experiments a vitamin K *deficiency* has helped inhibit the growth and spread of tumors.

If you have cancer, a nutritionally oriented physician may be able to help you in determining your vitamin needs.

Laxatives such as mineral oil may destroy the tiny bacterial flora that synthesize vitamin K in your large intestine, resulting in a nutritional imbalance. In fact, any medication—such as antibiotics and sulfa drugs—that influence your normal intestinal environment can also influence how much vitamin K your body is able to manufacture.

Because they lead to malabsorption of nutrients, ulcerative colitis and diarrhea also interfere with vitamin K synthesis. After a bout with either, it may be a good idea to eat yogurt regularly for a while, encouraging the growth and redistribution of the K-producing microflora.

If you are to be hospitalized for surgery, do everything possible to encourage the growth of those microflora beforehand, and eat lots of K-rich foods. As G. F. Pineo, M.D., St. Joseph's Hospital, Ontario, explains: "Vitamin K deficiency, often resulting in serious bleeding, may occur unexpectedly in the early postoperative period and in patients with renal failure. It is likely that the more rapid onset of vitamin K deficiency in our postoperative patients was due to a combination of multiple antibiotic treatment and poor oral [food] intake."[3]

A Practical Guide to Using Vitamin K

Other than bacterial synthesis, vitamin K is available primarily through foods. Good sources: green leaves of plants like kale and spinach; cauliflower, broccoli, and cabbage; and pork liver. Vitamin K is not usually destroyed by cooking. And don't forget to encourage bacterial synthesis by eating yogurt and other fermented dairy products!

How much vitamin K do you need? Little is known about the precise daily minimum need for humans. Supplements are not available over the counter. However, they are sometimes prescribed to help in blood clotting and to prevent internal blood clots. It is known that one's vitamin K needs increase with age, since susceptibility to circulatory disorders also increases.

How do you know if you are deficient in vitamin K? Perhaps the easiest way to tell is if you have the tendency to bruise easily, though that can be the symptom of other nutritional deficiencies as well. At any rate, a deficiency in vitamin K can be extremely dangerous, as one of the symptoms in an advanced inadequacy is the inability of blood to clot. Premature infants, whose intestinal bacteria are not yet established, and whose mothers have been taking anticoagulants, run the greatest risk of developing a vitamin K deficiency.[4]

Summary

Although little known and not available in commercial supplements, vitamin K is extremely important for the health of bones and blood.

You can encourage the growth of the microflora that synthesize vitamin K right in your body by eating yogurt or kefir. You can also include vitamin K in your diet by eating K-rich foods.

Pay special attention to your vitamin K needs if you are scheduled for surgery or taking any sort of medication that might interfere with your body's manufacture of K. Awareness of this little nutrient can keep your health "A-OK"!

Bioflavonoids

What Are the Bioflavonoids?

The bioflavonoids, a group of substances with many names, are water soluble and possess enough vitaminlike qualities that in some circles they are known as vitamin P. Uncovered by the Nobel prize–winning biochemist who also discovered vitamin C,[1] Albert Szent-Györgyi, these brightly colored nutrients are also known as citrin, vitamin C-2, flavones, flavonols, and flavonones.[2]

Let's take a brief look at some of the names used to identify the bioflavonoids, and what they mean: *Bioflavonoids* are nutrients with vitaminlike qualities; they are water soluble and always occur in combination with vitamin C. *Bioflavonoids* could be defined as compounds that perform biological functions in the human body. *CVP* is a short name that defines the combination of ascorbic acid with citrus bioflavonoids. *Citrin* is a flavone found primarily in citrus fruits. Within citrin are hesperidin and other bioflavonoids. *Hesperidin* is a bioflavonoid found in the skins and peels of citrus fruits. *Quercetin* and *rutin* are names for two individual members of the bioflavonoid family. Rutin, which occurs in buckwheat, is sometimes sold separately. *Trioexethylrutin* is a rutin-related flavonoid effective in the treatment of hemorrhoids. *Vitamin C complex* or *C-2* is used to describe the inseparable partnership of the flavones and vitamin C. *Vitamin P* symbolizes the positive effects that bioflavonoids have on the permeability of the capillaries.

Confused? Don't feel bad. Even the experts don't agree on what to call these substances, nor even on whether or not they deserve to be called vitamins.

Why the confusion? The controversy hovers around these questions: Does the bioflavonoid complex play an essential role in the metabolic processes of your body? How can a substance be labeled a vitamin when you can make as much as you need without getting it elsewhere?

So let's start by calling the bioflavonoids "semiessential." Then, tongue in cheek, let's say that these "semiessential" substances may prevent vascular disorders. (Those who really believe the bioflavonoids are "semiessential" will question the evidence that there exists a relationship between bioflavonoids and vascular health. To them, the healing effects of bioflavonoids, documented in controlled experiments, do not prove the substances to be essential.)

Other medical researchers argue that the effects of the bioflavonoids are so indirect—they keep vitamin C from oxidizing[3]—that they cannot be classified as a true vitamin.[4]

Still others acknowledge that vitamin P performs an important function in chelating (binding) harmful heavy metals and sweeping them out of the body.[5] Yet they question the stamina of the bioflavonoids, as these effects do not show up in every experiment.

As a result of the controversy bioflavonoids are stuck, at least for the time being, with the ambiguous classification, "semiessential food component,"[6] able to benefit a broad spectrum of disease conditions in therapeutic doses, as we shall soon see.

You should know the established facts about bioflavonoids, now that you're aware of the controversy surrounding them. The evidence is clearly in that they are a positive force in the health and energy of everything from insects to humans;[7] that they combat bacteria and help keep you safe from scurvy; that they keep vitamin C and epinephrine from oxidizing; that they may help you resist colds, flu, and respiratory ailments; and that they have great healing power in victims of capillary and vascular disorders.

Is the conventional medical opinion that the bioflavonoids should be called a "pseudovitamin" justified? Read on. The decision as to what to call them—in your foods, on your vitamin shelf, in your body—is up to you.

In this chapter, we'll call the bioflavonoids vitamin P, for simplicity's sake. This is the name originally ascribed to them for their effect on permeability, a factor in their most important action in your capillaries.[8] The "P" may also help you remember that peppers, plums, prunes, parsley, and papaya are some of your most valuable food sources of the bioflavonoids.

So we are back to the original question: what is vitamin P? Chemically, it is a carbon-hydrogen-oxygen compound that shares the spotlight with vitamin C. In fact, they are actually members of the same nutrient family, three members of which are the bioflavonoid compounds hesperidin, rutin, and a group called the pectinates. Like the members of the B-complex family, vitamin C and the bioflavonoids hang out together in the same foods, and they hang out together in your body as well, helping each other perform a number of essential functions. In other words, they share a synergistic relationship.[9]

How Does Vitamin P Work?

Bioflavonoids enhance the action of vitamin C. As a team, they work like this: vitamin C, the white knight of your cells, patrols the larger blood vessels in your body, while vitamin P's territory is the smaller blood vessels—the capillaries. Its main function here is to strengthen the capillaries and to aid in the absorption of nutrients. Bioflavonoids must be present before the vitamin C in your body can be absorbed and used properly.[10] And as we already stated, they keep vitamin C from oxidizing.[11]

Although vitamin C *can* work without its partner, it is far less effective when the bioflavonoids are not present. On the other hand, the bioflavonoids cannot work without vitamin C. Once again, nature has provided for us by combining these two friends in the most delicious foods for our optimum nutrition and health.[4]

Hesperidin, rutin, and the pectinates together encompass a broad and versatile range of activity that keeps your body's defense mechanisms strong at an elemental level: in the capillaries. Why are the capillaries so important? Through their walls flow the ingredients vital to cellular and tissue health, as well as the waste products that your body must excrete. And even though the capillaries are minute on an individual basis, together all the capillaries in your body would reach around our planet two and a half times![12]

One stratum of the walls of the capillaries is made of "nature's nylon"—collagen. We have already learned that one of the major ingredients used in the collagen manufacturing process is vitamin C. But we are learning now that vitamin P is also necessary. Hesperidin and rutin are especially vital to the strength of the collagen in the capillary walls. And the pectinates are vitamin C's lieutenants in patrolling your cells against invading viruses and bacteria.[13]

The bioflavonoids bind with copper, forming highly active copper-flavonoid chelates. ("Chelate" comes from a Greek word meaning "claw," which should help you visualize this process.) These copper-containing enzymes are able to protect the vitamin C in fruits and vegetables—and in your body—from oxidation. They also help increase the stability of capillary collagen, thus increasing the strength of your capillaries. How? As coenzymes, they catalyze the tissue lysine oxidases, strengthening the protein fibrils that are the components of collagen, thereby making the capillaries stronger, too.

Where Does Vitamin P Work?

By now, you should know enough about vitamin P to be able to answer that question. The bioflavonoids work in one extremely important place: the capillaries. When you consider that every one of the sixty-some trillion cells in your body is dependent on the network of blood vessels that bring in life-sustaining nutrients and carry away waste products, you can see why experts have claimed that "the combination of vitamin C and the bioflavonoids benefits every condition in which it has been tried and should be considered by physicians as 'supplemental therapy' of value in virtually all diseased states and specific in action with respect to some."[14]

In making certain that your diet contains plenty of bioflavonoids and vitamin C—in foods and in supplements—you are strengthening your body's front line of defense, the capillaries.

Who Needs Vitamin P?

Everyone needs plenty of foods containing the vitamin C–bioflavonoid family—they are essential for good health. Keeping the capillaries strong keeps our bodies strong and helps us resist disease. Vitamin P has a positive effect on a number of diseases and degenerative conditions in addition to its maintenance qualities. It can be beneficial for those who suffer from high blood pressure; strokes; atherosclerosis; blood flow and clotting disorders; diabetes; eye hemorrhage; glaucoma; allergies, colds, and infections; rheumatic fever, polio, and arthritis; bruising and bleeding gums, as well as the bleeding associated with hemophilia and tuberculosis; tumors and leukemic bleeding; varicose veins; and miscarriages and menstrual disorders.[15]

If the length of the above list surprises you, remember that almost any disease state of the human body can be upgraded by improving the state of the capillaries. In all the instances we named, the capillaries are, to some extent, failing.[16]

VITAMIN P FOR BLOOD PRESSURE

Bioflavonoids and vitamin C have been used as a team with some success in putting a stop to the bleeding that often accompanies hypertension, or high blood pressure. Dr. Boris Sokoloff,[17] reporting in the *American Journal of Digestive Diseases,* recalled a situation in which fifteen cases of such bleeding were treated with the bioflavonoids. This was chronic bleeding, complicated by the kidney inflammation that hypertensive victims so often suffer. In all but two of the patients, treatment with bioflavonoids stopped the bleeding quickly.

In another instance, someone who had suffered from high blood pressure for years developed bleeding in her uterus. A doctor treated her with 600 milligrams of bioflavonoids daily, and the bleeding ceased in just four days, with no recurrence.[18]

Bioflavonoids have also been used in the prevention of strokes. Their role in decreasing capillary fragility points the way to success, particularly in the treatment of patients who are victims of what the medical world calls "ministrokes." The *Journal of American Geriatrics* reported that in one experiment eighty-nine victims of ministrokes took a compound of 100 milligrams of bioflavonoids and 100 milligrams of ascorbic acid in capsules. An untreated control group of stroke patients also participated in the study. Over the next three to five years, there was a 17 percent reduction in the incidence of little strokes, which the doctors attributed to the C-complex therapy: only three of the test subjects had ministrokes. In the control group, eighteen had ministrokes, and eighteen severe strokes. Five of the severe strokes were fatal.[19]

In other experiments, some 75 out of 100 patients were protected from the possibility of stroke, apparently by bioflavonoid therapy, even though they all suffered from severe high blood pressure.[20]

Atherosclerosis is one of the leading "killer" diseases in our country. A number of studies have demonstrated that vitamin P is a "David" against this "Goliath" of a disease. In a Russian experiment, researchers fed rabbits a high-cholesterol regimen, at the same time giving them supplementary vitamin C and bioflavonoids. The result? A substantial reduction in the incidence of atherosclerosis.[21]

Around the same time, it was discovered that rutin and quercetin particularly act to lower cholesterol levels in the blood.[22]

Here's how the point was proved: researchers put groups of rats on diets that would normally induce heart disease. Some groups were also given vitamin P, and these rats lived much longer than the rats who got the fatty diets without bioflavonoids. In the rats who ate bioflavonoids, there was increased blood stability and improved circulation, as well as lowered cholesterol levels.[23]

And speaking of circulation, did you know that in certain cases bioflavonoids have been used to help regulate the blood flow of coronary and vascular disease patients? These patients are frequently prescribed anticoagulant drugs, and so there is always the possibility that as a side effect hemorrhage will result—the blood has become *too* free-flowing. Baltimore's Charles E. Brambel, M.D., in a study of 2,000 such patients, concluded that 5 percent of them were prone to complications involving bleeding. Yet with a four-times-daily bioflavonoid–vitamin C supplement, the hemorrhaging stopped in each case.[24]

VITAMIN P FOR DIABETICS

Vitamin P has been used to treat the complications arising out of diabetes, another debilitating condition that affects so many of us. One of the most common problems for diabetics is broken capillaries, particularly within the eyes, so it makes sense that vitamin P treatment would help combat the visual damage that can result.

In one experiment in which a doctor treated fifty such cases with bioflavonoids, there was a favorable response among all the patients observed. Even cases of long-standing retinal bleeding cleared up in a short time, with no recurrence of the problem. One patient had suffered for fifteen years![25]

Eye hemorrhage and glaucoma are other related conditions in which C-complex nutritional therapy has proved helpful.[26]

VITAMIN P FOR ALLERGIES, COLDS, AND INFECTIONS

Vitamin C has a great reputation for increasing your resistance to allergies, colds, and infections, and even for shortening the length of time you suffer from such afflictions. Doesn't it make sense that since vitamin P enhances the action of vitamin C, it too could help you as a remedy from the sneezing, sniffling misery of an allergy, cold, or flu?

Remember, one of vitamin P's most important functions is in quickening the manufacture and maintenance of the collagen in the walls of the capillaries. In this capacity it serves as vitamin C's right-hand vitamin in keeping cells strong and able to resist incoming histamines, viruses, and bacteria that can cause the allergy and cold symptoms we all know so well.

Those who suffer from severe allergies may find the bioflavonoids an effective preventative against anaphylaxis, which is the name given to an extremely violent allergic reaction that can result in death.[27] On a more mundane level, some hay fever sufferers swear by the inside pulp of an orange, lemon, or grapefruit—so rich in bioflavonoids—as the best antihistamine money can by. One longtime hay fever victim has found relief in pulp marinated in apple-cider vinegar and cooked with honey. She makes a whole jar at a time and keeps them in the refrigerator, ready at a moment's notice to help stop the sneezing, stuffiness, and discomfort of a hay fever attack.[28]

Just like vitamin C, the bioflavonoids may help increase your resistance to colds. One study in which half the group took bioflavonoids and vitamin C and half the group didn't provided impressive proof of the power of the C-complex family in resisting the viruses and bacteria that cause colds: the group who took the vitamins suffered 55 percent fewer colds in the course of a year than the untreated group. And the colds that did hit the treated group lasted an average of 3.9 days, compared to 6.7 days for the untreated group! Quite a savings, in both time and misery.

In another study, twenty-two cold- or flu-plagued patients took a 600 milligram dose of a C-complex combination every day and twenty of them were through with their infections and fevers in only eight to forty-eight hours. Yet neither vitamin C nor vitamin P showed such impressive results on its own.[29]

You may also be able to *avert* an oncoming cold or flu by taking large quantities of vitamin C plus bioflavonoids at the very first sniffle.[30]

VITAMIN P FOR RHEUMATIC FEVER, POLIO, AND ARTHRITIS

The bioflavonoids and vitamin C have been used with some success as part of a comprehensive treatment for rheumatic fever, polio, and arthritis.

At a seminar honoring bioflavonoid discoverer Albert Szent-Györgyi, several doctors recounted favorable response from rheumatic fever patients who were treated with bioflavonoids.[31]

At the same meeting, it was reported that patients with acute polio had also benefited from the bioflavonoids. Since the patients demonstrated "abnormal capillary fragility," they were given 600 milligrams of vitamin C and 600 milligrams of hesperidin daily, until their capillaries were strengthened. The result? Improved appetites and increased warmth in the afflicted limbs, showing that their blood circulation was more effective. The longer the treatment, the better the results.[32]

Other research demonstrates that people with low levels of the C-complex family may actually be more prone to the development of polio than those with adequate supplies.[33]

And what about the use of bioflavonoids with vitamin C in the treatment of arthritis—that crippling, painful condition that affects so many of us, particularly in later life?

Twenty-one acute rheumatoid arthritis patients at a hospital in Florida were treated with bioflavonoids and C. The doctor who conducted the experiment noticed improvement over the next two to six months, including less pain, fewer digestive problems, lower blood pressure, and more action in the joints. The dose? Three hundred milligrams of bioflavonoids daily.[34]

Bursitis, another painful joint condition, can also be helped with vitamin P. In one case, a thirty-eight-year-old patient was given 600 milligrams daily. In only twenty-four hours, his intense swelling and pain were almost gone. Only some tenderness remained. In seventy-two hours, even the lesion had almost disappeared.[35]

In a similar case, the victim took a combination of 100 milligrams of bioflavonoids and 200 milligrams of vitamin C every hour for sixteen hours a day, over a three-day period. The result? After only three days, the soreness in the joint was gone.[36]

VITAMIN P FOR BLEEDING

Isn't it logical that vitamin P's capillary-strengthening action would have some positive effect on conditions like bleeding gums, excessive bruising, even the more serious bleeding problems associated with hemophilia, tuberculosis, and leukemia?

If your gums bleed every time you brush your teeth, try enriching your diet with the bioflavonoids. You may find that the addition of just an orange or grapefruit on a daily basis will help improve the problem.

The same benefits work over a period of time for people who bruise easily. Bruises are capillary ruptures; they obviously happen more often if your capillaries are weak. Strengthen the capillary walls and your bruising problems may stop.

Dr. Thomas Dowd, who was the physician for the Philadelphia Eagles football team, put the team on a regimen of three citrus bioflavonoid capsules daily. After only a short time, the number of players who showed large bruises following a game decreased from a hefty 40 percent to a minuscule 5 percent.[37] If you bruise easily, you might try Dr. Dowd's treatment for a possible solution to your problem.

The profuse, uncontrollable bleeding that can be deadly for hemophiliacs can also be helped by regular bioflavonoid therapy. So can the bleeding that so often accompanies tuberculosis and leukemia. When the capillaries are under stress, no matter how serious the condition, vitamin P may be of some benefit.[38]

In several cases, the bioflavonoids have been used to stop heavy bleeding in hemophiliacs. One researcher found that 300 milligrams of bioflavonoids, 500 milligrams of vitamin C, and vitamin K were effective, even when liver therapy had failed to stop the bleeding.[39]

The capillaries are weakened in the treatment of leukemia: radiation and/or chemotherapy damages them severely and they become increasingly fragile. This unfortunate offshoot complicates the condition itself. Yet treated with bioflavonoids over long periods of time, leukemia patients have been helped.

In an experiment in which nine cases of advanced leukemic bleeding were treated, four of them showed prompt cessation. Over a period of four weeks, another stopped. Even the most advanced cases—the other four—gradually improved over a longer period of bioflavonoid therapy.[40]

TB hemorrhage, too, has been stopped with bioflavonoid therapy. Bleeding stopped in every one of 133 cases that were treated with 500 to 600 milligrams of bioflavonoids daily. In from two to three days, 100 percent improvement occurred, and with no side effects. Said Dr. William B. O'Brien, Superintendent of the Rhode Island State Sanatorium, where the experiment was undertaken, "It is my impression that this is a worthwhile drug and that it should be used routinely in the treatment of TB hemorrhage." He notes that the bioflavonoids reduced clotting time from four-to-seven minutes to three-to-four minutes in most cases.[41]

VITAMIN P FOR VARICOSE VEINS AND HEMORRHOIDS

If you suffer from varicose veins or hemorrhoids, try the bioflavonoids. As well as relieving some of the pain, they may reduce the severity of the problem. Rutin in particular may help prevent your ever developing varicose veins. In an experiment undertaken in France, women who suffered from varicose veins or hemorrhoids were treated intensively with bioflavonoids. They reported a relief from their pain, almost unanimously.[42]

In cases histories published in *Prevention* magazine, relief from hemorrhoids in as short a time as forty-eight hours after taking bioflavonoids was reported. One patient was practically on the operating table when his doctor decided to give the bioflavonoids a try, with remarkable success, as it turned out.[43]

BIOFLAVONOIDS FOR WOMEN

By now it should be clear that the bioflavonoids may help in any area of your body where the capillaries are fragile. Their activity has great implications in the treatment of those who suffer from habitual miscarriages, menstrual disorders, and postmenopausal problems.

A Cornell University researcher reports some success in using vitamin P to treat women who have a problem with habitual miscarriage. He treated 100 pregnant women who had histories of spontaneous abortion with large doses of both vitamin C and the bioflavonoids. A remarkable 91 percent of his patients were able to carry their babies to term after bioflavonoid therapy.[44]

If you suffer from irregular or painful menstrual periods, the bioflavonoids may be for you. Take them with vitamin C and see what happens. (Calcium therapy may also help, since much of the pain caused by cramps is actually caused by great losses of calcium in the menstrual fluid.)

A story in *Family Practice News* related that women who were suffering from excess menstrual discharge had been treated with vitamin P. Those treated noticed "good to excellent results."[45]

And finally, there is some evidence that bioflavonoids with vitamins C and E may even offer relief from hot flashes associated with menopause.

Remember, the bioflavonoids are water soluble; what your body doesn't need is excreted through the skin and urine. If you suffer from a condition in which they might be beneficial, there can be no harm in giving them a try.

VITAMIN P FOR DEPRESSION

One orthomolecular physician, in measuring the brain waves of volunteers who had taken rutin in 50 milligram doses, concluded that the bioflavonoid is a sedative. Now one of his favorite prescriptions for depression is 50 milligrams of rutin every morning.[46]

VITAMIN P FOR TUMORS

One final note: vitamin P has a decidedly strengthening effect on the capillaries of tumors in cancer patients. What does this mean for you, or for a loved one who has a tumor? It could mean help. In one experiment, fast-growing cancers were implanted in twenty-eight rats. Divided into three groups, one was not treated at all, another group was treated with 3 milligrams of rutin, and a third group received 3 milligrams of bioflavonoids. Group one died in seven hours, group two in twelve, and group three in twenty-one.

In the second stage of the experiment, the researchers gave the rats 5 milligrams of vitamin P before implanting the cancerous cells, and 5 milligrams afterward. The rats did not die.[47]

If you suffer from cancer, bioflavonoid therapy can't hurt you. And it may help.

A Practical Guide to Using Vitamin P

After all this convincing evidence of the almost universally beneficial effect of bioflavonoids on conditions from allergies to cancer, questions pop up. What are the best sources of bioflavonoids? What are the daily requirements? How can you tell if you are deficient in vitamin P?

It's not hard to find bioflavonoids in food. Excellent sources are grapes, rosehips, prunes, oranges, lemon juice, cherries, black currants, plums, parsley, grapefruit, cabbage, apricots, peppers, papaya, cantaloupe, tomatoes, broccoli, and blackberries.[48] With so many delicious foods to choose from, the typical mixed diet may supply as much as a gram of bioflavonoids daily.[49]

Here's a hint for getting the most bioflavonoids from your food: when you eat citrus fruit, don't remove all those white layers around the skin and each segment of fruit. You'll be tossing away your richest source of bioflavonoids. Garbage to the uninformed—good health to the wise![50]

And when you juice oranges or other citrus fruits, don't strain out the pulp. It contains as much as ten times the amount of vitamin P as the strained juice.[51]

How much vitamin P do you need every day? Since there is no government-established minimum daily requirement for bioflavonoids, the amount you need is somewhat controversial. Most nutritionists agree that 200 milligrams is a minimum—survival potency—while 900 milligrams may be the optimum amount, easily and deliciously yielded by one large orange.[52]

If the idea of an orange-a-day doesn't tantalize your taste buds, there are other delicious ways to include bioflavonoids in your diet, while adding variety at the same time. You could concentrate on apricots when they are in season, making honey-sweetened apricot sherbet for dessert, or serving just plain apricots and cream, or munching on an apricot for a snack. Or you could substitute kasha—a delicious buckwheat cereal rich in rutin—for your morning oatmeal, or for your evening brown rice, for that matter. You could sprinkle your salads with paprika, or include raw red peppers. In the summertime, a good cool-off rich in vitamin P is lemonade sweetened with honey. You can even turn it pink by mixing it with rosehips. In the winter, warm up with the reverse combination: rosehips tea with lemons. A spruicer-up on any menu is fruit salad, even richer in vitamin P if you use lemon juice to bring out the flavors of the fruits. With practically any entree, a garnish of parsley and lemons adds beauty *and* vitamin P, if you treat it as part of the dish and not just decoration. Another way to enjoy the bioflavonoids and get more energy than either coffee or tea provide is to take your "coffee break" with a "smoothie" of applesauce (from an unsprayed, unskinned organic apple), lemon juice, and honey.

If you are treating a specific condition with bioflavonoids and vitamin C, try this ratio: ten parts of ascorbic acid to one part bioflavonoids. It will give you the most effective results in terms of the C-complex's synergistic relationship. Luckily, supplement manufacturers are aware of this beneficial ratio; you can buy vitamins that are made with it in mind.

Remember, vitamin P and vitamin C are partners, and they almost always occur in foods together. Nature knows best!

Something else you should know: vitamin P is easily destroyed when it is boiled or exposed to air. So if you make a cooked dish with bioflavonoid-rich foods, you may be cheating yourself of nutrients.[53]

How do you know if you are deficient in vitamin P? Some good clues are bleeding gums and easily bruised skin—also symptoms of vitamin C deficiency.[54] If you have either of these problems, pay attention to the bioflavonoids in your foods. Try upping your consumption of citrus fruit. Or take a natural C supplement like rosehips in which the bioflavonoids occur, too.[55]

Summary

The bioflavonoids, also known as vitamin P, the capillary permeability factor, have a very specific function in a very specific part of your body: they insure the strength and proper function of the capillaries. With their partner vitamin C, the bioflavonoids help manufacture the intercellular cement that is a primary ingredient of your capillary walls. They also protect your cells against attack and invasion by viruses and bacteria.

Vitamin P has been used in treating a myriad of conditions, for in almost any disease, improvement of capillary function means improvement of overall health.

Vitamin P is easily obtained through a diet of fresh whole foods, particularly fruits and some vegetables. It is also available in supplements.

This brightly colored little nutrient still doesn't get the attention it deserves for its role in our health, but don't let that keep you from helping it help you by including it in your diet every day.

MINERALS

Calcium: Your Chief Mineral

What Is Calcium?

Minerals comprise just a small portion of your body weight, only 4 percent. Most of your weight is made up of hydrogen and oxygen (which together make the water in your tissues), carbon, and nitrogen. Calcium is the next most abundant element, chalking in at a hearty 2 percent. Phosphorus—calcium's bone-building partner—comes in second in the mineral tally with 1 percent. The remaining 1 percent of your weight is comprised of all the other minerals put together.[1]

So to say that calcium is your body's chief mineral is no exaggeration. To say that it is the principal component of your bones and teeth, where 99 percent of your calcium resides, is also not an overstatement. Without calcium and phosphorus, your bones would be soft and spongy; in fact, you would be unable to stand on your own two feet, so to speak. But don't get the wrong idea—the roughly 1,200 grams of calcium in your bones don't just sit there like rock; they are in constant motion.

How Does Calcium Work?

Every minute of the day, calcium moves in and out of your bones and teeth. Here is how it works: The bones' foundation is a protein base called the matrix. Within the matrix are collagen ("nature's nylon") cells that are in a constant state of flux, just like every other cell in your body: they are constantly breaking down and constantly being replenished. Attached to this "intercellular cement" is calcium, which accounts for the hardness of your bones. When the collagen cells disintegrate, the calcium in them flows into your cellular fluids and the bloodstream. When the collagen cells are replaced, the calcium is reabsorbed.

There is another reason for calcium's constant motion: if your foods are not supplying enough for the needs of the other tissues in your body, they draw calcium from your body's "bone bank" for their own use. If you have a plentiful supply of calcium, there are actually storage deposits of calcium in your bones—like a savings account. Under normal healthy conditions, up to 700 milligrams of calcium might be withdrawn from your "bone bank" and be redeposited, all in a single day. If you are under emotional or physical stress—as in an illness—the flow of calcium between your bones and your bodily fluids will be even greater.[2]

There is also a tiny amount of calcium (1 percent) that is not stored in your bones and teeth.[3] This amount may sound infinitesimal, but even so, your cells need it desperately as an important compound of the cellular membranes, vessels, and organelles (the cells' "energy factories"). Calcium is also a vital component of the liquid that bathes your cells, both inside the membranes and out. The watery part of your blood (called serum) also contains some of this 1 percent of your calcium supply.

As a matter of fact, the bloodstream needs calcium so much that your body is designed with homeostatic mechanisms to keep the calcium level stable throughout your life. If there is surplus calcium from your diet, the hormone calcitonin (manufactured in your thyroid and parathyroid glands) puts it away in your bones' "savings account" of calcium. If you don't have enough calcium in your diet, another hormone, parathormone (which the parathyroid also makes) makes a trip to your bone bank and draws out a deposit of calcium for your blood.[4]

Why is calcium so important that the bloodstream's supply must be kept stable? For one thing, it is one of the raw materials used in the manufacture of hormones like estrogen, androgen, and cortisone, produced in your sex glands and adrenal cortex, respectively. The principal raw material used in this manufacturing process is cholesterol.[5] But to break the cholesterol down to build hormones, you need calcium.[4] In another part of the hormone factory—the adrenal medulla (inside your adrenal glands)—the basic raw material is not cholesterol but proteins. But calcium is used here, too, not in actually making the hormones but in releasing them (adrenaline and noradrenaline) into your bloodstream when you need them to help you cope with stress.[6]

Calcium also plays an active role in your enzymatic system. Like many of the other minerals, calcium's part here is twofold: it is an active ingredient of some of your body's many enzymes, while for others it is a coenzyme—an enzyme stimulator. For example, both the impulse transmissions of your nervous system and the contractions of your muscles are controlled by calcium-stimulated enzymes.[7] In another arena, calcium helps your digestive system absorb fats by activating an enzyme in your pancreas called pancreatic lipase.[8]

Calcium must also be supplied before you can store glucose as glycogen in the "energy bank" of your muscles.[9] Glycogen is the starch trapped by ATP when your cells burn glucose; without this "energy bank," you would have to eat a meal every ten minutes to keep your body going. Glycogen serves yet another purpose: it must be present before your muscles can contract. So although most of us think of calcium first as the bone-builder of our bodies, it is at least as important to our muscles.

Calcium, along with several other minerals, also helps to maintain the pH of the blood, protecting it against overacidity.[10]

Every day, some of your body's calcium store—up to 400 milligrams under the best of conditions—is lost in your urine and feces.[11] This loss can be even greater if you do not pay attention to the intricate interrelationships between calcium, vitamin D, phosphorus, magnesium, and protein. If there is an imbalance, the result of malnutrition, poor nutrition, or just ignorance of your dietary needs, you can lose quite a lot of your valuable calcium supply. If you are under stress or ill, the loss can be even greater.[12]

Where Does Calcium Work?

Calcium is the prime component of your bones and teeth, as we already know. Yet throughout many areas of your body, it works at jobs that are just as important to your health as the strength of your skeletal system. Here are some of the places where calcium works.

• *Bones.* Your skeletal system needs a steady supply of calcium to keep your bones hard and durable. You may be lucky enough to have been well nourished in childhood and to have a strong skeletal system as a result. But if in your adolescence and adulthood you have insulted your system by eating a lot of sugar and refined carbohydrates, drinking alcohol to excess, or taking antacids, your bones will tell the story. All those activities destroy your stomach's hydrochloric acid. What does that have do to with your bones? Quite a lot. Calcium in your foods and supplements cannot be broken down unless your stomach has the hydrochloric acid to do it. Calcium's mineral partnerships are also vital. Even if you eat plenty of calcium and have the hydrochloric acid to utilize it, if you don't have enough vitamin D or magnesium, your bones will lose calcium.[13-19] On the other hand, if you eat too much phosphorus, your bones will also suffer.[20] And if your intake of protein is insufficient, you can't use the calcium you eat to build bones properly; the collagen matrix will be unable to maintain itself. In addition, you won't have the protein necessary to build hardworking calcium carriers in your bloodstream. As a result, large amounts of calcium will be lost from your bones.[21]

• *Nervous system.* Calcium is so important to your nervous system that no matter how low the calcium levels are in other parts of your body, they remain at a stable level in your spinal fluid.[22] Calcium keeps you calm by helping your nerves relax.[23, 24] Another important part of your nervous system—your brain—must have just the right proportions of calcium with magnesium and phosphorus to function correctly.[25, 26] Those hormones in the adrenal cortex that cannot be released without calcium—adrenaline and noradrenaline—are also vital to the health of your nervous system.

• *Muscles.* Without calcium your muscles would have no energy storage bank of glycogen. Calcium also plays a very direct role in the contraction of all your muscles, including your heart. After the muscles receive the word from the nerves to contract, calcium catalyzes the biochemical reaction that results in their carrying out the nerves' orders. After the contraction, cellular vessels recall the calcium stimulus, and your muscles relax.[27, 28]

• *Digestive system.* Calcium is one of the ingredients in your body's recipe for healthy digestive juices. It is a major ingredient in the recipe for bile, without which you could not break down your meals into nutrients, particularly the fats.[29] If you don't have enough calcium in your diet, the digestive system can suffer, developing muscle spasms that manifest as spastic constipation.[30]

• *Circulatory system.* Your circulatory system is particularly dependent on calcium in two ways. First, it helps your blood clot properly.[31-39] Second, the proper amount of calcium in your system protects you from high blood pressure in an indirect way: a calcium deficiency causes so much biochemical chaos that your body overproduces cortisone and aldosterone, both of which direct your kidneys to retain salt and water. High blood pressure is the result.[40]

• *Immune system.* Calcium helps keep your system clear of toxic heavy metals like lead and cadmium. When there is enough calcium in your diet, the spaces of the bone matrix—which we could visualize as chicken wire—contain calcium. But when inadequate calcium is provided, your body can be tricked into absorbing radium, uranium, lead, cadmium, or strontium to fill those empty spaces. Cancer may result.

Who Needs Calcium?

Everyone needs calcium. But if you are a woman, if you suffer from osteoporosis (fragile, porous bones), if you are in pain or under stress, if you have arthritis, muscle cramps, or menstrual cramps, if you are pregnant, have high blood pressure, or suffer from depression, you can certainly benefit by paying special attention to getting plenty of calcium-rich foods in your daily meals.

CALCIUM AND WOMEN

Women have a special need for calcium. Through menstrual fluid losses and in pregnancy, they are much more likely to lose unhealthy quantities of this mineral than are men. When a woman's need for calcium is not met, the common consequence is the development of osteoporosis in middle or old age. To illustrate: a woman who, at age twenty, is getting half the minimum amount of calcium—400 milligrams—in her foods and supplements, will have lost a third of her calcium supply by the time she reaches fifty-five.[41] At that point, she will be a prime candidate to join the 30 percent of American women who have suffered at least one bone fracture by that age.[42]

Osteoporosis is a subtle condition, difficult to track down in routine lab tests. The loss of calcium from bones becomes visible to the X ray only after it is acute: 60 percent of the bones' mineral content may be gone before it shows up.[43-45] The surgeon may discover that his patient has bones like eggshells—osteoporosis—only when he is repairing a fracture. Fortunately, your body may give you these warnings before your bones become so brittle that you suffer a fracture: backache, back muscle spasms, aching of the bones in the thighs, difficulty in performing simple acts that require twisting and bending. Even more fortunately, if you become aware that you are developing osteoporosis, you can take steps to recalcify your bones before it gets more serious. Improving your diet and taking therapeutic supplements containing calcium and phosphorus are the first steps in rebuilding your bones.

In any case, you must take in over 400 milligrams of calcium in your foods and supplements every day, or osteoporosis is almost certainly looming in your future. If you get up to 1,250 milligrams a day, your bones are likely to be dense and healthy, as compared even to the relatively sufficient amount of 750 milligrams daily.[46]

Women need more calcium for another reason. If you suffer from menstrual cramps, the reason may be that you are losing large amounts of your calcium store through the menstrual fluid. Try this, if menstrual cramps are an unpleasant feature of every month for you: ten days before your period is due, take calcium and its nutritional partners in supplements. Continue the treatment through the third day of your period. If your cramps are particularly painful, take calcium/magnesium tablets—one or two per hour—until they decrease. But remember, if you are nutritionally aware in the first place and eat plenty of whole, natural foods, there should be enough estrogen in your system to keep you from losing all that valuable calcium in the first place. Then you won't have cramps at all.[47]

Pregnancy is another time in a woman's life when she is likely to lose large amounts of calcium. If you are short on calcium when you are pregnant, both you and your baby may suffer. Tetany, a condition which may be deadly, may result from calcium deficiency in pregnancy. The symptoms are nervousness, irritability, numbness, tingling, cramps, spasms, and convulsions.[48] Particularly in the last two months of pregnancy, the serum blood levels of calcium in the mother may fall so low that the relationship between the muscles and the nerves is disturbed, and tetany can result.[49] Even while nursing, the mother loses so much calcium that if she doesn't watch her diet and take supplements, tetany can become a very real threat.[50]

And, of course, the pregnant woman must take in extra calcium so that her unborn baby can build its own reserves. Especially after birth, the baby needs plenty of calcium—its blood levels of the mineral fall in any case within the short time it takes for its parathyroid glands and kidneys to start functioning.[51, 52] And then if the baby is not breast-fed, receiving cow's milk (rich in phosphorus) or formulas instead, its parathyroid glands may not function properly; neonatal tetany can ensue.[53, 54] In breast milk, nature has provided just the right ratio of calcium and phosphorus, in a form that your baby can digest easily, so it is far preferable to anything you could buy in a store. Also, the baby can absorb two-thirds of the calcium in breast milk, while it absorbs only a quarter of the calcium in a commercial formula, due to the imbalance with other minerals.

Calcium and Bone Diseases

Calcium can be your chief helper in treating bone diseases, just as it can actually help rebuild the bones stricken by osteoporosis. Another common bone disease—osteomalacia (softening of the bones)—can be caused by damaged kidneys, because when the kidneys aren't working properly, they can't retain calcium.[55] The condition can also result from not getting enough vitamin D in sunshine and foods. The symptoms? Aching or easily broken bones, twitching muscles, cramps, spasms.[56] When the bones are infected or inflamed, other dangerous conditions result—osteitis, osteomyelitis, and osteitis deformans. Calcium can help here, too. In her books, Adelle Davis tells several dramatic stories of people with these diseases who were remarkably improved with calcium therapy.[57]

And if you break a bone, remember to eat plenty of protein and calcium-rich foods while it is healing. Paying attention to your diet will help rebuild the bone tissue where the bone broke, and more quickly. Another reason for getting lots of calcium when you suffer a fracture is that when a bone is immobilized in a cast, it loses even more of its calcium supply.[58] So a balanced calcium supplement can be a good idea if you are mending a fracture.

CALCIUM FOR PAIN AND STRESS

If you are in pain for any reason—perhaps you have the flu, for example—don't reach for the aspirin bottle, reach for the calcium. And when you are unhappy, working too hard, or have had an operation or an accident, calcium can make the road less rocky by keeping your stores of the mineral stable. Why? You may remember from our discussion earlier that calcium must be present for the production and the release of the hormones that help you fight stress. When you are in a lot of stress, as in any of the above situations, your calcium supply can be used up in a hurry. Your adrenal cortex is using it fast to keep producing the antistress hormones you need, and meanwhile the increased influx of hormones is speeding up your whole metabolism so that you need more of every other nutrient as well as calcium.

CALCIFICATION CAN BE A REAL DANGER

If you suffer a calcium deficiency, calcium is continually leaving your bones to supply the needs of other parts of your body. Not only do the bones degenerate under these conditions; the excess calcium that they release creates a real danger for the very tissues they are trying to help. When you have an excess calcium supply floating around in your blood because you've eaten a lot of calcium-rich foods, calcitonin does its job in depositing the calcium in your bones' storage bank. But when calcium is being withdrawn from the bones, this protective mechanism does not apply. Your body copes with the surplus calcium by depositing it in any convenient place, and the tissues of your body can develop dangerous calcium deposits as a result. Any areas in your body that are weak or even slightly damaged will attract the excess calcium like a magnet. In particular, your joints, muscles, heart, liver, pancreas, stomach, kidneys, and lungs may be damaged.[59]

For example, let's say that your joints are strained or overtired, or perhaps they have been damaged by bacteria, drugs, viruses, or accumulating toxic metal deposits. Any of these conditions will draw calcium deposits, which then lodge there. Painful arthritis can develop.[60, 61] Or if your smaller arteries are broken in places because they have built up fatty plaque deposits, or because you have high blood pressure, the calcium will be attracted to those broken spots. Arteriosclerosis—hardening of the arteries—will be the consequence.[62] When arteriosclerosis is a problem, the heart is automatically affected because it becomes harder to pump blood through the arteries. Also, the heart muscle itself will be weakened and may even be a target for the calcium deposits.[63]

If excess alcohol or other poisons have weakened your liver, it too will attract the floating particles of calcium, which will further hamper its work.[64] If you haven't paid enough attention to your diet, and your pancreas, stomach, kidneys, or lungs are weak because they haven't gotten the nutrients they need, calcium deposits will make a beeline for them, too.[65-67] Even your eyes and skin may be affected by calcium deposits, which manifest as cataracts and a condition called scleroderma (leathery skin), respectively.[68, 69]

This paradoxical situation in which a deficiency of calcium in your diet causes an excess supply in your bloodstream, withdrawn from your "savings account" in the bones, can also lead to kidney stones. Your kidneys will be trying very hard to get the excess calcium out of your system. But since you are deficient in calcium, you don't have enough magnesium either, and the kidneys are helpless. Why? Without enough magnesium, the pH of your urine is too alkaline to keep the calcium particles in solution. Instead of being excreted, the calcium joins with phosphoric or oxalic acid. These compounds are deposited as kidney stones made of either calcium phosphate or calcium oxalate.[70] Insufficient vitamin A or B_6 can also contribute to this process if you have a calcium deficiency.

Perhaps you already have kidney stones. Getting enough magnesium, as well as potassium, can help you get rid of them, or keep you from getting more. These two minerals keep your urine at the proper pH, so that it can work with the surplus of calcium.[71-73] Avoid eating gelatin, though, if you decide to try this treatment. Gelatin, if not eaten with foods rich in B_6, can help create more oxalic acid, which in turn can lead to the formation of more kidney stones.[74, 75]

If you suffer from arthritis, your doctor may have prescribed cortisone. Taking cortisone puts your body under a lot of stress, and calcium is lost from your bones as a result.[76, 77] Thus, in taking cortisone for the arthritis, you may be creating even more serious problems: calcification of soft tissues (including the already arthritic joints) and easily broken bones.

Luckily, making sure there is enough vitamin E in your diet is a good insurance policy against calcification. Why? Vitamin E keeps your cells and tissues strong and healthy enough that they will be able to resist the weakness and damage that invite harmful calcium deposits. So if you get enough vitamin E, you are much less likely to develop even the bruises that can eventually lead to calcification of joints and soft tissues. In addition, if you suffer from any of the conditions we have just described—which all result from excess calcium in the bloodstream withdrawn from the bones—vitamin E will help speed the repair of the injured tissues.[78, 79] Once again, we see how very important it is to eat a diet that contains *all* the essential vitamins and minerals.

CALCIUM FOR CRAMPS, SPRAINS, AND SPASMS

Calcium controls your muscles' responses to the nerves' stimuli. Thus, it is very important to have the proper level of calcium in your blood: either too much or too little can cause problems. Too much calcium can contribute to blocked breathing or cardiac failure; too little can cause tremors, cramps, spasms, and convulsions.[80]

In fact, even a slight deficiency of calcium—easily correctable with proper nutrition—can cause muscle cramps or spasms in your legs, feet, and toes, particularly at night.[81] It can even cause you to gnash your teeth in your sleep, which can mean unpleasant visits to the dentist and high bills. If you take a calcium supplement with magnesium and vitamin D right before you go to bed, you may find your cramps and/or teeth gnashing gone.[82] You will also get a good night's sleep—calcium is one of nature's most refreshing tranquilizers. It leaves you feeling awake the following morning, not drugged.

Your heart may beat irregularly if you are deficient in calcium. Luckily, this frightening condition is also easily correctable with an increased calcium intake.[83]

CALCIUM FOR NERVES AND FOR MENTAL HEALTH

Some other unpleasant warnings of calcium deficiency are nervousness, depression, headaches, and insomnia. We just cited calcium as one of nature's best tranquilizers, so it makes a lot of sense that when you don't get enough of it, you become irritable, flighty, belligerent, or quarrelsome.

Calcium deficiency may also play a major role in chronic depression and certain types of schizophrenia. In fact, victims of schizophrenia have benefited from injections of calcium, enjoying short periods of clarity.[84] Calcium is so vital to the antistress mechanisms in our bodies that if there isn't enough, mental disease or disturbance can manifest.[85, 86]

A Practical Guide to Using Calcium

What foods are your best calcium bets? While many foods contain minute quantities of calcium, dairy products are the only really rich sources of this bone-building mineral.[87] Milk is one of the very best ways to feed your bones—a quart gives you 1,000 milligrams of calcium[88] that is properly balanced with phosphorus and magnesium.[89] Some people have trouble digesting milk. If you fall into this category, try a more easily absorbed dairy product like buttermilk, yogurt, acidophilus milk, or kefir, in which the protein is predigested and the calcium more dissolved.[90]

You may think that by eating cheese you are fulfilling your daily calcium quota, yet unless you eat sweet milk cheeses, you are mistaken.[91] Surprisingly, most cheeses are not particularly good calcium sources, with the exception of unprocessed Swiss and Parmesan.

Sesame seeds, torula yeast, carob flour, and sea vegetables all contain calcium, yet most of us don't eat large enough quantities of these foods to count them as really good calcium sources.

How much calcium do you need on a daily basis? According to the National Academy of Sciences, 800 milligrams daily is sufficient for a healthy adult. For women who are pregnant or breast-feeding their babies, however, 1,200 milligrams daily is required.[92]

Since most of us are under some stress, and calcium is so important in the production and release of our antistress hormones, it is probably a good idea to take in more than the 800 milligrams daily that is recommended. Some nutritional authorities have suggested that we take as much as two grams (2,000 milligrams) a day, especially if we are sick or under a lot of stress.

The RDA of calcium for infants is from 360 to 540 milligrams. There are 300 milligrams in a quart of mother's milk, but not all of it is absorbed. However, a baby is able to absorb even less of the calcium in a formula. If you must feed your child a formula, at least find out from an orthomolecular physician how to add calcium lactate at feeding time to balance out the surplus phosphorus in the formula.[93, 94] Also find out if the formula contains glucose, maltose, or fructose, which may keep your baby from absorbing the calcium the formula does contain.

For children, the RDA for calcium is 800 milligrams for ages one through ten, and 1,200 milligrams for ages eleven to twenty. But children depend on calcium to help them combat stress just as adults do; if your child is ill or in a stressful situation, give him more calcium.

Your need for calcium may vastly increase under particular conditions. For example, if you suffer from osteoporosis, you will want to up your intake of therapeutic calcium in supplements, with the correct ratio to magnesium and vitamin D, of course.[95] If you suffer from arthritic spurs, your doctor may prescribe a short-term megadose of calcium, balanced with all the nutrients that may help you.[96] Sometimes large doses (from 2–4 grams) of calcium lactate or calcium gluconate can help in emergency situations involving muscle spasms or convulsions.[97]

If you decide you need to take a calcium supplement, dolomite is a particularly good one, because it is balanced with magnesium in the ratio your body needs.[98] Bone meal is too heavy on the phosphorus side to give any big boost to your calcium levels.[99] Calcium lactate is an especially concentrated supplementary source of calcium, and calcium gluconate is good too. From three and a half teaspoons of calcium lactate, you can get one gram of calcium; from seven and a half teaspoons of calcium gluconate, the same amount.[100, 101]

Throughout our discussion of calcium, we have hinted at its special relationships with several other nutrients. In particular, calcium works hand in hand with vitamin D and magnesium. Vitamin D is extremely important in escorting calcium from your intestine into your bloodstream.[102] It is also a coenzyme that catalyzes others into bringing calcium into the matrices of your bones and teeth. Your kidneys need vitamin D before they can filter out valuable calcium from your bloodstream and return it to your system.[103, 104]

Vitamin D and calcium are so important to each other that vitamin D is now added to milk (also to prevent rickets). But the type of vitamin D added is synthetic—not at all the same vitamin D you get from sunshine or fish liver oil—and may not work as effectively with calcium as the natural kind. If you work indoors, you are especially prone to low vitamin D levels, which can completely throw awry your means to absorb calcium.[105, 106]

Yet you must be careful in taking supplements of vitamin D. Since it is a fat-soluble vitamin, your body can build up a dangerous accumulation.[107-109] The symptoms of vitamin D poisoning are weakness, headaches, diarrhea, vomiting, and dehydration.[110] Too much vitamin D in relation to calcium can cause as many problems as too little: your bones can lose calcium and your soft tissues can calcify as a result. Vitamin D poisoning can be deadly. Luckily, it can also be reversed simply by eliminating the overdosage of supplementary D.[111-113]

Magnesium is another of calcium's partners. It helps you absorb vitamin D, and also changes calcium into a soluble state.[114] If there isn't at least 600 to 900 milligrams in your daily diet,[115] your whole calcium-vitamin D-magnesium relationship will be thrown out of balance.[116] The ratio of magnesium to calcium should be roughly one part magnesium to two parts calcium.[117] It is especially wise to get your magnesium through supplements: our chemicalized farming methods have resulted in a scarcity of this valuable mineral in our foods.

Zinc, iron, selenium, and sulfur must also be present in the proper amounts for your body to use its calcium supply properly.[118] Fluorine, too, helps your body absorb calcium,[119] as do the B-complex vitamin family and vitamins A, C, and E.[120, 121]

But calcium has more partners than simply vitamins and minerals. To break down the calcium in the foods you eat, your digestive system must have the proper enzymes, the right amount of bile, and an adequate supply of hydrochloric acid. A simple way to help your digestive system absorb not only calcium but also vitamin D is to take two tablespoons of lecithin-rich natural fats like soy, safflower, sunflower, or peanut oil every day.[122] To further aid your stomach in breaking down calcium and absorbing it into the bloodstream, complete proteins and lactose are also necessary.[123, 124]

On the other hand, there is a long list of factors that are antagonists to your body's absorption and utilization of calcium. A low-protein diet is one. If there aren't enough complete proteins in your diet, there won't be protein transporters like albumin in your bloodstream to transport calcium to your skeletal system. Instead, the valuable calcium in your foods will be treated as a waste product, or deposited in your soft tissues.[125] Furthermore, the enzymes in your stomach that help break calcium down for the bloodstream are dependent upon protein for their production.[126] Protein also must be present to make the collagen that holds the calcium in your bones. If you eat a lot of high-protein foods like eggs, sprouts, soy products, nutritional yeast, and milk powder, you will be able to absorb 15 to 20 percent of the calcium you eat, as opposed to the 5 percent you will be able to utilize if your diet is low in protein.[127]

However, a high-protein diet can also be detrimental to your body's use of its calcium supply. Too much protein in your system will cause you to lose calcium through the urine just as will too little, and a deficiency will be the result.[128-130] If you are on a high-protein diet for a medical reason (perhaps you have hypoglycemia, for example), take extra calcium in supplements to compensate for the loss.

Sugars other than milk sugar are also enemies to your ability to utilize calcium. While lactose actually helps you absorb the calcium in your foods,[131] any other form of sugar will obstruct calcium's movement into your bones. Why? It keeps your body from producing the hydrochloric acid necessary to break down calcium.[132] As a sugar, alcohol is especially dangerous. Not only does it affect your production of hydrochloric acid, it also adversely affects your magnesium supply. When magnesium is lost in the urine, so is calcium.[133]

The phytic acid in certain foods can also antagonize your absorption of calcium: phytic acid and calcium bind to form a compound that your body treats as a waste product because it is indigestible. Whole grain cereals, peanuts, and soybeans can all have this effect, to some degree. Oxalic acid has the same quality: spinach and chocolate are among the offenders here. Yet another situation in which you cannot properly use the calcium in your diet is if your liver is not making emulsifiers to work with the fatty acids in the foods you eat. When not emulsified properly, these fats can combine with calcium to make insoluble "soaps" that are also indigestible.[134]

As we noted above, deficiencies in either magnesium or vitamin D will cause you to lose calcium.[135-138] Most of us routinely lose calcium because our foods are so short on magnesium. In turn, one of magnesium's nutritional partners is B_6, so a B_6 deficiency can indirectly cause a calcium deficiency.[139, 140] A copper deficiency—fortunately quite rare—can do the same thing.[141]

Most of us get far more phosphorus than calcium in our diets, which is dangerous because too much phosphorus brings the calcium levels in the blood down, and your body starts withdrawing it from the "savings account" in your bones. Even foods that we consider healthful—yeast, liver, wheat germ, lecithin—contain far more phosphorus than calcium. It is worth mentioning again that this imbalance makes bone meal an unsatisfactory calcium supplement.[142]

We have also seen that pregnancy and lactation make huge demands on the mother's calcium reserves. During pregnancy, the fetus receives four times the amount of calcium from the mother as she would have lost in nine months' worth of menstrual fluids. The mother's losses increase dramatically while she is nursing her baby. Even after menopause, women need more calcium than men. The estrogen shortage impedes the body's ability to absorb calcium, and urinary losses are the consequence.[143, 144]

More calcium antagonists: antacids that destroy hydrochloric acid;[145] aspirin, which causes you to excrete calcium through the urine, as well as causing digestive problems and impeding the ability of your blood to clot;[146] mineral oil, which stands in the way of calcium absorption and causes vitamin D losses at the same time.[147-155] Even the mineral oil that many cosmetics list as an ingredient can be taken through your skin to the bloodstream, where it presents a problem for the calcium that is trying to reach your bones.

Still more conditions under which calcium may be lost: consuming large quantities of fluids (common advise for patients with kidney stones) washes it out through the kidneys, along with its friends magnesium and vitamin B_6;[156] undergoing renal dialysis can cause an extreme calcium deficiency;[157] a large amount of exercise combined with copious fluid intake results in a mass exodus of calcium through the sweat and urine.[158]

There are so many conditions under which calcium's absorption may be blocked, or calcium lost, that one wonders how it is that *any* of us get enough calcium! Here are some more: if you are an epileptic, the drugs that have been prescribed for you (anticonvulsive elements) can break down vitamin D and damage your calcium supply.[159] Thyroid medication also poses a threat,[160] as do cortisone or ACTH treatment, two common therapies for inflammatory diseases. Stress is one of the most pervasive of calcium's enemies, placing demands on your supply of the mineral that your body may not be able to meet.[161]

Being immobilized is also dangerous to your calcium levels. Astronauts in peak condition lost 200 milligrams of calcium in their urine every day they were confined to the tight space of an orbiting capsule.

Even when you are debilitated in a major way—a heart attack, for example—you should get up and walk around as soon as your physician sees fit. Thus you can avoid the complications of a severe calcium deficiency.[162, 163] The same advise applies to you if you have suffered a bone fracture and are immobilized in a cast. Not being able to move the injured limb combined with the fracture's needs for extra calcium to heal makes excessive demands on your calcium supply, and even two and a half grams of supplementary calcium every day would not be too much in such a situation. If you are in a wheelchair or bedridden, you should be very attentive to your calcium needs, because you are losing a lot through being immobilized.[164, 165]

If you suffer from kidney damage, you also have a special need for calcium. Normally your kidneys can return to your system up to 99 percent of the calcium that they filter out of the bloodstream.[166] Yet if they are damaged, they may not be able to filter out the calcium that you need.

If your diet is low in protein or fat, if you have a severe infection (especially one accompanied by a fever), or if you suffer from heavy metal poisoning, be advised to up your calcium intake.[167-170]

Can you take too much calcium? The answer is yes, and these are the consequences: your blood levels of magnesium will go down, your levels of zinc will suffer, your blood may even lose its ability to coagulate properly. If your child is getting too much calcium, it may retard his or her growth.[171]

Albumin transports both calcium and magnesium through your bloodstream, and they compete for its time. If there is too much calcium, the albumin will be so busy that it won't have time to carry magnesium, and you will lose it.[172] This imbalance poses a real threat since most of us don't get enough magnesium in our foods anyway.[173] Be especially aware of the dangerous imbalance of calcium and magnesium in baby formulas and in prescribed ulcer diets.[174, 175]

Diarrhea will be your first visible result of acute magnesium deficiency.[176] Luckily, you can stop this deficiency in time with a magnesium supplement, or with a balanced supplement of all three of the interrelated nutrients calcium, magnesium, and vitamin D.[177] The more serious symptoms of an imbalance between these nutritional partners—tremors and muscle spasms—can be successfully corrected with a megadose—500 milligrams—of magnesium.[178] As with any other megadose treatment, however, first get your physician's advice. In this case it is particularly important to consult your doctor because the very same symptoms signify an excess of calcium.[179]

Too much calcium can also have an adverse affect on your supply of zinc. Some elements in foods—like the calcium phytate in grains and cereals—form an indissoluble bond with zinc that prevents its proper absorption. It is noteworthy that calcium and zinc supplements should be taken separately, if you take both.[180]

Too much calcium can also impede the ability of your blood to clot.[181] If surplus calcium floods the bloodstream, hemorrhage may result. If you are scheduled to have an operation, be sure to make certain that the calcium you take is balanced with all the other nutrients to avoid the possibility of hemorrhage.

In extreme cases of calcium overdose, there are emergency treatments involving chelation therapy. Chelation therapy is an injection of a substance like fluoride or oxalate that binds the excess calcium so that it can be carried out of your bloodstream through the kidneys.[182]

At a meeting of the Federation of American Societies for Experimental Biology it was concluded that many American women are deficient in calcium and iron and men consume way too much salt.[183]

Summary

Calcium is your chief mineral, making up 2 percent of your body's weight. Ninety-nine percent of the calcium in your body lies in your bones and teeth, where it is involved in continual movement as the collagen-containing bone matrix repairs and maintains itself.

The other 1 percent of your calcium supply is very important to your body's cells, particularly active in your hormone and enzyme systems, as well as your nervous, muscle, and digestive systems. Your circulatory and immune systems also need adequate calcium to operate efficiently.

Women have a special need for calcium, as they are more prone to lose quantities of the mineral (through pregnancy, lactation, and menstruation) than are men. One unfortunate common result of calcium deficiency in women is osteoporosis—porous, brittle bones.

Calcium is a valuable therapy in bone disease or fracture; pain and stress; cramps, sprains, and spasms; and some mental disorders—even simple irritability. Adequate calcium is absolutely necessary to avoid the many complications that can come from calcium deposits in the soft tissues of the body. This "misdirected" calcium—removed from the reserves in the bones because there is not enough supplied in the diet —can lodge in any soft tissue that is even slightly damaged.

Calcium-rich foods are mainly in the dairy group: milk, buttermilk, yogurt, acidophilus milk, and kefir. Cheeses like Swiss and Parmesan are also good. Sesame seeds, torula yeast, carob flour, and sea vegetables also supply some calcium.

The RDA for calcium for adults is 800 milligrams. For pregnant or lactating women, the RDA is 1,200 milligrams. For infants and children, the range is from 360 for babies to 1,200 for those in puberty and adolescence.

Greater amounts of calcium may be required for particular conditions like osteoporosis, muscle spasms, or bone fractures. In supplements, make sure that the calcium is balanced with magnesium, as in dolomite.

Calcium enjoys nutritional partnerships with magnesium and vitamin D. Its antagonists are many. To name a few: a low-protein diet, a very-high-protein diet, a diet rich in sugar, foods that contain phytic or oxalic acid, deficiencies in vitamin D or magnesium, pregnancy and lactation, antacids, aspirin, mineral oil, kidney problems, anticonvulsive drugs, cortisone therapy, thyroid medication, stress, immobility, and infection.

Too much calcium can cause problems such as magnesium or zinc deficiency and inability of your blood to coagulate. Luckily, there are treatments that enable your body to excrete an acute excess of calcium, your chief mineral.

Chromium: A Mineral from the Fountain of Youth

What Is Chromium?

Until Drs. Klaus Schwartz and Walter Mertz pioneered research on the nutrient qualities of chromium, most of us thought of the mineral as something to be used only in plating the trims of our cars. Little did we know that chromium is not only in the earth all around us, but is also contained in minute but vital quantities throughout our bodies.

If you were to dig around for chromium in the earth's crust, you would find it in the rocks that also contain molybdenum (another nutrient your body needs in trace amounts). If you were to look for chromium in the air, you would find far too much of it hanging over cities where coal is burned in industry.

Schwartz and Mertz also found out that in every billion parts of blood in our bodies, there are twenty parts of chromium. They called it a "vitaminlike" mineral because it takes part in so many of the biochemical reactions of our metabolism, making sure the food we eat is transformed into energy for our cells. They called it "essential," because it is absolutely necessary for the proper functioning of our bodies, which cannot manufacture it themselves.[1]

How Does Chromium Work?

Now that we have a rough idea of what chromium is, let's look at how it works. We know that it works in our metabolic system, but how?

After you eat food, your body changes the carbohydrates, fats, and proteins the food contains into a simple fuel for energy called glucose. For your energy systems to work properly, each cell must receive glucose from the bloodstream. All the elements for proper glucose metabolism—of which insulin is one—must be present for the fuel to get from the blood to your cells, to give you energy.

Insulin, a key element for proper glucose metabolism, works hand in hand with a vitaminlike substance called the Glucose Tolerance Factor (GTF), so named because it was discovered in connection with the Glucose Tolerance Test. This is the test for insulin deficiency, determining how quickly insulin takes glucose from the blood to the cells. It is called the Glucose Tolerance Test because it tells you how much sugar your metabolic system can handle without going haywire.

Chromium is vital to GTF; in fact, it resides in the center of GTF. GTF, in turn, is vital to insulin, because without its coworker, insulin cannot transport glucose from your bloodstream to your cells. Therefore, chromium is an essential ingredient in the magical process we call metabolism. Your body cannot manufacture GTF, but enough chromium in your system stimulates its synthesization by helpful bacteria in your intestines. But as usual, a complete nutritional program is essential: niacin and three amino acids—glutamic acid, glycine, and cysteine —are other nutrients that must be present if GTF is to be synthesized.[2] One great source of GTF is brewer's yeast; it may be easier to take a tablespoon a day of that powerful stuff than to try to help your bacteria set up a chemistry lab in your intestine.

If there is not enough GTF to partner with insulin in getting the glucose from your bloodstream to your cells, your body has to use chromium from your chromium reserves (which we'll discuss later) to help metabolize foods properly. As the blood is filtered through the kidneys, about 20 percent of this mobilized chromium is lost through urination.[3] Thus, the more sugar you eat, the more your body needs the GTF to work with your insulin, and the more stored chromium you lose if your diet does not contain enough. This can be a true problem, for your chromium stores are quite limited and can actually be depleted very early in life on the average American diet.

Anything you eat that is quickly converted into excess glucose— such as sugar and other refined foods—can just as quickly exhaust your supplies of chromium, as they are continually being mobilized to help your insulin cope with the sudden surges of blood sugar levels that come from eating simple and refined carbohydrates. This discovery is a recent breakthrough that has important implications concerning the role sugar and refined foods seem to play in the development of heart disease. We'll discuss it at length later.

Where Does Chromium Work?

Although it is present only in tiny quantities, chromium is found throughout your body. Relatively large amounts are stored in your stomach, kidneys, muscles, fatty tissues, skin, and hair. It is especially important to the well-being of your heart, white blood cells, liver, protein production system, brain, immune system, and adrenal glands. But before we look at the reasons, let's discuss the place where chromium is most largely concentrated: the placenta. As a fetus, you needed all the trace minerals in a high concentration; perhaps you even exhausted your mother's supply of chromium. But as a result, when you were born, you had a large supply of chromium (unless your mother was chromium-deficient or you were very premature). The quantity you were born with diminished steadily for the first ten years or so.[4] From that point on, if you had been eating natural foods grown in chromium-sufficient soil, the amount of chromium in your body remained about the same (except for pregnant women, who are drained of their chromium supplies by their developing babies): about 6 milligrams. How much is 6 milligrams, you ask? A quarter of a teaspoon of chromium is roughly 1,000 milligrams. So 6 milligrams is a very small—yet very vital—quantity indeed.

Where in your body does this 6 milligrams of chromium work hardest? Obviously, it is important to every cell since it is the center of the GTF molecule, which helps glucose move from blood to cell. But chromium is especially important in the following places.

• *Heart.* If there is not enough chromium for efficient glucose metabolism, your heart will suffer because the liver will be unable to use glucose in its manufacture of glycogen. Glycogen, a storage form of glucose, is important because your muscles need it to contract properly. The muscle that needs the most glycogen is your heart. In fact, it is no coincidence that no matter how depleted the rest of your chromium stores are, your heart is the last of your organs that will give up its supply.[5]

Chromium also plays a key role in mobilizing excess fat in the blood —fat that can cause atherosclerosis. If chromium is lacking, the liver cannot properly remove the fat and use it to synthesize such elements as fatty acids, phospholipids, cholesterol, and lipoproteins, because chromium is needed for the liver to make these conversions.[6] Thus, the excess fat stays in the blood, where it will eventually clog the heart's arteries.

• *Immune system.* Your immune system also has a special need for chromium. One of the immune system's vital mechanisms for resisting invading viruses and bacteria—the white blood cells—contains a fair amount of chromium if you are in good health. Stress can use up the white blood cells' chromium supply quickly; thus, you are more likely to get sick when you are worn down by stress and fatigue.

• *Liver.* As we have already noted, chromium is an essential ingredient in the liver's production of glycogen, necessary for the proper contraction of your muscles. Chromium is also needed for the liver to do its job metabolizing the excess food fats it takes from the bloodstream. If chromium is deficient, your liver can't make lecithin to break down the cholesterol and fatty proteins in the blood, nor will it be able to lower your cholesterol. This can have serious implications: fatigue, overweight, premature aging, and atherosclerosis can be the unfortunate results.

• *Protein production system.* You need chromium in order to produce the new proteins that keep your body from degenerating into a state of rapid premature aging. In children, adequate chromium insures proper growth, protein synthesis, and efficient glucose metabolism.[7] A sufficient supply of chromium can improve your energy level no matter what your age.[8]

• *Brain.* If your chromium stores are inadequate, the insulin supply cannot be used properly. One result: a glucose deficiency in the brain. The symptoms? Trauma to both the nervous and endocrine systems, fatigue, dizziness, anxiety, insomnia, a craving for alcohol. Other more dramatic symptoms are blurred vision, jitters, depression, panic, phobias, and a tendency to suicide.

Much of your body's chromium supply is concentrated in your brain: a hint of how important it is to your mental health. Some studies indicate that a chromium deficiency, along with a deficiency in its GTF-partner, vitamin B_3, may be directly related to several types of schizophrenia.

• *Adrenal glands.* Chromium is also found in a relatively large amount in your adrenal glands, which with the brain's pituitary gland help you cope with stress.[9] Chromium is also an activator of vitamin C, another important element in the proper functioning of these glands.

Who Needs Chromium?

Those with hypoglycemia or diabetes, heart disease, high cholesterol levels, poor eyesight, mental illness, and susceptibility to infections may all have a special need for chromium. So might those of us
who are exposed to heavy pollutants, who are recovering from surgery,
who are pregnant, or who suffer from arthritis.

CHROMIUM FOR BLOOD SUGAR DISORDERS

Chromium is so important in helping glucose travel from the bloodstream to the cells that adequate amounts may really help your condition if you suffer from hypoglycemia or diabetes. In fact, there is evidence that one contributing factor in the development of a blood sugar
disorder is an imbalance or malfunction of your chromium-insulin
mechanism. If you suffer from hypoglycemia, your problem is that you
produce too much insulin, with a corresponding quick drop in blood
sugar. Perhaps your body is responding to a diet of refined carbohydrates (sugar and white flour), which do not supply enough chromium
for proper metabolism. If you have eaten such nonfoods for a long time,
your pancreas may simply be worn out from overproducing insulin to
cope with them, and at the same time your stores of chromium may be
depleted. The end result may be that your pancreas has exhausted itself
trying to keep up with your diet, and can no longer produce insulin at
all. You may then find yourself at the next stage of blood sugar disorder:
diabetes.

In both hypoglycemia and diabetes, the problem is that your cells
are not receiving the fuel (glucose) necessary to make energy for your
body to work. Eventually, every organ in your body will have a hard
time functioning under such conditions. Both these blood sugar disorders—endemic to the age of refined foods—are usually accompanied by
a chromium deficiency.[10]

Both GTF and chromium supplements have helped people who
suffer from blood sugar disorders.[11, 12] They have actually helped lower
the doses of insulin that diabetic children were taking. Chromium-GTF
therapy has helped some older patients end their dependence on insulin altogether.[13] In fact, in some experiments with chromium therapy,
it has taken only a few months to get the metabolism in formerly
diabetic adults to function properly again.[14] It is more complicated to
reverse diabetes in children.

While we are on the subject of diabetes and hypoglycemia, we
should note that in our industrialized society of processed and refined
foods these previously uncommon diseases have become rampant.
These figures may help tell us why: at the turn of the century, whole

wheat bread and only a marginal amount of sugar (five to ten pounds per year) were items in the average American diet. Today, most Americans eat very high amounts of white flour products, while sugar consumption per person has reached the unhealthy amount of two pounds a week![15] It is no surprise that blood sugar disorders are increasingly and tragically common.

CHROMIUM FOR HEART DISEASE

We have already touched briefly on the importance of chromium to the liver in removing excess fats and cholesterol from the blood. This function has a direct bearing on the healthiness of the heart. If the excess fats are not removed from the body by the liver, they remain in the bloodstream, where they can eventually lead to atherosclerosis.

Chromium is also necessary for the liver to make the phospholipid lecithin. Lecithin is an emulsifier that keeps fats and cholesterol broken into tiny particles that your blood can handle. Without it, they would form life-threatening globules that could stick to your arteries. The fatty acids are necessary to the energy requirements of your cells, and for the construction of your cellular membranes and nerve sheaths. But if they form globules because your liver isn't making enough lecithin, they can become a contributing factor in atherosclerosis, sticking to the arterial walls and narrowing the space in which your blood flows.

As we already know, atherosclerosis is a killer disease, bringing with it high blood pressure and heart damage, developing into hardening of the arteries, and eventually increasing your susceptibility to blood clots, thrombosis, or infarction. The connection between heart disease and diabetes has puzzled researchers until recently, when the research on chromium provided a key.

Eating refined carbohydrates (which are eventually converted into fat), creates an excess glucose supply which eventually depletes the chromium supply of your body. Thus the liver cannot take excess fats out of the bloodstream, nor can it make the emulsifier lecithin. As a consequence, a good supply of chromium is not only necessary for normal blood sugar metabolism, it is also necessary for normal fat and cholesterol metabolism. The two functions are vitally connected: when the blood sugar metabolism goes haywire, so can the fat and cholesterol metabolism. That is why so many diabetics also end up with heart disease.

But there is hope. Several medical experiments have used chromium to effectively treat the high cholesterol levels connected with atherosclerosis.[16, 17] Using chromium therapy alone, cases of heart disease have been reversed within a few months. Cholesterol levels throughout the experiments fell from between 16 and 28 percent. On younger patients, the treatment worked most quickly.[18]

In one experiment, every one of the patients on chromium therapy, all of whom were considered heart attack risks, benefited. All of them experienced a drop in serum cholesterol levels, with fewer cholesterol-transporting proteins in the blood. One patient's cholesterol levels fell by 26 percent in a mere seven weeks.[19]

Eating chromium-rich whole foods like nuts and brewer's yeast can reduce your risk of heart attack or degenerative heart disease by enhancing your liver's ability to deal with fats in the bloodstream. And it's a delicious way to keep yourself in good health!

CHROMIUM FOR IMPROVED EYESIGHT

One side effect of atherosclerosis is cataracts. Why? If you have fatty deposits on your arteries, your eyes don't get enough blood. When circulation in the eyes is bad, the lenses become opaque and cataracts develop.[20] Those chromium-rich foods that keep your cholesterol levels low can also help you maintain your eyesight through a healthy old age.[21]

Nearsightedness (myopia) can also be a result of depleted chromium stores. Both vitamin C and chromium are necessary for your eyes to focus clearly. Since chromium is an activator of C, it can also help you metabolize any vitamin C you take. Together, chromium and vitamin C have been used to improve the eyesight of myopic patients.

CHROMIUM IN MENTAL ILLNESS

We have already seen that much of your chromium supply is stored in your brain—symbolic, perhaps, of its importance as an antistress agent and its importance to your mental health. When you suffer from a blood sugar disorder like diabetes or hypoglycemia, your brain may not get enough glucose, which can result in the subtle and/or dramatic symptoms listed above. Several types of schizophrenia may be attributable in part to chromium and vitamin B_3 deficiencies.[22] Perhaps in the future our mental hospitals will be treating patients with brewer's yeast instead of chemicals and electroshock therapy!

CHROMIUM AND TOXIC METAL POISONING, ARTHRITIS, AND CANCER

Chromium can also help protect your body from the toxicity of pollution or heavy metal poisoning, because it activates that pollution-protector, vitamin C. It also helps keep your immune system strong when you are exposed to pollution, maintaining your resistance to infections and bacteria.

In fact, insuring yourself of an adequate chromium intake can be beneficial in treating any disease—such as rheumatoid arthritis or even cancer—that involves viral infections. Rheumatoid arthritis often involves such infections and/or metal deposits in the joint fluid, while some forms of cancer are virus- or toxin-related. More good reasons for taking chromium daily: laboratory tests with animals showed that those who received enough chromium had a stronger resistance to infection, while at the same time demonstrating a remarkably longer life span.[23]

CHROMIUM FOR POSTOPERATIVE PATIENTS AND PREGNANT WOMEN

Two short-term situations in which your chromium needs are increased are after you have had an operation and when you are pregnant. After surgery, you are always more vulnerable to infections; chromium can help you resist them. Be aware that if you do suffer a postoperative virus, your blood's supply of chromium can decrease by a third, and you will need to replenish it with lots of good food, or chromium supplements.[24]

A pregnant or lactating woman may lose up to two-thirds of her chromium supply to her developing fetus, with the amount of chromium in her white blood cells cut in half. During lactation, the loss goes on. If you are pregnant or nursing your baby, then, note that you need an extra supply of chromium, either in a good supplement or, better yet, brewer's yeast.

A Practical Guide to Using Chromium

Why are most Americans deficient in chromium? The answer can be simply and neatly put: refined foods.

A worldwide analysis of chromium deficiency showed up some interesting statistics. Absolutely not a trace of chromium could be found in 23 percent of the Americans over fifty who were tested. In dramatic contrast, 98.5 percent of people from other countries were found to have chromium in their bodies. Americans had only half as much chromium in their bodies as Africans; only a quarter as much as those tested in the Middle East; only a fifth as much as Orientals. Even teenagers in our overfed but malnourished society show signs of chromium depletion.[25]

Why are we Americans so deficient of this trace mineral? True, our soils may be as depleted as our bodies. Yet, what we put into our bodies may have more to do with it. White flour contains only 13 percent of the chromium of whole wheat flour; polished white rice, only 25 percent of the chromium of brown rice.[26] Our refined oils contain no chromium. And even raw sugar contains 83 percent more chromium than the refined white product! Not only do these foods not *supply* chromium, they contribute to the loss of the chromium supply you were born with, because they use up some of your chromium stores in their metabolism. And our refined diet not only robs us of our chromium, it literally robs us of our health: witness the tragic rise in heart disease and blood sugar abnormalities (diabetes and hypoglycemia) in our country since World War II.

So what do these unfortunate facts have to do with "A Practical Guide to Using Chromium"? This: the first and best way to increase your intake of chromium is to eat whole, natural foods, avoiding refined products whenever possible. Natural foods provide over six times the chromium found in a refined-foods diet, and you need the chromium they supply to replace the average 1 microgram of chromium each of us loses in our urine every day. Adequate chromium must be supplied on a daily basis or you can completely deplete yourself of this vital trace mineral in just a number of years.

What are the best food sources of chromium? Try whole wheat flour, brewer's yeast, nuts, black pepper (although too much can irritate your stomach lining), all whole grain cereals except rye and corn, fresh fruit juices, dairy products, seafoods, chicken, root vegetables, legumes, leafy vegetables, and mushrooms. If you cook your food in stainless steel pots, you may be adding a chromium bonus to your delicious meal of fresh, whole foods.

Two tablespoons a day of brewer's yeast—straight if you can enjoy the flavor, mixed in juice or milk or yogurt if you can't—is an excellent insurance policy for getting enough chromium, as well as other trace minerals like selenium.

Or you may get your chromium through supplements, particularly if you are pregnant or nursing, or suffer from a specific condition that may be helped by chromium. However, be aware that pure chromium supplements—as chromic acetate or chromic oxalate—are difficult to digest; you absorb less than 1 percent of the supplement in most cases. A more usable form of chromium is found in brewer's yeast.

How much chromium do you need? Although the FDA has not made any definite policy concerning the amount of chromium necessary on a daily basis, from 50 to 200 micrograms are suggested by other government studies.[27] Trace mineral experts back the higher figure of 200 micrograms, and that for someone whose basic chromium supply is still somewhat intact. The average American's diet of refined foods contains only 50 to 80 micrograms of chromium, and only half of that is absorbed.[28]

It is important to remember that your body has no way of holding on to chromium, as it does with some of the other minerals like sodium and magnesium.[2] If you don't eat properly, your chromium supplies will almost definitely be depleted.

It is possible to get too much chromium. An adult may be able to tolerate over 50 times the average amount suggested (up to 10 milligrams), but any metal can be toxic if you take too much of it. However, in the case of chromium, it is much more likely that you would be poisoned by the chromium that accumulates in your lungs if you live near a coal-burning industry, or from cigarette smoke, than by the chromium in your food or supplements. Just to be safe, though, if you are treating heart disease, rheumatoid arthritis, diabetes, or cancer with chromium, or have increased your intake because you are pregnant or must undergo surgery, do so only under your physician's guidance.

How do you know if your chromium levels are low? If you are under stress or have been living on a diet of refined foods (or both), you can be almost certain that they are. If you are pregnant or suffer from hypoglycemia or diabetes, you are almost surely deficient in chromium. If you fall into one of these categories, a hair analysis would be useful in diagnosing the severity of your deficiency. Or try upping your intake and see if you feel more energetic. Your energy levels are a key in detecting a deficiency, because of chromium's role in the metabolism of food.[29]

Summary

Vitaminlike chromium is absolutely necessary to your growth, energy level, and overall health. Because of its vital role in glucose metabolism and its importance to your immune system, it is one of your basic protectors against disease. You are born with a life supply of only 6 milligrams, which if not replenished by a healthy diet of wholesome natural foods, you could lose completely by the time you are thirty.

Chromium is found in minute amounts throughout the body, but is most important to your heart, liver, and brain. Your entire glucose metabolism system is in part based on insulin's partnership with a substance called GTF, which contains chromium. Chromium deficiencies can lead to abnormal glucose tolerance and lack of energy, hypoglycemia, and diabetes.

Since your liver uses chromium in its conversion of fats to energy, chromium is vital for keeping cholesterol levels low and your heart healthy. Chromium is also vital to your body's production of new proteins, lack of which can lead to premature aging. Your white blood cells must have chromium to fight bacteria, viruses, toxins, arthritis, aging, and cancer. To counteract stress, your adrenal glands must have their supply of chromium. Your brain needs chromium to keep sugar levels up and to avoid mental symptoms that can culminate in schizophrenia.

Trace mineral experts suggest that you take at least 200 micrograms of chromium daily to keep your system working properly. If you are pregnant or lactating or suffer from any of the disease conditions we discussed in this chapter, you may need more. Remember, you absorb only half of the chromium your food supplies, even less of the chromium supplied by supplements.

Brewer's yeast is an excellent source of chromium, more assimilable than chromium supplements. Something we forgot to mention above is that molasses, honey, maple syrup, and dark brown sugar also supply some chromium. However, if you eat too much of these sweets you will be doing more harm than good, as your insulin will use even more chromium than these sugary foods supply in handling so much glucose. Complex carbohydrates like whole grains are better chromium sources because they won't flood your bloodstream with more sugar than it can handle. Fresh fruits, dairy products, and meat are also good sources of chromium, a tiny mineral that can help keep you younger longer.

Iodine: Microscopic Might

What Is Iodine?

Iodine, an active ingredient of seaweed and fish, is present only in compounds in your body, and in infinitesimal quantities, making up only 0.0004 percent of your total body weight.[1] Unlike some of the other trace minerals, it is not a metal. But this fact makes its activity no less vital to your total well-being, as we shall see.

How Does Iodine Work?

The speed of all your body's activities is controlled by iodine. How could such a tiny element, and in such small quantities, accomplish such a large task? Iodine, most of which is stored in your thyroid gland, is used in making hormones vital to your overall metabolism. These hormones control the speed at which your blood absorbs carbohydrates, which are your body's energy fuel, from the food in your intestine. They also regulate the rate at which those carbohydrates are converted into glucose. Finally, they control how fast your body burns its fuel (oxidizes it) in the cells via cellular respiration. This synopsis makes it perfectly clear that without iodine our bodies could neither grow nor function.

The main hormone involved in regulating the metabolism is thyroxine, of which iodine is an integral part. Your cells are stimulated by this hormone to oxidize glucose properly, so that there will be sufficient energy for all the cellular functions.[2] Thyroxine is vital in maintaining your cells' energy mechanisms (cellular respiration) at a proper, steady rate.

Let's follow the iodine in your food through the bloodstream into the thyroid gland and see what happens from there. Although other glands—your salivary glands and those in the stomach lining—also take iodine from the bloodstream, they don't keep it, and they don't make hormones with it. On the other hand, your thyroid gland is your body's major storehouse of iodine, where it is being used to continuously make a supply of hormones.

The thyroid gland takes iodine out of your bloodstream at a voracious rate. In fact, iodine is literally "pumped" into the cells of the thyroid at a speed twenty-five times greater than it could seep in through the cell membranes. But if the pump mechanism is to work properly, you must have the right amount of potassium inside the walls of the cells, and the right amount of sodium outside. This sodium/potassium relationship, if it is in balance, creates an electrochemical pressure that pushes the iodine through the thyroid gland's cellular walls.

The amount of iodine that your thyroid receives through this pumping action is controlled by the anterior pituitary, or hypophysis gland, in your brain.[3] As thyroxine in your blood flows through the pituitary gland, a feedback mechanism measures the quantity. Your thyroid gland then gets messages from the pituitary gland about how much more thyroxine the metabolism needs to operate at peak efficiency. The thyroid absorbs the iodine it needs, at which point it combines it with the amino acid tyrosine to make the hormone thyroxine.

But wait—it's not really that simple. Before it can be combined with tyrosine, the iodine must first be converted into an active form. Enter the enzyme iodine peroxidase, which is protein-based (as all enzymes are). Thus, if there aren't enough proteins available to make iodine peroxidase, the iodine will remain in its inactive form—iodide—and will be completely useless to your thyroid in making thyroxine. The amino acid tyrosine, too, is dependent on adequate protein, and so are the other enzymes that help iodine and tyrosine combine to make thyroxine. So high-quality protein is necessary to the thyroxine-manufacturing process, or inactive iodide will simply back up in your thyroid and your bloodstream.[4, 5]

Other vitamins and minerals are also needed to make thyroxine: vitamins B_6 and C help your thyroid gland use the tyrosine properly;[6] manganese and choline must be present for the thyroxine hormone to form.[7]

Assuming that the enzyme iodine peroxidase, the amino acid tyrosine, the proteins needed to produce them, the iodine itself, and vitamins B₆, choline, and C are all there, what happens when the thyroxine is produced?

Your thyroid gland releases the hormone into the bloodstream, and the bloodstream takes it to every cell in your body to quicken respiration. This function is controlled by another hormone—called the thyrotropic hormone—produced in your anterior pituitary gland.

Once the thyroxine is in the bloodstream, it is protected from oxidation (destruction by free radicals) by vitamin C.[8, 9] At the same time, enzymes in your liver inactivate the old thyroxine hormones, breaking them down so that they can be excreted through the urine. Without this safety mechanism—which can malfunction if the necessary enzymes are not produced in your liver—excess thyroxine could cause your cellular respiration process to race completely out of control.[10] Thus, a healthy balanced metabolism depends not only on adequate iodine, but also on adequate vitamin C and enzyme-building proteins.

Although your body has mechanisms to conserve many of its other vital nutrients, such as iron, no such hemeostatic mechanism exists for the conservation of iodine.[11] The system is designed so that your thyroid is extremely efficient in absorbing the iodine it needs from your bloodstream, but it uses it quickly and sends it out again as a component of thyroxine. Some iodine is released when you have used and broken down the thyroxine, but the blood carries it to the kidneys, from which the urine carries it right out of your body. Therefore, you must constantly replenish your supply of iodine through food, even if you were born with a normal amount.

You need thyroxine (and therefore iodine) for more than just the metabolism of carbohydrates; it is also essential to the metabolism of fats. Thyroxine gives your cells the energy to break down and convert into usable form the fatty acids in your blood. As we shall soon see, this process has invaluable implications for those who suffer from high cholesterol levels.

Where Does Iodine Work?

As we have just seen, iodine works mainly in the thyroid gland in the production of the vital hormone thyroxine. But thyroxine—and therefore iodine—works in every cell of your body. It has special functions in these particular places:

• *Protein production system.* Ribosomes are manufactured by the body cells; they are in the protein family.[12] The ribosomes need thyroxine to make proteins properly.[13] Without thyroxine, childhood growth cannot occur and maintenance of healthy adult tissues cannot take place. Thus, an iodine deficiency can keep a child from growing properly, or cause the degeneration of tissues in an adult.

• *Immune system*. Vitamin A needs adequate thyroxine to be properly synthesized from the carotene you eat in food.[14] Since A is vital to the immune system, with an iodine deficiency you may find your resistance to infections lowered.

• *Heart*. Thyroxine helps your cells metabolize the fats in the bloodstream, keeping large fatty globules from building up in the circulatory system. By making sure there is enough iodine in your diet to metabolize fats properly, you are in effect taking out an insurance policy against atherosclerosis and arteriosclerosis, two killer heart diseases.

Thyroxine also has a role in lowering your serum cholesterol levels and therefore protecting your heart and arteries; it activates the liver's production of cholesterol, for which fats from your blood are required ingredients.[15]

Who Needs Iodine?

Everyone needs iodine, but under certain conditions extra iodine can be extraordinarily beneficial. Some of these conditions, like goiter (thyroid malfunction), are a direct result of iodine deficiency. Others, like heart disease, arthritis, impotence, and cancer, are conditions in which a variety of nutrients can be helpful, including iodine. And, of course, in pregnancy, all the nutritional elements are needed in larger-than-normal quantities.

Goiter is a direct result of iodine deficiency. The thyroid is unable to produce sufficient thyroxine, and as a result the metabolism is slowed. If the problem is not corrected at that stage, it can be too late, for degeneration of the thyroid tissues occurs, and the result is hemorrhaging of such proportions that the dead tissue cells lie stagnant in a pocket of blood.[16] Healing does take place, but with fibrous, brittle scar tissue rather than healthy, thyroxine-producing cells. To compensate, the thyroid gland enlarges itself, and the unsightly condition known as goiter becomes visible on the neck. Of the different varieties of goiter, the one directly related to iodine deficiency is called endemic goiter, so named because it usually prevails in regions of iodine-deficient soils.

Iodine therapy by itself can do nothing for the condition, once it has developed. It cannot make the scar tissue around your thyroid gland disappear, and it certainly can't help you make new thyroxine-producing tissue. However, vitamin E in therapeutic doses may be able to help the scar tissue dissolve. It may also be able to help your body make the new blood vessels necessary for the production of new cells. You should eat a lot of complete proteins if you try this route—they are necessary as raw materials in the replenishment of cells.

To repair your thyroid, try eating egg yolks, dairy products, nutritional yeast, wheat germ, sprouts, and tofu, along with daily supplements of iodine and vitamin E. A suggested therapeutic amount of vitamin E for this purpose is 600 to 1,000 units daily. Complement it with 1 to 3 milligrams of iodine, and you may experience a perceptible increase in the amount of thyroxine in your bloodstream, and relief from goiter.[17]

Alas, many victims of goiter and their physicians don't know about this nutritional therapy. As a result, endemic goiter often develops into an even more serious type of goiter called toxic, or exopthalmic goiter. (Exopthalmic means "bulging eyes," one of the unfortunate symptoms.) Besides bulging eyes, the symptoms include a greatly enlarged thyroid, trembling fingers and hands, rapid heartbeat and pulse, a metabolism that is wildly out of control, heavy perspiration, irritability, emaciation, anemia, and high blood sugar (a prediabetic state).[18] Women are far more susceptible to exopthalmic goiter than men.

The nutritional therapy described above cannot help victims of exopthalmic goiter; it is too late. Conventional treatment for the condition involves destruction of the thyroid tissues through X-ray irradiation, which suppresses the thyroid's activity and can increase the risk of cancer. Luckily, a nutritional therapy that is less toxic than irradiation does exist: it requires administration (by a physician) of quantities of iodide. Paradoxically, this treatment slows, rather than speeds up, the absorption of iodine by the thyroid gland.[19, 20] This strange therapy is an excellent example of how the body can react to megadoses of an isolated nutrient.

IODINE FOR HEART DISEASE

If you have heart disease, or wish to prevent heart disease, keep in mind that iodine has a very beneficial role in your body's metabolism of fats. Not only does it help your cells utilize the fats you eat, it also helps the liver convert the fatty substances in your blood into cholesterol for the production of bile and of your sex and adrenal cortex hormones.[21]

If your cells cannot properly utilize the fatty substances in the blood, or if the liver cannot properly convert the fats into substances that your body needs, the blood and arteries can become clogged with large particles of unmetabolized fat. If there are enough of these particles, they will eventually glob together to form fatty deposits of plaque on the walls of your arteries. Atherosclerosis—which has its own side effects: high blood pressure, hardening of the arteries, and heart disease—can be the result. Adequate iodine—along with adequate amounts of all the other nutrients we have discussed—can help your cells burn up the fats you eat, thus lowering your risk of developing heart disease, or possibly influencing your condition in a positive way if you already have it.

For example, in one experiment potassium iodide was administered to heart disease patients in the form of twelve drops of a 10 percent solution in milk, three times daily. Within a month, their serum cholesterol levels showed a significant drop, their lecithin levels (lecithin is produced by your liver to emulsify fats) rose, and they reported less heart pain (angina).[22] The experiment is a positive testimony to the beneficial effect of iodine in heart disease.

IODINE FOR ARTHRITIS, IMPOTENCE, AND CANCER

If your thyroid cannot function properly because of an iodine deficiency, stress is the result. Thus, an inadequate amount of iodine can indirectly cause the stress disease arthritis, and before the discovery of a vaccine for polio, also seemed to increase the susceptibility to that disease as well.[23] And because thyroxine is necessary for your liver to produce the cholesterol needed to manufacture your sex glands hormones, impotence can also be the result of an iodine deficiency.[24]

An unhealthy thyroid gland also bears a relationship to cancer. For one thing, the thyroid extract used in conventional therapy for hypothyroidism has been known to increase the likelihood of cancer of the thyroid, and of other cancers as well.[25, 26] In a hyperactive thyroid, the administration of radioactive iodine to destroy thyroid tissue can also increase the incidence of cancer.[27] These are good arguments for making sure you eat an iodine-rich diet in the first place, so that neither of those conditions have a chance to develop! Something else to be aware of is that even if you don't have a hypo- or hyperactive thyroid gland, an iodine deficiency can cause your thyroid gland to absorb the radioactive iodine present in fallout. With a normal iodine supply, the thyroid will not absorb that pollutant.[28, 29]

In fact, additional iodine can protect you from the radioactive iodine that could be a by-product of nuclear bomb testing. Supplementary iodine—as little as 5 milligrams daily—can help your thyroid excrete the radioactive iodine it does absorb. Thus, in more ways than one, it can be an effective weapon against cancer.

IODINE IN PREGNANCY AND FOR CHILDREN

During pregnancy, the mother needs abundant amounts of all the nutritive elements so that she is able to nourish both herself and her fetus properly. If you get enough iodine during pregnancy, you will probably be able to avoid the tragedy of a myxedemic baby—a child with low thyroid function. Be sure to use iodized salt, and eat sea vegetables and fish, whole grain breads, muffins, and crackers.

If your child should have a low thyroid function, you can help by making sure that there is plenty of iodine in his or her food in the early years. The deficiency of thyroxine in a child can cause cretinism,[30, 31] a condition in which a child is not only mentally retarded but also dwarfed, all because his system does not have enough thyroxine, i.e., iodine. Fortunately, cretinism can be reversed if iodine therapy is begun shortly after birth. Otherwise, the sad mental and physical defects of infantile iodine deficiency could be permanent.[32]

A Practical Guide to Using Iodine

How much iodine do you need every day? How can you enjoy getting it in delicious, wholesome foods? What other nutrients help in your absorption and utilization of iodine? Which ones hinder it? How can you tell if you are deficient? On the other hand, can you get too much?

Many Americans suffer from prolonged iodine deficiencies, partly because of iodine deficiencies in the soils in which our food is grown, partly because of our heavy consumption of foods from which iodine has been refined. In addition, the Food and Drug Administration has set a very low legal limit—twenty times under the amount needed daily for healthy maintenance of the thyroid gland—for over-the-counter iodine. By contrast, in Japan, where almost all of the food either comes from or is grown near the sea (where the soils are enriched by iodine-bearing rains), there are no thyroid problems except for those caused by genetic disorders or physical damage.

Iodine is added to salt to compensate for the lack of it in foods grown on deficient soils. And yet, if one tried to meet one's daily iodine requirements with salt, far more serious problems than iodine deficiency would be the result!

The RDA for iodine is 150 micrograms, but some nutritionists believe that 3 milligrams a day of this trace mineral is necessary to prevent serious thyroid disorders. A healthy intake for both children and adults is probably 150 to 500 micrograms daily. Except in coastal areas where the food is naturally rich in iodine, most of us would do well to make sure that we get that amount by eating iodine-rich foods or by taking supplements.

What if you prefer to receive your nutrients in foods? You may wish to join the wave of the future by learning to cook with sea vegetables. Even though you may not be at the stage at which you enjoy a heaping serving of hiziki or wakame on your plate, you can enhance the iodine content of your diet by cooking homemade soups with kelp, or including dulse in your salads. You can also try some of the flavor-enhancing kelp salt mixes on the market, or take kelp tablets for a more concentrated effect.

Fresh (not frozen) seafood is also a good source of iodine, as is garlic. Dried mushrooms are good, too, if they were grown in soil rich in iodine. Other decent iodine sources include leafy greens, celery, tomatoes, radishes, carrots, onions, and mushrooms (try them in a salad with a garlic dressing!), bananas, strawberries, oranges, and grapefruit. Milk, eggs, meat, and whole grains also supply some iodine.[33, 34]

Other nutrients are necessary for your thyroid gland to make thyroxine from the iodine in your diet. Let's review them: as you may remember, high-quality protein helps the thyroid produce enough iodine peroxidase to convert the iodine into an active form, which will combine with the amino acid tyrosine (also dependent on protein) to make thyroxine. Vitamins B_6 and C help your thyroid gland use the tyrosine efficiently. Manganese and choline are also necessary for the formation of thyroxine. Vitamin C also helps keep thyroxine from being destroyed by free radical oxidation in the bloodstream. So to insure that your body can *use* the iodine in your diet, be sure to get plenty of these other nutrients as well.

On the other hand, there are certain foods, like peanuts, untoasted soy flour, and vegetables of the cabbage family, that are antagonists to your absorption of iodine.[35-38] In fact, they contain elements that keep you from absorbing it at all. So if you are trying to beef up your intake of iodine, you might avoid combining iodine-rich foods with these.

How can you tell if you are deficient in iodine? A sluggish feeling —due to the fact that your thyroid is not producing enough thyroxine for your metabolism to work at normal speed—is one clue. Other symptoms are a bad complexion[39] and unhealthy looking hair, teeth, and nails. If your thyroid function degenerates into official hypothyroidism, in which perhaps only one-quarter of the thyroxine your body needs is present,[40] you may suffer from chronic fatigue, forgetfulness, lack of interest in sex, impotence, overweight, and irritability. Should you notice any of these symptoms, consult your physician. He or she may suggest a prescribed iodine supplement which, in the early stages of thyroid malfunction, could solve your problem.

Can you get too much iodine? Probably not. Of all the nutrients, iodine is most easily excreted through the urine, with small amounts also excreted in the feces, sweat, and hair.[41] Less iodine is lost from organically bound sources (as in foods such as kelp) because your body absorbs it better than it does iodine in potassium iodide supplements. There have been no documented cases of iodine poisoning.[42, 43] However, be aware that if you suddenly deluge your perfectly normal thyroid gland with large amounts of supplementary iodine, you can inhibit its ability to produce thyroxine.

Summary

Iodine, a natural element from the sea that is also present in soils in which our food is grown, is essential in the manufacture of the important hormone thyroxine. Thyroxine controls the speed at which your blood takes the food from your intestines to the cells, where it is used for energy. It is vital not only in glucose metabolism, but also in the metabolism of fats.

Iodine is particularly important to your heart, your immune system, and your system of protein synthesis. In adequate amounts, it can keep you from developing goiter—malfunction of the thyroid gland. Iodine deficiency can increase your risk of developing heart disease, arthritis, impotence, or cancer. In children, it can cause myxedema, resulting in retardation of mental and physical development.

A normal, healthy adult or child needs from 150 to 500 micrograms of iodine daily. Foods from the sea or grown near it are an excellent source, as is garlic, while some vegetables, fruits, and dairy products also contain small amounts.

The FDA prohibits the marketing of iodine is large supplements; but kelp tablets—many per day—may be useful in supplementing your diet if necessary. For supplements as treatment for a specific condition, see your physician.

Iron: Vital and Dangerous

What Is Iron?

The dictionary defines iron as "a ductile, malleable, silver-white metallic element, used in making tools," etc. How does this simple definition apply to the iron that is so often touted as vital to preventing fatigue and "poor blood" in our bodies?

Iron is a vital bodily element that is used in making a very important tool—hemoglobin—that carries oxygen to the cells via the bloodstream. Readily available in nearly every variety of food, it is also widely accessible in over-the-counter supplements. We all know that we need iron to think, to act, even to stay alive. But how many of us know that too much iron can be extremely dangerous to our health?

How Does Iron Work?

When we think of iron, we think of energy and strength, and rightly so. Iron energizes our cells by transporting to them oxygen from the air we breathe through our lungs via hemoglobin, the substance that makes blood red.[1]

Hemoglobin is made of protein (globin) and a pigment that is actually an iron-rich compound (heme). Chemically, there are four iron atoms in each molecule of hemoglobin. Each atom is capable of carrying one oxygen molecule through the bloodstream.[2]

It sounds simple, yes? In fact, it is a vast and skillfully engineered operation. One red blood cell contains 270 *million* hemoglobin molecules. Multiply 270 million by four and you will see that each red blood cell is capable of transporting—through its iron atoms—over a billion molecules of oxygen. Then imagine that a healthy adult has about 35 *trillion* red blood cells. Without the iron in the hemoglobin in these countless red blood cells, the body could not receive enough oxygen to stay alive.[3]

Iron also plays a reverse role in the nourishment of every cell in your body. After the hemoglobin has delivered the oxygen to the cells in your tissues, it picks up the waste product—carbon dioxide—and carries it back to your lungs, which breathe it out into the air. Thus, iron is necessary for the transport of oxygen to your cells, enabling them to burn glucose for energy, and for the transport of poisonous carbon dioxide away from the cells when the glucose has been burned.

An easy way to observe this process in your own body is to notice the veins in your arms and hands. They are blue: why? Because it is through the veins that blood carrying carbon dioxide returns to the lungs. On the other hand, the blood that is carrying oxygen to the cells —arterial blood—is bright red. If you cut a vein, however, the blood immediately appears to be red because it mixes with the oxygen present in air.

This phenomenon explains why "blue" babies and persons who have been poisoned by cyanide have a blue appearance: they lack oxygen molecules carried by the iron atoms in their hemoglobin. Those who have been asphyxiated by carbon monoxide also look blue. The iron in their hemoglobin has bonded with carbon monoxide, a tighter bond than is formed with oxygen; so tight, in fact, that the iron atoms are unable to deposit their deadly load. Thus, they are unable to carry oxygen, and suffocation is the result.[4]

Iron is also at work in a substance called myoglobin, which contains one iron atom per molecule. Myoglobin carries oxygen from the blood to the enzymes in the muscle cells, which produce energy. Without the oxygen-binding iron atom in myoglobin, the muscles would be unable to work.[5]

Iron works in yet another way, helping to synthesize an enzyme called ATP, one of your body's most important enzymes. ATP (adenosine triphosphate) works in the process that breaks down glucose—the energy substance that results from the breakdown of carbohydrates and excess fats and proteins.

ATP is like electricity in that it "stores" energy that can then be switched on when you need it. Without it, your energy supply of glucose would be utilized all at once, and you would have to eat constantly for a steady supply. Your muscles' store of ATP guarantees that you will have enough energy to move and breathe. How does iron figure into this picture? It is the part of your cells' enzymes that carries the electrons that break down glucose to produce ATP.[6-9]

In our discussion of how iron works it is interesting to note that your body actually recycles this valuable mineral. When red blood cells break down, the iron is released from the heme and attaches itself to other proteins. As a result, it is too large for the kidneys' membranes to filter it out through to the urine.[10]

This "old" iron in its new protein-compound forms (called ferritin and hemosiderin[11, 12]) is stored in the spleen, liver, and bone marrow —conserved for use in future times.[13] In fact, your body so efficiently conserves and recycles iron that if it is overloaded with the substance, it cannot rid itself of the excess. Luckily there is a built-in "safety catch" in the intestinal wall that, under normal conditions, keeps us from absorbing more iron than we need.[14]

Where Does Iron Work?

Our discussion above has already answered the question of *where* iron works:

• *Bloodstream.* The four iron atoms in hemoglobin carry oxygen to the body's cells and carry waste products from them.
• *Muscles.* Myoglobin's single atom of iron carries oxygen to the enzymes of the muscle cells, which then produce energy.
• *Metabolic system.* Within the enzymes of the cells, iron carries the electrons that break down glucose to produce ATP.

Who Needs Iron?

If we are to believe Madison Avenue, we are all desperately in need of iron in the form of One-A-Day Vitamins Plus Iron.[15] And yet, we have just seen that iron is recycled and conserved in our bodies in a most efficient way. The fact is, there are only a few specific situations that call for any more iron than most of us receive in our daily fare.

If you are anemic, you *may* need additional iron, but not always, as we shall see. If you are pregnant, an iron supplement may also be in order.[16] Other times when an iron supplement may be necessary are when you have lost blood through an accident, donation, or unusually heavy menstruation, and during periods of major muscular growth.

We all associate anemia with iron deficiency, and in fact there is a type of anemia that is caused by a lack of sufficient iron for hemoglobin synthesis (or if there is enough for the hemoglobin, by insufficient iron for the myoglobin and the enzyme processes detailed above).[17] The result? Chronic fatigue, shortness of breath, perhaps constant headaches, pale skin, and opaque and brittle nails.

The common reactions of a doctor who observed these symptoms in his patient would be 1) to give a test that would determine if the hemoglobin were low, and 2) to prescribe massive doses of supplemental iron. In some cases, this would be the proper treatment. The number of erythrocytes (red blood cells) would be restored to normal levels, and the problem would be corrected.

But—and this is a big but—nutritional research by biochemists within the past fifty years has determined that there are several types of anemia, not all necessarily precipitated by a deficiency in iron. In fact, there are a number of delicately balanced biochemical factors that can precipitate an anemic condition which will not be helped by supplemental iron.

For example, if there are genetic defects or damage to the bone marrow, where production of red blood cells takes place, iron cannot correct the problem.[18] If there is a deficiency of B_{12}, also needed to produce red blood cells, pernicious anemia may result;[19] an inadequate amount of vitamin E could result in the rapid destruction of red blood cells by oxidation and a form of anemia would develop;[20] there could be insufficient protein for the synthesis of the globin (protein) portion of the hemoglobin compound. Mineral deficiencies in cobalt, copper, zinc, or magnesium could be the cause of some types of anemia, as all those minerals are necessary for the synthesis of hemoglobin, as are folic acid, pantothenic acid, and B_6.[21-24]

To help you visualize the total picture of how red blood cells are manufactured (now that you know how many diverse nutrients are necessary to the process), you should know that in order to prevent anemia, your body must make nearly two and a half million erythrocytes per second. It must then keep each of these red blood cells alive for 120 days.[25]

In essence, anemia is a condition in which the red blood cells are prevented—by any one or a combination of the factors we have mentioned—from transporting sufficient oxygen to the cells. Obviously, an iron deficiency is only one of these factors.

How do you know if a deficiency of iron is the cause of your anemic condition? If the condition was precipitated by a major loss of blood, you can almost be certain that iron will help cure it. In other cases, a hemoglobin test is not sufficient for determining that iron is the element you need. In addition to that test, your doctor should also measure the serum iron levels. If they are adequate in spite of the low levels of hemoglobin, the anemia is being caused by something else. Another test can measure the iron-binding capacity of the iron carrier transferrin; yet another—the Atomic Absorption Spectograph—can reveal the iron content of your tissues.[26] An analysis of your hair can also be useful.

If these laboratory tests seem complicated and expensive, here is a simple at-home test, advised by the *British Medical Journal*. Eat a quantity of beets. If your urine turns red, you are deficient in iron.[27]

Why is it so important to be certain that your anemia really is due to iron deficiency before embarking on a regimen of supplements? Two reasons: 1) there is a real danger of taking too much iron, and 2) if you treat an anemia with iron when the root cause lies elsewhere, disaster could be the result.

Why is too much iron so dangerous? As you will remember, your body does have a safety mechanism built in to the intestinal wall that prevents you from absorbing excess iron. Yet, even this ingenious defense mechanism can be overpowered by a high intake of the mineral. Your body binds the excess iron in protein compounds called ferritin and hemosiderin and stores it in the liver, spleen, and bone marrow. When there is too much iron, first the ferritin storage protein is saturated. Then debilitating and sometimes fatal diseases called hemosiderosis and hemochromatosis can ensue. Hemosiderosis is the condition in which there are excess deposits of hemosiderin in the liver and spleen; in hemochromatosis, the iron/protein compound has been deposited in all the body's tissues. Sometimes a genetic incapacity may cause these diseases, but most often the cause is excessive iron intake.

The symptoms of excessive iron are, oddly enough, quite similar to the symptoms of anemia: headaches, shortness of breath, increasing fatigue, dizziness, weight loss, and a gray-bronze skin tone after the iron has been deposited throughout the tissues.[28]

Be aware that these conditions have a real possibility of manifesting as a direct result of long-term use of iron supplements, in oral or injected form. As small a dose as 900 milligrams of iron tablets taken at once can be fatal.[29] Children who have eaten iron tablets thinking they were candy have actually died.[30]

There are other conditions that can lead to hemosiderosis and hemochromatosis. Blood transfusions over a long period of time (often given to patients suffering from aplastic anemia, in which there is an insufficiency of red blood cells because of bone marrow damage; or those suffering from hemolytic anemia, the abnormal destruction of red blood cells) can cause toxic accumulations of hemosiderin in the liver, with the resulting destruction of that organ.[31]

Cirrhosis of the liver caused by excessive drinking or blood transfusions can in turn cause excessive deposits of iron in the liver and spleen. Disorders of the pancreas and diabetes can also result in excessive iron deposits.[32] Conversely, excessive iron can damage the pancreas, resulting in diabetes.[33]

In fact, the accumulation of excess iron can severely damage all your organs. Enough iron can be deposited in the heart muscle to cause cardiac arrest; the deposits are large enough to be seen during an autopsy.[34]

In hemosiderosis or hemochromatosis, the iron deposits oxidize valuable vitamin C, destroying your primary defense against scurvy.[38] If iron is deposited in your joints, painful arthritis can occur. If excess iron lodges in your brain, you may develop schizophrenia.[39] If your child has too much iron in his or her system, he or she may be hyperactive, or autistic.[40] Breathing polluted air can bring an accumulation of iron to your lungs, resulting in siderosis. Surplus iron in the stomach and intestines has been implicated in cancers of those organs. Interestingly enough, in test animals who were subjected to carcinogens, the presence of iron compounds visibly quickened the development of cancer.[41]

Thus, one should avoid taking iron supplements for an anemia that is not caused by iron deficiency, because excessive iron in the system can be very dangerous.

The other reason to avoid treating an anemic condition with iron unless it is definitely a result of iron deficiency is that iron therapy treatment could complicate an anemia that was actually caused by another factor.

For example, an anemia characterized by gross abnormalities in the bone marrow—interfering with the proper synthesis of red blood cells—can arise from a vitamin E deficiency.[35] The worst possible treatment for this condition would be to take iron. Not only would the bone marrow go unrepaired, but iron actually destroys vitamin E![36]

IRON FOR PREGNANT WOMEN

Your stores of iron are significantly depleted by pregnancy, for in effect some of them are being transferred to the growing fetus.[37] So pregnancy is one situation in which taking an iron supplement would be advisable.

Be aware that not only do you run the risk of developing iron-deficiency anemia when you are pregnant; there is also the possibility of developing folic-acid deficiency anemia. Because refining foods destroys so much folic acid, as does stress, and because it is water soluble in the first place, easily excreted through the urine and pores, you are likely to be deficient, particularly under the stress of pregnancy.[42-45] A lack of folic acid impairs the full development of the red blood cells, in both you and your growing baby.

You should remember, if you are pregnant, that excess iron lowers your levels of vitamin E. If you don't have enough vitamin E for yourself and your baby, neither of you will have enough oxygen, either. If your baby isn't getting enough oxygen, it could be premature, late, malformed, or mentally retarded—or you may even miscarry.[46-49] One sad possibility is that your baby could be born anemic, which was just what you were trying to prevent by taking iron supplements.[50]

IRON AFTER BLOOD LOSS AND DURING MUSCULAR GROWTH

Another situation in which your need for iron might truly be increased is if you have suffered a blood loss through accident, excessive donation of blood, or heavy menstrual flow. In these circumstances a substantial number of blood cells have been lost and iron is absolutely necessary to rebuild the supplies.

Around the ages of fifteen and sixteen, during periods of major muscular growth, the need for iron is also increased. Iron-rich foods help in the increasing production of myoglobin at this time. Since only about 10 percent of the body's iron is in myoglobin, however, large supplements are not necessary.

So you see, there are in reality only a few times when supplemental iron would be in order. If it seems that we have spent an inordinate amount of time on the circumstances in which supplemental iron is *not* necessary, it is because it seems necessary to counteract so much of the myth and advertising propaganda surrounding this element, which in excess can be quite dangerous to your health.

A Practical Guide to Using Iron

What foods should you eat to guarantee a steady supply of iron? Should you ever take iron supplements, and if so, in what dosages? How can you insure that the iron you eat is properly absorbed for full utilization? What are the symptoms of deficiency? If, on the other hand, you are suffering from an *excess* of iron, what can you do to detoxify yourself?

If you are healthy, there are about 7 grams of iron in your system.[51] Your hemoglobin contains two-thirds of that 7 grams, and a tenth of that amount is found in your myoglobin. The energy enzymes of your cells hold roughly a hundredth of the amount in the hemoglobin. The rest of the iron in your body may be flowing through your bloodstream, as molecules of transferrin; or it could be stored for future needs in the spleen, liver, and bone marrow in compounds of ferritin or hemosiderin.

What about stored amounts? In the liver alone, there may be up to 700 milligrams of iron.[52] Lesser amounts deposit in the spleen and bone marrow. Remember, before you start taking any kind of iron supplement, ask your physician to help you determine that these deposits are truly depleted!

Nearly every food you eat contains iron. Even refined foods are "enriched" with iron. The most concentrated sources of iron are animal livers. Unfortunately, however, the liver is also the waste-filtering organ and any hormone or chemical to which the animal was exposed will also concentrate there. Egg yolks are another good source, containing more iron than even the muscle meats. They are an especially good source of iron for vegetarians, since meat contains more of this element than fruits or vegetables. (The iron in meat is also more easily absorbed into your body.[53])

Good vegetable sources of iron include green leafy plants, dried beans, peaches, apricots, dates, prunes, cherries, figs, raisins, and black-strap molasses. Supplementary foods that are good sources of iron are yeast and wheat germ, also rich in B vitamins and vitamin E. Yeast is one of the most accessible sources of iron for babies and ulcer patients.[54]

Of all the major food groups, only the dairy group contains a negligible amount of iron. Also, the iron in grains and spinach is not as available to you as that from other sources. Their phytic and oxalic acids render their iron insoluble; much is lost in the feces.

If you must take iron in supplements for any of the conditions we discussed above, here are some tips for getting the most out of the supplement with the least danger of developing toxicity: take small doses; with the iron take larger doses of the vitamins and other minerals that help you absorb and utilize iron and prevent toxicity (more on that to come); try to find a source of organically grown meats and eat the livers in order to benefit from the heavily concentrated iron. The shorter time it takes to correct your iron deficiency, the less risk you run of creating a toxic condition.

The type of supplement called ferrous fumarate tends to be less harsh than ferrous gluconate. Read the labels when purchasing your supplement. Avoid the types of supplements that contain iron in the form of either ferrous sulfate and ferrous chloride, which are not beneficial to your health. If you are taking iron in a multivitamin/mineral tablet, check the dosage. Do not take more than 18 milligrams of iron a day (and give none to your children) unless you are under the direct supervision of a (preferably orthomolecular) physician.

What are the official daily requirements for iron (all of which are available through food)? For children, 8 to 12 milligrams; for teenagers, 10 to 15 milligrams; for adult males, 10 milligrams; for females in their reproductive years, 18 milligrams. Pregnant women need 30 to 60 milligrams per day.[55]

If you are taking iron supplements for an anemic condition and your hemoglobin levels are not raised by 2 grams per 100 milligrams of blood every three weeks, you may need other nutrients along with the iron, or you may not need the iron at all.[56]

How can you guarantee the proper absorption of iron from your food? Other minerals and vitamins play a part in the amount of iron you are able to use. Certain natural elements synthesized by your body also play a role.

For example, while copper is necessary for the absorption of iron, too much copper actually lowers iron levels and causes anemia.[57] There is an intricate play here between copper and the trace minerals molybdenum, manganese, and zinc—a deficiency in any of them can raise copper levels, resulting in iron deficiency. Keep in mind that these days copper is very easy to come by: it is in our water pipes, thus in our drinking and cooking water. It is also usually present in multivitamin/-mineral supplements. Too much copper can be dangerous for a variety of reasons. On the other hand, if you are deficient in copper, a lack of zinc or manganese can cause excess storage of iron. But an excess of zinc or manganese can limit iron's absorption.[58] Balancing trace minerals is a complicated matter even for biochemists; the best approach for the individual is to eat a wide variety of fresh, whole foods, preferably organically grown.

Refined foods contain abundant phosphorus in the form of phosphates, which can hinder the absorption of iron—another good reason for sticking to whole unprocessed foods. Fortunately, when there is an oversupply of phosphorus, it combines with calcium. This process helps keep your iron free for absorption.[59]

And speaking of calcium, for *it* to be broken down for use, hydrochloric stomach acid is necessary. This vital substance depends on the B vitamins B_1, B_2, B_3, pantothenic acid, and choline.[60] Anything you eat or drink that has an alkaline quality—sugar, white bread, pasta, crackers, cakes and cookies, white rice, alcoholic beverages—can lessen the hydrochloric acid and reduce its effectiveness. B_{12}—the lack of which may produce pernicious anemia—also depends on hydrochloric acid for proper absorption.

Diuretics such as coffee, tea, and alcohol can interfere with your absorption of iron simply because they cause so many other nutrients to pass quickly through the kidneys. Interestingly enough, too much plant fiber (cellulose) can also interfere with iron absorption, while protein is vital for iron's utilization in the body.

Vitamin C increases your ability to absorb iron, as well as the rate of hemoglobin production. It also protects you against toxic elements like lead, cadmium, and aluminum, all of which interfere with iron absorption.[61, 62]

Iron absorption is hindered by vitamin E, and vice versa. It is best to take iron eight to twelve hours after taking vitamin E, if you must take iron supplements. And remember, excess iron has the ability to diminish your tissues' vitamin E stores.[63]

How can you tell if you are deficient in iron? The symptoms of iron deficiency are the symptoms of anemia: chronic tiredness, lack of endurance, shortness of breath, etc. If you suspect an iron deficiency, it is advisable that your physician conduct an entire battery of tests (detailed above) before you start taking supplements.

But what if your problem is an *excess* of iron? We already know how dangerous too much iron can be—what can be done? Fortunately there are ways to rid your body of toxic excesses of iron, and to repair the tissues the deposits have damaged or destroyed. There are certain elements that can actually reduce the excess iron to a form that the kidneys can eliminate.

Chelation therapy, for example, is a process in which a patient is intravenously infused with a solution containing elements that will bind (chelate) toxic heavy metals and remove them from the body. L-histadine, an amino acid, is the substance used in chelating iron. Deferoxamine mesylate and 2,3 dihydroxybenzoic acid are also useful in chelating iron and helping the body rid itself of excess amounts.[64] Penicillamine, used in chelation of copper, may also be effective in removing iron.[65]

If you suffer from iron toxicosis, there are several other vitamins and minerals that can help you get rid of the excess iron. Zinc helps lower iron levels, for example, and there is some evidence that it can free arthritic joints of excess iron.[66] Vitamin B6 and magnesium are also helpful in the endeavor to reduce high iron levels.[67] If you want to guard against the dangers of iron deposits, make sure your diet includes plenty of the B vitamins, vitamins C and E, and protein.[68] Taking adequate amounts of E is also a good preventative against the deposits' causing cancer.[69]

Studies conducted on 37 volunteers resulted in the conclusion that the consumption of tea and coffee, especially in conjunction with a meal, tends to inhibit iron absorption. It was interesting to note that coffee consumed one hour before a meal was not as effective in preventing iron absorption as when taken with the meal.[70]

Summary

Without the oxygen-carrier iron, we could not live. The hemoglobin in our red blood cells, the myoglobin in our muscles, the enzymes tied in with energy release all depend on iron to function properly.

Perhaps because iron is so important to the trillions of cells in our bodies, we have sophisticated methods for conserving and recycling iron. In our modern era, this capacity is a double-edged sword in that we are actually in danger of building up excess amounts of iron throughout our tissues, which can be extremely dangerous.

Iron is readily available to us in all kinds of foods, the dairy food group being the only real exception. As a result, most of us are able to obtain the iron we need simply by eating. For those of us who need extra iron—those with iron-deficiency anemia, those who are pregnant, those who have suffered heavy blood loss or who are in a period of rapid muscular development—iron supplements may be in order. Even so, a definite need should be determined first, and the delicate and precariously balanced nutritional environment of our bodies taken well into consideration before supplementary iron is introduced.

Magnesium: The Mastermind Mineral

What Is Magnesium?

Magnesium is a light, pliable, silver-white metallic element that is present in the earth, in plants, and in human and animal bodies. In plants, it is an important component of the chlorophyll molecule, which not only makes plants green, but also helps them make carbohydrates.[1] The human body contains only four to five teaspoons of magnesium, yet the mineral is so vital to the muscles, cells, bones, blood, digestion, metabolism, and reproductive and immune systems, that it truly deserves its reputation as a nutritional "mastermind."

Only .05 percent of your body weight is composed of magnesium.[2] Of that tiny amount, 70 percent is located in your bones, where it is calcium's partner, while the other 30 percent circulates in your bloodstream and in the cells of your tissues, particularly nerve cells. Every day, you lose magnesium in your urine—from 100 to 300 milligrams—

which the RDA of 350 milligrams can barely replace.[3] Luckily, most whole foods supply some magnesium, so it is not difficult to get an adequate amount of the mastermind mineral.

How Does Magnesium Work?

Magnesium is necessary to the life of every cell in your body, because it is a key player in the cellular metabolic processes. It is also needed by your cells to produce proteins to replenish and replace themselves. Furthermore, it is one of your body's most important coenzymes, a helper in the numerous biochemical processes catalyzed by enzymes in all your cells each day. One of its most important functions as a coenzyme is in its relationship to ATP (adenosine triphosphate), an important energy compound in metabolism.[4-6] Their working relationship is strengthened by a chemical bond through which the two are actually chelated to one another.[7] Without magnesium, ATP would be helpless, unable to trap glucose from the energy processes of your cells and save it for your future energy demands.

Magnesium also has important interrelationships with other vitamins and minerals: calcium, and vitamins D, B_1, folic acid, B_6, C, and E. It is calcium's partner within your skeletal system, helping calcium move from your bones to your blood whenever you contract your muscles or perform other important work.[8] In that capacity, it is also a partner to vitamin D. Within the vitamin B family, it is a principal coworker, helping to synthesize thiamine (B_1) and folic acid, and activating vitamin B_6.[9] In fact, all the enzymes that contain B_6 must have magnesium to function.[10] So do the enzymes that contain inositol and pantothenic acid.[11] It helps your body use the other members of the vitamin B family properly, as well. It is also the mineral activator of vitamins C and E.[12] In fact, its work throughout your body is so comprehensive that it is easy to understand why it is found in greater quantities within your cells than any other mineral except potassium.[13]

Magnesium also maintains working relationships with some of the hormones in your body: aldosterone, the other adrenal hormones, your sex hormones, cortisone, and parathormone. Aldosterone, which cannot be synthesized without magnesium, is vital in maintaining a balance of minerals within your body.[14] The other hormones made in your adrenal cortex also depend on an adequate supply of magnesium for their production, because cholesterol, from which they are in part synthesized, cannot be manufactured without magnesium.[15] Magnesium also functions as an important coenzyme in your sex organs to make sex and steroid hormones.[16]

Cortisone is one such steroid hormone. If you have arthritis or rheumatism and have taken synthetic cortisone for your condition, you might be interested to know that you can avoid its dangerous side effects by beefing up your own cortisone production with an adequate intake of magnesium and other nutrients.

Parathormone, manufactured by your parathyroid glands, is also dependent on magnesium through the mastermind mineral's relationship with vitamin D. Without magnesium, vitamin D can't perform its work in your body; one result is the improper function of your parathyroid gland in producing parathormone.[17] The visible result of this malfunction would be falling hair and easily broken nails.[18]

As we have already discovered, magnesium is yet another nutrient that must be present before you can manufacture the building materials for new cells. These building materials are a variety of different compounds of proteins, all constructed from twenty-three amino acids. Magnesium is a coenzyme in the protein-production process,[19] and it is also glutamine's coworker in dispersing the proteins from the food you eat into amino acids.[22]

Magnesium is at work in several different locations at the protein construction site. In addition to the ones we just mentioned, it is also a key worker in synthesizing the genetic "brains" of the process, RNA and DNA. DNA functions as the architect of the cells, holding the genetic information that enables them to construct the right products, and RNA carries DNA's instructions to the work site. Both are dependent upon magnesium, among other nutrients, for proper synthesis. Since all your cells, enzymes, and hormones (with the exception of the adrenal cortex and sex hormones) are made of protein, magnesium is a vital component in your body's ability to maintain and rebuild healthy tissue.[20, 21]

There is a constantly flowing waste product from the protein production process: ammonia. Believe it or not, that tireless worker magnesium is part of the crew removing it from your body. Its job on the clean-up crew is to transform this toxic by-product into urea, which is a harmless compound that takes its exit through the urine.

Indefatigable magnesium is also stationed at the membranes of your cell, in the form of electrically charged ions that speed nutrients in and waste products out. This function is another example of the mastermind's partnership with ATP.[23, 24]

The pressure within and without those cellular membranes is also somewhat dependent on magnesium. Those same magnesium ions can be found floating freely in the intra- and extracellular fluids, helping keep the pressure right.[25]

Magnesium also works to keep your blood from clotting, helps to maintain its proper pH, and is a body temperature and weight regulator par excellence. More on that, below.

Where Does Magnesium Work?

It might be obvious that magnesium works everywhere in your body. But to make the range of its activities even more graphic, let's take a look at what it does in your muscles, cells, nervous system, bones, digestive system, metabolic system, reproductive system, protein production process, blood, and immune system.

• *Muscles.* Because of magnesium's synergistic partnership with ATP, your body's "spark plug," your muscles could not work without it unless you ate constantly to supply a steady flow of energy. As it is, ATP traps some of the glucose burned in cellular metabolism and saves it for your future energy needs. In addition, your muscles need magnesium in partnership with calcium for proper relaxation after each contraction.[26] Without magnesium, they would be plagued by problems: tics, cramps, spasms, and convulsions.[27-29] Since the heart is a muscle, magnesium's action here has broad-reaching implications for your very life.[30]

• *Cells.* We've seen how hardworking magnesium is at the cellular level. Yet there are functions that we haven't even mentioned; for one, with ATP, magnesium breaks up globs of fat into fatty acids that your cells can use both for energy and for the construction and maintenance of their membranes. (Coenzyme A plays a role here, too.[31])

• *Nervous system.* Magnesium's part in breaking down fatty globules into useful fatty acids helps your nerves as well. The sheaths around them are composed of myelin, which is a compound of cholesterol, lecithin, and fatty acids—all of which depend on magnesium, among other nutrients, for their manufacture within your body.[32] Without magnesium, your nerves can become quite literally ragged, to your great disadvantage![33]

In fact, your whole nervous system needs magnesium, from your nerves to your spinal cord to your brain. The nerves themselves need a balance of magnesium, calcium, potassium, and sodium to transmit their electrical impulses efficiently.[34, 35] And because of magnesium's part in synthesizing myelin, they may become supersensitive to pain without it.[36, 37] Magnesium can have such a calming effect on your nervous system that in intravenous doses, it is anesthetizing.[38, 39]

Do you have trouble learning, or remembering what you've learned? Perhaps you have a magnesium deficiency. The brain's hippocampus, which regulates your memory and your absorption of information, needs magnesium.[40] Magnesium's calming qualities extend to this realm, too, and can be particularly helpful if you suffer from anxiety —even confusion or psychosis.[41, 42]

• *Bones.* Seventy percent of your body's magnesium stores lie in your bones. In fact, without magnesium, you couldn't even stand up; your bones would be too soft to support you. Your bones and teeth need magnesium so much that they are even rather greedy about it—they will not give up their supply even when the rest of your body is in great need of magnesium.[43-47] In addition, your skeletal system, like most other parts of your body, needs a constant supply of new building material (proteins) to keep itself in good repair. If magnesium is not present in adequate quantities to do its multiple jobs in making new proteins, the cells in your skeletal system will suffer. Weak bones or even osteoporosis, in which the bones are porous and brittle, may be the unfortunate complication.

• *Digestive system.* Magnesium is a coenzyme, and one place where enzymes and their respective coenzymes work hardest is in your digestive system. Enzymes help you digest and absorb all the foods in your daily meals,[48] and they must have coenzymes like magnesium to do it. In addition, with ATP, magnesium helps your stomach manufacture hydrochloric acid, so necessary to break down your foods into glucose for energy.[49] The bile that your liver contributes to aid in your digestion, especially of fats, is made of cholesterol, so it too depends on magnesium. In fact, magnesium is so important to your overall digestive processes that you may suffer from something like spastic constipation if you don't get enough of it.

Interestingly enough, it is in the digestive system that magnesium begins its work in helping your body synthesize RNA and DNA. With the pancreatic enzyme deoxyribonuclease, magnesium works to dissolve the molecules of DNA in your foods into nucleotides. These are absorbed from your intestine into your cells to be used in the synthesis of new RNA and DNA.[50]

• *Metabolism.* Glycogen is the principal form of carbohydrate stored in animal cells. Your liver makes this starch out of glucose so that you will have a storehouse of fuel in the muscles when your body needs it. Yet the transformation of glucose into glycogen, and its conversion into energy, cannot take place without magnesium.[51] In fact, as we mentioned before, without magnesium plants could not manufacture the carbohydrates that you eat in the first place.

The magnesium-ATP partnership is another vital component of your metabolic process. Without magnesium, ATP would also be unable to store energy for the future: you would use the glucose in your body all at once, and would have to eat like a hummingbird (continuously) to survive. Coenzyme A is another component in your body's metabolism. Magnesium is essential to its synthesis as well.[52] In fact, magnesium and ATP can combine to manufacture coenzyme A, and coenzyme A and magnesium in turn can work together to form ATP. But magnesium is vital to both of these energy mechanisms.

• *Reproductive system.* Without magnesium, you would be unable to produce estrogens and progestins if you are a female, or androgens if you are male, because magnesium must be present for sex hormones to be synthesized.

• *Protein building.* You must have magnesium before you can break down the proteins you eat into the basic amino acids, from which you can then construct the new proteins necessary for the regeneration and maintenance of your cells and tissues. As we have already discovered, magnesium is a tireless worker in several different phases of protein production.

• *Blood.* In the bloodstream, magnesium is also busy. First, magnesium ions keep protein molecules in the bloodstream dissolved by interacting with the ions of protein.[53] This activity keeps your blood from clotting. Second, magnesium keeps your blood at the proper degree of alkalinity, while regulating the slightly acid pH of other parts of the body (stomach fluids and urine) at the same time.[54] Third, like all the other cells of your body, your blood cells depend on magnesium for new proteins and B_6, which cannot be utilized without it.

• *Immune system.* When your immune system is attacked by bacteria or viruses, magnesium swings into action with a blood protein (properdin) to put an end to the invaders.[55]

You should be able to see that we weren't exaggerating a bit when we stated that magnesium works everywhere. Getting plenty of this ubiquitous mineral in a wide variety of foods is one of the nicest things you can do for yourself!

Who Needs Magnesium?

Magnesium has been used therapeutically for a wide variety of acute and degenerative conditions, as well as for promoting beauty and health. Here are the medical situations in which magnesium therapy might be helpful: arthritis; constipation; prostate problems; menstruation and pregnancy; undulant fever; nervous irritability; Parkinson's disease, polio, multiple sclerosis; muscle cramps, tremors, and epilepsy; heart disease and hypertension; kidney and liver problems; diabetes; osteoporosis; anemia; and infections and cancer. If you are fortunate enough not to have any of these conditions, you might consider upping your intake of magnesium just to give your skin a better tone, or to keep your eyesight strong.

MAGNESIUM FOR ARTHRITIS

Magnesium can help to regenerate your adrenal glands so that they are able to produce enough cortisone. If you suffer from rheumatoid arthritis, it may enable you to cut back on your dependence on the synthetic variety of this steroid. Prescribed cortisone can bring in its wake a number of devastating side effects—including magnesium deficiency—that are unknown to the naturally produced variety. Magnesium does not cure arthritis, but an adequate intake can provide your body with an added tool to help itself.

MAGNESIUM FOR CONSTIPATION AND DIGESTIVE PROBLEMS

So many of your digestive processes—including the production of hydrochloric acid and bile—are dependent upon magnesium that it is no wonder that you can find yourself with digestive problems like spastic constipation if you aren't getting enough. If you suffer from a magnesium and B6 deficiency—and the two go hand in hand—you may be plagued with nausea and vomiting, indigestion, flatulence, abdominal pain, and cramps.[56] Beginning a regimen of magnesium/B6 supplementation under your doctor's supervision can put an end to these unpleasant symptoms. Even routine vomiting or nausea such as some of us experience from motion sickness or pregnancy can be successfully stopped with magnesium/B6 therapy.

MAGNESIUM FOR MEN AND WOMEN

We already know that magnesium plays an important role within the reproductive system, primarily as a prerequisite for the manufacture of sex hormones. But magnesium can play an even bigger part in your sex life if you suffer from irregular menstruation, sterility, or prostate problems, or if you are pregnant.

If you suffer from irregular menstrual cycles or sterility, try supplementing your diet with magnesium, in addition to concentrating on foods rich in the mastermind mineral. Because it is so important in your production of sex hormones, you may find that additional magnesium regulates your cycles, or even enables you to conceive a child. If you are a man and have prostate problems, perhaps magnesium can help here as well. Since the prostate produces part of the seminal fluid, getting enough magnesium to nourish this important gland might also help you if you are sterile. At any rate, it can help cure any prostate problems you might have.[57]

In pregnancy, additional quantities of all the nutrients are needed. But if you don't get enough magnesium while you are carrying a child, the results can be serious: your newborn could suffer from calcium deposits in its heart and other muscles; convulsions; or even be stillborn.[58] For yourself during pregnancy, adequate magnesium is an important preventative against miscarriage or painful contractions of the uterus toward the end of your term.[59] With calcium, it also guards you against eclampsia (postnatal convulsions and coma), a condition which can be fatal.[60]

MAGNESIUM FOR UNDULANT FEVER

Along with large doses of manganese and vitamin B_6, magnesium can cure undulant fever, a condition transmitted by pets and other domestic animals.[61]

MAGNESIUM FOR YOUR NERVES

Do your nerves feel ragged? Are you especially sensitive to the slightest pain or noise? Do you suffer from insomnia, especially after drinking? It could be that your nervous system is crying out for more magnesium.

We've already seen that a magnesium deficiency can quite literally make your nerves ragged because there is not enough magnesium in your system to synthesize the nerve sheaths, made of a substance called myelin. Thus, making sure you get plenty of magnesium, along with the other nutrients, of course, can help you overcome nervous irritability and hypersensitivity to pain and noise. It can even change your personality! If you have found that you must take a tranquilizer before bedtime, or even during the day, additional magnesium might be of great benefit, both in calming you down and in helping you sleep at night, as it is a natural tranquilizer with no side effects and no possibility of addiction.[62-66]

If you are the parent of a hyperactive child, magnesium could be your salvation. Try introducing natural foods like green leafy vegetables, legumes, whole grains, nuts, seeds, fresh fruits, and carob candies into your child's diet, and watch him or her calm down. Meanwhile, a magnesium-rich supplement like dolomite might help your own nerves.

MAGNESIUM FOR NEUROMUSCULAR CONDITIONS

Several neuromuscular diseases that can be crippling for life are directly related to magnesium deficiency. Among them are polio and multiple sclerosis, both of which have been treated successfully with magnesium supplements.[67, 68] Victims of palsy, Parkinson's disease, and epilepsy have also noted significant improvement of their conditions with magnesium treatments. In fact, in one experiment in which thirty children suffering from epilepsy were treated with 450 milligrams of magnesium daily (with no anticonvulsant drugs), twenty-nine of them responded favorably. (It turned out that the one who didn't was also suffering from a B_6 deficiency.) Some of the improvements were dramatic: one boy who had a ten-year history of the condition and was thought to be mentally retarded demonstrated remarkable mental clarity, and his epileptic seizures subsided.[69]

Magnesium therapy can also be helpful in less serious conditions such as muscle cramps or spasticity. In fact, magnesium deficiency itself can be responsible for these neuromuscular afflictions, which manifest in tics, tremors, or even severe muscle spasms and convulsions.[70-72]

MAGNESIUM FOR HEART DISEASE AND CIRCULATORY PROBLEMS

To most of us, the heart is such a central and important organ that we forget that it is a muscle. And as a muscle the heart can be helped by magnesium therapy just like the others in your body: magnesium can keep your heart free of disease, and it can help you "hold the line" if you already suffer from a heart condition. Unfortunately, magnesium deficiency is so prevalent in our culture—mainly because of our over-consumption of refined foods and "nonfoods"—that even children and young persons show signs of degeneration in this most important muscle due to a lack of magnesium and other nutrients.[73]

Since magnesium, ATP, and calcium all work together to make your heart muscle contract in a regular rhythm, one of the first signs of a magnesium deficiency is an irregular heartbeat.[74, 75] If the deficiency progresses, calcium deposits may form on the heart muscle, the result of a calcium/magnesium imbalance.[76] If this happens, the heart cannot contract properly. Another symptom of magnesium deficiency that manifests in the heart is related to magnesium's role in the synthesis of cortisone, which is a key element in the metabolic process of the cardiovascular system.[77]

You may remember that magnesium is also important in breaking down the fats you eat into fatty acids that can be useful in building body parts like nerve sheaths and cellular membranes. If those fats are not broken down properly, they begin to collect in deposits, which lodge on damaged arterial points. Thus, a magnesium deficiency can increase your risks of contracting the two major degenerative heart diseases: atherosclerosis and arteriosclerosis. Another point to remember in this regard is that magnesium is necessary for the synthesis of lecithin, which also helps break down those fats.[78-80]

If you eat a lot of saturated fats (found in animal protein and hydrogenated oils), drink coffee, drink alcohol, and smoke—as so many of us do—you may be a special candidate for magnesium deficiency. Coffee and alcohol flood nutrients out of your body via the urine; a diet heavy in fat puts extra stress on all your fat-metabolizing mechanisms, including magnesium; while smoking causes stress that in turn causes blood cholesterol levels to rise and magnesium levels to fall.[81] If you insist upon engaging in a self-destructive life-style, at least supplement your diet with nutrients to combat the damage you are doing to yourself. Taking plenty of fat-mobilizing minerals can at least help keep your lecithin production on par, as shown in tests with laboratory animals who were fed intravenous lecithin: the deposits of fat on the walls of their arteries was significantly reduced.[82-85] So give your body a chance with magnesium supplements, which can help it produce the lecithin it needs.

In arteriosclerosis, the arteries harden because free-floating calcium particles (the result of a calcium/magnesium imbalance) stick to the fatty deposits in the arteries, which then become hard or calcified. Working to rebalance your calcium/magnesium levels can stop this process.

Both atherosclerosis and arteriosclerosis engender yet another dangerous complication: high blood pressure. Your arteries become smaller as they become clogged with hardened fatty deposits, and they lose their elasticity as well. This can be dangerous to both your heart and your kidneys, because the same fatty deposits that have lodged and hardened in your cardiovascular arteries have also blocked your kidney tubules. When the kidney tubules are blocked, they don't get enough oxygen from the blood. Your body has a protective mechanism for dealing with just such a situation, on a *temporary* basis—it raises your blood pressure to deal with the lack of oxygen (the pressor factor). Combined with the rise in blood pressure that has already occurred because of the rigidity of the arteries, the setting off of this would-be safety mechanism can be extremely dangerous.[86]

There are some other ways in which magnesium deficiency can lead to high blood pressure or other circulatory problems. For example, when there is not enough magnesium in your system, your kidneys are very vulnerable to damage by sharp crystalline oxalic acid, which can result in hypertension.[87, 88] Furthermore, with inadequate magnesium to dispel protein molecules in your bloodstream, blood clots may form in your heart or brain.[89, 90] As a result, your blood and oxygen supplies could be blocked, with death or disablement a likelihood.

Spasms of an artery caused by a lack of magnesium can be the direct cause of angina pectoris or even a heart attack. Fortunately, magnesium therapy can effectively treat these problems, even for patients who have already had a heart attack.[91, 92] It makes sense that eating magnesium-rich foods *now* may prevent the development of heart disease later: in people who died of heart attacks, autopsies revealed roughly 42 percent less magnesium in their heart muscle than in people who died of other conditions.[93]

MAGNESIUM FOR YOUR KIDNEYS

We hinted above that a magnesium deficiency can have dire effects on your kidneys, partially because of the hypertension it creates. Blood rushing at high pressure through your tiny kidney tubules can actually cause them to burst in places. The body tries its best to repair itself, but when the proper nutrients are lacking, its best is rigid scar tissue, which clogs the tubules. And if one reason you are nutrient-deficient in the first place is that you drink too many diuretic substances—coffee, tea, alcohol—your kidneys can weaken as well. A combination of scar tissue and weakness impedes your kidneys' capacity to "save" valuable minerals from your bloodstream and reabsorb them for future use, so your loss of nutrients becomes even more devastating. Inflammation of the kidney tissue itself (nephritis) may come as a result of the stress of malfunction. Wild seizures may ensue. Fortunately, magnesium therapy can stop the seizures, yet the therapy should mark the beginning of some sort of nutritional rehabilitation program if the condition is not to recur.[94, 95]

If kidney stress continues, nephrosis (tissue degeneration) results. Now your kidneys are damaged and cannot reabsorb nutrients at all, so gigantic quantities of magnesium are lost. A calcium/magnesium imbalance allows calcium deposits to lodge on the kidney cells; in fact, low levels of magnesium can result in twenty-five times more calcium on your kidneys than on the kidneys of a healthy person.[96, 97] And as if that weren't enough, a magnesium deficiency also allows calcium kidney stones to form: not only is there a surplus of calcium, but as a result of the magnesium deficiency there is not enough citric acid to keep the calcium ions suspended in your urine.

Luckily, magnesium therapy can help rejuvenate the kidneys. In fact, in people with a history of kidney stones, large doses of magnesium have prevented the formation of new ones.[98] It's a good idea to start eating magnesium-rich natural foods before you have the painful occasion to develop kidney stones, however![99]

For people whose kidney problems have progressed to the point where they must receive dialysis treatments, supplementary magnesium can help, not only in replacing the large quantities of magnesium lost in the treatments, but also in stabilizing the serum phosphate levels, which can rise to dangerous heights in dialysis.[100]

MAGNESIUM FOR DIABETES

Magnesium can be beneficial in several ways to diabetics. Because diabetes is so often complicated by heart and kidney disease, supplementary magnesium can be an insurance policy for the diabetic's heart and kidneys. Magnesium is also vital to the health of the pancreas, which in the diabetic's case can no longer produce insulin. With B_6, magnesium helps the pancreas metabolize the amino acid tryptophane. Without magnesium, the process cannot take place, and a dangerous toxic substance—xanthurenic acid—is synthesized instead. Because xanthurenic acid can damage the pancreas in a very short time (forty-eight hours), for the diabetic it can be deadly. For the rest of us, it can actually shut off the insulin supply and cause diabetes.[101]

Two other ways in which adequate magnesium can be of help to the diabetic are in regulating the pH throughout the body and in breaking down the fats in the blood. Both these areas present problems to the diabetic: acidosis can occur quickly because the waste products of fat metabolism, called ketones, can accumulate, and they are very acid.[102] Sufficient magnesium keeps the pH of every part of the body at the right degree of alkalinity or acidity and can help prevent diabetic acidosis. A related fat-metabolism problem in diabetes—lipemia—in which there is too much fat in the blood, can also respond to adequate magnesium. In this case, magnesium functions as a coenzyme with the lipoprotein lipases to dispel the extra fat.[103]

MAGNESIUM FOR BONES AND TEETH

Because your bones and teeth are made in part of magnesium, obviously they suffer from any deficiency of the mineral. As we have already noted, their high need for magnesium makes them stingy; if other parts of the body need it, they simply refuse to give up their share.[104-108] In acute deficiency, however, they do become more generous, and subsequently suffer for it, because they are giving up not only magnesium but calcium as well. When this occurs, osteoporosis—characterized by porous, easily fractured bones—is the end result. Eggshell bones that break under the weight of the body—the mere possibility is enough to engender a craving for magnesium-rich foods.

Magnesium therapy—in doses from 750 milligrams to 1,250 milligrams—can be helpful to those who are already suffering from osteoporosis.[109] It can also serve to restore the vital calcium/magnesium balance within the body, which if out of equilibrium can result in very serious problems, characterized mainly by calcium deposits in the muscles, arteries, joints, and weak places in the tissues. The same imbalance can impede your healing powers in case of fractures, and can cause rickets in children, or osteomalacia (bone deformities) in adults.

MAGNESIUM FOR ANEMIA

We usually think of anemia as being caused by iron deficiency, but that is not always the case. If your body is not absorbing B_6 from your diet properly, there is an automatic reduction in the number of red blood cells and the amount of hemoglobin in your blood.[110, 111] If you have this type of anemia, taking iron won't help; in fact, it will hurt, because the combined magnesium/B₆ deficiency (which is usually the case) will cause you to absorb excess amounts of iron, which can scar tissue and attract calcium deposits.[112, 113] Too much iron in your body can result in these unsavory conditions: heart problems; rheumatoid arthritis; liver cirrhosis; scurvy (because vitamin C is destroyed); low levels of vitamin E; iron deposits in the lungs and pancreas, with resulting respiratory and digestive problems; and histapenia (a form of schizophrenia).[114, 115] The only cure for an anemia caused by a deficiency of vitamin B₆ is therapy with B₆ and magnesium, which must be present for your body to use B₆ efficiently.[116]

YOUR LIVER NEEDS MAGNESIUM, TOO

For much the same reasons that your heart and kidneys suffer from a lack of magnesium, your liver also suffers. When there is not enough magnesium for protein production, there are not the necessary materials available to your body for tissue maintenance and repair. There is also an excess of fats, because magnesium is necessary to break them down before they can become the fatty acids your body can use. So your liver suffers, especially if you are a heavy drinker, vulnerable to liver cirrhosis and meanwhile washing great quantities of magnesium out of your system. It should come as no surprise that a degenerated and scarred liver is one result of magnesium deficiency, especially when combined with heavy drinking.[117] A damaged liver also means the loss of amino acids necessary for building the proteins your body needs for maintenance.[76]

MAGNESIUM FOR EYES, SKIN, HAIR, AND NAILS

If you are magnesium deficient, your eyes and skin may tell the story. If there is a magnesium/calcium imbalance, there are excess fats and calcium floating in the bloodstream, and circulation may be reduced. For your eyes, the outcome may be cataracts.[118]

Your skin needs a lot of protein to replace its cells. If your diet lacks adequate magnesium, it can't, and wrinkles will form.[119] If you have psoriasis, your skin has an even greater than normal magnesium need, and magnesium therapy can be quite beneficial.[120] If you find your hair falling out at an alarming rate, or your nails breaking easily, you probably need magnesium to help build some protein for your thyroid gland; you have the symptoms of an improperly functioning thyroid.[121]

MAGNESIUM FOR OTHER CONDITIONS

Magnesium deficiency combined with low protein in the diet can be very dangerous because it means that your body has very few resources on which to draw for building vital proteins. Such a situation could manifest in a refusal of wounds to heal or a high vulnerability to infections, or worse, cancer. In countries where the diet is extremely low in magnesium—Central America and southern Africa, for example—kwashiorkor, a protein-deficiency disease, is quite common.[122] One of its morbid consequences is cystic fibrosis, in which the pancreas is destroyed (and the body unable to digest food as a consequence),[123, 124] another is cancer.[125] Don't follow the logic of this presentation too closely, however: a magnesium deficiency does not always cause kwashiorkor before it causes cancer. If you let your tissues starve for protein-building substances like magnesium, you are opening the gate to lowered immunity and increased susceptibility to viral diseases, of which cancer, in some forms, is one.

A Practical Guide to Using Magnesium

Now that you've seen how important magnesium is, you're probably wondering what foods you should include in your diet to get your daily quota and, for that matter, what the daily quota is. You should also be aware of magnesium's nutritional partners, as well as its antagonists, so that you can make the most of the magnesium in your foods.

One of the best foods you can eat for your body's magnesium needs is green leafy vegetables, preferably organically grown. Magnesium is a strong component of plant foods like kale, endive, chard, beet greens, alfalfa sprouts, and celery—it is responsible both for their carbohydrate composition and for their greenness itself. In this category of magnesium-rich greens we do not include spinach; it is high in oxalic acid, which impedes the body's absorption of magnesium. Nuts and seeds—peanuts, pecans, almonds, cashews, Brazil nuts, and hazelnuts; sunflower, pumpkin, and sesame seeds—all contain significant amounts of magnesium. So one quite delicious way to supply your body with magnesium is to make salads of leafy greens, with a sprinkling of nuts and seeds for texture, taste, and magnesium. Add a bit of avocado or raw slivered turnips and your magnesium intake will be even higher.

Whole grains also contain a good amount of the mastermind mineral. A particularly good source is leavened bread made of whole wheat or a mixture of grains: the leavening process transforms the grains' phytic acid, another inhibitor of magnesium utilization. Whole wheat, bran, wheat germ, oatmeal, barley, rye, corn, brown rice—all can be ingredients in delicious homemade bread. Add some nuts and seeds and you are getting an even richer supply of magnesium.

Within the higher protein foods, magnesium is also to be found in bounteous supply. Complement your grains with beans, peas, or lentils, and not only will you be getting all the amino acids to supply complete proteins, you will also be getting magnesium. Organic eggs and raw milk are excellent unpolluted magnesium sources; beef, pork, poultry, fish, and other seafoods also contain magnesium, yet its nutritional benefits may be offset by the chemical and hormonal content of these foods. Your best bet, if you like meat, is to find a source of organically grown products.

You can even enjoy getting some of your daily magnesium through snacks like oranges, grapefruit, peaches, apricots, pineapple, apples, figs, and dates. Combine them with nuts and seeds for a delicious between-meal munch and boost your intake even more. Hungry for sweets? Carob nuts or candies, honey, and blackstrap molasses all contain some of the magnesium your body likes so much.[126]

MAGNESIUM'S NUTRITIONAL PARTNERS

Magnesium and calcium are great friends. However, their intake must be balanced: your body needs roughly twice as much calcium as magnesium. If you take magnesium in foods or supplements at the same time you take calcium, you may experience a rather pleasant tranquilizing side effect: both these minerals are extremely important to the peace of your nerves. In fact, together they can help you get a good night's sleep.

As we said above, you must be careful that your intake of calcium and magnesium is balanced, or you may find yourself magnesium-deficient. This condition can come about if your diet contains too much calcium, or too little. Calcium and magnesium are both transported by molecules of protein in your blood called albumin. If all these mineral transporters are busy carrying calcium, they can't also take the magnesium to the places where it's needed; it may be lost through the urine as a result.[127] On the other hand, if your diet contains too little calcium, the kidneys will filter out valuable magnesium for excretion through the urine in a noble effort to maintain the precious calcium/magnesium balance. Women should be especially aware of this fact; in menstruation and pregnancy, a great deal of calcium is lost, causing magnesium to be lost as well.

Some more of magnesium's nutritional cohorts include vitamins B_6, C, and natural A and D, phosphorus, and protein.[128] Without these elements, the magnesium you take in through foods or supplements cannot work properly in your body. And remember, nearly all the B vitamins, as well as C and E, need magnesium for their own proper functioning.[129-131]

MAGNESIUM'S ANTAGONISTS

Equally important in menu planning is to know what inhibits your absorption of magnesium: excess alcohol, tea, and coffee; oxalic acid and phytic acid; excess milk; a low-protein diet as well as a high-protein diet; excess cholesterol, vitamin D, and salt.

Alcohol is one of magnesium's prime antagonists, causing tremendous quantities to be lost in the urine. In fact, this loss of magnesium is a prime cause of the delirium tremens ("DT's") that alcoholics frequently suffer. Diuretics like coffee, tea, and cola also wash magnesium out of your system before your body can use it, as do any prescribed diuretic drugs, of course. Magnesium isn't the only important mineral lost; when so much fluid passes through the kidneys that they cannot filter out what the body needs, many vital minerals become waste products.

Oxalic acid—contained in spinach, chocolate, rhubarb, and other foods—forms a mineral compound with magnesium that makes it impossible for the body to use it. Phytic acid—found in cereals and unleavened breads, corn, rice, soybeans, and peanuts—does the same thing.[132, 133] Obviously it is not suggested that you avoid these foods entirely, as they contain a number of nutrients that are not bound up by oxalic or phytic acid. But leaven your breads to get the most mineral utilization from the whole grains in them.

Surprisingly enough, commercially produced pasteurized milk with synthetic vitamin D also inhibits your absorption of magnesium. The synthetic D is extremely active as a chelating (binding) agent, and magnesium is one element with which it binds, sweeping it unused through your system.

If you eat a diet low in protein, your magnesium needs may suffer accordingly. Protein is necessary for your blood to make the albumin it needs to transport both magnesium and calcium. If the transporter is lacking, the magnesium cannot be taken to where you need it, and exits through the urine instead.[134] But if you eat too much protein on a regular basis, you will also develop a magnesium deficiency, because so much will be required to process your food proteins into building materials.[135] By the same token, a high-cholesterol diet will put great demands on your magnesium supply, as great quantities of the mineral will be necessary to break the fats into fatty acids.[136, 137]

Too much salt in your diet can also indirectly contribute to a magnesium deficiency. Magnesium must be balanced with potassium as well as calcium. If you eat too much sodium, you lose potassium through the urine, and as a result the potassium/magnesium balance is thrown out of whack, with ensuing deficiencies of both minerals. A good magnesium supplement can actually raise your levels of potassium, too,[138] while a potassium supplement is useless without complementary magnesium. The best idea is to take supplements of both minerals: your intake of magnesium and sodium together should equal your intake of potassium.

Other conditions that are magnesium antagonists are stress, kidney problems, inflammatory diseases, and vomiting and diarrhea. Emotional or physical stress increases the rate at which your body's metabolic reactions occur, so your stores of vital nutrients can be used up very fast. So it's a good idea to get more of all the nutrients, perhaps through supplements, during stressful periods of your life.

Any disease creates a certain physical stress, but some conditions create especially large deficiencies of magnesium. If your kidney tissues are inflamed, they cannot properly process out the magnesium from the fluids that pass through them, and much is lost. Conditions that affect your hormone-producing thyroid, parathyroid, and adrenal glands can also result in large magnesium losses. Arthritis, too, can mean magnesium loss, because the drugs used to treat it (cortisone and aspirin) are antagonists.

Fluoride, a common addition to our drinking water, is yet another enemy of magnesium, chelating it into an unusable compound that is rejected as a waste product.[139] Ironically, this fluoride is supposed to protect our teeth against decay, yet it results in a loss of one of the very minerals our teeth most need for the hard enamel that *keeps* them from decay.[140] Much of our tap water is a chemical soup these days, so for more reasons than simply fluoride content, drinking pure spring water might be a good idea.

HOW MUCH MAGNESIUM DO YOU NEED?

Here are the U.S. government's recommendations for magnesium intake for various age groups:[17]

Infants	60 to 70 milligrams
Ages 1 to 3	120 to 140 milligrams
Ages 4 to 6	170 to 190 milligrams
Ages 7 to 10	220 to 240 milligrams
Ages 11 to 14	350 milligrams
Ages 15 to 18	400 milligrams
Ages 19 and over	350 milligrams
Pregnant and lactating women	450 milligrams

Since our foods are particularly low in magnesium because of our chemical farming practices,[141-144] since you lose from 100 to 300 milligrams daily in your urine,[145] and since you absorb only about half of the magnesium that *is* present in your foods,[146] it might not be a bad idea to take in more magnesium than the government recommends. In fact, for a healthy adult, 450 to 650 milligrams of magnesium might be a more realistic figure for maintaining that health.[147] The nutritionist Adelle Davis proposed 600 to 900 milligrams as an acceptable amount of magnesium for the maintenance of optimum health.[148, 149] (She also blamed our widespread dependence on tranquilizers on the just-as-widespread magnesium deficiency.[150])

Since everyone is biochemically different, your own need for magnesium is different, too. But getting somewhere within the range of the advisable amounts can be a big first step on the road to better health. Be sure there is some magnesium in every meal you eat; since it is easily excreted in the urine and perspiration, you need a steady supply throughout your day.[151]

Also keep in mind that any magnesium your body can't use will be excreted through the kidneys. In fact, the only conditions under which you could get too much magnesium are if you were suffering from kidney failure or for some reason took a huge quantity intravenously. A more likely danger is that if you took too much magnesium in supplements, your bones' calcium metabolism would be thrown out of balance; this could not occur if you were taking the amounts outlined above—even in the upper ranges. But the very real threat to most of us is that we get too little, or that our magnesium levels are out of balance with the interrelated nutrients calcium, phosphorus, and potassium.

MAGNESIUM IN SUPPLEMENTS

The most important thing to remember in taking magnesium supplements is that magnesium and calcium must be balanced. Thus, magnesium oxide is an excellent supplement, if you make sure that you are getting the right amount of calcium from other sources. Dolomite is a good source of magnesium and calcium in balanced form, but it is hard for your stomach to break it down into utilizable nutrients. Bone meal contains far too little magnesium in ratio to calcium, and is not a particularly good way to supplement for magnesium.

Since magnesium is an alkaline element, it is a favorite component in commercial antacids, which neutralize hydrochloric stomach acid. Keep in mind, however, that you need your hydrochloric acid for proper digestion—without it your stomach cannot dissolve proteins or destroy bacteria contained in your food. In fact, trying to neutralize your stomach acid only results in your digestive system working harder.

For the above reason, it is not a good idea to take magnesium supplements with your meals, as you do most of your other vitamin and mineral supplements. They might interfere with your digestion. Try supplementing for magnesium with your between-meal snacks, or before bedtime, instead. However, if you want to include a magnesium supplement at mealtime for the sake of convenience, there are two that would be better than others under those conditions: magnesium chloride (the chloride is acid and gives some equilibrium to the magnesium's alkalinity),[152] and magnesium oxide, which has a lesser degree of alkalinity than some of the other magnesium supplements.

ARE YOU MAGNESIUM DEFICIENT?

Magnesium deficiency is not easy to diagnose, yet studies have shown that it is a plague among Americans, particularly the ill and elderly.[153-161] Because your bones give up their magnesium store in cases of acute deficiency, you may not eat any magnesium at all and tests for your serum and cerebrospinal fluid magnesium levels will be normal. Only after your deficiency has reached truly dangerous levels (when over 50 percent of the bones' magnesium has been leached out) will the tests show anything at all awry[162] and even at that point lab tests of your bones will show them to be normal![163-165] There is one quick test for magnesium deficiency, which your physician might undertake if you are suffering from a serious illness that could be related to a deficiency of magnesium: a large quantity of magnesium is injected; if over 90 percent of that quantity is then detected in urine tests, your magnesium levels are normal.[166]

The most easily detected symptoms of magnesium deficiency—i.e., most visible to you—are falling hair and easily broken nails. What those two signs can mean is that you have a thyroid problem: not enough parathormone is being produced.[167] And the direct cause of the problem is probably low levels of magnesium.

Summary

Magnesium is an important component of the earth, of plants, and of your body. Though there are only four to five teaspoons of magnesium throughout your whole system, that tiny amount is responsible for an enormous quantity of physiological functions, without which you would not survive. In fact, magnesium controls so many of your body's functions that it is fairly known as the "mastermind" mineral.

Magnesium has a star role in your cellular metabolic processes. It is a versatile and tireless worker in your body's protein production process. In addition, it is one of your body's most important coenzymes, particularly in relation to two important energy mechanisms, ATP and coenzyme A. Magnesium is also a valuable nutritional partner with calcium, and vitamins D, B_1, folic acid, B_6, C, and E. It is also necessary for your body's production of aldosterone, the adrenal hormones, cortisone, and parathormone.

Magnesium works in your muscles, your cells, your nervous system, your bones, your digestive system, your metabolism, your reproductive system, your protein production system, your blood, and your immune system.

It can be helpful if you suffer from arthritis; digestive problems; irregular menstruation, prostate problems, or sterility; undulant fever; nervous disorders; neuromuscular disease; heart disease and circulatory problems; kidney problems; diabetes; disorders of the bones and teeth; anemia; liver problems; low-protein disease; and infections. It can also be helpful as a cancer preventative.

Eat plenty of green leafy vegetables, seeds, nuts, grains, and beans to make sure that you meet your magnesium requirements of from 350 to 900 milligrams daily, if you are a healthy adult. Enjoy wholesome fruit-and-nut snacks for an additional magnesium boost. Avoid alcohol, coffee, tea, salt, excess milk, and fluoride to get the most magnesium mileage from your foods and supplements. Eat a moderate amount of protein, and watch out for fatty foods!

Remember, magnesium's principal partner is calcium, and your body needs a delicate balance of these two minerals: about twice as much calcium as magnesium. If you take magnesium supplements, try to balance them with the right amount of calcium in supplements or in your daily diet.

Oxalic acid and phytic acid bind magnesium into an unusable form, so be careful about your consumption of spinach, chocolate, rhubarb, and unleavened breads in combination with magnesium-rich foods. Also keep in mind that if you are sick or under any other form of stress, your needs for all the nutrients, including magnesium, are greatly increased.

With adequate magnesium, you have a wonderful protector against all forms of today's degenerative diseases. This protector is available in all sorts of easily accessible delicious natural foods. Give the "mastermind" of your body a chance to keep "all systems go" by including magnesium-full unrefined foods in every one of your daily meals. Your health can only be the better for it.

Manganese: The Activator

What Is Manganese?

Manganese is a hard, brittle, grayish-white metallic element that is plentiful in our earth, air, and water. In our bodies, it is a trace mineral, called so because it is present in only minute amounts. Yet these tiny amounts are hugely important: manganese works with several major vitamins, activating the enzymes that help your body take the vitamins from the foods you eat and put them to their proper work.

We said that manganese is a plentiful element, yet we must counterbalance that statement with the unfortunate fact that most Americans have at least a borderline manganese deficiency. Why? For one thing, nowadays much of our food is grown in soil farmed with chemicals, and this has an adverse effect on mineral content. For another thing, most of us routinely eat foods that have had many of the vital trace minerals and other nutrients refined out of them at the processing plant. If we were to eat a diet of whole, natural foods with plenty of vegetables, beans, and fruits, manganese deficiency would not concern us at all.

How Does Manganese Work?

Manganese may be a trace mineral, but its activities add up to much more than this term would imply. Besides activating vitamins and enzymes to do their stuff, manganese helps clear your body of poisons, helps build proteins, and helps synthesize RNA, fatty acids, and thyroxine. In addition, it stimulates glandular secretions that influence all phases of human sexuality, and plays a key role in blood sugar metabolism.

First let's discover how manganese works with vitamins and enzymes. B-vitamin family members choline, biotin, and thiamine (B_1) depend on manganese as a coworker. So does vitamin C. One ingredient of the choline compound in your bile is manganese; thus, your liver couldn't function without it. Nor could choline perform its work elsewhere. Biotin and thiamine are true wonder-workers in many areas of your body; yet without manganese, they couldn't work any wonders at all because both depend on enzymes that mighty manganese puts into motion. Vitamin C is the "white knight" of your cells, fighting infections and pollutants, yet its service would be stilled if manganese weren't there to activate the enzymes that send it out to combat.

Aside from helping vitamin C battle the pollutants in your system, manganese plays its own part as a warrior against poisons in your bloodstream, in particular against ammonia. You may think of ammonia as strictly a product for mopping the floor, but it is also a product of the energy process of your cells, produced when they break down proteins. However, it is little different from the ammonia you use in housecleaning in that it is extremely poisonous—a thousandth of a milligram in one quart of blood would kill you. Thus, your body must have a surefire way of reckoning with this deadly waste product, which is being produced even as you read this page. That's where manganese comes into the picture; it activates the enzyme arginase, which is a key element in your body's mechanism to rid itself of ammonia.[1, 2] The process is fairly simple: ammonia is mixed with carbon dioxide to create a harmless compound, urea. If all the elements that put this protective mechanism into gear—like manganese and arginase—are there, urea is formed and swept through the bloodstream to the kidneys, from which it exits in your urine.[3]

Another important arena in which manganese performs its enzyme-activating function is your cells, which need it for both growth and maintenance.[4] Here manganese is the ringleader of an enzyme family called the peptidases. Their job is to disassemble the proteins in your food into amino acids, the raw materials for the proteins you need to repair and maintain all the tissues of your body.[5] Inside the cells, another enzyme family is hard at work making the long amino-acid chains that constitute those proteins. This family, too, is spurred into activity by manganese.

To make RNA, you need manganese. Visualize your cells as a construction site where new proteins are constantly being built by enzyme families. RNA is vital to all the workers. It takes all the information from DNA—the genetic architect in the center of this construction site (the nucleus of the cells) who knows just what kind of proteins are being built—and transmits it to the ribosomes where the proteins are actually being constructed from amino acids.[6, 7] Thus, in a way, you are the person you are because of manganese, and you certainly couldn't be the person you are without it, because you wouldn't be able to continually replace the cells that die of natural causes every day of your life. Your tissues would shrivel and die without manganese the activator.

Another place manganese is active is in the manufacture of the fatty acids and cholesterol so important to your nerves, brain, liver, and sex glands. Here we are talking not about the excess fats and cholesterol that can make deposits on your arteries, causing a whole battery of dangerous problems, but about the fatty acids and cholesterol that are the building blocks for your cellular walls and the sheaths that protect your tender nerves. The same cholesterol is much needed by your brain, by the bile that your liver produces, and in the manufacture of adrenal cortex and sex hormones.

Because it *is* so important in the production of sex hormones, manganese is responsible for your being the person you are in yet another way: that you are at all! Without an adequate supply of manganese, your parents could not have conceived you, your mother would have lacked the instinct—not to mention the breast milk—to nourish you; in short, manganese activated you from before the very beginning!

Without enough manganese, levels of sex hormones are low and RNA may be lacking. Ovulation, breast milk, and the maternal instinct we take so much for granted depend in part on manganese's enzyme-activating activity.[8, 9] Manganese helps keep the seminal tubes and semen production at peak health and efficiency. A shortage of this little mineral can be responsible for loss of interest in sex or even impotence.

Manganese is also part of the total blood sugar metabolism picture. It seems to play quite a large role in your body's ability to burn its fuel (glucose) efficiently, or to store it for the future.[10] How? The beta cells in your pancreas need manganese to make insulin; insulin takes the glucose from your blood into every cell in your body. So manganese is essential if insulin is to be produced and glucose transported to the cells.

After the glucose reaches your cells, it is burned in several different stages, a process called oxidative phosphorylation. Manganese is essential for this process, in which at some of the stages the ATP enzyme "traps" some of the energy and squirrels it away for future needs.[11, 12]

Where Does Manganese Work?

Even though our bodies need only tiny amounts of manganese, the places where this manganese is put to work are all-encompassing.

• *Blood.* Manganese is one of the essential ingredients in the formation of new blood cells in your bone marrow, medical researchers believe. In its activating role, mighty manganese stimulates vitamin K to clot your blood properly.[13] With its comineral zinc, manganese has been used to successfully raise low blood pressure, an oft-observed side effect of hypoglycemia.[14]

• *Skeletal system.* You know that your bones and teeth, cartilage and tendons, need calcium and magnesium. But did you know that manganese, too, is essential to their correct structure?[15] Sometimes the great activator, administered in therapeutic doses, can even help treat bone and cartilage malformations in growing youngsters.[16]

• *Brain and nerves.* Manganese activates substances essential to the well-being of your brain and nerves. Your brain needs manganese-activated choline and ATP to make acetylcholine, a chemical compound that causes muscle action by transmitting nerve impulses.[17] Acetylcholine encourages your body to discharge norepinephrine and epinephrine (adrenaline), those important hormones that help you cope with fear and anger.

Another of manganese's work sites in the neurological system is in the synthesis of dopamine, which helps nerves transmit messages.[18] The enzyme cyclic APM, also involved as a neurotransmitter, is catalyzed by manganese.[19]

• *Immune system.* Two very special agents in your immune system are vitamin C and histamine. Both need manganese to work. Manganese-activated enzymes are vitamin C's lieutenants in fighting toxic invaders and abnormal cells. Histamine is released by manganese-stimulated calcium.

• *Protein production system.* You might say that manganese is the foreman of the protein production factory of the cells, because it activates the two enzyme families employed there. One family breaks down your food proteins into amino acids, which are the "raw materials" with which the other family builds the amino-acid chains that comprise the proteins so important for cellular construction and maintenance.

Manganese is an activator at important areas all through your body —your blood, skeletal system, brain and nerves, immune system, and protein production system. Making sure there is enough manganese in your daily diet is one way to keep all these systems "go."

Who Needs Manganese?

Answering the question, "Who needs manganese?" after explaining how and where it works is like putting together the pieces of a jigsaw puzzle. Because of its role in the metabolism of blood sugar and fats, you can guess that an adequate supply would be helpful to those suffering from hypoglycemia, diabetes, or heart disease. Because it is so necessary to the brain and nerves, you might also guess that it could be beneficial to those suffering from mental disorders or neuromuscular diseases. And because of its importance to the immune system, it is only logical to suppose that it might be useful in combating cancer and a number of other conditions.

MANGANESE FOR BLOOD SUGAR DISORDERS

Manganese therapy can benefit those who suffer from diabetes or hypoglycemia. In fact, manganese deficiency may be a pervasive symptom of diabetes: in one test of 122 diabetics of all ages, low levels of manganese was a common denominator. An identical control group who did not suffer from blood sugar metabolism disorders showed manganese levels twice as high as the diabetics! Fortunately, the diabetics were helped with manganese therapy.[20]

Manganese deficiency may be related to blood sugar disorders for two reasons. First, for the beta cells of the pancreas to produce insulin, you need manganese. That much we know. But the second reason is a bit more complicated. One of the reasons there is so much diabetes and hypoglycemia today is that we eat refined foods.[21] Products made with white sugar or flour overload your bloodstream with glucose, causing your pancreas to make a great deal of insulin all at once to metabolize the fuel. (In contrast, complex carbohydrates like those contained in whole grains allow glucose to enter your bloodstream slowly, so that the pancreas can produce insulin at a reasonable rate.) As a result of overwork, the pancreas can lose its ability to produce insulin at all, and first hypoglycemia, then diabetes, is the dire consequence. Since the manganese naturally contained in whole foods is lost when they are refined, a diet of refined foods does not supply enough manganese to help the pancreas produce insulin in the first place. It's a double-edged sword.

MANGANESE FOR HEART DISEASE

Like some of the other trace minerals, manganese is important in your metabolism of fats. If you lack manganese, the fats in your bloodstream cannot be converted into the tools your body needs—like cellular walls and protective nerve sheaths. Instead of being put to good use, the fats float around in your blood, clumping together in larger and larger particles that are attracted to damaged spots in your arteries, where they lodge, forming dangerous deposits and plaque. Manganese also helps your liver produce the fat-emulsifier lecithin, which is synthesized in part by manganese-activated choline. Thus, without manganese, you may be more susceptible to atherosclerosis, arteriosclerosis, and a damaged heart and arteries. Luckily, manganese therapy has proven itself to be a viable heart treatment, restoring the health of some patients even after they have had heart attacks.[22]

Manganese helps your liver put the fats in your blood to good use. You could see it this way: the more efficient your liver is in taking the fatty acids out of your blood and making them into cholesterol and lecithin and other vital compounds necessary for your nerves, cell membranes, and sex and adrenal cortex hormones, the less fat there is floating around in your arterial bloodstream, waiting to cause you trouble. And manganese helps your liver itself in the same way by assuring that fatty deposits don't build up there, either, which would lead to cirrhosis.[23]

And speaking of cirrhosis of the liver, here's a special message to drinkers: you need manganese more than others. Not only does alcohol raise blood sugar so rapidly that over time it is a leading cause of blood sugar disorder; it is also a major factor in the development of liver cirrhosis. Both of these conditions can be improved by adequate intake of manganese.

MANGANESE FOR MENTAL DISORDERS

We have already learned that manganese activates choline and ATP, both key components of several of the brain's most important neurotransmitters.[24] If these nerve messengers work at cross-purposes, or do not work efficiently, schizophrenic behavior may be the outward result. Dr. Carl Pfeiffer of the Brain Bio Center is largely responsible for discovering another way in which an inadequate supply of manganese can lead to schizophrenia, based on the delicate manganese/copper relationship in your body.

Did you know that manganese at proper levels protects you against high levels of copper? Why is that important? High levels of copper in your body destroy histamine, an important agent in your immune system. One result of low histamine levels is a type of schizophrenia called histapenia. Luckily, nutritional therapy with manganese is effective in treating this condition, because adequate manganese drives the copper levels back down. At the same time, calcium is activated, which stimulates the release of histamine. Thus, histapenia can be reversed through properly balanced nutritional therapy.

Keep in mind, however, that only a rigorously trained orthomolecular physician would be able to effect this treatment properly. You see, the manganese/calcium relationship is of such delicate balance that if *too much* manganese is given, the calcium's activity is inhibited. The result? Symptoms of histapenia may be accelerated rather than inhibited.

This latter approach with too much manganese can be helpful in the treatment of another form of schizophrenia, histadelia. This form of schizophrenia is characterized by over-high levels of histamine. With excessive amounts of manganese, calcium in the patient's body is inactivated, and the histamine levels are lowered.

Be aware that while a lack of manganese can contribute to a state of mental disorder like schizophrenia, it can also cause quite real defects in your perceptual senses. Your eyesight and hearing can be genuinely impaired by inadequate manganese, with resulting dizziness, ear noises, even blindness and deafness.[25]

MANGANESE AND NEUROMUSCULAR DISEASES

You need manganese for the function of your neurotransmitters— those important little messengers that carry commands from your nerves to your muscles.[26] Inadequate manganese can impair your neuromuscular system. To prove it, researchers withheld manganese from the diets of test animals. They observed these symptoms: inability to sit, stand, and walk, loss of balance, and neglect of offspring.[27] (Remember how important manganese is to the maternal instinct?) Complete failure of muscle coordination—called ataxia—is one result of manganese deficiency in humans. Particularly dangerous to tiny, newly formed neuromuscular systems, ataxia can mean paralysis and convulsions for infants.[28]

We have already discovered that manganese activates acetylcholine and several of the B vitamins. Because of that key role, without manganese a slow deterioration of muscular health, called myasthenia gravis, can develop. Conversely, manganese therapy can improve the condition of patients of this debilitating disease—whose muscles have often lost so much of their strength that their eyelids must be kept open with cellophane tape.[29]

In multiple sclerosis, it is the nervous system that has degenerated; its messages to the muscles are blocked. This "hit-and-run" disease usually strikes young people, sometimes to leave just as suddenly and sometimes to remain as their companion for life. Luckily, manganese therapy has proved helpful to victims of this disease.

Manganese has also been used to treat tardive dyskinesia and Parkinson's disease. Trembling and loss of muscular coordination are symptoms of both these conditions. In Parkinson's disease, the victim has lost the ability to make the manganese-dependent neurotransmitter dopamine.[30] The documented reports of physicians who have noticed an almost 100 percent improvement in their Parkinson's patients after treatments with 30 to 60 milligrams of manganese daily make perfect sense; manganese is essential to the synthesis of dopamine.[31]

MANGANESE FOR CANCER AND OTHER DEGENERATIVE DISEASES

Manganese can help you minimize the risk of developing cancer. Here it plays its role in several ways: first, as a component of the enzyme superoxide dismutase. In this role, manganese helps keep your cells safe from destruction by free radical oxidation. (Vitamin E and selenium help in the same way.) If your cells are subjected to conditions like heavy pollutants or inadequate nutrition, oxidation can destroy them like wildfire, resulting in general deterioration of tissue health and therefore accelerating susceptibility to carcinogenic elements.

The second way in which manganese can increase your resistance to cancer lies in its part in the synthesis of RNA. If your intake of manganese is inadequate, RNA cannot be properly made. Its genetic information may be incomplete, with the result that your cells will make abnormal proteins and enzymes and will be abnormal and unhealthy themselves. RNA and DNA can also be damaged by free radical oxidation, which manganese helps prevent. Particularly if DNA is damaged, an uncontrollable melee of cellular proliferation can take place, eventually culminating in the condition we call cancer.

The third way in which manganese can help minimize your risk of developing cancer is related to those cancers caused by viruses. What is a virus? In effect, it is a protein-coated molecule of RNA or DNA that causes cells to produce new viruses rather than healthy cells. Vitamin C and histamine are very strong agents in your immune system that are there to destroy viruses and abnormal cells, among other toxic elements. As you will remember, vitamin C needs manganese-activated enzymes to work efficiently, while the release of histamines is also stimulated by manganese. Thus, enough manganese in your system can help these two protectors keep "riding the ranges" of your immune system, destroying anything that doesn't really belong there.

Manganese therapy can help victims of two other degenerative conditions, in particular. It has been used successfully in treating patients who were poisoned by toxic substances, again because it activates vitamin C, which helps rid your body of toxins. In one experiment, manganese-deficient animals died when researchers exposed them to a poisonous substance called hydralazine. In the same test, animals whose diets contained adequate manganese survived.[32]

Manganese therapy has also helped victims of lupus erythematosus, again because it activates vitamin C. Lupus erythematosus is a condition in which the collagen ("intercellular cement") that makes your skin, blood vessels, and tissues elastic, is destroyed. Vitamin C is a vital component of collagen. Thus, it makes sense that manganese has sometimes helped victims of this condition, which is sometimes thought to be incurable.[33] Young women, who are most susceptible to the ravages of lupus, should be especially aware of getting enough manganese in their diets.

A Practical Guide to Using Manganese

Believe it or not, your best food source of manganese is tea. Yet trying to get your daily quota of manganese from tannin-rich tea would be as senseless as trying to get your iodine from salt. Better sources of manganese on a daily basis would be nuts—almonds and peanuts in particular—seeds like sesame and pumpkin seeds, and whole grains. (Be sure to refrigerate your nuts and seeds; they quickly go rancid.) For hypoglycemics, buckwheat is an excellent choice of a manganese source because it also contains magnesium. Both can help your condition.

If they are grown organically in a soil rich in minerals, green leafy vegetables can supply you with manganese, as can broccoli, rhubarb, carrots, potatoes, peas, and beans. If you like fruits, choose pineapple, blueberries, or raisins for a hefty hit of manganese. Cloves and ginger also contain significant amounts of the mighty little mineral activator.

Except for organ meats like liver, animal foods supply only small amounts of manganese. Thus, you can't expect much from meat, seafoods, poultry, or dairy products. In fact, if you eat the typical modern American diet of meat, refined flour and sugar products, and processed vegetables and fruits, you are probably one of the millions of Americans who is manganese deficient.

HOW MUCH MANGANESE DO YOU NEED?

Well then, how much manganese *do* you need every day? You should try to replace at least the amount you lose—about 3.8 milligrams daily—through excretions in your bile, urine, perspiration, and hair.[34-37] Making sure you get at least that amount will insure that you have a survival level of manganese—essential to activating all the enzymes and minerals that keep your body running efficiently. Although there is no official RDA for manganese, trace-mineral experts suggest that up to 7 milligrams a day might be more sensible, even for the healthiest of us.[38, 39] You might find your body running more than efficiently—and energetically.

Of course, there are many nutritional variables that influence your manganese needs. If you eat foods containing a lot of calcium and phosphorus, for example, extra manganese is necessary to balance them.[40]

WHAT ARE THE SYMPTOMS OF DEFICIENCY?

There have been no documented cases of manganese deficiencies in humans, but don't be fooled—that doesn't mean they don't exist. Current hospital tests may not be sophisticated enough to detect manganese deficiency, but many of us are actually chronic sufferers.[41] Even though it may not show up on a lab test, this deficiency does show up in many symptoms of ill health in our country. Trace-mineral experts such as Dr. Henry Schroeder believe that Americans probably simply subsist on extremely low amounts of this mineral. In particular, if you are an older male you may be suffering a deficiency.[42]

Manganese supplements are available, but as with any other concentrated form of a nutrient, you should use them with the utmost care. Too much manganese in large concentrated doses may inhibit your body's means of storing and using iron. As we have seen, manganese therapy can help a variety of conditions from blood sugar disorders to neuromuscular disease, but any sort of nutritional therapy is best undertaken under the prescription and supervision of an orthomolecular physician.

Besides possibly causing an iron deficiency and elevated blood pressure, a high oral dose of manganese has no toxic side effects. Be aware, however, that manganese can lower your supply of infection-fighting histamine because in excess it blocks the activity of calcium, from which histamine is released. All nutritional relationships depend on proper balance. In this case, the zinc/manganese relationship is also precarious; zinc levels can be detrimentally lowered by excess manganese as well.[43]

CAN YOU GET TOO MUCH?

You are unlikely to ever suffer manganese toxicosis (poisoning) unless you happen to work in a mine or dry battery factory and inhale a lot of manganese oxide dust. In that case, you may notice weakness, motor difficulties, and psychological problems.[44] If you are severely poisoned, apathy, loss of strength and appetite, headaches, pneumonia, muscular rigidity and tremors, and schizophrenia could result.[45-47]

The first step in curing industrial manganese toxicosis is to remove the victim from the source of manganese. The relatively unconventional chelation therapy, in which a chelator (an agent that bonds with the toxic metal) is intravenously administered in a succession of treatments, can detoxify the condition by sweeping the bonded metal through the bloodstream and out of the body. Large doses of vitamin C can have the same effect.[48]

Summary

Manganese is a trace mineral that helps give you energy, proper growth, a healthy metabolism, a good muscle system, a normal sex life, and good mental health. Because of our agricultural practices and the food we eat, most of us get by on very low levels of manganese.

Manganese activates a number of important enzymes and the vitamins choline, biotin, thiamine, and vitamin C. It keeps your body clear of poisonous ammonia, helps build proteins for growth and maintenance, and helps metabolize fatty acids and cholesterol as well as glucose. It is particularly vital to your blood, your skeletal and metabolic systems, and your brain and nerves. Your immune system, in which vitamin C and histamine fight poisonous invaders and cellular aberration, is dependent upon manganese's activating properties.

Manganese can be helpful in treating blood sugar disorders, heart disease, mental disorders, neuromuscular disease, and lupus erythematosus. For several different reasons, it is a valuable weapon in the nutritional arsenal against cancer.

Your best food bets for getting plenty of manganese are nuts, seeds, and whole grains. Leafy and other vegetables, as long as they were grown in mineral-rich soil, are also good sources. Meat, dairy foods, poultry, seafood, and refined and processed foods contain very little manganese.

Remember, manganese is an activator. It activates all sorts of other nutritional elements to bring your body into harmonious good health. Make sure that your diet contains plenty—and if you are especially careful to eat lots of fresh, natural foods, it will—and you may find your energy levels, health, and overall well-being activated and reactivated by this vital trace mineral.

Phosphorus: The Body's Factotum

What Is Phosphorus?

Phosphorus is a solid, nonmetallic element that glows in the dark when it is exposed to air. This glowing quality gives it its name, derived from the Greek, meaning "carrier of light." The second most abundant mineral in your body, which contains from one and a half to two pounds of it, it is truly a mineral "factotum," which we could define as "the element employed to do all kinds of work." And that's just what phosphorus does, in your bones, nerves, muscles, energy system, cells, brain, liver, digestive system, and circulatory system.

How Does Phosphorus Work?

Phosphorus is an integral component of the phospholipids—essential constituents of all of your cells. Without phospholipids, your cells would literally collapse: these fat-soluble compounds are in part responsible for upholding the structural stability of your cellular walls, as well as of the mitochondria—the energy-producing units which each cell contains. Phospholipids are also important transporters of fatty acids, and help your body use them properly. In addition, they are in themselves a valuable store of fatty acids, although they are so valuable to your body in their other capacities that unless you are truly on the brink of starvation, they are not used for nourishment. Even so, if your body reaches the point at which it *is* using phospholipids for food, death will occur anyway, because you cannot survive without them.

Phosphorus is an important part of your genetic materials, DNA and RNA. Without phosphorus, not only would your cells be unable to reproduce themselves to maintain the tissues in your body, you yourself would be unable to have children. Your cells would also be unable to construct all the materials necessary for the health of your body: proteins, enzymes, and hormones.[1]

Phosphorus-rich compounds are also an integral part of the fluids in your body that break down the foods you eat and carry the nutrients to your cells. Not only are these compounds present in your saliva, the enzymes of your stomach and pancreas, your gastric juices, and your bile, they are also crucial to maintaining the varying degrees of acidity and alkalinity in each of these digestive juices. And once your food has been broken down into compounds that your bloodstream can absorb, phosphorus is at work maintaining the proper pH there, too. It performs the same function in your intra- and extracellular fluids, as well as your urine.

Phosphorus cannot work properly without maintaining healthy interrelationships with several other vitamins and minerals. Maintaining the proper pH of the various parts of your body is not a one-nutrient job; in this capacity phosphorus works with calcium, magnesium, sodium, and potassium.[2] The phosphorus compounds that we mentioned above may be formed with sodium, potassium, iron, or hydrogen.[3, 4] To use the phosphorus in your diet, zinc and manganese are necessary.[5] If you take in too much phosphorus, valuable calcium will be lost.[6-8]

Other nutrients need phosphorus just as much as phosphorus needs other nutrients. Vitamins B_1 (thiamine), B_2 (riboflavin), and B_3 (niacin) cannot be properly used by your body unless phosphorus is also present.[9, 10] One of the body's most important phospholipids, lecithin, is made from two of the other B vitamins—choline and inositol—in combination with phosphorus.[11, 12] Valuable phospholipids like lecithin, as well as phosphorus-containing enzymes, must be present before your body can adequately use vitamins A, D, E, and K, all of which are fat soluble.

Phosphorus also maintains working relationships with the twenty-three amino acids that compose the proteins in your food and are used for construction of proteins in your body. The compounds that phosphorus and the amino acids make are used in several different areas: manufacturing RNA and DNA; stabilizing cellular membranes; and carrying fatty acids, fat-soluble vitamins, and hormones through the bloodstream. One of your body's most important enzymes—ATP (an important energy compound in metabolism)—is also formed from a phosphorus/protein combination.

By now you may suspect that phosphorus has more functions than any other mineral in your body. If so, you are right. It also combines for energy storage with carbohydrates, and for phospholipid synthesis with fats.

Where Does Phosphorus Work?

Your body demands phosphorus for a long list of life-sustaining activities. Here are some of the places where phosphorus is most active.

• *Bones and teeth*. Phosphorus is one of the minerals that makes your skeletal system hard and strong. In fact, it is so important to your bones and teeth that from 80 to 85 percent of your phosphorus is stored there in a compound with calcium, called calcium phosphate. Without calcium phosphate, you would be unable to stand up, because your skeletal system would be just a soft, spongy mass of collagen.

• *Collagen synthesis*. The previous statement is just a bit misleading; in fact, without phosphorus your body could not make collagen— the "intercellular cement" that is sometimes called "nature's nylon." Three-quarters of your bone structure is collagen, and so is most of your cartilage, tendons, organ-supporting tissue, skin, and eyes.

• *Nerves*. Your nerves need phosphorus, too. Without it, they could not send the messages necessary for every one of your thoughts and movements. Phospholipids are an important component of the sheaths, made of myelin, that protect your nerves. Without myelin, your nerves could not transmit their impulses. Your nerves contain about 1 percent of your body's store of phosphorus.

• *Muscles*. One of the messages sent by your nerves to your muscles is the message to contract. But without phosphorus, the muscles couldn't carry out the nerves' command. As a component of the enzyme ATP, phosphorus is especially important to your muscles, which depend on ATP's ability to trap glucose from the oxidation process in your cells and store it in the form of the starch glycogen for your muscles' future energy demands. But before your muscles can use the stored glycogen to contract, they have to change it back to the fuel glucose; for this process, phosphorus is necessary.

• *Metabolism*. Many of phosphorus's functions take place in the realm of the metabolic process. We have already hinted at some of these functions, which are connected to phosphorus's place in the energy compound ATP. ATP could be called the "master enzyme," because it catalyzes so many of the biochemical reactions of the other enzymes of your body. Proper metabolism of nutrients at the cellular level depends on ATP.

ATP also traps some of the energy released when your cells burn glucose so that your body will have energy stored up for later needs. (Without ATP, you would have to eat almost continuously to supply fuel for your body.) The chemical bonds responsible for ATP's ability to trap this energy are actually made of phosphorus and oxygen. Their chemical composition is phosphorus-oxygen-phosphorus (POP, for short). These chains of phosphorus and oxygen POP open to catch energy, and when your body is ready to use it, they POP open again to release it from its storage form, glycogen.[13]

• *Cells.* Your cells need phosphorus to bring them nutrients. As we already know, they also need it for their very stability—without phosphorus, their walls would collapse, and they would also be unable to produce nutrients within their energy factories, the mitochondria. More than that, they would be unable to replenish themselves as they die off, because phosphorus must be present before RNA or DNA can be synthesized.

• *Brain.* Phosphorus constitutes a vital component of your brain in the form of phospholipids. In fact, these phosphorus–fatty acid compounds compose roughly a third of your brain's dry weight.

• *Liver.* Your liver is a factory for turning the fats you eat into fatty acids and fatty acid compounds for your body to use.[14] Roughly three-quarters of its manufactured products are phospholipids, including lecithin, which is an important fat emulsifier.[15-17]

• *Digestive system.* Phosphorus helps you digest your food by keeping your digestive fluids at the right degree of acidity or alkalinity. We touched on this above: the various fluids need different degrees of pH to perform their jobs properly. For example, your saliva has to be alkaline for the foods you chew to be broken down without being destroyed. For the same reason, the enzymes in your pancreas, stomach, and duodenum must also be maintained at an alkaline pH. Yet the actual gastric juices in your stomach are acid (and kept that way by hydrochloric acid); this helps you disintegrate especially heavy foods into nutrients, as well as destroying any bacteria that might have accompanied your meal. Bile from your liver helps you digest the fats in your food, but your liver cannot make it without a good supply of phosphorus. So without phosphorus, you would be unable to make nutrients for your body from the foods you eat, and all your delicious meals would be for naught!

• *Circulatory system.* We all know how dangerous excess cholesterol can be to the circulatory system. Yet in the "cholesterolphobia" that has swept our country in recent years, the fact that our bodies actually *need* fats, and the truth that the liver manufactures up to a cup of cholesterol daily, has been largely ignored. The important thing about the fats that you eat is that they be broken down properly into assimilable forms for important building materials. Phosphorus, in the form of lipoproteins, helps your bloodstream carry along tiny particles of fats and, in the form of phospholipids, *keeps* them tiny, in which state they cannot form the harmful deposits on arteries and organs that we so rightly fear. The lipoproteins—composed of phosphorus/protein compounds—also carry along vital fat-soluble hormones and vitamins.

• *Eyes.* Your eyes, too, have a special need for phosphorus. For one thing, they depend on collagen for support, as do all of your inner organs as well. For another thing, they need phosphorus to nourish and maintain the health of the cornea, the external coating that protects the iris and the eyeball itself.[18]

Now that we know where phosphorus works throughout the body, it is easy to see that it truly deserves its reputation as the mineral "factotum."

Who Needs Phosphorus?

Luckily, phosphorus deficiency is rare; in fact, so much phosphorus is added to our foods as phosphates when they are processed or refined that you actually run the risk of getting too much, if you live on refined foods. (Phosphorus is one of the very few nutrients—sodium being another—that might be oversupplied on a diet of refined and processed foods.)

Some people are phosphorus deficient, however, and others suffer from diseases that could be helped by additional phosphorus, or the proper balance between phosphorus and calcium. Among these conditions are bone and tooth disorders; cramps and aching muscles; conditions that are related to circulating calcium and phosphorus; bursitis; collagen disease; heart disease; gallstones; tetany; liver cirrhosis; anemia; and susceptibility to viruses and cancer.

The bone disorders that result from insufficient phosphorus—hypophosphatemia (similar to rickets) in children; osteomalacia (soft, demineralized bones) in adults—are complicated by a mineral imbalance between phosphorus and calcium.[19] Any imbalance among the minerals vital to healthy bones (calcium, magnesium, and phosphorus) can result in the bones losing their minerals to the blood, and this can result in osteoporosis (brittle, porous bones). Up to 60 percent of your bones' minerals may be lost before an X ray can detect osteoporosis, and some other lab tests bear normal results even when your bones have lost more![20-25] In fact, if your bones have lost up to 60 percent of their mineral content, you may already have suffered from a fracture or two just because they are no longer strong enough to support the weight of your body.

Phosphorus can help your broken bones heal more rapidly, if you make sure that you are getting the right amounts of calcium, magnesium, and natural vitamin D in your diet as well. The proper balance of these minerals and vitamin D can also help your children's teeth come in strong and stay that way, if you watch their consumption of sugar. Awareness of your own balanced intake of phosphorus and its nutritional partners can save you from the miseries of tooth decay and gum disease (pyorrhea).[26]

The key word here is *balance.* An imbalanced intake of the bone-building minerals can cause you enormous problems; you should know that getting *too much* phosphorus in relation to its partners can actually cause you the same problems as getting too little. Osteoporosis and bad teeth, aching muscles and bones, difficulty in making movements that require muscular pliability—all are symptoms of a mineral imbalance that could involve an excess of phosphorus, or a lack of it.[27]

One example of such a mineral imbalance, and its dangerous results, is when your body is getting too little calcium and too much phosphorus—a fairly common occurrence. Calcium is leached from your bones to supply the other parts of your system with the calcium they need, yet this process may actually cause an excess of calcium in your bloodstream. Combined with excess phosphorus in the diet, big problems can develop. Your kidneys will be unable to handle all the calcium and phosphorus coming through, and your urine may be too alkaline to keep the compound that forms—calcium phosphate—in suspension. The result? Painful kidney and bladder stones, which can grow to gigantic proportions. The conventional remedies for these stones may be even worse than the stones themselves, because they create even more acute mineral imbalances. The only lasting treatment for calcium phosphate stones is a diet in which the nutritional elements involved are very carefully balanced.[28-32]

Another danger of an imbalance between calcium and phosphorus is osteoarthritis. The precursor of this painful condition is a diet that supplies too much phosphorus and not enough calcium; osteoarthritis has at times been cured by correcting the imbalance (changing to a diet that supplies two times more calcium than phosphorus).[33] Over a period of time, such a carefully monitored attempt at rebalancing mineral levels brings gradual but certain improvement: the nutritionist Adelle Davis documented amazing recoveries even among patients who suffered from joints immobilized by arthritic spurs and fused vertebrae.[34]

In fact, any area of your body is subject to the ravages of mineral imbalance. If calcium is released into the bloodstream because of a disequilibrium with its mineral partners, it can build up in the form of dangerous deposits on your soft tissues, including your muscles. Bursitis is the result. Or it may damage your tendons, ligaments, skin, blood vessels and arteries—even the valves of your heart.[35]

If your diet or nutritional supplement does not supply enough phosphorus, your body will be unable to make its "intercellular cement," collagen, and this will adversely affect the health of your bones, cartilage, tendons, ligaments, skin, organ-supporting tissue, and eyes. Various diseases—all related to inadequate collagen production—can result: rheumatic fever, kidney tubule inflammation, scleroderma (skin that has a leathery look and feel), and rheumatoid arthritis.[36] As a matter of fact, the first signs of rheumatoid arthritis (joints that ache) may appear as the simple consequence of calcium and phosphorus being leached from your bones.[37]

Another dangerous sign that the phosphorus balance with other minerals in the body is not right is heart disease. An inadequate supply of phosphorus means that your liver cannot make the phospholipids necessary to keep the fats in your blood dispersed into tiny particles that float freely through the bloodstream. If there is an insufficient store of the phospholipid lecithin, for example, the particles of fat will glob together and pose a very real danger to the walls of your arteries and blood vessels. Since 1935, lecithin's powers as an emulsifier have been known,[38] and in fact it has been used widely in manufacturing chocolate and other substances because it keeps the texture smooth. In the same way, it keeps the fats in your bloodstream flowing along at a smooth and even pace, preventing any sort of clumping together that could cause atherosclerosis. Vivid proof of the necessity of lecithin's activity is seen when autopsies of heart disease patients are performed: their lecithin levels are generally low.[39]

Lecithin also helps your liver produce bile at an even rate. Bile helps you break down the fats and cholesterol in your meals and also helps them move through your digestive system properly. The result of an inadequate flow of bile is the production of painful gallstones from the cholesterol that would normally have been used to make bile.[40] To put it simply, if there is not enough phosphorus in your system, you cannot produce the lecithin needed to make bile; thus, you will be unable to metabolize fats properly. The results? Fatigue, perhaps overweight, perhaps even gallstones.[41]

For infants, an imbalance between calcium and phosphorus can result in a dangerous condition called tetany. Too much phosphorus— a danger posed by infant formulas containing cow's milk, which contains more phosphorus than calcium—can lower the child's store of calcium, and this serious neuromuscular disease can ensue. The child may be besieged by wild, quick nerve spasms that actually lock his or her muscles.[42] Again, we reiterate that balance between calcium and phosphorus is of the utmost importance. For example, a child suffering from low phosphorus levels may be treated for the resulting rickets with phosphorus, but then develop tetany because there is too much phosphorus and not enough calcium in his or her system. Children with malfunctioning parathyroids can also develop tetany, again because the calcium and phosphorus levels are not in balance. The levels of vitamin

D come into play here—either too much or too little can influence the delicate calcium/phosphorus balance. An infant's tiny kidneys do not have the same resources as an adult's for maintaining mineral balances, so if you must feed your child formulas containing cow's milk, try to do the work for his or her little kidneys by diluting the milk with a calcium supplement like calcium lactate.[43]

Too much phosphorus can cause a problem for adults in the guise of liver cirrhosis. Here again, lecithin plays an important role. It is this phosphorus-based emulsifier that keeps fatty deposits from clogging your liver and rigidifying large portions of it into useless scar tissue.[44]

Too *little* phosphorus—though rare—is responsible for a certain type of anemia that comes about through abnormalities of the cellular membranes. You may remember that one of phosphorus's many functions is to keep these walls stable. If there is not enough phosphorus, the walls of the red blood cells, among others, disintegrate. Their count in your blood is significantly lowered, and since they are responsible for carrying oxygen through the bloodstream, your supply is limited.[45]

All the cells in your body depend on phosphorus to keep their walls structurally sound, so of course a deficiency affects your white blood cells, too. Thus, if there is not enough phosphorus in your system, your immunity to bacteria and viruses may be lowered.[46] This includes, of course, your susceptibility to virally caused cancers as well as to the common cold.

Tests have demonstrated that for some reason a cell that has been invaded by cancer loses its phosphorus more readily than a normal cell. These findings have far-reaching implications for the potentiality of phosphorus as a cancer preventative.[47]

An interesting footnote to the phosphorus story: many of the pesticides sprayed on the plants we eat, and on the plants that livestock animals eat, contain arsenic compounds. Curiously enough, the structure of a molecule of arsenic is so similar to the structure of a molecule of phosphorus that your body can actually mistake one for another. Thus, if your intake of pesticides is large (and they are most heavily concentrated in animal foods like meat and dairy products), your body could make the possibly deadly mistake of substituting arsenic in functions for which it really needs phosphorus.[48] This odd but useful fact is yet another good reason to eat foods grown without chemicals whenever you can.

A Practical Guide to Using Phosphorus

Luckily, phosphorus is readily available to us in foods—perhaps in excess. Yet the important balance that must be maintained between calcium and other nutrients, including its many antagonists, can keep our bodies from using it properly. This section will help you learn how to get the most phosphorus from the foods you eat, how to keep it in balance with calcium, and how to avoid impeding your absorption of it.

So many foods provide you with phosphorus that it is actually difficult to avoid getting enough, no matter what you eat. Protein foods like meat, poultry, fish, eggs, dairy products, whole grains, nuts, and seeds supply phosphorus in abundance. So many processed foods contain phosphate additives that you can actually get too much. The important thing to remember is that your phosphorus intake must be balanced with calcium.

Vitamin D is important to your body's ability to absorb and utilize both phosphorus and calcium. So sunshine, milk, yeast, wheat germ, and lecithin can actually raise your phosphorus levels; again, we emphasize that you must make sure you are getting adequate calcium (and magnesium) to make the delicate interrelationships of the bone-building minerals most efficient within your body.

Vegetables that contain phosphorus include legumes, whole grains, celery, carrots, cauliflower, string beans, cucumbers, chard, cabbage, and pumpkins. Fruits also contain a healthy supply of your body's factotum.

Those who have a problem with their weight may wish to emphasize lecithin-rich foods like eggs and liver, which can help mobilize the fats in your bloodstream. The same approach can be useful if you suffer from atherosclerosis or liver cirrhosis. (Eggs have received a lot of bad press in the recent wave of "cholesterolphobia"; however, we reiterate that there is nothing to fear from one of nature's most perfect foods. The point to be made concerning cholesterol is that it is the *quality* of the fats in your diet that is important.)

As far as phosphorus intake goes, the point to be made is this: if you eat whole, natural foods, with attention to getting enough *calcium,* you will not have to worry about phosphorus deficiency, nor will you be plagued by the more common problem of mineral imbalance. If you eat a diet heavy in refined and processed foods, you will have to worry— about getting an *excess* of phosphorus and seriously jeopardizing its precarious balance with calcium and magnesium.

THE PARTNERS OF PHOSPHORUS

You need roughly twice as much calcium as you do phosphorus, and about the same amount of magnesium in your foods as phosphorus.[49] These two minerals share an extremely important relationship with your body's "jack-of-all-trades," because together the three help build your bones and keep them strong.[50] As we've already mentioned, it is important to get vitamin D (through sunlight—far superior to the synthetic variety) to help your body absorb and utilize its bone-builders properly.[51-56] Fats supplied in the form of oil or cream along with your phosphorus-rich foods will help your body use the mineral even more efficiently.

THE ANTAGONISTS OF PHOSPHORUS

The following conditions can inhibit or impede your body's absorption and/or utilization of phosphorus: too much iron in your cookware or your diet; aluminum deposits from your deodorant, antacid, or cookware; vitamin E deficiency; diuretics; alcohol; coffee, tea, or cola; stress; X rays, thyroid medication, cortisone, and aspirin; any other drug; too little vitamin D, or too much; too little calcium, or too much; too much sugar; too much protein; diabetes; starvation; and excess exercise.

Whew! Phosphorus has so many enemies that one wonders how anyone could ever suffer from an excess. Let's take them one by one. A surplus of iron binds phosphorus into phosphates that your body treats as waste products and discards in the feces.[57] The same thing happens when there is aluminum in your system, which can come from aluminum cookware, baking powder, deodorants, and antacids. A special word here regarding antacids: because of their destructive effect on hydrochloric acid, which your stomach needs to digest its food, they can obstruct your stomach's ability to absorb calcium. Too little calcium can adversely affect your phosphorus levels, as you already know. By the same token, excessive use of antacids can also keep your stomach from absorbing phosphorus. A diet of wholesome natural foods can give you plenty of these nutrients and may also end your antacid habit.

Another antagonist of phosphorus, ironically, is calcium, either too little or too much. Anything but the proper amount (the ratio of calcium to phosphorus should be two to one) will result in an imbalance. Be especially aware of this problem if you are in the habit of taking bone meal or calcium supplements without the magnesium and natural vitamin D necessary for your body to utilize the calcium properly. Vitamin E deficiency can also result in a loss of phosphorus in the urine.[58] So can diuretics—and this category is not limited to prescribed diuretics; it also includes the most common diuretic substances like coffee, tea, and cola drinks. Drinking alcohol causes you to lose great quantities of magnesium, which must be present for you to use the phosphorus in your foods. So the phosphorus is lost as well. Stress—physical or emotional— speeds up your metabolism, which means that your body is using all of the nutrients you supply at a greater-than-normal rate. Illness or immobilization especially cause large losses of phosphorus, along with its partner calcium.[59, 60] X rays, thyroid medication, cortisone, and aspirin, among other drugs, are significant stress producers that can cause phosphorus losses.[61-63] Be especially aware of the combined effects of immobilization (confinement to a wheelchair, bed, or even a cast) and taking drugs—the two are devastating to your phosphorus/calcium levels.[64]

The right amount of vitamin D must be present if you are to use phosphorus most efficiently. But too much vitamin D can be just as detrimental to your phosphorus supply as too little. Excess synthetic vitamin D, in particular, causes you to excrete both phosphorus and calcium in your urine. Since they try to keep your mineral levels in balance, the kidneys react to too little calcium in your body by discarding valuable phosphorus as a waste product.[65, 66] At this point it seems redundant, but once again we hammer home just how important it is to balance the bone-builders.

Some people are naturally prone to phosphorus deficiency: those who do not have the proper enzymes to use the mineral, for example, and pregnant women, who are not only under physical stress, but also are donating some of their phosphorus supplies to their unborn children. Alcoholics or barbiturate abusers are begging for all sorts of nutritional problems, including a phosphorus deficiency. If you eat a lot of sugar, you are also asking for problems, one being that you will lose large amounts of phosphorus.[67] A high-protein diet also results in phosphorus deficiency. For the diabetic, acidosis may cause the kidneys to discard phosphorus in order to maintain the proper alkalinity of the blood. This next phosphorus antagonist seems obvious: starvation. Yet in our era of crash dieting and anorexia nervosa, perhaps it is not too much to say that starvation causes a deficiency in phosphorus (except in the phospholipids), as well as in every other nutrient.[68]

Some physical conditions cause your body to hang on to phosphorus, and this can cause mineral imbalances. Among these are nephritis, in which your kidneys are too inflamed to filter out nutrients through the urine, or to reabsorb them back into the bloodstream; and some bone disorders, in which your body tries to keep its phosphorus on purpose. Parathyroid or adrenal cortex glands that are not up to par is another condition under which your body will not be able to excrete excess phosphorus properly.[69]

WHAT ARE THE SIGNS OF PHOSPHORUS DEFICIENCY?

A phosphorus deficiency by itself is uncommon. Usually a phosphorus deficiency arrives hand in hand with a calcium deficiency—the two are loyal partners. So their symptoms are interrelated; in fact, almost identical. Here they are: decreased appetite, weight loss, or, paradoxically, overweight; fatigue; irregular breathing; ragged nerves;[70] anemia; and increased susceptibility to infections.[71, 72] As the double deficiency develops, you might notice aching bones, muscular weakness, and a real effort in breathing. However, such severe phosphorus deficiency is even more uncommon than a mild one, which is quite rare.

HOW MUCH PHOSPHORUS DO YOU NEED?

The government recommends the following amounts of phosphorus, depending on your age, on a daily basis:

Infants up to 5 months	240 milligrams
5 months to 1 year	400 milligrams
Children from 1 to 10	800 milligrams
Ages 11 to 18	1200 milligrams
Over 18	800 milligrams
Pregnant and lactating women	1200 milligrams

With phosphorus, the point of concern is not so much deficiency as it is excessive intake. Too much phosphorus is not known to be poisonous, but it definitely produces the adverse effect of calcium deficiency. The Food and Nutrition Board of the National Research Council warns that most of us get far too much phosphorus (much of it added to refined food in the form of phosphates) and not enough calcium. Two hormones, calcitonin and parathormone, try to keep your calcium/phosphorus levels in balance, but you can help them out at a basic level by not overloading your system with phosphorus in the first place.

If you have a baby and do not breast-feed it, be sure to supplement the formula you give him or her with calcium lactate. If you can breast-feed your baby, consider yourself and your child lucky—mother's milk contains phosphorus and calcium in just the right ratio. If you are a teenager or an adult who does not drink a quart or two of milk (or other dairy products) daily, a calcium supplement is a good idea. Only under the rarest of conditions would you take phosphorus supplements.

Summary

Phosphorus is probably the only element in your body that glows in the dark. It is this unique quality that gives it its name, yet its abundance of other qualities give it a place of prime importance in your body, in terms of the number of jobs it performs.

Phosphorus works in your body as an integral component of phosphorus/fat compounds called phospholipids. It is also an important part of your genetic materials, RNA and DNA. Phosphorus-rich compounds carry nutrients to your cells, as well as help all your digestive fluids break the foods you eat into body-building elements. Phosphorus even helps maintain your bodily fluids at the right pH.

Phosphorus has intertwining relationships with calcium, magnesium, sodium, potassium, iron, hydrogen, zinc, and manganese. It is essential if your body is to use its B vitamins properly, and the valuable fat-soluble vitamins, too. It also works with the twenty-three amino acids your body uses to make proteins. And one of its most important functions involves its working relationship with the power-plant enzyme ATP.

If you could somehow expose your inner body and stand in front of a mirror at the same time, you would see phosphorus shining as it worked in your bones and teeth, collagen, nerves, muscles, metabolic and cellular systems, brain, liver, and digestive and circulatory systems. You would even see it in your eyes.

Phosphorus deficiency is rare. An imbalance with its partner calcium is far more common, and causes serious problems: bone and tooth disorders, cramps and aching muscles, bursitis, calcium deposits on soft tissues, collagen disease, heart disease, gallstones, tetany, liver cirrhosis, anemia, and increased susceptibility to viruses and cancer.

Phosphorus is available to you in nearly every food you eat. In fact, if you eat a lot of refined foods, you are in danger of getting too much of it. The important thing is to remember to get enough of its partners, too, which can be somewhat more challenging. Plenty of sunshine and lots of calcium and magnesium (in the proper amounts: twice as much calcium as phosphorus, and roughly the same amount of magnesium as phosphorus) are the keys to balancing phosphorus for your best health. Avoid the antagonists of phosphorus, which constitute too great a list to recall here! The greatest antagonist of phosphorus's multitude of functions is *mineral imbalance,* as we've said again and again. Bone up on the information in the chapters about calcium and magnesium, get your nutritional act together, and enjoy the years and years of excellent health that the perfect balance of minerals (along with all the other nutrients) can bring.

Potassium: Sodium's Partner

What Is Potassium?

Even where poor farming practices such as the use of chemical fertilizers have leached most minerals out of the soil, there is one that remains abundant. Potassium is present in chemical fertilizer;[1] it is present in the soil; and it is available in most growing plants. Its prevalence in our food sources should make it an easy mineral to get enough of.

Yet many people don't consume as much potassium as their bodies require.

Why should a mineral so abundant in nature—even where the soil has been tampered with—be in short supply in our bodies?

First of all, because we use quite a bit of it. Not nearly as much as we use of calcium, by far the most predominant mineral in the body, or of phosphorus, the number-two mineral; these are the mortar of which our bones are built, and so are present in large quantities to keep us standing upright. But potassium runs a close third: normally, our body contains about 300 grams—nine ounces—of potassium; about 5 percent of our total mineral weight.[2, 3]

Too many of us carry less than this. The reason is familiar. Nature affords us an abundance of whole, unrefined foods. Even our commercial farmers supply good, potassium-rich fruits and vegetables. But instead of enjoying these foods close to their natural state, many of us opt for the so-called convenience of refined, processed foods. Stripped of most vitamins and minerals, processed foods can't meet our nutritional requirements. Potassium is one of the missing minerals.

Food processing poses another problem in terms of our body's potassium needs. Not only does it discard the potassium in nature's original package; it also increases the body's potassium requirements. This is because, by adding salt to foods already depleted of potassium, it throws off the crucial balance between sodium and potassium in the body. These two minerals work together: if you consume too much of one, you will need more of the other to balance it.

Our ancestors, unless they lived near the ocean, had relatively few sources of salt. While potassium is prevalent in plants, sodium is relatively scarce on the land. So, just as animals still do today, early humans might have had to walk for miles to find a "salt lick," a natural source of sodium that could balance all the potassium they consumed by eating a diet consisting mostly of green leaves and fruit. We know that animals that eat grass and leaves may take in twenty times as much potassium as sodium. No wonder they, like us, evolved to enjoy the taste of the occasional salty food they might encounter! Without that salt craving, we would never have eaten enough sodium to balance the huge amount of potassium nature offers.[4]

But now that industrial food processing and long-established trading patterns have made salt readily available in large quantities whenever we want it, we are paying a high price for the wisdom nature taught us over long eons of potassium abundance and sodium scarcity: we eat so much salt, our problem is getting enough potassium. If we don't consume these two minerals in about equal proportions, our bodies have to find ways to compensate.

This isn't easy. Because of the conditions under which we evolved, most of our sodium/potassium balancing mechanisms are designed to *excrete* the expected excess of potassium and *retain* presumably scarce sodium.

BALANCING MECHANISMS

Potassium may be excreted both through the kidneys and through the sweat glands, which have been likened to "little kidneys."[5] Generally, in order to keep the body's potassium level constant, unless our stores are depleted, we excrete about as much potassium as we consume. When we eat potassium-rich foods, their potassium is absorbed, along with most other nutrients, through the walls of the intestines, which release it into the bloodstream for fast delivery into the cells. If too much accumulates in the blood, or the buildup is too rapid— as measured by the kidneys, the blood's filter—production of the hormone aldosterone is stimulated in the cortex of the adrenal gland. Aldosterone, in turn, acts on the kidneys, ordering them to excrete potassium faster than usual.[6] At the same time, the aldosterone, which also helps regulate sodium metabolism, induces the kidneys to retain sodium, in an effort to maintain the crucial balance between these two minerals.[7]

Now let's take a look at exactly how potassium and sodium function in tandem.

THE SODIUM/POTASSIUM PUMP

In every cell in your body, a mechanism called the sodium/potassium pump helps carry nutrients into the cells and waste products out.[8] Here is how it works. The cells expend a great deal of energy almost constantly pumping their contents to keep most potassium inside the cell and most sodium outside it, in the intercellular fluid. When sodium leaks in, it is pumped out. When potassium leaks out, it is pumped back in. If not for the sodium/potassium pump, there would be equal amounts of sodium and potassium ions both inside and outside the cell; water containing both minerals would diffuse through the pores of the cell walls until sodium- and potassium-containing solutions were thoroughly mixed. In fact, this is what happens when a cell dies, and its sodium/potassium pump is no longer working.[9]

Sodium and potassium ions are electrically charged particles. Their separation in different concentrations inside and outside the cell causes the cell membrane to become polarized: the sodium solution outside the cell is positively charged relative to the more negatively charged potassium solution inside the cell. This electrical polarization helps nutrients to flow into the cell and waste products to be eliminated into the surrounding fluid, eventually to find their way into the bloodstream for elimination from the body.[10]

There are two factors that prevent sodium from diffusing into the cell from outside, attracted by the negative charge inside the cell and by the lower concentration of sodium there: the sodium/potassium pump, and the fact that the cell membrane's pores do not readily admit sodium. When a cell dies, sodium slowly seeps in; some potassium diffuses out; the electrical polarization of the membrane diminishes to zero; and the flow of nutrients in and wastes out ceases.[11, 12] And something else happens. When the sodium/potassium pump stops working, more particles enter the cell than leave it. Water flows in with them, since water tends to diffuse across a membrane toward the side where particles are most concentrated, seeking equilibrium.[13]

A shortage of potassium inside a living cell can cause a similar, dangerous situation. If potassium is not concentrated enough inside the cell, the sodium/potassium pump is hard pressed to keep out enough sodium. Along with the sodium comes too much water, and the cell becomes waterlogged—possibly to the point of bursting. This, in turn, causes a drop in blood pressure as water seeps from the bloodstream into the interstices between cells to replace the water that has disappeared into the cells.

POTASSIUM IN THE ENDOCRINE AND DIGESTIVE SYSTEMS

Without the sodium/potassium pump common to all cells, no other vital biochemical pumping actions could take place. For example, cells in the thyroid gland are specialized to actively collect iodide from the blood.[14] The sodium/potassium pump makes possible this iodine pump. Without it, we could not produce thyroid hormones, which require concentrated iodide. Thyroid hormones help regulate glucose metabolism.

Similarly, the intestines actively pump glucose through their walls and into the bloodstream, for quick energy utilization.[15] The action of this pump, too, depends on the polarization created by the sodium/-potassium pump.

POTASSIUM AND pH

The sodium/potassium balance plays a part in another vital regulatory mechanism. This mineral duo is used by the body to regulate the acidity of the various body fluids. Some of these—such as stomach and scalp secretions and urine—must be kept acid. Others—saliva, intestinal secretions, and blood—must stay slightly alkaline. If the urine should become too alkaline, the result can be kidney stones, bladder stones, or even death. If the blood becomes too acid, as can happen in diabetes, depressed nerve functioning and dehydration can lead to coma.

Since the pH of these fluids is so important, the body has several mechanisms for controlling it. The key to one of these is the potassium/-sodium partnership.[16] The kidneys excrete sodium when the body is too alkaline; they excrete potassium when it is too acid.[17] Sometimes, the latter process can go too far. The acidosis—blood acidity—of diabetes is caused by the presence of too many acidic ketone bodies in the blood. In an effort to correct the blood's pH, the kidneys keep throwing off potassium. To do so, they must release water, too. Hence, potassium deficiency and dehydration—the basic causes of diabetic coma.[18-20]

One good argument for getting plenty of potassium in your diet is the danger of overalkalinity. Diabetics are at risk of overalkaline urine when they over-excrete potassium.[21] If you or anyone in your family has ever had kidney stones, it is especially important for you to know that taking in extra potassium can help protect you against the formation of future stones by increasing urine acidity.[22]

HOW YOUR MUSCLES USE POTASSIUM

You couldn't move a muscle without potassium. To do prolonged work, the muscles store extra energy in the form of a starch called glycogen. Glycogen is produced in the liver with the help of potassium.[23]

The proteins that make up much of the substance of your muscles also could not be formed without potassium.

And finally, in order to be able to contract, the muscles must receive a message from the nerves. This message can be relayed up and down the length of the muscle cells because each cell membrane is polarized—due to the differential concentration of potassium and sodium.[24] The message—in the form of a brief shower of positive calcium ions—briefly depolarizes the membrane of the muscle cell at the point where it arrives. Immediately, this depolarization is passed along the cell membrane to the adjacent section, and then the next, so the message to contract is passed along the length of the muscle fiber.

POTASSIUM AND YOUR NERVES

The transmission of messages along the length of nerve fibers—whether they are located in your brain, your spine, or your peripheral nervous system—works in a similar way. Many people, when they try to picture the way nerves carry messages, visualize water flowing through plumbing pipes, or electrons through electrical wires. These aren't the right analogies. It might be better to imagine a row of closely lined-up synchronized swimmers—as in a Busby Berkeley musical—who, one at a time, gracefully stroke in such a way that their bodies rotate 360 degrees in the water without ever changing position or swimming forward or backward. Just as one swimmer returns to her starting orientation, the next one strokes and turns. From a distance, a turning impulse appears to have rippled down the line; yet no swimmer has actually moved from her place. In our analogy, the turning of the first swimmer represents a brief pause in the action of the sodium/-potassium pump at one end of the nerve. For a split second, sodium enters the cell freely at that point and potassium exits, causing that portion of the cell membrane's polarity to drop and the electrical charge outside the cell membrane to reverse to negative—just as, to return to the swimming pool, we see the first swimmer's back instead of her face for a moment. This negative charge halts the sodium/potassium pump in the next tiny segment of the cell just as the first segment's pumping action—and polarity—returns to normal. The message—in the form of a ripple of reversed charge along the outside of the cell membrane—passes rapidly down the length of the nerve cell without any lengthwise movement of the cell or its contents.[25]

You can infer from the importance of the action of potassium and sodium in nerve impulse transmission how potassium depletion can cause depressed functioning of the nervous system.

Lack of potassium can affect our brain cells through yet another mechanism. The brain consumes a surprisingly large portion of the body's energy stores in the form of glucose. For glucose to be converted to energy, it must be oxidized. Two minerals work together to transport the necessary oxygen to the sites where it is needed: phosphorus and potassium.[26] Since the brain controls almost all life functions and activities directly or indirectly, the necessity of potassium cannot be overstated. Without potassium in the communication process and in helping supply energy to the brain, your brain's functioning would grind to a halt.

Potassium, then, works in tandem with sodium in the metabolism of each cell; in specialized pumps in the endocrine and digestive systems; in transmitting messages through the nervous system and along the muscle fibers; and in maintaining the pH of the circulatory, urinary, and digestive systems. And it works with phosphorus to help provide energy for the brain. That leaves very few systems that are unaffected by this important mineral.

Who Needs Potassium?

Everyone, therefore, needs potassium, and in healthy quantities. But some conditions demand extra. These include colic in babies; muscle cramps or weak muscles in children or adults; the blood sugar disorders diabetes and hypoglycemia; and cases of high blood pressure, heart disease, and stress.

In the case of colic, a tiny dose of potassium can often save parents long, sleepless nights and babies months of misery. There are reports of as little as a gram of potassium in the form of an injection quickly solving the problem of colic.[27] You have already seen the reason why: potassium activates the "glucose pump" in our intestinal walls. If a tiny baby's system doesn't deliver enough potassium, digestion doesn't quite work. This is a common cause of colic. A small amount may be all that is needed to prime the glucose pump.

Did you ever wake up in the night with a cramp in the leg— particularly after an afternoon of jogging or other strenuous exercise? Extra potassium in your diet may help prevent this problem, and may also help increase your energy levels and muscle tone, because of the importance of potassium in efficient use of your muscles.

While potassium can be a boon to athletes, it can save the lives of older people. Potassium deficiency can cause cramps in such vital muscles as those that line the digestive tract.[28-30] Normally, the churning and pushing of these muscles moves foods along the digestive tract. Constipation and painful gas are only the immediate symptoms of inefficient peristaltic action. Paralysis of the digestive tract inhibits digestion of all nutrients, and can lead both to serious undernutrition and severe and agonizing elimination problems.

When potassium deficiency is the cause of muscle cramps, whether of the extremities or of the internal muscles, the cure is simple, inexpensive, and enjoyable: eat more fresh fruits and vegetables. Even very weak or partially paralyzed muscles have responded quickly to increases in potassium intake.[31]

And don't forget: the heart is also a muscle. If potassium deficiency causes this muscle to cramp, the result can be a heart attack.[32-35] It is foolish to take that risk, when prevention is a simple matter of eating correctly. Some researchers have speculated that potassium deficiency may explain the deteriorated heart tissue observed in autopsies of heart attack victims.[36-44] We do know that slow and irregular heartbeats have been corrected by increased potassium intake.[45] This expedient may also help lower blood pressure, another risk factor in heart disease.[46-51] And, together with magnesium, adequate potassium can help prevent the formation of blood clots that can threaten heart, lungs, and brain alike.[52]

A diet high in potassium, together with potassium chloride supplements, can help save your life if you are a diabetic. You have seen how acidosis can lead to potassium depletion, coma, and even death.[53, 54] Besides protecting your nervous system from this shock, supplemental potassium can help prevent heart disease and high blood pressure. Diabetics are at high risk for these problems because every time they take insulin, their blood sugar levels plummet while their blood pressure and pulse rates increase. Two to five grams of potassium chloride just before—or even after—each insulin injection can help minimize these effects, and may also help prevent insulin shock.[55-57] Because it is so important in glucose metabolism, speeding absorption through the intestines and, more important for the diabetic, aiding glycogen formation and storage in the liver and muscles and glucose utilization by the brain, potassium is the perfect complement to insulin therapy.[58]

Even if you are not diabetic, you may find potassium helpful in regulating your blood sugar levels. Much has been said about chromium and hypoglycemia, but few people are aware that potassium may help maintain the blood sugar levels of hypoglycemics. Next time you're tempted by the three o'clock doldrums to reach for a candy bar or a cup of coffee, try instead taking 2 to 5 grams of potassium chloride with a glass of water. Regular potassium supplements will leave you on a much more even keel than the emotional roller coaster caused by sugar or caffeine.[59]

So whether you are trying to soothe a colicky infant, cure a chronically constipated senior citizen, improve the prowess of an athletic adolescent, overcome the irritability and apathy of hypoglycemia, or prevent the complications of diabetes and heart disease, extra potassium is the best bet for you and your whole family.

A Practical Guide to Using Potassium

Adding potassium to your diet is easy. Green leafy vegetables are an excellent source—but be sure not to soak them in water or boil them, since potassium is very water soluble. Rinse them quickly, or steam them if they need cooking, to retain the most nutrients—and even when you steam, save the mineral-rich cooking water for soup stock. High-potassium fruits include bananas, cantaloupe, avocados, dates, prunes, dried apricots, and raisins. Be careful with dried fruits, though —eating too much, too fast, can give you a sugar overdose.

Plant protein foods are also generally good sources of potassium. Whole wheat flour, wheat germ, and other whole grains are good sources, as are soybeans, kidney beans, and most legumes, as well as nuts and seeds.

Not quite as high in potassium as plant sources are the animal proteins—meat, fish, and dairy products. Fish and other seafood are good sources. Of these, swordfish has about the highest potassium content. But again, be careful: as with dried fruits, overdoing animal protein can be counterproductive and can end up depleting potassium stores.

HOW MUCH POTASSIUM DO YOU NEED?

If you eat correctly, you needn't worry about your potassium intake. You will be consuming easily the 2 to 4 grams you need each day to replace the amount lost in your urine.[60] However, eating correctly means limiting your salt intake. Processed foods, a heavy hand with the salt shaker, or even reliance on antacids, can cause you to excrete as much as nine times the normal amount of potassium.[61] Illnesses, medicines, stress, or other conditions that affect potassium metabolism can also cause deficiencies. In such cases, therapeutic doses range from 5 to 20 grams daily.

POTASSIUM'S ANTAGONISTS

A high-sodium diet is not the only condition that can disrupt your sodium/potassium balance. Too much sugar or other refined carbohydrates can cause potassium loss, too. Even high-protein diets,[62-64] often prescribed for hypoglycemics, have been implicated. Medicines such as diuretics, aspirin, cortisone, and antibiotics also increase potassium requirements, as do prolonged diarrhea and vomiting, illness, or any stress. If you can't avoid one or more of these conditions, be sure to add extra potassium to your diet.[65]

Your doctor may not have prescribed diuretics, but you may be taking one or more anyway without realizing it. Coffee, tea, cola, and alcohol are all strong diuretics. If you drink much of any of them, your kidneys cannot help discarding quite a bit of potassium with the extra urine you pass. Alcohol poses a double threat to your potassium stores: not only is it a diuretic, but it also causes magnesium deficiency, another factor implicated in potassium losses.[66]

Illness and all forms of stress deplete your body's potassium stores, just as they do those of other nutrients. When sickness results in diarrhea or vomiting, potassium from gastric and intestinal secretions is lost.[67] Liver disease or kidney damage leave people particularly likely to suffer from potassium depletion, since these organs are so important in potassium metabolism.[68, 69] But any illness—indeed, any stress—increases aldosterone production. Stress, therefore, causes your kidneys to save sodium and lose potassium. This problem is exacerbated when hospitalized victims of serious accidents or surgery patients—surely examples of people under severe stress—are given high-sodium intravenous solutions, since sodium accelerates potassium losses still further.[70] The answer in this case is simply the addition of potassium dihydrogen phosphate to the IV mix.[71]

Aspirin and cortisone are two commonly used drugs that lower potassium levels. Arthritics—who often take both—are at double risk. Both drugs can have a side effect contrary to their intended purpose.

Because they increase the body's retention of sodium, they can attract water to the joints—and thereby increase the pain of arthritis instead of alleviating it. To help prevent swollen, watery joints, it's not a bad idea for arthritics who take these drugs to supplement the diet with 1 to 9 grams of potassium daily.

Antibiotics, prednisone, and digitalis—all very commonly prescribed drugs—can lower potassium levels,[72] especially when taken over long periods of time. Again, if you must take any of these potent drugs, be sure to get enough potassium in your diet, and consult your doctor about supplements.

SYMPTOMS OF POTASSIUM DEFICIENCY

Because potassium is so ubiquitous in the body, deficiency results in a wide range of symptoms.

Protein, remember, cannot be produced without potassium, so if you find injuries take a long time to heal, or your skin and other tissues seem "worn out," you may be suffering from potassium deficiency. If you know a child who seems to be growing too slowly, the cause may be the same: an inability to produce enough protein resulting from potassium deficiency.[73]

Has your doctor prescribed a low-salt diet or diuretic for edema (water-swollen tissues)? Because sodium and potassium work together, an increase in potassium intake might be as effective. If you're pregnant, it could also be safer: a low-salt diet during pregnancy can reduce blood pressure too much, carrying the risk of eclampsia.

Skin and hair problems can be among the first signs that you need more potassium. In teens, acne can signal overindulgence in sugary junk foods that increase potassium needs. In adults, dry skin may be your first clue to potassium deficiency.[74] Animal studies indicate that thinning hair, too, may result from potassium deprivation.[75] If you suffer from any of these symptoms, check your diet. Do you eat a variety of fresh fruits and green leafy vegetables, whole grains and other plant proteins every day? If not, you know what to do.

Don't forget potassium's importance to the functioning of the nervous system. Lethargy and insomnia are typical early signs of lack of potassium. If they are not remedied, poor reflexes and dysfunction of the whole neuromuscular system may be down the road.[76] Colicky babies, too, can end up with emotional and nervous problems. Besides sometimes being caused by potassium shortage, colic itself is a stress that can deplete any remaining potassium stores.

Malfunctioning muscles can be a reminder at least to carry dried apricots, dates, seeds, and nuts with you as a handy pick-me-up. Especially if you're already getting enough exercise, weakness, cramps, or flabby muscles are indications you may be neglecting your potassium needs.[77, 78] It's time to change your eating habits long before cramps progress to partial paralysis,[79, 80] which can happen in severe cases of potassium deficiency.[86, 87] Internal organs can be damaged or permanently scarred from lack of potassium.[81-83]

If it's the muscles of the digestive tract that are slowing you down with intestinal spasms or severe constipation,[84] try adding potassium-rich foods like whole grains, legumes, prunes, and other dried fruits to your diet, perhaps along with a potassium supplement if your doctor agrees, instead of using commercial laxatives. These foods combine the biochemical stimulation of potassium with the physical stimulation of fiber, and should improve your peristaltic action promptly. If the deficiency becomes acute, paralysis of the intestinal muscles is possible, and very serious.[85, 86]

Then there are the already mentioned problems that potassium deficiency causes by allowing the urine to become too alkaline. In a relatively alkaline medium, calcium and phosphorus bind together to form kidney or bladder stones instead of floating freely as they do in normally acid urine.[87-89] If you want to stop producing stones, supplement your diet with potassium, because prolonged deficiency can result in paralysis of the urinary tract (urethra),[90-91] swelling, lesions, and scarring of the kidneys,[92] and ultimately, complete dysfunction of the urinary system.[93]

To sum up, you should see your doctor for tests of your potassium levels if any of the following signs of potassium deficiency apply to you: loss of the ability to maintain and repair tissues, or in children, slow growth; swollen tissues and joints; skin disorders; nervous or emotional problems; soft, flabby, or cramped muscles; intestinal spasms or constipation; or urinary difficulties. A simple change in your diet may quickly solve what now appear to be intractable, long-term problems.

TOO MUCH POTASSIUM?

You probably need not fear getting too much potassium. Hyperkalemia, as excess potassium retention is called, is rare, because the body so easily throws off excess potassium in the urine. The only circumstances in which it has been noted are in cases of kidney damage, uremia (excess uric acid), Addison's disease, and, occasionally, in patients fed intravenous solutions containing too much potassium and in those with terminal conditions.[94] When it does occur, hyperkalemia can damage the heart and even cause death. Fortunately, an electrocardiogram can quickly detect this problem.[95]

POTASSIUM'S MINERAL PARTNERS

We have already seen how important the potassium/sodium partnership is for the most fundamental metabolic functions of each cell: intake of nutrients and excretion of waste. To keep these two minerals in harmonious balance, it is important to consume as much or more potassium than you do sodium each day. If you can't resist the salt shaker, at least fill yours with a half-sodium, half-potassium mixture (such as Morton Lite Salt). This will ensure that your heavy hand with the salt will not top the scale too far in favor of sodium.

Another mineral partner of potassium is magnesium. Merely adding magnesium to your diet can help you retain potassium and increase its levels in your body.[96, 97] But retaining magnesium itself can be tricky, since magnesium has another partner, calcium. The secret of making magnesium work for you is this: for every gram of magnesium you take, you need two grams of calcium, whether in your diet or in mineral supplements.[98, 99]

It may sound complicated, but don't bother getting out your calculator yet. The proportions you need are roughly those found in a good, varied diet of whole, natural foods; and supplements containing both calcium and magnesium in the right two-to-one proportion are readily available.

Summary

Potassium is one of nature's most bounteous elements, and farmers add to the bounty by fertilizing with potassium-rich substances. But unfortunately our modern refining and processing methods rob most of our foods of potassium before they even reach our tables.

In our bodies, potassium is the third most prevalent mineral, following calcium and phosphorus. If you are healthy, your body contains about 300 grams of sodium's partner.

Together, sodium and potassium form an electrical pump that speeds nutrients into every cell of your body, and speeds wastes out. Thus they are vital to the functioning of all of your trillions of cells, as well as in maintaining the proper acid/alkaline balance of all your body fluids.

Potassium is particularly vital to the workings of your digestive and endocrine systems, your muscles, your brain, and your nerves. Obviously, we all need it (in delicate balance with sodium), but to those with muscle cramps, heart disease, or diabetes, additional potassium can be a real boon.

In general, vegetables, fruits, and other plant foods are far richer sources of potassium than animal foods. In fact, it is easy to obtain the

2 to 4 grams that you need daily by eating plenty of whole, unrefined, and fresh food, as long as you don't take too much salt. For therapeutic purposes, 5 to 20 grams daily may be recommended.

High-protein, high-sodium, or high-sugar diets all increase your need for potassium. Illnesses that involve diarrhea and vomiting, as well as use of common medications such as aspirin, cortisone, antibiotics, diuretics, prednisone, or digitalis, can spell disaster for your potassium stores. So can any stress. It is a good idea to take extra potassium supplements under these circumstances.

You may be suffering from a potassium deficiency if you have any of the following symptoms: "worn out" tissues, swelling, skin disorders, nervous and emotional problems, poorly toned muscles, digestive problems, or urinary difficulties. Check with your physician, who will prescribe a supplement if you are low in potassium. And eat lots of fruits and vegetables!

Few of us suffer from having too much potassium. For one thing, our kidneys are programmed to excrete any surplus. Yet under certain conditions, hyperkalemia can be a problem that poses a mortal but preventable danger, particularly to the heart.

Sodium and magnesium are potassium's two principal nutritional partners; phosphorus is a lesser third partner. Since magnesium depends on calcium for your body to absorb it properly, calcium comes into play as well. The best insurance for a healthy interrelationship of these minerals—not to mention the rest of the nutrients your body needs every day—is to eat a hearty balanced diet of whole, natural foods, with little sugar, salt, or processed products. Mineral supplements are also available. Awareness of your nutritional needs, and attention to them, is your guarantee of glowing, energetic health.

Micromight Selenium

What Is Selenium?

Scarce, powerful selenium, named for the mysterious goddess of the moon, Selene, is one of your body's most vital nutrients.[1] If you were to eat it as it exists in the earth, you would die. Yet as it comes to us transformed into one of the nutrients in our foods, it is necessary not just for our good health, but for life itself.[2-4]

Selenium is a water-soluble nonmetallic element that is found in many foods. Yet like so many of the other trace minerals, the amount of selenium in your food is dependent on the richness and health of the soil in which the food was grown. The rich, dark farmlands of South Dakota are rich in selenium, while those in Ohio are quite poor. Why the disparity? One large factor is the amount of old volcanic ash in the soil, which gives it a lot of selenium. In fact, the most selenium-rich farmlands were probably the sites of prehistoric volcanic eruptions.[5]

In any case, one reason that selenium is so scarce a nutrient is that over the years it has been depleted from our soils—by loss of topsoil, by overplanting, and by modern chemical farming methods. Another reason it is scarce is that it is literally processed out of refined foods. Its scarcity in our soils and foods is reflected by its scarcity in our bodies.

How Does Selenium Work?

Selenium's primary function in your body is as an antioxidant, important in protecting your trillions of cells from destruction by oxygen. In fact, it is absorbed by every cell except those of your fatty tissues. It plays its vital role mainly through the enzyme system.

The enzymes in tiny particles of your cellular fluid (called mitochondria) make an energy chain of fast-moving electrons, on which your muscles depend for stamina and general strength. In particular, two of these energy-producing enzymes are dependent on selenium to function properly. One is called coenzyme Q: low levels of selenium result in a deficiency of this enzyme, without which there is a break in the "energy chain." The name of the other enzyme that depends so much on selenium is glutathione peroxidase, which contains four atoms of selenium in each molecule.[6]

Why is glutathione peroxidase so important? It protects you from dangerous elements called "free radicals" (which you will remember from our discussion of another antioxidant, vitamin E) that damage or destroy cells by oxidation. And what is oxidation? Simply put, it is a chemical reaction in which oxygen combines with another substance, steals an electron, and "burns up" the substance, reducing it to water and carbon dioxide. A chain reaction may ensue, as each broken cell produces another free radical. That is what happens to your cells when a free radical—a broken fragment of a molecule, highly activated because of an abnormal imbalance in its atomic electrons—attacks.

Where do free radicals come from? They can be formed by radiation; toxic substances like chemicals, drugs, pollutants, or overheated oils; or even by rancid vitamins A, D, and E. In addition, free radicals can be produced within your cells when they contain either too much or too little oxygen.

Another source of free radicals of more concern to us in our discussion of selenium is accidents within the chain of energy-producing enzymes in the mitochondria. This is where coenzyme Q and glutathione peroxidase come back into the picture.

Along the energy chain, a whole series of special enzymes, coenzyme Q included, pass along electrons one at a time. If anything goes amiss within these lightning-fast chemical reactions, a free radical—that is, a particle with an uneven number of electrons—can go sparking off to oxidize anything it hits. Glutathione peroxidase exists to disintegrate these highly activated particles before they destroy your cells.[7]

If you do not have sufficient selenium in your body to produce and maintain both coenzyme Q and glutathione peroxidase, a vicious cycle of cell oxidation may be the result. If coenzyme Q is weak or missing from the energy chain, accidents in which a free radical spins off are much more likely to occur, for there is literally a missing link in the energy process. And if glutathione peroxidase is weak or missing because of a lack of selenium, it cannot deactivate the free radical, thus cannot prevent it from destroying your cells.

The results of free radical oxidation are vast: not only can it mean cellular death, it can mean DNA and RNA alteration or destruction; protein alteration (it welds them together into abnormal compounds that in the skin, for example, would cause a leathery appearance); it can destroy the gelatinous material (made of mucopolysaccharides) that glue your cells together and also lubricate your joints.[8] Similarly, it can damage the collagen and elastin that compose the basic structure of your bones, cartilage, ligaments, skin, eyes, and the tissue that supports your internal organs.[9] And finally, it can attack and destroy the fat-soluble vitamins A, D, E, and K.

Because of its role as an antioxidant, selenium is very important in preventing a wide variety of degenerative diseases, in protecting your immune system, and even in ridding your body of toxic metals.

Where Does Selenium Work?

Now that we have seen where selenium works on a microscopic level, let's take a look at the larger picture of this mighty trace mineral's activity. Selenium is at work in every cell of your body, but its functions are of special importance in the following places.

• *Heart.* One contributory factor in the development of cardiovascular disease is free radical oxidation in the blood vessels and the heart muscle itself. When a free radical attacks a muscle cell, the genetic material contained in the DNA of that cell can change. The result is an abnormal proliferation of cells that bond together to form plaque. These deranged cells may then begin to manufacture cholesterol, other fats, and collagen. In turn, the plaque attracts calcium deposits.[32] Soon the plaque has grown and is bulging into the artery, getting in the way of the blood that is trying to flow through. Blood pressure rises. The result? Atherosclerosis if the plaques are simply fatty; arteriosclerosis if they are also fibrous and calcified.

Heart disease may be the result of a diversity of conditions, yet the presence of adequate amounts of selenium can minimize the damage simply because it protects your cells from free radical oxidation.

Selenium protects you from high blood pressure in another way: it is necessary for the manufacture of the active, hormonelike substances called prostaglandins. A prostaglandin called prostaglandin A2 is vital in controlling your blood pressure.[10] Prostaglandin E2 helps keep your blood from clotting. Thus, selenium works to lessen your risk of strokes or heart attacks from clots or high blood pressure.

• *Red blood cells.* Along with vitamin E, selenium-based glutathione peroxidase protects the walls of your red blood cells.[11] A deficiency in either E or selenium can cause these cells to break down, resulting in a type of anemia that neither iron nor vitamin B_{12} can cure.

In another capacity, selenium is responsible for helping transferrin retrieve the iron from your broken hemoglobin when the red blood cells die—after 120 to 130 days.[12]

• *Fibroblasts.* Fibroblasts are cells that produce the collagen for your tissues and for the cells that make up the matrices of your bones and teeth.[13] Selenium protects the fibroblasts from oxidation.

• *Eyes.* Selenium is vital in protecting your eyes against cataracts. Peroxides resulting from cell destruction by oxidation are apt to damage the proteins in the lenses of your eyes, and the fats in the cell membranes.[14] The concentration of selenium in the eye lenses of people with cataracts is at a level six times less than in those of the same age without cataracts.[15]

• *Protein production.* Selenium is necessary for your body to produce protein compounds essential for proper maintenance and repair.[16] Damaged RNA and DNA caused by oxidation can mean defective protein compounds, which for a child can result in stunted growth or even the protein-deficiency disease kwashiorkor.

• *Immune system.* Selenium stimulates the immune system, offering protection against infection.[17] An important part of the immune system are scavenger cells called macrophages, which literally eat toxic particles, bacteria, and viruses.[18] They also produce interferon—the special coded protein substance that keeps viruses from multiplying.[19] Viruses—really foreign DNA or RNA molecules that invade the cells—cause the cells to reproduce the virus rather than normal RNA and DNA.[20] Selenium enters the picture in its role as protector of the macrophages' DNA, RNA, and membranes, and even more important by stimulating the production of coenzyme Q[21] and glutathione peroxidase, which protect both the macrophages and the interferon.

Selenium also protects vitamin A, another warrior against infection, from oxidation.[22-31]

While we are on the subject of where selenium works, we should also discuss where it is stored. Your greatest stores of selenium are to be found in your vital organs: the heart, liver, spleen, kidneys, and sex glands (particularly if you are a man).[32-36]

Who Needs Selenium?

While everyone needs selenium on an everyday basis, there are certain situations in which the human need for selenium may be increased, or in which additional selenium may be helpful in the treatment of a disease.

If you are a male, your selenium needs are greater than if you are female. If you suffer from heart disease or muscular disorders, additional selenium may help you. The same can be said if you suffer from cataracts, diabetes, cystic fibrosis, liver necrosis, iron deficiency anemia, joint problems, heavy metal poisoning, or cancer.

SELENIUM FOR MEN

Men need more selenium than women. Since the testicles hold large quantities of this mineral and a great deal of it is lost through the seminal fluid, the supply must be constantly maintained.[37] Selenium can help keep a man free of prostate problems since, as we mentioned earlier, it allows production of prostaglandins.[38] Two other aspects of the male need for selenium: adequate amounts may help prevent impotence and sterility;[39] selenium can protect the testicles from deterioration due to cadmium buildup.[40]

SELENIUM FOR A HEALTHY HEART

Heart disease patients may find a helper in selenium, too. Since it is vital to the cells' ability to protect themselves from free radical oxidation, selenium is necessary both in protecting the artery walls from plaque (as we discussed above), and in helping prevent further plaque formation.[41] The mineral has also been used with vitamin E to help relieve the pain of angina pectoris, which occurs because the tissues in and around the heart muscle are not receiving enough oxygen.[42] Another interesting connection between selenium and the heart is that a lack of selenium can cause or accelerate deterioration of the nerve fibers in the brain (Purkinje fibers) that tell the heart when to beat.[43, 44] Another weakening effect on the heart that a selenium deficiency has is related to free radical oxidation. If there is not enough coenzyme Q (which needs selenium) to keep the cells in the heart muscle from oxidizing, cells will be destroyed and the heartbeat will weaken.[45, 46] Your heart holds a large store of coenzyme Q—more than any other tissue in your body, in fact, if it is healthy—and for good reason.

Since selenium is vital to the immune system, it also plays a role in protecting your heart against bacteria- and virus-based diseases such as rheumatic heart disease, diphtheria myocarditis, bacterial endocarditis, and meningococcal carditis.[47]

The elasticity of the heart muscle is due in part to a healthy supply of glutathione peroxidase. The enzyme keeps the fats in the cell membranes from oxidation that could transform your healthy cells into tough, fibrous scar tissue.[48] Collagen, another ingredient in the recipe for a healthy heart, is made by fibroblasts, which need selenium for their synthesis.[49, 50]

Rx for a healthy heart: plenty of selenium in your daily diet. And if you already suffer from heart disease, consider the addition of selenium in supplements to possibly help prevent further degeneration.

SELENIUM FOR EYES

We have already stressed how vital selenium seems to be in the prevention of cataracts. The eyes are a literal repository of selenium: during an average life span of eighty-five years, the concentration of selenium in the lenses of the eyes multiplies four times. Yet, if you have cataracts, your selenium levels will show a *decrease*.[51] Certainly there are other contributing factors in the development of cataracts—diabetes, stress, and other nutritional deficiencies—yet research points to a shortage of antioxidants as a primary cause. Oxidation can destroy or damage the proteins in the lenses of the eye, and the invaluable cellular membrane fats. That is why selenium is so important in keeping your eyesight clear, and your eyes cataract-free.

SELENIUM FOR BLOOD SUGAR DISORDERS

Both diabetics and hypoglycemics have a need for increased selenium intake.[52] Why? Because the regulation of carbohydrate metabolism depends in part on glutathione peroxidase. For your cells to have the energy they need, glucose must be oxidized in the mitochondria. It is glutathione peroxidase that protects the organelles and coenzyme Q from free radical destruction, and thus keeps your cellular energy factories able to oxidize glucose. Another reason people with blood sugar disorders need plenty of selenium is that the production of insulin, which carries the glucose from the bloodstream to your cells, depends upon selenium and sulfur, among other elements.[53]

The beta cells of the pancreas manufacture insulin. But if your pancreas has been damaged by free radical oxidation, the beta cells can't make insulin properly. Also, if your pancreas is unhealthy or damaged, you can't make all the digestive enzymes you need to break down your foods into nutrients and glucose. Selenium helps protect your pancreas from the ravages of free radical oxidation. For diabetics and hypoglycemics, it may be able to help in terms of proper carbohydrate metabolism and pancreatic health.

SELENIUM FOR CYSTIC FIBROSIS

Cystic fibrosis is a condition characterized by a sticky mucus which clogs the lungs and digestive tract. At the same time, the pancreas is damaged—in some cases reduced to a dysfunctional mass of scar tissue. The cause of the disease, which usually attacks children, may be oxidation damage of the cell membranes of the pancreas.

Effective in some cases as a nontoxic natural therapy for cystic fibrosis is treatment with a combination of the antioxidants vitamin E and selenium. In fact, vitamin E alone has been used in treatment since 1956, when it was used in an experiment at the Johns Hopkins University School of Medicine. Even children who had suffered from cystic fibrosis for ten years or more showed noticeable improvement with vitamin E therapy. Later studies have shown that a combination of vitamin E, selenium, and manganese can be an even more powerful therapeutic tool.

SELENIUM FOR LIVER DISEASE

The liver, like the pancreas and indeed like all your major organs, is dependent on selenium to prevent free radical oxidation of its cells. Selenium has proved to be effective in treating liver necrosis (literally, liver death), caused by a deficiency of either selenium, vitamin E, or the amino acid cystine. In preventing the condition, selenium has shown itself 250,000 times more effective than cystine; 500 times more potent than vitamin E.[54] In addition, an adequate amount of selenium lightens the detoxification chores of the liver. Since it works in your immune system to clear out toxic debris, it is the liver's partner in ridding your body of waste products.

SELENIUM FOR ANEMIA

In an indirect way, selenium can keep you from developing iron-deficiency anemia, or even help you recover from it. It is needed in the production of transferrin, vital to the iron recycling process that takes place when old red blood cells die. Without enough transferrin, there may not be enough iron available to your new red blood cells, and anemia may be the result.

SELENIUM FOR JOINT DISEASE

Remember, selenium has a role in protecting the mucopolysaccharides that "oil" your joints. It also helps keep the collagen strong (through its function in the synthesis of fibroblasts) and protected from free radical oxidation. Thus, adequate intake of selenium can help prevent the development of rheumatoid arthritis, and in some cases has been used in slowing its progression.[55] In acute cases, 1,000 micrograms of selenium with at least 600 units of vitamin E has been effective in reducing the swelling and pain. The key lies in its antioxidant abilities, and in stepping up the production of glutathione peroxidase. It may be just as effective in treating osteoarthritis as well.[56]

SELENIUM FOR MUSCULAR DYSTROPHY

Muscular dystrophy, in which the muscles waste into paralysis, may be caused by selenium and vitamin E deficiencies. In part, it may possibly be the result of a coenzyme Q deficiency and the ensuing inability to move the muscles because of lack of the energy that proper enzyme action sparks.[57] One muscular dystrophy patient, having been told that there is no cure for the disease, embarked on his own self-help program in which he took 2,000 units of vitamin E daily, 3,000 units of C, and for selenium, ate tuna fish and cottage cheese. As a result, he dramatically lowered his CPK (creatine phosphokinase) count (which is the test for muscular dystrophy) from 610 to 140—from a full-blown case to a borderline condition. Simultaneously, his triglyceride count fell from 130 to 68, and his cholesterol count plummeted from 240 to 186.[58]

SELENIUM FOR HEAVY METAL POISONING

Selenium acts to prevent the accumulation in your body of toxic deposits of heavy metals like cadmium (contained in cigarette smoke). In this role, it is an important protector against modern-day pollution.

How does it work? Chemically, it creates a bond with the metal, thus rendering it less harmful and helping your body to eliminate it.[59-62] You can actually reduce the risk of being poisoned by the high mercury levels contained in some fish by eating your fish dinner with high-selenium foods like asparagus or mushrooms. If you smoke or are frequently around others who do, you are inhaling a vast amount of cadmium, which can cause high blood pressure, among other effects.

Alcohol, too, contains cadmium.[63] Selenium has proved extremely effective (100 times more than zinc or other chelating agents) in removing cadmium deposits from your body.[64] Other metals that it can help you excrete are silver, thallium, and excessive copper.[65]

Be aware that some nutritional authorities believe that buildups of lead and cadmium cause disturbances in brain chemistry, which may result in mental illness.[66] Carl Pfeiffer of the Brain Bio Center in New Jersey has conducted research that hints at the usefulness of selenium in treating mental disturbances.[67]

SELENIUM FOR CANCER

Some forms of cancer are the result of free radical oxidation that destroys or damages the part of the DNA that regulates cell multiplication. When that happens, the cells can begin to multiply abnormally, damaging the healthy tissue until your whole body is invaded by these wildly proliferating cells. Since selenium can protect you from free radical oxidation, one way to minimize your risk of developing this type of cancer is to eat selenium-rich foods like whole grains or their products with each meal.

If you already have cancer, selenium may be useful in slowing its progression. A way to get it in even more concentrated doses than in foods is to take brewer's yeast or supplements.

Just as selenium protects you against toxic metal poisoning, it can also protect you against radiation, whether you are exposed to it through the environment or more directly through medical treatments. A particularly effective form of selenium for this purpose is selenoaminoacid compounds (selenium plus amino acids).[68, 69] Selenium also protects you against compounds called epoxides, as it breaks them down. What are epoxides? Formed when an enzyme named aryl hydrocarbon hydroxylase binds with a carcinogenic substance, epoxides could be called the immediate cause of cancer. The carcinogens cause your body to produce them, and then cancer may ensue.[70]

Macrophages—those garbagemen of the bloodstream—are capable of keeping your body clear of tumor cells. Also, since they produce interferon, they can help eliminate the viruses that cause some forms of cancer.[71] But to do their job properly, they need adequate selenium.[72]

It is interesting to note the results of recent studies: cancer occurs at a much higher rate in low-selenium areas than in areas that are selenium-rich.[73, 74] Tests on animals and humans suffering from cancer show them to be suffering from selenium deficiency as well.[75] In turn, people with a selenium deficiency may be much more likely to develop cancers of the breast, colon, bladder, lung, ovary, pancreas, and prostate. Conversely, if your intake of selenium is adequate, that alone may minimize your risk of developing these types of cancers.[76] As the research evolves, selenium is proving itself to be a very effective weapon against cancer.

A Practical Guide to Using Selenium

SELENIUM IN FOOD AND SUPPLEMENTS

Selenium is available in both foods and in supplements. Remember, the selenium content of food is highly dependent on the selenium content of the soil in which the food was grown. Thus, you may be interested in buying foods grown in soil with rich organic matter and no pesticides rather than foods grown on land poor in topsoil and farmed with heavily chemical methods.

What foods are naturally rich in selenium? Liver is an excellent source, but remember, since it is also the detoxifying organ, animal liver can contain high concentrates of any hormones or chemicals the animal was fed. Try to find a source for organic meats if you like liver. Tuna and eggs are excellent selenium sources, for they also contain sulfur, which helps your body absorb and utilize selenium.

In general, animal foods are better selenium sources than plant foods. Depending on the soil in which they were grown, whole grains, mushrooms, asparagus, broccoli, onions, and tomatoes can be decent sources of selenium. According to the selenium content of the food the cows ate, dairy products can give you trace amounts of the mineral.[77, 78] Processed, refined foods and those grown in mineral-deficient soils contain little if any selenium.

Though there is no official RDA for selenium, the Food and Nutrition Board recommends an intake of at least 150 micrograms daily. Since there is so much uncertainty about the selenium content of soils and therefore of foods, it would be a safe bet to get some of your selenium through a supplement. The Food and Nutrition Board has established that 50 to 150 micrograms of supplemental selenium will insure good health; your health would probably not suffer if you were to take up to 500 micrograms daily. In this age of ecological imbalance, the average American diet contains only 35 to 60 micrograms of selenium on a daily basis. Therefore supplementation seems absolutely necessary.

Up to 2,000 micrograms of selenium per day have been used by physicians as therapy for specific conditions, with no symptoms of toxicity. Be aware that different selenium compounds have different toxicity levels, however; selenium that is organically bound is much safer than the inorganic type, and also more potent.[79] Selenium yeast, in particular, has an extremely low toxicity. Since selenium is water soluble, an overdose will be excreted. But as with any kind of therapy, it is wise to take megadoses only under a physician's supervision.

For babies, breast milk is an excellent source of selenium. In fact, it contains six times more selenium and twice as much vitamin E as cow's milk. Selenium and vitamin E deficiencies of infant formulas may account for a quarter of the roughly 35,000 infant deaths in our country each year.

For children, it is probably best that their selenium comes through food rather than supplements as long as their teeth are developing. Studies suggest that selenium supplements may be linked to an increased number of dental caries in children under ten.[80] Selenium may also be responsible for changes in the chemical composition of the tooth enamel as it develops. Whole, natural foods are their best source of the mineral.

SELENIUM'S PARTNERS AND ANTAGONISTS

Selenium is vitally interconnected with other nutrients in your diet, particularly vitamin E. Since they perform many of the same functions and actually enhance each other (in terms of retention and action), you should try to take them together. You may find that by doing so you will need smaller doses of each.[81]

Selenium also interacts with the amino acids that contain sulfur, in two ways. First, the presence of sulfur lessens any possible poisonous effect of selenium. Second, as antioxidants, they work synergistically, and may be capable of promoting your life span. In one experiment with mice, sulfur and selenium proved capable of adding 20 to 30 percent to their expected life span.[82, 83] Eggs are a good natural source of a combination of sulfur-containing amino acids and selenium.

On the subject of mineral relationships, it is important to note that several minerals interfere with your body's utilization of selenium. Among these are zinc, copper, and nickel, which increases the excretion of selenium. Avoid taking copper in multimineral supplements as you probably already get a sufficient amount—if not too much—through the copper in your water pipes. Of course, the intake of heavy metals can also cause great selenium loss since your body uses the selenium to rid itself of toxic heavy metal deposits. Smokers, take note! Lead, cadmium, mercury, silver, and thallium are particularly dangerous.

Your supplies of both selenium and its partner vitamin E may be depleted by a large intake of polyunsaturated oils. If you eat too much oil (more than two tablespoons of polyunsaturated fats daily, one teaspoon at a time), your system will be so saturated that the selenium and vitamin E that normally protects the fatty acids in the cell membranes from oxidation will wind up instead protecting the excess fatty acids in the food! Ironically, by switching from animal fats to polyunsaturated oils for the benefit of your heart, you could cause yourself heart disease by creating a selenium deficiency.

SIGNS OF SELENIUM DEFICIENCY AND EXCESS

How do you know if you are getting too little—or too much—selenium? The signs of selenium deficiency are a lack of energy (the result of a shortage of coenzyme Q), development of degenerative disease (which can also be due to many other factors), and accelerated aging, produced by free radical oxidation.

Can you get too much selenium? To develop selenosis (selenium poisoning), your daily intake would have to be from 2,400 to 3,000 micrograms. Since the average daily intake from foods is on the low side, and the supplemental intake usually from only 50 to 150 micrograms, you run little risk of developing selenosis. However, since each person is different biochemically, the safest thing to do is to stay within the 50 to 150 microgram range. Luckily, excess selenium is readily excreted.

Possibly the greatest risk of selenium poisoning comes from continued large doses or industrial overexposure.[84] If you work around photocopy machines all day, you should know that they contain selenium plates, releasing selenium into the environment.[85] A good antidote to this situation is to eat a diet that emphasizes both high-protein foods and sulfur-rich foods like eggs, fish, meat, cabbage, and brussels sprouts.[86]

The symptoms of selenosis are loss of olfactory (smell) sense, a sore throat, respiratory problems, and an upset stomach. Further symptoms include a skin rash, brittle hair and nails, irritability and exhaustion.[87] In an extreme toxic state, symptoms include loss of teeth, pneumonia, fatal pulmonary edema, myelitis (inflamed spinal cord and bone marrow), and progressive paralysis.[88]

If you suffer from milder selenium poisoning caused by industrial pollutants or oversupplementation, your wisest course is to remove yourself from the polluting source, or stop taking selenium in such great quantities. Remember, if you suffer from a condition in which a larger intake of selenium might be helpful, be sure to embark on a program of supplementation only under your doctor's supervision.

Summary

One of the scarcest and most poisonous of minerals as it exists in nature, selenium is also one of the most vital trace minerals to your health. Its most important role is as an antioxidant, protecting your cells from free radical oxidation.

It plays its role mainly in the synthesis of the protective enzyme glutathione peroxidase, the molecules of which are built on four selenium atoms. Selenium also helps maintain healthy levels of coenzyme Q. Both glutathione peroxidase and coenzyme Q have a big part in keeping oxidation of cellular membranes from taking place. Selenium also stimulates the immune system, keeping you protected from invading viruses and bacteria. Furthermore, it chelates with toxic metals and helps remove them from your body.

Selenium is especially important to your heart, your red blood cells, white blood cells, fibroblasts, eyes, and protein production system. It also protects fat-soluble vitamins A, D, K, and E from oxidation.

Men need more selenium than women. But deficiencies of this little wonder-worker in either sex may lead to kwashiorkor, muscular dystrophy, blood sugar disorders, liver necrosis, arthritis, anemia, cataracts, infections, heavy metal poisoning, and even cancer.

Though there is no official RDA for selenium, the Food and Nutrition Board suggests an intake of 150 micrograms daily. Since the average American diet, due to depleted soils and refined foods, contains only 35 to 60 micrograms, supplementation is probably a good idea. It is also a good idea to eat plenty of selenium-rich foods like liver, tuna, whole grains, mushrooms, asparagus, broccoli, onions, tomatoes, and garlic. Brewer's yeast is an excellent supplemental food rich in selenium, and is one of your best weapons against heart disease and cancer.

Sodium

What Is Sodium?

Sodium is a metallic element that occurs in nature only in the combined state, i.e., as sodium chloride—salt. Salt is a universal taste, one of the four that your tongue's taste buds recognize instantly. Salt is necessary to the metabolism of both humans and animals: animals will walk for miles to find the salt to counterbalance all the potassium they eat in the form of vegetation. But we humans have only to look as far as the dinner table to find more-than-ample salt to meet our needs.

We all know that our bodies need salt. What many of us don't know is that most foods contain sodium chloride naturally. In fact, it is quite possible to get the 50 to 200 milligrams of sodium[1] that we need on a daily basis—even the 400 milligrams that we might need if we drink a lot of fluids—without adding a particle of salt to our food. Yet even if we ourselves don't add salt to our food at the dinner table, our industrialized food processing system will have already added the salt for us, to mask a bad flavor, to preserve the food in order that it might have a longer shelf life, or to give the food a taste to replace the one that was lost in the refining process. Even commercially produced baby foods contain added sodium—not to please baby's still innocent taste buds, but to please mother's. As a result, most of us suffer from an overload of sodium; few of us have to worry about a deficiency of this most necessary but heartily overprovided mineral. In fact, the average American consumes 3 to 7 grams of sodium each day.[2]

How Does Sodium Work?

Sodium accounts for only about 2 percent of your body's entire mineral makeup. Yet that 2 percent of the mineral content is very important: sodium is present mainly in the fluid that surrounds each and every cell of your body. With potassium, it is responsible for speeding nutrients into your cells, and speeding waste products out; thus, it is a vital ingredient in the metabolic processes of every cell. Your cells work hard to maintain exactly the proper balance of sodium and potassium, for only with sodium outside the cellular walls, and potassium inside, can the unique pumping action that quickens these life-sustaining energy processes work.

How *does* it work? Tiny, electrically charged particles called ions are responsible. When sodium's ions feel the magnetic force of potassium's ions through the cellular wall that separates them, an electrical wave of energy is produced that results in the sodium/potassium pump that draws nutrients into, and waste products out of, your cells.[3]

But the sodium/potassium pump does more than simply feed and clean up after your cells. It also supervises and stabilizes their delicate fluid pressure, keeping them from becoming waterlogged or dehydrated. It pulls water in from the bloodstream to keep the extracellular fluids at a constant level. At the same time, it draws surplus water out of the cells and returns it to the bloodstream.[4] This mechanism is also what keeps your blood pressure stable. If the cells were to become waterlogged, for example, your blood pressure would become dangerously low. On the other hand, dehydration could be fatal, as blood pressure would rise.

At the same time, the sodium/potassium balance itself must be regulated, or the whole intricate mechanism will fail. This job falls to the kidneys, which are helped by a hormone called aldosterone, produced by the adrenal glands located above them. (In turn, the adrenal glands are stimulated by ACTH, which is produced by your pituitary gland.) As long as your body needs the sodium in your bloodstream, ACTH stimulates aldosterone to instruct your kidneys to filter out sodium from the blood that continually passes through their tiny tubules and to return it for recycling. When there is too much sodium in the bloodstream, the kidneys simply filter it out and excrete it from the body through the urine. Then when sodium is needed again, the hormones go to work and instruct your kidneys not to let the sodium leave your body.

This mechanism, like all the others in the intricately designed organism we call our body, was designed for us when we were simply people living on simple natural foods. In other words, it was designed to handle fairly subtle fluctuations in the sodium/potassium balance, not to handle the wildly varying levels of sodium that come from eating salty, industrialized foods like potato chips and Big Macs. Under the best of conditions, the kidneys work hard, regulating not only the sodium/potassium balance but also the delicate interrelationships of all the other minerals—in fact, each of us passes five quarts a day, sixty-five times a day, through our kidneys. Throwing excessive quantities of sodium into the system starts a vicious cycle in which the two organs are trying desperately to maintain the proper balance between sodium and its partner. For unfortunately, our kidneys were designed to handle a diet that contains excess *potassium*, not excess sodium; in trying to eliminate the salt, huge amounts of potassium—no longer so readily available in our refined, processed foods and so the more valuable—are also lost (up to nine times as much on a high-sodium diet as on a low-sodium diet). Even when there isn't too much salt in your system, your kidneys are programmed to excrete potassium—up to 240 milligrams daily. A diet that induces this wild attempt at rebalancing the two, even though the kidneys are trying their best, results in dangerously large potassium losses and, over time, can actually wear out your kidneys.

On the other hand, your kidneys are programmed by years of evolutionary experience to hang on to sodium. Thus, if your body seems to need sodium, the kidneys can actually reabsorb into the bloodstream all but about 10 milligrams daily. The whole system works just beautifully, unless you happen to be eating thirty-five times more sodium than you need!

And don't be deceived, you *do* need sodium. Besides its function as half of the sodium/potassium pump, as fluid pressure regulator, and in fact as blood pressure regulator, it also works to maintain the pH of your blood. More than that, it works with potassium, proteins, phosphates, carbonates, and other minerals to keep all your tissues at the proper degree of alkalinity or acidity: different body parts have different degrees of pH, so it is no small job.[5]

Another of sodium's functions is in partnership with calcium. We all know how important calcium is; as a matter of fact, it is your body's chief mineral, one of nature's most effective calming agents, necessary for muscle contraction and relaxation, and for the construction of healthy bones. Yet without sodium, you would not be able to use the calcium in your body. It is sodium that keeps calcium dispersed throughout your bloodstream, ready for any of your tissues that need it. With sodium, calcium is even one of the components of the extracellular fluids—it helps its partner regulate the liquids as they are pumped in and out of the cells.

Where Does Sodium Work?

We have just seen how sodium works at the very basic levels of cellular activity. Now let's look at the larger picture of where sodium is at work throughout your body system.

• *Nerves.* The transmission of nerve impulses depends on the sodium/potassium pump. Short halts in the pumping action in the nerve cells actually create a wave of energy by which the nerve impulses travel from one cell to the next (see the chapter on potassium for a more complete explanation). In short, the nerve messages are carried by an electrical wave that is created by reversing the magnetic energy between sodium and potassium within the nerve cells.[6]

• *Muscles.* Without sodium, your muscles could not contract. When a muscle cell receives a message from a nerve cell, there is a sharp, short halt in the action of the sodium/potassium pump. Just as when a nerve impulse is traveling along the nerve cells, at this point sodium crosses the cellular walls, crowding the potassium out. This influx of sodium causes the cell to release calcium, which in turn stimulates the process that culminates in a muscle contraction. Almost immediately, the action of the sodium/potassium pump has resumed, with sodium outside and potassium within the cellular walls, and the muscle relaxes.[7] Sodium, then, is necessary for your very heart to beat!

• *Metabolism.* Within your metabolic system, sodium is part of another kind of pump. This pump is located in the cells of the wall of your intestine—the ones that absorb your food after it is digested. Its purpose is to speed the glucose—your body's fuel—through the walls of the intestine to your bloodstream. But since glucose has no electrical charge of its own, sodium ions do the work.[8] Without this "sugar pump" you would not enjoy the energy pickup that a good meal—especially one of unrefined carbohydrates like whole grains and vegetables—gives you.

• *Cells.* We know that sodium's most basic function—as part of the sodium/potassium pump—takes place within the cells. With chloride, sodium is also the tireless transporter of nutrients between cells,[9] carrying them through the blood and other extracellular fluids of the body. (That's why those fluids—blood, tears, perspiration, urine—are salty.)

Sodium and chloride make a great team, as sodium is the most positive of the ions in the blood; chloride, the most negative.[10]

• *Blood*. Sodium is one of the minerals necessary for maintaining the blood's pH balance, which is slightly alkaline.

• *Digestive system*. Sodium also plays a part here. Too much salt (especially in antacids) causes your stomach to make too much hydrochloric acid. Yet just the right quantity must be present for hydrochloric acid to be produced for the digestion of the foods you eat. The antacid manufacturers would have us believe that acid in the stomach is something to be avoided, yet without hydrochloric acid, you would be unable to break down the heavier foods you eat (like proteins) into nutrients, nor would you be able to destroy any bacteria that might accompany your food.[11]

Who Doesn't Need Sodium?

Yes, we all need sodium, just as we need all of the other vital minerals. But in this section we are not going to talk about how supplementary sodium can help you prevent stress, hypertension, cholesterol buildup, heart disease, muscular weakness, kidney damage, liver damage, or pancreas dysfunction. We are going to talk about how too much sodium—present in almost all of our diets—can *cause* these problems.

An imbalance of sodium and potassium puts your body under a great deal of stress. Not only must your hormonal system and your kidneys overwork in trying to regulate the balance, physical or emotional stress actually confuses them into retaining sodium. Extra aldosterone is manufactured in stressful situations, giving your kidneys the message to retain sodium and throwing the body into a more stressful state. This mechanism is complicated even more if you are eating too much salt in the first place. Certain physical conditions can cause the same dangerous reaction: low blood sugar, for example, or conditions such as arthritis for which cortisone is prescribed, send the body into a state of stress that results in sodium retention and potassium loss.[12] High blood pressure may be the result: there is too much salt in the extracellular fluids. If your heart has been weakened by pumping blood through at high pressure, the blood flow to your kidneys is affected. They respond to the reduced flow with the production of renin, an enzyme that constricts the blood vessels in an effort to *raise* your blood pressure. The kidneys don't know any better—"If there isn't enough blood coming through, the pressure must be low," they reason. Ironically, one side effect of renin's activity is that more aldosterone is produced, and more sodium retained by the kidneys![13] And at this point, the kidneys keep more than sodium, they also retain water and urea, the toxic by-product of protein production. Thus, your body retains more salt, your blood pressure is even higher, and you are accumulating toxic wastes to boot!

Acute or chronic stress can actually cause the breakdown of your aldosterone-producing adrenal glands. At this point, there's another problem. There's no one there to tell your kidneys when to recycle the sodium, and the kidneys let too much go out as a waste product. The sodium that leaves the body this way carries water with it—water that your tissues need. They begin to dehydrate, your sodium/potassium pump can no longer work, and there is a dangerous decline in your blood pressure.[14]

EXCESS SODIUM AND HYPERTENSION

We've already hinted that excess sodium causes hypertension (high blood pressure). There's no question about it: a great number of comparative studies of people who use no salt and those who use great quantities have proved that high salt equals high blood pressure. And if you look around the world at the geographical incidence of hypertension, the pattern will become clear: high salt equals high blood pressure!

The United States rates right up there with Japan in these studies as one of the world's greatest salt-consuming countries, and it has one of the highest incidences of hypertension among its citizens. (A whopping 20 to 40 percent of our population is prone to the development of hypertension, estimates claim.) The Japanese eat even more salt than we do (soy sauce has 1,029 milligrams of sodium per tablespoon), and their rate of hypertension is correspondingly higher.

If you need more proof of the correlation between high salt intake and hypertension, you will be interested to know that it is an established medical fact that high blood pressure decreases with lowered salt intake. Logically, taking supplements of potassium chloride daily also helps, though in excess it can annoy the gastrointestinal system and further endanger the kidneys, if they are already damaged.

And here's more proof in the case against excess salt: a diet high in sodium may also raise cholesterol levels.[15] Thus, it is implicated in heart disease in at least two ways: it makes the heart work harder by pumping blood through at a high pressure, and it may cause fatty deposits on arteries by contributing to raised serum cholesterol levels. The arterial diseases that may result contribute to a vicious cycle by causing high blood pressure. It is no coincidence that autopsies of American stroke patients reveal that their bodies contain much more sodium than those of people who expired from something else.

High blood pressure can be uncomfortable—causing headaches, faintness, constipation, and ear noises. It can also be deadly, and is—to 250,000 Americans annually. To drive this point home we could say that hypertension is responsible for one death out of every eight, every year.

Among the living, there are 23 million of us with hypertension, one of every ten American adults. In addition, even children now suffer from this life-threatening condition. A recent Boston medical survey revealed that possibly 8 percent of our children are afflicted.[16]

One commonly prescribed medication for high blood pressure is a diuretic. Be aware that diuretics can be dangerous to your health. First, they make your kidneys process overly large quantities of fluid, with which they discard valuable potassium and a number of other minerals that your body needs, as well as the offending sodium. Second, they bring with them a long list of side effects ranging from anemia to fainting to impotence, and including palpitations, angina, hepatitis, diarrhea, pancreas inflammation, arthritis, lethargy, depression, and nightmares.[17]

You can spare yourself and your family the enormous misery of high blood pressure by decreasing the salt in your diet. There are two easy and quite delicious ways to do this: first, cut out, or at least cut down, the amount of refined and processed foods you eat. Second, eat as much whole, fresh, unrefined natural food as you can possibly incorporate into your diet and life-style. You will find a bonus in switching to a diet of natural foods: they taste so good that their natural flavors, with little or no salt added, will speak for themselves!

EXCESS SALT AND MUSCULAR WEAKNESS OR FATIGUE

An imbalance in the sodium/potassium ratio—i.e., excess salt—can cause cramps, fatigue, and muscular weakness. It can even make your heartbeat irregular, which is no surprise, since your heart is a muscle. (And conversely, lowered salt intake or additional potassium can return your heartbeat to normal.[18]) If you are an athlete, be aware that taking salt tablets or eating a high-protein diet can cause problems with your sodium/potassium balance, creating potassium deficiency. That's why you may be plagued with cramping muscles or even pain in your chest or an irregular pulse after you work out. In one experiment, doctors found potassium deficiency (hypokalemia) in 30 percent of the 116 track runners that they examined after a long workout. Astronauts were also found to develop the condition, symptomized in their case by irregular heartbeats—a result of potassium deficiency brought on by stress.[19] Karen Krautzcke, a professional tennis player in excellent physical condition, died while jogging when her heart stopped due to potassium deficiency.[20]

The irony is that many athletes think that they need to take extra salt to replace what is lost in their perspiration when they exercise. But the truth is, what is being lost is not sodium, but potassium. In fact, *Runner's World* has advised its readers that taking salt tablets can actually encourage sodium deficiency because it impedes your production of aldosterone. A better idea than salt tablets is a glass of freshly squeezed fruit or vegetable juice, which gives you balanced quantities of sodium and potassium and perks you up almost instantly. Salt tablets, on the other hand, do not reach your tissues for a long time after you take them.

EXCESS SALT AND LIVER DAMAGE

When your kidneys wear out from the strain of trying to balance sodium/potassium levels in a body that contains too much salt, your liver is damaged as well. Because your kidneys can no longer protect your body from excessive amounts of sodium, the liver may swell and lose its ability to filter out toxic wastes from your bloodstream. At the same time, the body must try to handle the poisons that the liver cannot filter out; your lungs, in particular, will be hurt by the decreased oxygen supply.

EXCESS SALT AND PANCREAS DAMAGE

If there is too much salt in your system, your pancreas may suffer because it is no longer able to produce enzymes necessary for you to digest your food properly. Over time, the tissue swelling caused by excess sodium can turn your pancreas into a mass of scar tissue, so that your body no longer gets any of the nutrients it needs.[21] Too much salt and too little potassium are also precursors of the blood sugar disorders hypoglycemia and diabetes.[22]

A Practical Guide to Using Sodium

Unless you are a strict vegan, perspire profusely, or are under a great deal of stress, you do not need to worry about getting enough salt in your diet. For most of us, the concern should be directed in the opposite way: are we getting too *much*? If you eat a diet heavy in refined and processed foods, and routinely add salt to your meals at the table, as most of us do, the answer to that question is most likely, "Yes."

All foods contain some sodium naturally. But refined foods contain sodium in enormous quantities. Here are some examples:

FOOD	SODIUM CONTENT
Egg McMuffin	914 milligrams
TV dinner (fried chicken)	1,152 milligrams
Dill pickle	1,137 milligrams
Big Mac	1,510 milligrams
Instant broth (one pkt.)	818 milligrams

Even a serving of cottage cheese, which most of us consider to be unrefined food, contains a whopping 457 milligrams of sodium!

After eating any of the foods above, you might feel that you need an antacid. More salt is added to your meal, without your even knowing it.

Rolaids (1 tablet)	53 milligrams
Alka-Seltzer (2 tablets)	521 milligrams
Bromo-Seltzer	717 milligrams

Even the water you use to dissolve the antacid adds sodium to your already besieged system: some soft water contains as much as 12 milligrams of sodium per glass![23]

No wonder the "average" American salt intake is from 6 to 18,000 milligrams daily.[24] Even some children take in up to 10,000 milligrams of salt a day. In contrast, the suggestion of the National Research Council is that we need only from 50 to 200 milligrams of salt in our diets (or 1 gram for every 2.2 pounds of water consumed).[25] Even for those of us who drink fluids copiously or perspire a lot, the recommended amount is only 400 milligrams—only a third of the amount of salt in one commercially produced dill pickle!

SODIUM'S PARTNERS

But we mustn't forget that sodium is a vital nutrient. Just like the other minerals, it has complex interrelationships with nutrient "partners." Potassium is its most obvious partner; we have already stressed the necessity of a balanced relationship here. In turn, potassium and magnesium are interrelated: if there is not enough magnesium in your system, your kidneys will respond by excreting large amounts of valuable potassium through the urine. Alcoholics, who almost routinely suffer from magnesium deficiency, are particularly prone to this problem, the result of which is a sodium excess, no matter how little salt is eaten.[26] Too much protein in the diet can also upset the delicate sodium/potassium balance, as can too many carbohydrates, particularly refined carbohydrates (which invariably contain a lot of salt).[27]

Two more of sodium's partners are calcium and vitamin D. These elements, in addition to pantothenic acid, can help your kidneys eliminate surplus sodium.[28] An important factor to remember if you are trying to encourage your body to discard sodium is that with every bit of sodium your kidneys excrete, water that your tissues need is lost as well. That's why eating salty foods makes you thirsty: it's an ingenious way in which your body tells you that it needs replenishment of the water excreted with the excess sodium. (And that's why drinking seawater to quench your thirst will result in death from dehydration more quickly than not drinking water at all.[29])

With the widespread availability of salt, it is hard to imagine that anyone could suffer from sodium deficiency. Yet certain conditions can produce it: long-term diarrhea and/or vomiting, strict vegan diets, and profuse perspiration are examples of situations under which you might develop a sodium deficiency that can be corrected by taking salt.

Conditions that involve more chronic sodium deficiency all entail physical stress. We have already discovered that stress can create conditions under which your body retains sodium, yet it can also create a deficiency. Here's why. When they are under stress, the adrenal glands first produce too much aldosterone, which results in sodium retention. But prolonged stress wears the adrenal glands out, so that after some time, as in pregnancy or illness, they no longer are able to produce the aldosterone necessary to tell your kidneys to retain sodium.[30] Since they don't receive messages from aldosterone to the contrary, your kidneys discard sodium in the urine, and a deficiency is the result.

Examples of stressful situations that can cause sodium deficiency are exposure to toxic chemicals, infections, digestive difficulties, allergies, and injuries or accidents. Even pregnancy causes a form of prolonged stress which may result in low-salt syndrome. (And doctors are demonstrating an increasing awareness of this possibility by no longer prescribing low-sodium diets for their pregnant patients.)

If you find yourself in any of the above situations, be on the lookout for sodium deficiency. The symptoms? Wrinkles and sunken eyes (due to tissue dehydration); flatulence, diarrhea, nausea, and vomiting (because your stomach does not have enough sodium to make hydrochloric acid for digestion); confusion and fatigue (because of insufficient circulation of fluids in your brain); low blood pressure; irritability; difficulty breathing; and heightened allergies.

At the same time, there are symptoms that you cannot detect right away. These include the buildup of mineral deposits on the walls of your arteries (because sodium is not there to keep calcium dissolved in your bloodstream), and toxic waste backups throughout your system (because as your kidneys try to reabsorb sodium, they also keep urea). Other symptoms of severe sodium deficiency are muscle cramps. That may not sound too dangerous, but if the cramp happens to be in your heart, it can be deadly. In fact, any or all of your organs can suffer if your muscles aren't contracting properly due to sodium deficiency. Your muscles can atrophy if your case is very severe, with tissue degeneration due to poor blood circulation the result.

Summary

Our bodies need salt, which is freely available in a natural form in nearly every food we eat. Salt is necessary for a variety of important functions. With potassium, it forms a pump that speeds nutrients into and waste products out of your cells. At the same time, it regulates the cellular fluid pressure, which affects your blood pressure. With a number of other nutrients, it also controls the varying degrees of pH balance throughout the different parts of your body. Sodium also keeps particles of calcium suspended in your bloodstream, ready for any of your tissues' needs.

Sodium is vital to the ability of your nerves to transmit impulses to your muscles, and to your muscles' ability to contract. Within your metabolic system, sodium helps pump glucose through the walls of the intestine into your bloodstream. In your cells, sodium is part of the sodium/potassium mechanism. In the fluids of your body, sodium works with chloride to transport nutrients between cells. In the digestive system, sodium helps produce hydrochloric acid, which in turn helps you digest your foods.

Yes, we all need sodium, but most of us get too much. Too much sodium results in potassium deficiency and even more serious problems, such as stress, hypertension, muscular weakness and fatigue, liver damage, and pancreas disease. Of these, hypertension is the most dangerous and is in fact one of the leading killer diseases in our country today. One out of every ten Americans may be predisposed to high blood pressure, which is rearing its ugly head even in the lives of our children.

Very few of us need to worry about getting too little salt. Yet most of us do need to be concerned about getting too much. Your body needs only from 55 to 400 milligrams of sodium to perform its daily functions, yet many of us eat from 7,000 to 20,000 milligrams daily. That adds up to about thirty-five times the amount of salt we need!

Sodium maintains important partnerships with potassium, calcium, vitamin D, and pantothenic acid. Its antagonists include prolonged diarrhea and vomiting, strict vegan diets, profuse perspiration, prolonged or acute stress, pregnancy, and chronic illness. The symptoms of sodium deficiency—though much more rare—can be just as serious as the symptoms of sodium excess.

Be aware that if you eat a lot of refined and processed foods, your daily consumption of sodium is almost certainly too high. Foods contain sodium naturally, just as natural foods have their own distinctive and delicious tastes which do not need to be either masked or enhanced by the addition of salt. Switching off a diet of refined foods in favor of a more balanced diet of natural foods will mean not only an almost automatic reduction in your salt intake, it will also mean the awakening of your taste buds to the delightful flavors that nature has provided for our health and enjoyment.

Zinc

What Is Zinc?

Zinc is a familiar, bluish-gray metal, in widespread use in industry and in medicine. It serves as a coating for iron; it galvanizes pipes; it is an ingredient in household burn and baby ointments; and it helps speed healing of the eyes when included in eye solutions. But perhaps its most important uses are those your own body finds for it.

Tiny traces of this mineral can make the difference between life and death; between normal growth, and dwarfism or perennial sexual immaturity. There are dozens of complex biochemical operations in which zinc is of paramount importance. Yet the entire body contains only about a half teaspoon of zinc. Because so little of it is needed, it is called a trace mineral. This trace, however, is crucial. The *Seventh Revised Edition of U.S. Recommended Dietary Allowance* stresses, "Zinc is required for normal health and functioning in man and animals; life is incompatible with a severe deficiency."[1]

Fortunately, most animals find it easy to obtain enough zinc. It is liberally distributed in the soil in most areas and therefore in most plants that grow in the soil, and it is in the meat of animals that eat those plants.

But it is not everywhere. It is this fact that led to the discovery of the importance of zinc in the human diet. While it had been known since 1934 that animals required zinc, it was only in 1961 that three scientists published a paper linking human abnormalities such as dwarfism, hypogonadism (failure of the sexual organs to mature properly), and learning disabilities in children to zinc deficiency.[2] These disabilities, health authorities had noted, occurred particularly frequently, and together, in certain parts of Iran and Egypt.

It turned out that these areas had two features in common that explained their high percentage of people who failed to mature properly. Iran and Egypt, countries located in a part of the world often designated the cradle of civilization, have sustained continuous human settlement for countless generations. Year after year, century after century, human beings have tilled the soil there to bring forth wheat and other grains from which to produce bread, the staff of life. Finally, after long years, the soil has become depleted. In certain areas, there is so little zinc left that people who eat only locally grown produce cannot absorb enough for proper growth. And the areas of zinc-deficient soil correlate with the areas of increased frequency of dwarfism.

Another factor exacerbating local zinc deficiencies, it was discovered, is a preference in many parts of these countries for eating unleavened as opposed to leavened bread. (The Jewish tradition of eating matzo—unleavened bread—on Passover, which celebrates the Hebrews' exodus from Egypt, may recall this Egyptian custom.) Unleavened bread, unfortunately, contains a compound called phytate that inhibits zinc absorption. Phytates, which occur in the bran portion of whole grains, are destroyed by the leavening process. In regions where bread is not allowed to rise and the soil has been overworked without replenishment for too long, zinc deficiencies are so severe that a relatively high frequency of serious deformities results.

Iran and Egypt are not the only countries where zinc deficiencies are common. Wherever the soil is eroded or the diet is incomplete, zinc deficiencies appear. In the United States, they are not so severe as to result in noticeably increased incidence of dwarfism and hypogonadism; nonetheless, even though we eat mostly leavened bread, our preference for making it with refined instead of whole grain has combined with soil depletion due to mechanized farming and other poor agricultural practices to lead to widespread borderline zinc deficiency.

How Does Zinc Work?

At the molecular level, zinc plays a role in our bodies similar to that of the skeleton for the organism as a whole: each molecule in each cell retains its structure in part because of the rigidity of the mineral zinc.[3]

At the level of cell and protein reproduction upon which all growth depends, zinc is fundamental. It is needed for the synthesis of the two proteins that store the cells' blueprints for reproduction—DNA and RNA.[4] A number of minerals are involved in the process of protein manufacture carried out by RNA: zinc, calcium, iron, magnesium, and manganese all work together so that RNA can accurately reproduce each of the thousands of proteins needed by the body.[5, 6]

Among these proteins are the hormones that regulate growth and sex. Zinc helps stimulate production of these essential hormones. The process seems to begin, oddly enough, in the retina of the eye—which distinguishes light with the aid of zinc. The presence of light triggers a neural signal from the retina to the hypothalamus, a gland in the brain, to stimulate the production of hormones that in turn trigger hormone production in the pituitary gland. It is the pituitary which produces growth hormone, but one more level of chemical signaling is required for the production of sex hormones: the pituitary produces gonadotrophic hormones which stimulate your ovaries or testes to produce the female and male sex hormones. You can see why zinc deficiency leads to distorted growth and sexual immaturity—the symptoms first noted in Egypt and Iran.

In women, there seems to be yet another gland involved in regulating production of the sex hormones. The pineal gland, a tiny pineconeshaped gland in the brain, is a repository of zinc. Like the hypothalamus, it too is light dependent. Light seems to prevent it from secreting a hormone that inhibits the activity of the ovaries. So during the day, when sunlight streams into the eyes, the ovaries can go ahead and produce estrogen and progesterone, the female sex hormones.

Your body runs on the energy supplied by the foods you eat—mostly in the form of carbohydrates. Carbohydrates are stored in the body with the aid of insulin. But for insulin itself to be stored, zinc must be bound to it. If your diet is too low in zinc, your body may neither store insulin nor use it well. As a result, the complications of zinc deficiency can be similar to the complications of diabetes: problems metabolizing carbohydrates, circulatory problems, and liver and kidney damage.

Enzymes are the catalysts of all chemical changes in the body, but they do not operate at all times: they are activated by the nucleotides adenosine monophosphate (AMP) and guanosine monophosphate (GMP), which make up part of the DNA and RNA molecules. Together with calcium and sodium, zinc is needed to spark these nucleotides into action. Once activated by AMP and GMP, there are at least eighty enzymes that require the presence of zinc ions as a coenzyme.

One of these eighty, for example, is the carboxypeptidase enzyme. Carboxypeptidase helps break down proteins into their component amino acids during digestion. It is produced by the pancreas, and incorporates the zinc ions needed for its operation as part of its structure.[7]

Another enzyme dependent on zinc as a coenzyme is carbonic anhydrase, present in the red blood cells. Carbonic anhydrase regulates the production of bicarbonate from carbon dioxide and water. This promotes the rapid exchange of carbon dioxide for oxygen between the blood and the cells. This exchange is the essential life function of cell respiration, without which no cell—and no breathing organism—would survive. In addition, zinc-containing carbonic anhydrase regulates the buffering function of bicarbonate, keeping the blood's pH at the proper level of acidity.

The regulation of the blood's pH—making it more acid when it becomes too alkaline and vice versa—is an example of a homeostatic mechanism: a means of balancing opposing tendencies to maintain the correct equilibrium for the continued functioning of the organism. Zinc ions are important in other homeostatic mechanisms in addition to the regulation of blood pH. They help regulate the amount of copper in your body. Copper can be toxic in too-large quantities, although, like zinc, it is a necessary trace mineral. Zinc ions help produce histamine, which lowers copper levels. In addition, zinc itself can chelate both iron and copper when they are in surplus in your blood, binding to them and removing them from circulation. Zinc ions also stimulate the removal of other toxic metals.

The kidneys are a part of this process. One of the functions of the kidneys is to maintain the proper mineral balance in the blood, removing toxic metals when too much of any accumulate. Zinc prevents the kidneys from doing this too quickly and removing minerals your body needs. Yet if zinc levels fall too low, the kidneys cannot function properly at all, and toxic minerals may build up in the blood.

To sum up the many roles of zinc: at all biochemical levels, it is important. At the molecular level, zinc helps stabilize the shape of each molecule. It is needed for the synthesis of DNA and RNA, and for activation of the nucleotides AMP and GMP, so that enzymes can in turn be activated. Similarly, it is itself a coenzyme with at least eighty specific enzymes—that is, they cannot operate without zinc ions. It is crucial in the production of growth and sex hormones, and in cell respiration. It is also needed for several vital homeostatic mechanisms, helping balance, for example, blood acidity, and levels of copper, iron, and other minerals. You cannot live without zinc.

Where Does Zinc Work?

Zinc acts throughout the body, but some systems are especially dependent on it. Knowing about these should motivate you to get enough in your diet, so let's take a look at where zinc works especially hard.

• *Protein production system.* Every cell in your body must construct the proteins it needs for maintenance and reproduction, and for any special functions it performs such as hormone or enzyme secretion. Zinc sees to it that the RNA in each cell correctly transmits the pattern for construction of each protein, so that amino acids—the building blocks of protein—are strung together in the right sequence. We obtain these amino acids from the proteins we eat, and zinc plays a role here, too, as we have seen. As a coenzyme of the pancreatic enzyme carboxypeptidase, zinc is needed to separate food proteins into amino acids in the intestines.

• *Blood cells.* Zinc has a number of functions in the blood. As a coenzyme of carbonic anhydrase, it buffers the blood and assists in transporting oxygen and carbon dioxide to and from each cell. It is so important to the functioning of the red blood cells that 80 percent of the zinc in the blood is in the red blood cells' hemoglobin. Without it, the red blood cells rupture and cell respiration becomes impossible. Zinc also plays a role in blood clotting. And in addition, zinc enables mucopolysaccharides to be formed. Mucopolysaccharides are a component of the antigens that determine your blood type.

The white blood cells, or leukocytes, are the body's first defense against disease. Zinc helps one type of white blood cell, in particular, play its role in the immune system. When you are injured, or when you are acutely ill, polymorphonuclear leukocytes, also known as neutrophils, go into action. They release a hormone called LEM (leukocyte endogenous mediator), and LEM transports zinc to your liver. The liver uses zinc in the production of a number of protective compounds.

Another type of white blood cell, the lymphocytes, reside in the thymus or lymph nodes and help the body fight viruses and other microbes by releasing antigens. Lymphocytes cannot be reproduced without zinc. Zinc, then, is every bit as important in protecting your body against disease as are vitamin C or vitamin A—yet few people think of taking zinc supplements when they must cope with illness or other stresses.

• *Circulatory system.* The blood plasma is the body's transportation system. Composed mostly of water, plasma carries blood cells, platelets, food and waste particles, any microorganisms that find their way into the body, and so on. Most of the zinc in the blood plasma is bound to the water-soluble protein albumin.

Plenty of zinc in your diet can help as part of an overall prevention program to protect you against stroke, high blood pressure, and heart attack. It does this in several ways. It helps keep your artery walls in good repair, so that they do not attract as much fatty plaque buildup. And inside each cell, zinc keeps fatty acids from being oxidized by free radicals. Proper fatty acid assimilation, too, prevents cholesterol from building up in the arteries. Zinc also helps keep fatty acids from agglomerating in the blood plasma and endangering your arteries or clogging up your peripheral circulation.

• *Liver.* In the liver, zinc helps in breaking down fatty acids and in creating cholesterol, one of the materials used in building nerve sheaths and cell membrane walls. Zinc, therefore, protects your liver just as it does your arteries: because it helps metabolize fatty acids, zinc prevents fat deposits from accumulating. This means that zinc is important in the prevention of cirrhosis of the liver. If you drink much alcohol, beware: alcohol, which contributes to cirrhosis, also causes you to excrete zinc along with other minerals, and thereby removes one of the best defenses against cirrhosis.

• *Bones and joints.* Zinc deficiency can prevent the bones from growing to their full length, and can also cause painful bones and joints.

Besides being necessary in the production of growth hormone, zinc keeps children's bones growing properly by assuring that enough blood reaches the head of the long bones. Two bone diseases, Perthe's disease and Osgood Schlatter's disease, have been linked to zinc deficiency.

To prevent arthritic or pyroluric joint pains, the joints must be properly lubricated. Zinc can help lubricate the joints against the pains of arthritis because of its role in the synthesis of mucopolysaccharides. These compounds are components of the gelatinous fluid that lubricates your joints.

Osteoporosis, or soft, mineral-poor bones, which causes so many elderly women, especially, to be prone to hard-to-heal broken hips and other fractures, can be the indirect result of zinc shortages. Zinc deficiencies prevent the full absorption of calcium from food. It works like this: zinc, as we have noted, is needed in the production of histamine. Histamine not only lowers blood copper levels, it also helps the stomach produce enough hydrochloric acid to absorb calcium from your food. And without enough calcium, bones become soft, brittle, and very breakable.

• *Eyes.* We have already shown that the retina requires zinc to transmit its complex messages about incoming light to the brain. Like the retina, the lens cornea and the iris of the eye also need zinc both in their formation and in their daily functioning. In children, zinc deficiency can lead to poor vision and, often, a characteristic sideways glance.

• *Neuromuscular system.* It would be hard to overstate the importance of zinc to the nervous system. Two diseases involving nervous system degeneration, multiple sclerosis and Wilson's disease, seem to involve low zinc levels. In multiple sclerosis, the fatty portions of the nerve sheaths degenerate, making it more difficult for the nerves to carry messages to the muscles. Wilson's disease, a hereditary syndrome leading to brain degeneration and muscular rigidity, is characterized by the accumulation of copper in the brain, liver, kidney, and cornea of the eye—remember zinc's role in chelating excess copper.

Zinc is used by the nerve cells that regulate the body's homeostatic functions. And since histamine helps the nerves carry their messages, zinc may be said to be vital for the transmission of nerve impulses through a watery medium.

• *Immune system.* We have already seen some of the roles zinc plays in the immune system. As we know, it is needed to produce histamine, one of the most important functions of which is to dilate the capillaries so that blood—carrying infection-fighting white blood cells —can rush to the scene of an injury or infection. And zinc is carried to the liver by LEM when you are sick or injured for use in the production of other substances that help fight infection.

To carry out these life-saving activities, the liver needs a few other substances that zinc helps supply. The adrenal cortex—a major zinc repository—provides cortisone. The pancreas provides insulin—that is, if zinc has been available so the insulin can be stored for just such emergencies. Zinc, then, is a key infection-fighting nutrient, one that should never be neglected in the diet.

• *Metabolic system.* We have already outlined the ways zinc influences basic energy metabolism. It ignites the nucleotides AMP and GMP, which catalyze all the enzymes basic to energy use. It is a coenzyme in cell respiration. It helps transform carbohydrates into glucose, and as a requirement for insulin storage, it is important in the transport of glucose and its use by the cells. It is so basic to energy metabolism that life would be impossible without it.

Without zinc, then, you could neither fully digest nor reconstruct proteins; your blood and circulatory system would be impaired; your liver could not function properly; your eyes would not see; your nervous system would degenerate; your bones would not grow properly or sustain your weight; and your immune and metabolic systems would falter. It is obvious, now, why it is said that life is incompatible with a severe zinc deficiency.

Who Needs Zinc?

Obviously, everyone needs zinc. But there are certain times when extra zinc can be especially helpful. Anyone who suffers from high cholesterol, circulatory problems, cell rupture, accident or injury, viral disease, cancer, neurological diseases or psychological problems, blood sugar disorders, rheumatism, or arthritis, can almost surely be helped by extra zinc in their diets.

Because zinc is so crucial to growth—as the experience in Egypt and Iran demonstrated—no child should be subjected to a zinc-deficient diet. The symptoms of deficiency in children—delayed or improper growth and development, learning disabilities, distorted or diminished sense of taste and smell—can, however, be reversed. When the investigators in Iran and Egypt finally figured out what was transforming children in the area into dwarfs and slow learners, and supplemented their diets with zinc, many of the young subjects added as much as five inches to their height. Similar benefits accrue to children here whose problems are found to be caused by zinc deficiencies. But prevention would be a far preferable measure to therapeutic supplements after symptoms have become acute.

Prevention of zinc deficiency in children begins with pregnancy. Mothers-to-be should be sure their diet is rich in zinc, because if their bodies are lacking zinc, their infants are at increased risk for a long list of serious conditions, including malformed bones, cartilage, and teeth;

dwarfism; hypogonadism; and anemia. Worse, the child's brain and nerves may also suffer from the mother's zinc deficiency, possibly resulting in abnormal brain development, mental retardation, hyperactivity, epilepsy, schizophrenia, autism, or multiple sclerosis. Not surprisingly, the children of alcoholic mothers are at risk for a similar list of problems, since alcohol depletes the body's zinc reserves.

Zinc deficiency during pregnancy can ruin the reproductive organs of the offspring. Boys born to zinc-deficient mothers may have infantile sex organs their whole lives. Women with one type of schizophrenia, which causes zinc deficiency, cannot even bear male children: they always miscarry males before term. When pyroluric women give birth to girls, their daughters also show signs of zinc deficiency before reaching puberty, including problems with their reproductive systems.

Even if you consume enough zinc while you are pregnant, if you allow your children to indulge in a junk-food diet low in zinc, you may be letting them in for reproductive system problems in their teens. In girls, painful or irregular menstruation are often symptoms of zinc deficiency. These symptoms can frequently be alleviated by supplementing the diet with zinc in combination with vitamin B_6, which enables the body to use zinc properly. Zinc and vitamin B_6 have become a staple orthomolecular alternative to estrogen therapy for menstrual problems; they often work better than estrogen, and they certainly cause fewer side effects. In fact, ironically, one of the drawbacks of estrogen therapy—whether used to correct menstrual problems or as a method of birth control—is that it depletes the body's zinc stores. Of course, this can lead to side effects that include other physical or mental problems in addition to the original dysmenorrhea.

Boys, too, need zinc for their sex organs to mature properly. In fact, men need extra zinc all their lives. Zinc is essential in the production of sperm, and in the maintenance of the health of the prostate gland. Dr. Carl Pfeiffer, an expert on the role of minerals in the body, notes that zinc supplements can help the penis and testes grow to normal size in adolescent boys; can ameliorate prostatitis and prevent the development of prostate problems; can normalize semen secretion and help prevent impotency. Pumpkin seeds are a rich source of zinc. A handful each day can not only help prevent prostate problems, but can supplement the body's supply of zinc in men who are especially active sexually, since quite a bit of zinc is lost with each ejaculation of semen.

ZINC FOR THE CIRCULATORY SYSTEM

Everyone knows that high blood cholesterol levels increase the risk of heart disease. But few are aware that to lower blood cholesterol, it may be preferable to consume extra zinc than to consume less cholesterol! The reason is this: our livers manufacture cholesterol each day to meet the body's needs, and if we consume too little, the liver could respond by producing extra. But adequate zinc in the diet helps regulate the way the liver uses fats. Eggs are a good source of zinc as well as lecithin, a substance that emulsifies fats. Because eggs contain zinc and lecithin, two substances that help prevent cholesterol buildup in the blood, they are not the best food to cut out completely if you are trying to reduce your serum cholesterol levels.

In certain diseases, such as sickle cell anemia, the red blood cells can burst. Zinc deficiency therefore becomes a factor in this genetic condition, since so much zinc-rich hemoglobin is lost and excreted through the urine when red blood cells rupture. People who have inherited sickle cell anemia would be well advised to make sure they get plenty of zinc in their diets to make up the loss.

ZINC'S HEALING POWER IN ACCIDENT OR INJURY

Accident-prone people may want to take extra zinc. The liver, as we have seen, uses zinc to cope with accidents and other emergencies. But since no one ever knows when an accident will happen, extra zinc in the diet makes good sense as accident insurance for everyone.

You may know when surgery is coming up. If you are preparing for an operation, it's a good idea to build up your zinc reserves. Whether your body is traumatized by an accidental injury or the deliberate incisions of an operation, thousands of your cells will die in the process. Somehow, your body must evacuate all the debris of dead cells and the microorganisms they attract, and zinc is a member of the cleanup team. Zinc-containing white blood cells called phagocytes gobble up and remove dead cells, accumulated bacteria, viruses, and other waste matter before they can do any damage. This leaves room for restoration and new growth. In addition, zinc helps carry oxygen to the tissues and insures that your blood will clot when exposed to air. So to speed healing, be sure to prepare for your operation or for healing after an accident by increasing your zinc intake.

In case of accidents involving fire, zinc is triply important. Burn victims excrete great quantities of zinc through their urine, and their white blood cells and liver use up still more as they mobilize all their resources to fight off infection. As a result, serum zinc levels in burn victims may tumble to one-third or less of normal levels. Zinc supplementation in the case of burns is an absolute necessity.

ZINC FOR VIRAL DISEASE AND CANCER

Your immune system cannot function without zinc. Two situations in which it must function well is when the body is attacked by virus, and when it is defending itself against cancer. There are three viral infections that are known to produce zinc deficiencies—hepatitis, encephalitis, and mononucleosis. But whenever the immune system is called into play, extra zinc is useful. Without adequate zinc, the lymphocytes break down and cannot resist infection.

Some forms of cancer are known to be caused by viruses; in other cases, viruses are suspected agents. As a necessary ingredient in the synthesis of DNA and RNA, zinc can help repair the damage when a virus, which is nothing but a bit of DNA or RNA encased in a shell, invades the cell and takes over its reproductive system. In any event, many researchers theorize that cancer represents a problem of the body's immune system. Extra zinc can help strengthen that system.

ZINC FOR NEUROLOGICAL AND PSYCHOLOGICAL PROBLEMS

We have already discussed the significance of zinc deficiency in such serious degenerative diseases of the nervous system as multiple sclerosis (which involves degeneration of the nerve's fatty myelin sheath) and Wilson's disease (which causes cirrhosis of the liver, psychic disturbances, and muscular tremor, rigidity, and spasms).

Another nervous system disorder in which zinc deficiency is sometimes implicated is epilepsy, which is manifested as cerebral seizures that may result in altered mental states and uncontrollable muscle spasms. In cases where epilepsy is accompanied by zinc deficiency, a combination of zinc, magnesium, and vitamin B_6 has proved therapeutic.

Zinc also works sometimes to alleviate emotional problems with no apparent organic cause. Observing that the pineal gland and the hippocampus—the center of emotions in the brain—both concentrate large quantities of zinc, orthomolecular physicians theorize that increasing the zinc supply to these areas may increase the brain's ability to regulate the emotions. They therefore often prescribe zinc in combination with vitamin B_6 when they encounter emotional difficulties in their patients. These experiments have frequently been rewarded with positive changes in outlook and emotional stability.

Dr. Alan Cott, who noticed that some of the symptoms of autism were similar to those of zinc deficiency, pioneered in treating autistic children with zinc and B_6, and was delighted to find he was able to rescue a number of such children from their trancelike state. His success has been repeated elsewhere, and has led to further exploration of the role of zinc deficiency in autism.

We often think of adolescence, pregnancy, and menopause as being, invariably, psychologically traumatic passages from one life stage into the next. We assume they will be accompanied by emotional turbulence, since they represent irrevocable life changes. But much of the emotional turmoil experienced by adolescents, pregnant or postpartum women, and menopausal women may actually be symptoms of zinc deficiency, since the body's need for zinc increases at these times. Senility, too, may sometimes result from zinc deficiency. Zinc supplements might be more appropriate therapy for the trauma of life's passages than the antidepressants and tranquilizers that are currently the most common remedy.

Schizophrenia, too, once thought to be an emotional disorder, is now sometimes proving amenable to nutritional therapies of various kinds. Sometimes food allergy is shown to cause a person's schizophrenic symptoms; in other cases, nutritional deficiencies prove to be the root problem. In several types of schizophrenia, loss of zinc is the culprit. In one of these, porphyria chelates zinc and carries it out of the body with the urine. In another, a chemical substance called kryptopyrrole does the same. Pyrolia, too, is characterized by zinc deficiency leading to schizophrenic symptoms, an inability to carry male children to term, and acute zinc deficiency in pyrolia daughters as they attain adolescence.

In other cases of schizophrenia, the cause is believed to be a buildup of heavy metals such as copper in brain tissues. Here, too, zinc supplements can be helpful, because of zinc's importance in keeping copper levels down. Where it works, zinc is the ideal treatment, since it removes the cause of the disorder rather than merely treating its symptoms.

ZINC FOR BLOOD SUGAR DISORDERS

Zinc can help normalize blood sugar levels, and is therefore important in preventing and sometimes alleviating diabetes or hypoglycemia. Because it is needed for insulin storage and utilization, zinc added to the diet can help you prevent adult-onset diabetes, the incidence of which is on the rise. If you already have this disorder, zinc therapy can help your body use the insulin you receive, and can help prevent a common complication of diabetes, kidney failure due to fatty deposits in the kidney tubules.

Low blood sugar, too, can sometimes be helped by increasing the intake of zinc and other trace minerals important in carbohydrate metabolism, such as chromium. If you suffer from hypoglycemia—symptoms of which may include irritability, tired spells, dizziness, and chronic fatigue—it is very important to be sure your mineral intake is adequate and balanced. Correcting your condition by improving your diet and making sure you get enough exercise is important, since hypoglycemia can develop into diabetes.

ZINC FOR RHEUMATISM AND ARTHRITIS

If you have rheumatism or arthritis, you will be happy to learn that zinc may help you in two ways. As an ingredient of the mucopolysaccharides that are needed in the jellylike substance that eases joint motion, extra zinc may help boost production of these materials. In addition, by homeostatically balancing the levels of other minerals, zinc may reduce heavy metal deposits in the tissues surrounding your joints. For whichever reason, rheumatologists have found that a number of their patients lose joint stiffness and inflammation and gain increased freedom of movement when they are given 220 milligrams of zinc sulfate three times a day.

A Practical Guide for Using Zinc

For the normal adult, daily zinc requirements are only 20 to 25 milligrams. Infants need far less: 0.7 to 5 milligrams.[8] However, adolescents, pregnant women, and older people may have much higher requirements. And of course, anyone who shows signs of zinc deficiency should be sure to obtain more than the minimum daily requirement.

This means you must consume foods containing three times your requirement, because our bodies can only absorb about a third of the zinc in our foods.[9] But zinc is not toxic, and any you don't need will be easily excreted through the urine, so there is little danger in consuming too much. The only caveat is this: because zinc works in tandem with other minerals and can chelate some of them, if the body's other mineral needs are not also taken into account when zinc intake is increased, then an overabundance of zinc may lead to imbalances of other minerals. The trick is to get as much as you need of all the minerals necessary to good health.

How can you get enough zinc in your diet? If you eat meat, organ meats are an excellent source: the liver, heart, and kidneys of the animals you eat will strengthen the corresponding organs of your own body, since animals' bodies concentrate zinc where it is most needed, just as ours do. Eggs, poultry, and seafood are also good sources. Milk also contains zinc (though it may not be well absorbed from milk because of milk's high calcium levels). Excellent vegetable sources include peas, soybeans, mushrooms, whole grains, and most nuts and seeds, notably pumpkin seeds.

SYMPTOMS OF ZINC DEFICIENCY

If your food has little taste or smell, or if cooking smells seem distorted and turn you off, you are very likely in need of zinc supplements. Zinc deficiencies also show up in the skin: stretch marks are an indication that elastin, the fibers that make your skin springy and strong, is not incorporating enough zinc and copper to keep your skin smooth. A serious type of acne, acanthosis, also results from zinc deficiency. So does psoriasis, an intransigent dermatitis that just won't heal, even with medication. In newborn infants, hereditary acrodermatitis enteropathica, in which zinc deficiency leads to infections at each body orifice, must be quickly treated with zinc supplements to prevent death.

Here is a simple test for zinc deficiency: take a look at your fingernails. Are there little white spots on them, or are they opaque instead of translucent? If so, you'd be well advised to stock up on pumpkin seeds, and perhaps take a zinc supplement for good measure. What about your hair? If it's been getting more brittle or losing its color, think about adding zinc to your diet before you run to the drugstore to try a new hair conditioner. Your teeth and gums need zinc, too: if your gums bleed, if the enamel on your teeth is wearing away, a zinc deficiency may be the problem.

The symptoms you can't see may be the most serious, however, The fatty sheaths around each nerve and your cell membranes may need repairs they won't get if you neglect to eat a zinc-rich diet. Your cells may not be able to reproduce all the proteins they need for maintenance and repair of tissues. Your arteries may attract plaque deposits because of lack of zinc to help repair damaged spots in the arterial walls. Fatty deposits in the liver may lead to disabling cirrhosis, and scar tissue may build up in the kidneys until they, too, can no longer function fully. You can't afford to neglect zinc.

ZINC'S PARTNERS

There is good reason why doctors who prescribe zinc supplements tell their patients to take vitamin B$_6$ along with it. Pyridoxine enables the tissues to absorb and use zinc; without B$_6$, the zinc you absorb into the bloodstream from your foods will just stay there, and can cause serious imbalances of iron and copper, resulting in anemia and other symptoms of iron and copper deficiency.

We have said that zinc is needed to stimulate growth, but it cannot do so without manganese. Manganese is also needed, together with chromium and zinc, in the utilization of insulin.

When serving zinc-rich foods, don't forget that whole grains, because they contain phytates, inhibit zinc absorption. High levels of calcium have the same effect. (So rather than sprinkling seeds and nuts on your cereal or yogurt, you might make a point of eating them alone sometimes as a between-meal snack.) On the other hand, vitamin A and phosphorus increase the efficiency with which your body uses zinc.

Another factor to be aware of is that iron in the intestines inhibits the absorption of zinc's partner manganese—so take a break sometimes from cooking in that heavy cast-iron skillet.

However, don't worry about these complications too much. If you include several sources of zinc in your menu each day—which is not difficult, since nature provides plenty of them—and if you eat fresh and whole rather than processed foods, you should have no trouble meeting your zinc requirements.

Summary

Although your body contains and needs only a small amount of zinc, that amount is responsible for many vital biochemical functions. Unfortunately, many of us are zinc deficient because our foods are refined and also because our soils no longer contain zinc. An increased occurrence of degenerative disease is one result of this widespread zinc deficiency.

Zinc is at work throughout our bodies. At the cellular level, zinc must be present before RNA and DNA can be synthesized. With calcium, iron, magnesium, and manganese, zinc enables RNA to work properly in the production of proteins for cellular regeneration and maintenance. The cellular molecules depend on zinc for structural stability.

Zinc also plays an important role in the body's production of growth and sex hormones, and in its utilization of the hormone insulin. As a coenzyme, zinc catalyzes many important activities: it sparks the energy sources AMP and GMP, which activate all enzymatic activity; it helps carboxypeptidase break down the proteins you eat into amino acids; and it must be present for carbonic anhydrase to speed the exchange between carbon dioxide and oxygen within your cells. In addition, zinc is an important element in your body's homeostatic functions, keeping your blood at a proper acidity, producing the histamine needed, chelating excess toxic metals from your body, and helping your kidneys maintain a healthy balance of minerals.

Zinc works in your protein production system, your blood cells, your circulatory system, your liver and kidneys, your muscles, bones, joints, and eyes, your immune system, your metabolic system, and your nerves. Each of these areas of your body will suffer if your zinc supply is inadequate.

Everybody needs zinc—men, women, and children. It plays an active role in the development of sex glands and organs, and for men continues to play a role in the production of semen and sperm. For pregnant women it is especially important to eat zinc-rich foods, as a zinc-deficient mother can produce a child hampered by problems connected to that deficiency. Zinc deficiency in children is responsible for slow growth, learning disabilities, and failure of the sex organs to mature properly.

Adequate zinc can also lower your cholesterol levels; keep your red blood cells from rupturing; help you heal from accident, injury, surgery, or burn; keep your immune system strong against viruses and cancer; and effectively treat emotional and mental disturbances ranging from depression to schizophrenia. Zinc's chelating effects on iron and copper come into play here, particularly in those cases of schizophrenia that are now thought to be caused by heavy metal deposits in the brain.

Zinc can also help you if you suffer from a blood sugar disorder like diabetes or hypoglycemia, or from rheumatism and arthritis. In fact, zinc is such an important factor in balancing the activity of the other minerals in your body that an adequate intake of zinc may be an excellent insurance policy against all sorts of nutritional imbalance.

Adults need 20 to 25 milligrams of zinc daily, with more required by pregnant women, teenagers, and the elderly. Any surplus zinc you take will be excreted in your urine, and since you do not absorb all the zinc present in your food, it's a good idea to get more zinc than the authorities recommend.

You can find zinc in organ meats, whole grains, mushrooms, and seeds like sunflower seeds and pumpkin seeds. Your body will tell you if you aren't getting enough: you may develop stretch marks, skin problems, brittle hair and fingernails, or unhealthy teeth and gums. There are more serious symptoms of deficiency which are not quite so visible: unrepaired membranes and tissues, circulatory diseases, and scar tissue or fatty deposits in the liver or kidneys.

For zinc to work properly, B$_6$ must be present as well. Vitamin A and phosphorus at a meal with zinc-rich foods will also help your body use the zinc efficiently. On the other hand, calcium-rich foods and the phytates found in whole grain fiber inhibit your absorption of zinc.

NOTES

PROTEIN

1. Richard Lyons, "Diet May Be a Link to 10 More Deaths," *The New York Times*, November 23, 1977.
2. N. Glick, "Low-Calorie Protein Diets," *FDA Consumer*, March 1978, p. 7.
3. Dr. Virginia Livingston, Interview by Gary Null on "Natural Living," WBAI, New York.
4. Gary Null, *The New Vegetarian* (New York: Delta, 1978).
5. H.J. Freeman and Y.S. Kim, "Digestion and Absorption of Protein," *Annual Review of Medicine* 29 (1978):99–116.
6. Nutrition Foundation, Inc., "Present Knowledge of Protein," *Present Knowledge of Nutrition*, 3rd ed., New York, 1967.
7. C.H. Robinson and M.R. Lawler, *Normal and Therapeutic Nutrition*, 15th ed., (New York:Macmillan, 1977).
8. E. D. Wilson, et al., *Principles of Nutrition*, 4th ed., Ch. 6, p. 56 (New York:John Wiley and Sons, 1979).
9. Hara Marano, "The Problem with Protein," *New York*, March 5, 1979.
10. Wilson, op cit.
11. G. Inoue, et al., "Studies on Protein Requirements of Young Men Fed Egg Protein and Rice Protein with Excess and Maintenance Energy Intakes," *Journal of Nutrition* 103 (1973):1673–1687.
12. Judy Dyer, "High-Protein Challenges Cholesterol as Villain," *Vegetarian Times*, April 1980.
13. N.S. Scrimshaw, "An Analysis of Past and Present Recommended Dietary Allowances for Protein in Health and Disease," Shattuck Lecture— Strengths and Weaknesses of the Committee Approach: Part I, *New England Journal of Medicine* 294 (January 15, 1976):136.
14. D.M. Hegsted and Y. Chang, "Protein Utilization in Growing Rats at Different Levels of Intake," *Journal of Nutrition* 87 (1965):19.
15. M.V. Krause and M.A. Hunscher, "Proteins and Amino Acids," *Food, Nutrition and Diet Therapy* (Philadelphia:W.B. Saunders, 1972).
16. Wilson, op. cit.
17. M.I. Irwin and D.M. Hegsted, "A Conspectus of Research on Protein Requirements of Man," *Journal of Nutrition* 101 (March 1971):3, 385–430.
18. Scrimshaw, op. cit.
19. Ibid.
20. Irwin and Hegsted, op. cit.
21. L.A. Weller, et al., "Nitrogen Balance of Men Fed Amino Acid Mixtures Based on Rose's Requirements, Egg White Protein and Serum Free Amino Acid Patterns," *Journal of Nutrition* 101 (March 1971):1499–1508.
22. J.C. Waterlow, "Observations on the Mechanism of Adaptation to Low Protein Intakes," *The Lancet*, November 23, 1968.

23. Krause and Hunscher, op cit.
24. N.S. Scrimshaw, "An Analysis of Past and Present Recommended Dietary Allowances for Protein in Health and Disease," Shattuck Lecture—Strengths and Weaknesses of the Committee Approach: Part II, *New England Journal of Medicine* 294 (January 22, 1976):4.
25. D.S. Miller and P.R. Payne, "Assessment of Protein Requirements by Nitrogen Balance," Symposium Proceedings: Biochemical Assessment of Protein Needs, *British Journal of Nutrition* 28(1969).
26. J.S. Garrow, "Protein Nutrition and Wound Healing," Symposium Proceedings: Biochemical Assessment of Protein Needs, *British Journal of Nutrition* 28 (1969).
27. Robinson and Lawler, op. cit.
28. Wilson, op. cit.
29. Robinson and Lawler, op. cit.
30. Ibid.
31. Krause and Hunscher, op. cit.
32. "Vegetarianism: Can You Get By Without Meat?" *Consumer Reports*, June 1980 p. 357.
33. M.G. Hardinge and H. Crooks, "Non-Flesh Dietaries," *Journal of the ADA*, Vol. 43, No. 6 (December 1963):552–553.
34. Wilson, op. cit.
35. Robinson and Lawler, op. cit.
36. Kathleen M. Henry and S.K. Kon, "The Nutritive Value of Proteins: General Considerations," Symposium on the Nutritive Value of Proteins, 112th Scientific Meeting, Royal Free Hospital School of Medicine, London, England, *British Journal of Nutrition*, Vol. 17, (October 12, 1957):78–84.
37. F.M. Lappé, *Diet for a Small Planet* (New York: Ballantine, 1971).
38. M.G. Stephenson, "Textured Plant Proteins Products: New Choices for Consumers," *FDA Consumer* 18(April 1975).

CARBOHYDRATES

1. Nutrition Foundation, Inc., *Present Knowledge in Nutrition*, 3rd Edition, New York, 1967.
2. Ibid.
3. G.M. Gray, "Drugs, Malnutrition and Carbohydrate Absorption," *American Journal of Clinical Nutrition* 26(1973):121.
4. R. Levine, "Carbohydrates," Ch. 3, *Modern Nutrition in Health and Disease*, R.S. Goodhart and M.E. Shils, ed., (Philadelphia: Lea & Febiger, 1973).
5. William Dufty, *Sugar Blues* (Radnor, Pa.: Chilton, 1975).
6. I. Tamir, et al., "Serum Lipids During Short-term High Glucose and High Sucrose Feeding in Infants," *Pediatrics* 50 (1972):89.
7. *Fructose*, Bureau of Foods, FDA, Contract No. FDA 223-75-2090, October 1976.
8. A.E. Bender and K.B. Damji, "Some Effects of Dietary Sucrose," *World Review of Nutrition and Dietetics*, 15(1972):104–155.
9. Gray, op. cit.
10. Ibid.
11. Ibid.
12. A. Jeanes and J. Hodge, ed., *Physiological Effects of Food Carbohydrates*, American Chemical Society Symposium Series, Washington, D.C., 1975.

13. Eleanor Baker and D.S. Lepkovsky, *Bread and the War Food Problem,* Riverside: College of Agriculture, University of California, June 1943 as quoted in Beatrice Trum Hunter *Consumer Beware,* (New York: Simon and Schuster, 1971).

14. Ibid.

15. I.M. Sharman and Pamela J. Richards, "Commercial Breads as Sources of Vitamin E for Rats Determined by the Hemolysis Test," *British Journal of Nutrition* 14(1960):85 as quoted in Hunter.

16. *Lockwood's Technical Manual: Flour Milling* (London: Crosby Lockwood, 1948) as quoted in Hunter.

17. Advertisement, *Baker's Weekly,* January 17, 1966, p. 51 as quoted in Hunter.

18. Quoted in "Breakfast Cereals," *Consumer Reports,* May 1961, p. 238 as quoted in Hunter.

19. "Quote Without Comment," *Consumer Reports,* June 1965, p. 274 as quoted in Hunter.

20. Beatrice Trum Hunter, *Consumer Beware* (New York: Simon and Schuster, 1971).

21. H. Sharon, *Complex Carbohydrates* (Reading, Mass.:Addison Wesley, 1975).

22. H.N. Shultz, ed., *Symposium on Foods; Carbohydrates and their Roles* (Westport, Conn.: AVI Publishing Co. 1969).

23. G. Borgstrom, *Principles of Food Science* (New York:Macmillan, 1968).

24. Ibid.

25. H. Zamcheck and S.A. Broitman, "Nutrition in Diseases of the Intestines," Ch. 28, Sect. B, *Modern Nutrition in Health and Disease,* R.S. Goodhart and M.E. Shils eds. (Philadelphia: Lea & Febiger, 1973).

26. C.H. Robinson and M.R. Lawler, eds., *Normal and Therapeutic Nutrition,* 15th ed. (New York:Macmillan, 1977).

27. Levine, op. cit.

28. Ibid.

29. G.M. Gray, "Carbohydrate Digestion and Absorption:Role of the Small Intestine," *Physiology in Medicine,* Vol. 292, No. 23(1976):1225.

30. Ibid.

31. Shultz, op. cit.

32. Borgstrom, op. cit.

33. *Fructose,* op. cit.

34. Dufty, op. cit.

35. Hunter, op. cit.

36. Dufty, op. cit.

37. Hunter, op. cit.

38. Dufty, op. cit.

39. *Fructose,* op. cit.

40. Bender, op. cit.

41. *Fructose,* op. cit.

42. Borgstrom, op. cit.

43. Hunter, op. cit.

44. Ibid.

45. Ibid.

46. Ibid.

47. Ibid.

48. Ibid.

49. Gary Null, "The Dulcet Dogfight Over Saccharin," *Let's Live,* October 1977.

50. J. Pekkanen and M. Falco, "Sweet and Sour," *Atlantic Monthly,* July 1975.

51. J.L. Hess, "Harvard's Sugar-Pushing Nutritionist," *Saturday Review*, 1978.
52. Pekkanen, op. cit.
53. Ibid.
54. Ibid.
55. "Carbohydrate Preference in Normal and Malnourished Rats," *Nutrition Reviews*, Vol. 31, No. 5 (May 1973).
56. Ibid.
57. Levine, op. cit.
58. Ibid.
59. Ibid.
60. Ibid.
61. L. MacDonald, "Sucrose," *Science*, Oxford, September 9, 1971.
62. Levine, op. cit.
63. Ibid.
64. Ibid.
65. Tamir, op. cit.
66. Ibid.
67. Gray, "Drugs, Malnutrition and Carbohydrate Absorption."
68. Ibid.
69. K.D. Buchanan, "Hormonal Control of Carbohydrate Metabolism," *Journal of Clinical Pathology*, Vol. 22 supplement.
70. Shultz, op. cit.
71. Ibid.
72. Ibid.
73. Levine, op. cit.
74. Ibid.
75. Ibid.
76. T.L. Cleave, *The Saccharine Disease* (New Canaan, Conn.: Keats Publishing 1975).
77. "Effect of Dietary Factors on Carcass Composition of Rats," *Nutrition Reviews* 28(March 1970).
78. A.R. MacRae, et al., "Studies on Carbohydrate Digestibility and Weight Gain Response in Rats Fed Dietary Sucrose, Glucose or Fructose," *Nutritional Metabolism* 17 (1974).
79. A.S. Leon, et al., "Effects of a Vigorous Walking Program on Body Composition, and Carbohydrate and Lipid Metabolism in Obese Young Men," *American Journal of Clinical Nutrition* 33 (1979).
80. Covert Bailey, *Fit or Fat* (Boston:Houghton Mifflin, 1977).
81. Ibid.
82. Ibid.
83. Ibid.
84. Ibid.
85. Ibid.
86. K.K. Makinen, "The Role of Sucrose and Other Sugars in the Development of Dental Caries, A Review," Vol. 22, No. 3.
87. A.L. Scheinen and K.K. Makinen, "The Effects of Various Sugars on the Formation and Chemical Composition of Dental Plaque," *Proceedings of the Nutrition Society* 32 (December 1973).
88. *Fructose*, op. cit.
89. T.H. Grenby, et al., "Effects of Sweets Made with and without Sucrose on the Dental Plaque and the Correlation Between the Extent of Plaque and Human Dental Caries Experience," *Journal of Oral Biology*, 19 (1974).

90. L.E.A. Folke, et al., "Effect of Dietary Sucrose on Quantity and Quality of Plaque," *Scandanavian Journal of Dental Research* 80 (1972).
91. Tamir, op. cit.
92. *Fructose*, op. cit.
93. Makinen, op. cit.
94. *Fructose*, op. cit.
95. John Yudkin, "Sugar and Disease," *Nature* 239 (September 22, 1972).
96. Bender, op. cit.
97. F. Grande, "Sugar and Cardiovascular Disease," *World Review of Nutrition and Dietetics* 22 (1975).
98. Yudkin, op. cit.
99. R.A. Ahrens. "Sucrose, Hypertension and Heart Disease: A Historical Perspective," *American Journal of Clinical Nutrition* 27 (1974).
100. Bender, op. cit.
101. Ibid.
102. L.M. Dalerup and N. Visser, "Influence of Extra Sucrose in the Daily Food on the Life Span of Wistar Albino Rats," The Netherlands Institute of Nutrition, Amsterdam.
103. J. Yudkin, "Dietary Sucrose and the Behavior of Blood Platelets," *Proceedings of the Nutrition Society* 29 (1969).
104. Ibid.
105. Ahrens, op. cit.
106. R.E. Hodges and N.A. Krehl "The Role of Carbohydrates in Lipid Metabolism," *American Journal of Clinical Nutrition* 17 (1965).
107. J. Yudkin, "Sucrose, Insulin and Coronary," *American Heart Journal* 80 (1970):6.
108. Veikko A. Koivisto, et al., "Carbohydrate Ingestion Before Exercise: Comparison of Glucose, Fructose, and Sweet Placebo," *Journal of Applied Physiology* 51, 4(1981):783–78.
109. Ibid.
110. Gina Kolata, "Dietary Dogma Disproved," *Science,* April 1983.
111. Gina Kolata and Toni Goldfarb, "In Praise of Pasta and Beans," *American Health,* Vol. 2, No. 3(June 1983).
112. Hodges and Krehl, op. cit.
113. S. Mukherjee, et al., "Effect of Low Dietary Levels of Glucose, Fructose and Sucrose in Rat Lipid Metabolism," *Journal of Atherosclerosis Research* 10 (1969).
114. J.L. Kelsay, "Diets High in Glucose or Sucrose and Young Women," *American Journal of Clinical Nutrition* 27 (1974).
115. M.A. Antar, et al., "Interrelationship Between the Kinds of Dietary Carbohydrate and Fat in Hyperlipoproteinemic Patients," *Atherosclerosis* 11 (1970).
116. S. Reiser, "Metabolic Effects of Dietary Carbohydrates: A Review," American Chemical Society Symposium Series, 1974.
117. Ibid.
118. M. Murakami, "Effect of Sugar in Atherosclerosis in Nonhuman Primates," *Japanese Circulation Journal* 37 (September 1973).
119. K.R. Bruckdorfer, et al., "The Lipid Content of the Aorta of Rats Given Sucrose," *Proceedings of the Nutrition Society* 31 (1971).
120. C.D. Berdanier, et al., "Effects of Age, Strain and Dietary Carbohydrates on the Hepatic Metabolism of Male Rats," *Journal of Nutrition* 109 (1979).
121. *Apharmacy Weekly,* June 4, 1980.
122. Ahrens, op. cit.

123. I. MacDonald, "Sex Differences in Response to Dietary Carbohydrates," *Proceedings of the Nutrition Society* 35 (1976).
124. H.A. Schroeder, "Serum Cholesterol and Glucose Levels in Rats Fed Refined and Less Refined Sugars and Chromium," Dartmouth Medical School, 1969.
125. A. Keys, "Coronary Heart Disease: Overweight and Obesity as Risk Factors," *Journal of Internal Medicine* 77 (1972).
126. Nutrition Foundation, op. cit.
127. B.M. Rifkind, et al., "Effects of Short-term Sucrose Restriction on Serum-Lipid Levels, *The Lancet*, December 24, 1961.
128. Yudkin, "Dietary Sucrose and the Behavior of Blood Platelets," op. cit.
129. P.A. Akinyanju, et al., "Effect on an Atherogenic Diet Containing Starch or Sucrose on the Blood Lipids of Young Men," *Nature* 218 (June 8, 1968).
130. S. Szanto and J. Yudkin, "The Effect of Dietary Sucrose in Blood Lipids, Serum Insulin, Platelet Adhesiveness and Body Weight in Human Volunteers," *Postgraduate Medical Journal* 45 (1969).
131. K.R. Bruckdorfer, et al., "Does Dietary Lactose Produce Hyperlipaemia in the Rat?" *Proceedings of the Nutrition Society* 31 (September 1971).
132. Keys, op. cit.
133. Pekkanen, op. cit.
134. R.W. Stout, "The Role of Insulin in the Development of Atherosclerosis," *Advances in Metabolic Diseases* Supplement 2, 1973.
135. A.R.P. Walker, "Sugar Intake and Diabetes Mellitus," *S.A. Medical Journal* 51 (1977).
136. A.M. Cohen, A. Teitelbaum and B. Saliternik, "Genetics and Diet Factors in Development of Diabetes Mellitus," *Metabolism* 21 (March 1972):3.
137. Pekkanen, op. cit.
138. Ibid.
139. Walker, op. cit.
140. J. Yudkin and S. Szanto, "Hyperinsulinism and Atherogenesis," Letter to the Editor, *British Medical Journal*, date unknown.
141. Rifkind, op. cit.
142. Szanto and Yudkin, op. cit.
143. L.H. Opie, "Dietary Sucrose in Relation to the Development of Ischemic Heart Disease," *American Heart Journal* 89 (May 1975).
144. Ibid.
145. J.B. Bennett, "Physiological and Biochemical Changes in Impaired Glucose Metabolism," Vancouver Address, *The Academy of Orthomolecular Psychiatry*, May 21, 1974.
146. Ibid.
147. Stout, op. cit.
148. H. Keen, "Glucose Tolerance, Plasma Lipids and Atherosclerosis," *Proceedings of the Nutrition Society* 31 (1972):339.
149. Ibid.
150. Reiser, op. cit.
151. Ibid.
152. Ibid.
153. Jeanes and Hodges, op. cit.
154. "Sugar-Induced Diarrhea in Children," *Canadian Medical Association Journal* 109 (September 1, 1973):343.
155. Ibid.
156. G.A. Bray, "Effects of Oral Contraceptives on Carbohydrate Metabolism," *The Western Journal of Medicine*, Vol. 33, date unknown.

157. A. Sanchez, et al., "Role of Sugars in Human Neutrophilic Phagocytosis," *American Journal of Clinical Nutrition* 26 (1973).

158. "Dyspepsia," *Nature* 22 (September 1972).

159. J. Yudkin, "Infant Feeding and Diabetes," *Nature* 239 (1972):197.

160. Ibid.

161. J. Espinoza and N.S. Rosenzweig, "Effect of Aging in the Response of Rat Hepatic Glycolytic Enzyme Activities to Dietary Sugars," *American Journal of Clinical Nutrition* 26 (1973).

162. Ronald J. Prinz, et al., "Double Blind Study Implicates Sugar, Questions Feingold Diet," *Journal of Behavioral Ecology*, Biosocial Vol. 2, No. 1 (1981).

163. J. Kershner and W. Hawke, "Megavitamins and Learning Disorders: A Controlled Double Blind Experiment," *Journal of Nutrition* 109 (1979): 819–826.

164. J.A. Wacker, "The Dyslogue Syndrome—The ACLD Key," Texas Association for Children with Learning Disabilities, Symposium, Dallas, September 1975.

165. A.G. Schauss, "A Centrical Analysis of the Diets of Chronic Offenders, Part k" *Journal of Orthomolecular Psychiatry* 8 (1979):149–157.

166. Kershner, op. cit.

167. Personal interview.

168. "Diet and Colonic Cancer," *British Medical Journal* (March 2, 1974):3390–3401.

169. M.A. Howell "Diet as an Etiological Factor in the Development of Cancers of the Colon and Rectum," *Journal of Chronic Disease* 28 (1975):67–80.

170. Ibid.

171. "Diet and Colonic Cancer," op. cit.

172. M.V. Krause and M.A. Hunscher, *Food, Nutrition and Diet Therapy* (Philadelphia: W.B. Saunders, 1972).

173. *Merck Manual of Diagnosis and Therapy*, Merck, Sharpe and Dohme Research, Division of Merck & Co., 1961.

174. Kenneth Lamott, *Escape from Stress: How to Stop Killing Yourself* (New York: Putnam, 1974).

175. Krause and Hunscher, op. cit.

176. Zamcheck and Broitman, op. cit.

177. Leslie C. Thompson, *Intestinal Fitness: New Light on Constipation* (London: Thomson Publishers, Ltd., 1967).

178. Borgstrom, op. cit.

179. N.S. Painter and J.W. Wilson, *The Miracle* (Philadelphia: J.P. Lippincott, 1975).

180. F. G. Slaughter, *Your Body and Your Mind* (New York: New American Library, 1953).

181. Painter and Wilson, op. cit.

182. "Intestinal Disturbance Due to Psychic Factors, Allergy and Endogenous Infection," *Ciba Digestive Systems*, Section XII, 1973.

183. Painter and Wilson, op. cit.

184. Personal interview.

185. Zamcheck and Broitman, op. cit.

186. *Merck Manual*, op. cit.

187. Ibid.

188. H.S. Mitchell, et al., "Diseases of the Intestines," *Nutrition in Health and Disease* (Philadelphia: J.P. Lippincott, 1970).

189. Ibid.

190. *Merck Manual*, op. cit.

191. D.P. Burkitt, "Dietary Fiber and Pressure Diseases," *Journal of the Royal College of Physicians* 9 (January 1975):138–147.

192. D.P. Burkitt, "The Aetiology of Appendicitis," *British Journal of Surgery* 58(1971): 695–699.

193. D.P. Burkitt and N.S. Painter, "Dietary Fiber and Disease," *Journal of the AMA,* 229 (August 19, 1974):1068–1074.

194. Burkitt, "The Aetiology of Appendicitis," op. cit.

195. Burkitt, "Dietary Fiber and Pressure Diseases," op. cit.

196. Burkitt, "The Aetiology of Appendicitis," op. cit.

197. Burkitt, "Dietary Fiber and Pressure Diseases," op. cit.

198. Burkitt, "The Aetiology of Appendicitis," op. cit.

199. N.S. Painter and D.P. Burkitt, "Diverticular Disease of the Colon: A Deficiency Disease of Western Civilization," *British Medical Journal* 2 (1971): 450–454.

200. J.N. Finlay, et al., "Effect of Unprocessed Bran on Colon Function in Normal Subjects and in Diverticular Disease," *The Lancet* 1 (February 2, 1974):146–149.

201. Painter and Wilson, op. cit.

202. P.F. Plumley and B. Francis, "Dietary Management of Diverticular Disease," *Journal of the ADA* 63 (November 1973):525–530.

203. Painter and Wilson, op. cit.

204. Burkitt and Painter, op. cit.

205. Ibid.

206. Personal interview.

207. Krause and Hunscher, op. cit.

208. Thompson, op. cit.

209. Ibid.

210. Krause and Hunscher, op. cit.

211. Painter and Wilson, op. cit.

212. Ibid.

213. Personal interview.

214. Ibid.

215. Krause and Hunscher, op. cit.

216. Ibid.

217. Painter and Wilson, op. cit.

218. Personal interview.

219. Krause and Hunscher, op. cit.

220. Painter and Wilson, op. cit.

221. Burkitt, "Dietary Fiber and Pressure Diseases," op. cit.

222. Ibid.

223. Ibid.

224. Painter and Burkitt, op. cit.

225. Burkitt, "Dietary Fiber and Pressure Diseases," op. cit.

226. Burkitt and Painter, op. cit.

227. Painter and Wilson, op. cit.

228. Ibid.

229. Finlay, op. cit.

LIPIDS

1. C.H. Robinson and M.R. Lawler, *Normal and Therapeutic Nutrition,* 15th ed., (New York: Macmillan, 1977).

2. Ibid.
3. Ibid.
4. R.S. Goodhart and M.E. Shils, *Modern Nutrition in Health and Disease*, 5th ed. (Philadelphia: Lea and Febiger, 1973).
5. D.B. Lindsay, "Fatty Acids as Energy Sources," *Proceedings of the Nutrition Society* 34 (1975).
6. Ibid.
7. R.W. Stout, "The Physiology of Triglyceride Metabolism," *British Journal of Hospital Medicine*, September 1973, pp. 309–319.
8. G.J. Tortora and N.P. Anagnostakos, *Principles of Anatomy and Physiology*, 3rd ed., (New York: Harper & Row, 1981).
9. B. Ferderber, "Fats May Be Your Best Medicine," *Bestways*, April 1974, pp. 11–13.
10. D.A. Van Derp, "Essential Fatty Acid Metabolism," *Proceedings of the Nutrition Society* 34 (1975):279–285.
11. Ferderber, op. cit.
12. J.P.W. Rivers and A.G. Hassam, "Defective Essential Fatty Acid Metabolism in Cystic Fibrosis," *The Lancet*, October 4, 1975.
13. H. Hopkins, "Getting Specific About Fats and Oils," *FDA Consumer*, March 1976, pp. 13–14.
14. Ferderber, op. cit.
15. T.O. Von Lossonczy, et al., "The Effect of a Fish Diet on Serum Lipids in Healthy Human Subjects," *American Journal of Clinical Nutrition* 31 (August 1978):1340.
16. Goodhart and Shils, op. cit.
17. Ibid.
18. Ferderber, op. cit.
19. Beatrice Trum Hunter, *Consumer Beware* (New York:Simon & Schuster, 1971), Ch. 9.
20. Ibid.
21. Ibid.
22. Ibid.
23. R.W.D. Turner, "The Lipid Hypothesis," *Nature* 273 (June 8, year unknown).
24. E.R. Pinckney, "The Potential Toxicity of Excessive Polyunsaturates," *American Heart Association*, Vol. 85, No. 6 (June 1973).
25. Hopkins, op. cit.
26. B.H. Ershoff, "Effects of Diet on Fish Oil Toxicity in the Rat" *Journal of Nutrition* 71(May 1960).
27. G.L.S. Pawan, "Fat Metabolism," *The Practitioner* 212 (April 1974).
28. Pinckney, op. cit.
29. Barbara R. Landau, *Essential Human Anatomy and Physiology* (Chicago: Scott Foresman, 1980).
30. Pawan, op. cit.
31. Stout, op. cit.
32. R.H. Dowling, "The Enterohepatic Circulation of Bile Acids as They Relate to Lipid Disorder," *Journal of Clinical Pathology*, Vol. 26, No. 5, pp. 59–67.
33. N.B. Myant, "The Influence of Some Dietary Factors on Cholesterol Metabolism," *Proceedings of the Nutrition Society* 34 (1975):271–277.
34. Dowling, op. cit.
35. Tortora, op. cit.
36. Pawan, op. cit.
37. Ibid.

38. Tortora, op. cit.
39. Robinson and Lawler, op. cit.
40. M. Tzagournis, "Triglycerides in Clinical Medicine," *American Journal of Clinical Nutrition* 31 (August 1975):1437–1452.
41. Robinson and Lawler, op. cit.
42. L.M. Morrison, *The Low-Fat Way to Health and Longer Life* (New York: Prentice-Hall, 1958).
43. Ibid.
44. V. Licata, "Lecithin for the Modern Man," *Continental Health Research*, 1971.
45. Morrison, op. cit.
46. Interview with Ira Berry, Vice-President, Technical Services for Pharmaceutical Caps, Inc., Elizabeth, New Jersey.
47. Gary Null, "The Lecithin Rip-off" *Forum*, August 1979.
48. Morrison, op. cit.
49. Carlton Fredericks, "Let's Learn About Lecithin," *Nutrition News*, Vol. 11, No. 4 (April 1956).
50. Pat Lazarus, "Lecithin, Battling the Dangerous Cholesterol," *Let's Live*, 1979.
51. Ibid.
52. Interview with Ira Berry, op. cit.
53. Ibid.
54. Licata, op. cit.
55. Interview with Ira Berry, op. cit.
56. Fredericks, op. cit.
57. Janice Fillips, "On the Labels of Lecithin," *Whole Foods*, February 1979.
58. Interview with Ira Berry, op. cit.
59. Ibid.
60. Ibid.
61. Lazarus, op. cit.
62. Harold Schmeck, Jr., "Memory Loss Curbed by Chemicals in Foods," *Science Times (The New York Times)*, January 9, 1979.
63. Department of Nutrition and Food Science, Massachusetts Institute of Technology, Symposium on Dietary Choline Sources and Brain Function (date unknown).
64. Interview with Ira Berry, op. cit.
65. G.F. Wilgram, et al., "Abnormal Lipid in Coronary Arteries and Aortic Sclerosis in Young Rats Fed a Choline-Deficient Diet," *Science*, June 11, 1954.
66. MIT Symposium, op. cit.
67. Ibid.
68. Lazarus, op. cit.
69. Interview with Ira Berry, op. cit.
70. Fredericks, op. cit.
71. Lazarus, op. cit.
72. Schmeck, op. cit.
73. Lazarus, op. cit.
74. Ibid.
75. Morrison, op. cit.
76. Lazarus, op. cit.
77. Licata, op. cit.
78. "Phosphorus in Metabolism," Associated Concentrates Co., Woodside New York.

79. Ruth M. Feeley, et al., "Cholesterol Contents of Food," *Journal of the American Dietetics Association* 61 (August 1972).
80. "Soy Phospholipid as Cholesterol Lowering Agent," Associated Concentrates Co., Woodside, New York.
81. Feeley, op. cit.
82. Interview with Ira Berry, op. cit.
83. David W. Bartels, "Serum Triglycerides and Cholesterol," *Hospital Pharmacy* 14 (July 1979).
84. N.B. Myant, "Cholesterol Metabolism," *Journal of Clinical Pathology*, Vol. 26, No. 5 (date unknown).
85. E.G. Gruberg and S.A. Raymond, "Beyond Cholesterol," *Atlantic Monthly* May 1979.
86. G. Hepner, et al., "Hypocholesterolemic Effect of Yogurt and Milk," *American Journal of Clinical Nutrition* 32 (1979).
87. Myant, "Cholesterol Metabolism," op. cit.
88. David Reuben, "Peddling Sheer Nonsense," *Newsday*, 1978.
89. Von Lossonczy, et al., op. cit.
90. Feeley, op. cit.
91. "How Steroids Affect Lipid Metabolism," *Medworld News*, August 6, 1971.
92. Myant, "Cholesterol Metabolism," op. cit.
93. Ibid.
94. Ferderber, op. cit.
95. F.H. Mattson, et al., "Effect of Dietary Cholesterol on Serum Cholesterol in Man," *American Journal of Clinical Nutrition* 25 (June 1972).
96. Margaret Albrink, "Triglyceridemia," *Journal of the American Dietetic Association*, (date unknown).
97. Ibid.
98. Ibid.
99. A.M. Gotto, Jr., et al., "Dietary and Behavioral Treatment of Hyperlipidemia," *Comp. Ther.*, Vol. 4, No. 10 (October 1978).
100. Albrink, op. cit.
101. Tzagournis, op. cit.
102. "Soy Protein Drink is Reported to Reduce Cholesterol Levels." *The New York Times*, April 21, 1982.
103. W.E. Stchsens, "A New Concept of the Aetiology of Atherosclerosis," *Medical Journal of Australia* 2 (1974).
104. Gruberg and Raymond, op. cit.
105. Stehsens, op. cit.
106. Nancy Lyon, "Cholesterol," *Town & Country*, January 1977.
107. J.S. Lewis, et al., "Effect of Long-term Ingestion of Polyunsaturated Fat, Age, Plasma Cholesterol, Diabetes Mellitus, Supplemental Tocopherol upon Plasma Tocopherol." *American Journal of Clinical Nutrition* 26 (February 1973).
108. Ibid.
109. U.M. Donde, et al., "Effect of Contraceptive Steroids on Serum Lipids," *Fertility and Sterility*, Vol. 26, No. 1, January 1975.
110. Ibid.
111. M.K. Horwitt, et al., "Relationship Between Levels of Blood Lipids, Vitamin C, A and E, Copper Compounds and Urinary Excretions of Tryptophan Metabolites in Women Taking Oral Contraceptive Therapy," *American Journal of Clinical Nutrition* 28 (April 1975).
112. A.S. Trusell, "Diet and Plasma Lipids—A Reappraisal," *American Journal of Clinical Nutrition* 31 (June 1978).

113. Ibid.
114. Ibid.
115. Ibid.
116. Ibid.
117. Ibid.
118. Sir John McMichael "Fats and Arterial Disease," *American Heart Journal*, Vol. 98, No. 4(October 1979).
119. Dowling, op. cit.
120. A.J. DeBont, et al., "Influence of Alteration in Meal Frequency on Lipogenesis and Body Fat Content in the Rat," *Proceedings of the Society for Experimental Biology and Medicine* 149 (1975).

VITAMIN A

1. *Prevention* staff, *The Complete Book of Vitamins* (Emmaus:Rodale Press, 1977).
2. Eleanor Whitney and May Hamilton, *Understanding Nutrition* (St. Paul; Minn.:West Publishing Co., 1977).
3. J.P. Sweeney and A.C. Marsh, "Effect of Processing on Provitamin A in Vegetables," *Journal of the American Dietetic Association*, September 1971, pp. 238–243.
4. R.C.H. Rosse and A.H. Campbell, *Medical Journal of Australia*, August 19, 1961.
5. Robert E. Hodges, et al., Hematopoietic Studies in Vitamin A Deficiency," *American Journal of Clinical Nutrition* 31 (May 1978):876–885.
6. Ibid.
7. Robert M. Russell, et al., "Vitamin A Reversal of Abnormal Adaptation in Cirrhosis," *Annals of Internal Medicine* 88 (1978):622–626.
8. *Medical World News*, March 5, 1971.
9. Ibid.
10. Richard A. Chole and Cedric A. Quick, "Experimental Temporal Bone Histopathology in Rats Deprived of Dietary Retinol and Maintained with Supplemental Retinoic Acid." *Journal of Nutrition* 108 (1978):1008–1016.
11. T.L. Harris, *Proceedings of the Society for Experimental Biology and Medicine*, March 1947.
12. *Prevention* staff, op. cit.
13. Merrill S. Chermov, *American Journal of Surgery* 122 (1971).
14. Whitney and Hamilton, op. cit.
15. *Prevention* staff, op. cit.
16. Ibid.
17. Leonard E. Savitt and Maximillian E. Obermayer, "Treatment of Acne Vulgaris and Senile Keratoses with Vitamin A: Results of a Clinical Experiment," *Journal of Investigative Dermatology*, Vol. 14, No. 4 (April 1950), pp. 283–289.
18. *Clinical Medicine*, July 1959.
19. *Prevention* staff, op. cit.
20. B. Ahluvalia, et al., "Distribution of Labeled Retinyl Acetate and Retinoic Acid in Rat and Human Testes, A Possible Site of Retinyl Acetate Incorporation in Rat Testes," *Journal of Nutrition* 105 (1975):467–474.
21. *Prevention* staff, op. cit.
22. Ibid.
23. Ibid.

24. E. Bjelke, "Dietary Vitamin A and Human Lung Cancer," *Cancer* 15 (1975): 561–565.

25. Ibid.

26. David M. Smith, et al., "Vitamin A (Retinyl Acetate) and Benzo(a)pyrene-induced Respiratory Tract Carcinogenesis in Hamsters Fed a Commercial Diet," *Cancer Research* 35 (January 1975):11–16.

27. Mildred S. Rodriguez and M. Isabel Irwin, "A Conspectus of Research on Vitamin A Requirements of Man," *Journal of Nutrition*, Vol. 102, No. 7 (July 1972):pp. 911–968.

28. "The Use and Abuse of Vitamin A," Joint Committee Statement of American Academy of Pediatrics and the Committees on Drugs and Nutrition," *Nutrition Reviews*, Supplement, July 1974, pp. 41–42.

29. Ibid.

30. Ibid.

31. Ruth Adams, *The Complete Home Guide to All the Vitamins* (New York: Larchmont Books, 1972).

32. *Prevention* staff, op. cit.

33. Isabel Gal, et al., "Effects of Oral Contraceptives on Human Plasma Vitamin A Levels," *British Medical Journal*, May 22, 1971, pp. 436–438.

34. "Effect of Oral Contraceptives on Plasma Vitamin A," *Journal of the American Dietetic Association* 72 (May 1978).

35. John R. Duncan and Lucille S. Hurley, "An Interaction Between Zinc and Vitamin A in Pregnant and Fetal Rats," *Journal of Nutrition* 108 (1978): 1431–1438.

36. "Vitamin A: A Health Hazard?" *Natural Foods Merchandiser*, Vol. 5, No. 7 (July 1983).

B COMPLEX

1. Henry Borsook, *Vitamins* (New York: Pyramid, 1968), p. 71.

2. Roger J. Williams, *Nutrition Against Disease* (New York:Bantam, 1971).

3. Ibid.

4. Ibid.

5. Ibid.

6. Frank S. Butler as quoted in Ruth Adams and Frank Murray, *Body, Mind and the B Vitamins* (New York: Larchmont Books, 1972).

7. Drs. George Watson and W.D. Currier as quoted in *Prevention* staff, *The Complete Book of Vitamins*, (Emmaus: Rodale Press, 1977).

8. Gregory Stefan, *In Search of Sanity* (New Hyde Park: University Books, 1966).

9. Abram Hoffer and Humphrey Osmond, *How to Live with Schizophrenia* (Secaucus, N.J.: University Books, 1966).

10. Malathi Damodaran, et al., "Vitamin B-Complex Deficiency and Visual Acuity," *British Journal of Nutrition* 41(1979):27.

11. Eleanor Whitney and May Hamilton, *Understanding Nutrition* (St. Paul, Minn.:West Publishing Co., 1977).

12. Ibid.

13. Paul Jay Friedman and Robert E. Hodges, "Tongue Color and B-Vitamin Deficiencies," *The Lancet*, May 28, 1977, pp. 1159–1160.

14. Russell Wilder, "A Brief History of the Enrichment of Flour and Bread," *Journal of the American Medical Association*, Vol. 162, No. 17, December 22, 1956.

15. Ruth Adams and Frank Murray, *Body, Mind and the B Vitamins* (New York: Larchmont Books, 1972).
16. Ibid.
17. Ibid.
18. C.H. Robinson and M.R. Lawler, *Normal and Therapeutic Nutrition*, 15th ed., (New York: Macmillan, 1977).
19. Ibid.
20. M.K. Gaitonde, et al., "The Effect of Deficiency of Thiamine on the Metabolism of [U¹⁴C] Glucose and [U¹⁴C] Ribose and the Levels of Amino Acids in the Brain," *Journal of Neurochemistry* 22 (1974):53–61.
21. T. Kositawattanakul, et al., "Chemical Interactions Between Thiamine and Tannic Acid, II. Separation of products," *American Journal of Clinical Nutrition* October 1977, pp. 1686–1691.
22. Michael Lesser, *Nutrition and Vitamin Therapy* (New York: Grove Press, 1980).
23. Dr. Myron Brin as quoted in *Prevention* staff, *The Complete Book of Vitamins* (Emmaus: Rodale Press, 1977).
24. "The Thiamine Status of Australian People," Summary of a Report to the National Health and Medical Research Council, the *Medical Journal of Australia*, February 25, 1978, p. 232.
25. E. Cheraskin, et al., "The 'Ideal' Daily Vitamin B₁ Intake," *Journal of Oral Medicine*, Vol. 33 No. 3(July–September 1978), pp. 77–79.
26. B.R. Forker and A.F. Morgan, "Effect of Adrenocortical Hormone on the Riboflavin Deficient Rat," January 29, 1954 (journal unknown).
27. Ibid.
28. Whitney and Hamilton, op. cit.
29. Ibid.
30. Robinson and Lawler, op. cit.
31. Ibid.
32. N. Sanpitake and L. Chayutimonkul, "Oral Contraceptives and Riboflavin Nutrition," *The Lancet*, May 4, 1974, pp. 836–837.
33. Leonard J. Newman, et al., "Riboflavin Deficiency in Women Taking Oral Contraceptive Agents," *American Journal of Clinical Nutrition* 31 (February 1978):247–249.
34. Marianna K. Fordyce and Judy A. Driskell, "Effects of Riboflavin Repletion During Different Developmental Phases on Behavioral Patterns, Brain Nucleic Acid and Protein Contents, and Erythrocyte Glutathione Reductase Activity of Male Rats," *Journal of Nutrition* 105 (1975):1150–1156.
35. Ibid.
36. Bruce Mackler, "Studies of the Molecular Basis of Congenital Malformations," *Pediatrics*, Vol. 43, No. 6 (June 1969), pp. 915–926.
37. Ibid.
38. Newman, et al., op. cit.
39. E. Vanderween and J. Vanderween, *Remington Pharmaceutical Sciences* (Easton, Pa.: Mack Publishing Co., 1980), p. 958.
40. *Prevention* staff, op. cit.
41. W.J. Darby, et al., *Nutrition Reviews*, Vol. 33, No. 10 (October 1975):289.
42. *Prevention* staff, op. cit.
43. Ibid.
44. Adams and Murray, op. cit.
45. *Prevention* staff, op. cit.
46. E. Cheraskin, et al., *International Journal for Vitamins and Nutritional Research*, Vol. 46, No. 1 (1976), pp. 58–60.

47. *Prevention* staff, op. cit.
48. Cheraskin, *International Journal for Vitamins and Nutritional Research,* op. cit.
49. Adams and Murray, op. cit.
50. *Prevention* staff, op. cit.
51. Dr. Miles Atkinson as quoted in *Prevention* staff, op. cit.
52. Darby, et al., op. cit.
53. Adams and Murray, op. cit.
54. Darby, et al., op. cit.
55. *Prevention* staff, op. cit.
56. Williams, op. cit.
57. Ibid.
58. *Prevention* staff, op. cit.
59. Ibid.
60. Dorothy M. Morre, et al., "Effects of Vitamin B-6 Deficiency on the Developing Central Nervous System of the Rat. Gross Measurements and Cytoarchitectural Alterations," *Journal of Nutrition,* Vol. 108, No. 8 (August 1978), pp. 1250–1259.
61. Michael H. Brophy and Pentti K. Silteri, "Pyridoxal Phosphate and Hypertensive Disorders of Pregnancy," *American Journal of Obstetrics,* Vol. 121, No. 8 (April 15, 1975).
62. Brophy and Silteri, op. cit.
63. Ibid.
64. Sheila C. Vir and A. H. G. Love, "Vitamin B6 Status of the Hospitalized Aged," *American Journal of Clinical Nutrition* 31 (August 1978): pp. 1383–1391.
65. *Modern Medicine,* June 15–20, 1979.
66. Stanley Gershoff, "Vitamin B6 and Oxalate Metabolism," *Vitamins and Hormones* 22 (1964).
67. Ibid.
68. John M. Ellis, *Vitamin B6: The Doctor's Report* (New York: Harper & Row, 1973).
69. A. Hoffer, "Treatment of Hyperkinetic Children with Nicotinamide and Pyridoxine," *Journal of the Canadian Medical Association* 107 (July 22, 1972).
70. "Vitamin Is Linked to Nerve Damage," *The New York Times,* August.
71. Platon J. Collipp, et al., "Pyridoxine Treatment of Childhood Bronchial Asthma," *Annals of Allergy,* Vol. 135, No. 2 (August 1975), pp. 93–97.
72. Richard W. Vilter, et al., "Interrelationships of Vitamin B12, Folic Acid and Ascorbic Acid in the Megaloblastic Anemia," *American Journal of Clinical Nutrition* 12 (February 1963):130–141.
73. Ibid.
74. Ibid.
75. Tibor L. Kopjas, "Effect of Folic Acid on Collateral Circulation in Diffuse Chronic Arteriosclerosis," *Journal of the American Geriatrics Society,* Vol. 14, No. 11, pp. 1187–1192.
76. "Folic Acid and the Nervous System," *The Lancet,* October 16, 1976, p. 836.
77. Adams and Murray, op. cit.
78. Carl C. Pfeiffer, *Mental and Elemental Nutrients* (New Canaan, Conn.: Keats Publishing, 1975).
79. Ibid.
80. Ibid.

81. "2 Vitamins Slow Damage to the Heart," *The New York Times*, November 7, 1979.
82. Pfeiffer, op. cit.
83. Ibid.
84. *Prevention* staff, op. cit.
85. Ibid.
86. Ibid.
87. Robinson and Lawler, op. cit.

VITAMIN C

1. Linus Pauling, *Vitamin C, the Common Cold, and the Flu* (San Francisco: W.H. Freeman & Co., 1976).
2. Michael C. Alfano, et al., "Effect of Ascorbic Acid Deficiency on the Permeability and Collagen Biosynthesis of Oral Mucosal Epithelium," *Annals of the New York Academy* of Science 258 (1975):253–263.
3. Roberto J. Moran and Harry L. Greene, "The B Vitamins and Vitamin C in Human Nutrition," *American Journal of Diseased Children* 133 (March 1979):308–314.
4. Ibid.
5. Pauling, op. cit.
6. Linus Pauling, "The Controversy Over Vitamin C (Ascorbic Acid) to Prevent or Relieve the Common Cold," *Executive Health*, Vol. VIII, No. 6 (1971).
7. Ibid.
8. Ibid.
9. Pauling, *Vitamin C, the Common Cold, and the Flu*, op. cit.
10. Ibid.
11. Ruth Whitney, "The Great Vitamin C Controversy and Dr. Robert Cathcart," *High Sierra Times*, January 19, 1977.
12. Michael H.M. Dykes and Paul Meier, "Ascorbic Acid and the Common Cold," *Journal of the American Medical Association* 231 (March 10, 1975): 1073–1079.
13. T.W. Anderson, et al., "Vitamin C and the Common Cold," *Journal of the Canadian Medical Association* 107 (September 23, 1972):503–508.
14. *New England Journal of Medicine*, January 1974.
15. Pauling, *Vitamin C, the Common Cold, and the Flu*, op. cit.
16. E. Regnier, *Review of Allergy* 22 (1968):835, 948.
17. Dykes and Meier, op. cit.
18. Pauling, *Vitamin C, the Common Cold, and the Flu*, op. cit.
19. Ibid.
20. Robert Cathcart, "Using Vitamin C to Treat Viral Diseases," *Today's Living*, August 1977.
21. Pauling, *Vitamin C, the Common Cold, and the Flu*, op. cit.
22. *Prevention* staff, *The Complete Book of Vitamins* (Emmaus: Rodale, 1977).
23. I.B. Chatterjee, "Evolution and the Biosynthesis of Ascorbic Acid," *Science*, December 1973, pp. 1271–1272.
24. Ibid.
25. *Prevention* staff, op. cit.
26. Irwin Stone, *Vitamin C: The Healing Factor* (New York:Grosset & Dunlap, 1972).
27. E. Ginter, "Vitamin C. Deficiency and Gallstone Formation," *The Lancet*, November 27, 1971.

28. Ibid.
29. W.J. McCormick as cited in Stone, op. cit.
30. *Prevention* staff, op. cit.
31. Ibid.
32. Chatterjee, op. cit.
33. T.C. Hindson as cited in *Prevention* staff, op. cit.
34. Mark Vrana, *New England Journal of Medicine*, Vol. 285, No. 1.
35. David H. Klasson as cited in *Prevention* staff, op. cit.
36. Fred Klenner, Ibid.
37. Winston Whei-Yang Kao, "Primary and Secondary Effects of Ascorbate on Procollagen Synthesis and Protein Synthesis by Primary Cultures of Tendon Fibroblasts," *Archives of Biochemistry and Biophysics* 173(1976):638–648.
38. Robert B. Greenblatt, "The Management of Habitual Abortion," *Annals of New York Academy of Sciences*, pp. 713–719.
39. *Journal of Orthomolecular Psychiatry*, Vol. 5, No. 1.
40. Carl C. Pfeiffer, *Mental and Elemental Nutrients* (New Canaan: Keats Publishing, 1975).
41. Faye Boquist, "Chemist Claims Vitamin Can Cure Drug Habit," *San Jose Mercury*, West Valley Section B, January 10, 1978.
42. Ibid.
43. Ibid.
44. Ibid.
45. *The Washington Post*, January 1, 1975.
46. Hugo Theorell, *The New York Times*, July 16, 1973.
47. Stone, op. cit.
48. Ibid.
49. Carl F. Shaffer, "Ascorbic Acid and Atherosclerosis," *American Journal of Clinical Nutrition*, Vol. 23, No. 1(January 1970): pp. 27–30.
50. Ibid.
51. Ewan Cameron and Linus Pauling, *Cancer and Vitamin C* (Menlo Park, Calif.:Linus Pauling Institute of Science and Health, 1979).
52. *Prevention* staff, op. cit.
53. Stone, op. cit.
54. Irwin Stone, "Cancer Therapy in the Light of the Natural History of Ascorbic Acid," *Journal of the International Academy of Metabology*, Vol. III, No. 1 (March 1974).
55. Ibid.
56. Pauling, *Vitamin C, the Common Cold, and the Flu*, op. cit.
57. Mark N. Grant, "Vitamin C Seen Mustering Interferon to Fight Viruses," *Medical Tribune*, February 2, 1977, p. 21.
58. Ibid.
59. Cameron and Pauling, op. cit.
60. Ibid.
61. Ibid.
62. Solomon Garb, *Cure for Cancer: A National Goal* (New York: Springer Publishing Company, 1968).
63. Ibid.
64. Pauling, *Vitamin C, the Common Cold, and the Flu*, op. cit.
65. Stone, *The Healing Factor*, op. cit.
66. H.S. Loh and C.W.M. Wilson, "Cigarette Smoking and Cadmium," *The Lancet*, February 26, 1972, p. 491.
67. M.R. Spivey Fox, "Protective Effects of Ascorbic Acid Against Toxicity of

Heavy Metals," *Annals of the New York Academy of Science* 258 (1975): 144–149.
68. Ibid.
69. *Prevention* staff, op. cit.
70. Stone, *The Healing Factor*, op. cit.
71. M.L. Riccitelli, "Vitamin C Therapy in Geriatric Practice," *Journal of the American Geriatric Society*, Vol. 20, No. 1 (January 1972), pp. 34–41.
72. Ibid.
73. Stone, *The Healing Factor*, op. cit.
74. Ibid.
75. Ibid.
76. Dietrich Hornig, "Distribution of Ascorbic Acid, Metabolites and Analogues in Man and Animals," *Annals of the New York Academy of Science* 258 (1975):103–115.
77. Stone, *The Healing Factor*, op. cit.
78. Ibid.
79. Cameron and Pauling, op. cit.
80. John H. Weisburger, "Vitamin C and Prevention of Nitrosamine Formation," *The Lancet*, September 17, 1977, p. 607.
81. Sidney S. Mirvish, "Blocking the Formation of N-Nitroso Compounds with Ascorbic Acid in vitro and in vivo." *Annals of the New York Academy of Science* 258 (1975):175–180.
82. Constance Spittle, "Atherosclerosis and Vitamin C," *The Lancet*, December 11, 1971.
83. Ibid.
84. Norman M. Sulkin and Dorothy F. Sulkin, "Tissue Changes Induced by Marginal Vitamin C Deficiency," *Annals of the New York Academy of Science* 258 (1975).
85. E. Ginter, "Atherosclerosis and Vitamin C," *The Lancet*, June 3, 1972, p. 1233.
86. Emil Ginter, "Cholesterol: Vitamin C Controls Its Transformation to Bile Acids," *Science*, February 1973, pp. 702–704.
87. Spittle, op. cit.
88. Constance Spittle, "Vitamin C and Deep-Vein Thrombosis," *The Lancet*, July 28, 1973, p. 199.
89. Ibid.
90. A. Henschel, *American Journal of Tropical Medicine* 24:259–265.
91. *Home and Garden Bulletin* No. 72, USDA, Washington, D.C.
92. Mary S. Eheart, *Journal of the American Dietetic Association*, Vol. 60, pp. 402–406.
93. Constance Spittle, "Seasonal Variation of Vitamin C Intake," *Canadian Journal of Nutrition*, March 1974.
94. *Consumer Reports*, August 1976, pp. 436–442.
95. Ibid.
96. Ibid.
97. Pfeiffer, op. cit.
98. Ibid.
99. S.H. Rubin, *Federation Proceedings*, Vol. 36, No. 6.
100. Alfred E. Harper, "The Recommended Dietary Allowances for Ascorbic Acid," *Annals of the New York Academy of Science* 258 (1975):491–495.
101. A. Hoffer, "Ascorbic Acid and Toxicity," *New England Journal of Medicine*, Vol. 285, No. 11 (September 9, 1971).
102. Ibid.

103. Ibid.
104. Man-Li S. Yew, "Biological Variation in Ascorbic Acid Needs," *Annals of the New York Academy of Science* 258 (1975):451–455.
105. Lewis A. Barness, "Safety Considerations with High Ascorbic Acid Dosage," *Annals of the New York Academy of Science* 258 (1975):523–527.
106. Ibid.
107. Ibid.
108. Ibid.
109. Terence W. Anderson, "Large-Scale Trials of Vitamin C," *Annals of the New York Academy of Science* 258 (1975):498–503.
110. Pauling, *Vitamin C, the Common Cold, and the Flu,* op. cit.
111. Ibid.
112. Ibid.
113. *Prevention* staff, op. cit.
114. H.S. Loh and C.W.M. Wilson, "Iron and Vitamin C," *The Lancet,* October 2, 1971, p. 768.
115. Moran and Greene, op. cit.
116. Ibid.
117. Catharyn Elwood, *Feel Like a Million* (New York: Pocket Cardinal Books, 1965).
118. F. Bicknell and F. Prescott, *Vitamins in Medicine* (Los Angeles:Regent House, 1953).
119. Pauling, *Vitamin C, the Common Cold, and the Flu,* op. cit.
120. Geoffrey Taylor, "Vitamins in Illness," *British Medical Journal,* February 3, 1973, p. 292.
121. Stone, *The Healing Factor,* op. cit.
122. H.L. Newbold, *Mega-Nutrients for Your Nerves* (New York:Berkeley, 1975).
123. Pfeiffer, op. cit.
124. Ibid.
125. Michael Briggs, "Vitamin-C Induced Hyperoxlauria," *The Lancet,* January 17, 1976, p. 154.
126. Charles D. Gerson, "Ascorbic Acid Deficiency in Clinical Disease Including Regional Enteritis," *Annals of the New York Academy of Science* 258 (1975).
127. Ibid.
128. Ibid.
129. "Vitamin C Cures Impotence—in Just Four Days," *The Boston Globe,* June 21, 1983.
130. John H. Weisburger, "Vitamin C, Vitamin E and the Prevention of Gastric Cancer: Discussion, Micronutrient Interactions: Vitamins, Minerals and Hazardous Elements," *Annals of the New York Academy of Sciences,* Vol. 355 (December 1, 1980).

VITAMIN D

1. C.H. Robinson and M.R. Lawler, *Normal and Therapeutic Nutrition.* 15th ed. (New York: Macmillan, 1977).
2. *Prevention* staff, *The Complete Book of Vitamins* (Emmaus: Rodale Press, 1977).
3. Robinson and Lawler, op. cit.
4. Ibid.

5. Mark R. Haussler, "Vitamin D: Mode of Action and Biomedical Applications," *Nutrition Reviews*, Vol. 32, No. 9 (September 1974).
6. Jack W. Coburn, et al., "Advances in Vitamin D Metabolism as they Pertain to Chronic Renal Disease," *American Journal of Clinical Nutrition* 30 (July 1977):1082–1086.
7. Dilnawaz and Elsie M. Widdowson, "Vitamin D in Human Milk," *The Lancet*, January 22, 1977, pp. 167–168.
8. Steven L. Teitelbaum, "Morphological Effects of Vitamin D and Its Analogs on Bone," *American Journal of Clinical Nutrition* 29 (November 1976): 1300–1306.
9. Coburn, et al., op. cit.
10. Committee on Nutritional Misinformation, "Hazards of Overuse of Vitamin D," *Nutrition Reviews*, Vol. 33, No. 2 (February 1975).
11. W.H. Taylor, "Renal Calculi and Self-Medication with Multivitamin Preparations Containing Vitamin D," *Clinical Science* 42 (1972):515–522.
12. "The Need for Vitamin D Supplement," *The Lancet*, May 19, 1973, p. 1097.
13. *Prevention* staff, op. cit.
14. Sara B. Arnaud, et al., "Components of 25-hydroxyvitamin D in Serum of Young Children in Upper Midwestern United States," *American Journal of Clinical Nutrition* 30 (July 1977):1082–1086.
15. Ibid.
16. Robinson and Lawler, op. cit.
17. Eleanor Whitney and May Hamilton, *Understanding Nutrition* (New York: West Publishing Co., 1977).
18. Committee on Nutritional Misinformation, op. cit.
19. Ibid.
20. Henry Borsook, *Vitamins* (New York: Pyramid, 1968).
21. L.E. Reeve, et al., as cited in John O' Rourke, "Vitamin D: How Much Do We Need?" *Let's Live*, March 1983.

VITAMIN E

1. Dr. Jeffrey Bland as cited in *Prevention* staff, *The Complete Book of Vitamins* (Emmaus: Rodale Press, 1977).
2. Ibid.
3. *The Wall Street Journal*, March 13, 1973.
4. Wilfrid E. Shute, *The Vitamin E Book* (New Canaan, Conn.:Keats Publishing, Inc., 1975).
5. Ibid.
6. Ibid.
7. Ibid.
8. Ibid.
9. Wilfrid E. Shute, *The Health Preserver* (Emmaus: Rodale Press, 1977), p. 25.
10. Samuel Ayres, Jr. and Richard Mihan, "Leg Cramps (Systremma) and Restless Legs' Syndrome," *California Medicine*, Vol. 111, No. 2, (August 1969) pp. 87–91.
11. Shute, *The Vitamin E Book*, op. cit.
12. Ibid.
13. Shute, *The Health Preserver*, op. cit.
14. Ibid.
15. *Prevention* staff, op. cit.
16. Shute, *The Vitamin E Book*, op. cit.
17. Shute, *The Health Preserver*, op. cit.
18. D. Warshauer, et al., "Effect of Vitamin E and Ozone on the Pulmonary

Antibacterial Defense Mechanisms," *Journal of Laboratory Clinical Medicine*, Vol. 83, No. 2 (February 1974).
19. Ibid.
20. Dr. A.L. Tappel as quoted in Shute, *The Vitamin E Book*, op. cit.
21. Ayres, op. cit.
22. Shute, *The Vitamin E Book*, op. cit.
23. Ibid.
24. *Prevention* staff, op. cit.
25. Shute, *The Health Preserver*, op. cit.
26. Ibid.
27. Shute, *The Vitamin E Book*, op. cit.
28. Shute, *The Health Preserver*, op. cit.
29. Ibid.
30. Ibid.
31. Ayres, op. cit.
32. Patrick J. Leonard and Monty S. Losowsky, "Effect of Alpha-Tocopherol Administration on Red Cell Survival in Vitamin E-Deficient Human Subjects," *American Journal of Clinical Nutrition* 24 (April 1971):388–393.
33. Shute, *The Vitamin E Book*, op. cit.
34. Raymond Killeen, *Journal of the American Medical Association*, Vol. 70 No. 9.
35. Philip M. Farrell, et al., "The Occurrence and Effects of Human Vitamin E Deficiency," *Journal of Clinical Nutrition* 60 (July 1977):233–241.
36. Ibid.
37. C. Raychaudhuri and I.D. Desai, "Ceroid Pigment Formation and Irreversible Sterility in Vitamin E Deficiency," *Science* 173 (September 1971):1028.
38. *Prevention* staff, op. cit.
39. Henry Borsook, *Vitamins* (New York: Pyramid, 1968).
40. Dr. A.L. Tappel as quoted in Shute, *The Vitamin E Book*, op. cit.
41. Philip L. Harris and Norris D. Embree, *American Journal of Clinical Nutrition*, December 1963.
42. Douglas Rotman, "Unsaturated Fat and Vitamin E Deficiency," *The Lancet* (September 25, 1971):1028.
43. Dr. Bland as quoted by *Prevention* staff, op. cit.
44. Ibid.
45. *Prevention* staff, op. cit.
46. Lloyd A. Witting and Lok Lee, "Recommended Dietary Allowance for Vitamin E: Relation to Dietary, Erythrocyte and Adipose Tissue Linoleate," *American Journal of Clinical Nutrition* 28 (June 1975):577–583.
47. Takaaki Fujii, et al., "Pathophysiological Study of Iron Deficiency Anemia in Adolescence," *Keio Journal of Medicine*, Vol. 17, No. 3 (September 1968).
48. Samuel Ayers Jr., "Natural vs. Synthetic Vitamins," *Journal of the American Medical Association* Letters, Vol. 225, No. 9 (August 27, 1973) p. 1124.
49. Myron Winick, "Setting the Facts Straight on Vitamins E and K," *Modern Medicine*, October 15–30, 1978.
50. M.K. Horwitt, "Therapeutic Uses of Vitamin E in Medicine," *Nutrition Reviews*, Vol. 38, No. 3 (March 1980).
51. Shute, *The Vitamin E Book*, op. cit.

VITAMIN K

1. "Osteocalcin A Vitamin K-Dependent Calcium-Binding Protein in Bone." *Nutrition Reviews*, Vol. 37, No. 2 (February 1979).
2. P. Hilgard. "Cancer & Vitamin K" p. 403, *The Lancet*, August 20, 1977.

3. G.F. Pineo, *Canadian Medical Journal* 109 (November 3, 1973):880–883.
4. J.I. Rodale and Staff, *The Complete Book of Vitamins*, p. 491.

BIOFLAVONOIDS

1. Jean Weininger and George M. Briggs, "M. Bioflavonoids" *Modern Nutrition in Health and Disease*, edited by Robert Goodhart and Maurice E. Shils (Philadelphia: Lea and Febiger 1980).
2. J.I. Rodale, ed., *The Health Builder: An Encyclopedia of Health Information from the Preventive Point-of-View* (Emmaus: Rodale Books, Inc., 1959).
3. Adelle Davis, *Let's Get Well: A Practical Guide to Renewed Health Through Nutrition* (New York: Harcourt, Brace and World, Inc., 1965).
4. Weininger and Briggs, op. cit.
5. Ibid.
6. Joachim Kuhnau, "The Flavonoids, a Class of Semi-Essential Food Components; Their Role in Human Nutrition," *World Review of Nutrition and Dietetics*, Vol. 24, as cited by Weininger and Briggs, op. cit.
7. Ibid.
8. Abram Hoffer and Morton Walker, *Nutrients to Age without Senility* (New Canaan: Keats Publishing Inc., 1980).
9. Sheldon C. Deal, *New Life Through Nutrition* (Tucson: New Life Publishing, 1974).
10. Ibid.
11. Earl Mindell, *Earl Mindell's Vitamin Bible: How the Right Vitamins and Nutrient Supplements Can Help Turn Your Life Around* (New York: Rawson Wade Publishers, Inc., 1979).
12. Rodale, op. cit.
13. Deal, op. cit.
14. Rodale, op. cit.
15. Michael Lesser, *Nutrition and Vitamin Therapy* (New York: Grove Press, Inc, 1980).
16. Rodale, op. cit.
17. Catharyn Elwood, *Feel Like a Million: How Proper Nutrition Can Revitalize Your Life* (New York: Pocket Cardinal Books, 1965).
18. Ibid.
19. Linda Clark, *Get Well Naturally: Nature's Way to Health* (New York: ARC Books, Inc., 1965).
20. Ibid.
21. Roger J. Williams, *Nutrition Against Disease* (New York: Bantam Books, 1973).
22. Ibid.
23. Ibid.
24. Rodale, op. cit.
25. Elwood, op. cit.
26. Carlton Fredericks and Herbert Bailey, *Food Facts and Fallacies: The Intelligent Person's Guide to Nutrition and Health* (New York: ARC Books, 1968).
27. Ibid.
28. Mark Bricklin, *The Practical Encyclopedia of Natural Healing* (Emmaus: Rodale Press, Inc., 1976).
29. Rodale, op. cit.
30. Lesser, op. cit.

31. Rodale, op. cit.
32. Ibid.
33. Edward E. Marsh, *How to Be Healthy with Natural Foods* (New York: Arco Publishing Company, 1968).
34. Elwood, op. cit.
35. Ibid.
36. Ibid.
37. Lesser, op. cit.
38. Elwood, op. cit.
39. Ibid.
40. Ibid.
41. Ibid.
42. Bricklin, op. cit.
43. Ibid.
44. Rodale, op. cit.
45. Bricklin, op. cit.
46. Lesser, op. cit.
47. Elwood, op. cit.
48. Hoffer and Walker, op. cit.
49. Weininger and Briggs, op. cit.
50. Davis, op. cit.
51. Ibid.
52. Carlton Fredericks, *Look Younger, Feel Healthier* (New York: Grosset & Dunlap 1972).
53. Elwood, op. cit.
54. Deal, op. cit.
55. Elwood, op. cit.

CALCIUM

1. Frank Murray, *Program Your Heart for Health* (New York: Larchmont Books, 1977).
2. Ibid.
3. Ibid.
4. Carl C. Pfeiffer, *Zinc and Other Micro-Nutrients* (Old Greenwich, Conn.: Devin Adair, 1973).
5. A. White, et al., *Principles of Biochemistry* (New York:McGraw Hill, 1968).
6. Ibid., p. 952.
7. Ibid., p. 887.
8. Ibid., p. 471.
9. Ibid., p. 437.
10. Ibid., p. 795.
11. William Longgood, *The Poisons in Your Food* (New York:Pyramid, 1971).
12. W. Krehl, *American Journal of Clinical Nutrition* 11(1962):77.
13. B. Nordin, *The Lancet* 1(1961):1011.
14. M. Bogdonoff, et al., *Journal of Gerontology* 8(1953):272.
15. I. MacIntyre, *Journal of Chronic Diseases* 16(1963):201.
16. E. Barker, *Journal of Chronic Diseases* 11(1960):27.
17. W. Wacker, et al., *Medical Clinics of North America* 44(1960):1357.
18. C. Booth, et al., *British Medical Journal* 2(1963):141.
19. I. MacIntyre, et al., *Clinical Science* 20(1961):297.
20. Adelle Davis, *Let's Get Well* (New York:New American Library, 1972).

21. MacIntyre, *Clinical Science,* op. cit.
22. White, et al., op. cit.
23. Pfeiffer, op. cit.
24. E. Back, et al., *Archives of the Disabilities of Childhood* 37(1962):106.
25. Ibid.
26. Nutrition Search, Inc., *Nutrition Almanac* (New York:McGraw Hill, 1979).
27. White, et al., op. cit.
28. Philip Handler, *Biology and the Future of Man* (New York:Oxford University Press, 1970).
29. E. Kaplan, *Archives of Pathology* 34 (1942):1042.
30. Davis, op. cit., p. 148.
31. P. Chen, et al., *American Journal of Physiology* 180 (1955):632.
32. D. Bronsky, et al., *Journal of Laboratory and Clinical Medicine* 44 (1954): 774.
33. White, et al., op. cit., p. 893.
34. G. Dunning, *Journal of the American Dietetic Association* 42(1963):17.
35. B. Larson, *Journal of Dairy Science* 46 (1963):759.
36. Nutrition Search, Inc., op. cit., pp. 68, 69.
37. Davis, op. cit., pp. 136, 137.
38. F. Klenner, *Tri-State Medical Journal,* December 1957.
39. F. Klenner, *Tri-State Medical Journal,* July 1954.
40. H. Selye, *The Stress of Life* (New York: McGraw Hill, 1956).
41. Pfeiffer, op. cit.
42. Ibid.
43. H. Grusin, et al., *American Journal of Clinical Nutrition* 5 (1957):644.
44. L. Smith, et al., *Journal of Dairy Science* 45 (1962):581.
45. R. Fraser, et al., *Proceedings of the Royal Society of Medicine* 50 (1957):21.
46. D. Thorangkin, et al., *Journal of the American Dietetics Association* 35 (1969):23.
47. Davis, op. cit., pp. 246–248.
48. Thomas Clayton, ed., *Taber's Cyclopedic Medical Dictionary* (Philadelphia: F.A. Davis Co., 1970).
49. Isaac Asimov, *The Bloodstream* (New York: Collier Macmillan, 1976).
50. E. Kramer and W. Biebner, *The Medical Clinics of North America,* May 1952, p. 881.
51. H. Bakwin, *American Journal of the Disabilities of Childhood* 54 (1947):1211.
52. H. Bakwin, *Journal of Pediatrics* 14(1939):1.
53. I. Gittleman and J. Pincus, *Proceedings of the Society of Pediatric Residents,* May 1950.
54. Kramer and Leibner, op. cit., pp. 884, 885.
55. Krehl, op. cit.
56. Davis, op. cit., pp. 256, 257.
57. Ibid, p. 258.
58. Nutrition Search, Inc., op. cit., p. 136.
59. Davis, op. cit.
60. S. Morgules, et al., *Journal of Biological Chemistry* 124 (1938):767.
61. S. Ames, *Journal of Biological Chemistry* 169 (1947):503.
62. Davis, op. cit., pp. 55, 116.
63. Ibid, pp. 46, 64, 115, 116.
64. L. Maynard, et al., *Journal of Nutrition* 64 (1958):85.
65. White, et al., op. cit., p. 896.
66. Davis, op. cit., pp. 292, 293.
67. Pfeiffer, op. cit., p. 96.

68. White, et al., op. cit., p. 900.
69. Hans Selye, Calciphylaxis (Chicago: University of Chicago Press, 1962).
70. Davis, op. cit.
71. R. Womersley, et al., *Journal of Clinical Investigation* 34 (1955):456.
72. D. Black, et al., *Clinical Science* 11 (1952):397.
73. W. Blahd, et al., *Metabolism* 2 (1953):218.
74. H. Archer, et al., *British Medical Journal* 1 (1958):175.
75. J. Crawhill, et al., *The Lancet* 2 (1959):806.
76. L. Lutwak, et al., *Borden's Review of Nutritional Research* 23 (1962):45.
77. S. Krane, et al., *Journal of Clinical Investigation* 35 (1956):84.
78. B. Tuchweber, et al., *American Journal of Clinical Nutrition* 13 (1963):238.
79. M. Cantin, et al., *Experimental Medical Surgery* 318 (1962):20.
80. White, et al., op. cit., p. 888.
81. R. McCollister, *American Journal of Clinical Nutrition* 12 (1963):415.
82. Nutrition Search, Inc., op. cit., p. 118.
83. Pfeiffer, op. cit., p. 97.
84. Ibid., pp. 90–92.
85. White, et al., op. cit., p. 952.
86. Thomas, op. cit., p. C-26.
87. Davis, op. cit., pp. 319, 320.
88. Ibid. pp. 261, 320.
89. Pfeiffer, op. cit., pp. 94, 95.
90. Davis, op. cit., p. 261.
91. Ibid, pp. 319, 320.
92. Pfeiffer, op. cit., p. 93.
93. E. Kaplan, *Archives of Pathology* 34 (1942):1042.
94. L. Gardner, et al., *Pediatrics* 5 (1950):228.
95. Davis, op. cit.
96. Gardner, op. cit.
97. Kramer and Leibner, op. cit.
98. Nutrition Search, Inc., op. cit., p. 104.
99. Davis, op. cit., p. 320.
100. Kramer and Leibner, op. cit., p. 882.
101. Davis, op. cit., p. 320.
102. Murray, op. cit., p. 323.
103. *Nutrition Reviews* 16 (1958):148.
104. R. Smith, et al., *American Journal of Clinical Nutrition* 14 (1964):98.
105. Ibid.
106. A. Helmer, et al., *Studies Institutum Divi Thomae* 1 (1937):83, 207.
107. J. Bauer, et al., *Journal of the American Medical Association* 130 (1946): 1208.
108. L. Eising, *Journal of Bone and Joint Surgery* 45A (1963):69.
109. P. Davies, *Annals of Internal Medicine* 53 (1960):1250.
110. Murray, op. cit.
111. Bauer, et al., op. cit.
112. Eising, op. cit.
113. Davies, op. cit.
114. Pfeiffer, op. cit.
115. M. Seelig, *American Journal of Clinical Nutrition* 14 (1964):342.
116. Murray, op. cit.
117. Seelig, op. cit.
118. Pfeiffer, op. cit.
119. Nutrition Search, Inc., op. cit.

120. A. Morgan, *California Agricultural Experimental Station Bulletin*, 1959, p. 769.
121. Seelig, op. cit.
122. Davis, op. cit.
123. Morgan, op. cit.
124. Seelig, op. cit.
125. D. Kushner, *American Journal of Clinical Nutrition* 4 (1956):561.
126. Davis, op. cit., p. 255.
127. H. Newbold, *Mega-Nutrients for Your Nerves* (New York: Berkeley Publishing Corp., 1980).
128. R. Smith, et al., *American Journal of Clinical Nutrition* 14 (1964):98.
129. Pfeiffer, op. cit., pp. 95, 96.
130. Seelig, op. cit.
131. F. Lengemann, et al., *Journal of Nutrition* 68 (1959):443.
132. Davis, op cit., p. 259.
133. Gary and Steve Null, *Alcohol and Nutrition* (New York: Pyramid, 1977), p. 59.
134. White, et al., op. cit.
135. P. Ackerman, et al., *Journal of Gerontology* 8 (1953):451; 8 (1954):446.
136. Krehl, op. cit.
137. J. Crawford, et al., *American Journal of Physiology* 180 (1955):156.
138. Bogdonoff, op cit.
139. Seelig, op. cit.
140. Davis, op. cit., p. 259.
141. Emanuel Revici, *Research in Physiopathology as the Basis of Guided Chemotherapy* (New York: D. Van Nostrand Co., 1961).
142. Davis, op. cit., pp. 254, 320.
143. *Nutrition Reviews* 9 (1951):100.
144. I. Lutwak, *New York State Journal of Medicine* 63 (1963):590.
145. L. Valberg, et al., *British Journal of Nutrition* 15 (1961):473.
146. Davis, op. cit., p. 33.
147. G. Becker, *American Journal of Digestive Disorders* 19 (1952):344.
148. A. Frazer, et al., *Nature* 148 (1942):167.
149. A. Curtis, et al., *Journal of the American Medical Association* 113 (1949): 1785.
150. A. Curtis, et al., *Archives of Internal Medicine* 63 (1939):54.
151. A. Mahle, et al., *Gastroenterology* 9 (1947):44.
152. D. Javert, et al., *American Journal of Obstetrics and Gynecology* 42 (1941): 409.
153. R. Jackson, *Journal of Nutrition* 7 (1934):607.
154. M. Elliott, et al., *Proceedings of the Society of Experimental Biological Medicine* 43 (1940):240.
155. G. Thiele, *Southern Medical Journal* 35 (1942):920.
156. Davis, op. cit.
157. Pfeiffer, op. cit.
158. White, et al., op. cit., p. 813.
159. Pfeiffer, op. cit., p. 97.
160. Davis, op. cit., p. 207.
161. Krehl, op. cit.
162. Pfeiffer, op. cit., p. 91.
163. White, et al., op. cit., p. 895.
164. Lutwak, *Borden's Review of Nutritional Research*, op. cit.
165. B. Nordin, *British Medical Journal* 1 (1962):145.

166. Chen, et al., op. cit.
167. F. Sargent, et al., *American Journal of Clinical Nutrition* 4 (1956):466.
168. L. Eales, *American Journal of Clinical Nutrition* 4 (1956):529.
169. H. Zimmerman, *American Journal of Clinical Nutrition* 4 (1956):482.
170. W. Kolff, *Nutrition Reviews* 11 (1953):193.
171. Pfeiffer, op. cit., p. 94.
172. *Nutrition Reviews* 10 (1952):306.
173. Murray, op. cit., p. 329.
174. Back, op. cit.
175. G. Bruce, et al., *Journal of Nutrition* 76 (1962):23.
176. Davis, op. cit., p. 149.
177. Ibid., p. 141.
178. Ibid., p. 149.
179. Pfeiffer, op. cit., pp. 93, 94.
180. Ibid., p. 92.
181. Ibid., p. 93.
182. White, et al., op. cit., p. 934.
183. "Diet in U.S. Held Faulty," *The New York Times,* April 20, 1983.

CHROMIUM

1. J.I. Rodale and Staff, *The Complete Book of Minerals for Health* (Emmaus: Rodale Press, 1972).
2. Carl C. Pfeiffer, *Mental and Elemental Nutrients* (New Canaan, Conn.:Keats Publishing, Inc., 1975).
3. Henry Schroeder, *The Trace Elements and Man* (Old Greenwich, Conn.:Devin Adair, 1973).
4. Ibid.
5. Ibid.
6. Rodale, op. cit.
7. Schroeder, op. cit.
8. Ibid.
9. Pfeiffer, op. cit.
10. Schroeder, op. cit.
11. Paavo Airola, *Hypoglycemia: A Better Approach* (Phoenix: Health Plus, 1977).
12. Schroeder, op. cit.
13. Pfeiffer, op. cit.
14. Airola, op. cit.
15. Pfeiffer, op. cit.
16. Schroeder, op. cit.
17. Pfeiffer, op. cit.
18. Schroeder, op. cit.
19. Ibid.
20. Ibid.
21. Ibid.
22. Pfeiffer, op. cit.
23. Schroeder, op. cit.
24. Pfeiffer, op. cit.
25. Schroeder, op. cit.
26. Ibid.
27. Ibid.

28. Ibid.
29. Ibid.

IODINE

1. Nutrition Search, Inc., *Nutrition Almanac* (New York:McGraw Hill, 1979).
2. John Holum, *Elements of General and Biological Chemistry* (New York: John Wiley and Sons, Inc., 1972).
3. A. White, et al., *Principles of Biochemistry* (New York: McGraw Hill, 1968).
4. Ibid.
5. C. Tui, *Journal of Clinical Nutrition* 1 (1953):232.
6. M. Gasmami, et al., *Journal of Chronic Diseases* 16 (1963):363.
7. J. Forbes, *Endocrinology* 35 (1944):126.
8. Gasmami, et al., op. cit.
9. *Nutrition Reviews* 4 (1946):259.
10. R. Kark, *American Journal of Medical Science* 222 (1951):154.
11. Henry Schroeder, *The Trace Elements and Man* (Old Greenwich, Conn.:Devin Adair, 1973).
12. Holum, op. cit.
13. Nutrition Search, Inc., op. cit.
14. H. Guthrie, *Introductory Nutrition* (St. Louis: C.V. Mosby, Co. 1971).
15. Nutrition Search, Inc., op. cit.
16. R. Follis, *Proceedings of the Society of Experimental Biological Medicine* 100 (1959):203.
17. Ibid.
18. Clayton Thomas, ed., *Taber's Cyclopedic Medical Dictionary* (Philadelphia: F.A. Davis Co., 1970).
19. Schroeder, op. cit.
20. White, et al., op. cit.
21. Nutrition Search, Inc., op. cit.
22. G. Pearce, et al., *Science* 116 (1953):254.
23. White, et al., op. cit.
24. *Nutrition Reviews* 8 (1950):196.
25. J. Benson, et al., *Cancer Research* 16 (1956):135.
26. *Nutrition Reviews* 8 (1950):141.
27. Benson, op. cit.
28. M. Eisenbud, et al., *Science* 146 (1962):370.
29. *Consumer Reports* 27 (1962):139.
30. J. Forbes, et al., *Journal of the American Pharmacological Association* 37 (1948):509.
31. V. Srinivasan, et al., *Journal of Nutrition* 61 (1957):87.
32. Nutrition Search, Inc., op. cit.
33. K. Saxena, et al., *Science* 138 (1962):430.
34. Pearce, op. cit.
35. J. Matovinovic, *Journal of the American Medical Women's Association* 17 (1962):571, 646.
36. Srinivasan, et al., op. cit.
37. *Nutrition Reviews*, op. cit.
38. J. Van Wyk, et al., *Pediatrics* 24 (1959):752.
39. Schroeder, op. cit.
40. White, et al., op. cit.
41. Schroeder, op. cit.

42. Srinivasan, et al., op. cit.
43. Nutrition Search, Inc., op. cit.

IRON

1. Isaac Asimov, *The Bloodstream* (New York: Collier Macmillan, 1976): p. 38.
2. Ibid.
3. Ibid., p. 39.
4. Ibid., p. 45.
5. Ibid., p. 52.
6. Ibid., pp. 42, 43.
7. A. White, et al., *Principles of Biochemistry* (New York:McGraw Hill, 1968).
8. John Holum, *Elements of General and Biological Chemistry* (New York: John Wiley and Sons, Inc., 1972).
9. Asimov, op. cit., pp. 51, 52.
10. White, et al., op. cit., p. 749.
11. Asimov, op. cit., p. 52, 53.
12. Clayton Thomas, ed., *Taber's Cyclopedic Medical Dictionary* (Philadelphia: F.A. Davis Co., 1970).
13. Ibid.
14. White, et al., op. cit., p. 748
15. Henry Schroeder, *The Trace Elements and Man* (Old Greenwich, Conn.: Devin Adair, 1973).
16. Ibid.
17. E. Beutler, *American Journal of Medical Science* 234 (1957):517.
18. Thomas, op. cit., pp. A-76, 77.
19. Nutrition Search, Inc., *Nutrition Almanac* (New York:McGraw Hill, 1979).
20. W. Krehl, et al., *Borden's Review of Nutritional Research* 24 (1963):50.
21. Thomas, op. cit., p. E-59.
22. Carl C. Pfeiffer, *Zinc and Other Micro-Nutrients* (New Canaan, Conn.: Keats Publishing, Inc., 1968): p. 209.
23. M. Shils, *American Journal of Clinical Nutrition* 15 (1964):133.
24. Thomas, op. cit., p. E-59.
25. Ibid.
26. C. Pfeiffer and B. Aston, *The Golden Pamphlet* (Princeton: Brain Bio Center, 1980).
27. W. Watson, et al., *British Medical Journal* 1 (1963):971.
28. Pfeiffer, op. cit., p. 61.
29. *Journal of the American Medical Association* 184 (1963):992.
30. J. Hines, et al., *American Journal of Clinical Nutrition* 14 (1964):137.
31. White, et al., op. cit., p. 749.
32. R. Goodhart and M. Shils, *Modern Nutrition in Health and Disease* 5th ed. (Philadelphia: Lea and Febiger, 1973).
33. Pfeiffer, op. cit., p. 61.
34. Ibid., p. 59.
35. Krehl, op. cit.
36. J. Waddell, et al., *Journal of Biological Chemistry* 80 (1928):431.
37. Schroeder, op. cit.
38. Pfeiffer, op. cit.
39. Pfeiffer and Aston, op. cit.
40. Pfeiffer, op. cit.
41. F. Adamstone, *American Journal of Cancer* 28 (1935):540.

42. B. Cooper, et al., *Journal of the Canadian Medical Association* 85 (1961): 987.
43. R. Vilter, et al., *Journal of Laboratory and Clinical Medicine* 32 (1948):1426.
44. R. Thompson, et al., *Quarterly Journal of Medicine* 20 (1951):187.
45. K. Gough, et al., *Quarterly Journal of Medicine* 32 (1963):243.
46. R. Verzar, International Congress on Vitamin E, 1955.
47. R. Bayer, *Wiener Medicalische Wachschrift* 109 (1959):271.
48. C. Tedeschi, et al., *American Journal of Obstetrics and Gynecology* 71 (1956):16.
49. M. Horwitt, et al., *American Medical Association Archives of Neurology* 1 (1959):312.
50. Adelle Davis, *Let's Get Well* (New York: New American Library 1972).
51. Asimov, op. cit.
52. White, et al., op. cit.
53. Nutrition Search, Inc., op. cit., p. 71.
54. Davis, op. cit, p. 231.
55. Asimov, pp. 58, 59.
56. Pfeiffer, op. cit., p. 60.
57. Davis, op. cit., p. 232.
58. Pfeiffer, op. cit., pp. 36, 73, 203, 208.
59. White, et al., op. cit.
60. M.V. Krause and M.A. Hunscher, *Food, Nutrition, and Diet Therapy* (Philadelphia: W.B. Saunders Co., 1972).
61. Linus Pauling, *Vitamin C and the Common Cold* (New York: Bantam Books, 1970).
62. Pfeiffer, op. cit., p. 178.
63. Davis, op. cit., p. 228.
64. Pfeiffer, op. cit., p. 64.
65. Ibid., p. 201.
66. Ibid., p. 51.
67. Shils, op. cit.
68. *Nutrition Reviews* 10 (1952):299.
69. Adamstone, op. cit.
70. T.A. Morck, et al., as cited in *Nutrition Research Newsletter*, Vol. 2, No. 4 (April 15, 1983).

MAGNESIUM

1. A. White, et al., *Principles of Biochemistry* (New York:McGraw Hill, 1968).
2. Nutrition Search, Inc., *Nutrition Almanac* (New York: McGraw Hill, 1979).
3. White, et al., op. cit.
4. J. Stewart, et al., *Journal of Comparative Pathology* 66 (1956):1.
5. Paavo Airola, *How to Get Well* (Phoenix:Health Plus, 1974).
6. Carl C. Pfeiffer, *Zinc and Other Micro-Nutrients* (New Canaan, Conn.: Keats Publishing, Inc., 1978).
7. White, et al., op. cit., pp. 389–390.
8. Pfeiffer, op. cit., p. 102.
9. White, et al., op. cit., pp. 1021, 1036.
10. H. Martin, et al., *Journal of Clinical Investigations* 26 (1947):216.
11. White, et al., op. cit., p. 511.
12. W. Philpott and D. Kalita, *Brain Allergies* (New Canaan, Conn.:Keats Publishing, Inc., 1980).

13. White, et al., op. cit., p. 779.

14. Nutrition Search, Inc., op. cit. p. 73.

15. Clayton Thomas, ed., *Taber's Cyclopedic Medical Dictionary* (Philadelphia: F.A. Davis, Co., 1970).

16. White, et al., op. cit., pp. 523–524.

17. F. Murray, *Program Your Heart for Health* (New York: Larchmont Books, 1977) pp. 312–313.

18. Thomas, op. cit., p. P-26.

19. G.Y. Nelson, et al., *Journal of the American Dietetics Association* 38 (1961): 437.

20. White, et al., op. cit. pp. 563–564, 570–571.

21. Ibid., p. 678.

22. Ibid., p. 536.

23. Isaac Asimov, *The Bloodstream* (New York: Collier Macmillan, 1976).

24. White, et al., op. cit., p. 781.

25. Ibid., p. 778.

26. White, et al., op. cit., p. 850.

27. Nutrition Search, Inc., op. cit.

28. E. Back, et al., *Archives of the Disabilities of Childhood* 37 (1962):106.

29. White, et al., op. cit., p. 1015.

30. D. Kushner, *American Journal of Clinical Nutrition* 4 (1956):561.

31. J.R. Bronk, *Chemical Biology* (New York:Macmillan, 1973).

32. Thomas, op. cit., p. M-77.

33. W. Krehl, *Nutrition Reviews* 11 (1953):225.

34. Back, op. cit.

35. White, et al., op. cit., p. 888.

36. Pfeiffer, op. cit., p. 9.

37. R. Stern, *American Journal of Surgery* 39 (1938):495.

38. Pfeiffer, op. cit., pp. 102–103.

39. White, et al., op. cit., p. 1015.

40. Pfeiffer, op. cit.

41. R. Williams and D. Kalita, *A Physician's Handbook on Orthomolecular Medicine* (New Canaan, Conn.:Keats Publishing, Inc., 1979), p. 78.

42. R. Randall., et al., *Annals of Internal Medicine* 50 (1959):257.

43. I. MacIntyre, *Journal of Chronic Diseases* 16 (1963):201.

44. E. Barker, *Journal of Chronic Diseases* 11 (1960):27.

45. W. Wacker, et al., *Medical Clinics of North America* 44 (1960):1357.

46. C. Booth, et al., *British Medical Journal* 2 (1963):141.

47. I. MacIntyre, et al., *Clinical Science* 20 (1961):297.

48. M. Seelig, *American Journal of Clinical Nutrition* 14 (1964):342.

49. White, et al., op. cit., p. 330.

50. Adelle Davis, *Let's Get Well* (New York:New American Library, 1972):319.

51. Murray, op. cit., p. 328.

52. White, et al, op. cit., pp. 642ff.

53. Ibid., p. 125.

54. Murray, op. cit., p. 328.

55. Thomas, op. cit., p. P-150.

56. R. Hodges, et al., *American Journal of Clinical Nutrition* 11 (1962):180, 187.

57. Nutrition Search, Inc., op. cit., p. 74.

58. Pfeiffer, op. cit., pp. 105–106.

59. Pierre Muller, First International Symposium on Magnesium Deficit in Human Pathology, 1971.

60. Pfeiffer, op. cit., p. 105.

61. Davis, op. cit., p. 127.
62. Airola, op. cit., p. 275.
63. R. Horton, et al., *Journal of Clinical Endocrinology* 22 (1962):1187.
64. J. Hammerstein, et al., *New England Journal of Medicine* 256 (1957):897.
65. S. Hanna, et al., *The Lancet* 2 (1960):172.
66. Editorial, *Journal of the American Medical Association* 174 (1960):69.
67. Nutrition Search, Inc., op. cit., p. 74.
68. S. Stone, *Disturbances of the Nervous System* 11 (1950):131.
69. L. Barnet, *Journal of Clinical Physiology* 1 (1959):26.
70. Nutrition Search, Inc., op. cit.
71. Back, op. cit.
72. White, et al., op. cit.
73. Davis, op. cit., p. 67.
74. Carlton Fredericks, *Prevention*, May 1974.
75. Pfeiffer, op. cit., p. 97.
76. Ibid., p. 94.
77. Thomas, op. cit., p. A-37.
78. K. Blaxter, et al., *Journal of Comparative Pathology* 64 (1954):157, 176.
79. L. Greenberg, et al., *American Journal of Clinical Nutrition* 6 (1958):635.
80. A. Steiner, *Journal of Applied Nutrition* 16 (1963):125.
81. A. Keys, et al., *Journal of Nutrition* 69 (1967):39.
82. L. Morrison, *Journal of Laboratory and Clinical Medicine* 39 (1952):550.
83. L. Horlick, *Circulation* 10 (1954):30.
84. R. Rosenmann, et al., *Journal of the American Medical Association* 169 (1959):1286.
85. R. Labecki, *American Journal of Clinical Nutrition* 6 (1958):325.
86. A. Grollman, et al., *American Journal of Physiology* 157 (149):21.
87. N. Olsen, et al., *Journal of Nutrition* 53 (1954):317.
88. J. Crawhall, et al., *The Lancet* 2 (1959):806.
89. Nutrition Search, Inc., op. cit., p. 74.
90. P. McAllen, *British Heart Journal* 17 (1966):5.
91. I. Bersohn and P. Oelofse, *The Lancet* 1 (1957):1020.
92. Malkiel-Shapiro, et al., *Medical Proceedings* 2 (1956):455.
93. A. Heggtveit, *Prevention*, November 1976.
94. Randall, op. cit.
95. Nutrition Search, Inc., op. cit., p. 75.
96. L. Maynard, et al., *Journal of Nutrition* 64 (1958):85.
97. I. MacIntyre, et al., *Biochemistry Journal* 70 (1958):456.
98. F. Kohler and C. Uhle, *Journal of Urology*, November 1966.
99. Davis, op. cit., p. 208.
100. Pfeiffer, op. cit., pp. 96–97, 105.
101. J. Biehl, et al., *Proceedings of the Society of Experimental Biological Medicine* 85 (1954):389.
102. Thomas, op. cit., pp. D-27, A-24, K-5.
103. White, et al., op. cit., p. 476.
104. MacIntyre, *Biochemistry Journal*, op. cit.
105. Barker, op. cit.
106. Wacker, op. cit.
107. Booth, op. cit.
108. MacIntyre, *Biochemistry Journal*, op. cit.
109. D. Thorangkin, et al., *Journal of the American Dietetics Association* 35 (1959):23.
110. S. Snyderman, et al., *Federation Proceedings* 9 (1950):371.

111. Hodges, et al., op. cit.
112. T. Kinney, et al., *Journal of Experimental Medicine* 102 (1955):151.
113. J. Hines, et al., *American Journal of Clinical Nutrition* 14 (1964).
114. Pfeiffer, op. cit., pp. 60, 61.
115. J. Waddell, et al., *Journal of Biological Chemistry* 80 (1928):431.
116. M. Shils, *American Journal of Clinical Nutrition* 15 (1964):133.
117. Thomas, op. cit., p. C-77.
118. J. Maxwell, et al., *Proceedings of the Royal Society of Medicine* 33 (1940): 777.
119. Davis, op. cit., p. 262.
120. Nutrition Search, Inc. op. cit., p. 74.
121. A. Costa, International Congress on Vitamin E, 1955.
122. Nutrition Search, Inc., p. 74.
123. J. Davis, *The Lancet* 1 (1948):317.
124. E. Holmes, et al., *The Lancet* 1 (1938):395.
125. J. Brock, *Nutrition Reviews*, 13 (1955):17.
126. Nutrition Search, Inc., op. cit., pp. 73–74.
127. *Nutrition Reviews* 10 (1952):306.
128. Nutrition Search, Inc., op. cit., p. 98.
129. White, et al., op. cit.
130. Philpott and Kalita, op. cit., p. 63.
131. Nutrition Search, Inc., op. cit.
132. Pfeiffer, op. cit., p. 103.
133. Murray, op. cit.
134. Kushner, op. cit.
135. Nutrition Search, Inc., op. cit., p. 74.
136. C. Bunce, et al., *Journal of Nutrition* 76 (1962):20.
137. J. Vitale, *Journal of Biological Chemistry* 228 (1957):573.
138. Pfeiffer, op. cit., p. 114.
139. Nutrition Search, Inc., op. cit.
140. J.I. Rodale, *The Complete Book of Minerals for Health* (Emmaus: Rodale Press Inc. 1972).
141. Nelson, op. cit.
142. Stewart, op. cit.
143. C. Stevens, et al., *Journal of Nutrition* 64 (1958):67.
144. C. Cohn, *Nutrition Reviews* 20 (1962):321.
145. White, et al., op. cit.
146. Nutrition Search, Inc., op. cit.
147. H. Grusin, et al., *American Journal of Clinical Nutrition* 5 (1957):644.
148. Davis, op. cit.
149. Seelig, op. cit.
150. Davis, op. cit.
151. Grusin, op. cit.
152. Airola, op. cit.
153. S. Wallach, et al., *Journal of Laboratory and Clinical Medicine* 59 (1962): 195.
154. R. Horton, et al., *Journal of Clinical Endocrinology* 22 (1962):1187.
155. MacIntyre, *Journal of Chronic Diseases*, op. cit.
156. Barker, *Journal of Chronic Diseases*, op. cit.
157. Wacker, *Medical Clinics of North America*, op. cit.
158. J. Elkinton, *Clinical Chemistry* 3 (1957):309.
159. E. Flink, *Journal of the American Medical Association* 160 (1956):1406.
160. Hammerstein, op. cit.

161. Randall, op. cit.
162. Pfeiffer, op. cit.
163. Grusin, op. cit.
164. L. Smith, et al., *Journal of Dairy Science* 45 (1962):581.
165. R. Fraser, et al., *Proceedings of the Royal Society of Medicine* 50 (1957):21.
166. Pfeiffer, op. cit., p. 105.
167. Thomas, op. cit.

MANGANESE

1. Henry Schroeder, *The Trace Elements and Man* (Old Greenwich, Conn.: Devin Adair, 1973).
2. Carl C. Pfeiffer, *Zinc and Other Micro-Nutrients* (New Canaan, Conn.: Keats Publishing Inc., 1978).
3. Isaac Asimov, *The Bloodstream* (New York:Collier Macmillan Publishers, 1976).
4. J.I. Rodale, *The Complete Book of Minerals for Health* (Emmaus: Rodale Press, 1972).
5. Pfeiffer, op. cit., pp. 68, 73.
6. Schroeder, op. cit., p. 140.
7. Pfeiffer, op. cit., p. 66.
8. Schroeder, op. cit.
9. Pfeiffer, op. cit.
10. Rodale, op. cit.
11. Pfeiffer, op. cit., p. 39.
12. Philip Handler, *Biology and the Future of Man* (New York:Oxford University Press, 1970).
13. Pfeiffer, op. cit., p. 72.
14. Ibid., p. 25.
15. Ibid., p. 68.
16. L. Anderson, et al., *Cooper's Nutrition in Health and Disease* (Philadelphia:J. P. Lippincott Co., 1968).
17. Pfeiffer, op. cit., p. 67.
18. Nutrition Search, Inc., *Nutrition Almanac* (New York:McGraw Hill, 1979).
19. Pfeiffer, op. cit., p. 71.
20. Ibid, p. 67.
21. Handler, op. cit.
22. Pfeiffer, op. cit., p. 66.
23. Pfeiffer, op. cit., p. 67.
24. Ibid.
25. Nutrition Search, Inc., op. cit., p. 76.
26. Pfeiffer, op. cit., p. 67.
27. Rodale, op. cit.
28. Nutrition Search, Inc., op. cit., p. 76.
29. Linda Clark, *Know Your Nutrition* (New Canaan, Conn.:Keats Publishing Co., 1973), pp. 166, 167.
30. Nutrition Search, Inc., op. cit.
31. Pfeiffer, op. cit., p. 66.
32. Schroeder, op. cit., p. 39.
33. Ibid.
34. M. Chaney and M. Ross, *Nutrition* (Boston: Houghton Mifflin Co., 1971).
35. Pfeiffer, op. cit., p. 68.

36. Schroeder, op. cit., p. 47.
37. Ibid.
38. M. V. Krause and M.A. Hunscher, *Food, Nutrition, and Diet Therapy* (Philadelphia: W.B. Sanders Co., 1972), p. 116.
39. Linus Pauling, *Vitamin C and the Common Cold* (New York: Bantam Books, 1970).
40. Nutrition Search, Inc., op. cit.
41. Pfeiffer, op. cit.
42. Ibid.
43. Nutrition Search, Inc., op. cit.
44. Ibid.
45. Ibid.
46. Schroeder, op. cit.
47. Pfeiffer, op. cit.
48. Pauling, op. cit.

PHOSPHORUS

1. Isaac Asimov, "The Genetic Code" (New York:New American Library, 1962), pp. 117, 145.
2. Carl C. Pfeiffer, *Zinc and Other Micro-Nutrients* (Old Greenwich, Conn.:Devin Adair 1973), p. 99.
3. Ibid. p. 100.
4. Nutrition Search, Inc., *Nutrition Almanac* (New York:McGraw Hill, 1979), p. 84.
5. H. Newbold, *Mega-Nutrients for Your Nerves* (New York:Berkley Publishing Corp., 1980), p. 180.
6. Isaac Asimov, *The Bloodstream* (New York: Collier Macmillan, 1976).
7. Nutrition Search, Inc., op. cit., p. 77.
8. Newbold, op. cit., p. 172.
9. Ibid., p. 180.
10. Nutrition Search, Inc., op. cit., p. 77.
11. D. Zilversmit, et al., *American Journal of Clinical Nutrition* 6 (1958):235.
12. B. Rosenfeld, et al., *Canadian Journal of Biochemistry and Physiology* 35 (1957):845.
13. Garrett Hardin, *Biology: Its Principles and Implications* (San Francisco: W.H. Freeman and Co., 1966), pp. 78–81.
14. Adelle Davis, *Let's Get Well* (New York: New American Library, 1972), p. 50.
15. D. Davies, *Clinical Science* 17 (1958):563.
16. E. Ahrens, et al., *Journal of Experimental Medicine* 90 (1949):409.
17. J. Leathes, *The Lancet* 1 (1925):1019.
18. A. White, et al., *Principles of Biochemistry* (New York:McGraw Hill, 1958), pp. 890, 898.
19. Ibid, p. 895.
20. H. Grusin, et al., *American Journal of Clinical Nutrition* 5 (1957):644.
21. L. Lutwak, et al., *Borden's Review of Nutritional Research* 23 (1962):45.
22. N. Vinther-Paulsen, *Geriatrics* 8 (1953):76.
23. V. Nordin, *British Medical Journal* 1 (1962):145.
24. L. Smith, et al., *Journal of Dairy Science* 45 (1962):581.
25. R. Fraser, et al., *Proceedings of the Royal Society of Medicine* 50 (1957):21.
26. J.I. Rodale, *The Complete Book of Minerals for Health* (Emmaus: Rodale Press, 1972), p. 65.

27. Davis, op. cit., p. 254.
28. M. Wohl and R. Goodhart, *Modern Nutrition in Health and Disease* (Philadelphia: Lea and Febiger, 1955).
29. E. Shorr, et al., *Journal of the American Medical Association* 144 (1960): 1549.
30. R. Spellman, et al., *Journal of Urology* 73 (1955):1660.
31. C. Higgins, *Journal of Urology* 68 (1952):117.
32. Davis, op. cit. p. 208.
33. A. Hogan, et al., *Journal of Nutrition* 41 (1950):203.
34. Davis, op cit., p. 108.
35. White, et al., op cit., p. 896.
36. Ibid., p. 891.
37. Nutrition Search, Inc., op cit., p. 78.
38. W. Downs, *American Medicine* 41 (1935):460.
39. D. Aldersberg, et al., *Clinical Chemistry* 1 (1955):18.
40. N. Watanabe, *Archives of Surgery* 85 (1962):136.
41. Ibid.
42. B. Kramer and I. Leibner, *Medical Clinics of North America,* May 1952, pp. 880–885.
43. Ibid.
44. Clayton Thomas ed., *Taber's Cyclopedic Medical Dictionary* (Philadelphia: F.A. Davis Co., 1970), p. C-77.
45. Pfeiffer, op. cit., p. 100.
46. Ibid.
47. J.I. Rodale, *The Health Builder* (Emmaus:Rodale Press, 1957), p. 664.
48. Henry Schroeder, *The Trace Elements and Man* (Old Greenwich, Conn.:Devin Adair, 1973), p. 7.
49. Newbold, op. cit. p. 172.
50. Ibid.
51. F. Murray, *Program Your Heart for Health* (New York:Larchmont Books, 1977), pp. 312, 313.
52. Schroeder, op. cit., p. 169.
53. G. Buckley, et al., *American Journal of Clinical Nutrition* 2 (1954):396.
54. R. Mitchell, *Archives of the Disability of Childhood* 35 (1960):385.
55. A. DelGiudice, *Summary* 12 (1960):21.
56. M. Horwitt, et al., *American Medical Association Archives of Neurology* 1 (1959):312.
57. Nutrition Search, Inc., op cit., p. 77.
58. L. Weissberger, et al., *Journal of Biological Chemistry* 151 (1943):543.
59. Davis, op. cit., p. 320.
60. J. Deitrick, et al., *American Journal of Medicine* 4 (1948):3.
61. L. Hurley, et al., *Journal of Biological Chemistry* 151 (1952):583.
62. B. Ershoff, *Nutrition Reviews* 13 (1955):33.
63. B. Ershoff, *Metabolism* 2 (1953):175.
64. W. Krehl, *American Journal of Clinical Nutrition* 11 (1962), p. 77.
65. White, et al., op cit., pp. 894, 895.
66. Kramer and Leibner, op cit.
67. Pfeiffer, op. cit., p. 100.
68. Thomas, op. cit., p. P-76.
69. Ibid.
70. Nutrition Search, Inc., op. cit., p. 78.
71. Thomas, op. cit., p. P-77.
72. Pfeiffer, op. cit., p. 100.

POTASSIUM

1. J. Stewart, et al., *Journal of Comparative Pathology* 66 (1956):10.
2. Nutrition Search, Inc., *Nutrition Almanac* (New York:McGraw Hill, 1979), p. 78.
3. Carl C. Pfeiffer, *Zinc and Other Micro-Nutrients* (New Canaan, Conn.:Keats Publishing, Inc., 1978), pp. 110, 111.
4. Adelle Davis, *Let's Get Well* (New York: New American Library, 1972), p. 216.
5. Henry Schroeder, *The Trace Elements and Man* (Old Greenwich, Conn.:Devin Adair, 1973), p. 33.
6. Ibid.
7. Nutrition Search, Inc., p. 79.
8. Davis, op. cit., p. 216.
9. Isaac Asimov, *The Bloodstream* (New York: Collier Macmillan, 1976), p. 123.
10. Davis, op. cit.
11. Ibid.
12. Asimov, op. cit.
13. Davis, op. cit., pp. 211, 216, 236.
14. A. White, et al., *Principles of Biochemistry* (New York: McGraw Hill, 1968), p. 923.
15. Philip Handler, *Biology and the Future of Man* (New York: Oxford University Press, 1970), pp. 254, 255.
16. Schroeder, op. cit., p. 24.
17. White, et al., p. 793.
18. *Nutrition Reviews* 10 (1952):163.
19. R. Womersley, et al., *Journal of Clinical Investigation* 34 (1955):456.
20. F. Moore, et al., *Metabolism* 4(1955):379.
21. Stewart, op. cit.
22. Pfeiffer, op. cit., pp. 110, 111.
23. Nutrition Search, Inc., op. cit., pp. 78, 79.
24. Ibid.
25. Asimov op. cit., pp. 123 124.
26. Nutrition Search, Inc., op. cit., pp. 78, 79.
27. *Nutrition Reviews* 14 (1956):295.
28. D. Streeten, et al., *Journal of Physiology* 118 (1952):149.
29. D. Leithauser, *Surgical Gynecology and Obstetrics* 86 (1948):543.
30. H. Zintel, *American Journal of Clinical Nutrition* 3 (1955):501.
31. M. Ziegler, et al., *The Lancet* 2 (1961):511.
32. *Nutrition Reviews* 14 (1956) op. cit.
33. Streeten, op. cit.
34. D. Black, et al., *Clinical Science* 11 (1952):397.
35. Pfeiffer, op. cit., p. 109.
36. White, et al., op. cit., p. 802.
37. G. Rouser, *American Journal of Clinical Nutrition* 6 (1958):681.
38. N. Anstall, et al., *The Lancet* 1 (1959):814.
39. K. Blaxter, et al., *Journal of Comparative Pathology* 64 (1954):157, 176.
40. *Nutrition Reviews* 18 (1960):262.
41. R. Gilbert, et al., *Annals of Internal Medicine* 25 (1946):928.
42. E. Egeli, et al., *American Heart Journal* 59 (1960):527.
43. J. Bryant, *Proceedings of the Society of Experimental Biological Medicine* 67 (1948):557.
44. P. McAllen, *British Heart Journal* 17 (1955):5.

45. Pfeiffer, op. cit., p. 110.
46. A. Keys, et al., *The Biology of Human Starvation* (Minneapolis: University of Minnesota Press, 1951).
47. Bryant, op. cit.
48. E. del Castillo, *Medicine* 6(1945):471.
49. N. Keith, et al., *American Heart Journal* 27(1944):817.
50. N. Keith, et al., *Proceedings of the Staff Meeting of the Mayo Clinic* 21 (1946):385.
51. E. Sharpey-Achafer, *British Heart Journal* 5 (1943):80, 85.
52. McAllen, op. cit.
53. Moore, op. cit.
54. J. Holler, *Journal of the American Medical Association* 131(1946):1186.
55. K. Guggenheim, *Metabolism* 3 (1954):44.
56. Egeli, op. cit.
57. K. Emerson, *Nutrition Reviews* 6 (1948):257.
58. Holler, op. cit.
59. Egeli, op. cit.
60. White, et al., op. cit., p. 804.
61. Womersley, op. cit.
62. Pfeiffer, op. cit., p. 113.
63. Nutrition Search, Inc., op. cit., p. 79.
64. Pfeiffer, op. cit., p. 113.
65. Davis, op. cit., p. 215.
66. Nutrition Search, Inc., op. cit., p. 79.
67. White, et al., op. cit., p. 803.
68. Pfeiffer, op. cit., p. 108.
69. Davis, op. cit., p. 216.
70. Roger J. Williams, *Nutrition Against Disease* (New York: Bantam Books, 1980), pp. 156, 157.
71. Pfeiffer, op. cit., p. 101.
72. Ibid.
73. White, et al., op. cit., p. 804.
74. Nutrition Search, Inc., op cit., p. 79.
75. White, et al., op. cit., p. 804.
76. Pfeiffer, op. cit., p. 110.
77. Davis, op. cit., p. 236.
78. White, et al., op. cit., p. 802.
79. Pfeiffer, op. cit., p. 110.
80. White, et al., op. cit., p. 802.
81. McAllen, op. cit.
82. Moore, op. cit.
83. *Nutrition Reviews* 16 (1958):90.
84. Streeten, op. cit.
85. Leithauser, op. cit.
86. Zintel, op. cit.
87. Womersley, op. cit.
88. Black, op. cit.
89. W. Blahd, et al., *Metabolism* 2(1953):218.
90. Leithauser, op. cit.
91. Zintel, op. cit.
92. White, et al., op. cit., pp. 803, 804.
93. Davis, op. cit., pp. 262, 263.
94. White, et al., op. cit., pp. 802, 803.

95. Ibid.
96. Pfeiffer, op. cit., p. 114.
97. Davis, op. cit., p. 101.
98. D. Kushner, *American Journal of Clinical Nutrition* 4 (1956):561.
99. C. Carr, *Proceedings of the Society for Experimental Biological Medicine* 89 (1955):546.

SELENIUM

1. Carl C. Pfeiffer, *Zinc and Other Micro-Nutrients* (Old Greenwich, Conn.:Devin Adair, 1973), pp. 85, 86.
2. O. Levander and V. Morris, *Journal of Nutrition,* Vol. 100(9), 1970, pp. 1111–1118.
3. R. Passwater and P. Welker, *American Laboratory,* Vol. 3(4), 1971, pp. 36–40.
4. O. Levander and C. Baumann, *Toxicology and Applied Pharmacology* 9 (1966):98–115.
5. Pfeiffer, op cit., p. 84.
6. Richard Passwater, *Selenium as Food and Medicine* (New Canaan:Conn.: Keats Publishing, Inc., 1980).
7. Pfeiffer, op. cit.
8. Passwater, op. cit.
9. Ibid.
10. Ibid.
11. A. White, et al., *Principles of Biochemistry* (New York:McGraw Hill, 1968), p. 1055.
12. S. Gross, *Seminars in Hematology,* Vol. 13(3), 1967, pp. 187–199.
13. White, et al., op. cit., pp. 873, 875, 891.
14. Clayton Thomas, ed., *Taber's Cyclopedic Medical Dictionary* (Philadelphia:F.A. Davis Co., 1970).
15. Pfeiffer, op. cit.
16. Ibid.
17. Passwater, op. cit.
18. Thomas, op. cit., p. R-36.
19. Passwater, op. cit.
20. Thomas, op. cit.
21. D. Frost and R. Van Poucke, *Trace Substances in Environmental Health,* ed. by Hemphill (Columbia: University of Missouri, 1973).
22. H. Getz, et al., *American Review of Tuberculosis* 64 (1951):381.
23. White, et al., op. cit., p. 1055.
24. T. Moore, *Biochemistry Journal* 34 (1940):1321.
25. T. Berenshtein, *Zdravookh. Belorussia,* Vol. 18(10), 1972, pp. 34–36.
26. Nutrition Search, Inc., *Nutrition Almanac* (New York:McGraw Hill, 1979).
27. Passwater, op. cit.
28. P. Whanger, *Proceedings of the Symposium on Selenium Tellurium in the Environment* (Pittsburgh: Industrial Health Foundation, 1976), pp. 234–252.
29. R. Chen, et al., *Pharmacological Research Commentary,* Vol. 6(6), 1974, pp. 571–579.
30. O. Levander, et al., *Journal of Nutrition,* Vol. 107(3), 1977, pp. 378–382.
31. Henry Schroeder, *The Trace Elements and Man* (Old Greenwich, Conn.:Devin Adair, 1973).
32. G. Schrauzer and D. White, *Bioinorganic Chemistry* 8(1978):303–318.

33. M. Scott, *Proceedings of the Symposium on Selenium Tellurium in the Environment* (Pittsburgh: Industrial Health Foundation, 1976), p. 25.
34. Pfeiffer, op cit., p. 86.
35. M. Scott, *Annals of the New York Academy of Science* 138 (1966):82–89.
36. F. Murray, *Program Your Heart for Health* (New York:Larchmont Books, 1977).
37. Pfeiffer, op. cit.
38. Thomas, op. cit.
39. Passwater, op. cit.
40. S. Gunn, et al., in *Selenium in Biomedicine,* ed. by Muth, Oldfield and Weswig (Greenwich, Conn.: AVI, 1967).
41. R. Passwater, *Supernutrition for Healthy Hearts* (New York:Dial Press, 1977).
42. Ibid.
43. *The Wall Street Journal,* March 13, 1973.
44. Henry Gray, *Anatomy, Descriptive and Surgical* (New York: Bounty Books, 1977).
45. B. Chipperfield, *Clinical Chimica Acta* 31 (1971):459–465.
46. E. Edwin, et al., *Biochemistry Journal* 125 (1971):407.
47. Alan Nourse, *Family Medical Guide* (New York: Harper & Row, 1973).
48. J.I. Rodale and Staff, *The Complete Book of Minerals for Health* (Emmaus: Rodale, 1972).
49. White, et al., op. cit.
50. W. McKeehan, et al., *Proceedings of the National Academy of Science,* Vol. 73(6), 1976, pp. 2023–2027.
51. Pfeiffer, op cit.
52. H. Newbold, *Mega-Nutrients for Your Nerves* (New York: Berkley Publishing, 1980).
53. Pfeiffer, op. cit.
54. Murray, op. cit.
55. J. Aaseth, et al., *Second International Symposium on Selenium in Biology and Medicine,* Texas Tech University, Lubbock, Texas, May 1980.
56. H. Nitowsky, et al., *American Journal of Clinical Nutrition* 4 (1956):397.
57. Murray, op. cit.
58. Passwater, op. cit.
59. Ibid.
60. H. Parrish, *Journal of Chronic Diseases* 14 (1961):339.
61. White, et al., op. cit.
62. M. Garner and A. Spector, *Proceedings of the National Academy of Science,* Vol. 77(2), 1980.
63. Schroeder, op. cit.
64. Passwater, op. cit.
65. Pfeiffer, op. cit.
66. Carl Pfeiffer and B. Aston, *The Golden Pamphlet* (Princeton: Brain Bio Center, 1980).
67. Pfeiffer, op. cit.
68. G. Colombetti and S. Munti, *Proceedings of European Biophysics Conference* 2 (1971), pp. 45–53.
69. R. Badiello, et al., *International Journal of Radiation Biology,* Vol. 20(1), 1971, pp. 61–68.
70. Passwater, op. cit.
71. G. Nelson, et al., *Fundamental Concepts of Biology* (New York: John Wiley and Sons, Inc., 1970).

72. Passwater, op. cit.
73. Pfeiffer, op. cit.
74. McKeehan, op. cit.
75. W. Blanc, et al., *Pediatrics* 22 (1958):494.
76. Passwater, op. cit.
77. Pfeiffer, op. cit.
78. Passwater, op. cit.
79. Schrauzer, op. cit.
80. Pfeiffer, op. cit.
81. Passwater, op. cit.
82. United States Patent Office, USSN 39, 142, USSN 97, 011.
83. Passwater and Welker, op. cit.
84. Passwater, op. cit.
85. Pfeiffer, op cit.
86. R. Vracko and E. Benditt, *American Journal of Pathology* 75 (1974):204–207.
87. E. Benditt and M. Benditt, *Proceedings of the National Academy of Science* 70(1973):1753–1756.
88. Thomas, op cit., p. M-67.

SODIUM

1. Philip Chen, *Mineral Balance in Eating for Health* (Emmaus: Rodale Press, 1969).
2. M.V. Krause and M.A. Hunscher, *Food, Nutrition and Diet Therapy* 5th ed. (Philadelphia: W.B. Saunders Co., 1972).
3. Corinne H. Robinson and Marilyn R. Lawler, *Normal and Therapeutic Nutrition*, 15th ed., (New York: Macmillan, 1977).
4. Eleanor Whitney and May Hamilton, *Understanding Nutrition* (St. Paul: West Publishing 1977).
5. Ibid.
6. Philip Handler, *Biology and the Future of Man* (New York:Oxford University Press, 1970).
7. Adelle Davis, *Let's Eat Right to Keep Fit* (New York:New American Library, 1970).
8. Ibid.
9. Robinson and Lawler, op. cit.
10. White, et al., op. cit.
11. Thomas Clayton, ed., *Taber's Cyclopedic Medical Dictionary* (Philadelphia: F.A. Davis Co., 1970).
12. Adelle Davis, *Let's Get Well* (New York:New American Library, 1972).
13. Handler, op. cit.
14. Davis, *Let's Get Well*, op. cit.
15. Carl C. Pfeiffer, *Zinc and Other Micro-Nutrients* (Old Greenwich, Conn.: Devin Adair 1973).
16. F. Murray, *Program Your Heart for Health* (New York:Larchmont Books, 1977).
17. Ibid.
18. Ibid.
19. Ibid.
20. Pfeiffer, op. cit.
21. Davis, *Let's Get Well*, op. cit.

22. Ibid.
23. Murray, op. cit.
24. Nutrition Search, Inc., *Nutrition Almanac* (New York:McGraw Hill, 1979).
25. Chen, op. cit.
26. Pfeiffer, op. cit.
27. Isaac Asimov, *The Bloodstream* (New York: Collier Macmillan, 1976).
28. Davis, *Let's Get Well*, op. cit.
29. Asimov, op. cit.
30. Davis, *Let's Get Well*, op. cit.

ZINC

1. Carl C. Pfeiffer, *Zinc and Other Micro-Nutrients* (Old Greenwich, Conn.:Devin Adair, 1973).
2. Carl Pfeiffer and B. Aston, *The Golden Pamphlet* (Princeton: Brain Bio Center, 1980).
3. Pfeiffer, op cit.
4. K. Hambridge, *et al., Pediatric Research* 6 (1972).
5. Pfeiffer, op cit.
6. Hambridge, et al., op cit.
7. R. Burch and J. Sullivan, *Medical Clinics of North America*, Vol. 60, No. 4(July 1976).
8. Pfeiffer and Aston, op cit.
9. Nutrition Search, Inc., *Nutrition Almanac* (New York:McGraw Hill, 1979).

BIBLIOGRAPHY

Adams, Ruth, *The Complete Home Guide to All the Vitamins* (New York: Larchmont Books, 1972).

Adams, Ruth and Frank Murray, *Body, Mind and the B Vitamins* (New York: Larchmont Books, 1972).

Bailey, Herbert, *Vitamin E: Your Key to a Healthy Heart* (New York: ARC Books, Inc., 1971).

Cameron, Ewan and Linus Pauling, *Cancer and Vitamin C* (Menlo Park, Calif.: The Linus Pauling Institute of Science and Medicine, 1979).

Cheraskin, Emanuel, W. Marshall Ringsdorf and Emily L Sisley, *The Vitamin C Connection: Getting Well and Staying Well with Vitamin C* (New York: Harper & Row, 1983).

Ellis, John M. and James Presley, *Vitamin B6: The Doctor's Report* (New York: Harper & Row, 1973).

Klenner, Fred R., *The Key to Good Health—Vitamin C* (Chicago: Graphic Arts Research Foundation, 1971).

Kunin, Richard A., *Mega-Nutrition* (New York: New American Library, 1981).

Lesser, Michael, *Nutrition and Vitamin Therapy* (New York: Grove Press, Inc., 1980).

Nutrition Search, Inc., *Nutrition Almanac* (New York: McGraw Hill, 1979).

Pauling, Linus, *Vitamin C, the Common Cold, and the Flu* (San Francisco: W.H. Freeman and Company, 1976).

Pfeiffer, Carl C., *Mental and Elemental Nutrients* (New Canaan, Conn.: Keats Publishing, Inc., 1975).

Pfeiffer, Carl C., *Zinc and other Micro-Nutrients* (Old Greenwich: Devin Adair, Inc., 1973).

Prevention staff, *The Complete Book of Vitamins* (Emmaus: Rodale Press, Inc., 1977).

Rodale, J.I. and Staff, *The Complete Book of Minerals for Health* (Emmaus: Rodale Press, Inc., 1972).

Schroeder, Henry A., *The Trace Elements and Man* (Old Greenwich, Conn.: Devin Adair, 1973).

Shute, Evan V., *The Heart and Vitamin E* (New Canaan, Conn.: Keats Publishing, Inc., 1977).

Shute, Wilfrid E., *The Vitamin E Book* (New Canaan, Conn.: Keats Publishing, Inc., 1975).

Shute, Wilfrid E., *Vitamin E for Ailing and Healthy Hearts* (New York: Jove, 1969).

Stone, Irwin, *The Healing Factor* (New York: Grosset & Dunlap, 1972).

Underwood, Eric J., *Trace Elements in Human and Animal Nutrition,* 4th ed. (New York: Academic Press, 1977).

Watson, George, *Nutrition and Your Mind* (New York: Bantam Books, 1972).

Williams, Roger J., *Nutrition Against Disease* (New York: Bantam Books, 1971).

Williams, Roger J., *You Are Extraordinary* (New York: Pyramid, 1971).

INDEX